BEHAVIOR MODIFICAT
WITH WOMEN
Edited by Elaine A. Blechman

"This volume should help therapists of both sexes to raise critical questions about their management of clinical problems in women, and certainly will stimulate many readers toward a more comprehensive view of the origins and consequences of gender differences in daily behaviors and misbehaviors."
—Frederick H. Kanfer

"An important book for all mental health professionals, especially since the majority of clients seeking treatment are women. . . . Interwoven throughout the book is Blechman's intriguing question: Is it more effective to treat individual women who are experiencing problems, or to focus on the societal environment that may be fostering women's problems?"
—Rosemery O. Nelson

Although women outnumber men as recipients of behavioral treatments, clinicians and researchers rarely consider gender when they design and evaluate the short- and long-term outcomes of interventions. The contributors to this volume challenge the prevailing assumption that the application of behavioral techniques is unaffected by value judgments, and provide important guidelines for the assessment and treatment of life problems and clinical disorders common to women seeking therapy. A primary tenet of the book is the existence of two distinct worlds: male and female. Knowledge of these worlds is a prerequisite for the design of effective, long-lasting behavioral interventions for women.

The book opens with a review of the basic issues pertaining to treatment: the nature of sex roles, gender differences in competence, and gender biases in assessment. Dr. Blechman proposes an operational definition of competence and sets forth a testable theory of environmental influences on the acquisition of competent behavior. Life problems prevalent among women are the focus of Part II. Among those examined are health maintenance, lack of assertiveness, marital and family conflicts, sexual dysfunction, wife abuse, and parenting difficulties. Each is discussed in terms of etiology, assessment, prevention, and treatment. The third section covers clinical disorders common in women, including depression, physiological and reproductive disorders, anxiety, fears and phobias, and weight disorders. The volume closes with a consideration of the particular problems of four previously neglected female populations—delinquents, aging and alcoholic women, and mentally retarded mothers.

Unique in its thorough, systematic coverage, the book's review of recent research findings and its practical recommendations for treatment are vital for clinicians and students in family and marital therapy, clinical psychology and psychiatry, and physicians who work with problems in women.

BEHAVIOR MODIFICATION WITH WOMEN

BEHAVIOR MODIFICATION WITH WOMEN

Edited by

ELAINE A. BLECHMAN

Wesleyan University

THE GUILFORD PRESS

New York   London

© 1984 The Guilford Press
A Division of Guilford Publications, Inc.
200 Park Avenue South, New York, N.Y. 10003

Printed in the United States of America

LIBRARY OF CONGRESS CATALOGING IN PUBLICATION DATA

Main entry under title:

Behavior modification with women.

 Bibliography: p.
 Includes indexes.
 1. Women—Mental health. 2. Sex role. 3. Behavior
modification. 4. Behavior therapy. I. Blechman,
Elaine A.
RC451.4.W6B43 1984   615.8′51   82-15655
ISBN 0-89862-625-0

This book is affectionately dedicated to my husband,
ARTHUR BECK.

CONTRIBUTORS

JAMES F. ALEXANDER, PhD, Department of Psychology, University of Utah, Salt Lake City, Utah

BEVERLY M. ATKESON, PhD, Department of Psychology, University of Georgia, Athens, Georgia

DAVID H. BARLOW, PhD, Department of Psychology, State University of New York at Albany, Albany, New York

J. GAYLE BECK, PhD candidate, Department of Psychology, State University of New York at Albany, Albany, New York

ELAINE A. BLECHMAN, PhD, Department of Psychology, Wesleyan University, Middletown, Connecticut

KAREN S. BUDD, PhD, Meyer Children's Rehabilitation Institute, University of Nebraska Medical Center, Omaha, Nebraska

KAREN S. CALHOUN, PhD, Department of Psychology, University of Georgia, Athens, Georgia

IRIS GOLDSTEIN FODOR, PhD, Department of Educational Psychology, School Psychology Program, New York University, New York, New York

JOHN P. FOREYT, PhD, Baylor College of Medicine, Houston, Texas

ELLEN FRANK, PhD, Western Psychiatric Institute and Clinic, Department of Psychiatry, University of Pittsburgh School of Medicine, Pittsburgh, Pennsylvania

MARVIN R. GOLDFRIED, PhD, Department of Psychology, State University of New York at Stony Brook, Stony Brook, New York

G. KEN GOODRICK, PhD, Baylor College of Medicine, Houston, Texas

STEPHEN GREENSPAN, PhD, Boys Town Center for Study of Youth Development, Boys Town, Nebraska

ALAN S. GURMAN, PhD, Department of Psychiatry, University of Wisconsin Medical School, Madison, Wisconsin

EMILY FRANCK HOON, PhD candidate, Department of Clinical Psychology, University of Florida, Gainesville, Florida

BELINDA A. JOHNSON, PhD, Brown University Health Services, Providence, Rhode Island

MARJORIE H. KLEIN, PhD, Department of Psychiatry, University of Wisconsin Medical School, Madison, Wisconsin

HARRY D. KROP, PhD, Psychology Service, Veterans Administration Medical Center, Gainesville, Florida

MARSHA M. LINEHAN, PhD, Department of Psychology, University of Washington, Seattle, Washington

MARIAN L. MACDONALD, PhD, Department of Psychology, University of Massachusetts, Amherst, Massachusetts

BARBARA S. MCCRADY, PhD, Brown University/Butler Hospital, Providence, Rhode Island

IVAN W. MILLER, III, PhD, Section of Psychiatry and Human Behavior, Brown University–Butler Hospital, Providence, Rhode Island

WILLIAM H. NORMAN, PhD, Section of Psychiatry and Human Behavior, Brown University–Butler Hospital, Providence, Rhode Island

WENDY J. PADAWER, PhD candidate, Department of Psychology, State University of New York at Stony Brook, Stony Brook, New York

BARBARA DUFFY STEWART, MPH, Western Psychiatric Institute and Clinic, Department of Psychiatry, University of Pittsburgh School of Medicine, Pittsburgh, Pennsylvania

STEPHANIE B. STOLZ, PhD, Department of Health and Human Services, U.S. Public Health Service, Kansas City, Missouri

CYD C. STRAUSS, MS, Department of Psychology, University of Georgia, Athens, Georgia

ELLIE T. STURGIS, PhD, Department of Psychiatry and Human Behavior, University of Mississippi Medical Center, Jackson, Mississippi

JODI THAL, MA, Department of Educational Psychology, School Psychology Program, New York University, New York, New York

JANET R. WARBURTON, PhD, Western States Family Institute, Salt Lake City, Utah

JOHN P. WINCZE, PhD, Division of Biology and Medicine, Brown University, Providence, Rhode Island

PATRICIA A. WISOCKI, PhD, Department of Psychology, University of Massachusetts, Amherst, Massachusetts

ACKNOWLEDGMENTS

The nucleus of this book is a set of papers presented to a largely female audience at the Association for Advancement of Behavior Therapy (AABT) in 1980 by Marsha Linehan, Iris Fodor, Barbara McCrady, Alan Gurman and Marjorie Klein, and me. Each of these contributors has waited a long time to see his or her words in print and I appreciate their patience. David Barlow, who was president of AABT that year, and the symposium discussant, mentioned the problem of hurried dissemination of untested behavioral treatment packages in his presidential address. Several contributors to this volume echo his concerns. I am grateful that Cyril Franks, who is among the founders of the behavior therapy movement, and Violet Franks, who edited the first book in which a chapter on behavioral treatment of women appeared (Franks & Burtle, 1974), encouraged me to put this book together. After Al Gurman and I met at the Psychotherapy with Women conference, he introduced me to The Guilford Press and shared his expertise about editing books. Seymour Weingarten, whose son was born when the book was started, was exceedingly patient through the delays and frustrations that surprised me but not him. My assistant, Lyn Hanson, typed and retyped, and predicted with prescient accuracy when the project would be done. Her advice and thoughtfulness were invaluable. From start to finish, my daughter, Reva, was proud of me, something that not every mother of a college student can claim. Although my husband, Arthur, works in the publishing industry, his contributions were practical and spiritual rather than literary. He did far more than his share of the household chores, and only rarely did he mention that he had forewarned me not to edit a book. I thank you all.

E.A.B.

REFERENCE

Franks, V., & Burtle, V. (Eds.). *Women in therapy: New psychotherapies for a changing society.* New York: Brunner/Mazel, 1974.

PREFACE

In 1979, Annette Brodsky and Rachel Hare-Mustin invited me to write a chapter on behavior modification with women for a joint APA-NIMH conference on Psychotherapy with Women (Blechman, 1980a). I was leary about the assignment since I had never really thought that biological sex or psychological gender made much difference in the way behavior modification was practiced, or in the way it should be practiced. Before accepting the task, I sampled six issues of that year, from each of three prominent behavioral journals, all of which were still in my to-be-read pile. I found that women were all of the clients, or the majority of clients, in 80% of the articles concerned with intervention. In not one of these articles did the authors consider sex or gender relevant to the design of treatment, or to the evaluation of its effectiveness. As I began to write that first chapter, and as other invitations to write on the topic developed (Blechman, 1980a, 1980b, 1981), I discovered other trends.

Although behavioral interventions for anxiety reduction and pain control have been tested on many women, these interventions have not been directed toward the forms of anxiety and pain most common among women. Thus behavioral strategies for improved coping with dysmenorrhea, premenstrual symptoms, pregnancy, labor, and menopause have received little systematic development. Although empiricism is espoused by all subspecialties of behavior modification, packaged behavioral treatments which lack objective, repeated evaluation are widely disseminated, mostly to women. All over the United States, profit-making programs that "use behavior modification" promise that women will lose weight, be more assertive, be less fearful, and be better parents. These programs, however, neither check fidelity to supposed behavioral principles, nor test short-term and long-term specific and general effects. Efforts to police the dissemination of behavioral procedures, both to safeguard the consumer and to protect the reputation of the discipline, have not received widespread support.

Although most behaviorists assert that dysfunctional behavior is acquired and credit the social environment with production and maintenance of psychopathology, many interventions aimed at women are of the skill training variety. Behavioral programs designed to prevent dysfunction by altering the settings in which women work, study, and live are hard to find. Unfortunately, it is rather easy to find studies in which women are subjected to procedures which ameliorate their presenting complaints while enhancing their powerlessness. Demonstrations of short-term change which served an important purpose when there was a need to convince people about the efficacy of behavior modification are no longer necessary. Instead, evidence of generalization of change over time, settings, and response classes, is required to disarm those who view behavior modification as dangerously effective and short-sighted.

Behaviorists will have to find a way to make subtle environmental changes which are acceptable to women and to men, if they are to achieve generalized therapeutic change. Skill training of the disabled woman is insufficient for generalization of individual improvement and unfeasible as a method of enhancing the psychological well-being of large numbers of women. Tharp and Wetzel (1969) changed the practice of behavior modification with children by demonstrating how the natural environment of predelinquent boys is the gateway to generalization of change. They were able to modify the natural environment by training cooperative parents and teachers to understand and use principles of behavior modification. Perhaps this book will change the practice of behavior modification with women; it certainly provides ample information about the role that the natural environment plays in the etiology and treatment of maladaptive behavior. It is unlikely that only one approach to engineering of the natural environment will emerge from this book; each contributor approaches this challenge from a slightly different vantage point and draws different conclusions.

When I first wrote about behavior modification with women, I made much of the value-free technology of behavior modification. Both time and Alan Gurman have changed my mind. From the vantage point of the woman consumer, behavior modification is no more value free than any other form of psychological or medical intervention. The egalitarian argument that the basic mechanisms of behavior do not differentiate between the sexes has a fatal flaw. The same mechanisms operate in two different social environments, one male, one female. For better and for worse, the world treats women differently from men.

The broad aim of this book is to bring to the attention of behaviorists, the existence of what Jesse Bernard (1981) calls the female and male worlds. These environmental differences have been ignored for too long by a discipline that credits the environment with ultimate control over behavior. Every major area of disordered behavior in women is considered in this book. The one unfortunate exception is the absence of a chapter on psychotic disorders. Each of the central chapters reviews relevant theory and empirical research, considers issues of etiology, assessment, and treatment, and ends with recommendations for clinicians. The introductory chapters provide detailed coverage of concepts and methods central to the study of behavior modification with women. This book has been planned for two groups of readers: those who are knowledgeable about women's issues but unfamiliar with behavior modification, and those who are expert in behavior modification and concerned about women's issues. Because the contributors have provided ample background information about their areas of interest, and have considered in detail issues rarely discussed before in the behavioral literature, this book should prove useful to students, researchers, and clinicians.

REFERENCES

Bernard, J. *The female world.* New York: Free Press, 1981.

Blechman, E.A. Behavior therapies. In A.M. Brodsky & R.T. Hare-Mustin (Eds.), *Women and psychotherapy.* New York: Guilford, 1980.(a)

Blechman, E.A. Ecological sources of dysfunction in women: Issues and implications for clinical behavior therapy. *Clinical Behavior Therapy Review,* 1980, 2, 1–16.(b)

Blechman, E.A. Competence, depression, and behavior modification with women. In M. Hersen, R.M. Eisler, & P.M. Miller (Eds.), *Progress in behavior modification* (Vol. 12). New York: Academic, 1981.

Tharp, R.G., & Wetzel, R.J. *Behavior modification in the natural environment.* New York: Academic, 1969.

CONTENTS

PART I: BASIC ISSUES, 1

CHAPTER 1. WOMEN'S BEHAVIOR IN A MAN'S WORLD:
SEX DIFFERENCES IN COMPETENCE   3
Elaine A. Blechman

Overview, 3; Background, 4; Competence Is Relative Success at Achievement and Interpersonal Tasks, 7; Validation of the Construct of Competence with School-Aged Children, 11; The Unexplained Decline in Women's Achievement Competence, 14; Problem-Solving Skill, Activity Structure, and Competence, 20; Conclusions and Recommendations, 26; Acknowledgments, 27; References, 27

CHAPTER 2. UNRAVELING THE NATURE OF SEX ROLES   34
J. Gayle Beck and David H. Barlow

Overview, 34; Background, 35; Development of the Checklist, 37; The Display of Sex-Typed Motor Behavior by Adults: Social Responses, 42; The Display of Sex-Typed Motor Behavior by Children, 47; Clinical Assessment of Sex-Role Motor Behavior, 52; Conclusions and Recommendations, 54; References, 57

CHAPTER 3. BEHAVIORAL ASSESSMENT OF WOMEN
CLIENTS   60
Marian L. MacDonald

Overview, 60; Background, 62; Behavioral Assessment's Emergence and Rationale, 68; A Review of Behavioral Assessment Strategies, 73; Conclusions and Recommendations, 88; References, 89

CHAPTER 4. DISSEMINATION OF BEHAVIORAL
INTERVENTIONS WITH WOMEN: NEEDED—A
TECHNOLOGY   94
Stephanie B. Stolz

Issues in Dissemination of Behavioral Interventions, 95; An Explicit Technology?, 99; An Implicit Technology of the Adoption of Innovations, 101; Conclusion, 106; Acknowledgments, 107; References, 107

PART II: PROBLEMS OF LIVING, 109

CHAPTER 5. SEXUALITY   113
Emily Franck Hoon, Harry D. Krop, and John P. Wincze

Overview, 113; Background, 114; Behavioral Model of Sexual Functioning: The Advantage for Women, 116; The Assessment Process for Women Expressing Sexual Distress, 118; Female Sexual Problems and Common Treatment Approaches, 124; Conclusions and Recommendations, 135; References, 139

CHAPTER 6. INTERPERSONAL EFFECTIVENESS IN
ASSERTIVE SITUATIONS   143
Marsha M. Linehan

Overview, 143; Background, 144; Interpersonal Behavior, Psychopathology, and Women, 145; Assertive Behavior: The Topographical View, 148; Assertive Behavior: A Functional View, 149; Maximizing Effectiveness: Assertive Skill, 153; The Content of Assertive Training Programs, 154; Assessment of Assertion Skill, 159; Intervention Strategies, 160; Conclusions and Recommendations, 162; References, 163

CHAPTER 7. MARRIAGE AND THE FAMILY: AN
UNCONSCIOUS MALE BIAS IN BEHAVIORAL
TREATMENT?   170
Alan S. Gurman and Marjorie H. Klein

Overview and Background, 170; Behavioral Views of Marital and Family Dysfunction, 171; Behavioral Marriage and Family Therapy in Practice, 174; Assessing the Outcomes of Behavioral Marriage and Family Therapy, 181; Conclusions and Recommendations, 185; Acknowledgments, 186; References, 186

CHAPTER 8. PARENTING: TRAINING MOTHERS AS
BEHAVIOR THERAPISTS FOR THEIR CHILDREN   190
Cyd C. Strauss and Beverly M. Atkeson

Overview, 190; Background, 191; Causal Factors, 197; Maintenance and Generality of Treatment Effects, 199; Cost Effectiveness of Treatment, 201; Family Variables' Influence on Treatment, 204; Assessment Issues, 208; Conclusions and Recommendations, 211; Acknowledgments, 212; References, 213

CHAPTER 9. HEALTH MAINTENANCE: EXERCISE AND
NUTRITION   221
John P. Foreyt and G. Ken Goodrick

Overview, 221; Background, 221; Exercise and Women's Health, 222; Correcting Misconceptions and Reservations about Exercise, 225; Establishing the Exercise Habit, 229; Behavioral Techniques to Develop Exercise Habits, 231; Nutrition and Women's Health, 234; Behavioral Self-Management of Diet, 237; Conclusions and Recommendations, 240; Acknowledgments, 242; References, 242

CHAPTER 10. PHYSICAL AGGRESSION: TREATING THE VICTIMS 245

Ellen Frank and Barbara Duffy Stewart

Overview, 245; Background of the Problem of Rape Victimization, 246; Behavioral Treatment of Rape Victims, 251; Background of the Problem of Wife Abuse, 265; Current Approaches to Treatment of Abuse, 267; Conclusions and Recommendations, 269; References, 270

PART III: DISORDERS COMMON AMONG WOMEN, 273

CHAPTER 11. DEPRESSION: A BEHAVIORAL–COGNITIVE APPROACH 275

William H. Norman, Belinda A. Johnson, and Ivan W. Miller, III

Overview, 275; Background, 276; Assessment of Depression, 281; Behavioral–Cognitive Formulations of Depression, 285; Conclusions and Recommendations, 299; References, 301

CHAPTER 12. PHYSIOLOGICAL AND REPRODUCTIVE DISORDERS 308

Karen S. Calhoun and Ellie T. Sturgis

Overview, 308; Background, 308; Physiological Disorders, 310; Reproductive Disorders, 323; Conclusion, 334; References, 335

CHAPTER 13. ANXIETY-RELATED DISORDERS, FEARS, AND PHOBIAS 341

Wendy J. Padawer and Marvin R. Goldfried

Background, 342; Anxiety-Related Disorders in Women, 347; Conclusions, 364; Acknowledgments, 365; References, 365

CHAPTER 14. WEIGHT DISORDERS: OVERWEIGHT AND ANOREXIA 373

Iris Goldstein Fodor and Jodi Thal

Overview, 373; Background, 374; Social Conditioning of Acceptable Body Types, 377; Treatment of Overweight and Anorexia, 379; The Basic Self-Control Program, 381; New Directions in Behavioral Treatment of Overweight, 385; Anorexia: The Obsession with Thinness, 386; Expanded Behavioral Treatment for Weight Disorders, 388; Conclusions and Recommendations, 393; References, 394

PART IV: NEGLECTED POPULATIONS, 399

CHAPTER 15. FEMALE DELINQUENTS   401
Janet R. Warburton and James F. Alexander

Overview, 401; Background: Stereotypes and Data, 402; Explanatory Models, 406; Treatment Approaches, 412; Modifying Family Relationship Patterns, 416; Social and Political Implications of Intervention with Female Delinquents, 419; Conclusions and Recommendations, 422; References, 423

CHAPTER 16. WOMEN AND ALCOHOLISM   428
Barbara S. McCrady

Overview, 428; Background, 429; Identification of Drinking Problems in Women, 431; Remaining in Treatment, 433; Behavioral Assessment, 434; Behavioral Interventions with Women Drinkers, 439; Evaluation of Treatment Outcome for Women Alcoholics, 444; Conclusions and Recommendations, 446; References, 447

CHAPTER 17. AGING WOMEN   450
Patricia A. Wisocki

Overview, 450; Background, 451; Empirical Data about the Elderly, 454; Selected Clinical Problems of Elderly Women, 461; Behavioral Interventions with the Elderly, 465; Conclusions and Recommendations, 470; References, 470

CHAPTER 18. MENTALLY RETARDED MOTHERS   477
Karen S. Budd and Stephen Greenspan

Overview, 477; Background, 477; Research on Mentally Retarded Parents, 482; Factors Contributing to Inadequacies of Mentally Retarded Parents, 486; Behavioral Interventions with Mentally Retarded Mothers, 489; Conclusions, 501; Acknowledgments, 502; References, 503

AUTHOR INDEX   507
SUBJECT INDEX   531

I

BASIC ISSUES

The first four chapters of this book treat theoretical and practical issues central to behavior modification with women. Competence—its operational definition and validation—is the topic of Chapter 1. Because little is known about the behavior of competent women, skill training with women clients relies excessively on unproven assumptions. The strategy that is proposed for measuring competence can be used to identify competent women, to set treatment goals, and to measure the general effects of treatment for dysfunctional behavior. Using this strategy, interventions can be designed for women clients which narrow the gap between them and more competent women, while ameliorating their behavior deficits and excesses. It is assumed that competence can be improved by a variety of behavioral strategies and that women achieve competence through traditional and modern life-styles. At the same time, work and marriage have significant effects on women's competence which need to be anticipated when behavioral interventions are designed.

Considerable criticism has been directed at behaviorists who have modified the motor behavior of effeminate boys. In Chapter 2 Beck and Barlow, active researchers on sex-role motor behavior, provide a thoughtful discussion of these issues. Rather than infer psychological androgyny from self-report measures, Beck and Barlow show how an objective measure can be used to assess motor behavior and to improve women's behavioral flexibility. At a time when speculation about the consequences of behavioral flexibility for species survival is a popular topic, Barlow's motor-behavior checklist provides an empirical method of testing the effects of behavioral flexibility. For the behaviorists who doubt the effects of sex and gender on behavior, Beck and Barlow describe the links between anatomy and behavioral destiny.

In Chapter 3 MacDonald provides a thorough review of the strategies of behavioral assessment, together with a detailed consideration of how bias can creep into the assessment process. Her novel and unified approach to sex-fair behavioral assessment is consistent with the positions of many contributors to this volume. In the treatment of depression, and sexual dysfunction, sex-fair assessment can be used to select from available treatment strategies. In the treatment of other disorders

1

such as obesity, sex-fair assessment may reveal the inadequacies of popular treatment strategies and the need for innovation.

Effective prevention and treatment of women's behavior problems
requires dissemination of technological innovations to consumers and
to professionals. In Chapter 4 Stolz argues for a technology of dissemination which uses basic principles of generalization of behavior to
spread information among people. In fact, Stolz suggests that the same
scientific rigor be applied to dissemination of behavior modification as
is now used to evaluate its efficacy. Applied researchers have begun to
design their treatments with generalization in mind; Stolz urges them
to take the next step and to plan for dissemination in the early stages
of treatment design. Many of the criticisms of behavior modification
with women expressed in subsequent chapters of the volume acquire
new meaning after Stolz's chapter is read. Criticisms seem to fall into
two categories: Ineffective or unproven treatments are disseminated too
quickly, and effective treatments are disseminated too slowly or distorted
during the adoption process. Stolz's chapter suggests how applied researchers, clinicians, and consumer groups can respond to valid criticism
by improving the diffusion of technical knowledge about treatment of
women.

1

WOMEN'S BEHAVIOR IN A MAN'S WORLD: SEX DIFFERENCES IN COMPETENCE

ELAINE A. BLECHMAN

OVERVIEW

The world tends to treat a woman differently from a man, even when the two have similar capabilities. Around puberty, and again at marriage, women's social environments become more structured; this interferes with the acquisition and maintenance of problem-solving skills and impairs women's achievement and interpersonal competence. The by-products of reduced competence are life crises, poor physical health, psychopathology, and dysphoric mood. The individual woman's learning history determines the extent to which the highly structured female world impairs her competence, and it determines what by-products of incompetence will affect her. A valid measure of competence and a model of the acquisition of competence are badly needed. Their absence accounts for several problems in contemporary behavior modification with women.

Most behavioral interventions with women focus on the incidental by-products of incompetence, attempting, for example, to alleviate depression or improve parenting behavior. The effects of intervention on the woman's competence at work and at home tend to be ignored. It is impossible to determine whether an intervention that remediated a woman's specific presenting problem, improved or impaired her competence. Most behavioral interventions with women, which are of the skill-training variety, treat specific skill deficits as if they are unrelated

Elaine A. Blechman. Department of Psychology, Wesleyan University, Middletown, Connecticut.

to the way the woman leads the rest of her life. Although behaviorists acknowledge the pernicious effects of the social environment on problems common among women, they direct most of their energies to the short-term skill training of individual women. Evidence that women with disparate skill deficits have a common deficit in competence might convince some behaviorists to engineer life settings that promote competence in women and prevent the numerous ill-effects of incompetence.

This chapter provides an operational definition of competence and describes how competence can be measured in child and adult populations. Evidence gathered among school-aged children is presented to support the construct validity of this definition. The decline of achievement competence among adolescent women is discussed, relevant social learning theories of depression are reviewed, and a model of the acquisition of competence is proposed.

BACKGROUND

Normality and adjustment are no longer idealized by the public or by social and behavioral scientists. Competence has gained acceptance as a goal at work and school, and even in psychological treatment. There are a number of conceptual definitions of competence in the general psychological and behavioral literatures. Each definition has its strength, but none lends itself to the measurement of competence in people of different ages, abilities, and life circumstances.

COMPETENCE AS MASTERY OF CULTURALLY RELEVANT TASKS

The most popular descriptions of competence come from the anthropological and sociological literatures, and equate competence with mastery of culturally relevant tasks (Connolly & Bruner, 1974; Inkeles, 1968; LeVine, 1967; Ogbu, 1981; White, 1979). As Ogbu (1981) pointed out, when competence is not measured by culturally relevant tasks, absurd conclusions result. For example, when children's performance is measured only on tasks relevant to life in a middle-class suburb, lower-class children will be found incompetent, even though they survive in surroundings that would defeat middle-class children.

COMPETENCE AS MASTERY OF CHALLENGING TASKS

In the psychological literature, competence, which has been called mastery, effectance, and achievement motivation, is measured by performance at challenging laboratory tasks (Harter, 1975, 1977; Harter & Zigler, 1974; Molnar & Weisz, 1981). Sex differences in performance and in preference for challenging tasks, favoring boys, have often been found; how early these differences emerge is unclear (e.g., Harter, 1977; Molnar & Weisz, 1981). The sex difference in mastery behavior appears to be influenced by the social setting. Harter (1975) reported that boys (but not girls), played longer at unsolvable than at solvable tasks. Girls, however, played longer at unsolvable tasks when an experimenter was present than when the experimenter was absent.

COMPETENCE AS MASTERY OF DAILY LIFE PROBLEMS

The best-defined concept of competence is found in the clinical psychology literature. Zigler and Phillips (1960) measured the ability of psychiatric patients to cope with the demands of daily life; they defined this ability as premorbid social competence and conceived of it as a broad though imperfect bench mark of developmental maturity. They measured premorbid social competence by combining scores for age, intelligence, education, occupation, employment history, and marital status. In numerous studies this formula has predicted outcome of psychiatric hospitalization better than any other available information (Zigler & Levine, 1981). This formula which uses the products of behavior to assess how well the individual copes, predicts success in psychiatric treatment, but not satisfaction with one's accomplishments. Achenbach and Zigler (1963) reported that among adult patients, dissatisfaction, or the disparity between real and ideal self-image, increased with premorbid social competence.

Women generally score higher on premorbid social competence than men, perhaps because when first hospitalized, women are older, better educated, married, and employed at higher prestige jobs (Zigler & Levine, 1981). This sex difference in premorbid social competence might come about because more inadequacy is tolerated among women than among men (Farina, Garmezy, & Barry, 1963); women's performance in marriage and community life, and at work, may be judged by lower standards. On the other hand, the sex difference in premorbid social competence might be an artifact, attributable to the fact that low-paying,

feminine, clerical positions score somewhat higher on occupational prestige measures than low-paying, masculine, laborer jobs.

COMPETENCE AS ANDROGYNOUS SEX TYPING

An interest in activities generally favored by one's own sex was considered a prerequisite of psychosexual adjustment by psychodynamic trait
theorists (Fenichel, 1953; Freud, 1923/1961; Jahoda, 1977), and early social
learning theorists (Bandura & Walters, 1963; Gewirtz & Stingle, 1968;
Miller & Dollard, 1941; Sears, 1957). After social learning theory revi-
sionists challenged the concept of psychosexual adjustment and the
centrality of same-sex typing (Bandura, 1969, 1977a, 1977b; Gewirtz,
1969; Maccoby, 1966; Maccoby & Jacklin, 1974; Mischel, 1966, 1970, 1973),
Bem (1974) devised a self-report inventory which quantifies same-sex
and opposite-sex interests and abilities. Androgynous people, who have
a broader range of interests and abilities than either same-sex or opposite-sex typed individuals, are presumed to be particularly competent.
This presumption has gained empirical support. Androgynous subjects
reported the fewest, and undifferentiated subjects reported the most,
socially undesirable traits (Kelly, Caudill, Hathorn, & O'Brien, 1977).
When men and women role-played situations requiring the appropriate
expression of commendatory or refusal assertiveness, androgynous subjects were most effective on rated skill components for both situations,
and undifferentiated subjects were the least effective (Kelly, O'Brien,
& Hosford, 1981). Among high school students, androgyny was associated with better psychological adjustment for females, while masculine
sex typing was associated with better adjustment for males (Massad,
1981).

COMPETENCE AS SOCIAL SKILL

The mastery motivation literature, which was discussed earlier, equated
competence with mastery of challenging laboratory tasks, most of which
were of an impersonal, cognitive nature. The recent behavioral literature
equates competence with mastery of real-life, interpersonal problems
(Foster & Ritchey, 1979; McFall, 1982). It is easy to determine when an
individual has succeeded at a cognitive, laboratory task, such as solution
of a set of anagrams. Determination of success at real-life, interpersonal
problems is more difficult; consensus about a "positive effect" (Foster

& Ritchey, 1979) is not readily achieved. Recognizing that objective criteria for social effectiveness are unavailable, and that short-term effectiveness may not predict long-term results, Wolf (1978) recommended that experts or peers judge the effectiveness of a given pattern of behavior. Or, a pattern of behavior might be presumed effective if it is frequently demonstrated by people known to be successful on relevant dimensions. Wolf's social validation approach presumes that it is possible to isolate an effective pattern of behavior for each task in question. McFall (1982) on the other hand, assumes that success at a task can be achieved in many different ways, by many different skills; he calls this the principle of equifinality.

REQUIREMENTS FOR AN OPERATIONAL DEFINITION OF COMPETENCE

The concepts reviewed above suggest three directions for an operational definition of competence and its validation:

   1. Measure success at challenging culturally and subculturally relevant tasks. A measure of competence at achievement and interpersonal relationships takes into account domains that are important to both sexes, and bridges the concerns of the mastery and social-skills literatures.
   2. Quantify task outcome rather than instrumental behavior. Criteria are available for successful task outcomes, but not for successful instrumental behavior. The principle of equifinality suggests that the number of patterns of successful instrumental behavior may be infinite. Premorbid social competence, an extremely well-defined concept applicable to psychiatric patients, is measured by outcomes at common life tasks.
   3. If the measure of competence has construct validity, people who score high on competence will have androgynous interests.

COMPETENCE IS RELATIVE SUCCESS AT ACHIEVEMENT AND INTERPERSONAL TASKS

If competence (C) is to be defined as relative success at pertinent interpersonal and achievement tasks, then terms in this simple formula need to be defined: $C = A + I$. Success at achievement (A) is the mean of objective indices of current performance at school (for children and adolescents), and at work (for adults). Objective measures of achievement include salary, occupational prestige ratings, achievement test scores, and school grades. Success at interpersonal tasks (I) is the mean of subjective, self- and other-evaluations of the individual's current performance on relevant interpersonal dimensions (e.g., friend, family member, co-worker).

Since competence has been defined as *relative* success, standards of comparison are needed. These can be derived by gathering achievement and interpersonal scores from a group of peers, and using relative standing in the group to assess competence. Thus scores might be gathered from classes of schoolchildren, or from adults who reside in the same neighborhood. Competence has been defined as success at *pertinent* interpersonal and achievement tasks. Within limits, this definition permits the measurement of children and adults, of literate college students, and of mute psychiatric patients. Thus scholastic achievement tests would be used to score the achievement success of school-aged children, while occupational prestige ratings would be used to score the achievement success of adults. Since scores are to be gathered from a group of peers, the individual's competence relative to similarly measured peers will be easy to derive. In order to compare the competence scores of individuals measured with different instruments, achievement and interpersonal scores must be standardized using the mean and standard deviation of the peer group.

An interpersonal score has been included in the competence measure because peer ratings predict social adjustment (Roff, Sells, & Golden, 1972); inclusion of the interpersonal score insures that material well-being is not the sole criterion of competence. Self-ratings are included in the interpersonal score to insure that deviant or socially isolated individuals are not underestimated. An achievement score has been included in the competence measure because in industrialized societies, school achievement, income, and occupational status predict self-esteem and psychological adjustment (Blau & Duncan, 1967; Kohlberg, La-Crosse, & Ricks, 1970). The proposed operational definition provides a strategy for measuring competence, but does not dictate which of the available and relevant instruments should be used to derive achievement and interpersonal scores.

IS THIS DEFINITION OF COMPETENCE FAIR TO WOMEN?

Using this definition of competence, sex differences favoring men are very likely. There is no question about sex differences on the achievement score for adults. As a group, women earn 40% less than men in similar jobs. If achievement success is a major determinant of peer evaluations and of self-esteem, then men will also have higher interpersonal scores. Since women may compensate for their lower achievement scores with higher interpersonal scores, questions about sex differences in competence can only be answered by empirical research. Feminists may argue that this definition does no more than emphasize well-documented differences between the sexes. This argument ignores the fact that competence, measured in this manner, will vary within the sexes as well as between them. To the extent that this measure distinguishes between competent and less competent women, it will facilitate investigation of the acquisition of competence by women. Traditionalists may argue that this definition makes work a precondition for competence in women. This argument ignores the possibility that traditional and modern women may prove equally competent, the former because of their high interpersonal scores, the latter because of their high achievement scores (Friedan, 1981).

VALIDATION OF THE CONSTRUCT OF COMPETENCE

When discussing requirements for an operational definition, I noted that if a measure of competence has construct validity, then people who score high on competence will have androgynous interests. The proposed definition, which includes an achievement and an interpersonal score, is likely to detect competent people with androgynous interests. Common sense and available research suggest that if the competence measure has construct validity, then competent people will have other favorable characteristics. They should be relatively happy and healthy, high in self-esteem and moral judgment, and internal in locus-of-control. They should experience few life crises, job losses, disrupted marriages, major illnesses, and suicide attempts (Farina et al., 1963; Leavitt, Garron, & Bieliauskas, 1980; Lloyd, 1980; Slater & Depue, 1981).

The expectation that people who are competent at achievement and interpersonal tasks will have many fortunate life experiences is supported by considerable evidence. Peer nominations, observer ratings of interpersonal behavior, and ratings of role performance derived from structured interviews distinguish between depressed and nondepressed people, and between people who report many and people who report few, stressful life events (Lefkowitz & Tesiny, 1980; Lewinsohn & Libet,

1972; MacPhillamy & Lewinsohn, 1974; Paykel & Weissman, 1973; Rad-loff & Rae, 1979). Seeman (1966) and Duncan (1966) found that college women and men highly rated by their peers, had more positive self-concepts, outside contacts, and intellectual efficiency. Achievement test scores and income account for the majority of variance in numerous measures of life adjustment (Kohlberg, LaCrosse, & Ricks, 1970; Roff, Knight, & Wertheim, 1976; Steinberg, Catalano, & Dooley, 1981).

COMPETENCE AND SOCIOECONOMIC STATUS

This definition of competence incorporates income and occupational data used to construct measures of socioeconomic status (SES). Competence, however, differs from SES. Measures of SES are almost exclusively designed for adult male populations (Mueller & Parcel, 1981; Nock & Rossi, 1979). In contrast, the competence measure can be applied to both sexes, and to school-aged, adolescent, and adult populations. Unlike the measure of competence, measures of SES do not assess intangible interpersonal accomplishments. Measures of SES cannot discriminate within a homogeneous population; the competence measure, because it is standardized on a population of peers, can make fine intragroup distinctions. Thus the competence measure can be used to identify relatively competent members of a poor, urban neighborhood, and relatively incompetent members of a wealthy suburb. Measures of SES invariably find that women have less status than men, since women are more often unemployed, and earn considerably less than men (Featherman & Hauser, 1976), and since female occupations have less prestige than male occupations (Touhey, 1974). In contrast, the competence measure does not rely exclusively on work status.

INCOMPETENCE AND PSYCHOPATHOLOGY

If this definition of competence is valid, then individuals who are incompetent at interpersonal and achievement tasks are likely to demonstrate a disproportionately high incidence of psychopathology. A low rate of self-reinforcement (including few positive self-evaluations) appears to be characteristic of most psychopathological disorders (Gotlib, 1981). Psychiatric patients, particularly depressed and schizophrenic individuals, tend to be unpopular with peers (Boswell & Murray, 1981).

Cognitive deficits characteristic of schizophrenia tend to deflate achievement test scores (Lewine, 1981) and to limit employment prospects.

VALIDATION OF THE CONSTRUCT OF COMPETENCE WITH SCHOOL-AGED CHILDREN

A recent study (Blechman, 1982) tested the construct validity of the competence measure in order to improve intervention strategies for vulnerable children (Blechman, Kotanchik, & Taylor, 1981; Blechman, Taylor, & Schrader, 1981). Since the reader can refer to the full report for details, I have summarized statistical findings; the term significant findings refers to p values less than .05. To accomplish this study, teachers in four elementary schools in a city of 50,000 people were recruited; their schools represented all family income levels equally. One month after school began, the homeroom teachers sent letters to the parents of all 900 children in their classes inviting their cooperation. During the preceding spring the school system had administered the SCAT (School College Ability Test) and the STEP (Sequential Test of Educational Progress) tests (Educational Testing Service) to children in grades 2 to 5, and the Circus Test (Educational Testing Service) to children who were in grade 1. The peer-nomination questionnaire was administered to all children during a class testing session. Using class lists children circled names in response to eight questions such as "Who would you like to sit next to in class?," and "Who are the best artists?"

To provide independent tests of the competence construct, four questionnaires were administered to randomly selected subsets of classes. The validating questionnaires were the Children's Locus of Control Scale (Bialer, 1961); a short form of the Coopersmith Self-Esteem Scale (Coopersmith, 1967); a measure of children's sex-typed attitudes, the Children's Personal Attributes Questionnaire (Hall & Halberstadt, 1980); and the Peer Nomination Inventory of Depression (Lefkowitz & Tesiny, 1980). In addition, from the 43 classroom teachers, volunteers were sought to rate children on the same dimensions used by children to rate themselves and their peers.

CHARACTERISTICS OF THE STUDY SAMPLE

In the four elementary schools, nine second grades, eight third grades, six fourth grades, ten fifth grades, and ten sixth grades participated.

Competence scores could be constructed for 566 children of the 641 children who were allowed to participate. The sample included 296 girls and 270 boys ranging in age from 6 to 13 with a mean age of 9 years.

THE COMPOSITE ACHIEVEMENT AND PEER-NOMINATION SCORES

The Circus Score for young children is the equivalent of the STEP score for older children, but there is no equivalent of the older children's SCAT score. The aptitude (SCAT) and performance (STEP) scores were highly and significantly correlated, and age had a clear and expected effect on these scores. Therefore, the SCAT and STEP scores were transformed to z scores using the means and standard deviations of the child's grade. Then the two z scores were averaged, yielding a standardized academic performance score. Univariate ANOVAs showed that girls had significantly higher scores than boys, and that scores dropped as family size increased. Many significant intercorrelations among peer-nomination scores warranted a combined peer-nomination score. The peer-nomination scores were therefore transformed into standardized z scores using the means and standard deviations of the child's school grade and a total standardized peer-nomination score was calculated for each child. There were no significant differences by gender, family size, or number of parents for the combined peer-nomination score.

ASSIGNMENT TO THE FOUR COMPETENCE GROUPS

Pearson's r tested the association between the standardized academic performance score and the standardized peer-nomination score, and revealed a small but significant positive association, such that 8% of the variance in one could be predicted from knowledge of the other.

The distribution of composite achievement scores was split at the median as was the distribution of peer nomination scores, and each child was placed in one of four groups. The competent group included children who scored above the median on both dimensions. The incompetent group included children who scored below the median on both dimensions. The bookworm (high achievement, low interpersonal) and social butterfly (low achievement, high interpersonal) groups included children who scored above the median on one dimension and below the median on another. As a result, there were 175 children (105 girls, 70 boys) in the competent group, 168 children (86 girls, 82 boys) in the incompetent group, 110 children (60 girls, 50 boys) in the bookworm group, and 113 children (45 girls, 68 boys) in the social butterfly group. The four groups did not differ significantly in respect to number of parents heading the family. There were significant differences between groups in family size. Children from larger families were most likely to be in the incompetent group.

VALIDITY OF THE CONSTRUCT OF COMPETENCE

If the construct of competence is valid, then children in the competent group should score higher on all validating measures than the other groups, and children in the incompetent group should score lower than all other groups on all validating measures. The findings support this hypothesis. To test this hypothesis, separate ANOVAs had to be run since different subsets of the population took different validating tests. There was some overlap, because most children took more than one test, but not enough to require multivariate ANOVAs. Accordingly, univariate one-way ANOVAs (competent, incompetent, bookworm, social butterfly) were run on each validating measure; following significant Fs, a priori contrasts tested hypotheses about differences between groups and yielded these statistically significant findings. Children in the competent group scored higher than any other group on peer nominations and achievement, happiness, teacher nominations, feminine attributes, and internal locus of control. They scored lowest of all groups on depression. On self-nominations and on social self-esteem they scored at the grand mean, and below the social butterfly group. On occupational aspirations they scored below the bookworm group and above the incompetent and social butterfly, low achievement groups. Thus, the competent group who were extremely high achievers and very well liked, were happy, rarely depressed, frequently nominated by teachers for excellence, high in feminine interests, and internal in locus of control. They had relatively high occupational aspirations, average self-nominations, and social self-esteem. These competent children, like the high-achieving bookworms, had parents with high occupational prestige. Their mothers had the second highest occupational prestige ratings and their fathers had the highest prestige ratings of all groups.

The incompetent group scored lowest of the four groups on achievement, peer nominations, teacher nominations, femininity, internality, and happiness. They scored highest of all groups on depression. On self-nominations and social self-esteem, their scores were higher than only one group, the bookworms. The occupational aspirations of the incompetent group equaled the social butterfly group and fell below the competent and bookworm groups. In short, the children in the incompetent group had the most unfavorable scores on all measures except self-nominations, social self-esteem, and occupational aspirations. These incompetent children, like the social butterflies, had parents with low occupational prestige. Their mothers had the third lowest occupational prestige ratings and their fathers had the lowest prestige ratings of all groups.

These findings support the construct validity of this measure of competence. Children who had high interpersonal and achievement scores excelled on almost all of the independent validity measures. As expected, the competent children demonstrated an androgynous interest pattern. Given the continuing debate about the impact of working mothers, it is interesting to note that competent children had mothers who worked at high-prestige jobs, while incompetent children's mothers worked at low-status jobs or not at all. Research in progress employs a similarly constructed measure of competence with an adolescent and an adult population.

THE UNEXPLAINED DECLINE IN WOMEN'S ACHIEVEMENT COMPETENCE

In the study just reported, girls and boys were proportionately represented in the competent group; this finding is consistent with other evidence that during childhood, girls' achievement and interpersonal competence equals or exceeds that of boys (Bank, Biddle, & Good, 1980; Dweck, Davidson, Nelson, & Enna, 1978; Dweck & Goetz, 1978; Morgan, 1979). A dramatic and poorly explained change takes place during adolescence, when women's achievement competence declines, and women increasingly experience the accompaniments of incompetence, including life crises, physical and psychological complaints, dysphoric mood and attitudes. By the time of young adulthood, women, particularly married women, fare worse on all these dimensions than men.

ACHIEVEMENT INCOMPETENCE

When test scores are used to measure achievement, consistent sex differences do not emerge. Maccoby and Jacklin (1974) asserted that there are well-established sex differences in quantitative and visual–spatial ability which favor boys, and that girls' quantitative ability declines around age 14. Others contend that the magnitude of these differences is small (Hyde, 1981; Plomin & Foch, 1981), and that the differences are an ephemeral product of recent experience. According to deWolf (1981), the quantitative shift is entirely due to a changing interest pattern in high school, since math achievement has been found to be the same for both sexes when amount of math coursework is held constant.

Clear, consistent sex differences do emerge when occupational prestige ratings and salary levels are used to measure achievement competence. Women are the lowest paid, lowest status members of every trade and profession (Giraldo & Weatherford, 1978; Gottfredson & Swatko, 1979; Lenney, 1977). The occupation of homemaker is not found on any widely used scale of occupational prestige (Haug, 1974; Mueller & Parcel, 1981; Nilson, 1978). Only in part is this an artifact of the rating scales. Homemakers have little prestige in their own right; their social standing depends on the accomplishments of their fathers, husbands, and children.

Sex differences in occupational achievement are supported by observers' opinions. Etaugh and Brown (1975) found that no matter what women do, they are viewed as less skillful than men. Inwold and Bryant (1981) reported that in small, decision-making groups, the arguments made by men were more often accepted by the group than were the arguments made by women. This held true, even though women advanced as many proposals as men, and whether or not group members were familiar with one another. Women are generally given lower evaluations than men by job interviewers when the job candidates have similar or even identical qualifications; race, by comparison, has not been found to have such systematic biasing effects on employment decisions (Arvey, 1979).

Sex differences in occupational achievement are also supported by women's opinions about themselves. On a digit-guessing task, women stressed poor ability as a cause for failure, far more often than men (Pasquella, Mednick, & Murray, 1981). Women took less credit for successful performance at a teaching task than they were given credit for by observers (Beckman, 1973). Women attributed less competence to themselves after succeeding or failing at a social-sensitivity task (Schlenker, 1975). On a word-analogies task, there were no performance differences between men and women. However, compared to men, women felt worse, less competent, and less happy, after success and after failure. After success, women felt less satisfied, believed their scores were lower, expected to perform worse in the future, and rewarded themselves less (Curtis, 1981). Berg and colleagues (Berg, Stephan, & Dodson, 1981) use the term attributional modesty to describe women's self-derogatory attitudes. In three experiments, they found that women were particularly modest when they knew their attributions would be publicized, and when they anticipated that they would perform the same tasks in the future.

Restating these findings using the proposed definition of competence: Men are likely to achieve higher global competence scores than women, because of men's superior achievement competence. During childhood, there are few sex differences in achievement competence. During adolescence, when the focus is on educational achievement, sex differences emerge and favor men, particularly when quantitative and scientific accomplishment is measured. During young adulthood, and thereafter, when achievement is measured by occupational accomplishment, men surpass women. Of all adults, married women will have the lowest global competence scores, due to their low occupational achievement. Competence was defined in such a way that men and women could prove equally competent, although the source of their competence might differ. Interpersonal accomplishments might raise women's competence scores, and achievement accomplishments might raise men's competence scores. Yet the evidence suggests that in the real world, the interpersonal and achievement components of the competence score are never orthogonal. In Western industrialized countries, what people achieve at work determines how well they think of themselves, and how much they are respected and liked by others. Thus, a large sex difference in achievement competence may be accompanied by a smaller sex difference in interpersonal competence, both of which favor men. Certainly, the distributions of men's and women's competence scores overlap, so that large numbers of men and women are equally compe-

tent. Despite the overlap of distributions, there appear to be a disproportionate number of competent men and incompetent women.

CONCOMITANTS OF INCOMPETENCE

If the construct of competence proposed here is valid, then incompetent
people will experience an excess of stressful life events, poor physical
health, psychopathology, and dysphoric mood. Evidence suggesting
that there are a disproportionate number of incompetent women has
just been discussed. There is also evidence that the presumed accompaniments of incompetence more often befall women than men, and
married women more often than single women. During adolescence,
women's psychological adjustment and physical health begins to decline
(Baumrind, 1980). The physical disorders which predominate among
women and begin in adolescence include anorexia, obesity, agoraphobia,
and depression. By adulthood, women are disproportionately overrepresented among the consumers of every type of health care (Gove,
1980; Ilfeld, 1978; *President's Commission on Mental Health*, 1978). Among
adults, women report the most life crises, and married women, the most
depressive symptoms (Radloff & Rae, 1979). In general, marriage appears to improve men's quality of life, and to worsen women's (Bernard,
1973). Mortality rates are lower for married than for single men (Gove,
1980); and the disruption of marriage appears more stressful for men
than for women (Bloom, Asher, & White, 1978).

If sex differences in competence are originally caused by cultural
biases which advance men in the workplace (as the lack of marked sex
differences in educational achievement suggests), then the construct of
competence might be said to describe differences between environments
rather than differences between men and women. Unfortunately, the
environment leaves enduring marks on people. As a group, women
seem to suffer from more of the accompaniments of incompetence than
do men. They carry these from workplace to home, and from adolescence
to later life, in the form of poor psychological and physical health, and
an abundance of life crises. Thus the construct of competence describes
differences between people as well as between environments. In and of
itself, the construct of competence does not explain the decline in competence among adolescent women, nor does it explain the particular
handicaps of married women.

SOCIAL LEARNING THEORIES OF DEPRESSION

Contemporary learning theories of depression, which were formulated
to account for the process of adult depression, have been used to explain
sex differences in the incidence of depression. By extrapolation, these
theories are relevant to sex differences in competence. Each of the prominent theories assumes that a different, critical pattern of deficient behavior accounts for the manifestations of depression, and dictates the
ingredients of successful treatment. For Beck (1974) the critical pattern
involves cognitions about the world, one's self, and one's future. For
the revised, learned helplessness group (Abramson, Seligman, & Teasdale, 1978; Miller & Norman, 1979; Miller & Seligman, 1975; Seligman,
Abramson, Semmel, & vonBaeyer, 1979) the critical pattern involves
initiation of, and persistence at, frustrating tasks, along with congruent
attributions for task outcome. For Kanfer and Rehm (Kanfer & Hagerman, 1979; Rehm, 1977) the critical pattern involves self-regulation. For
Lewinsohn the pattern involves social behavior instrumental in the occurrence of pleasing events (Lewinsohn, 1974; Lewinsohn & Libet, 1972;
Lewinsohn, Mischel, Chaplin, & Barton, 1980).

Learned helplessness theory has been used to explain the onset of
depression in traditional women (Bart, 1975; Radloff & Monroe, 1978).
Yet learned helplessness theory and other social learning theories of
depression focus exclusively on social reinforcement of depressogenic
behavior patterns. For this reason they provide inadequate accounts of
the etiology of depression in women since they cannot explain the following circumstances. The peak years for incidence of depression in
women are in late adolescence (Eme, 1979; Weissman & Klerman, 1977);
if pathology occurs because parents and teachers reinforce feminine and
depressogenic behavior, depression should emerge earlier. Married and
formerly married women are particularly susceptible to depression (Radloff & Rae, 1979); there is no reason to believe that the consequences for
a woman's behavior are unique simply because she is married. The
learned helplessness paradigm seems at first to explain the etiology of
depression in women, just as the fear-of-failure paradigm seems to explain women's low salaries and underemployment (Riger & Galligan,
1980). As etiological explanations, the two paradigms have the same
flaw; they ignore environmental abuses and use fictitious personality
traits to account for women's difficulties.

Not all social learning models of adult behavior focus on pathology.
Social learning theorists have proposed accounts of general adult com-

petence and efficacy (Bandura, 1977a; Bandura, Adams, Hardy, & Howells, 1980; Mischel, 1973) that link public behavior, private cognitions
and affect, and external events. It is difficult to employ these theories
to explain sex differences in competence since these theories do not
postulate sex-linked differences in the social consequences of behavior,
they do not attempt to account for sex differences in competence, nor
do they integrate developmental data about the transitions from childhood to adolescence and adulthood.

According to Radloff and Rae (1979), social learning theories provide
only circular explanations of women's heightened susceptibility to
depression. Between 1971 and 1973, they questioned 2515 White adults
in Missouri and Maryland about psychological and physiological complaints, especially about symptoms of depression. They found that
women who were married, formerly married, or not married/not heads
of own households, were significantly more depressed than their male
counterparts. Among the widowed or never married/heads of own
households, men were as depressed as women. The same life events
were associated with depression in men and in women, including low
occupational status, low income, little education, social isolation, and
physical illness. Women, however, were exposed to about twice as many
precipitating conditions as men. Even when exposure to precipitating
conditions was held constant, women who were married, formerly married, or single/not heads of own households, were still more depressed
than their male counterparts.

Because controlling for exposure to precipitating life events did not
eliminate differences in depression between married women and men,
Radloff and Rae concluded that there probably is a sex difference in
susceptibility to depression which is partly biological and partly learned.
They proposed a two-factor sequential model to explain the etiology of
depression. One factor, susceptibility, is the product of the individual's
learning history. People who learn pessimistic cognitions and helpless
behavior, either directly or vicariously, are highly susceptible to depression. The second factor, precipitating conditions, represents life problems and crises. Susceptibility is latent until a precipitating condition
occurs which demands goal-oriented problem solving and persistent
action. The more susceptible the individual, the more likely the person
is to respond inadequately to the crisis and experience objective failure
and subjective distress. In a vicious cycle, helpless cognitions and behavior tendencies are strengthened by failure and distress, and the
chance of future exposure to precipitating conditions rises. Finally the

somatic dimension of depression sets in with disturbances of appetite and sleep.

As an explanation for sex differences in depression, Radloff and Rae's (1979) model is an improvement over other social learning theories which fail to provide a central role to adult environments in their models. However, Radloff and Rae's model applies only to depression; it does not account for the adolescent decrement in competence experienced by many women, nor does it account for the relative incompetence of married women.

PROBLEM-SOLVING SKILL, ACTIVITY STRUCTURE, AND COMPETENCE

If the acquisition of competence, and its by-products such as depression, are to be explained, then the individual's current behavior and characteristics of the surrounding environment must be considered (Blechman, 1980a, 1980b, 1981). Such a model can be summarized by the formula $C = P \times -S$, where C is the global competence score; P, the individual's current level of problem-solving skill; and S, the level of activity structure in the individual's daily activities. This model posits that competence increases with problem-solving skill and decreases with level of activity structure; and, problem-solving skill and activity structure affect one another.

LEVEL OF PROBLEM-SOLVING SKILL

Level of problem-solving skill can be assessed by the number of solutions an individual achieves when confronted with novel interpersonal and impersonal problems. The ideal test of problem-solving skill employs many samples of work and interpersonal problems which are confronted by people of the same age. The large item pool permits repeated testing. Scores are standardized using the mean and standard deviation for that age group. Since these are all characteristics of standardized intelligence tests, it is reasonable to use such tests to gauge level of problem-solving skill. No other measure predicts performance on so many different cognitive and interpersonal problems (Kohlberg, LaCrosse, & Ricks, 1970; Zigler & Trickett, 1978). Use of an intelligence test score to estimate problem-solving skill does not imply that intelligence is an enduring trait, unaffected by current situations. Nevertheless, reliability of intelligence test scores over time suggests that people tend to be exposed to new settings that are similar to the ones they now inhabit.

A well-constructed achievement test is criterion-referenced; it samples problems that have been taught in a school curriculum and is only appropriate for students. A well-constructed intelligence test which includes novel problems that challenge the individual's general skills, can be administered to nonstudent adults as well as to children. The intelligence-test score will probably be a significant predictor of children's and adolescent's global competence scores, given the usual positive correlation between achievement and intelligence test scores (Thorndike & Hagen, 1977).

The process of problem solving has been equated by Kendler (1979) with the number and quality of hypotheses that the individual generates and tests when confronted with a problem. Hypotheses are, of course, less amenable to measurement than problem solutions. Tumblin and Gholson (1981) have provided a nonmediational and parsimonious analysis of complex problem solving. They distinguish between response-set hypotheses—simple rules about cause and effect (equivalent to stimulus–response associations)—and prediction hypotheses—complex rules about cause and effect. They assume that prediction hypotheses are composed of response-set hypotheses, and that complex problem solving is learned in the same manner as stimulus–response associations.

DEVELOPMENT OF COMPLEX PROBLEM-SOLVING SKILL

The popular explanation of the development of complex problem-solving skill, credits contingent social reinforcement of partial problem-solving efforts. This hands-on explanation of problem-solving learning involves operations such as these. The problem solver is rewarded with attention and affection for partial and complete solutions to problems; the problem solver is similarly rewarded for experimentation with new problem-solving strategies; complex problem-solving sequences are cued with instructions and verbal examples. Maccoby and Jacklin (1974) explored the hands-on explanation of sex differences in a variety of skill domains and found no evidence of differential socialization practices. The hands-on hypothesis actually embodies a paradox. When parents, teachers, siblings, or peers actively reinforce successful problem-solving behavior, their presence is likely to become a discriminative stimulus for problem-solving efforts, so that only dependent–independent behavior results. This is what Harter (1975) found among girls, who preferred difficult problems only when the experimenter was present. Another shortcoming of the hands-on hypothesis concerns the nature of complex problem solving. Social-reinforcement agents probably cannot discriminate between successful and unsuccessful approximations to many solutions, nor can they respond contingently to a process that is largely covert.

THE FEMALE WORLD

The sociologist Jesse Bernard has recently written about the radically different social environments of men and women. "At school, . . . at church, at work, at play, boys and girls, and men and women, are governed by different norms, rules of behavior, and expectations; they are subject to different eligibility rules for rewards and different vulnerability to punishments. *Sometimes the differences are as great as the differences, if not between species, at least between countries"* (Bernard, 1981, p. 4; emphasis added). Bernard also recounts how responsive women's behavior is to momentary environmental contingencies. "The research literature by men (and by women who have been trained by men) portray women as basically passive and dependent. This portrayal does in fact reflect the way women tend to behave vis-à-vis men or in the presence of men, so that the passive–dependent image seems entirely valid from the perspective of the male world. . . . Actually of course, if women *were* passive and dependent they could hardly survive" (Bernard, 1981, p. 22, *sic*). Bernard's male and female worlds are distinguished by the kinds of activities in which the occupants engage themselves. Differential reinforcement contingencies are a by-product of sex-typed activity patterns; women are expected to excel at feminine activities, men at masculine activities. Masculine and feminine sex-typed activities occur in different social contexts, and they have corresponding effects on problem-solving skills.

ACTIVITY STRUCTURE

An operational definition of sex-typed activities and preliminary evidence of their effects on problem-solving behavior comes from the developmental research of Carpenter, Huston, and colleagues. They found

(Carpenter & Huston-Stein, 1980) that girls spent more time than boys in preschool activities that were highly structured by teacher feedback or availability of adult models, while boys spent more time in less structured activities. Comparisons across classrooms showed that in structured classrooms, children were more compliant, showed less novel behavior, and spent more time in organized activities. A replication and extension (Carpenter, Huston, & Neath, 1981) measured the structure of individual play activities by direct observation of amount of adult availability, individual feedback, and group feedback during each activity. Once again, boys participated more in unstructured activities, and girls participated more in structured activities. All children showed more compliant behavior as the level of activity structure increased, and they issued more requests for help and more bids for recognition in structured activities. In unstructured activities, there was more aggression, leadership attempts, initiation, and peer commands.

Carpenter and colleagues concluded from these two studies that sex-typed socialization occurs through participation in play experiences which represent different psychological environments. This conclusion represents the nucleus of a hands-off explanation of sex differences in competence. Having found natural covariations between behavior and activity structure, Carpenter, Huston, and Holt (1981) experimentally manipulated children's participation in activities that varied in level of structure. Children were selected for participation because they showed extremes of sex-typed behavior, either responsiveness to adults and bids for recognition, or responsiveness to peers and a high rate of leadership attempts. In a counterbalanced, reversal, within-subjects design, each of eight children was placed in high- and low-structure activities for 2 weeks at a time. The predicted effect of activity structure on behavior was observed. There was a consistent carry-over from mandatory activities to a free-play period. Finally a 2-year longitudinal analysis of activity participation (Carpenter, Petrowsky, Powell, & Huston, 1981) demonstrated consistency in children's preference for a particular level of activity structure.

LEVEL OF ACTIVITY STRUCTURE

Level of activity structure might be defined as the proportion of waking hours spent in highly structured leisure or work activities. The level of structure of an individual's activities would be determined from direct observation of the availability in that activity of a live expert or model, and of verbal, individual, and group feedback. An expert is a person whose advice is openly solicited; a model is a person whose behavior is openly imitated. An activity would be classified as high in structure if more than one half of the time spent at the activity involves interaction with an expert or model, or receipt of individual or group feedback. All other activities would be classified as low in structure.

This operational definition of activity structure builds on Carpenter and Huston's work, and allows for classification of adult, as well as child, activity. Using this rubric, most psychotherapy hours would be classified as high in structure. Time spent in most classrooms, would be classified as high in structure. Most solitary activities would be classified as low in structure. The amount of direct supervision a worker receives per hour would determine how high in structure the workplace is for that person. The amount of specific advice, suggestions, criticisms, and demands that a housewife receives at home, per hour, from children, husband, and other people, determine how high in structure the household is for her. This operational definition of activity structure samples all of the individual's waking hours and all of the settings in which the individual spends time. Direct observation of events in those settings, rather than inferences, are used to estimate level of activity structure.

THE INTERACTION BETWEEN PROBLEM-SOLVING SKILL AND ACTIVITY STRUCTURE

This model depicts competence as the result of an interaction between problem-solving skill and activity structure, such that competence increases with level of problem-solving skill, and decreases with level of activity structure. Low levels of activity structure should enhance existing problem-solving skill by providing the individual with ample opportunity to attack problems through trial and error, and to directly experience the natural consequences of the problem-solving effort. High levels of structure should inhibit existing problem-solving skill by making the presence of other people, and their guidance, discriminative stimuli for problem-solving efforts. The converse should also hold true; people with little problem-solving skill are likely to seek out activities with high levels of structure; people with much problem-solving skill are likely to seek out activities with low levels of structure. This model does not apply to people whose basic human needs for physical safety, shelter, and sustenance are not satisfied.

The same high level of structure may be provided by the overindulgent laissez-faire family (in which parents set few goals for their children, and solve many problems for them), as is provided by the authoritarian family (in which parents tell children how to solve many problems). This high level of structure is consistent with the problem-solving deficits of children reared in both family types (Locke, Shaw, Saari, & Latham, 1981). In contrast, the authoritative family, in which parents encourage children to independently accomplish age-appropriate tasks, and tolerate the conflict that occurs when children are frustrated by their failures, may provide a lower level of activity structure than either the authoritarian or the laissez-faire family (Lewis, 1981). The presumption that a low level of activity structure enhances problem solving is confirmed by evidence that authoritative families rear children with superior moral judgment (Haan, Smith, & Block, 1968; Holstein, 1972; Leahy, 1981).

MANIPULATIONS OF ACTIVITY STRUCTURE AND PROBLEM-SOLVING SKILL

When the tasks an individual is confronted with are held constant, a reduction in activity structure should increase problem-solving skill. In addition, manipulations of problem-solving skill should affect preferred activity structure. When the individual learns new problem-solving skills, access to less structured settings often becomes available.

INCREASED ACTIVITY STRUCTURE ACCOUNTS FOR THE DECLINE IN ACHIEVEMENT COMPETENCE OF ADOLESCENT WOMEN, AND FOR THE LOW COMPETENCE OF MARRIED WOMEN

If this model of competence is to prove useful, it must account for the decline of achievement competence among adolescent women, and the preponderance of incompetence among married women. Both can be accounted for by dramatic increases in activity structure when a girl reaches puberty and when she marries. Early in adolescence, compared to their male peers, girls enter more structured, less challenging courses at school, receive more restrictions on physical movements, more advice and more exemptions from unstructured activities (Hull & Schroeder, 1979; Whalen & Flowers, 1977). During adolescence, young women experience protective structure in the form of exclusion from dangerous work, from travel in dangerous areas, and from military combat.

Parents' fears about pregnancy and rape, their concerns about their daughters' marriageability, and adolescent women's recurrent menstrual distress, all contribute to the sudden increase in structure during adolescence. For example, it is estimated that about half of adolescent women (Widholm, 1979) experience severe menstrual discomfort each month because of increased levels of uterine prostaglandins (Reid & Yen, 1981). Menstrual complaints account for more absences by adolescent and young adult women from work and school, than any other single cause (Kistner, 1971). The family, friends, teachers, and physician of a young woman suffering from severe menstrual complaints offer more advice, suggest more restrictions on activity, and solve more problems for the woman than they did before menarche (Lennane & Lennane, 1973). The best available evidence on adult activity structure comes from psychotherapy process studies which indicate that compared to equally troubled men, women receive more help and more tolerance for inadequate behavior (Davidson & Abramowitz, 1980; Haccoun & Lavigueur, 1979; Hammen & Peters, 1978; Stein, DelGaudio, & Ansley, 1976).

Marriage introduces a second increase in activity structure into women's lives. The core responsibilities of married women—household maintenance, cooking, childcare, entertaining—are services performed at others' requests, and to please other people. It seems very likely that in most cases, these tasks have high levels of activity structure. Employed as well as unemployed married women are likely to experience high levels of activity structure. In 52% of all American married couples, both husband and wife are wage earners; in only 12% is the housework shared equally by both spouses (Klemesrud, 1982). Self-selection into marriage by women who prefer highly structured activities may also occur.

CONCLUSIONS AND RECOMMENDATIONS

The competence model presents several low-level hypotheses for future empirical tests:

1. Competence should increase with level of problem-solving skill and decrease with level of activity structure. This relationship

should hold true in correlational research which measures a group of individuals on all three variables, and in experimental research which manipulates one variable and observes the effects on the other two.

2. Average sex differences in competence should be found among men and women who have been systematically exposed to structured and unstructured environments.

3. Developmental research should find a significant increase in the structure of women's activities after puberty and after marriage.

4. The value of the construct of competence lies in its associations with important life events. It should be the case that as competence increases, physical and psychological well-being improve, and life crises diminish.

Applications of the competence model to the clinical domain can only be a topic for speculation. A competence measure used in combination with measures of specific problem behaviors could be used to assess treatment outcome for the whole woman. Treatments might be designed to boost the competence score directly (through manipulations of achievement or interpersonal status), or indirectly (through manipulations of problem-solving skill or activity structure). Given the interdependence of problem-solving skill and activity structure, the most widespread and enduring benefits should result from treatments which attend both to skill training and to environmental change.

ACKNOWLEDGMENTS

Preparation of this chapter was partly supported by NIMH Grant 31403. Correspondence and conversations with Lenore Radloff and Jan Carpenter contributed to the formulation of this chapter.

REFERENCES

Abramson, L. Y., Seligman, M. E. P., & Teasdale, J. D. Learned helplessness in humans: Critique and reformulation. *Journal of Abnormal Psychology*, 1978, *87*, 49–74.

Achenbach, T., & Zigler, E. Social competence and self-image disparity in psychiatric and nonpsychiatric patients. *Journal of Abnormal and Social Psychology*, 1963, *67*, 197–205.

Arvey, R. D. Unfair discrimination in the employment interview: Legal and psychological aspects. *Psychological Bulletin*, 1979, *86*, 736–765.

Bandura, A. Social learning theory of identificatory processes. In D. A. Goslin (Ed.), *Handbook of socialization theory and research*. Chicago: Rand-McNally, 1969.

Bandura, A. Self-efficacy: Toward a unifying theory of behavioral change. *Psychological Review*, 1977, *84*, 191–215. (a)

Bandura, A. *Social learning theory*. Englewood Cliffs, N.J.: Prentice-Hall, 1977. (b)

Bandura, A., Adams, N. E., Hardy, A. B., & Howells, G. N. Tests of the generality of self-efficacy theory. *Cognitive Therapy and Research*, 1980, *4*, 39–66.

Bandura, A., & Walters, R. *Social learning and personality development*. New York: Holt, Rinehart & Winston, 1963.

Bank, B. J., Biddle, B. J., & Good, T. L. Sex roles, classroom instruction and reading achievement. *Journal of Educational Psychology*, 1980, *72*, 119–132.

Bart, P. B. *Unalienating abortion, demystifying depression, and restoring rape victims.* Paper presented at the American Psychiatric Association, Anaheim Calif., 1975.

Baumrind, D. *Are androgynous individuals more effective persons and parents?* Unpublished manuscript, University of California, Berkeley, 1980.

Beck, A. T. The development of depression: A cognitive model. In R. J. Friedman & M. M. Katz (Eds.), *The psychology of depression: Contemporary theory and research*. Washington, D.C.: Winston, 1974.

Beckman, L. Teachers' and observers' perceptions of causality for a child's performance. *Journal of Educational Psychology*, 1973, *65*, 198–204.

Bem, S. L. The measurement of psychological androgyny. *Journal of Consulting and Clinical Psychology*, 1974, *42*, 155–162.

Berg, J. H., Stephan, W. G., & Dodson, M. Attributional modesty in women. *Psychology of Women Quarterly*, 1981, *5*, 711–727.

Bernard, J. *The future of marriage*. New York: Bantam, 1973.

Bernard, J. *The female world*. New York: Free Press, 1981.

Bialer, I. Conceptualization of success and failure in mentally retarded and normal children. *Journal of Personality*, 1961, *29*, 303–320.

Blau, P. M., & Duncan, O. D. *The American occupational structure*. New York: Wiley, 1967.

Blechman, E. A. Ecological sources of dysfunction in women: Issues and implications for clinical behavior therapy. *Clinical Behavior Therapy Review*, 1980, *2*, 1–18. (a)

Blechman, E. A. Behavior therapies. In A. M. Brodsky & R. T. Hare-Mustin (Eds.), *Women and psychotherapy. An assessment of research and practice*. New York: Guilford, 1980. (b)

Blechman, E. A. Competence, depression, and behavior modification with women. In M. Hersen (Ed.), *Progress in behavior modification* (Vol. 12). New York: Academic, 1981.

Blechman, E. A. *Identification of high-risk children*. Unpublished manuscript, Wesleyan University, 1982.

Blechman, E. A., Kotanchik, N., & Taylor, C. J. Families and schools together: Early behavioral intervention with high risk children. *Behavior Therapy*, 1981, *12*, 308–319.

Blechman, E. A., Taylor, C. J., & Schrader, S. M. Family problem solving versus home notes as early intervention with high-risk children. *Journal of Consulting and Clinical Psychology*, 1981, *49*, 919–926.

Bloom, B. L., Asher, S. J., & White, S. W. Marital disruption as a stressor: A review and analysis. *Psychological Bulletin*, 1978, *85*, 867–894.

Boswell, P. C., & Murray, E. J. Depression, schizophrenia, and social attraction. *Journal of Consulting and Clinical Psychology*, 1981, *49*, 641–647.

Carpenter, C. J., Huston, A. C., & Holt, W. *The use of selected activity participation to modify sex-typed behavior*. Paper presented at Annual Meeting of the Association for Behavior Analysis, Milwaukee, 1981.

Carpenter, C. J., Huston, A. C., & Neath, J. F. *Feminine and masculine behaviors associated with activity structure*. Paper presented at Annual Meeting of the Association for Behavior Analysis, Milwaukee, 1981.

Carpenter, C. J., & Huston-Stein, A. Activity structure and sex-typed behavior in preschool children. *Child Development*, 1980, *51*, 862–872.

Carpenter, C. J., Petrowsky, K., Powell, L. K., & Huston, A. C. *Longitudinal analysis of activity participation and associated behavior in children from ages 3 to 5.* Paper presented at Annual Meeting of the Association for Behavior Analysis, Milwaukee, 1981.

Connolly, K. J., & Bruner, J. S. Competence: Its nature and nurture. In K. J. Connolly & J. S. Bruner, (Eds.), *The growth of competence*. London: Academic, 1974.

Coopersmith, S. *The antecedents of self-esteem*. San Francisco: Freeman, 1967.

Curtis, R. Success and failure, gender differences, and the menstrual cycle. *Psychology of Women Quarterly*, 1981, 5, 702–710.

Davidson, C. V., & Abramowitz, S. I. Sex bias in clinical judgment: Later empirical returns. *Psychology of Women Quarterly*, 1980, 4, 377–395.

deWolf, V. A. High school mathematics preparation and sex differences in quantitative ability. *Psychology of Women Quarterly*, 1981, 5, 555–567.

Duncan, C. B. A reputation test of personality integration, *Journal of Personality and Social Psychology*, 1966, 3, No. 5, 516–524.

Dweck, C. S., Davidson, W., Nelson, S., & Enna, B. Sex differences in learned helplessness: II. The contingencies of evaluative feedback in the classroom; III. An experimental analysis. *Developmental Psychology*, 1978, 14, 268–276.

Dweck, C. S., & Goetz, T. E. Attributions and learned helplessness. In J. Harvey, W. Icke, & R. Kidd (Eds.), *New directions in attribution research* (Vol. 2). Hillsdale, N.J.: Erlbaum, 1978.

Eme, R. F. Sex differences in psychopathology: A review. *Psychological Bulletin*, 1979, 86, 574–595.

Etaugh, C., & Brown, B. Perceiving the causes of success and failure of male and female performances. *Developmental Psychology*, 1975, 11, 103.

Farina, A., Garmezy, N., & Barry, H. Relationship of marital status to incidence and prognosis of schizophrenia. *Journal of Applied Social Psychology*, 1963, 67, 624–630.

Featherman, D. L., & Hauser, R. M. Sexual inequalities and socioeconomic achievements in the U.S., 1962–1973. *American Sociological Review*, 1976, 41, 462–483.

Fenichel, O. *The collected papers of Otto Fenichel*. New York: Norton, 1953.

Foster, S. L., & Ritchey, W. L. Issues in the assessment of social competence in children. *Journal of Applied Behavior Analysis*, 1979, 12, 625–638.

Freud, S. [The ego and the id.] In J. Strachey (Ed. & trans.), *The standard edition of the complete psychological works of Sigmund Freud* (Vol. 19: 1923–1925). London: Hogarth, 1961. (Originally published, 1923.)

Friedan, B. *The second stage*. New York: Summit Books, 1981.

Gewirtz, J. L. Mechanisms of social learning: Some roles of stimulation and behavior in early development. In D. A. Goslin (Ed.), *Handbook of socialization theory and research*. Chicago: Rand-McNally, 1969.

Gewirtz, J. L., & Stingle, K. G. Learning of generalized imitation as the basis for identification. *Psychological Review*, 1968, 75, 374–397.

Giraldo, Z. I., & Weatherford, J. M. *Life cycle and the American family: Current trends and policy implications*. Institute of Policy Sciences and Public Affairs, Duke University, 1978.

Gotlib, I. H. Self-reinforcement and recall: Differential deficits in depressed and nondepressed psychiatric inpatients. *Journal of Applied Psychology*, 1981, 90, 521–530.

Gottfredson, G. D., & Swatko, M. K. Employment, unemployment, and the job search in psychology. *American Psychologist*, 1979, 34, 1047–1060.

Gove, W. R. Mental illness and psychiatric treatment among women. *Psychology of Women Quarterly*, 1980, 4, 372–376.

Haan, N., Smith, M., & Block, J. Moral reasoning of young adults: Political social behavior, family background, and personality correlates. *Journal of Personality and Social Psychology*, 1968, 10, 183–201.

Haccoun, D. M., & Lavigueur, H. Effects of clinical experience and client emotion on therapists' responses. *Journal of Consulting and Clinical Psychology*, 1979, 47, 416–418.

Hall, J. A., & Halberstadt, A. G. Masculinity and femininity in children: Development of the Children's Personal Attributes Questionnaire. *Developmental Psychology*, 1980, *16*, 270–280.

Hammen, C. L., & Peters, S. D. Interpersonal consequences of depression: Responses to men and women enacting a depressed role. *Journal of Abnormal Psychology*, 1978, *87*, 322–332.

Harter, S. Mastery motivation and need for approval in older children and their relationship to social desirability response tendencies. *Developmental Psychology*, 1975, *22*, 186–196.

Harter, S. The effects of social reinforcement and task difficulty on the pleasure derived by normal and retarded children from cognitive challenge and mastery. *Journal of Experimental Child Psychology*, 1977, *24*, 476–494.

Harter, S., & Zigler, E. The assessment of effectance motivation in normal and retarded children. *Developmental Psychology*, 1974, *10*, 169–180.

Haug, M. R. Social class measurement and women's occupational roles. *Social Forces*, 1974, *52*, 86–98.

Holstein, C. E. The relation of children's moral judgment level to that of their parents and to communication patterns in the family. In R. Smart & M. Smart (Eds.), *Readings in child development and relationships*. New York: Macmillan, 1972.

Hull, D. B., & Schroeder, H. E. Some interpersonal effects of assertion, nonassertion, and aggression. *Behavior Therapy*, 1979, *10*, 20–28.

Hyde, J. S. How large are cognitive gender differences? A meta-analysis using w^2 and d. *American Psychologist*, 1981, *36*, 892–901.

Ilfeld, F. W. Psychologic status of community residents along major demographic dimensions. *Archives of General Psychiatry*, 1978, *35*, 716–724.

Inkeles, A. Society, social structure, and child socialization. In J. A. Clausen (Ed.), *Socialization and society*. Boston: Little, Brown, 1968.

Inwold, R. H., & Bryant, N. D. The effect of sex of participants on decision making in small teacher groups. *Psychology of Women Quarterly*, 1981, *5*, 532–542.

Jahoda, M. *Freud and the dilemmas of psychology*. New York: Basic, 1977.

Kanfer, F. H., & Hagerman, S. *The role of self-regulation in depression*. Unpublished manuscript, University of Illinois, 1979.

Kelly, J. A., O'Brien, G. G., & Hosford, R. Sex roles and social skills: Considerations for interpersonal adjustment. *Psychology of Women Quarterly*, 1981, *5*, 758–766.

Kelly, J. A. Caudill, S., Hathorn, S. & O'Brien, C. G. Socially undesirable sex-correlated characteristics: Implications for androgyny and adjustment. *Journal of Clinical and Consulting Psychology*, 1977, *45*, 1186–1187.

Kendler, T. S. Toward a theory of mediational development. In H. W. Reese & L. P. Lipsitt (Eds.), *Advances in child development and behavior* (Vol. 13). New York: Academic, 1979.

Kistner, R. W. *Gynecology, principles, and practices*. Chicago: Year Book, 1971.

Klemesrud, J. Working women: Easing burden. *The New York Times*, February 6, 1982, p. 21.

Kohlberg, L., LaCrosse, J., & Ricks, D. The predictability of adult mental health from childhood behavior. In B. Wolman (Ed.), *Handbook of child psychopathology*. New York: McGraw-Hill, 1970.

Leahy, R. L. Parental practices and the development of moral judgment and self-image disparity during adolescence. *Developmental Psychology*, 1981, *17*, 580–594.

Leavitt, F., Garron, D. C., & Bieliauskas, L. A. Psychological disturbance and life event differences among patients with low back pain. *Journal of Consulting and Clinical Psychology*, 1980, *48*, 115–116.

Lefkowitz, M. M., & Tesiny, E. P. Assessment of childhood depression. *Journal of Clinical and Consulting Psychology*, 1980, *48*, 43–50.

Lennane, K. J., & Lennane, R. J. Alleged psychogenic disorders in women: A possible manifestation of sexual prejudice. *The New England Journal of Medicine*, 1973, *288*, 288–292.

Lenney, E. Women's self-confidence in achievement settings. *Journal of Consulting and Clinical Psychology*, 1977, *84*, 1–13.

LeVine, R. A. *Dreams and deeds: Achievement motivation in Nigeria.* Chicago: University of Chicago Press, 1967.

Lewine, R. R. J. Sex differences in schizophrenia: Timing or subtypes? *Psychological Bulletin*, 1981, *90*, 432–444.

Lewinsohn, P. M. A behavior approach to depression. In R. J. Friedman & M. M. Katz (Eds.), *The psychology of depression: Contemporary theory and research.* New York: Wiley, 1974.

Lewinsohn, P. M., & Libet, J. Pleasant events, activity schedules, and depression. *Journal of Abnormal Psychology*, 1972, *79*, 291–295.

Lewinsohn, P. M., Mischel, W., Chaplin, W., & Barton, R. Social competence and depression: The role of illusory self-perceptions. *Journal of Abnormal Psychology*, 1980, *89*, 203–212.

Lewis, C. C. The effects of parental firm control: A reinterpretation of findings. *Psychological Bulletin*, 1981, *90*, 547–563.

Lloyd, C. Life events and depressive disorder reviewed. *Archives of General Psychiatry*, 1980, *37*, 541–548.

Locke, E. A., Shaw, K. N., Saari, L. M., & Latham, G. P. Goal setting and task performance: 1969–1980. *Psychological Bulletin*, 1981, *90*, 125–152.

Maccoby, E. Sex differences in intellectual functioning. In E. Maccoby (Ed.), *The development of sex differences.* Stanford, Calif.: Stanford University Press, 1966.

Maccoby, E. E., & Jacklin, C. N. *The psychology of sex differences.* Stanford, Calif.: Stanford University Press, 1974.

MacPhillamy, D. J., and Lewinsohn, P. M. Depression as a function of levels of desired and obtained pleasure. *Journal of Abnormal Psychology*, 1974, *83*, 651–657.

Massad, C. M. Sex role identity and adjustment during adolescence. *Child Development*, 1981, *52*, 1290–1298.

McFall, R. M. A review and reformulation of the concept of social skills. *Behavioral Assessment*, 1982, *4*, 1–33.

Miller, I. W., & Norman, W. H. Learned helplessness in humans: A review and attribution-theory model. *Psychological Bulletin*, 1979, *86*, 93–118.

Miller, N. E., & Dollard, J. *Social learning and imitation.* New Haven, Conn.: Yale University Press, 1941.

Miller, W. R., & Seligman, M. E. P. Depression and learned helplessness in man. *Journal of Abnormal Psychology*, 1975, *84*, 228–238.

Mischel, W. A social-learning view of sex differences in behavior. In E. Maccoby (Ed.), *The development of sex differences.* Stanford, Calif.: Stanford University Press, 1966.

Mischel, W. Sex-typing and socialization. In P. H. Mussen (Ed.), *Carmichael's manual of child psychology* (Vol. 2). New York: Wiley, 1970.

Mischel, W. Toward a cognitive social learning reconceptualization of personality. *Psychological Review*, 1973, *80*, 252–283.

Molnar, J. M., & Weisz, J. R. The pursuit of mastery by preschool boys and girls: An observational study. *Child Development*, 1981, *52*, 724–727.

Morgan, S. R. The learning disabilities population: Why more boys than girls? *Journal of Clinical Child Psychology*, 1979, *8*, 211–213.

Mueller, C. W., & Parcel, T. L. Measures of socioeconomic status: Alternatives and recommendations. *Child Development*, 1981, 52, 13–30.

Mueller, C. W. & Pope, H. Marital instability: A study of its transmission between generations. *Journal of Marriage and the Family*, 1977, 39, 83–94.

Nilson, L. B. The social standing of a housewife. *Journal of Marriage and the Family*, 1978, 40, 541–548.

Nock, S. L., & Rossi, P. H. Household types and social standing. *Social Forces*, 1979, 57, 1325–1345.

Ogbu, J. U. Origins of human competence: A cultural-ecological perspective. *Child Development*, 1981, 52, 413–429.

Pasquella, M. J., Mednick, M. T. S., & Murray, S. R. Causal attributions for achievement outcomes: Sex-role identity, sex and outcome comparisons. *Psychology of Women Quarterly*, 1981, 5, 586–594.

Paykel, E. S., & Weissman, M. M. Social adjustment and depression: A longitudinal study. *Archives of General Psychiatry*, 1973, 28, 659–663.

Plomin, R., & Foch, T. T. Sex differences and individual differences. *Child Development*, 1981, 52, 383–385.

President's Commission on Mental Health. Washington, D.C.: U.S. Government Printing Office, 1978.

Radloff, L. S., & Monroe, M. M. Sex differences in helplessness: With implications for depression. In L. S. Hansen & R. S. Rapoza (Eds.), *Career development and counseling of women*. Springfield, Ill.: Thomas, 1978.

Radloff, L. S., & Rae, D. S. Susceptibility and precipitating factors in depression: Sex differences and similarities. *Journal of Abnormal Psychology*, 1979, 88, 174–181.

Rehm, L. P. A self-control model of depression. *Behavior Therapy*, 1977, 8, 787–804.

Reid, R. L., & Yen, S. S. C. Premenstrual syndrome. *American Journal of Obstetrics and Gynecology*, 1981, 139, 85–104.

Riger, S. & Galligan, P. Women in management: An exploration of competing paradigms. *American Psychologist*, 1980, 35, 902–910.

Roff, J. D., Knight, R., & Wertheim, E. A factor-analytic study of childhood symptoms antecedent to schizophrenia. *Journal of Abnormal Psychology*, 1976, 85, 543–549.

Roff, M., Sells, S. B., & Golden, M. M. *Social adjustment and personality development in children*. Minneapolis: U. of Minneapolis Press, 1972.

Schlenker, B. R. Self-presentation: Managing the impression of consistency when reality interferes with self-enhancement. *Journal of Personality and Social Psychology.*, 1975, 32, 1030–1037.

Sears, R. R. Identification as a form of behavior development. In D. B. Harris (Ed.), *The concept of development*. Minneapolis: University of Minnesota Press, 1957.

Seeman, J. Personality integration in college women. *Journal of Personality and Social Psychology*, 1966, 4, 91–93.

Seligman, M., Abramson, L., Semmel, A., & vonBaeyer, C. Depressive attributional style. *Journal of Abnormal Psychology*, 1979, 88, 242–247.

Slater, J., & Depue, R. A. The contribution of environmental events and social support to serious suicide attempts in primary depressive disorder. *Journal of Abnormal Psychology*, 1981, 90, 275–285.

Stein, L. S., DelGaudio, A. C. & Ansley, M. Y. A comparison of female and male neurotic depressives. *Journal of Clinical Psychology*, 1976, 32, 19–21.

Steinberg, L. D., Catalano, R., & Dooley, D. Economic antecedents of child abuse and neglect. *Child Development*, 1981, 52, 975–985.

Thorndike, R. L., & Hagen, E. P. *Measurement and evaluation in psychology and education*. New York: Wiley, 1977.

Touhey, J. C. Effects of additional men on prestige and desirability of occupations typically performed by women. *Journal of Applied Social Psychology*, 1974, *4*, 330–335.

Tumblin, A., & Gholson, B. Hypothesis theory and the development of conceptual learning. *Psychological Bulletin*, 1981, *90*, 102–124.

Weissman, M. M., & Klerman, G. L. Sex differences and the epidemiology of depression. *Archives of General Psychiatry*, 1977, *34*, 98–111.

Whalen, C. K., & Flowers, J. V. Effects of role and gender mix in verbal communication modes. *Journal of Counseling Psychology*, 1977, *24*, 281–287.

White, B. L. *The origins of human competence: The final report of the Harvard preschool project.* Lexington, Mass.: Heath, 1979.

Widholm, O. Dysmenorrhea during adolescence. *Acta Obstetrica Gynecologia Scandinavica Supplement*, 1979, *87*, 61–66.

Wolf, M. M. Social validity: The case for subjective measurement *or* How applied behavior analysis is finding its heart. *Journal of Applied Behavior Analysis*, 1978, *11*, 203–214.

Zigler, E., & Levine, J. Premorbid competence in schizophrenia: What is being measured? *Journal of Consulting and Clinical Psychology*, 1981, *49*, 96–105.

Zigler, E., & Phillips, L. Social effectiveness of sympatomatic behavior. *Journal of Abnormal Psychology*, 1960, *61*, 231–238.

Zigler, E., & Trickett, P. K. IQ, social competence, and evaluation of early childhood intervention programs. *American Psychologist*, 1978, *33*, 789–798.

2

UNRAVELING THE NATURE OF SEX ROLES

J. GAYLE BECK
DAVID H. BARLOW

OVERVIEW

Although social scientists have examined sex *differences* in behavior for many years, this line of investigation contributed little information about the social processes which create and maintain sex *roles*. As Unger pointed out (1979a), the study of sex differences has typically aimed to explain, rather than describe, dissimilarities between males and females. Explanations of human sex differences often assume biological causality, although the causal hypothesis is rarely subjected to direct test. Attempts to explain observable differences in behavior, in biological terms, ignore the psychological significance of noted sex differences and the social processes which create and maintain these differences. Recent work (e.g., Unger, 1979a) has challenged the traditional assumption of a close correspondence between biological and psychological sex, adding to the intellectual turmoil surrounding the topic of sex roles. Controversy and confusion about basic definitions is fueled by changing social values about women, men, masculinity, and femininity and by an increasing awareness among behavioral and social scientists that our science may not be value-free. The purpose of this chapter is to provide an alternative approach to the study of sex-role processes. Specifically, rather than focusing upon group differences drawn along biological lines of anatomy, this chapter will present a viewpoint which emphasizes specific behavioral components of the complex construct known as sex roles. This viewpoint will be illustrated through the presentation of a checklist which assesses sex-role motor behavior or, more specifically, patterns

J. Gayle Beck and David H. Barlow. Department of Psychology, State University of New York at Albany, Albany, New York.

of sitting, standing, and walking. Examples are given from a number of areas, including social responses, developmental patterns, and clinical assessment of these behaviors. Throughout these examples, the importance of objective assessment of specific components of this complex construct is stressed, noting the possibility that these components may not overlap with each other. Additionally, broader issues, such as the role of behavioral flexibility in adaptive functioning, are discussed.

BACKGROUND

For the purposes of this chapter, *sex roles* are behaviors that are judged appropriate for individuals using social definitions of their sex (Unger, 1979b). For example, one female may be described by herself and others as a "masculine woman," due to her occupation as a truck driver, her manner of walking with long, smooth strides, and her deep tone of voice. Another female may be described as "feminine," due to her occupation as a typist, her manner of sitting with her legs crossed at the ankle, and her high-pitched voice. Both of these examples are stereotypic caricatures, that illustrate the limit-setting nature of sex roles. Sex roles outline the limits of permissible behavior for individuals who are categorized by their biological sex. Sex roles vary widely within and between cultures, as do the consequences for transgression. In contrast, biological or anatomical features which are identified as male or female are subject to little cultural variation; these are referred to by the term *sex* in this chapter. An individual's *gender* refers to his or her psychological self-definition as either masculine or feminine. Thus, sex roles depend upon both sex and gender; a variety of social processes contribute to norms that regulate role performance. A complex interaction of biological characteristics, psychological factors, and social customs creates and maintains sex roles. In beginning to examine the nature of sex roles from a behavioral perspective, it seems important to explore components of this interactional process.

THE MEASUREMENT OF MASCULINITY AND FEMININITY

Early attempts to measure sex roles consisted of self-report inventories which construed masculinity and femininity as mutually exclusive and opposite ends of a single continuum (Hathaway & McKinley, 1943;

Strong, 1943; Terman & Miles, 1936). These inventories were constructed without a clear operational definition of sex roles and, in some ways, are representative of the study of sex differences. A major, recent advance in the field has been the construction of sex-role inventories in which masculinity and femininity are measured according to an orthogonal two-dimensional model; that is, since masculinity and femininity are conceptualized as independent dimensions, an individual may possess both types of qualities (Bem, 1974; Constantinople, 1973; Spence, Helmreich, & Stapp, 1975). While these instruments have provided a great deal of informative data, they suffer from sources of bias common to self-report measurement including tendencies to emphasize certain characteristics over others (Mischel, 1973) and to provide socially desirable responses (Edwards, 1957). In addition, self-report inventories measure only one aspect of the complex interactive processes which constitute sex roles. From a behavioral perspective, these inventories tap one of several, independent response systems. The construct of sex roles (Barlow, 1977), like the construct of fear (Lang, 1968), comprises several, independent, response systems, all of which cannot be assessed with one measurement strategy. For example, in the treatment of individuals with phobias, therapeutic change does not always occur simultaneously in the cognitive, behavioral, and physiological response systems; this lack of correspondence has been termed "desynchrony" (Rachman & Hodgson, 1974; Sartory, Rachman, & Grey, 1977) and seems to have important implications for treatment outcome (Barlow & Mavissakalian, 1981). Within the area of sex roles, similarly there is reason to believe that the multiple response systems cannot all be assessed with the same measurement device and do not covary. Therefore, self-report inventories of sex roles must be augmented.

BEHAVIORAL MEASUREMENT OF SEX ROLES

One hallmark of the behavioral approach is objective, repeated measurement of the specific components of presenting target problems and complex variables, in relationship to the larger social context (Barlow, 1980). Behaviorists are in a unique position to unravel the nature of sex roles, given this emphasis upon specifying components of a complex variable and designing measures relevant to each component. This approach can be used to operationalize the construct of sex roles through a careful analysis of constituent response systems and their interrelationships. As stated previously, the bulk of the work on sex roles has employed self-report inventories and thus uses a verbal measure of the cognitive response system. Behavioral aspects of sex roles have been ignored or have been assigned secondary importance (e.g., to validate a self-report measure). A recently published, sex-typed motor behavior checklist (Barlow, Hayes, Nelson, Steele, Meeler, & Mills, 1979) pinpoints stereotypic masculine and feminine motor behaviors. A rater using this checklist, observes an individual and checks off any behavior displayed within a given time interval. The results are a masculine motor behavior score and a feminine motor behavior score that are consistent with an orthogonal, two-dimensional model (of masculinity and femininity). This checklist, which assesses motor behavior through direct observation, supplements self-report measures and adds information about another aspect of sex-role behavior. The next section of this chapter reviews a small but growing body of literature on this checklist and some important findings about the nonverbal aspects of sex-role processes. Nonverbal behaviors appear to be a unique influence on social roles, social functioning, and sex roles.

DEVELOPMENT OF THE CHECKLIST

The construction of this checklist came about during the clinical treatment of adult transsexuals, in response to the need for a reliable, valid measure of sex-role behavior. Several preliminary versions of the checklist were validated before publication. The latest version of the checklist (Barlow et al., 1979) contains 15 behaviors which are labeled masculine and 16 behaviors which are termed feminine; these behaviors are categorized into sitting, standing, and walking positions. As can be seen in Table 2-1, the checklist contains both gross stereotypical motor positions as well as more subtle behaviors. The items on this checklist were derived from Hewes's (1957) anthropological study of posture as well as from clinical observations of gender-disturbed adults, who frequently appear rigid in their verbal and motoric sex-role behavior (Green & Money, 1969). Thus, while checklist items do not describe all possible human postures, they were selected because they appear to capture the major, nonverbal, motoric aspects of sex roles.

The validity data were obtained for the checklist in the following manner (Barlow et al., 1979); 46 White subjects were selected as representatives of the following four categories: masculine females, feminine

TABLE 2-1. Feminine and Masculine Sex-Role Motor Behavior Checklist Items

Feminine	Masculine
Sitting	
Buttocks close to back of chair	Buttocks away from back of chair
Legs uncrossed or crossed at the ankles; knees held fairly close together	Legs uncrossed; knees and feet spread apart
Legs crossed at the knee	Legs crossed, foot on knee
Arm movements made from the elbow	Arm movements made with fingers together and fairly straight
Graceful hand motions, made with fingers relaxed and bent	Firm wrist (not bent)
Bent or limp wrist	
Standing	
Feet together (less than 4 inches)	Feet apart (more than 4 inches)
Arm movements made from the elbow	Arm movements made from the shoulder
Frequent arm movements (more than 5 per minute)	Hand(s) in pocket(s)
Bent or limp wrist	Firm wrist (not bent)
Walking	
Relatively small steps, legs not kicked out in front	Long strides, legs kicked out in front
Pronounced hip movement ("swish")	Minimum hip movements
Arm movements made from elbow	Arm movements made from shoulder
Frequent arm movements (more than 5 per minute)	Arms hang loosely from shoulders
Bent or limp wrist	Firm wrist (not bent)
Upper arms held fairly close to body	Feet straddle an imaginary line

females, masculine males, and feminine males. There were 12 subjects in each category except the latter, which contained 10 subjects (due to difficulty in locating representatives of this cell). Subjects were selected by the following procedure: Two raters, naive to the purpose of the study, rated passersby at a college campus on a 7-point scale, ranging from extremely masculine (-3) to extremely feminine ($+3$). No further details regarding the definition of "masculinity" or "femininity" were supplied to the raters. Criteria were developed to select representatives of the four categories by using these ratings. For the cells involving corresponding sex-role behavior and sex (e.g., feminine females), potential subjects had to receive a rating at the extreme end of the scale from both observers. For example, for inclusion in the study as a "feminine female," a woman had to receive ratings from both observers of +3 or +2. For cells involving cross-sex motor behavior (e.g., feminine males), slightly more liberal criteria were employed, due to the difficulty in locating extremely feminine males and extremely masculine females. For example, for inclusion as a "feminine male," a man had to receive ratings from both observers of +3, +2, or +1. Once individuals were located who met the criteria for one of the four cells, they were approached by a third experimenter and asked to participate in a study. Individuals who agreed (nearly all who were asked), were escorted to a nearby room, where they were observed while sitting, standing, and walking. Subjects were taped twice, once while aware that they were being recorded, and once at the very beginning while unaware. A 30-second sample of each behavior was recorded for both conditions. Later, the tapes were rated with the checklist by two trained raters, who were unaware of the purpose and method of the study. Raters indicated the presence or absence of each of the behaviors. The overall interrater agreement across all items on the checklist was .80; individual item reliabilities ranged from .66 to .96.

Given the construction of the scale, the total feminine score could range from zero to 16, while the total masculine score could range from zero to 15. These total scores were analyzed, as were subtotals for sitting, standing, and walking. As Figure 2-1 shows, the analysis of the total feminine scores revealed higher scores for both groups of females as compared with both groups of males; individuals in the feminine female category had significantly higher feminine scores than did those in the masculine female category, while no such difference was found between the two male groups. A significant difference was found across taping conditions; all four groups demonstrated significantly less "feminine" motor behavior when aware of the videotape recording. As Figure 2-2 shows, the analysis of the total masculine scores showed similar effects. Both groups of males had higher scores when compared with both groups of females; masculine females had higher masculine scores than did feminine females. Unlike the feminine total scores, no differences were found across the two videotaping conditions. Analysis of the subtotal scores revealed similar findings; on all three subtotal scores (sitting, standing, and walking), masculine and feminine females differed more in their motor behavior than did masculine and feminine males. The differences between the aware and unaware videotaping conditions were primarily accounted for by the feminine standing subtotal scores. In addition to providing preliminary validation data for the checklist, this study suggested that volunteers of both sexes decrease their feminine motor behavior when they are aware of being recorded and observed.

While this study provides preliminary evidence of the validity and reliability of the motor behavior checklist, much more work is needed to examine the psychometric properties of this instrument. The checklist adequately discriminated between biological males and females and between feminine and masculine females. The checklist's poor differen-

FIGURE 2-1. Mean feminine scores for all groups when they were either aware or unaware of being rated on sex-role motor behavior. (Feminine females, ff; masculine females, mf; masculine males, mm; feminine males, fm.) From "Sex Role Motor Behavior: A Behavioral Checklist" by D.H. Barlow, S.C. Hayes, R.O. Nelson, D.L. Steele, M.E. Meeler, and J.R. Mills, *Behavioral Assessment*, 1979, *1*, 119–138. Copyright 1979 by Pergamon Press, Ltd. Reprinted by permission.

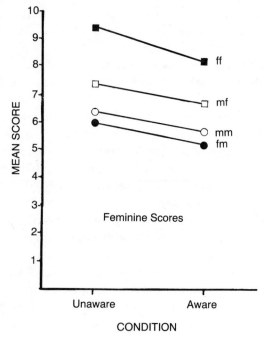

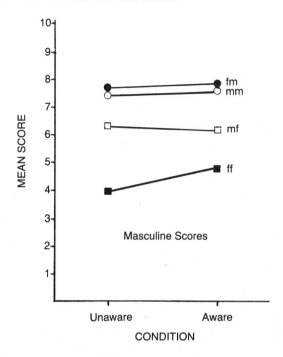

FIGURE 2-2. Mean masculine scores for all groups when they were either aware or unaware of being rated on sex-role motor behavior. (Feminine females, ff; masculine females, mf; masculine males, mm; feminine males, fm.)

tiation between feminine and masculine males can be explained in several ways. It could be that the raters who observed students on campus applied different standards of masculinity and femininity to males and females. Our informal observations suggest that males selected as feminine were tall, slender, and more flamboyantly dressed than masculine males. It is possible that the naive raters selectively attended to cues of dress, height, and general appearance when forming sex-role impressions of males. Or, perhaps the masculine checklist items do not include behaviors which appear feminine when displayed by a male, although they do distinguish masculine from feminine females. Finally, these motor behaviors may have different effects on the observer when demonstrated by a male or a female. A man who walks with a pronounced hip movement or sits with his legs crossed at the ankle may be perceived as feminine, solely on the basis of one or two motor behaviors. Thus, while his score on the checklist may not be significantly different from the score of a man who is perceived as motorically masculine, the few behavioral differences between these two men may be weighed heavily in an observer's sex-role judgments. These and other possibilities need to be examined in future studies on the validity of this checklist.

More investigation of social desirability effects on sex-role motor behavior is in order, since awareness of observation by other people apparently decreases feminine motor behaviors, especially feminine standing behaviors. While this awareness factor could confound the interpretation of some research data, the existence of this factor seems an important finding in and of itself. These preliminary data suggest that because feminine-typed motor behaviors are perceived by both sexes as less desirable, at least some people who are subject to obvious, careful scrutiny by others purposefully display fewer feminine behaviors. The social desirability of these motor behaviors could be related to what have been termed status signals. Henley (1973) explored the relationship between status variables and the nonverbal behavior of men and women; she found that differences in touching in public were closely related to the status of the toucher. That is, women, young people, and those perceived to be of lower economic status were likely to be touched more by others and were less likely to reciprocate the touch. It is possible that feminine motor behaviors are another such signal of lower status. Since women score lower than men on every measure of social standing, the display of feminine motor behaviors is often a valid index of less income, lower occupational prestige, and less physical and social power. Uncritical evaluation of feminine motor behavior with objectively low social power is likely to hinder the social effectiveness of men and women whose motor behavior is feminine. Nonverbal behavior, by providing clues about social status, may shape unfamiliar observers' perceptions and reactions. In sum, an apparent social desirability confound in the motor behavior checklist may have heuristic value for the study of sex roles.

THE DISPLAY OF SEX-TYPED MOTOR BEHAVIOR BY ADULTS: SOCIAL RESPONSES

The adult display of sex-typed motor behavior raises a number of interesting questions. Do people display the same amount of masculine and feminine motor behaviors across situations or time? What are others' perception of same-sex and cross-sex motor behavior? How does this perception affect social interactions? How socially effective are people who habitually display masculine, feminine, or mixed motor behavior? Are people aware of their nonverbal sex-role signals? Researchers have begun to address these questions. This work helps to unravel the complexities of nonverbal sex roles, as they relate to women and stereotypical feminine behavior.

One of the tenets of behaviorism is that behavior is situationally specific, dependent upon environmental contingencies which often change from situation to situation. One study has examined the specificity of sex-role motor behavior in preliminary fashion (Heckerman, Schoen, & Barlow, 1981). Twelve college students were selected on the basis of their scores on the Bem Sex Role Inventory (Bem, 1974); two subjects of each sex were categorized as either masculine typed (high masculine, low feminine Bem scores), feminine typed (high feminine, low masculine scores), or androgynous (high masculine and feminine scores). All subjects were observed both in a classroom situation and in their dormitory or apartment. The results of this study are somewhat confounded by the subject's awareness of observation (although they were unaware of the specific purpose of the observations). Eight of the 12 subjects (four men and four women), displayed more feminine motor behaviors at home than in class. There were no significant differences in the display of masculine motor behaviors across these two settings.

Interesting trends emerged in examining interactions between Bem scores and behavior at home and school. When data were plotted in histograms, men and women with feminine-typed Bem scores displayed more feminine than masculine motor behaviors at home, while their masculine-typed counterparts displayed more masculine than feminine motor behavior at home. Androgynous subjects showed approximately equal amounts of feminine and masculine motor behaviors at home. In the classroom, this pattern was altered somewhat; androgynous and masculine-typed subjects of both sexes displayed more masculine motor behaviors, while feminine-typed subjects displayed more feminine motor behaviors. This finding is of interest in light of Bem's theory that androgynous individuals display the greatest sex-role flexibility in their behavior across a variety of situations (Bem, 1975; Bem & Lenney, 1976; Bem, Martyna, & Watson, 1976). Masculine motor behaviors on the checklist, may be more highly valued and more often reinforced when displayed by individuals of both sexes in the college classroom. Given that our cultural standards for success differ according to the nature of the task and the sex of the worker (Taynor & Deaux, 1975), perhaps the college classroom is a culturally masculine setting to which individuals with greater behavioral flexibility adapt their behavior. In this vein, Kelly *et al.* (1977) have suggested that masculine-typed behaviors may have a higher probability of social reinforcement than feminine-typed behavior, and that these behaviors may be differentially reinforced depending on the sex of the actor. This hypothesis was indirectly supported by data reviewed earlier. In the original validation study of the checklist, it was found that when students were aware that their motor behavior was being observed, both sexes decreased their display of feminine motor behavior. It does appear, however, that sex-role motor behavior is situationally specific; further examination of a wider range of situations would seem fruitful as a method of analyzing cultural sex-role expectations. It might be interesting to examine single-sex situations in dorms or locker rooms as these environments would seem to contain slightly different sex-role contingencies from coed situations. This preliminary study does shed some light on the complex nature of sex-role behavior; it appears as if self-perception of sex role, as well as biological sex and situational demands contribute to the display of these nonverbal sex-role signals.

If sex-role motor behaviors are a function of both environmental and organismic (or person) variables and their interaction (Mischel, 1973), then it is important to investigate social reactions to each type of motor behavior. Hayes and Leonard (in press) addressed this issue in a recent study; the first part of the study presented videotapes of males and females whose sitting, standing, and walking behavior were either extremely masculine or extremely feminine as measured by the checklist. Two groups of naive observers viewed these tapes and rated the actors on six dimensions (masculinity, femininity, naturalness, sexual orientation, likeability, and confidence) using Likert-type scales. Several interesting findings resulted; both motor behavior and sex of the model influenced impressions of masculinity and femininity, supporting the validity of both the checklist and the manipulation. Consonant motor behavior/sex combinations (e.g., feminine females) were rated as more natural than dissonant combinations (e.g., masculine females). However, individuals of both sexes who displayed feminine motor behavior were rated as less natural than those displaying masculine motor behavior. Consonant motor behavior/sex combinations led to the impression of heterosexuality, while dissonant combinations were rated as less heterosexual for women, and homosexual for men. The likeability ratings revealed a somewhat different pattern. While males were liked more when they showed masculine rather than feminine motor behavior, motor behavior did not influence the ratings of likeability of the female models. All females were liked less than masculine males and more than feminine males. The raters' estimates of models' confidence paralleled the likeability ratings. Males and females displaying masculine motor behavior, and females displaying feminine motor behavior, were rated as highly confident, while males displaying feminine mannerisms were judged significantly less confident. In short, both biological sex, nonverbal behavior, and combinations of the two variables affect social perceptions.

The link between social perceptions and social behavior needs to be more clearly elucidated. Hayes and Leonard (in press) conducted a second experiment that begins to examine this issue. Four confederates (two female, two male) were trained to perform extremely masculine and feminine sex-role motor behavior, as defined by the checklist. These confederates were college age and dressed in a gender-consonant fashion. Each confederate, working in teams with a second experimenter, approached a fellow student in the University Student Union, with either extreme masculine or extreme feminine motor behavior, as defined by the checklist. A "foot in the door" technique was used (Freedman & Fraser, 1966); a student was approached by the confederate and asked to participate in a class project, by answering four questions. The students who agreed were then asked to complete a 200-item questionnaire. Since it was assumed (and found) that nearly all subjects would comply with the first request, the dependent variable was subjects' willingness to comply with the confederate's second request and to answer a 200-item survey. The 250 subjects included approximately equal numbers of males and females. The results were the same for men and women students. Irrespective of their sex, confederates displaying masculine motor behavior elicited significantly more compliance than confederates displaying feminine motor behavior (51% compliance vs. 32% compliance). Male and female confederates with masculine mannerisms elicited an equal amount of compliance. Female confederates with feminine motor behavior elicited slightly more compliance than did feminine male confederates; both elicited significantly less compliance than masculine confederates.

Data from the two studies by Hayes and Leonard present an interesting pattern. Masculine motor behavior elicited more compliance, yet women with masculine motor behavior were rated more masculine and unnatural in appearance. Motor behavior had little effect on the ratings of likeability and confidence for females. Males displaying feminine motor behavior were unlikely to elicit compliance, were evaluated harshly by others, and thought to be unnatural, unlikeable, unconfident, and homosexual. Other studies have shown similar effects despite their different purposes. For example, Shaffer and Wegley (1974) examined perceptions of a competent woman in a competitive situation. They presented male and female college students with a description of a highly successful female student. Two characteristics of the woman were varied—her preference for masculine or feminine sex roles and her degree of success orientation. Both male and female students rated the competent woman as less attractive as a work partner when she combined a preference for masculine roles with a high success orientation. Either characteristic by itself produced less devaluation. While this study examined more global social impressions than did the Hayes and Leonard study (in press), it is important to note the similarities between the two studies' findings. It seems that masculine women receive different social responses than feminine men. The latter exercise little authority, are negatively perceived, and accorded low status; the former, although less negatively evaluated, are likely to be avoided in work situations.

These data have implications for a variety of behavioral therapies. In assertion training there is a growing awareness that what is assertive for a male may be perceived as aggressive when displayed by a female (Linehan, Chapter 6, this volume). Rose and Tryon (1979) reported that observers of both sexes rated assertive women as more aggressive than equally assertive men. It would be fruitful to explore the relationship between observers' ratings of assertive behavior and self-ratings. Fontaine (1976) has reported that, compared to men, women attribute little of their success to ability and devalue their successes at sex-inappropriate tasks. Nonverbal gender signals, such as those measured by the checklist, seem to affect social responses that an individual receives from others which, in turn, may have an impact upon an individual's perception of her own social competencies. This type of analysis would be important in the unraveling of sex-role processes. Since sex roles are just beginning to be explored by social scientists, there is need for a valid, reliable behavioral assessment devices. The Barlow et al. (1979) checklist provides one such measure, at a microbehavior level, and the investigations which have been conducted thus far do seem to reveal findings which have profound implications for conducting therapy with women. For example, stereotypically feminine women whose unassertiveness is interfering with their functioning in work settings might be taught to display more verbal and nonverbal masculine behavior in this situation and yet retain feminine behavior with family and friends as part of their assertive training. Similarly, stereotypically masculine women who might be, for example, successful in a work setting but dissatisfied with the impressions they convey socially, might be taught to approximate more feminine behavior in social situations as one step toward increasing effectiveness in these settings. Precisely the same strategies could be used effectively with an equally large number of males. The speculative examples of the use of the checklist in therapy each illustrated the hypothesized adaptability of flexible sex-role behavior, or behavior androgyny, described in more detail below.

THE DISPLAY OF SEX-TYPED MOTOR BEHAVIOR BY CHILDREN

In many ways, the motor behavior checklist offers a unique measurement device to the field. The checklist does not suffer the problem of excessive subjectivity like some previous measures of sex-role behavior in children (i.e., the "It" Test; Brown, 1956), nor is it situationally limited, as are toy preference tests. In addition to providing a valid instrument for the assessment of nonverbal motor behaviors, the checklist taps a separate response system from the verbal/cognitive response mode which is assessed via self-report inventories of sex roles. As was discussed previously, one cannot assume that the various components of a complex construct covary or are synchronized, and this lack of correspondence can often have profound implications for therapy and for a complete understanding of the construct. The checklist thus permits further exploration of these interrelationships, and provides an objective measurement tool which can be repeated across situations. In addition, the checklist can be employed with people who are not able to complete a pencil-and-paper measure; children are one such population. There has been some preliminary work involving the display of sex-typed motor behaviors by children of varying ages. This work provides additional validation for the checklist, and information about the processes involved in sex-role socialization. Volumes have been written about sex-role socialization (e.g., Maccoby & Jacklin, 1974; Money & Ehrhardt, 1972; Sears, Rau, & Alpert, 1965), yet it seems as if further study of sex-role processes in children may help to identify unknown sources of influence in the development of adult sex roles.

Before reviewing research on children's motor behavior, it is useful to summarize other reports of sex-role behavior in children. Rekers and his colleagues (Rekers, Lovaas, & Low, 1974; Rekers, Willis, Yates, Rosen, & Low, 1977) have operationally defined nine "feminine" gestures which are frequently displayed by gender-disturbed boys. Among these are bent or limp wrist, frequent arm movements (termed "flutters"), and walking or standing with a flexed elbow. It is interesting to note that some of these gestures correspond with items on the Barlow *et al.* (1979) checklist, although the two sets of motor behaviors were constructed for different purposes. Normative data have also been collected demonstrating that some of these behaviors operationalized by Rekers and his colleagues differentiate between boys and girls (Rekers, Amaro-Plotkin, & Low, 1977). Comparisons between normal boys and girls and gender-disturbed children displaying stereotypical, inflexible, opposite sex-role behavior have not been done. Other researchers (Jenni & Jenni, 1976) have noticed sex differences in the postures that are used to carry books, which became more exaggerated as older children were observed, from kindergarten to high school. These differences were also noted in a variety of geographical locations in the United States and in Central America. A recent study (Klein & Bates, 1979) has shown sex differences in young children on three motor behaviors (leg separation, pelvis roll, and trunk-limp independence); these data partially validated the observations made by Birdwhistell (1970) and other social scientists (Hewes, 1957; Mehrabian, 1972) concerning postural differences between the sexes.

One study has been completed that examines developmental patterns in the display and knowledge of sex-role motor behaviors employing the motor behavior checklist (Hayes, Nelson, Steele, Meeler, & Barlow, 1981). Three hundred and eight children served as subjects for this project; 25–30 subjects of each sex were randomly selected from grades K, 2, 4, 6, 8, 10, and 12 (approximately ages 5, 7, 9, 11, 13, 15, and 17, respectively) of several public schools. Subjects were observed individually while sitting, standing, and walking in their usual fashion and were also asked to perform these behaviors as a member of the opposite sex would do them (e.g., "Try to walk as boys/girls do"). These conditions were employed in order to differentiate between children's display of nonverbal sex-role signals and their knowledge of these behaviors. One hypothesis was that children first display these behaviors before they are recognized as sex-typed (a nativist perspective; e.g., Moss, 1967). Alternatively, these behaviors may first be seen as sex-typed by children and subsequently displayed (a cognitive–developmental perspective; e.g., Kohlberg, 1966). The children's motor behavior was rated by three observers who were present in the experimental room.

The results of this study indicate that beginning around the 4th grade (age 9), clear differences emerge in the motor behavior of boys and girls. These differences become especially prominent in the later high school years (grades 10–12, ages 15–17). Differences in sitting style (both feminine and masculine) became evident in the 2nd grade (age 7); differences in walking style emerge slightly later, in the 4th grade (age 9), and continue throughout high school. Differences in standing style became evident in the 10th and 12th grades (ages 15 and 17). It appears that once differences in motor behavior were first observed, they continued to be displayed in all of the older grade levels. These differences were observed in young children for sitting and walking behaviors, but were not seen for standing behaviors until the high school years. A difference score was computed between each child's motor behavior score during the "natural" and "cross-sex" instructions. The analysis of these difference scores showed some significant changes occurring as early as kindergarten (age 5), but the clear and consistent ability to modify motor behavior on demand did not emerge until 4th grade (age 9). By high school, large changes in sex-role motor behavior were produced when subjects were instructed to act like a member of the opposite sex. In examining the subtotal scores for sitting, standing, and walking separately, it was found that specific motor behavior patterns were able to be changed consistently on demand at about the same time that these motor behaviors were beginning to be displayed differently by the sexes.

Children's display and knowledge of sex-role motor behaviors seem to develop at about the same time, with clear differences emerging between the sexes on both dimensions around age 7. While more work needs to be conducted in this area, it appears as if the development of these sex-role signals pertains to the acquisition of behavioral flexibility. For example, it has been reported that some gender-disturbed children do not alter their sex-role motor behavior (e.g., Rekers, Willis, Yates, Rosen, & Low, 1977), even when strong negative contingencies are applied in the natural environment on these behaviors. The ability to vary motor behaviors depending upon the situation could be seen as one type of behavioral flexibility. In fact, this ability could be termed "behavioral androgyny" (Barlow et al., 1979), paralleling Bem's formulation of "psychological androgyny" (Bem, 1974, 1975) which is conceptualized as the ability to display both masculine and feminine personality characteristics flexibly according to situational demands. In this context, behavioral androgeny can be seen as the useful ability to adapt degrees of masculine and feminine motor behaviors to social and environmental demands. This flexibility may be necessary to some degree for adaptive sex-role functioning, given the observation that gender-disturbed children and adults frequently and rigidly display cross-sex mannerisms, despite consistent punishment.

It also seems relevant to explore the correspondence between motor behavior and other sex-role behaviors, such as toy preference (e.g., Green 1976; Green, Fuller, Rutley, & Hendler, 1972), to ascertain the relationship among the various components which comprise childhood sex roles. Display and knowledge of sex-role motor behaviors may represent an independent response system which develops differently from other nonverbal behavior. Children aged 4 to 7 comprehend and respond appropriately to a variety of nonverbal gestures that do not involve sex-role messages, although there is a pronounced positive effect of schooling on the understanding of role-free nonverbal gestures (Michael & Willis, 1968). The contribution of schooling to sex-role motor behaviors is hinted at by the Hayes *et al.* (1981) study which found sex differences only after several years of school. However, young children seem to display sex differences on some of the motor behavior patterns which differentiate adult women and men. For example, boys age 6 and older interacted with other boys at greater distances than did female pairs (Aiello & Aiello, 1974). This finding is consistent with evidence in the literature on personal space, that women claim a small amount of space (Lott & Sommer, 1967; Edney & Jordan-Edney, 1974; Leibman, 1970).

One clinical study comments on the relationship between a child's gender identity and the child's sex-typed motor behavior, and shows how social reinforcement shapes both processes. Hay, Barlow, and Hay (1981) successfully treated a 10-year-old boy with gender identity confusion using covert modeling techniques. This child was referred because his rigid, stereotypically feminine behaviors (nonverbal mannerisms, toy preferences, dress choice) were punished by peers. Direct observation confirmed that the boy sat, stood, and walked in a decidedly girlish way, and used many of the feminine gestures described by Rekers and his colleagues (Rekers, Lovaas, & Low, 1974). Treatment targeted each of these behaviors separately and employed covert modeling of more masculine motor behaviors. In these covert sequences, the boy was instructed to imagine his favorite male television character (the Bionic Man), performing each behavior (sitting, standing, and walking), and to imagine himself imitating these gestures; this sequence was followed by imagined social reinforcement from the boy's peers. Each specific behavior changed in a masculine direction as the covert procedure was applied to it. In addition, the boy's parents reported an increase in his frequency of choosing male playmates and masculine play activities as treatment proceeded. It is important to note that treatment was not aimed at the reduction of this child's pretreatment feminine behavior, but rather the goal was to expand his behavioral repertoire to include both masculine and feminine gestures. Inclusion of masculine motor behaviors permitted this child greater behavioral androgyny. As a result of treatment, this child learned to predict the typical social response to feminine and masculine motor behaviors in different situations. At the completion of treatment, the boy reported that peers teased him less and that he was more effective with peers. This increased popularity is consistent with the findings of the Hayes and Leonard (in press) analogue study, which revealed that men showing extreme feminine motor behavior were perceived by others as less likeable than men demonstrating masculine gestures. Positive social feedback from peers and family, real and imagined, helped this boy view his own behavior in a positive light and balance the demands of his family and school with his own gender role preferences. Perhaps a similar process occurs spontaneously in children who are behaviorally androgynous at a younger age. Investigation of familial contributions to this process seem in order.

As seen in the above examples, the motor behavior checklist provides one measure of complex sex-role behaviors and yields useful information concerning childhood sex roles. Additionally, this measure has clinical utility and can increase our understanding of sex-role problems. For example, Chesler (1972) suggested that many symptoms of psychological problems involve either extreme acceptance or extreme rejection of conventional sex roles. Women often appear trapped, since stereotypically feminine behavior is acceptable but ineffective, while stereotypically masculine behavior is unacceptable but effective. This conflict, where it exists, may contribute to the higher prevalence of certain psychological disorders in women (e.g., depression, obesity, agoraphobia). If the hypothesis outlined above, concerning the relationship between an individual's acceptance of culturally typical sex roles and the experience of psychological problems, is correct, this would reveal a great deal of information concerning one of the mechanisms involved in maintaining certain behavioral disorders, as well as providing insight into both the beneficial and the destructive aspects of sex-role processes.

CLINICAL ASSESSMENT OF SEX-ROLE MOTOR BEHAVIOR

The motor behavior checklist offers clinically useful information. As with all behavior modification techniques and behavioral assessment tools, this checklist can be used to accomplish a variety of goals; that is, "it can be used to fortify existing sex roles and to maintain the current social status of women" (Blechman, 1980) or it can be used to promote equality between women and men. In our opinion, the technology of behavior therapy is value free with respect to social norms and can be adapted to the needs of individual clients. Objective assessment helps to avoid value-laden generalizations about individual clients. A thorough functional analysis of behavior often suggests the environmental and organismic conditions which contribute to a specific presenting problem. In the following examples, the motor behavior checklist is used as a dependent measure and to assess and specify what treatment is needed in working with adult clients.

Barlow, Reynolds, and Agras (1973) employed an early version of the checklist in the treatment of a 17-year-old boy who was diagnosed as transsexual. Because of his age, this client was not considered an appropriate candidate for sex-change surgery and decided to enter a treatment program to change his gender identity. A variety of assessment devices were used tapping specific aspects of the client's sex-role behaviors and sexual arousal patterns. At the onset of treatment, the client's motor behavior was rated as extremely and rigidly feminine; he displayed few masculine behaviors while sitting, standing, and walking. All observations were made without the client's awareness. Direct modification of sitting, standing, and walking behaviors was conducted via modeling, videotape feedback, and therapist reinforcement; each behavior was targeted separately and a multiple baseline across behaviors was employed. The client demonstrated a dramatic increase in masculine motor behaviors and a decrease in feminine movements during this intervention; he reported receiving much less ridicule from others and stated that he felt more at ease in public situations at the end of this intervention. After motor behavior changed, other concerns were targeted (e.g., social skills, sexual fantasy, and sexual arousal patterns);

during the second phase of treatment, newly acquired motor behavior remained stable. This case illustrates how complex role behavior can be defined, broken down into several components, and sequentially modified to produce clinically significant change.

The second clinical example involves a different use of the motor behavior checklist. Barlow, Mills, Agras, and Steinman (1980) compared the sex-role motor behavior of eight presurgical male-to-female transsexuals with eight women whose motor behavior was feminine. Two trained raters observed these people without their knowledge. Behavior ratings found more feminine and masculine motor behaviors among the women, although both groups showed few masculine behaviors. These data supplement clinical reports that male-to-female transsexuals caricature women, exaggerating the feminine role (Pauly, 1974; Walinder, 1967; Money & Primrose, 1968).

Leonard (1981) used this checklist in the treatment of a man with depressed affect, decreased activity level, and few social contacts. A functional analysis of behavior indicated that the client's social withdrawal was promoted by his feminine motor behavior, which frequently elicited verbal abuse or teasing by strangers in public. Specific motor behaviors were targeted, using modeling, practice, feedback, and therapist praise. As the client's motor behavior became less feminine, the frequency of public teasing decreased. Cognitive restructuring techniques were employed to alleviate his depression and to increase his activity level. By the end of treatment, the client reported an increase in social contacts and activity level, as well as a complete absence of verbal abuse when in public situations. His scores on the Bem Sex Role Inventory revealed changes in his self-description, even though this was not a specific target of treatment. This case suggests a more direct relationship between motor behavior and other components of a client's sex role than has previously been demonstrated. Synchrony between the motor behavior and verbal self-report response systems may be required for a long-lasting treatment outcome. Induction of response synchrony may be as important in the treatment of sex-role disturbances as it is in the treatment of phobic disorders (Rachman & Hodgson, 1974; Sartory, Rachman, & Grey, 1977).

As is evident from these examples, the motor behavior checklist is relevant to a variety of clinical situations, clients, and problems. A clinical researcher can use the checklist together with a single-case experimental design (e.g., Hersen & Barlow, 1976), to tease out situation-specific motor behavior effects and to gain experimental control over treatment.

For example, the checklist and a multiple baseline design across settings could be used to assess a client's sex-role motor behavior in different settings and to modify the maladaptive behaviors within each.

For a successful experimental approach to clinical sex-role problems, a functional analysis of behavior must follow the initial determination of the general presenting problem (Nelson & Barlow, 1981). A functional analysis reveals not only parameters of sex-role behaviors, but also social antecedents and consequences. Although client motor behaviors would be a central focus of the functional analysis, sex-role attitudes also need to be assessed. Environmental deficits must be given as much attention as client behavior deficits. Although this is an easy recommendation to make, translation into practice is difficult. As Blechman (1980) noted, most behavioral formulations of treatment for women ignore environmental deficits. An analysis of motor behavior should observe others' responses to her nonverbal sex-role behaviors, and make reasonable attempts to change prejudiced behavior, rather than its victims.

Clinical use of the checklist must aim to decipher the often complex and confusing interrelationships between clients' sex-role behavior and surrounding environmental pressures. Pressures to enact conventional sex roles take the form of punishment and praise; when these pressures are attended to by the client, they set limits on social effectiveness. Since behavioral androgyny seems adaptive, treatment goals should aim for this outcome. This may require sensitizing men to the social implications of their behavior, and desensitizing women.

CONCLUSIONS AND RECOMMENDATIONS

The motor behavior checklist sidesteps the traditional study of sex *differences*. The checklist is not intended to measure innate male and female differences; rather it focuses on aspects of sex-role behavior which are susceptible to environmental influences. The purposes of the checklist are practical rather than theoretical. At the same time, clinical and experimental use of the checklist could unravel the complexities of culturally prescribed behaviors. At present, components of sex roles can be measured by self-report inventories, such as the Bem Sex Role Inventory (Bem, 1974) or by the motor behavior checklist. Self-report and observational measures seem to tap partly independent components of sex roles. It is the interaction between the loosely related components of sex roles which defines the sex-role construct. Future research must explore the nature of interaction between components of the sex-role construct, since it is unclear how and when each component spontaneously develops during childhood and adolescence, and how much change these components undergo in adulthood. Exploration of the effects of self, peer, and adult feedback on components of the construct is also needed. Studies of interaction in the families of behaviorally flexible preteens and teenagers would provide useful information. Since conventional sex-role behaviors may be more crucial to the psychological well-being of men than of women, sensitivity to the different social circumstances of men and women should characterize future research on the topic.

People tend to vary their feminine and masculine motor behaviors from one setting to another. This may happen because of consistently different contingencies in the home as opposed to the classroom, or it may happen because people anticipate different reactions and modify their demeanor accordingly. There is a general tendency for people to act less feminine in public places than they do at home. This seems to be an adaptive tendency, since both sexes are considered less "natural" when displaying feminine motor behaviors, since males displaying feminine motor behaviors are rated as less "likeable" and less "confident," and since both sexes elicit significantly more compliance with masculine motor behaviors. Further investigations of the contributions of motor behaviors to social effectiveness are needed. The relative contributions to social effectiveness of the cognitive versus the motoric components of the sex-role construct deserves exploration. Finally, there may be unknown routes to the enhancement of social effectiveness which allow sex-role preference to remain unchanged. Information about these routes would increase the freedom of choice of unconventional clients. The relationship between sex-role preference and psychological disorder is the topic of much speculation.

Various chapters in this book endorse the view that the conventional feminine sex role is maladaptive. These include the Norman, Johnson, and Miller chapter (11) on depression, Padawer and Goldfried's chapter (13) on phobias and anxiety, Fodor and Thal's chapter (14) on obesity, and Linehan's chapter (6) on assertiveness. Barlow's motor behavior checklist provides an unobtrusive measure of conventional feminine behavior might might enrich discourse on the topic. For example, rather than assuming that depressed women are depressed because they are women and women are hyperfeminine, the checklist might be used to measure degree of rigid hyperfeminity. More depressed women should be more rigidly hyperfeminine, if conventional wisdom is accurate. Perhaps some women would benefit more from training in nonverbal behavior than in verbal assertiveness. The nucleus of such a tool is already available.

The central proposition in this chapter, the purported relationship between behavioral androgyny and adaptive functioning, requires further inquiry. There has been considerable investigation of "psychological androgyny" (Bem, 1974, 1975) through self-report inventories. Few pertinent inquiries of observed behavior can take place in the absence of an appropriate measure. Our ignorance about the relationship between behavioral androgyny and adaptive functioning limits clinical innovations and promotes endless philosophical debates. The checklist provides a simple but concrete way to measure flexibility. Future research must determine if this sort of behavioral flexibility is a necessary and sufficient condition for healthy human functioning or merely a trivial by-product.

Perhaps sex-typed motor behavior is neither all-important, nor trivial. Perhaps it contributes to (and is affected by) healthy daily functioning much like other skill repertoires. The ultimate importance of sex-typed motor behavior may reside in its permeability to clinical interventions. Since these behaviors are flexible, adaptive motor behavior can easily be taught, and if this tuition generalizes to other behavior domains, then we have added a broadly useful tool to our clinical storehouse.

From a behavioral perspective, the checklist offers the advantages of providing an objective measurement device which can be employed in a variety of settings, including clinical settings. As is suggested by Blechman (1980) when conducting therapy with women, it is critical to fully explore the conditions which control a client's problem behavior and to examine environmental deficits with the goal of providing therapeutic services that do not perpetuate situational factors harmful to women. Toward this end, Blechman recommends increased attention to skills training which will facilitate the woman's control over her behavior and environment. Nonverbal behaviors are a frequently forgotten component of social roles and as Weitz (1976) concludes, it is only when both verbal and nonverbal behaviors are combined that a complete understanding of social processes and social roles will be achieved. This understanding seems to be an integral ingredient in the development of effective skill training programs for women.

Throughout this process, it seems important to avoid the lure of justifying social myths. As Shields (1975) discusses in her examination of the evolution of the psychology of women, social scientists and psychologists in particular, have in the past frequently used their empirical tools and theoretical formulations to fortify social values concerning sex-role behavior. While behavioral treatment techniques and assessment devices do not in and of themselves promote specific social values, the use of these therapies and measures can be directed towards a number of goals. It thus seems important not only to explore the nature of sex-role behavior and to practice sex-fair therapy, but also to use the knowledge gained in these pursuits toward the achievement of equitable social systems.

REFERENCES

Aiello, J. R., & Aiello, T. D. The development of personal space: Proxemic behavior of children six through sixteen. *Human Ecology,* 1974, *2,* 177–189.

Barlow, D. H. Behavior therapy: The next decade. *Behavior Therapy,* 1980, *22,* 315–328.

Barlow, D. H. Assessment of sexual behavior. In A. R. Ciminero, K. S. Calhoun, & H. E. Adams (Eds.), *Handbook of behavioral assessment.* New York: Wiley, 1977.

Barlow, D. H., Hayes, S. C., Nelson, R. O., Steele, D. L., Meeler, M. E., & Mills, J. R. Sex role motor behavior: A behavioral checklist. *Behavioral Assessment,* 1979, *1,* 119–138.

Barlow, D. H., & Mavissakalian M. Directions in the assessment and treatment of phobia: The next decade. In M. Mavissakalian & D. H. Barlow, (Eds.), *Phobia: Psychological and pharmacological treatment.* New York: Guilford, 1981.

Barlow, D. H., Mills, J. R., Agras, W. S., & Steinman, D. L. A comparison of sex-typed motor behavior in male-to-female transsexuals and women. *Archives of Sexual Behavior,* 1980, *9,* 245–253.

Barlow, D. H., Reynolds, E. J., & Agras, W. S. Gender identity change in a transsexual. *Archives of General Psychiatry,* 1973, *28,* 569–576.

Bem, S. L. Sex-role adaptability: One consequence of psychological androgyny. *Journal of Consulting and Clinical Psychology,* 1975, *31,* 634–643.

Bem, S. L. The measurement of psychological androgyny. *Journal of Consulting and Clinical Psychology,* 1974, *42,* 155–162.

Bem, S. L., & Lenney, E. Sex typing and the avoidance of cross-sex behavior. *Journal of Personality and Social Psychology,* 1976, *33,* 48–54.

Bem, S. L., Martyna, W., & Watson, C. Sex-type and androgyny: Further explorations of the expressive domain. *Journal of Personality and Social Psychology,* 1976, *34,* 1016–1023.

Birdwhistell, R. *Kinesics and context: Essays on bodily motion communication.* Philadelphia: University of Pennsylvania Press, 1970.

Blechman, E. A. Behavior therapies. In A. M. Brodsky & R. T. Hare-Mustin (Eds.), *Women and psychotherapy.* New York: Guilford, 1980.

Brown, D. Sex role preference in young children. *Psychological Monographs,* 1956, *70* (14, Whole no. 421).

Chesler, P. *Women and madness.* Garden City, N.Y.: Doubleday, 1972.

Constantinople, A. Masculinity–feminity: An exception to a famous dictum. *Psychological Bulletin,* 1973, *80,* 389–407.

Edney, J. J., & Jordan-Edney, N. L. Territorial spacing on a beach. *Sociometry,* 1974, *37,* 92–104.

Edwards, A. L. *The social desirability variable in personality assessment and research*. New York: Dryden, 1957.

Fontaine, C. M. *Cognitive and self-reward patterns in an achievement situation as a function of task outcome, sex, and achievement motivation*. Paper presented at the meeting of the Eastern Psychological Association, New York City, April 1976.

Freedman, J. L., & Fraser, S. C. Compliance without pressure: The foot-in-the-door technique. *Journal of Personality and Social Psychology*, 1966, *4*, 195–202.

Green, R. One hundred ten feminine and masculine boys: Behavioral contrasts and demographic similarities. *Archives of Sexual Behavior*, 1976, *5*, 425–446.

Green, R., Fuller M., Rutley B. R., & Hendler, J. Playroom toy preferences of fifteen masculine and fifteen feminine boys. *Behavior Therapy*, 1972, *3*, 425–429.

Green, R., & Money, J. *Transsexualism and sex reassignment*. Baltimore: Johns Hopkins Press, 1969.

Hathaway, S. R., & McKinley, J. C. *The Minnesota Multiphasic Personality Inventory*. New York: Psychological Corp., 1943.

Hay, W., Barlow, D. H., & Hay, L. R. Treatment of stereotypic cross-gender motor behavior using covert modeling in a boy with gender identity confusion. *Journal of Consulting and Clinical Psychology*, 1981, *49*, 388–394.

Hayes S. C., & Leonard S. R. Sex related motor behavior: Effects on social impressions and social cooperation. *Archives of Sexual Behavior*, in press.

Hayes, S. C., Nelson, R. O., Steele, D. L., Meeler, M. E., & Barlow, D. H. The development of the display and knowledge of sex related motor behavior in children. *Child Behavior Therapy*, 1981, *3*, 1–24.

Heckerman, C. L., Schoen, S., & Barlow, D. H. Situational specificity of sex role behavior: A preliminary investigation. *Behavioral Assessment*, 1981, *3*, 43–54.

Henley, N. M. Status and sex: Some touching observations. *Bulletin of the Psychonomic Society*, 1973, *2*, 91–93.

Hersen, M., & Barlow, D. H. *Single case experimental designs: Strategies for studying behavior change*. New York: Pergamon, 1976.

Hewes, G. W. The anthropology of posture. *Scientific American*, 1957, *196*, 123–132.

Jenni, D. A., & Jenni, M. Carrying behavior in humans: Analysis of sex differences. *Science*, 1976, *188*, 859–860.

Kelly, J. A., Caudill, M. S., Hathorn, S., & O'Brien, C. G. Socially undesirable sex-correlated characteristics: Implications for androgyny and adjustment. *Journal of Consulting and Clinical Psychology*, 1977, *45*, 1185–1186.

Klein A. R., & Bates, J. E. *Gender typing of game choices and qualities of boys' play behavior*. Unpublished manuscript, 1979. (Available from J.E. Bates, Department of Psychology, Indiana University, Bloomington, Ind. 47401.)

Kohlberg L. A cognitive-developmental analysis of children's sex role concepts and attitudes. In E. Maccoby (Ed.), *The development of sex differences*. Stanford, Calif.: Stanford University Press, 1966.

Lang, P. J. Fear reduction and fear behavior: Problems in treating a construct. In J. M. Shlien (Ed.), *Research in psychotherapy* (Vol. 3). Washington, D.C.: American Psychological Association, 1968.

Leibman, N. The effects of sex and race norms on personal space. *Environment and Behavior*, 1970, *2*, 208–246.

Leonard, S. Sex related motor behavior change: A demonstration of empirical clinical practice. *Behavioral Assessment*, 1981, *3*, 403–410.

Lott, D. F., & Sommer, R. Seating arrangements and status. *Journal of Personality and Social Psychology*, 1967, *7*, 90–95.

Maccoby, E., & Jacklin, C. *The psychology of sex differences*. Stanford, Calif.: Stanford University Press; 1974.

Mehrabian, A. *Nonverbal communication*. Chicago: Aldine-Atherton, 1972.

Michael, G., & Willis, F. N. The development of gestures as a function of social class, education, and sex. *Psychological Record*, 1968, *18*, 515–519.

Mischel, W. Toward a cognitive social learning reconceptualization of personality. *Psychological Review*, 1973, *80*, 252–283.

Money, J., & Ehrhardt, A. *Man and woman: Boy and girl*. Baltimore: Johns Hopkins University Press, 1972.

Money, J., & Primrose, C. Sexual dimorphism and dissociation in the psychology of male transsexuals. *Journal of Nervous and Mental Disease*, 1968, *147*, 472–486.

Moss, H. Sex, age, and state as determinants of mother–infant interaction. *Merrill–Palmer Quarterly*, 1967, *13*, 19–36.

Nelson, R. O., & Barlow, D. H. Behavioral assessment: Basic strategies and initial procedures. In D.H. Barlow (Ed.), *Behavioral assessment of adult disorders*. New York: Guilford, 1981.

Pauly, I. B. Female transsexualism: Part II. *Archives of Sexual Behavior*. 1974, *3*, 509–526.

Rachman, S., & Hodgson, R. I. Synchrony and desynchrony in fear and avoidance. *Behaviour Research and Therapy*, 1974, *12*, 311–318.

Rekers, G. A., Amaro-Plotkin, H. D., & Low, B. P. Sex-typed mannerisms in normal boys and girls as a function of sex and age. *Child Development*, 1977, *48*, 275–278.

Rekers, G. A., Lovaas, O. I., & Low, B. P. The behavioral treatment of a "transsexual" preadolescent boy. *Journal of Abnormal Child Psychology*, 1974, *2*, 99–115.

Rekers, G. A., Willis, T. J., Yates, C. E., Rosen, A. C., & Low, B. P. Assessment of childhood gender behavior change. *Journal of Child Psychology and Psychiatry*, 1977, *18*, 53–65.

Rose, Y., & Tryon, W. Judgments of assertive behavior as a function of speech loudness, latency, content, gestures, inflection, and sex. *Behavior Modification*, 1979, *3*, 112–123.

Sartory, B., Rachman, S., & Grey, S. An investigation of the relation between reported fear and heart rate. *Behaviour Research and Therapy*, 1977, *15*, 435–438.

Sears, R., Rau, L., & Alpert, R. *Identification and child rearing*. Stanford, Calif.: Stanford University Press, 1965.

Shaffer, D. R., & Wegley, C. Success orientation and sex role congruence as determinants of the attractiveness of competent women. *Journal of Personality*, 1974, *42*, 586–600.

Shields, S. A. Functionalism, Darwinism, and the psychology of women. *American Psychologist*, 1975, *30*, 739–754.

Spence, J. T., Helmreich, R., & Stapp, J. Ratings of self and peers on sex role attributes and their relation to self-esteem and conceptions of masculinity and femininity. *Journal of Personality and Social Psychology*, 1975, *32*, 29–39.

Strong, E. K. *Vocational interests of men and women*. Stanford, Calif.: Stanford University Press, 1943.

Taynor, J., & Deaux, K. Equity and perceived sex differences: Role behavior as defined by the task, the mode, and the actor. *Journal of Personality and Social Psychology*, 1975, *32*, 381–390.

Terman, L. M., & Miles, C. *Sex and personality: Studies in masculinity and femininity*. New York: McGraw-Hill, 1936.

Unger, R. K. Toward a redefinition of sex and gender. *American Psychologist*, 1979, *34*, 1085–1094. (a)

Unger, R. K. *Female and male: Psychological perspectives*. New York: Harper & Row, 1979. (b)

Walinder, J. *Transsexualism: A study of forty-three cases*. Göteborg, Sweden: Scandinavian University Books, 1967.

Weitz, S. Sex difference in nonverbal communication. *Sex Roles*, 1976, *2*, 175–184.

3

BEHAVIORAL ASSESSMENT OF WOMEN CLIENTS

MARIAN L. MACDONALD

OVERVIEW

The field of behavioral assessment has virtually exploded in the past decade. Ten years ago, those of us teaching behavioral assessment could not find texts to adopt for our courses (Evans, 1982). Today, many fine texts are available, some as second editions, and two major behavioral assessment journals are well under way. It is no longer fair to regard behavioral assessment as a new field; it is a young field, but one that has come ot age.

We must, then, evaluate the field critically, and make judgments on the basis of product, not promise. From this perspective, the picture is a disappointing one: There is no technology for doing what the old "differential diagnoses" were supposed to do—identify the problem and indicate the appropriate intervention; there is no heuristic or pragmatic taxonomy bringing order to behaviors, to situations, or to their inter-actions; and there is no compelling evidence that behavioral assessment data are any more successful at predicting real life behavior than were the traditional assessment data before them.

For feminists, the picture is an even more disappointing one. There has been essentially no attention given to feminist issues in the behavioral assessment literature.

With no feminist behavioral assessment literature to draw on, one might wonder what a behavioral assessment chapter in a feminist text could hope to do. Frankly, the author has puzzled over this question on more than one occasion. What such a chapter *cannot* do seems a

Marian L. MacDonald. Department of Psychology, University of Massachusetts, Amherst, Massachusetts.

question more easily answered. With no grounding literature, it cannot specify how women clients and subjects can be fairly assessed. Even more basically, in the absence of data directly bearing on gender bias, it cannot develop a tenable *scientific* argument supporting the thesis that gender bias in behavioral assessment does, in fact, exist.

What a feminist behavioral assessment chapter could try to do, and what this chapter does try to do, is raise questions that come up *given the assumption that gender bias is in fact real*. Although a logical argument in support of this assumption could be made and indeed will be made shortly in this chapter, it must not be forgotten that logical arguments can easily be wrong and/or discounted. It is empirically based arguments that are needed; with this in mind, more than anything else this chapter is intended to serve as a feminist call to arms. Toward this end, the chapter provides first clarifying contextual–historical background (an overview of assessment as a form of measurement and a review of behavioral assessment's emergence and rationale); this is followed by a summary–critique of the six most common behavioral assessment strategies (behavioral interviewing, self-monitoring, questionnaires, psychophysiological measures, naturalistic observation, and controlled observation). The chapter's purposes are to highlight behavioral assessment's strengths and weaknesses as an intervention aid and evaluation tool, and especially to sensitize readers to areas of potential gender bias warranting study in a research context, and caution in a clinical one. The chapter begins with an anecdotal example.

We have all heard stories of willing women who have been refused employment on loading docks. The employer's argument has typically been given as the women's inability to lift heavy objects. Had we observed one of the employer's test situations, we might have seen stacks of 100-pound bags to be lifted, bags which all but the most muscular of women—the superwomen in this context—were incapable of lifting. Given this situation, why is it concluded that the women have a deficiency rather than the bags? Had the bags been 500-pound ones, neither the women nor the men would have been able to lift them; doubtless the conclusion under these circumstances would have been not that the people (women and men) "were unable" to lift them, but rather that the bags "were too heavy" to lift.

The point of this example is that what we observe or measure, the way we observe or measure it, and most especially the attributions we make and the conclusions we draw from what we have observed or measured are all influenced by cultural expectations and assumptions.

Cultures are constructed realities. There is no dictum in nature demanding that bags be constructed so that they will weigh 100, as opposed to 25 or 500 pounds. Where cultural "realities" have been built around men, they, and the assessments which grow from them, will be biased against women. It is the thesis of this chapter that the major source of gender bias in behavioral assessment is found in our repeatedly measuring women from the cultural perspective of a man's world.

BACKGROUND

Both behavioral assessment, and traditional assessment before it, have evaluated women in the context of a culture constructed around men. It is important to recognize, however, that this shared bias is not a problem embedded in the logic or mathematics of measurement theory, but instead resides directly in the assessment technologies that have been developed using that theory. Sowell (1981) addresses this distinction with a case in point:

> Equality is such an easily understood concept in mathematics that we may not realize it is a bottomless pit of complexities anywhere else. That is because in mathematics we have eliminated the concreteness and complexities of real things. When we say that two plus two equals four, we either don't say two *what* or we say the same what after each number. But if we said that two apples plus two apples equals four oranges, we would be in trouble. (p. 13)

Rather than creating bias itself, measurement theory provides a vehicle for generating solutions to the problems of gender bias, and it provides one method for detecting gender bias that occurs in specific tests. For these reasons, a review of psychometric theory—measurement theory as it is relevant to psychological assessment—is critical in the present context.

All psychological assessment is rooted in observations (Anastasi, 1982). Exactly what is observed, and how it is observed, is not, of course, determined randomly. Specific observations take place within a framework provided by an assessment system. And systems of assessment are based on sets of assumptions about two things (McReynolds, 1975).

The first set of assumptions involves a conceptualization of what people "are like" or what the relevant controlling dimensions of human behavior are. At the most general level, these assumptions address whether behavior is controlled by factors external to the person (e.g., environmental pressures), or internal to the person, (e.g., inherited features), or by a complex interaction between internal and external influences. Also dictated by these assumptions, however, are the specific dimensions of importance (e.g., ward atmosphere, authoritarianism, level of assertion, expectation) that can be considered within the general categories of internal, external, or interactive factors. Clearly, selection is involved at both the general–categorical and the specific–dimensional assumptive levels; it is conceivable, if it is believed that there are gender differences in which specific selections are appropriate, that there might be biases in selecting factors systematically that are more relevant to the functioning of one gender than the other. One might wonder, for example, whether assertion is as relevant to the functioning of women as it is to men, and why assertion is considered to be so much more important to measure than is nurturance. On the more general level, one might wonder whether the physical *and social* environments confronted by women and men exert identical degrees of influence over their behaviors; if not, one might wonder which gender's "reality" gets embedded in the assessment system's assumptive network.

It should be noted that in the set of assumptions about what people "are like," there may be a premise positing a fundamental superiority of one gender relative to the other. It has been argued that a fundamental superiority of men historically has been posited in psychology and consistently pervades psychological assessment, so that when systematic sex differences result on tests, they are interpreted as evidence of women's inferiority rather than as evidence of test bias (see Unger, 1979). It would appear, then, that the loading-dock example at the outset of this chapter cannot be dismissed as a straw man.

The second set of assumptions grounding any assessment system involves specifying which particular observables—signs, cues, or behaviors—are to be taken as indices of the designated controlling dimensions. Again, these assumptions may specify behaviors systematically more common or more appropriate for one gender than the other. When one visits museums displaying "artwork," why are quilts and crewel embroidery seen so rarely?

The point under discussion is that the products of assessment systems are very powerfully influenced by various assumptions which underlie them. Perhaps the clearest illustration of how these assumptions operate, as well as where they initially come from, can be found in astrology, which was the first well-developed system of assessment (McReynolds, 1975).

Astrology developed within a culture viewing behavior as determined at the moment of birth by the complex interactions of the wishes of a cadre of immortal gods. The gods' wishes at any given moment were signified, it was believed, by the positions heavenly bodies held relative to one another. As a consequence, careful records were kept of the various stars' positions, and assessments were conducted by studying the relative positions of the stars at the moment of an individual's birth. The product of this assessment system was the individual horoscope.

The cultural assumptions which were predominant when astrology developed clearly had a profound impact on the system's assumptions about what should be measured and how one should measure it. In reviewing the scores of assessment systems found in the three millennia since the development of astrology, McReynolds (1975) has noted repeatedly a close correspondence between popular assessment systems of given times and the cultural assumptions about human behavior predominant during those times. He observed especially that when cultures regarded external factors as controlling human behavior, assessment systems were built to measure those relevant external factors, but that when cultures regarded internal factors as controlling, assessment systems were constructed to measure them. As will become evident in the next section of this chapter, behavioral assessment developed in large measure to accommodate a radical shift in views about what causes human behavior and, in fact, this shift in focus remains behavioral assessment's most distinguishing feature. For the moment, however, the point to underscore is that assessment technologies have historically reflected, rather than enlightened, the cultures and cultural assumptions surrounding them. If one regards contemporary American culture as biased against women, it would seem logically reasonable, following McReynolds (1975), to regard behavioral assessment as reflecting, and perpetuating, that bias.

While assessment systems, and the cultural realities giving rise to them, dictate what should be measured, it is the logic and mathematics of measurement theory which addresses how whatever it is that should be measured can be measured well. Measurement theory draws heavily on statistics, which is a fortunate result of dealing with observables, for with observables there can be agreement on whether phenomena are present. As a consequence of the potential for agreement, the reliability of coding observables can be studied. With reliable coding, how often a phenomenon occurs can be counted. And with counting, assessment can become quantitative.

Quantitative assessment systems, of which behavioral assessment is one example, are bound by two principles. The first, which will be considered in greater detail shortly, is that numbers, be they counts, ratings, or any type of score, have no quantitative meaning in isolation (Freedman, Pisani, & Purves, 1978). Abstract numbers acquire meaning as quantities only when they are compared to other scores. The second principle, of great importance in the assessment of women, is that scores are comparable *if and only if* they have been derived under the same standard conditions (Wiggins, 1973). Since scores are a joint function of what's being measured and the conditions of measurement, differences in conditions will make scores for what's being measured noncomparable. In illustration of this point, consider the following example.

You and a friend wear exactly the same ring size. Your friend is planning a December trip to Hawaii; you give her some money and ask her to buy you a coral ring while she is there. She returns with the ring, you slip it on, and it is too large. Why? Because when your friend made the purchase, she measured its size under hot, humid conditions, and December weather is cold where you live. The difference in assessment conditions, here the temperature and humidity, made the derived scores, here ring sizes, noncomparable.

"Identical testing conditions" is one of those phrases much more easily said than done. Anastasi (1982) has identified three things which must be held constant in the testing situation if scores are to be comparable; the first is the conditions under which behavior is observed. An obvious example can be found in the interview situation: "Show me how you irritate your husband" might elicit a very different role play, even given the same *in vivo* behavior, than would the instruction "Tell me what you're saying just before your husband gets irrational." More subtle examples may be found in Behavioral Avoidance Tests, where research assistants' sex-role stereotypes might influence the nature of the demand characteristics communicated to their subjects before testing. The general point to note is that whenever observables are derived under different testing conditions, specifically conditions where differences systematically favor one gender over the other, gender bias will make those scores noncomparable.

The second condition Anastasi (1982) has identified as one which must be held constant for scores to be comparable is the way in which observed behavior is scored. Under some circumstances, such as with multiple-choice or true–false self-report tests, it is easy to guarantee a uniform response-to-numerical-score strategy. Under other circumstances, however, such as ones in which observed behavior is rated by judges whose judgments are influenced by sex-role stereotypes, consistent observable-behavior-to-rated-score procedures, especially across genders, may be much more difficult to arrange (Moon & MacDonald, 1982).

The final condition Anastasi (1982) identified as one which must be held constant if scores are to be comparable is the way in which assessed scores are given quantitative meaning. As has been noted, numerical scores do not convey quantitative value when taken singly, they acquire value only when they are compared with other scores. Another way of saying this is that scores are made quantitatively meaningful by placing them within some larger frame of reference, one which reveals whether their value is large or small, given that frame of reference. To argue that 10 is a larger or higher score than 5, for instance, we must be sure that the scores did not come from two different tests with 10 and 5 questions, respectively.

Frames of reference afford quantitative value to scores by providing an empirical basis for comparison. Probably the most familiar frame of reference is found in normative data (Haynes, 1978). The normative data strategy for generating a frame of reference requires that a large, representative sample, called a standardization sample, be tested under identical (standard, hence the sample name) conditions. The resulting distribution of scores is used to give individual scores quantitative value by translating them into standard scores which express how far above or below the standardization sample's mean they are, in standard deviation units:

$$(\text{Raw score} - \text{Sample mean})/\text{Sample standard deviation}$$

With this strategy, the standardization sample's mean is used as a point of reference, and the largeness or smallness of individual scores can be seen by determining how far they are from the average score, relative to how far away from the average most scores would be expected to fall.

The normative data strategy can be quite useful for identifying individuals who depart markedly from the average or the "norm" on some dimension (e.g., number of observed Research Diagnostic Criteria of the Depressive Syndrome; see Spitzer, Endicott, & Robins, 1978) or for determining whether the frequency of a person's behavior has become indistinguishable from the average frequency, or the norm (Kazdin, 1977). It is critical to note, however, that individual scores may be referred to normative sample's distributions for meaning only when there is no reason to believe there is any systematic difference between that individual or their conditions of measurement and the individuals in or conditions of measurement for the standardization sample. It would be inappropriate, for example, to assign value to a woman's score relative to scores from a standardization sample comprised only of men. If we regard men and women as different cultural groups in this context, Anastasi's (1976) comments regarding culture-fair testing become most relevant:

> For man, culture permeates nearly all environmental contacts. Since all behavior is thus affected by the cultural milieu in which the individual is reared and since psychological tests are but samples of behavior, cultural influences will and should be reflected in test performance. It is therefore futile to try to devise a test that is *free* from cultural influences. . . . It is unlikely, moreover, that any test can be "fair" to more than one cultural group, especially if the cultures are quite dissimilar. . . . Every test tends to favor persons from the culture within which it was developed. . . . It is therefore to be expected that on tests developed within the majority American culture, for example, persons reared in that culture will generally excel. (pp. 345–356)

Furthermore, if normative data have been generated by a standardization sample comprised of equal numbers of women and men, it is essential to compute separate male and female distributions and compare their summary statistics. If there are differences between the distributions' means or standard deviations, cross-gender comparisons are not legitimate. Whether the differences arise from veridical differences between women and men, or from test-embedded gender bias differentially favoring or influencing one gender or the other, is psychometrically indeterminate from such data, and conclusions that one gender is superior to, or more variable than, the other on such grounds are not legitimate (Anastasi, 1976; MacDonald, 1982).

A second method for generating score frames of reference involves comparing a single score to other scores obtained by the same individual at different points in time. This reference source, quite common in behavioral assessment, is the basis of single subject designs. The strategy has proven quite useful for determining whether interventions result in any measureable effects. Moreover, since performances by the individual woman provide the entire source for the frame of reference, when standardization is insured, this strategy is immune to gender bias effects.

A third strategy for generating frames of reference is available, but has been used only rarely (Haynes, 1978); it is appropriate whenever a finite set of behaviors can be identified as comprising a specifiable content domain. The approach has been used most often in criterion-referenced testing (Gleser, 1963). With this approach, the components of successful performance in a situation are identified and tests are constructed to sample systematically each component (MacDonald, 1978). Scores are referenced by indicating what percentage of the critical performance components have been mastered.

It might seem at first that this third strategy, which compares against performance rather than person standards, would be the strategy most immune to gender bias test effects. It must be recognized, however, that this strategy has as its performance criterion performances which occur in culturally constructed "realities." Recollection of the loading-dock example will illustrate the grave potential for gender bias hidden within this approach.

In summary, psychological tests result from the marriage of an assessment system and measurement theory. Unfortunately, this union has several points of entry for gender bias. Regarding measurement theory, because scores have no quantitative meaning in isolation and acquire value only in comparison with scores derived under the same conditions, whenever testing conditions vary systematically with the tested person's gender, gender bias in testing will occur. Moreover, even when these conditions are successfully held constant across genders, gender bias in the informing assumptions of the parent assessment system will work to one sex's disadvantage.

BEHAVIORAL ASSESSMENT'S EMERGENCE AND RATIONALE

No chapter on the behavioral assessment system would be complete without a presentation of behavioral assessment's emergence and rationale. Such a review is of particular importance in this context, for it will suggest that behavioral assessment has more potential than did its predecessors to be responsive to feminist concerns. Before reviewing behavioral assessment's history, however, a central point should be emphasized. Behavioral assessment's focus is *not* on behavior: it is on behavior *as it occurs in its situational context* (O'Leary, 1979). Behavior theorists have argued that behavior varies as a function of, and cannot be measured apart from, the situation which surrounds it (Mischel, 1968; Peterson, 1968) ever since the classic studies of Hartshorne and May (Hartshorne & May, 1928; Hartshorne, May, & Shuttleworth, 1930) and Endler and Hunt (1966, 1968, 1969). Unfortunately, however, behavioral assessment has often been done in a way that overemphasizes the measurement of behavior, and underemphasizes the measurement of the behavior's surrounding situations (Hersen, 1976). As a result, behavioral assessment suffers from a serious deficiency: an articulated taxonomy of behavior-relevant situational parameters has not yet been identified. Nonetheless, the behavioral assessment system rests on a fundamental commitment to viewing behavior and the environment as inherently inextricable. While this commitment has not been translated fully into available technology, it does allow the behavioral assessment system to be sensitive to social forces' impacts on behavior. As a consequence, behavioral assessment's technology is potentially much more compatible with feminist approaches to therapy than were the trait and type technologies preceding it.

Prior to the emergence of behavior therapy two decades ago (Ullmann & Krasner, 1965), psychology was dominated by a model of behavior holding that observed actions were primarily a function of person variables known as traits. Traits were defined as "organized dispositions within the individual which are assumed to have some generality in their manifestations across a variety of stimulus situations" (Wiggins, 1973, p. 320); they were recognized clearly as hypothetical and, in fact, were regarded as unobservable in principle (Loevinger, 1957).

The assessment paradigm which grew out of this tradition had as its task the accurate measurement of those unobservable person variables which predicted overt behavior. Test performances were attributed primarily to the person and minimally to the assessment context, and they were regarded as signifying inferred traits hypothetically related to them (Goodenough, 1949).

Intelligence testing was one contribution from the trait tradition which was, and remains, a remarkable empirical achievement (Mischel, 1968). During the first half of this century, the success intelligence testing enjoyed gave psychologists hope that measures of other person variables might be equally successful (Anastasi, 1982). Within clinical psychology, work on additional person variable tests began in earnest with the impetus of two social pressures: the armed forces' need for rapid, reliable methods to screen inductees during the First and Second World Wars, and researchers' need for objective methods to describe psychiatric samples in studies of drug effects (Hathaway & Meehl, 1951; Hathaway & McKinley, 1951). In response to both needs, tests such as the Minnesota Multiphasic Personality Inventory (MMPI) (Hathaway & McKinley, 1951) were developed carefully, against psychiatric diagnoses as a criterion. Despite an enormous amount of effort, directed first toward scale refinement, and later toward detecting variables which might be obscuring test–criterion relationships, however, validity correlations between test scores and psychiatric diagnoses remained disappointingly low (Mischel, 1968; Wiggins, 1973).

Low test–criterion correlations may result from imperfections in a test. They may also result, however, from imperfections in a test's criterion. The repeated failure of efforts to raise correlations by improving the psychometric properties of the tests led some researchers to suspect the value of the criterion; they reasoned that low correlations might be resulting from problems with psychiatric diagnoses.

Attention turned first to the reliability of diagnoses. Ash (1949) conducted a study in which 52 male outpatients were evaluated by at least two psychiatrists on the basis of a conference interview. He found marked evidence of unreliability—for specific diagnostic categories, the highest index of concordance was 44%. Even within major diagnostic categories which, by virtue of their breadth required fewer discriminations, agreement was a modest 67%. Sandifer, Pettus, and Quade (1964), suspecting that Ash's (1949) results might be attributable to the inexperience of some of his clinicians, evaluated the agreement among 14 senior diagnosticians examining 91 first admissions to a psychiatric facility. Their results were no less discouraging. The probability of a second diagnosis in agreement with the first was, on average, about 57% (Sandifer et al., 1964). Similar results from a host of studies, each of which attempted to isolate and remediate some human error deflating agreement (Blashfield, 1973; Cohen, Harbin, & Wright, 1975; Doering, 1934; Nathan, Andberg, Behan, & Patch, 1969), led to a serious, general skepticism about the possibility of reliably assigning diagnoses as summaries of underlying person variables.[1]

It has been argued that low reliability does not preclude a nomenclature's validity in principle, and researchers considered this possibility

---

[1] Evidence of low reliabilities for psychiatric diagnoses eventually resulted in the development of a new taxonomy based more closely on observable behaviors. Early work with this new taxonomy (DSM-III) suggests that it may be applied reliably (Spitzer, Endicott, & Robins, 1978) and therefore supports its potential value as a descriptive, although not explanatory, schema (see Nelson & Barlow, 1981; Nelson & Hayes, 1981).

as an explanation for test–criterion failures. However, studies directly evaluating the validity of psychiatric diagnoses were less than encouraging. Zigler and Phillips (1961) examined behavior profiles for 793 persons with one of four major diagnoses: manic–depressive psychosis, psychoneurotic, character disorder, and schizophrenia. They discovered marked overlap; there were similarities in the overt behavior of all 793 persons, regardless of their diagnostic classifications. Even the most salient behavioral features presumed to signify underlying diagnostic categories (e.g., depression, tension, drinking, hallucinations) failed to discriminate adequately between the four diagnostic categories. Peter Nathan and his colleagues (Nathan, 1969; Nathan, Gould, Zare, & Roth, 1969; Nathan, Robertson, & Andberg, 1969; Nathan, Zare, Simpson, & Andberg, 1969) conducted extensive studies of the behavior of 924 psychiatric patients assigned to one of five diagnostic categories: psychosis, psychoneurosis, personality disorder, acute brain disorder, and chronic brain disorder. Although some observable behaviors did differentiate the major categories in their work, there was considerable overlap. Moreover, for diagnostic subcategories within the larger classifications, the overlap in observed behaviors was substantial. On the basis of their data, Nathan, Gould, Zare, and Roth (1969) concluded that "study of the diagnostic process revealed only limited differential diagnostic validity for many of the most common signs and symptoms of psychopathology" (p. 370). The utility of viewing behavior as caused primarily by underlying, unobservable person variables was being seriously questioned.

A different strategy in search of objective differences between different diagnostic categories was reported by Eisler and Polak (1971). These investigators tabulated the frequency of occurrence of specific life stressors, such as economic loss, divorce, and death in the family, for 172 persons whose diagnoses would suggest life-stress differences: Diagnostic categories were schizophrenic, depressive, personality disorder, and transient situational personality disorder. Their data yielded no differences between groups in either frequency, or type, of stressors experienced.

In 1969, and again in 1976, Jerome Frank reviewed the body of studies evaluating various aspects of psychiatric diagnoses. Both reviews led him to conclude that psychiatric nosology suffered from serious deficiencies as a classification system:

> The review of this research leaves one with the uncomfortable feeling that the results of all the studies that have used psychiatric diagnosis as a

dependent or independent variable are of questionable validity. The data reviewed herein suggest that an entirely new system of classification is needed, *one which can encompass the many variables that define psychological functioning and behavior.* (Frank, 1969, p. 167; emphasis added)[2]

Disappointment with the reliability and validity of psychiatric nomenclature and with diagnoses' irrelevance to treatment planning (Goldfried & Pomeranz, 1968), in concert with critiques of other trait-based testing also showing repeatedly low correlations between tests and behavioral criteria (Mischel, 1968; Peterson, 1968), gave rise to more than mere questioning of the specific diagnoses and traits which failed to relate to observable behavior. A fundamental distrust of the assumptions underlying type and trait tests, and the model of behavior justifying them, emerged. Inspired by the effectiveness of treatments based on an alternative, learning-based model of behavior presented in Wolpe's (1958) influential *Psychotherapy by Reciprocal Inhibition,* and by the effectiveness of treatments following a Skinnerian approach (Ullmann & Krasner, 1965), a group of psychologists began to reject the assumption that behavior is determined by underlying, global person variables and instead regard behavior as strongly influenced by the individual's environment (O'Leary, 1979).

The implications for assessment of this shift were profound. Whereas the task of trait assessment had been to gather information exclusively about unobservable person variables, since behavior was thought to be caused by them, behavioral assessment's task became that of gathering information about observable behavior and its situational context. Traditional assessment had regarded test performance as of only incidental importance, assuming value only as it signified underlying attributes. Since behavioral assessment's focus was on observable behavior in context, however, test performance became of central importance in that it supplied a meaningful sample of situationally bound behavior (Goldfried & Kent, 1972). In recent years, behavioral assessment has broadened its conception of situational contexts to include both objective situational parameters and subjective, cognitive ones imposed by the behaver (Hollon & Bemis, 1981; Nelson & Hayes, 1979),

---

[2] Frank's (1969) conclusion was directed toward the adequacy of psychiatric diagnoses as a scientific taxonomy. Of additional importance to feminists is psychiatric diagnosing as a social act. Whether systematic gender bias pervades diagnostic categories remains an unresolved question (Brodsky & Hare-Mustin, 1980), but at least one study has documented that given identical *perceived* diagnoses, *assigned* diagnoses will be influenced by diagnosticians' personal biases (Cohen, Harbin, & Wright, 1975).

so that behavior is regarded as a joint function of environmental and personal, but not personological, variables (Ekehammer, 1974; Mischel, 1973). The assumption remains, however, that behavior is controlled by its situational context so that assessment requires the measurement of both behavior and its situational medium directly.

There are several additional distinguishing features of behavioral assessment (see *Behavioral Assessment,* Vol. 1; Haynes, 1978; Nelson & Hayes, 1981). First, there is a strong commitment to maintaining a close association between assessment and intervention (Stuart, 1969). The goal of assessment is not just description, but description as it informs the effecting of clinical change. Second, the clear specification or "pinpointing" of behavioral and situational parameters is strongly emphasized, and whenever possible, that "pinpointing" should involve only current and public events (O'Leary, 1979). Third, there is a clear emphasis on quantification (Haynes, 1978). And finally, there is an appreciation for behavior in the natural environment as the ultimate, rather than intermediate, assessment criterion (MacDonald, 1978).

While behavior in its natural context is the ultimate criterion, the preponderance of behavioral assessment in both clinical and research contexts does not involve the direct observation of natural situation–response complexes (Nay, 1977; Swan & MacDonald, 1978). When direct observation occurs, it usually occurs under contrived circumstances. And in fact, the preponderance of behavioral assessment involves some variant of the self-report.

A REVIEW OF BEHAVIORAL ASSESSMENT STRATEGIES

As has been noted, behavioral assessment's primary function is to inform intervention efforts. Assessment information is useful, then, to the extent that it aids clinical decisions. There is no dearth of decisions to inform: Clinicians are faced with a series of choice points from therapy's beginning through its end. Among the most frequently recurring decisions are the following: (1) whether there is a need for psychological services; (2) given a need for psychological services, what the nature of the legitimizing problem(s) is; (3) what type of intervention is most likely to be effective, given the legitimizing problem(s); (4) what the client's commitment to the most probably effective treatment will be; (5) whether the treatment engenders any unwanted negative side effects; (6) whether, and when, treatment or events collateral to it have produced sufficient positive change to warrant termination; and (7) whether gains leading to termination are maintained at follow-up. Although clinical judgments are made at each of these choice-points, behavioral assessment technologies have been developed to address primarily only the latter two. Nonetheless, all of these decisions are ones that must be made, whether or not behavioral assessment technologies are used to help make them. It is unfortunate that a more comprehensive technology has not been developed, for although no assessment technology can ever completely eliminate subjectivity, assessment technology can serve to reduce it. In the absence of assessment technologies, then, sheer human judgment—with all its unchecked subjectivity and potential for gender bias—provides the sole basis for clinical decisions.

The remainder of this chapter will review the six most common behavioral assessment strategies. Critiques of specific measures within strategies will not be provided. Readers with a particular interest in a specific measure are referred to the subject index of this volume, the journals *Behavioral Assessment* and *Journal of Behavioral Assessment*, and one of the several excellent texts providing critical reviews (Barlow, 1981; Ciminero, Calhoun, & Adams, 1977; Cone & Hawkins, 1977; Haynes, 1978; Haynes & Wilson, 1979; Hersen & Bellack, 1981; Keefe, Kopel, & Gordon, 1978; Mash & Terdal, 1976, 1981).

BEHAVIORAL INTERVIEWS

Behavioral interviews are the most frequently employed (Haynes, 1978) and least frequently researched (Linehan, 1977) behavioral assessment strategy (Morganstern & Tevlin, 1981). They serve multiple functions including determining whether psychological intervention is warranted, identifying persons appropriate for specific outcome studies, determining which behavioral and circumstantial parameters should be addressed by interventions, and evaluating intervention effects both posttreatment and at follow-up (see Haynes & Jensen, 1979).

It is surprising that interviews have been rarely researched, given their popularity. However, perhaps the interview's greatest strength has also served as the primary deterrent to its systematic evaluation: Interviews are flexible, and maximally responsive to the individual client. Flexibility, while allowing broad applicability, precludes standardization. Without standardization, interview data are noncomparable across interviewers, and times.

In addition to their flexibility, interviews have a second great strength in that they provide an invaluable opportunity to build a working relationship with the client. For both reasons, interviews will no doubt retain their popularity. Feminists should remain informed, however, that while some research suggests that interviews successfully detect clinical problems (Beiman, O'Neill, Wachtel, Fruge, Johnson, & Feuerstein, 1978; Herjanic, Herjanic, Brown, & Wheatt, 1977; Kleinman, Goldman, Snow, & Korol, 1977; Vogler, Weissback, & Compton, 1977), other research raises serious doubts about the interview's objectivity (Hay, Hay, Angle, & Nelson, 1979). At this point, it would seem unwise to base any clinical decision solely on interview data, particularly if the interview is conducted or reported by a nonfeminist colleague.

One of the earliest, and still most frequently cited, behavioral interview outlines was provided by Kanfer and Saslow (1969). Their strategy includes seven components: (1) an initial analysis of the client's problem situation, during which problematic behavioral excesses and deficits in all three response modes (overt-motoric, cognitive, and physiological), as well as nonproblematic behavioral assets, are identified in their situational contexts; (2) a clarification of the problematic situation, including study of specific contextual factors such as consequential behavior of those who view the client's behavior as problematic, and likely responses of those who might be affected by client change; (3) a motivational analysis in which contingencies that might be resulting in the problematic behavior are identified, as are reinforcers potentially capable of producing behavior change; (4) a developmental analysis during which biological, sociological, and behavioral factors that may have led to the problem situations are determined; (5) an analysis of the client's skill at self-control, in which methods, limitations, and conditions of self-control strategies are evaluated; (6) an analysis of the client's social network, particularly as it might impinge on the client's change; (7) an analysis of the client's cultural environment, during which information is elicited concerning subcultural norms and restrictions as they relate to the client's behavior.

Among the major strengths of Kanfer and Saslow's (1969) suggested strategy is its encouragement of breadth in gathering information. Without breadth, areas which are not initially recognized as problematic but which are functionally related to presenting problems might remain undetected (see Lazarus, 1971).

As assessment tools, however, interviews are susceptible to multiple sources of error and bias (Haynes & Jensen, 1979; Morganstern & Tevlin,

1981), including gender bias. Unfortunately, however, they stand as the only available method for detecting what is specifically in need of change. Nelson and Barlow (1981), noting that target behavior selection is highly subjective, offer four philosophical guidelines which should influence this decision: (1) Behavior should be altered if it is dangerous to the client or to others in the environment; (2) target behaviors should be altered so as to maximize the client's reinforcers; (3) undesirable behaviors should be decreased not through punishment, but by super-imposing desirable behaviors over them; (4) target behaviors should maximize the flexibility of the client's skills for achieving long-term individual and social benefits. Particularly when working with women, for whom culturally supported behaviors may be personally damaging (Brodsky & Hare-Mustin, 1980; MacDonald, 1982), target selection must proceed with considerable reflection.

SELF-MONITORING

Interview data are necessarily retrospective. As a consequence, they are highly dependent on characteristics, included culturally transmitted gender biases, of the observer (Wiggins, 1973). Nonretrospective data, immune from distortions inherent in recollection (Linehan, 1977), would clearly be preferable. Once a target behavior has been selected, nonretrospective data may be collected through self-monitoring.

With adult clients, self-monitoring is widely used; "with this procedure, which is generally labeled self-monitoring, self-recording, or self-observation, individuals may be asked to record the occurrence of a specified behavior, as well as the events which precede and follow the behavior" (Ciminero, Nelson, & Lipinski, 1977, p. 195). The popularity of self-monitoring is not based on its ease of execution. On the contrary, self-monitoring is often an arduous task for clients (Mahoney, 1977). This cost, however, is more than outweighed by its benefits as a procedure yielding nonretrospective data, about areas particularly selected for the individual client, in a manner which can easily include all the components necessary for a functional analysis of behavior.[3] Moreover, when extended through treatment, self-monitoring provides immediate feedback to both client and clinician on intervention effects.

---

[3] Functional analysis of behavior is the generic name for the process through which the environmental conditions eliciting and maintaining a defined problem are specified (Skinner, 1938).

Self-monitoring requires first defining the target behavior in sufficient detail to enable the client to discriminate between occurrences and nonoccurrences of the behavior, and then devising a method for recording occurrences of the behavior as well as the events which precede and follow it. For behaviors that occur at a manageable rate and for a relatively constant duration (e.g., cigarette smoking, between-meal snacking, escapes from aversive social interactions at work), and where rate of occurrence is a probable intervention target, it is desirable to have each instance of the antecedent–behavior–consequence sequence recorded. For other behaviors of variable duration where duration is of primary concern (e.g., number of hours spent working, number of minutes spent in relaxed foreplay, duration of spousal arguments), the amount of time spent engaging in the behavior should be recorded as well. Where high-rate behaviors are of interest, time-sampling procedures (where the client is asked to record only during certain time blocks of the day), interval recording procedures (where the client is asked to record only whether the behavior did or did not occur at successive half-hourly or hourly intervals during the day), or situation sampling procedures (where the client is asked to record frequencies only in certain specified situations) may be useful. Ciminero, Nelson, and Lipinski (1977) have suggested an innovative procedure for circumstances involving very-high-rate–fixed-duration behaviors: spot checking. With this procedure, the client keeps a timer with her and sets it to sound after variable intervals; when the timer sounds, the client simply records whether or not the behavior is occurring and notes the surrounding circumstances.

Once a recording procedure is established, some method for keeping track of the data must be devised. Care should be taken to develop a method which is perceived as workable by the client (Mahoney, 1977). Some clinicians, when interested only in frequencies of occurrence, have found portable counters (golf wrist counters; mechanical grocery store counters) to be effective (Ciminero, Nelson, & Lipinski, 1977; Lindsley, 1968). It is perhaps most common to use a paper-and-pencil form, sometimes utilizing an index card.

Mahoney (1977) has developed a five-step outline for instituting self-recording. His sequence includes: (1) giving the client explicit definitions and examples of target events and explaining their possible relevance to the problem(s) at hand; (2) giving explicit self-monitoring instructions in exactly how to self-record; (3) demonstrating how to self-record using a sample form; (4) asking the client to repeat the target definitions and self-monitoring instructions, and providing corrective feedback if necessary; (5) insuring the client's understanding by asking her to record several hypothetical trial instances conceived and described by the clinician.

Once collected, self-monitoring data should be charted in some fashion so that they are given a frame of reference: Where simple frequencies have been recorded, a graph (with frequencies plotted on the ordinate, and equivalent blocks of time such as days plotted against the abscissa) may be constructed; with time-sampling and spot-checking, the percentage of intervals or spot-checks during which the behavior occurred can be plotted (with percentage on the ordinate and days on the abscissa); where duration is of primary concern, the length of each response should be charted (with duration on the ordinate and response instances on the abscissa).

Self-monitoring has been well-researched, and it has been noted that under some circumstances, self-monitoring can be quite reactive (Haynes, 1978).[4] In the self-monitoring literature, when reactivity has been noted, it has been interpreted variably as a threat to the procedure's validity and a demonstration that self-monitoring can function as an intervention procedure producing measurable change (Haynes, 1978).

Nelson (1977) has thoughtfully analyzed the conditions which influence whether self-monitoring will be reactive. A major factor is the client's motivation to alter the behavior being recorded. When clients express a desire to change the self-recorded behavior before the fact, reactivity is much more likely to occur. Moreover, the direction of the change is likely to be determined by whether the behavior is viewed as a positive or negative one. Behaviors viewed by the client as positive are likely to accelerate, while behaviors viewed as negative are likely to decelerate as a function of self-monitoring. There is some evidence to suggest that the nature of the behavior's obtrusiveness or distinctiveness may influence its susceptibility to self-monitoring-induced change. Other factors which have been linked to enhancing self-monitoring's reactivity include: (1) establishing a priori performance goals, particularly when reinforcement is made contingent on achieving them; (2) recording the monitored response prior to, rather than after, its occurrence; (3) using an obtrusive, rather than unobtrusive, recording device; (4) recording one, rather than several, behaviors at a time; (5) conducting continuous, rather than intermittent, self-recording.

---

[4] Reactivity refers to changes in the topography of a behavior which are caused by the assessment procedure used to measure it (Cronbach, 1970).

Reactive effects may be beneficial when self-monitoring is intended or regarded as an intervention. When self-monitoring is intended as an assessment strategy, however, reactivity introduces a distortion which threatens validity; in an assessment context, self-monitoring's reactivity must be minimized. Nelson (1977) has suggested two procedures as especially useful for maximizing self-monitoring accuracy (i.e., concordance between self-recorded and other-recorded results): (1) Self-monitoring will be more accurate when self-observers are aware that their accuracy is being monitored, and (2) self-monitoring is more accurate when reinforcement is made contingent on accuracy rather than levels of the observed behavior.

Self-monitoring is a highly flexible approach of demonstrated utility. It is particularly well suited for establishing the magnitude and situational parameters of target behaviors, once they have been selected, and for providing continuous feedback about the nature of intervention effects.

QUESTIONNAIRES

Originally self-report tests were developed as efficient, standardizable substitutes for extended interviews (Anastasi, 1982). Certainly within behavioral research, and increasingly within behavioral clinical practice, written questionnaires are gaining popularity. Especially for the areas of assertion and other social behaviors, fears, psychophysiological disorders, drinking patterns, sexual orientation, depression, and marital interaction, self-report tests have been used as preintervention assessment devices, as research instruments in the study of specific behavior problems, and as measures to evaluate intervention effects (Haynes, 1978).

There is some irony in the increasing use of questionnaires within behavioral assessment, for it was dissatisfaction with self-report tests developed around trait notions, and their failure to evidence strong relationships with observed behavior, that to a great extent gave initial impetus to the development of the behavioral assessment approach (Wiggins, 1973). Nonetheless, as behavior therapy has become increasingly involved with complex, multifaceted response classes (MacDonald, 1978) and cognitive variables (Hollon & Bemis, 1981; O'Leary, 1979), the use of questionnaires has become more common.

Within traditional psychology, there is a massive body of literature addressing psychometric properties which are prerequisites for acceptable questionnaires. Although developed in the context of trait measures, these principles are equally applicable for behavioral tests (Haynes, 1978; MacDonald, 1978). There are marked differences between the trait and behavioral approaches which must be kept in mind, however, when adapting these principles (Cone, 1981). Behavioral questionnaires are designed to tap behavior directly, not the inferred attributes presumably causing the behavior; they ask respondents to collaborate as retrospective observers of their own behaviors and environments. Behavioral tests reflect an appreciation of situational specificity, most often including items asking what a person does under specified circumstances. Finally, there is a difference in the value of the criterion. Within the trait approach, low correlations between test scores and behavioral criteria were often interpreted as the behavioral criterion's imperfection as an index of the true criterion (the unobservable trait) underlying it. In behavioral assessment, however, repeatedly low test–behavioral criterion correlations are sufficient justification for discarding the test.

Unfortunately, it is rare for the psychometric properties of behavioral questionnaires to have been studied (Bellack & Hersen, 1977; Haynes, 1978) or for tests to have been developed with these psychometric principles in mind (MacDonald, 1978). Moreover, following the correspondence point of view (Wiggins, 1973) and perhaps because they ask directly about behavior, behavioral questionnaires have often been assumed to provide veridical reflections of naturalistic motoric behavior, an assumption which has proven empirically untrue (Haynes, 1978).

Properly developed behavioral questionnaires are designed through several phases. The sequence involves: (1) specifying the behavioral criterion a priori; (2) generating stimulus situations empirically related to the behavioral criterion; (3) selecting those situations which are relevant both to the behavioral criterion and to the target population to be assessed; (4) generating response pools for each time; (5) establishing empirical scoring criteria for various responses; (6) constructing the questionnaire using a standardized format; (7) evaluating the internal properties of the questionnaire, including reliability; (8) evaluating the external properties of the questionnaire, including validity (MacDonald, 1978). Within behavioral assessment, reliability refers to score consistency across factors (e.g., time and scorers) where there is no reason to suspect behavior change. Without some demonstration of reliability, it cannot be argued that test scores reflect anything substantive. Test validity refers to demonstrated relationships between test scores and some directly observable behavioral criterion. Even with measures of cognitive variables, test scores must evidence significant relationships to public phenomena for them to be regarded as scientifically meaningful (O'Leary, 1979).

When deciding whether to use a self-report test, whether in a clinical or research context, it is useful to review the manner in which it was developed. This is especially true when assessing women, since gender bias may intrude at any test development stage. As examples, the behavioral criterion may have been established using situations encountered, or responses made, more frequently by men. Women may not have been included among the sample generating stimulus situations, or situations particularly relevant to women may have been selected out. Women may not have been included in the sample generating response alternatives. And gender bias may influence the manner in which scores are assigned to response options or the manner in which scores are given quantitative value.

Even with well-developed tests, some potential limitations on their utility for women should be kept in mind. First, the relationship of questionnaire responses to actual behavior is always an important one. Regardless of how much a test looks as if it should be valid, face validity should not be taken as evidence of empirical validity assessed against observed behavior. Moreover, validity when used with men should not be taken as evidence of validity when used with women. Also, questionnaires often ask respondents to rate what they do rather than to describe or report it. It is not safe to assume that the respondent's conception of what she is rating (e.g., arousal; assertion) coincides with the investigator's; indeed, it is not safe to assume that conceptions of usual rating qualifiers (e.g., often, sometimes, seldom) will be identical across respondents (Mischel, 1968). It is useful, then, to clarify the meaning of all rated dimensions and rating qualifiers before gathering self-report data. Moreover, motivational variables influencing the respondent's interest in presenting a socially desirable picture (Crowne & Marlowe, 1964) may distort the accuracy of the reported information. And especially for women, self-reports may be based more on internalized notions of how one "ought" (is required) to behave than they are on actual behavior (MacDonald, 1982).

Despite these areas warranting caution, questionnaires represent an approach with enormous potential within behavioral assessment. They are extraordinarily efficient to both administer and score. They are easily standardized so that normative data may be generated on large samples of women with relative ease. Moreover, for some variables, particularly cognitive and sexual ones (Freund & Blanchard, 1981; Hollon & Bemis, 1981), they provide the most direct, ethical avenue of access. As Haynes (1978) has noted:

> The potential validity of questionnaires has probably been underestimated by behaviorally oriented interventionists. There is an increasing amount of research data which supports the hypotheses that under some conditions (with specific populations, specific behaviors, or with specific question-naires) questionnaires can accurately predict or covary with behavior meas-ured by other instruments and in other situations. If observed covariations between questionnaire and observation derived data are found, there is little doubt that in many cases questionnaires would be the measurement instrument of choice because of their efficiency. (p. 342)

PSYCHOPHYSIOLOGICAL MEASURES

For some behaviors such as fear, sexual arousal, and psychophysiological disorders, psychophysiological measurement procedures provide a crit-ical data base. This form of measurement involves "the quantification of biological events as they relate to psychological variables" (Kallman & Feuerstein, 1977, p. 329). Biological events studied are predominantly, although not exclusively, those controlled by the autonomic nervous system; some of the more usual measured responses are electrical activity of muscles, heart rate, blood pressure, peripheral temperature, skin conductance, and vaginal blood volume (Geer, 1977; Haynes, 1978).

Psychophysiological measurement instrumentation is relatively ex-pensive. Perhaps because of its expense and its complexity, psycho-physiological measurement is conducted almost exclusively in research rather than clinical contexts. In light of the expense and complexity inherent in this measurement approach, some researchers have sug-gested that it be used sparingly, only when it provides information uniquely available through psychophysiological means, or when it taps some aspect of a physiological response which can be directly modified with beneficial effects, or when it is unusually sensitive to the effects of nonbiological intervention (Kallman & Feuerstein, 1977). Other research-ers have argued, however, that especially because of its objectivity, psychophysiological measurement should be employed more frequently (Haynes, 1978). With continued progress in simplifying and miniatur-izing instrumentation, and with increasing interest in the field of be-havioral medicine, the latter suggestion may well prevail (Ray & Raczynski, 1981).

The basic principle of physiological recording instrumentation is one of translation: An input transducer, constructed so as to react electrically to a certain type of biological/physical electrical or mechanical action, is connected through an amplifier (enlarger) to an output transducer which changes the enlarged electrical signal into either visual or auditory form. With additional instrumentation, it is possible to join the output transducer directly to a computer, rather than some visual or auditory recording device, enabling on-line analyses for any preprogrammed aspect of the physiological response (Kallman & Feuerstein, 1977).

Psychophysiological recording devices are designed to be sensitive to minor electrical or physical changes. This sensitivity, necessary for ensuring sensitivity to the responses they must detect, also makes them susceptible to influences from seemingly minor alterations in the recording situation (e.g., lighting, room temperature); the recording procedure (e.g., instructions to the subjects, type and site of attachment of electrodes); and the recorded organism (e.g., eyeblinks, phase of the menstrual cycle). Artifacts traced to these environmental, instrumentation, or organismic sources introduce measurement error which reduces reliability. Situational specificity and individual response stereotypy (Lacey & Lacey, 1970) further limit the amount of generalization that is warranted beyond the situation, procedure, individual, and time under study (Ray & Raczynski, 1981).

At present, "neither the reliability nor the validity of psychophysiological assessment has been firmly established by traditional criteria" (Kallman & Feuerstein, 1977, p. 359). However, intrasubject, repeated measures tests of reliability, for individual responses measured under standard conditions, appear to be quite satisfactory. Attempts to validate psychophysiological measures against other tests have met with mixed results (Ray & Raczynski, 1981), perhaps because the two types of tests cannot be administered concurrently. There is unfortunately little research assessing the degree of relationship between biological responses and motoric behavior. Such data will hopefully be collected as more sophisticated telemetric recording devices become widely available.

NATURALISTIC OBSERVATION

Naturalistic observation is often considered the paragon of behavioral assessment. While difficult to negotiate with noninstitutionalized persons, data generated via naturalistic observation are regarded generally as the ultimate behavioral criterion for any behavioral assessment device. In principle, measures are valid to the extent that they accurately reflect unconstrained behavior as it unfolds in the uncontrolled environment. Naturalistic observation is the procedure through which this ultimate criterion is quantified.

Observation requires an initial selection of specific behaviors to observe, a selection which may be influenced by gender bias. Behaviors are often selected on the basis of their importance to the client or to social judges (e.g., spouses or teachers) in the client's environment. On occasion, informal observations are conducted to identify behaviors which might profitably be counted more formally. Infrequently, observers will select behaviors on the basis of a published behavior code (Wildman & Erickson, 1977).

Once behaviors to observe have been selected, they are clearly and explicitly defined. Category definitions should be written in terms of observables; wherever possible, visual or descriptive examples should be provided. Definitional clarity is a major determinant of interobserver agreement: Where definitions are ambiguous or include inferential observee-attributions, interobserver agreement will be lowered (Hawkins & Dobes, 1977).

After behavior categories have been defined, a format for recording the occurrence or nonoccurrence of the behaviors, as defined, must be established. A number of formats have proven successful. Perhaps the simplest method is to prepare a sheet of paper listing each behavior category alongside spaces to be marked upon the behavior's occurrence. Event recorders have also been reported as useful (Baltes, 1978).

Ordinarily naturalistic observation involves selecting the situations in which the preselected behaviors will be recorded, and selecting the length of observation-recording cycles. The length of observation intervals should be influenced by the frequency of the behavior; since occurrence rather than frequency is recorded, unless short observation intervals are used with high rate, short duration behaviors, information and sensitivity to differences in rate will be lost. With less frequent behaviors, longer observation intervals will be satisfactory. Recording intervals should be sufficiently long to allow observers to note all the behavior categories. Except with markedly complex codes, 5 to 10 seconds should be sufficient for experienced raters.

Most often, the adequacy of naturalistically observed data has been judged by the extent to which independent observers have agreed when making simultaneous observations. Interobserver agreement is a form of reliability; it reflects consistency across scorers. Two types of error—timing errors and interpretive errors—appear to be responsible for most failures in observer agreement (Wildman & Erickson, 1977). Timing errors may be reduced by insuring that observe–record intervals coincide precisely. Interpretive errors may be reduced by adequate observer training.

Kent and Foster (1977) reviewed factors in addition to inadequate training which might result in consistent interpretive errors. Errors appear to become more likely as codes and coding tasks become more complicated, and less likely when observers know that reliability is being assessed.

Several methods for computing reliability have been suggested. Agreement reliability, in which the number of agreements about the occurrence and nonoccurrence of the behavior is divided by the total number of observation intervals, is the most commonly employed. With very low- and high-rate behaviors, it is more appropriate to divide the number of occurrence agreements by the number of occurrence agreements and disagreements, and the number of nonoccurrence agreements by the number of nonoccurrence agreements and disagreements, respectively; otherwise, meaninglessly high coefficients in the presence of critical disagreements could occur. Additional indices of reliability include the φ-coefficient and Cohen's (1969) kappa, which adjusts for agreement resulting from chance.

At first, it may seem unnecessary to consider the validity of naturalistic observation; as Wiggins (1973) has noted, it is easy to forget that one must validate validity criteria. However, since observation involves the selection of both aspects of behavior and observational circumstances, as well as interpretive judgements concerning the behavior's occurrence, demonstrations of validity are as important as with any behavioral assessment method. With behaviors that affect the behaver's physical environment, the validity of naturalistic observations refers to the degree of correspondence between observations and objective, physical evidence of response occurrences (Webb, Campbell, Schwartz, & Sechrest, 1966). With behaviors that affect the behaver's social environment, the validity of naturalistic observations is suggested by their degree of correspondence with the perceptions of natural judges in the environment (Wiggins, 1973). Wildman and Erickson (1977), reviewing the observational literature, have identified three factors potentially limiting observational data's validity. The first, as with self-monitoring, is reactivity: The mere factor of the observer's presence may be sufficient to result in the "guinea pig effect" (Selltiz, Jahoda, Deutsch, & Cook, 1964) or the "role selection effect" (Webb *et al.*, 1966). The second is a form of calibration slippage (Campbell & Stanley, 1963) known as "observer drift" (Johnson & Bolstad, 1973; O'Leary & Kent, 1973) that may develop as observers work together over time. A third threat to validity is presented by observer bias: Observers' expectations and biases about what they are observing, as well as their perceptions of their supervisor's expectations about what they are observing, have been found to be related to frequencies they record (Kent & Foster, 1977).

An additional threat to validity is found in selection errors. Especially with social behavior constructs, the behaviors selected for observation, or the behaviors as defined for observational purposes, may be unrelated to the behavior construct as socially defined. This is a particular risk when women are assessed using behaviors selected or defined by nonfeminists or behaviors selected or defined on the basis of observations of men. Whenever possible, naturalistic observations of women should include study of known contrasted groups of women (Anastasi, 1982) to establish the validity of the behaviors selected, as defined.

There are always methodological concerns with assessment strategies; naturalistic observation is no exception. Nonetheless, given behavioral assessment's explicit commitment to observed behavior in the natural environment, naturalistic observation will no doubt retain its status as the most desirable data source.

CONTROLLED OBSERVATION

In general, accurate assessment requires having control over a host of potentially influential contextual variables. For better or worse, in naturalistic observation, experimental control is limited to the selection of observed situations and behaviors. In controlled observation, assessment is conducted under special circumstances created by the observer:

> The advantages of controlled observation should be evident. Stimulus control ensures the relevance of the behavior observed by increasing the probability that the response class of interest will be emitted during the period of observation. Limitation of the environment decreases the range of possible responses the subject might make and thereby makes it more likely that the behavior observed will be easily classified within a preplanned system of coding. Perhaps most important, the standardization of the stimulating environment minimizes the influence of extraneous factors which tend to decrease generalizability across different times and different oc-

casions. From the standpoint of classical reliability theory, the controlled experiment is the technique par excellence of behavior observation. (Wiggins, 1973, p. 298)

Controlled, rather than naturalistic, observation is particularly desirable, then, when the behaviors of interest are low frequency, or when intra- or intersubject comparisons are intended, necessitating standardization across assessment occasions.

Controlled observation has been employed widely in behavioral assessment, especially since the publication of Lang and Lazovik's (1963) classic phobia outcome study incorporating a Behavioral Avoidance Test. As a method, it represents a hybrid of naturalistic observation and questionnaire tests; as a consequence, it shares the pitfalls noted in previous sections for both methods.

Typically, controlled observation involves presenting one or more situational test items and instructing subjects to respond to them as they would if the situations were occurring in their natural environments. Often responses are observed and coded according to preestablished coding schema. Scores are assigned to coded behaviors on the basis of judgmental, and occasionally empirical (see MacDonald, 1978), criteria.

Controlled observations have been employed for a host of problematic situations including heterosocial skills, mother–child interactions, wife–husband communication, public speaking anxiety, specific social skills such as assertion, alcohol consumption, and various specific phobias such as acrophobia and fear of flying (Haynes, 1978).

Nay (1977) identifies five categories of controlled observation which he terms analogues, in recognition of their status as simulations of respondents' natural environments. The first category is paper-and-pencil analogues in which respondents are asked to write how they would respond if experiencing each of several situations presented in written form; while notably efficient, this method's format departs markedly and obviously from the natural environment it is designed to tap. The second category is audiotaped analogues. In this approach, audiotaped descriptions of various stimulus situations are presented, and respondents are expected to make a verbal response. Videotaped analogues, the third category, are similar to audiotaped analogues except that test items are presented in a videotaped, rather than audiotaped, format. The fourth category is illustrated by the Behavioral Avoidance Test; in this and other examples of enactment analogues, critical stimuli (objects or persons) from the respondent's natural environment are brought into the laboratory and presented in a structured fashion, and the respondent's reactions to the critical stimulus in the controlled format are observed and coded. The final analogue category of role play replaces the enactment analogue's critical person stimulus with an experimental confederate.

The most frequently voiced criticism of controlled observation is that it will be perceived as unrealistic. Aronson and Carlsmith (1968) argue, however, that a lack of realism is not inherent in the methodology and that at least experimental realism can be achieved "if the situation is realistic to the observer, if it involves [her], if [she] is forced to take it seriously, if it has an impact on [her]" (Aronson & Carlsmith, 1968, p. 22).

As is true with any measure, it is most appropriate to base objections on data. Most unfortunately, less than a dozen studies have empirically addressed the relationship between analogue and naturalistic performances. There are indications, however, that with analogues developed following psychometric principles and administered in standardized format, relationships to naturalistically observed behavior are highly significant (Kern, in press; MacDonald & Tyson, 1982).

CONCLUSIONS AND RECOMMENDATIONS

Behavioral assessment developed largely in response to two things: a disagreement with alternative paradigms' conceptions of what causes behavior, and a dissatisfaction with alternative paradigms' relevance to the clinical context. Behavioral assessment's essential function is to assist in the making of clinical decisions. Each of the major behavioral assessment strategies—behavioral interviewing, self-monitoring, psychophysiological measurement, questionnaires, naturalistic observation, and controlled observation—is directed toward measuring behavior in its situational medium. This attention to situational influences on behavior, which represents a recognition that behavior may result from environmental rather than personal variables, makes behavioral assessment potentially more compatible with feminist approaches to therapy than any other available assessment paradigm.

Despite its comparative strengths, behavioral assessment is by no means exempt from gender bias. As is true with all assessment systems, cultural assumptions—including those embedding gender bias—exert marked influences on what behavioral assessors look for, and how they interpret what their assessments seem to find. As was noted with each different strategy, subjectivity is invariably involved at some point—if not during instrument application, then during the process through which the variable measured was selected for study. And, subjectivity brings with it the opportunity for gender bias to significantly influence and distort results.

Behavioral assessment's commitment to the study of behavior in its sociopolitical–environmental context, however, makes it *potentially* more compatible with feminist therapy than its rivals. Without data, and direction, and professional consciousness-raising, however, this potential will not be translated into technology. From this author's perspective, what is needed at this point is data—solid, nondismissable, compelling data—to invite and shape that technology. Given data, and given interpretations of those data from feminist perspectives, less biased assessments of women will become more possible.

REFERENCES

Anastasi, A. *Psychological testing* (4th ed.). New York: Macmillan, 1976.

Anastasi, A. *Psychological testing* (5th ed.). New York: Macmillan, 1982.

Aronson, E., & Carlsmith, J. M. Experimentation in social psychology. In G. Lindzey & E. Aronson (Eds.), *The handbook of social psychology* (2nd ed.). Reading, Mass.: Addison-Wesley, 1968.

Ash, P. The reliability of psychiatric diagnoses. *Journal of Abnormal and Social Psychology*, 1949, 44, 272–276.

Baltes, M. Pesonal communication, 1978.

Barlow, D. H. (Ed.). *Behavioral assessment of adult disorders*. New York: Guilford, 1981.

Beiman, J., O'Neill, P., Wachtel, D., Fruge, E., Johnson, S., & Feuerstein, M. Validation of a self-report/behavioral subject selection procedure for analog fear research. *Behavior Therapy*, 1978, 9, 169–177.

Bellack, A. S., & Hersen, M. Self-report inventories in behavioral assessment. In J. D. Cone & R. P. Hawkins (Eds.), *Behavioral assessment: New directions in clinical psychology*. New York: Brunner/Mazel, 1977.

Blashfield, R. An evaluation of the DSM-II classification of schizophrenia as a nomenclature. *Journal of Abnormal Psychology*, 1973, 82, 382–389.

Brodsky, A. M., & Hare-Mustin, R. T. (Eds.). *Women and psychotherapy: An assessment of research and practice*. New York: Guilford, 1980.

Campbell, D. T., & Stanley, J. C. *Experimental and quasi-experimental designs for research*. Chicago: Rand-McNally, 1963.

Ciminero, A. R., Calhoun, K. S., & Adams, H. E. (Eds.). *Handbook of behavioral assessment*. New York: Wiley, 1977.

Ciminero, A. R., Nelson, R. O., & Lipinski, D. P. Self-monitoring procedures. In A. R. Ciminero, K. S. Calhoun, & H. E. Adams (Eds.), *Handbook of behavioral assessment*. New York: Wiley, 1977.

Cohen, J. A coefficient of agreement for nominal scales. *Educational and Psychological Measurement*, 1969, 20, 37–46.

Cohen, E. S., Harbin, H. T., & Wright, M. J. Some considerations in the formulation of psychiatric diagnoses. *Journal of Nervous and Mental Disease*, 1975, *160*, 422–427.

Cone, J. D. Psychometric considerations. In M. Hersen & A. S. Bellack (Eds.), *Behavioral assessment: A practical handbook* (2nd ed.). New York: Pergamon, 1981.

Cone, J. D., & Hawkins, R. P. (Eds.). *Behavioral assessment: New directions in clinical psychology*. New York: Brunner/Mazel, 1977.

Cronbach, L. J. *Essentials of psychological testing* (3rd ed.). New York: Harper & Row, 1970.

Crowne, D. P., & Marlowe, D. *The approval motive: Studies in evaluative dependence*. New York: Wiley, 1964.

Doering, C. R. Reliability of observaion of psychiatric and related characteristics. *American Journal of Orthopsychiatry*, 1934, *4*, 249–257.

Eisler, R. M., & Polak, P. R. Social stress and psychiatric disorder. *Journal of Nervous and Mental Disease*, 1971, *153*, 227–233.

Ekehammer, B. Interactionism in personality from a historical perspective. *Psychological Bulletin*, 1974, *81*, 1026–1048.

Endler, N. S., & Hunt, J. McV. Sources of behavioral variance as measured by the S-R Inventory of Anxiousness. *Psychological Bulletin*, 1966, *65*, 336–346.

Endler, N. S., & Hunt, J. McV. S-R inventories of hostility and comparisons of the proportions of variance from persons, responses, and situations for hostility and anxiousness. *Journal of Personality and Social Psychology*, 1968, *9*, 309–315.

Endler, N. S., & Hunt, J. McV. Generalizability of contributions from sources of variance in the S-R inventories of anxiousness. *Journal of Personality*, 1969, *37*, 1–24.

Evans, I. M. A review of *Multimethod clinical assessment* by W. R. Nay. *Behavioral Assessment*, 1982, *4*, 121–124.

Frank, J. Psychiatric diagnosis: A review of research. *Journal of General Psychology*, 1969, *81*, 157–176.

Frank, J. *Psychiatric diagnosis: A review of research*. Oxford: Pergamon, 1976.

Freedman, D., Pisani, R., & Purves, R. *Statistics*. New York: W. W. Norton, 1978.

Freund, K., & Blanchard, R. Assessment of sexual dysfunction and deviation. In M. Hersen & A. S. Bellack (Eds.), *Behavioral assessment: A practical handbook* (2nd ed.). New York: Pergamon, 1981.

Geer, J.H. Sexual functioning: Some data and speculations on psychophysiological assessment. In J.D. Cone & R.P. Hawkins (Eds.), *Behavioral assessment: New directions in clinical psychology*. New York: Brunner/Mazel, 1977.

Gleser, R. Instructional technology and the measurement of learning outcomes. *American Psychologist*, 1963, *18*, 519–522.

Goldfried, M. R., & Kent, R. N. Traditional versus behavioral personality assessment: A comparison of methodological and theoretical assumptions. *Psychological Bulletin*, 1972, *77*, 409–420.

Goldfried, M. R., & Pomeranz, D. M. Role of assessment in behavior modification. *Psychological Reports*, 1968, *23*, 75–87.

Goodenough, F. L. *Mental testing*. New York: Rinehart, 1949.

Hartshorne, H. & May, M. A. *Studies in deceit*. New York: Macmillan, 1928.

Hartshorne, H., May, M. A., & Shuttleworth, F. K. *Studies in the organization of character*. New York: Macmillan, 1930.

Hathaway, S. R., & McKinley, J. C. *The Minnesota Multiphasic Personality Inventory* (rev.). New York: Psychological Corp., 1951.

Hathaway, S. R., & Meehl, P. E. *An atlas for the clinical use of the MMPI*. Minneapolis: University of Minnesota Press, 1951.

Hawkins, R. P., & Dobes, R. W. Behavioral definitions in applied behavior analysis: Explicit or implicit. In B. C. Etzel, J. M. LeBlanc, & D. M. Baer (Eds.), *New devel-*

opments in behavioral research: Theory, method and application. In honor of Sidney W. Bijou. Hillsdale, N.J.: Erlbaum, 1977.

Hay, W. M., Hay, L. R., Angle, H. V., & Nelson, R. O. The reliability of problem identification in the behavioral interview. Behavioral Assessment, 1979, 1, 107–118.

Haynes, S. N. Principles of behavioral assessment. New York: Gardner, 1978.

Haynes, S. N., & Jensen, B. J. The interview as a behavioral assessment instrument. Behavioral Assessment, 1979, 1, 97–106.

Haynes, S. N., & Wilson, C. C. Recent advances in behavioral assessment. San Francisco: Jossey-Bass, 1979.

Herjanic, B., Herjanic, M., Brown, G., & Wheatt, T. Are children reliable reporters? Journal of Abnormal Child Psychology, 1977, 3, 41–48.

Hersen, M. Historical perspectives in behavioral assessment. In M. Hersen & A. S. Bellack (Eds.), Behavioral assessment: A practical handbook. New York: Pergamon, 1976.

Hersen, M., & Bellack, A. S. (Eds.). Behavioral assessment: A practical handbook (2nd ed.). New York: Pergamon, 1981.

Hollon, S. D., & Bemis, K. M. Self-report and the assessment of cognitive functions. In M. Hersen & A. S. Bellack (Eds.), Behavioral assessment: A practical handbook (2nd ed.). New York: Pergamon, 1981.

Johnson, S. M., & Bolstad, O. D. Methodological issues in naturalistic observation: Some problems and solutions for field research. In L. A. Hamerlynck, L. C. Handy, & E. J. Mash (Eds.), Behavior change: Methodology, concepts, and practice. Champaign, Ill.: Research, 1973.

Kallman, W. M., & Feuerstein, M. Psychophysiological procedures. In A. R. Ciminero, K. S. Calhoun, & H. E. Adams (Eds.), Handbook of behavioral assessment. New York: Wiley, 1977.

Kanfer, F. H., & Saslow, G. Behavioral diagnosis. In C. M. Franks (Ed.), Behavior therapy: Appraisal and status. New York: McGraw-Hill, 1969.

Kazdin, A. E. Assessing the clinical or applied importance of behavior change through social validation. Behavior Modification, 1977, 1, 427–452.

Keefe, F. J., Kopel, S. A., & Gordon, S. B. A practical guide to behavioral assessment. New York: Springer, 1978.

Kent, R.N., & Foster, S.L. Direct observational procedures: Methodological issues in naturalistic settings. In A.R. Ciminero, K.S. Calhoun, & H.E. Adams (Eds.), Handbook of behavioral assessment. New York: Wiley, 1977.

Kern, J.M. Relationships between obtrusive laboratory and unobtrusive naturalistiic behavioral fear assessments: "Treated" and untreated subjects. Behavioral Assessment, in press.

Kleinman, K. M., Goldman, H., Snow, M. Y., & Korol, B. Relationship between essential hypertension and cognitive functioning: II. Effects of biofeedback training generalized to nonlaboratory environment. Psychophysiology, 1977, 14, 192–197.

Lacey, J. I., & Lacey, B. C. Some autonomic-CNs interrelationships. In P. Black (Ed.), Physiological correlates of emotion. New York: Academic, 1970.

Lang, P. J., & Lazovik, A. D. Experimental desensitization of a phobia. Journal of Abnormal and Social Psychology, 1963, 66, 519–525.

Lazarus, A. A. Behavior therapy and beyond. New York: McGraw-Hill, 1971.

Lindsley, O. A reliable wrist counter for recording behavior rates. Journal of Applied Behavior Analysis, 1968, 1, 77–78.

Linehan, M. M. Issues in behavioral interviewing. In J. D. Cone & R. P. Hawkins (Eds.), Behavioral assessment: New directions in clinical psychology. New York: Brunner/Mazel, 1977.

Loevinger, J. Objective tests as instruments of psychological theory. Psychological Reports, 1957, 3, 635–695.

MacDonald, M. L. Measuring assertion: A model and method. *Behavior Therapy*, 1978, *9*, 889–899.

MacDonald, M. L. Assertion training for women. In J. P. Curran & P. M. Monti (Eds.), *Social skills training: A practical handbook for assessment and treatment*. New York: Guilford, 1982.

MacDonald, M. L., & Tyson, P. A. *External validities of several laboratory measures of assertion*. Manuscript submitted for publication, 1982.

McReynolds, P. (Ed.). *Advances in psychological assessment* (Vol. 3). San Francisco: Jossey-Bass, 1975.

Mahoney, M. J. Some applied issues in self-monitoring. In J. D. Cone & R. P. Hawkins (Eds.), *Behavioral assessment: New directions in clinical psychology*. New York: Brunner/Mazel, 1977.

Mash, E. J., & Terdal, L. G. (Eds.). *Behavior therapy assessment*. New York: Springer, 1976.

Mash, E. J., & Terdal, L. G. (Eds.). *Behavioral assessment of childhood disorders*. New York: Guilford, 1981.

Mischel, W. *Personality and assessment*. New York: Wiley, 1968.

Mischel, W. Toward a cognitive social learning reconceptualization of personality. *Psychological Review*, 1973, *80*, 252–283.

Moon, T. H., & MacDonald, M. L. *The realationship between the personality variable Machiavellianism and role-play measures of assertion*. Paper presented at the 16th Annual Meeting of the Association for Advancement of Behavior Therapy, Los Angeles, November 1982.

Morganstern, K. P., & Tevlin, H. E. Behavioral interviewing. In M. Hersen & A. S. Bellack (Eds.), *Behavioral assessment: A practical handbook* (2nd ed.). New York: Pergamon, 1981.

Nathan, P. E. A systems analytic model of diagnosis: V. The diagnostic validity of disordered consciousness. *Journal of Clinical Psychology*, 1969, *25*, 243–246.

Nathan, P. E., Andberg, M., Behan, P. O., & Patch, V. D. Thirty-two observers and one patient: A study of diagnostic reliability. *Journal of Clinical Psychology*, 1969, *25*, 370–375.

Nathan, P. E., Gould, C. F., Zare, N. C., & Roth, M. A systems analysis of diagnosis: VI. Improved diagnostic validity from median data. *Journal of Clinical Psychology*, 1969, *25*, 370–375.

Nathan, P. E., Robertson, P., & Andberg, M. M. A systems analytic model of diagnosis: IV. The diagnostic validity of abnormal affective behavior. *Journal of Clinical Psychology*, 1969, *25*, 235–242.

Nathan, P. E., Zare, N. C., Simpson, H. F., & Andberg, M. M. A systems analytic model of diagnosis: I. The diagnostic validity of abnormal psychomotor behavior. *Journal of Clinical Psychology*, 1969, *25*, 3–9.

Nay, W. R. Analogue measures. In A. R. Ciminero, K. S. Calhoun, & H. E. Adams (Eds.), *Handbook of behavioral assessment*. New York: Wiley, 1977.

Nelson, R. O. Methodological issues in assessment via self-monitoring. In J. D. Cone & R. P. Hawkins (Eds.), *Behavioral assessment: New directions in clinical psychology*. New York: Brunner/Mazel, 1977.

Nelson, R. O., & Barlow, D. H. Behavioral assessment: Basic strategies and initial procedures. In D. H. Barlow (Ed.), *Behavioral assessment of adult disorders*. New York: Guilford, 1981.

Nelson, R. O., & Hayes, S. C. Nature of behavioral assessment. In M. Hersen & A. S. Bellack (Eds.), *Behavioral assessment: A practical handbook* (2nd ed.). New York: Pergamon, 1981.

Nelson, R. O., & Hayes, S. C. Some current dimensions of behavioral assessment. *Behavioral Assessment*, 1979, *1*, 1–16.

O'Leary, K. D. Behavioral assessment. *Behavioral Assessment*, 1979, *1*, 31–36.

O'Leary, K. D., & Kent, R. N. Behavior modification for social action: Research tactics and problems. In L. A. Hamerlynck, L. C. Handy, & E. J. Mash (Eds.), *Behavior change: Methodology, concepts, and practice.* Champaign, Ill.: Research, 1973.

Peterson, D. R. *The clinical study of social behavior.* New York: Appleton-Century-Crofts, 1968.

Ray, W. J., & Raczynski, J. M. Psychophysiological assessment. In M. Hersen & A. S. Bellack (Eds.), *Behavioral assessment: A practical handbook* (2nd ed.). New York: Pergamon, 1981.

Sandifer, M. G., Jr., Pettus, C., & Quade, D. A study of psychiatric diagnosis. *Journal of Nervous and Mental Disease*, 1964, *139*, 350–356.

Selltiz, C., Jahoda, M., Deutsch, M., & Cook, S. *Research methods in social relations.* New York: Holt, Rinehart & Winston, 1964.

Skinner, B. F. *The behavior of organisms.* New York: Appleton-Century-Crofts, 1938.

Sowell, T. My turn: We're not really "equal." *Newsweek*, September 7, 1981, p. 13.

Spitzer, R. L., Endicott, J., & Robins, E. Research diagnostic criteria: Rationale and reliability. *Archives of General Psychiatry*, 1978, *35*, 773–785.

Stuart, R. B. Operant-interpersonal treatment of marital discord. *Journal of Consulting and Clinical Psychology*, 1969, *33*, 675–682.

Swan, G. E., & MacDonald, M. L. Behavior therapy in practice: A national survey of behavior therapist. *Behavior Therapy*, 1978, *9*, 799–807.

Ullmann, L. P., & Krasner, L. *Case studies in behavior modification.* New York: Holt, Rinehart & Winston, 1965.

Unger, R.K. Toward a redefinition of sex and gender. *American Psychologist*, 1979, *34*, 1085–1994.

Vogler, R. E., Weissback, T. A., Compton, J. V., & Martin, G. T. Integrated behavior change techniques for problem drinkers in the community. *Journal of Consulting and Clinical Psychology*, 1977, *45*, 267–279.

Webb, E. J., Campbell, D. T., Schwartz, R. D., & Sechrest, L. *Unobtrusive measures: A survey of nonreactive research in the social sciences.* Chicago: Rand-McNally, 1966.

Wiggins, J. S. *Personality and prediction: Principles of personality assessment.* Reading, Mass. Addison-Wesley, 1973.

Wildman, B. G., & Erickson, M. T. Methodological problems in behavioral observation. In J. D. Cone & R. P. Hawkins (Eds.), *Behavioral assessment: New directions in clinical psychology.* New York: Brunner/Mazel, 1977.

Wolpe, J. *Psychotherapy by reciprocal inhibition.* Stanford, Calif.: Stanford University Press, 1958.

Zigler, E., & Phillips, L. Psychiatric diagnosis: A critique. *Journal of Abnormal and Social Psychology*, 1961, *63*, 607–618.

4

DISSEMINATION OF BEHAVIORAL INTERVENTIONS WITH WOMEN: NEEDED—A TECHNOLOGY

STEPHANIE B. STOLZ

How can we get behavioral researchers and therapists to consider the special problems of women? How can we get behavioral therapists to use therapeutic techniques that are appropriate for women? These are questions raised by many of the chapters in this book. This chapter will examine the technology of knowledge dissemination to see what answers are available from research and theory.

The dissemination of scientific knowledge is often discussed in the context of the adoption of some specific technique or intervention package. In one classic study, for example, Fairweather, Sanders, and Tornatzky (1974) compared several techniques that were designed to get hospitals to adopt a particular style of posthospitalization living program for recovering mental patients. Their systematic nationwide study was an attempt to conduct an experimental analysis of key variables in the process of adopting new procedures for the care of former patients.

Research on the adoption of innovations goes back to early studies on the diffusion of new farm practices (Ryan & Goss, 1943), somewhat more recently it has been concerned with the adoption of new medical procedures (e.g., Coe & Bernhill, 1967) and the spread of acceptance of new retail products (Katz, Levin, & Hamilton, 1963), and currently includes research on the adoption of innovations by local governments (Pelz, 1981) and the adoption of mental health research results by government decision makers (Weiss & Weiss, 1981).

Although the great bulk of the literature in this area seems to focus

Stephanie B. Stolz. Department of Health and Human Services, U.S. Public Health Service, Kansas City, Missouri.

on the adoption and use of specific technologies (cf. Human Interaction Research Institute, 1976), Weiss and Weiss (1981) found that the decision makers they studied reported that they drew on research-based information not only for usable techniques but also for what Weiss (1977) has called "enlightenment," that is, for "bringing new ideas to public attention, framing or conceptualizing problems, keeping up with professional developments, finding out what is happening in other states or agencies, legitimating budget allocations, attacking established policies, or lobbying for new programs" (p. 846). From research, decision makers get information leading to new ideas, policies, and programs, but also, and perhaps more commonly, get information that supports, confirms, and justifies ideas, policies, and programs already decided on (Brown, 1981). In other words, knowledge dissemination can refer not only to the adoption of a particular technology but also to the adoption or confirmation of a particular idea, way of thinking, or reconceptualization of an issue (Larsen, 1980; Weiss, 1977).

For the social sciences as a whole, Weiss's generalization may be correct that "the conscious use of research to guide specific choices is a relatively uncommon event" (1980, p. 403). However, the nature of behavior modification research puts a special burden on the field to get its technology adopted, not merely to influence the gradual accumulation of insights, theories, concepts, and ways of looking at the world. Among the fundamental characteristics of behavior modification are that it is technological and that it is effective (Baer, Wolf, & Risley, 1968). In other words, research in behavior modification results not only in knowledge per se, but more importantly in procedures that can be replicated by people other than the developers, and the technology of behavior modification produces effects large enough to have practical value. Thus, although behavior modification research certainly may affect people's insights, theories, concepts, and views of the world, it should also alter what interventions people use, and how they do things, because behavior modification research will, by definition, have provided usable, practical, replicable, effective technology.

ISSUES IN DISSEMINATION OF BEHAVIORAL INTERVENTIONS

Some of the dissemination issues relating to behavior modification with women that are raised in this book do involve questions of "enlightenment" (Weiss, 1977) or "conceptual utilization" (Larsen, 1980), expressed as education of therapists and the general public, as well as resulting political action; other issues concern adoption of specific therapeutic technologies. McCrady (Chapter 16, this volume), for example, is concerned about conceptual change. She expresses concern that researchers and therapists do not consider the unique issues in treating substance-abusing women, including the special difficulties in detecting women's alcohol and drug problems and in engaging substance-abusing women in treatment. Her chapter provides many specific examples of these difficulties. Fodor and Thal (Chapter 14), similarly, feel that behavior therapists in their development of treatments for anorexia nervosa and overweight have inappropriately ignored how women are trained to think about their bodies in relation to eating and not eating. What McCrady and Fodor and Thal recommend is the diffusion of an idea, an approach—what Weiss and Weiss's (1981) decision makers might have seen as a new formulation of these problems or perhaps publicity for a new idea—in short, dissemination that results in education, the rethinking of a policy issue, and/or political action, rather than adoption of some specific technology (Larsen, 1980).

The dissemination of specific technologies, also discussed in this book, can, when successful, result in the widespread use of those technologies. Masters and Johnson's (1970) development of a short-term, directive treatment program for the remediation of sexual dysfunctions was widely adopted within a few years of its initial publication, according to Hoon, Krop, and Wincze (Chapter 5), and even resulted, they say, in the development of a new therapeutic specialty, sex therapy. Intelligence testing, intensively developed in response to the needs of the armed forces in World War I for rapid and reliable screening methods, has become extensively used and has, according to MacDonald (Chapter 3), formed the basis for the field of psychometrics. Assertion training for women is a behavioral technology that has been exceptionally widely disseminated in a relatively short period of time. Linehan (Chapter 6) notes that in the last 10 years, "almost every women's magazine in the U.S. has published at least one article on assertion," and various procedures labeled assertion training are offered to women by a wide range of sources, including therapists, management-training organizations, and community centers. Behavioral weight-loss programs have also been quickly adopted by the private sector and are now offered by many companies—despite their apparent failure to produce large weight loss and long-term maintenance of weight reduction (Fodor & Thal, Chapter 14).

Although assertion training, therapy for sexual dysfunction, and behavioral weight-reduction programs have been rapidly disseminated and widely adopted, other behavioral techniques discussed in this book have not as yet achieved widespread use. McCrady, for example, says that alternate skills training, which "seems to be crucial for alcoholic women" (p. 440), has not yet been systematically applied to them, nor, she contends, has behavioral marital therapy. The dissemination called for here is to researchers who might evaluate the efficacy of these approaches, and therapists who might use them.

Beck and Barlow (Chapter 2) urge that a recently developed motor behavior checklist, which they contend is preferable to existing techniques for measuring sex-role behaviors, should be used for basic social psychological research and as a behavioral assessment device in clinical behavior modification and behavior therapy. In this case, the intended dissemination is both to researchers who might use this instrument in basic research on sex-role problems, and to therapists who might use it in a variety of clinical situations to assess their clients and determine what treatment is needed.

Problems in getting clients to adopt particular procedures, that is, learn a particular behavior, are discussed in some of the chapters in this book. These problems are seen by the various authors as problems in behavior change, for which the technology of behavior modification is a recommended solution. Problems in dissemination, referred to in some of the chapters, are seen as problems in knowledge diffusion and the adoption of technology, as discussed earlier in this chapter.

However, problems in dissemination can also be comfortably conceptualized as problems in behavior change, for becoming "enlightened"—learning new attitudes—and adopting a new technology both call for changes in what people do. Furthermore, in my view, problems in behavior change can be conceptualized as problems in dissemination, in that the desired goal is to have the clients become aware of the procedures needed to change the target behavior (knowledge diffusion) and use the procedures to acquire the behavior (adoption of technology).

This analysis suggests that the technology of behavior change may have a contribution to make to our understanding of the technology of knowledge diffusion and the adoption of technology. Likewise, were there an effective technology of dissemination, including a technology of the adoption of technology, it might expand the technology of behavior change in areas such as getting clients to adopt particular procedures.

Although most discussions of therapeutic techniques are focused more on the techniques than on getting clients to use them, Strauss and

Atkeson (Chapter 8) discuss some methods of getting clients to use the procedures of parent training, such as providing therapy sessions only if the parents have completed assigned tasks, decreasing the fee for service for regular attendance at therapy sessions and for completion of homework, requiring specific behavior before therapy is allowed to progress, and praising the client for cooperation. These procedures use the technology of behavior modification to affect clients' adoption of the technology of behavior modification. What is needed is a technology to disseminate this information to practitioners and target members of the public.

Some examples in the earlier chapters in this book, where a need for dissemination is described, do not specify the technology necessary to effect this dissemination. For example, MacDonald (Chapter 3) would like psychologists who develop behaviorally focused paper-and-pencil tests to make greater use of the body of psychometric knowledge, but describes no method for bringing this about. Also, Budd and Greenspan (Chapter 18) report that one result of their survey was that therapists reported that mentally retarded clients often had difficulty understanding the responsibilities of being a parent, so that it was difficult to persuade them to get training in these responsibilities. Getting retarded parents to participate in parent training in which they would learn behavior we would label as "good judgment" is an interesting question, as yet unsolved, one that Budd and Greenspan see as a behavior-change question. As noted earlier in this chapter, this type of behavior-change question can also be conceptualized as a question in the adoption of technology, where the target behavior change is participation in parent training. In general, therapy is provided to those who come voluntarily as clients, and people are not normally given explicit training in volunteering. The question that Budd and Greenspan raise in regard to recruiting volunteers for parent training could be seen as a challenge to develop a technology of getting people to ask for technologies, which they would then adopt.

The most sweeping dissemination issue dealt with in this book is how to engineer social change, not just with respect to single issues like parent training, but more broadly in terms of public policy on the female sex role. For example, after discussing a variety of ways that women's anxieties and phobias might be dealt with in therapy, Padawer and Goldfried (Chapter 13) recommend social change as the fundamental intervention that would "ensure the psychological well-being of women" (p. 365), particularly through changes that would make sex-role stereotypes less rigid. Frank and Stewart (Chapter 10) contend that changes in society's tolerance of violent behavior will have to occur before it will be possible to establish programs for the primary prevention of rape and wife abuse. Many other chapters contain similar calls for social change and changes in public policy (e.g., Fodor & Thal; McCrady; Budd & Greenspan).

AN EXPLICIT TECHNOLOGY?

In the discussion of generality in their seminal article on the nature of applied behavior analysis, Baer, Wolf, and Risley (1968) made what is perhaps the most widely quoted statement in the literature of behavior modification: "Generalization should be programmed, rather than expected or lamented" (p. 97). In other words, a technology for the explicit production of generalization of behavioral changes should be developed; such a technology may indeed be well on the way to formulation (Stokes & Baer, 1977). The situation is similar for dissemination: "Dissemination is not to be spontaneous but is to be controlled and administered" (Knott & Wildavsky, 1980), or, in other words, a technology for the explicit production of knowledge diffusion and the adoption of technology should be developed. What is the status of the development of that technology? What is known from the literature on the diffusion of scientific knowledge that might be applied to the issues raised in this book, involving dissemination and adoption of specific therapy techniques as well as broad social change?

The most striking aspect of the literature on the diffusion of scientific knowledge is the near absence of empirical studies. The second most striking aspect is the absence of a generally accepted systematic theory, despite the general acknowledgment that the diffusion situation is an exceedingly complex one, involving a multiplicity of variables (Larsen, 1980; Stolz, 1981; Yin, 1981). One of the few systematic theoretical approaches (Pelz & Munson, 1981) is not called a theory even by its authors; rather, it is a "framework," which they organize around four "conceptual domains," specifically, the content of the innovation, the actors involved in applying the innovation, the stage in the innovating process (e.g., beginning to diagnose the problem and incorporating the solution), and the originality level of the specific innovation (i.e., the extent to which what is adopted is modified from its source). Using these four dimensions, Pelz and Munson (1981) develop an approach to the adoption of innovation which fulfills some of the goals of a useful theory, such as handling otherwise incongruous empirical observations. At the same time, although their framework does organize the field, their approach is so complex that it does little to reduce the difficulties that result from trying to deal with the literature in its unorganized state.

Related to the first two striking aspects of the literature on the diffusion of knowledge is a third characteristic, the lack of an effective technology of diffusion and adoption, of an effective set of interventions that would result in "enlightenment" or the adoption of technology—a lack even of some powerful variables on which a technology might be built (Stolz, 1981; Yin & Gwaltney, 1981). Salasin and Davis (1977) sum up the situation succinctly:

> The literature [on diffusion and utilization] . . . leaves a margin of opportunity for validating research. Much of the literature consists of asserted notions. A large portion consists of observations of experiences. There are, of course, many contributions from those who have scientifically observed change in process. The number of true experiments testing techniques facilitating knowledge transfer almost equals the number of ferns in the desert. (p. 430)

In the absence of a few strong variables or an effective technology, the literature in the area of the diffusion of innovations contains numerous lists of possibly effective variables, each of which appears to be weak (Roessner, 1980; Stolz, 1981). When an empirical study is done, the result is that another weak variable gets added to these lists, or, perhaps, the evidence for some variable or variables is slightly strengthened. The lists of variables are so numerous, in fact, that some publications contain lists of the lists (Human Interaction Research Institute, 1976). "One might gain the impression," Salasin and Davis say, "that there is something a bit short of consensus" (1977, p. 430).

In the areas dealt with by behavior modification, in contrast, the literature is organized by its reference to a few strong variables, particularly reinforcement and stimulus control. With these few theoretical principles, the apparent complexity of behavior dissolves (in most cases). In medicine, likewise, researchers' experience has been that until the cause of a disease was discovered, the disease was thought to be extremely complex, affected by a variety of environmental influences, and not subject to simple control techniques. Once the single causative agent is located, however, the apparent complexity dissolves, and control of the causative agent results in control of the disease (Thomas, 1979).[1]

For the diffusion of technological innovations, the causative agent, the strong variable, is yet to be located. Presumably such an agent will be found some day, and the expected reduction of complexity will result.

[1] I thank D. M. Baer for calling this example to my attention.

Until such an agent or agents are identified, until research reveals the variable or variables most influential, the only recourse for those interested in promoting dissemination is to focus on those variables that at a minimum have been shown to increase the probability that an innovation will be adopted.

My own review of the literature in this area and my case-study analysis (Stolz, 1981) suggest that the strongest single variable influencing the diffusion of innovation is personal interaction between the decision maker and a colleague who promotes the adoption of the innovation. The case studies suggested that individual contacts and individual personalities were crucial in determining whether a given technology would be adopted. A much more extensive study by Patton and his associates (Patton, 1978; Patton, Grimes, Guthrie, Brennan, French, & Blyth, 1977) involving interviews with decision makers, found similarly that the single most important element in the utilization process was what these authors called "the personal factor," which, in their research, was said to be "made up of equal parts of leadership, interest, enthusiasm, determination, commitment, aggressiveness, and caring" (Patton et al., 1977, p. 155). Patton et al. (1977) sum up their findings: *"The pattern is markedly clear: Where the personal factor emerges, where some person takes direct, personal responsibility for getting the information to the right people"* (p. 158; italics in original), adoption of the innovation occurs. Many other studies concur in emphasizing this variable (e.g., Glaser, 1973; Yin & Gwaltney, 1981).

To deal with the dissemination issues raised in the earlier chapters in this book, however, the recommendation that an aggressive, enthusiastic, determined, committed (and so on) individual be established as the colleague of each potential adoptor is not a very practical solution. Even though accomplishing such placements might be the single most effective way to disseminate and get adopted any innovation, this is not a technique that lends itself to widespread use. What, then, can be suggested as a feasible alternative?

AN IMPLICIT TECHNOLOGY OF THE ADOPTION OF INNOVATIONS

In other writings (Stolz, 1981), I have suggested the possibility that there may be an implicit technology of the adoption of innovations, that is, a set of feasible techniques implicit in the published literature but not collected anywhere as a list of techniques. This would be analogous to Stokes and Baer's (1977) implicit technology of generalization, a list of generalization techniques of varying utility which Stokes and Baer were able to draw out of the existing behavioral literature. Its translation to this problem takes the following form:

1. *Publish and hope.* The first "nonmethod" of generalization listed by Stokes and Baer (1977) was Train and Hope; its analogy in the dissemination field would be Publish and Hope. This may be the most common way of attempting to disseminate one's findings—and common also are articles complaining that decision makers do not read the research literature (e.g., Halpert, 1966), and that when they do, they do not make use of what they have read (e.g., Weiss, 1979). The National Institute of Mental Health, responding to this complaint, has fostered a special journal, *Innovations,* designed to make it easy for decision makers to read about innovations in human services through simple, attractive graphics, a readable style avoiding jargon, an emphasis on practical details, and so on (Larsen, 1978).

Many of the chapters in this book include material that could be described as an attempt to disseminate through Publish and Hope. Foreyt and Goodrick (Chapter 9) state explicitly that a purpose of their chapter is to get behavioral specialists who work in the area of health education, as well as a wide variety of persons in the helping professions, to adopt their behavioral exercise and nutrition treatment program. Similarly, Norman, Johnson, and Miller (Chapter 11) hope that clinicians reading their chapter will come to use behavioral formulations of depression and especially will use them in a way beneficial to women clients. Less explicitly, Strauss and Atkeson (Chapter 8), describing a number of techniques for getting clients to use the procedures they have learned in parent training, might be attempting through this publication to disseminate such information to therapists.

The absence of numerous adoptions, despite much publishing, suggests that Publish and Hope is at best a weak technique. Simply doing research and communicating it (and then hoping), while effective sometimes, is not effective very consistently, much as Train and Hope is only somewhat effective in obtaining generalization of learned behavior.

What about Stokes and Baer's (1977) other eight techniques? These also may have analogies in the area of the dissemination of innovations.

2. *Sequential implementation.* Sequential Modification, Stokes and Baer's (1977) second technique, involves initiating procedures to accomplish generality by systematic sequential modification in every nongeneralized condition in which generalization is desired (rather than simply hoping for generalization but not scheduling necessary consequences

in every relevant condition). The analogy in the area of dissemination and adoption might be Sequential Implementation, in which a program exemplifying adoption is established (once adoption has not occurred following publication), and then a determination is made as to whether further adoptions occur; the external establishment of model programs would eventually be repeated in all settings where such control is possible and internal adoptions do not otherwise occur.

MacDonald (Chapter 3), interested in getting behavioral psychologists to use sophisticated psychometric techniques in the development of assessment instruments, could make use of Sequential Implementation by using the psychometric techniques herself in the development of each paper-and-pencil test she creates, and by reevaluating and modifying with that technology the behavioral paper-and-pencil instruments now in use. Similarly, McCrady (Chapter 16) might make use of this technique to achieve her goal of having researchers evaluate the use of alternate-skills trainings for alcoholic women, by herself initiating evaluative research. If other researchers do not pick up on the line of research begun by McCrady, she could do additional studies until all relevant questions have been answered. The technique of Sequential Implementation calls for extraordinary expense, pluck, and commitment, because it requires that the disseminator eventually implement programs in every possible setting.

3. *Introduce to natural maintaining contingencies.* The next technique in Stokes and Baer's list, Introduce to Natural Maintaining Contingencies, would, in the adoption-of-innovation area, involve identifying naturally occurring reinforcers for the potential adoptors, so as to entrap them with these reinforcers into adopting the new technology. A natural consequence for getting parental cooperation with parent training may be improvement in the child's behavior, for example. Already noted above is the importance of the personal element in the decision to adopt. Presumably a key factor in making the personal element an important variable is the reinforcement provided to the potential adoptor by a colleague. In getting her colleagues who are developing behavioral paper-and-pencil tests to use appropriate psychometrics, MacDonald (Chapter 3) might find her own social consequences an important influence on their behavior.

4. *Implement sufficient exemplars.* The analogy to Stokes and Baer's (1977) Train Sufficient Exemplars would be Implement Sufficient Exemplars. This technique might promote the adoption of innovation through the establishment of some model programs. This technique is

similar to Sequential Implementation, but involves implementation in fewer settings, using the shrewdest possible choice of exemplars that best represent the dimensions of the problem (Baer, 1981). Unlike Sequential Implementation, Implement Sufficient Exemplars rests on the expectation that adoption by others will occur after only the right few examples are provided.

If this technique were used by MacDonald (Chapter 3) in attempting to get others to use psychometric techniques in behavioral test development, she might find that others began to use those techniques after she had made public her use of them in the development of the most representative few paper-and-pencil tests, for example. Likewise, Gurman and Klein (Chapter 7), critical of widely used assessment checklists, might develop their own checklists which define successful marriages in ways that are consistent with their values. Reported use of a few such checklists might stimulate others to develop their own instruments that would meet Gurman and Klein's standards. McCrady (Chapter 16) might conduct only a few, shrewdly chosen studies of the use of alternate-skills trainings for alcoholic women before she found others initiating similarly focused research.

Other issues raised in earlier chapters also lend themselves to the technique of Implement Sufficient Exemplars. For example, to get retarded parents to participate in parent training, an issue raised by Budd and Greenspan (Chapter 18), involvement of some retarded parents may well be an effective technique. One of the variables generally thought to promote the adoption of innovations is having potential adoptors view well-chosen model programs (Stolz, 1981), which is essentially the same technique as Implement Sufficient Exemplars.

5. *Implement loosely.* In obtaining the generalization of learned behavior, the technique of Train Loosely means to conduct teaching with relatively little restriction over the stimuli presented and the correct responses allowed, so as to maximize sampling of possibly relevant dimensions for transfer to other situations and other behavior (Stokes & Baer, 1977). Implement Loosely, the analogous dissemination/adoption technique, might refer to changing the intervention to suit local conditions, so that each adoption is somewhat different from the others, as well as from the initial model. Many writers in the area of the adoption of innovations suggest that enabling modification for local conditions is a highly important factor in facilitating adoptions (Fawcett, Mathews, & Fletcher, 1980; Rice & Rogers, 1980; Stolz, 1981), because rigid specification of procedures seems to mitigate against adoption.

Strauss and Atkeson (Chapter 8) list numerous methods to get clients to use the procedures of parent training; it is possible that enabling parents to modify the techniques to suit their home situation would be an additional method of promoting adoption of parent-training procedures. Health educators may be more likely to adopt Foreyt and Goodrick's (Chapter 9) behavioral exercise and nutrition program if they could modify details of the program, rather than being required to adopt it unchanged, as described in their chapter.

6. Stokes and Baer's (1977) sixth technique for obtaining generalization of learned behavior is to Use Indiscriminable Contingencies. This refers to designing the environment in such a way that the subject cannot discriminate in which settings the response will be reinforced or not reinforced, so that the behavior comes to occur in all settings, that is, generalizes. I have not been able to develop an analogy of this technique that is applicable to the adoption of innovations or the dissemination of knowledge.

7. *Program common stimuli.* The seventh technique, Program Common Stimuli, would, in the area of adoption and dissemination, deal with having common elements between some preliminary or model form of the program and the ultimate adoption. For example, to get parents to use the procedures of parent training at home, research described by Strauss and Atkeson (Chapter 8) tried having the parents use the procedures with their own children in the therapist's office, and, in other studies, in a model apartment with a homelike atmosphere. Such arrangements should enhance the likelihood that the parents would continue to use the new procedures, because of the common stimuli in parent-training and home settings.

To get retarded parents to participate in parent training, it might be possible to contact organizations of retarded parents (if such exist) and arrange for presentations at their meetings of examples of the parent-training procedures. This might be especially effective if members of the host organization participated in the demonstrations.

8. *Mediate dissemination.* Mediate Generalization, the eighth technique, calls for establishing a response as part of the newly learned behavior that is likely to be used in other problems as well, so as to result in generalization. To Mediate Dissemination might involve ensuring that those who will ultimately decide on adoption are among those who ask that a preliminary test of the adoption be conducted. If an organization of retarded parents asks that a demonstration of parent-training methods be provided for one of their meetings, this might fa-

cilitate those parents' later participation in parent training, which could be described as adoption of that methodology. Researchers who petition the government for additional funds to support research to develop psychotherapy to represent women's needs may be more likely later to conduct such research. Similarly, child-care facilities are probably more likely to be set up by employers who belong to a Chamber of Commerce that petitions the local government for funds to establish such facilities.

9. *Train to implement.* The analogy of Stokes and Baer's (1977) final technique, Train to Generalize, would be Train to Implement. This technique involves establishing training programs specifically focused on teaching people to acquire knowledge which has been disseminated, and thus to adopt innovations. Training courses are available at a few universities (e.g., Vanderbilt) which have explicit programming for policymakers, teaching them to adopt innovative technology.

Strauss and Atkeson (Chapter 8) used this technique in getting clients to adopt the procedures of parent training through explicit training on adoption, described in their chapter. MacDonald (Chapter 3) might develop courses to train those who develop behavioral paper-and-pencil techniques in the latest psychometric techniques.

These techniques comprise what might be an implicit technology of dissemination and the adoption of new techniques. The techniques were developed nonempirically, by analogy with known techniques for the generalization of learned behavior. Much remains to be done in the development of an actual (rather than implicit) technology of dissemination and adoption, most especially a review of the literature to see when these techniques or others have been used, how effective they are, and then later, empirical testing and evaluation of techniques needing further study.

CONCLUSION

This chapter began with two questions that are raised by the authors of other chapters in this book: How can we get behavioral researchers and therapists to consider the special problems of women? How can we get behavioral therapists to use therapeutic techniques that are appropriate for women? This chapter suggests that the answer to both these questions is that these goals will not be accomplished without a technology of knowledge dissemination and the adoption of innovations—knowledge dissemination so that researchers and therapists will consider the special problems of women, and the adoption of innovations so that therapists will use the appropriate therapeutic techniques.

ACKNOWLEDGMENTS

The opinions expressed here are the author's and do not necessarily reflect the views of the U.S. Department of Health and Human Services. I thank D. M. Baer for thoughtful comments on an earlier version of the manuscript.

REFERENCES

Baer, D. M. *How to plan for generalization.* Lawrence, Kans.: H & H Enterprises, 1981.

Baer, D. M., Wolf, M. M., & Risley, T. R. Some current dimensions of applied behavior analysis. *Journal of Applied Behavior Analysis,* 1968, *1,* 91–97.

Brown, B. S. Comments on *Policy research for policymakers.* A. Majchrzak (Chair), Symposium presented at the meeting of the American Psychological Association, Los Angeles, 1981.

Coe, R. M., & Bernhill, E. A. Social dimensions of failure in innovation. *Human Organization,* 1967, *26,* 149–156.

Fairweather, G. W., Sanders, D. H., & Tornatzky, L. G. *Creating change in mental health organizations.* New York: Pergamon, 1974.

Fawcett, S. B., Mathews, R. M., & Fletcher, R. K. Some promising dimensions for behavioral community technology. *Journal of Applied Behavior Analysis,* 1980, *13,* 505–518.

Glaser, E. M. Knowledge transfer and institutional change. *Professional Psychology,* 1973, *4,* 434–444.

Halpert, H. P. Communications as a basic tool in promoting utilization of research findings. *Community Mental Health Journal,* 1966, *2,* 231–236.

Human Interaction Research Institute. *Putting knowledge to use: A distillation of the literature regarding knowledge transfer and change.* Rockville, Md.: National Institute of Mental Health, 1976.

Katz, E., Levin, M. L., & Hamilton, H. Traditions of research on the diffusion of innovation. *American Sociological Review,* 1963, *28,* 237–252.

Knott, J., & Wildavsky, A. If dissemination is the solution, what is the problem? *Knowledge: Creation, Diffusion, Utilization,* 1980, *1,* 537–578.

Larsen, J. K. *Innovations: Summary report* (AIR-72300-11/78-PR). Palo Alto, Calif.: American Institutes for Research in the Behavioral Sciences, 1978.

Larsen, J. K. Knowledge utilization: What is it? *Knowledge: Creation, Diffusion, Utilization,* 1980, *2,* 421–442.

Masters, W. H., & Johnson, V. E. *Human sexual inadequacy.* Boston: Little, Brown, 1970.

Patton, M. W. *Utilization-focused evaluation.* Beverly Hills, Calif.: Sage, 1978.

Patton, M. W., Grimes, P. S., Guthrie, K. M., Brennan, N. J., French, B. D., & Blyth, D. A. In search of impact: An analysis of the utilization of federal health evaluation research. In C. H. Weiss (Ed.), *Using social research in public policy making.* Lexington, Mass.: Heath, 1977.

Pelz, D. C. *Quantitative case studies of urban innovations.* Unpublished manuscript, 1981. (Available from Center for Research in the Utilization of Scientific Knowledge, ISR, University of Michigan, Ann Arbor.)

Pelz, D. C., & Munson, F. C. *A framework for organization innovating.* Paper presented at Conference on Knowledge Use, University of Pittsburgh, March 1981.

Rice, R. E., & Rogers, E. M. Reinvention in the innovation process. *Knowledge: Creation, Diffusion, Utilization,* 1980, *1,* 499–514.

Roessner, J. D. Technological diffusion research and national policy issues. *Knowledge: Creation, Diffusion, Utilization,* 1980, *2,* 179–201.

Ryan, B., & Gross, N. C. The diffusion of hybrid seed corn in two Iowa communities. *Rural Sociology,* 1943, *8,* 15–24.

Salasin, S. E., & Davis, H. R. Facilitating the utilization of evaluation . . . A rocky road. In I. Davidoff, M. Guttentag, & J. Offutt (Eds.), *Evaluating community mental health services: Principles and practices* (DHEW Publication No. [ADM]77-465). Rockville, Md.: U.S. Department of Health, Education and Welfare, 1977.

Stokes, T. F., & Baer, D. M. An implicit technology of generalization. *Journal of Applied Behavior Analysis,* 1977, *10,* 349–367.

Stolz, S. B. Adoption of innovations from applied behavioral research: "Does anybody care?" *Journal of Applied Behavior Analysis,* 1981, *14,* 491–505.

Thomas, L. *The medusa and the snail.* New York: Viking, 1979.

Weiss, C.H. (Ed.). *Using social research in public policy making.* Lexington, Mass.: Heath, 1977.

Weiss, C. H. The many meanings of research utilization. *Public Administration Review,* 1979, *39,* 426–431.

Weiss, C. H. Knowledge creep and decision accretion. *Knowledge: Creation, Diffusion, Utilization,* 1980, *1,* 381–404.

Weiss, J. A., & Weiss, C. H. Social scientists and decision makers look at the usefulness of mental health research. *American Psychologist,* 1981, *36,* 837–847.

Yin, R. K. The case study as a serious research strategy. *Knowledge: Creation, Diffusion, Utilization,* 1981, *3,* 97–114.

Yin, R. K., & Gwaltney, M. K. Knowledge utilization as a networking process. *Knowledge: Creation, Diffusion, Utilization,* 1981, *2,* 555–580.

II

PROBLEMS OF LIVING

The six chapters in Part II deal with problems commonly experienced by adult women. The lives of adult women are fraught with complex, conflicting demands. They must act in an independent manner and yet avoid physical intimidation. They must play a central role in the rearing of children and in the success of a marriage, compete with men at work, and still be relaxed in intimate sexual relationships. The authors of this group of chapters recognize that prevention and clinical treatment may require solutions for problems of daily living.

At home and at work, women are often the guardians of other people's health and nutrition. Even so, Foreyt and Goodrick remind us in Chapter 9 that women rarely take sufficient responsibility for their own health. No authors in this book take a more adamant stand about the prevention of behavioral problems in women than Foreyt and Goodrick. While it is hard to disagree with the benefits of health maintenance that they describe, more evidence about the simplest way to encourage life-style change is needed. Fortunately, Foreyt and Goodrick present their intervention strategies in sufficient detail to permit implementation and further evaluation.

Assertiveness training has become a core behavioral treatment procedure for women. As Linehan demonstrates in Chapter 6, the applications of assertiveness training go far beyond women who complain of being mistreated by other people. As Hoon, Krop, and Wincze point out in Chapter 5, assertiveness training often helps women with sexual dysfunctions; and as Padawer and Goldfried show in Part III, Chapter 13, assertiveness training often helps excessively anxious women. A longstanding, unresolved problem in assertiveness and social skills training with women, concerns the design of skill repertoires. Without adequate knowledge about the behavior patterns of competent women, it is difficult to be certain that assertive-looking and assertive-sounding behaviors will achieve the goals that the client desires—advancement at work, a happier family life, better relationships with friends. Linehan confronts this problem by focusing on assessment and intervention strategies that train clients in interpersonal effectiveness, so that they can achieve the interpersonal outcomes they value. Some critics argue that assertiveness training procedures were popularized too quickly and distorted in the adoption process by inexperienced clinicians. Linehan's requirements for assessment of interpersonal difficulties and their remediation will serve as a guide to the perplexed who wish to avoid common problems in the application of this technology.

The specialty area of behavior modification with women is a relatively new one. In Chapter 7 Gurman and Klein take the position that behavioral marital therapy is not value free in its underlying assumptions or in its technology. In fact, they argue that behavioral marital therapy perpetuates traditional inequities in the division of labor between husbands and wives. For two reasons workers in the field cannot afford to ignore these criticisms. First, marital satisfaction appears to be central to the psychological welfare of many women, and married women appear to be at particularly high risk for depression and other behavior dysfunctions, such as agoraphobia. Second, an inequitable responsibility for household and child care, and resulting dissatisfaction, is not restricted to traditional marriages; there is convincing evidence of similar inequities in modern, two-worker marriages. Gurman and Klein's recent criticisms of the matching-to-sample approach to goal setting for marital interventions have already made an impact on the field; their discussion of the issue in this volume sparked a lively debate in print among several contributors.

Parent training may be the earliest form of applied behavior analysis to involve large numbers of women. As Strauss and Atkeson point out in Chapter 8, parent training, in the majority of cases, is mother training. Behaviorists have persuaded few fathers to participate in child rearing, despite the egalitarian dream of Skinner's *Walden Two* (1948). Strauss and Atkeson summarize evidence that depression impairs a mother's perception of her child's behavior, and they hint that some mothers' depression might lessen as their child-rearing skills improve. Since depression is most prevalent among married women, the preventive impact of on-the-job parent training deserves exploration. Compared to other areas of inquiry described in this book, parent training has been extensively investigated. This chapter will direct even the knowledgeable reader to unanswered questions and issues of clinical importance.

Rape and aggression by strangers and family members are, unfortunately, problems of daily living for many women. Frank and Stewart's review of epidemiologic data in Chapter 10 shatters stereotypes about women's protected status. They also dispute the belief that women seek physical intimidation, although no amount of evidence may disconfirm this popular prejudice. Since behavioral interventions aimed at victimized women are just now being developed and tested, Frank and Stewart

review self-help and insight-oriented approaches and present preliminary data from several clinical research projects including their own.

Hoon, Krop, and Wincze's chapter, like Chapter 12 in this volume
on physiological and reproductive disorders, answers skeptics' questions about the need for a book on behavior modification with women,
by emphasizing how little is known about normal female sexual behavior
and about the treatment of female sexual dysfunction. Along with the
chapters in this book on victimized women and obesity, this chapter
points out that the women's movement has had healthy effects on
women's attitudes and behavior, and hints at the need for behaviorists
to learn about prevention and intervention from peer self-help groups.
Hoon, Krop, and Wincze emphasize assessment, since problems of sexual dysfunction tend to have heterogeneous causes, and to respond to
available treatment procedures developed for nonsexual disorders.
While the chapter provides a thorough, practical review of sexual dysfunctions and their behavioral treatment, it also raises basic questions
about human behavior. Is treatment less effective when a woman is a
passive rather than an active participant? Is positive change less likely
to generalize if it has been induced by a mechanical device or a pharmacological substance rather than by the woman's own actions? Is altered pain sensitivity a precondition for increased sexual pleasure?

REFERENCE

Skinner, B. F. *Walden Two*. New York: Macmillan, 1948.

5

SEXUALITY

EMILY FRANCK HOON
HARRY D. KROP
JOHN P. WINCZE

OVERVIEW

Profound changes in views of human sexuality have come about during the past 85 years through advances in clinical practice and scientific enquiry. Changing viewpoints about human sexual conduct have affected the way in which all of us conceptualize our sexual well-being and indeed, our self-esteem. Compared to men, women appear to have confronted more dramatic conflict about their sexual practices, and more ambiguous definitions of good treatment for dysfunction. Behavior therapy appears to offer a structural model assessment procedure and a treatment methodology which may combat the adverse effects of ignorance and of religious and cultural biases.

This chapter reviews some of the history of attitudes toward female sexuality and explores the advantages of a behavioral approach to female sexual problems. The chapter emphasizes a behavioral model which facilitates assessment and treatment. Presentation of the model along with details of assessment and treatment provides the reader with a state-of-the-art understanding of behavioral intervention for women experiencing sexual difficulties.

Emily Franck Hoon. Department of Clinical Psychology, University of Florida, Gainesville, Florida.

Harry D. Krop. Psychology Service, Veterans Administration Medical Center, Gainesville, Florida.

John P. Wincze. Division of Biology and Medicine, Brown University, Providence, Rhode Island.

BACKGROUND

Western culture has throughout history placed restraints, prohibitions, and legal sanctions on various aspects of human sexual expression. Religious authorities have been among the prime influences in prescribing rules governing sexual conduct and, alas, religious dogma has often become law and has even dictated medical practice. As a result, the time prior to the 20th century is often considered an antisexual era. However, through the outspoken efforts of some scientists and clinicans around the turn of the century, restrictive sexual concepts were challenged and, more generally, some societal sexual values changed. It is important to understand that change did not bring a new set of values, replacing restriction with wild abandonment. Change was subtle, and at times led only to new problems. For example, Freud diagnosed many sexual practices not as sickness, but as neuroticism; through Freud's efforts, masturbation was viewed as a neurotic act rather than as a reflection of brain damage.

Freud's major contribution was his description of the role of sexuality in personality growth and development. Unfortunately, Freud was also a victim of his culture (as we all are) and his work led to the freeing of the sexual expression of men more than that of women. Thus, his concepts of "penis envy" and "vaginal orgasm" set limits on appropriate female sexual behavior. Although many of Freud's (1905/1962) original concepts of psychosexual development have been seriously challenged, his rigid definition of "healthy" female sexuality persists. In Freud's (1905/1962) view, female sexuality was compensatory—a poor facsimile of the male's sexuality—and thus her development could only be considered healthy if she accepted her inferiority and resolved her "penis envy." Despite the general acceptance of Freud's theories of psychosexual development, his ideas were mostly speculative. Not until the publication of Kinsey's systematic research (Kinsey, Pomeroy, Martin, & Gebhard, 1953) were there statistical data regarding female sexual behavior. Although Kinsey's studies certainly challenged many outdated concepts, his data did not alter the common belief that it is the male's responsibility to initiate sex and to maintain erection; if anything, he suggested that it is natural for men to be more sexually active than women. It was Masters and Johnson's (1966) illuminating data about female sexuality which disconfirmed the traditional notion of sexual dysfunction as the "tip of an iceberg," a reflection of a deep-seated emotional problem (LoPiccolo, 1980).

In *Human Sexual Inadequacy* (1970), Masters and Johnson defined sex as a learned skill. The need to learn to be sexual, that is, to learn appropriate techniques for deriving sexual satisfaction, was a revolutionary concept, especially for women who grew up believing that sex should be a totally spontaneous and natural activity (Barbach, 1980). Although the increased liberalization of sexual standards among women may not be sufficiently dramatic to warrant the label of revolution, we certainly have witnessed a sexual evolution during the last decade. Until recently, sex-role training of American girls has established passivity and dependency as desirable female attributes. These "female" characteristics have carried over to a woman's view of her own sexuality and have been highly resistant to change. In our society, both men and women have been taught that the male is the authority on sex (Barbach, 1980). With minimal instruction, each man is somehow expected to understand each woman's unique sexuality. Because women are "submerged in the mystical vision of sex" that arises out of this mutual lack of information, many women do not explore their sexual preferences, but expect a man to awaken them (Barbach, 1980, p. 7).

Ironically, the availability of psychologically accurate information about female sexuality, coupled with an emphasis on women's responsibility, have increased women's sexual expectations. The feminist ideal of women who assume responsibility for their own sexual satisfaction has taken pressure off penis-centered males while adding to women's performance anxiety.

As women have accepted the premise that "sex is a learned skill," they have also accepted the notion that sexual dysfunction may be learned. Masters and Johnson's (1970) short-term directive treatment program for sexual dysfunctions launched sex therapy as a psychotherapeutic specialty. Since 1970, sex therapy has gained widespread acceptance as a method of aiding couples and individuals in overcoming dysfunction and in enhancing sexual satisfaction. Since the two-week intensive (and expensive) treatment format developed by Masters and Johnson was prohibitive for most people, new treatment formats and therapeutic strategies had to be developed (Leiblum & Pervin, 1980). Although not self-described behaviorists, Masters and Johnson's approach incorporated many explicitly behavioral strategies and principles. During the past decade, there has been a plethora of publications by behavior therapists describing techniques for modifying sexual dysfunction and enhancing sexual satisfaction. This chapter reviews current sex therapy practices for women by emphasizing a behavioral analysis model of the assessment and treatment of female sexual problems.

BEHAVIORAL MODEL OF SEXUAL FUNCTIONING: THE ADVANTAGE FOR WOMEN

A functional Behavioral Analysis Model of sexual behavior was formulated by Wincze (1981) and emphasized a problem-oriented approach (Fowler & Longabough, 1975) which linked assessment and treatment. The model shown in Figure 5-1 places three common areas of sexual distress (i.e., sexual anxiety, sexual arousal, and orgasm/ejaculation) on a continuum and independently considers subjective, behavioral, and physiological involvement within each area. Medical and psychosocial antecedents and consequences of sexual distress are analyzed along with clients' interpretations of their problems.

While the advantages of a behavioral model compared to more dynamic models of human behavior have been well described (Bandura, 1969; Ullmann & Krasner, 1969), the advantages to women's sexual functioning are especially important. Since common knowledge about sexual behavior is imbued with ignorance and unscientific emotionality, clinical treatment is susceptible to bias and misjudgment. Information about female sexuality is particularly scanty, since the sexual behavior of females has been studied less than that of males. For example, electromechanical measures of male genital response have existed for over 100 years (Mountjoy, 1974), while comparable measures of female arousal have been available only since the mid-1970s. Because there is more ignorance about female sexuality, an objective and unbiased description of problems is needed more than a categorization of problems based on comparisons to normal behavior. The behavioral model provides such a framework for an objective description of problems. Within this model, each client's sexual problem is viewed as caused by an association of factors, each bearing a degree of responsibility which differs in proportion from one person to the other.

The task of assessment within a behavioral framework encourages the health-professional assessor to describe the problem and the antecedents and consequences of the problem rather than to determine

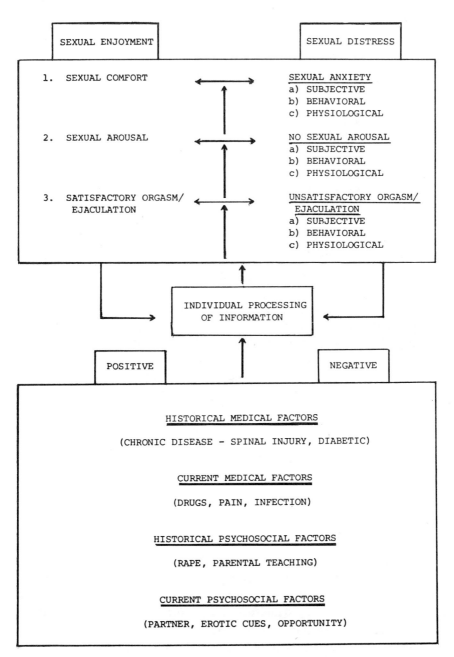

FIGURE 5-1. Behavioral model of sexual problems.

whether or not a person is sick (read dysfunctional). Cultural biases and misinformation about female sexuality are consequently less likely to hinder the assessment process.

THE ASSESSMENT PROCESS FOR WOMEN EXPRESSING SEXUAL DISTRESS

Because behavior therapy focuses on overt behaviors, assessment demands precise descriptions of the behavior in question, and of the context in which problem behavior occurs (Tollison & Adams, 1979). Assessment must determine whether a client is appropriate for sex therapy, the presence and degree of psychopathology in the individual, the degree of discord in the relationship, the individual's and the couple's motivation for treatment, and the likelihood of an organic etiology to the sexual problem. In their clinical assessment procedure, Lobitz and Lobitz (1978) evaluate whether (1) other relationship problems will interfere with sex therapy; (2) the couple's needs will be better met by marital therapy; and (3) the equilibrium in the couple's relationship will be upset by sex therapy. Despite taboos about disclosure of sexual behavior (Caird & Wincze, 1977; Hoon, 1978) assessment tools have been designed to tap attitudinal, behavioral, and physiological components of sexual behavior.

MEDICAL EXAMINATION

A complete gynecological examination and health history are the first steps in assessment. Diabetes, hypertension, abnormal thyroid function, vaginal infection, underdeveloped secondary sexual structures, a prolapsed uterus, painful vaginal or perineal scars, vaginal mucosal atrophy, imperforate hymen, and inadequate pubococcygeal muscle tone are conditions commonly implicated in female sexual dysfunctions. Since the use of alcohol and drugs which affect the central and peripheral nervous systems can interfere with normal sexual functioning, a relevant history should be obtained. It cannot be assumed, however, that the absence of medical problems directly related to sexual functioning eliminates all important physical conditions interfering with sexual response. Many indirect physical factors, such as lethargy, pain, body scars, and skin rashes, can alter the delicate balance between sexual desire and the desire to be left alone.

For the most part, the primary care physicians and a few specialists such as urologists, obstetricians, and gynecologists have been the initial resources for individuals seeking sexual help. The medical profession, however, has never been adequately prepared to respond to patients' sexual concerns. As a group, physicians have fewer sexual experiences than their graduate-school peers and most physicians who graduated before 1970 never had any formal training in human sexuality (Hunt, 1979). Although almost all medical schools now offer didactic course work in human sexuality, it is still possible for graduating medical students to have no formal training in this area. Since most medical students view the social and behavioral sciences as unimportant compared to the hard sciences and clinical clerkships, only the truly interested medical student graduates with more than an anatomical and biological understanding of human sexuality. Thus, most physicians are not sensitive or knowledgeable when they respond to a patient's complaint of sexual difficulty.

It is not surprising that physicians who are comfortable discussing sexual matters report a higher percentage of patients with sexual complaints than physicians who are disinterested or uncomfortable (Burnap & Golden, 1967; Lief & Karlen, 1976). Many physicians may still harbor pre-Kinsian attitudes toward women complaining of sexual problems, and those with contemporary attitudes may lack good interviewing skills. Recognizing the deficit in physician education, several new books have been written for physicians (Green, 1979; Masur, in press; Munjack & Oziel, 1980), but it is still likely that women seeking help for sexual problems will be met with little acceptance or understanding.

Fortunately, there are a number of professional resources in most large communities for patients complaining of sexual problems. While primary care physicians may have neither the time nor the skill to treat sexual problems, they play an extremely important role in screening sexual problems, since most women discuss this type of problem with their personal physicians before going to a sex therapist. The directive therapy model promoted by Masters and Johnson (1970) has helped to categorize sexual difficulties by describing the components of various problems. This workable and easily understood system has minimized dynamic interpretations and emphasized a more problem-oriented approach. Changes in the classification of sexual problems to a more directive therapy conceptualization have been reflected in the new DSM-III (*Diagnostic and Statistical Manual of Mental Disorders*, 3rd ed., 1980).

CLINICAL INTERVIEW

The clinical interview is the most common method of obtaining information about a sexual problem. The initial interview determines if sex therapy will be useful and enables the client to choose a therapeutic program. A decision to engage in sex therapy that is mutually made by client and therapist increases client commitment to therapy (Lobitz & Lobitz, 1978). Since the disclosure of private information is uncomfortable for most clients, the therapists can provide support by acknowledging that many people find it difficult to discuss sexual issues (Wincze, 1981). It is helpful to assure the couple that sex is an individual matter and that neither partner is necessarily expected to agree with the other's perceptions (Lobitz & Lobitz, 1978). Since an interview is not an inquisition, it should proceed on a friendly, conversational basis. The format can be modified in response to verbal and nonverbal signs of discomfort with general questions to anxious clients, and specific questions to relaxed clients (Wincze, 1981). It should be noted, however, that even with the most anxious patients detailed information is needed. The therapist's demeanor and ease in asking questions is more important than the exact question content. Topics to be covered include demographic information, specifics about the couple's or individual's current sexual functioning including the problem areas and previous attempts to resolve them, psychosexual history, relevant medical history, and current health status.[1]

During a second interview, the therapist shares initial impressions, gives clients the opportunity to challenge these impressions, and recommends treatment. When sex therapy is recommended and accepted, during the remainder of the interview the therapist collects information about predisposing background factors and about conditions which maintain the problem. Lobitz and Lobitz (1978) recommend covering the following areas:

    1. Sexual attitudes and behaviors of parents or other significant authority figures.

---

[1] A structured intake format can be obtained from the second author.

2. Source and content of early sexual information, for example, parents, peers, siblings, church, school, self.

3. Early sex play, same or opposite sex, with peers, siblings, adults.

4. Self-discovery of one's own sexuality, for example, erection, orgasm, menstruation, nocturnal emission.

5. Masturbation.

6. Social–sexual experience in adolescence, for example, dating, petting, intercourse.

7. Social–sexual values and any changes that occurred in them, particularly sexual responsivity, virginity, contraception, and male versus female role.

8. First intercourse.

9. First and subsequent social–sexual involvement with present partner.

10. Other significant social–sexual relationships.

11. Onset and course of sexual problem.

12. Attempts to change the problem either by self or by others.

QUESTIONNAIRES

Self-report questionnaires save interview time and are available in a variety of formats from a brief historical inventory to psychometrically sophisticated, standardized instruments. Although the results of many instruments are affected by response bias, motivated clients provide reasonably accurate accounts. The reliability and validity of data is improved when partners complete the same questionnaires. A client sometimes discloses information on a questionnaire which she refuses to discuss. LoPiccolo and Nowinski (1981) collect repeated questionnaire data: before an intake interview, before therapy (if there has been a waiting period), right after therapy ends, at 3-month and 1-year follow-ups. To avoid overwhelming clients, only the most relevant measures should be used. A list of commonly used measures follows. Unless otherwise noted, these measures have population norms and adequate reliability and validity. A comprehensive list of sexual assessment measures and their availability is provided in a recent review (Schiavi, Derogatis, Kuriansky, O'Connor, & Sharpe, 1979).

Multidimensional Measures

1. *Sexual Interaction Inventory* (SII) (LoPiccolo & Steger, 1974). This inventory of sexual adjustment and satisfaction takes 30 to 40 minutes

to complete. It includes 17 items which describe heterosexual behaviors; for each item the client rates satisfaction with current frequency and range of the behavior, pleasure, self-acceptance, accuracy of perception of partner's desires, acceptance of partner's responsiveness, disharmony, and dissatisfaction. The inventory's scores provide an 11-scale profile to identify aspects of a couple's reslationship that require therapeutic attention.

2. *Derogatis Sexual Function Inventory* (DSFI) (Derogatis, 1976; Derogatis & Meyer, 1979). This 245-item inventory takes 30 to 40 minutes to complete and assesses information, experience, drive, attitude, psychological symptoms, affect, gender-role definition, fantasy, body image, and sexual satisfaction. Extreme scores on the psychological symptom and affect subscales contraindicate sex therapy until the client's general mental health has improved. From the fantasy scale, which provides a window on sexual wishes and drive, the therapist can predict the success of imaginal therapy techniques. The one disadvantage of this questionnaire is that it has a very complicated and awkward scoring system. A therapist may, however, obtain valuable information without scoring the questionnaire.

Specific Measures

1. *Sex Knowledge and Attitude Test* (SKAT) (Miller & Lief, 1979). In this scale there are 71 true–false knowledge items; 35 items are rated on Likert scales and produce four attitude scores: heterosexual relations, sexual myths, abortion, and masturbation.

2. *Premarital Sexual Permissiveness Scale* (Reiss, 1967). The respondent rates degree of agreement to the appropriateness of 12 behaviors in the context of four levels of affection, from no affection to engagement.

3. *Dyadic Adjustment Scale* (Spanier, 1976). This inventory, consisting of 32 items rated on 6-point scales, is designed to assess the quality of a heterosexual relationship. The four subscales include satisfaction, consensus, cohesion, and affectional expression.

4. *Marriage Inventory* (Locke & Wallace, 1959). This commonly used scale measures conflicts and stability of a relationship. It consists of 15 items and a system of weighted scores, which reflect the values prevailing during development of the scale in the 1950s.

5. *Sexual Arousability Inventory* (SAI) (Hoon, Hoon, & Wincze, 1976). Clients rate 28 erotic experiences on 7-point Likert scales ranging from

slightly aversive to extremely arousing. Norms are available with this scale to compare a client's ratings of arousability.

BEHAVIOR ASSESSMENT

Because of the private nature of sexual behavior, observation via video-tape is questionable, even though it has reported benefits (Serber, 1974). Clinicians necessarily rely on self-report measures. Lange (as cited in Caird & Wincze, 1977) developed a retrospective behavioral measure for use each time the client comes to therapy. Using independent lists of 10 sexual behaviors, the client and her partner recall each activity they engaged in during the past week and which caused arousal or anxiety. More rigorous data collection can be accomplished by providing a daily record form on which clients note each sexual activity, its duration, ratings of pleasure, arousal, and anxiety for the activity, and subjective comments. Daily record keeping has therapeutic value. In a sexual log kept by women with desire phase problems, Gillespie and LaPointe (1979) asked clients to record date and time, cycle day, basal body tem-perature, sexual thoughts, and feelings of desire and arousal. With in-creased awareness of bodily responses and accompanying feelings and thoughts, the women became their own therapists by increasing their own exposure to the stimuli which caused arousal.

Because accurate record keeping can be a chore for the client, Lobitz and LoPiccolo (1972) require a refundable penalty deposit. Clients who keep all appointments, turn in daily record forms, and follow therapists' homework assignments, receive the entire deposit back. One violation results in a forfeit of one fifteenth of the deposit; subsequent violations result in increasingly larger forfeits. Since therapy ends after six viola-tions, clients are motivated to attend therapy and to keep accurate rec-ords.

PHYSIOLOGICAL MEASURES

Researchers and clinicians with access to equipment have supplemented self-report data with physiological measures, specifically genital meas-ures, which are activated during sexual arousal. The most frequently used measure for women at the present time involves a light-reflective photoplethysmographic approach (Hoon, 1978; Hoon, Wincze, & Hoon, 1976; Sintchak & Geer, 1975). Using a vaginal probe, women complaining of insufficient sexual arousal were assessed during erotic stimulation (videotape) before and after therapy. Before therapy the women experiencing sexual problems showed less responsivity than normal controls (Wincze, Hoon, & Hoon, 1976). However, after therapy, in spite of the women's self-reports of improvement, significant changes in genital arousability were not demonstrated (Wincze, Hoon, & Hoon, 1978). In a similar investigation, Morokoff and Heiman (1980) failed to find pretreatment differences between a clinical group and a nonclinical comparison group. Their posttreatment results were comparable to the earlier study: Vaginal differences were absent despite reports of increased pleasure and satisfaction within sexual relationships. Recent research by Beck, Sakheim, and Barlow (1982) indicates that the probe is subject to an unmeasurable amount of variance due to certain operating characteristics. In view of these findings, the failure to demonstrate sensitivity to therapeutic change, and the potential for causing anxiety to clients, use of the probe in routine clinical practice is not advised.

FEMALE SEXUAL PROBLEMS AND COMMON TREATMENT APPROACHES

This section describes the female sexual disorders which are most frequently encountered in clinical practice and the therapeutic approaches which have been used to effect behavior change. Female sexual distress is described according to the behavioral model presented earlier.

SEXUAL ANXIETY: DESCRIPTION

For females, the experience of sexual anxiety is often related to early sexual trauma and messages of prohibition and restraint. The resulting anxiety experience for women is often expressed as a phobic-like reaction. The fear can be very specific, such as fear of the male penis, or fear of exposing one's breasts, or it can be a more general fear of all aspects of sexual encounters. While men also experience phobic-like reactions to sexual encounters, men generally express a fear of performance failure rather than fear of sex itself.

Within the behavioral model, subjective sexual anxiety in women is represented by such statements as, "I dread sex and panic inside whenever I think of doing it." The behavioral manifestation of sexual anxiety is avoidance of sex, which is often cloaked in somatic complaints, annoyance with one's partner, unattractive physical appearance, and dissynchrony with a partner's bedtime habits. The physiological manifestations of sexual anxiety in women can resemble the racing heart and sweating palms of other phobic reactions, but they also may include actual genital muscle contractions as in vaginismus and dyspareunia.

Vaginismus involves involuntary spastic contraction of the vaginal and pelvic floor muscles and adduction of the thighs as a reaction to attempted or anticipated vaginal penetration. Intromission is either prevented or accomplished with difficulty, anxiety, and pain. Intercourse may be avoided for years, and other marital and sexual problems are likely. Vaginismus is not always accompanied by aversion to sexual stimuli, and many vaginismic women can experience orgasms (Lamont, 1976). About 10% of women referred for sexual dysfunctions suffer from vaginismus (Masters & Johnson, 1970), but this may be an underestimate (Lamont, 1976). Although the etiology of vaginismus has been variously explained by denial of womanhood, defense against pregnancy, or violation of an incest taboo, all authors agree that vaginismic women confronted by coital attempts, vaginal examination, or penetration are fearful and anxious. Kaplan (1974) interprets vaginismus as the conditioned association of pain and fear to real or fantasized vaginal penetration (Fertel, 1977). The unconditioned noxious stimulus may have been physical pain or psychological distress, including painful, local vaginal conditions. The conditioned phobic reaction leads to avoidance of most sexual encounters; anxiety avoidance further strengthens the phobic response.

Dyspareunia is defined in DSM-III as "pain in women from penetration or thrusting of the penis in the vagina . . . localized to the vaginal or lower pelvic area in the absence of physical disease." The factors that alone or together produce coital discomfort are anatomic, pathological, psychosomatic, and iatrogenic (Abarbanel, 1978). Congenital or developmental anatomic factors affect the introitus (the opening into the vagina) and the vagina. Common pathological factors are infections of the genital tract (e.g., yeast infections), skin disease, residue of pelvic inflammatory disease, malignant and benign growths, and disorders of the adjacent viscera. Physical or psychogenic iatrogenic factors induced by physicians include a surgically induced "shortened vagina," with a painful scar at the vaginal vault, and unpleasant attitudes of an examining physician. Psychological factors include real or imagined fears of pain and injury which result in avoidance of coitus. Insufficient foreplay or inept precoital techniques may result in insufficient arousal and lubrication for comfortable intercourse. A lack of privacy, and ignorance of the physiology of the sexual response, may perpetuate anxiety. Next to orgasmic difficulty, dyspareunia is the most common female sexual problem (Kaplan, 1974). Many women with dyspareunia are also anorgasmic; anorgasmia often develops before dyspareunia (Kaplan, 1974).

SEXUAL ANXIETY: TREATMENT

The treatment procedures for sexual anxiety in women will, of course, depend on the exact nature of the anxiety problem. Cognitive restructuring, progressive relaxation and systematic desensitization are all relevant to the treatment of sexual anxiety. Caird and Wincze (1974) have demonstrated in controlled studies that systematic desensitization can be an effective procedure for reducing sexual anxiety in women but will not necessarily affect other components of a woman's sexual problem. The reduction of sexual anxiety may help make an otherwise intolerable sexual relationship tolerable, but other treatment approaches may be necessary. Behavioral procedures have also been found helpful for the more specific anxiety-related conditions of vaginismus and dyspareunia.

Behavioral techniques are the preferred method of treatment for vaginismus. A 27-year-old woman who had been married 3 years without completing sexual intercourse experienced sexual pleasure with her husband but anticipated pain on penetration (Holroyd, 1970). Systematic desensitization treatment was provided; the hierarchy of eight fantasy scenes ranged from "patient with her hand on vagina" (low anxiety) to "penis insertion resulting in pain" (high anxiety). The woman had successful, comfortable intercourse after the seventh session; continued success was reported on a 6-month follow-up.

Most therapists prefer *in vivo* desensitization, alone or together with other techniques. Hypnosis has been combined with *in vivo* desensitization (Fuchs *et al.*, 1973). A gynecological examination under hypnosis began with an external process, proceeded to insertion of the client's finger into her vagina, to self-insertion of a Hegal dilator, and finally to the insertion of a series of gradually larger dilators by the physician. The criterion for success was the insertion of the husband's penis into the vagina. Fuchs and colleagues (1973) reported good results with 31 (of 34) women they treated.

Another approach to vaginismus involves acquisition of voluntary control over the vaginal muscles through contraction rather than through relaxation (Fertel, 1977). Kegel exercises are practiced daily until a maintenance level of strong, rapid contractions is achieved. Then, the partner begins to insert his finger to dilate the vagina and does not withdraw it until the patient can relax completely, at which time he adds an additional finger. These tasks culminate in intercourse using the female superior position with gradual penile insertion. A recent study has shed some doubt on the usefulness of Kegel exercises which are aimed at strengthening the pubococygeal muscles. Sultan (1980) demonstrated no change in muscle tension following a rigid exercise program.

Masters and Johnson (1970), often found sexual problems in the partners of vaginismic women. They require the husband's presence at the wife's pretreatment pelvic examination so that he can observe the vaginal spasm. Cooper (1969) described a vaginismus patient who was able to tolerate the largest dilator in comparative comfort but was still unable to achieve coitus. The husband was told that he was oversensitive to his spouse's discomfort and that if he could arouse her more fully, pain would diminish as his wife became more excited. He was encouraged to ignore complaints of pain, educated about sexual physiology, and persuaded to use the dilators which his wife had previously accommodated. Penile penetration was leisurely and unhurriedly accomplished immediately following the joint interview, with the wife reporting continued pleasure 10 months later.

Cooper's (1969) study was uncontrolled, however, and the value of the husband's presence during a pelvic examination described by Masters and Johnson is similarly untested. It is just as likely that the husband's presence could be deleterious to him by inflaming feelings of inadequacy. As in much of the area of sex therapy, case studies and uncontrolled research are the rule rather than the exception. Although dyspareunia is often the result of organic pathology, behaviorally oriented approaches have been successful. Annon (1974) suggests privacy and freedom from interruption during lovemaking, discusses fears, for example, fear of pregnancy, and gives information about preventive measures (e.g., artificial lubricants), and sexual positions.

Intense therapeutic approaches for dyspareunia include hypnosis (Kroger & Fezler, 1976), couple reeducation (Ellis & Abarbanel, 1973), and systematic desensitization (Lazarus, 1963; Holroyd, 1970; Ince, 1973). Brady (1966) used intravenous Brevital to facilitate relaxation during systematic desensitization and reported that on a 4-month follow-up four of his five patients had painless sexual intercourse after a maximum of 14 sessions. *In vivo* desensitization with vaginal self-dilators had also been successful (Cooper, 1969; Hastings, 1963).

Despite the "technical" success of behavioral therapy with vaginismus and dyspareunia, it must be pointed out that these dysfunctions are similar in nature to other phobias and thus can be easily exacerbated should the treatment itself invoke high levels of anxiety. The importance of the doctor (therapist)–patient–spouse relationship cannot be overemphasized. This combination is essential for treating these problems, whether in the case of women without partners seeking help for sexual anxiety or women entering therapy with available sexual partners.

SEXUAL AROUSAL PROBLEMS IN WOMEN: DESCRIPTION

Since there is wide variation in sexual interest among females, a woman who does not desire sexual activity is diagnosed (DSM-III) as suffering from a psychosexual disorder only if she is dissatisfied and experiences no other sexual dysfunction (Tollison & Adams, 1979). According to DSM-III, "psychosexual dysfunction with inhibited sexual excitement" refers to a lack of response to sexual stimulation, failure to find pleasure in sexual activities, lack of erotic feelings, and reports of anxiety, disgust, anger, or other negative emotions toward all sexual activity. These subjective, physiological and behavioral symptoms do not necessarily covary (Kaplan, 1977). Women may love their partners and desire sexual activity but feel nothing when sexual activity is initiated. Other women, who experience the physiological concommitants of arousal and have orgasms, are simply disinterested in sex. We use the term low sexual arousal to describe a lack of physiological excitation and lubrication; we reserve the term inhibited sexual desire for a lack of interest or a distaste for sexual activity. Estimates of the incidence of low sexual desire or arousal are as high as 40% of people requesting sex therapy (Kaplan, 1979; LoPiccolo, 1980). Although the majority of desire and arousal problems are psychological in etiology (Masters & Johnson, 1970), the disorder may be related to physical causes. Fatigue, overconsumption of alcohol, endocrine diseases and pathology, certain systemic diseases, and medication side effects are just some of the physiological factors which may decrease arousability. Guilt, shame, and anger inhibit sexual desire but anxiety is the emotion most frequently implicated as a deterrent to sexual desire (Burgess & Krop, 1978; Kaplan, 1977). The sources of anxiety include skill deficits, fear of poor performance and of commitment, and realistic and unrealistic anticipation of pain secondary to vaginismus or dyspareunia.

SEXUAL AROUSAL PROBLEMS: TREATMENT

When lack of information or a skill deficit is apparent, an educational approach to treatment is indicated. When anxiety is associated with a specific fear, such as the fear of nudity, it may be treated with systematic imaginal or *in vivo* desensitization. Conception anxiety calls for birth-control information. When diffuse anxiety is due to relationship conflicts, marital therapy may be required (Sorg, 1978).

Cognitive factors also affect sexual arousal (Rook & Hammen, 1977). Many women misperceive internal and external cues of sexual arousal and have limited expectations regarding their own arousability. Bodily awareness and accurate labeling of the physiological concomitants of sexual arousal can be rehearsed by clients in daily exercise. Gillespie and LaPointe (1979) asked clients to record self-statements about sex, so that treatment techniques could be matched with negative cognitions. Many low-arousal women respond to a narrow range of sexual stimuli. When they determine what events are arousing, they can increase their exposure to preferred activities and increase the range of arousing stimuli. Erotic literature and fantasy training may help this endeavor.

Short-term therapy gains for women reporting sexual desire problems are difficult to maintain, often because of failure to deal with the functional role of low desire within the relationship (Kaplan, 1979). Maintenance of change may also be obstructed by the failure of the client or couple to continue therapeutic activities after treatment ends, and by reluctance to accept responsibility for sexuality and internalize change (LoPiccolo, 1980). Successful treatment of low desire and arousal requires a gradual weaning process and a maintenance program which teaches clients to resolve conflicts without therapeutic support.

In spite of isolated reports of success in treating women experiencing low sexual desire, this problem when unaccompanied by anxiety remains difficult to treat. Speculation about a hormonal basis for low desire has not yet been supported by published reports.

ORGASMIC PROBLEMS: DESCRIPTION

Orgasmic problems in women also have subjective behavioral and physiological manifestations. Subjectively, a woman experiencing orgasmic
problems may be very anxious, bored or angry; behaviorally, she may
avoid sexual contacts because of the problem; and physiologically, she
may experience no orgasmic pleasure at all. Difficulty in achieving orgasm from sexual stimulation is the most frequent problem presented
by women seeking sex therapy (Masters & Johnson, 1970; Sotile, Kilmann, & Scovern, 1977). Attainment of orgasm during intercourse may
be interpreted to mean either orgasm caused solely by penile–vaginal
friction during penetration, orgasm experienced during penetration with
the aid of additional clitoral stimulation, or orgasm that occurs at some
time during a sexual encounter which includes intercourse. Statistics on
the attainment of orgasm in a normal population differ according to the
method of data collection, the population surveyed, and the definition
of orgasmic attainment. From 12% (Butler, 1976) to 53% (Hunt, 1974) of
women report an orgasm always or almost always; from 5% (Fisher,
1973) to 25% (Kinsey, 1953) report an orgasm never or almost never;
from 7% to 30% (Tavris & Sadd, 1977) report never experiencing orgasm.
Kaplan (1974) postulates that the ability to achieve orgasm in response
to a wide range of stimulation is normally distributed in a bell-shaped
curve. At one extreme are those women unable to climax in response
to any stimulation and those who only experience orgasm through masturbation. On the far extreme are those who achieve orgasm through
fantasy alone. The definition of orgasm was shaped by the Freudian
view that vaginally induced orgasms are the only correct female pleasure, and that clitorally induced orgasms are immature (Freud, 1905/1962).
The unfortunate result is the notion that the man is responsible for his
partner's climax. It is no wonder that women and men were enthusiastic
about the report that all orgasms are elicited by clitoral stimulation
(Masters & Johnson, 1966).

According to most current classification of sexual dysfunctions, orgasm inadequacy can be either primary or situational. The woman with
primary orgasmic dysfunction has never experienced orgasm. We use
the term *preorgasmic* for these women, as it points to their potential and
suits a behavioral framework. Women who rarely experience orgasm or
climax only in response to restricted types of stimulation, experience
situational orgasmic dysfunction (Masters & Johnson, 1970). Inadequate
information is almost always a factor in orgasmic inadequacy. A preor-

gasmic woman may be unaware of what stimulation is most pleasing to her. When she cannot identify her own needs, it is unlikely that she can communicate those needs to her partner. On the other hand, a situationally orgasmic woman may be aware of the effective stimuli but may wish to expand her ability to climax to a less restrictive set of circumstances, or she may wish to become more consistently orgasmic. Therefore, it is important to determine precisely what occurs during sexual activity and to uncover expectations regarding the consistent attainment of coital orgasm or simultaneous orgasm through penile thrusting alone (Oziel, 1978). Thus, the clinician needs to ascertain current and past sexual techniques and therapeutic goals.

When a couple lacks sufficient information, they generally lack adequate sexual stimulation techniques as well. An inability to assertively communicate sexual needs and desires may plague the woman who can climax during masturbation but not during sexual encounters with her partner. Sexual skill building and practice in sexual communication are called for in these circumstances. Although sexual arousal and inhibited orgasm are separate and independent dysfunctions, inhibited arousal generally undermines orgasmic ability (Burgess & Krop, 1978). Since sexual arousal can be easily affected by both cognitive and environmental factors such as lack of privacy, career and family obligations, and financial worries, orgasmic attainment requires optimal conditions. Anxiety may play a major role in the development and maintenance of orgasmic inadequacy. Among the origins of anxiety are traumatic experiences which instill fear and avoidance of sexual activities, pain associated with intercourse because of a transient medical problem, or inadequate arousal and lubrication. Many women who overevaluate their orgasms experience increased anxiety. The condition of orgasm watching (Kaplan, 1974), spectatoring (Masters & Johnson, 1970), or the effort syndrome (Hunt, 1974) is characterized by a determination to achieve excellence, and conscious striving for greater ecstasy. Clients must be informed of the paradox that the harder one tries, the less likely it is that the orgasm reflex will occur. Cognitive strategies such as thought stopping and attending to current, pleasurable feeling may help these clients (Ascher & Clifford, 1976). Kaplan (1974) uses erotic fantasy to distract the client, while Masters and Johnson (1970) recommend pleasuring of the woman by her partner during which orgasm is not the objective. Considering that women are taught to simultaneously seduce and limit sexual interaction, it is not surprising that the loss of control during orgasm threatens women who associate feelings of arousal with promiscuity. It is helpful to proceed slowly and allow the client to maintain control of the therapeutic pace in such cases (LoPiccolo & Nowinski, 1981).

Relationship difficulties make major contributions to lack of arousal and inadequate orgasm, especially in cases of situational orgasmic inadequacy (Oziel, 1978; Snyder, LoPiccolo, & LoPiccolo, 1977). The most obvious example of this is the woman who is consistently orgasmic with a lover, but not with her husband. In such a case, more than brief sex therapy may be required to ameliorate her problems with her husband. Anger, resentment, inadequate communication, failure to find a partner attractive, and lack of trust may all interfere with the arousal process. One sensitive relationship problem which frequently occurs with inadequate orgasm is orgasm faking. Because female orgasms are variable and often subtle, they lend themselves to deception. A faked orgasm is often produced as a tribute to a partner's virility, to ward off humiliation (Rosenbaum, 1970), or as a means of terminating a frustrating experience while protecting a partner from feelings of failure (Barbach, 1980). In a recent survey, 58% of the nonclinical female respondents reported that they sometimes faked orgasms (Butler, 1976). One's inclination may be to encourage a woman to "come clean" and confess her subterfuge to her partner in the interest of improving communication in the couple. However, pretended orgasms are sometimes adaptive, and a woman's knowledge of her own situation is frequently better than her therapist's. It is not necessarily an obstacle to therapy when a woman judges her circumstance to be too sensitive to reveal a deception (Barbach, 1980). Such a pretense may not be revealed during initial assessment unless the client has the opportunity to speak alone with the therapist or respond privately on a questionnaire. Women with relationship difficulties have responded best to sex therapy when it is combined with prolonged therapy focused on relationship and communication issues (Kaplan, 1974; Kilmann, 1978; McGovern, Stewart, & LoPiccolo, 1975).

ORGASMIC PROBLEMS: TREATMENT

Behavior therapy for orgasmic inadequacy aims to:

1. Heighten sexual arousal so that the woman is approaching the orgasmic level when coitus commences.

2. Enhance the client's awareness of and pleasure in her vaginal sensation.

3. Maximize clitoral stimulation.

4. Rehearse the verbal and motor responses frequently associated with orgasm.

5. Enhance the sexual skills and techniques of the client's partner (Tollison & Adams, 1979).

Once the goals of therapy have been established, a decision must be made about the prohibition of intercourse. Masters and Johnson (1970), Kaplan (1974), and others authoritatively introduce sensate focus exercises, making it clear that orgasmic release for either partner is not the focus of the interaction. This prohibition interrupts a maladaptive, nonreinforcing chain of events if the couple has been attempting coitus, while allowing them to rediscover the pleasures of other sensual experiences. The demand for response can also be removed without prohibition by reducing the frequency of intercourse or allowing intercourse at a separate time from sensate focus and other assigned activities (Ascher & Clifford, 1976). In addition to banning genitally focused activities, the therapist may want to provide information about the psychological and physiological stimulation required to bring women to climax. When a client is unnecessarily restricted in her enjoyment of sexuality by her religious beliefs, a religious adviser might discuss theological dogma with her (Jehu, 1980).

Masturbation is the most reliable method of reaching orgasm (Burgess & Krop, 1978; Hite, 1976; Masters & Johnson, 1970). LoPiccolo and Lobitz's (1972) masturbatory training program can be adapted to the individual clients needs:

1. The client examines her genital area visually with a mirror and flashlight, identifying anatomical features with the aid of a diagram.

2. She explores her genitals tactually, but is not instructed to become aroused.

3. She identifies the most sensitive areas.

4. She manually stimulates her genitals using a lubricant, concentrating on identified pleasurable areas.

5. She is told to prolong the stimulation until "something happens" or she becomes tired or sore.

6. If orgasm is not reached in step (5) client continues to self-stimulate with the aid of a vibrator.

7. The client's partner is allowed to be present for a masturbatory session. This disinhibits her to displaying arousal and orgasm

in his presence, and he learns what kind of stimulation she likes.

8. The partner manipulates the client as she has demonstrated in step (7).

9. The couple engages in intercourse with simultaneous manual or vibrator stimulation of the client's genitals.

Clients who harbor childhood fears about masturbation, will not benefit from masturbation training until they examine their attitudes toward masturbation. Many women who reject the term masturbation, can accept the idea of self-exploration as a means of discovering something about their bodies that they can then teach to their partners (Annon, 1974).

Kegel exercises (Kegel, 1952) may be prescribed as an adjunct to therapy. These exercises are designed to strengthen the pubococcygeal muscles which purportedly heightens sexual pleasure and orgasmic ability. The exercises give the woman a feeling that she is constructively working on her problem and increase her awareness of genital sensations. To find the pubococcygeal muscle, the client stops her urine flow midstream without closing her legs. Once it is located, the client can contract the muscle at anytime. Most women are instructed to contract and hold the muscle for a slow count of 3 for 10 times at first. A second exercise consisting of rapid contracting and releasing, nicknamed the "flutter," is also repeated 10 times at first. As described above, the Kegel exercise technique has not been supported by controlled research and positive results using this technique may be due to therapist enthusiasm or other placebo effects.

Once a couple elicits an orgasmic reponse in the woman through one or more means, they should experiment with other methods to avoid strict stimulus control. They might try oral caressing, oils, and various coital positions. In side-by-side, rear entry, and female astride positions, either partner can reach the genitals for manual or vibration stimulation during penile thrusting. When a couple feels stuck on a particular method of inducing orgasm in the female, they can try that method to bring her almost to orgasm and then switch to another form of stimulation. For example, when she is about to climax using a vibrator, her partner can begin to stimulate her orally or manually. In this way, one form of stimulation is gradually substituted for another, moving earlier and earlier in the time sequence until the second form of stimulation is effective alone. By randomly altering modes of stimulation, the orgasmic response can be generalized to the widest possible range of stimuli, and the narrow stimulus control problems of the situationally dysfunctional women can be avoided (Ascher & Clifford, 1976).

Zeiss, Rosen, and Zeiss (1977) have reported two cases in which they successfully employed fantasy to aid in the transition to intercourse-related orgasm. The fantasies involved vaginal insertion of the partner's penis. An intermediate step included insertion of a safe phallic object. A gradual reduction in self-stimulation and greater reliance on penile thrusting resulted in coital climax. While sex therapy has helped some women to have orgasms during intercourse, reasons for dependence on clitoral manipulation vary. Therefore, it is best for a couple to develop stimulation patterns suited to their own needs (Ascher & Clifford, 1976).

CONCLUSIONS AND RECOMMENDATIONS

Despite the tremendous growth of professional interest in the treatment of sexual dysfunction during the past decade, research on the effectiveness of sex therapy with women has not kept pace. In a recent literature review, Hogan (1978) noted that most of the research consists of case studies, uncontrolled or poorly controlled "demonstrations" of therapeutic effects, or badly confounded clinical studies. As LoPiccolo (1977) points out, much of the literature is further weakened by a failure to clearly specify the characteristics of the patients, in terms of personality, relationship, or biological correlates of dysfunction. Similarly, little attention is paid to therapist characteristics associated with success or failure. Although these factors are important in evaluating the effectiveness of sex therapy for all dysfunctions, they appear to be even more significant in the evaluation of sex therapy with women. Our review of the literature suggests that the format of sex therapy still reflects many of the traditional biases of a male-oriented culture (Golden & Golden, 1976). These biases are reinforced in popular sex and marriage manuals where females are seen as the cause for most sexual problems (Peterson & Peterson, 1973). The adult sex-education literature as well continues to depict men as the superior sex (Gordon & Shankweiler, 1976). In a field, therefore, primarily dominated by men[2] it is essential to conduct research on patient–therapist interaction variables.

[2] According to the latest National Register (AASECT, 1979), 67% of all certified sex counselors and therapists are males.

Now that sex therapy is no longer a fad and is, in fact, a professionally accepted therapeutic area, it is time for researchers to provide scientifically acceptable answers to the basic questions asked of all psychotherapy: "*What* treatment, by *whom*, is most effective for *this* individual with *that* specific problem, and under *which* set of circumstances?" (Paul, 1967). During the 1970s there were continued methodological improvements in sex therapy outcome studies, but as Levine (1979) points out, these studies, despite their multiple documentation, are based upon limited conceptions of success. For example, although a client being treated for vaginismus may report success in terms of penile penetration, she may still have a dysfunctional sex life. Another issue may be related to the women's perception of success. For example, does a woman who learns to relax via the induction of Brevital (Brady, 1966) feel that treatment was successful even though drugs were required to help her become sexually functional? Several issues critical to the clinical practice of sex therapy have not been explored. Issues involved in treating dysfunctional women without partners, treating women who have extremely negative attitudes toward masturbation, and the effectiveness of passive versus active patient involvement in therapy need to be investigated.

Levine (1979) suggests that there are three perspectives from which to view success in sex therapy. From the first perspective, success involves the reversal of a previously specified component deficit (e.g., desire, arousal, orgasm, or emotional satisfaction). For example, the author who describes the treatment outcome of 15 preorgasmic women need only clearly define preorgasmic dysfunction and then provide us with a count. A second perspective involves the reversal of all of a client's component deficits. The treatment of a preorgasmic woman would not be considered a success unless she experienced desire, achieved orgasm, and found sex emotionally satisfying. As implied above, we suspect that many women with vaginismus continue to have component deficits even after painless intromission is achieved. Success according to a third perspective is defined as the reversal of all component deficits in both partners; obviously this perspective will produce the lowest rates of success, but will be the most meaningful for clients.

It is time to get serious about sex therapy research, to replace single-case studies and Masters-and-Johnson-type studies which lack outcome criteria for female dysfunctions (Zilbergeld & Evans, 1980). Hogan (1978) recommends that treatment outcome studies utilize factorial designs to include *client variables* (e.g., type of dysfunction, type of marital problem); *treatment components* (e.g., masturbation, sensate focus, marital therapy); and *mode of therapy* (e.g., individual, conjoint, group). To these variables, we would recommend adding therapist characteristics, including gender. Only with factorial designs will researchers answer the question, "What treatment, by whom, is most effective for a given client with a specific dysfunction under certain circumstances?"

This chapter's emphasis on techniques of treatment may conjure up a mechanistic view of sexuality. Yet sex must be viewed as a spectrum of experiences whose impact is determined by personal needs, desires, and values (Zussman & Zussman, 1979). Sex therapy can provide new ways of relating and feeling as well as new methods of intercourse. Ideal sexual expression has a celebrative, renovative function in a loving, sharing relationship.

As long as our competitive culture evaluates responsiveness, potency, and orgasms, psychological stress will impede sexual functioning (Jacobs & Whiteley, 1975). Education is the most economical and humane way to prevent the common and tragic sexual dysfunctions of women. Many sexual difficulties can be traced to miseducation, lack of reliable and valid information, prejudice, and irrational beliefs (Caird & Wincze, 1977; Jacobs & Whiteley, 1975). If a mother's messages are the most important determinants of a girl's feelings toward sexuality and her body, educational programs might help young mothers share their enthusiasm for life and love with their daughters (Barbach, 1975). Daughters whose mothers encourage them to see beyond traditional-role confines will be less inhibited, more optimistic, more independent, and happier with themselves and their partners. Only then will women in our culture experience the full range of their sexual and emotional potential.

RECOMMENDATIONS FOR THERAPISTS

Health professionals dealing with sexual problems have to be careful to assess and treat their patients without prejudice and misunderstanding. This statement is, of course, applicable to the treatment of any medical or psychological disorder but must be underscored when dealing with sexual issues. As we pointed out in the introduction, the study of human sexual behavior is confused by volatile emotions and misunderstandings, which can lessen the quality of professional care. This seems to be especially true of the treatment of women's sexual problems. Women seem to have suffered disproportionately from the restrictive attitudes of professionals and of society, and there is decidedly less scientific information available describing female sexual functioning than there is describing that of males.

Because of the relative poverty of information on female sexuality and on women in sex therapy, most concrete guidelines and recommendations cannot distinguish between the treatment of males and females. For example, there is no evidence that female patients relate better to female therapists when dealing with sexual problems. The attitude and skill of the therapist is probably more important than gender. Nonetheless, the following recommendations may be of some help in dealing with female clients:

> 1. The therapist should assume that the female client has difficulty in talking about sexual issues. Men are more likely to have discussed sexual issues with male friends than females with female friends.
> 2. The therapist should assume that the female client has misunderstandings and false expectations about her own or her partner's sexual response. Because of the relative lack of female discussion with peers about sex and restrictions on female sexuality, there exists more room for distortions.
> 3. The therapist should assume that the female client has been profoundly inhibited in her expression of sexuality by parental, religious, and cultural restrictions. In spite of the more liberated presentation of female sexuality in the media, women still get a more restrictive message about sexual behavior.

By adopting these three guidelines, the therapist might err in a conservative direction but will not harm the client. Neglect of these guidelines could create a danger by intimidating and overwhelming a female client and hindering the doctor–patient communication. Although these guidelines apply to some men, they are especially important for women.

Detailed guidelines for the conduct of sex therapy for men and women can be found elsewhere (Caird & Wincze, 1977; Leiblum & Pervin, 1980) and are beyond the scope of this chapter. The purpose of this chapter has been to describe a behavioral model and the assessment and treatment procedures that follow from the model. Of all available approaches, the behavioral model seems to provide the basis for the most objective treatment of women's sexual problems.

REFERENCES

Abarbanel, A. R. Diagnosis and treatment of coital discomfort. In J. LoPiccolo & L. LoPiccolo (Eds.), *Handbook of sex therapy*. New York: Plenum, 1978.

Annon, J. S. *The behavioral treatment of sexual problems: Brief therapy*. New York: Harper & Row, 1974.

Ascher, M. L., & Clifford, R. E. Behavioral considerations in the treatment of sexual dysfunction. In M. Hersen, R. Eisler, & P. Miller (Eds.), *Progress in behavior modification* (Vol. 3). New York: Academic, 1976.

Bandura, A. *Principles of behavior modification*. New York: Holt, Rinehart & Winston, 1969.

Barbach, L. *Women discover orgasm: A therapist's guide to a new treatment approach*. New York: Free Press, 1980.

Barbach, L. *For yourself: The fulfillment of female sexuality*. Garden City, N.Y.: Doubleday, 1975.

Beck, J. G., Sakheim, D. K., & Barlow, D. H. *Operating characteristics of the vaginal photoplethysmograph: Some implications for its use*. Unpublished manuscript, 1982. (Available from authors at State University of New York, Albany, N.Y.)

Brady, J. P. Brevital-relaxation treatment of frigidity. *Behaviour Research and Therapy*, 1966, *4*, 71–77.

Burgess, D., & Krop, H. *The relationship between sexual arousability, heterosexual attitudes, sexual anxiety, and general anxiety in women*. Paper presented at the Southeast Regional American Association of Sex Educators, Counselors, and Therapists, Asheville, N.C., October 1978.

Burnap, D., & Golden, J. Sexual problems in medical practice. *Journal of Medical Education*, 1967, *42*, 673–680.

Butler, C. A. New data about female sexual response. *Journal of Sex and Marital Therapy*, 1976, *2*, 40–46.

Caird, W., & Wincze, J. Videotaped desensitization of frigidity. *Behavior Therapy and Experimental Psychiatry*, 1974, *5*, 175–178.

Caird, W., & Wincze J. *Sex therapy: A behavioral approach*. Hagerstown, Md.: Harper & Row, 1977.

Cooper, A. J. An innovation in the behavioral treatment of a case of nonconsummation due to vaginismus. *British Journal of Psychiatry*, 1969, *115*, 721–722.

Derogatis, L. R. Psychological assessment of the sexual disabilities. In: J. K. Meyer (Ed.), *Clinical management of sexual disorders*. Baltimore: Williams & Wilkins, 1976.

Derogatis, L. R. & Meyer, J. K. A psychological profile of the sexual dysfunction. *Archives of Sexual Behavior*, 1979, *8*, 201–223.

Diagnostic and statistical manual of mental disorders (3rd ed.). Washington, D.C.: American Psychiatric Association, 1980.

Ellis, A., & Abarbanel, A. *The encyclopedia of sexual behavior*. New York: Aronson, 1973.

Fertel, N. S. Vaginismus: A review. *Journal of Sex and Marital Therapy*, 1977, *3*, 113–121.

Fisher, S. *The female orgasm*. New York: Basic, 1973.

Fowler, R., & Longabough, R. The problem-oriented record problem definition. *Archives of General Psychiatry*, 1975, *32*, 831–834.

Freud, S. *Three essays on the theory of female sexuality*. New York: Avon, 1962. (Originally published, 1905.)

Fuchs, K., Hoch, Z., Paldi, E., Abramovici, H., Brandes, J. M., Timor-Tritsch, I., & Kleinhaus, M. Hypnodesensitization therapy of vaginismus: *In vitro* and *in vivo* methods. *International Journal of Clinical and Experimental Hypnosis*, 1973, *21*, 144–156.

Gillespie, H. G., & LaPointe, C. A short-term cognitive and behavioral treatment and approach to sexual desire phase dysfunction. *Highland Highlights*, Asheville, N.C., February 1979.

Golden, J. S., & Golden, M. A. You know who and what's her name: The woman's role in sex therapy. *Journal of Sex and Marital Therapy*, 1976, 2, 6–16.

Gordon, M., & Shankweiler, P. J. Different equals less: Female sexuality in recent marriage manuals. In C. Gordon & G. Johnson (Eds.), *Readings in human sexuality*. New York: Harper & Row, 1976.

Green, R. (Ed.). *Human sexuality: A health practitioner's text* (2nd ed.). Baltimore: Williams & Wilkins, 1979.

Hastings, D. W. *Impotence and frigidity*. Boston: Little, Brown, 1963.

Hite, S. *The Hite report*. New York: Macmillian, 1976.

Hogan, D. R. The effectiveness of sex therapy: A review of the literature. In J. LoPiccolo & L. LoPiccolo (Eds.), *Handbook of sex therapy*. New York: Plenum, 1978.

Holroyd, J. Treatment of a married virgin by behavior therapy: Report of a case. *Obstetrics and Gynecology*, 1970, 36, 469–472.

Hoon, E. F., Hoon, P. W., & Wincze, J. P. An inventory for the measurement of female sexual arousability. *Archives of Sexual Behavior*, 1976, 5, 291–300.

Hoon, P. W. The assessment of sexual arousal in women. In M. Heisen, R. Eisler, & P. Miller (Eds.), *Progress in behavior modification* (Vol. 7). New York: Academic, 1978.

Hoon, P. W., Wincze, J. P., & Hoon, E. F. Physiological assessment of sexual arousal in women. *Psychophysiology*, 1976, 13, 196–204.

Hunt, M. *Sexual behavior in the 1970's*. New York: Dell, 1974.

Hunt, M. Where sex is concerned the doctor is out. *Playboy*, July 1979.

Ince, L. P. Behavior modification of sexual disorders. *American Journal of Psychotherapy*, 1973, 3, 446–451.

Jacobs, M. J., & Whiteley, J. M. Approaches to sexual counseling. *The Counseling Psychologist*, 1975, 5, 3–8.

Jehu, D. *Sexual dysfunction: A behavioral approach to causation, assessment and treatment*. New York: Wiley, 1980.

Kaplan, H. S. *The new sex therapy*. New York: Brunner/Mazel, 1974.

Kaplan, H. S. Hypoactive sexual desire. *Journal of Sex and Marital Therapy*, 1977, 3, 3–9.

Kaplan, H. S. *Disorders of sexual desire*. New York: Simon & Schuster, 1979.

Kegel, A. H. Sexual functions of the pubococcygeus muscle. *Western Journal of Surgery*. 1952, 60, 521–524.

Kilmann, P. R. The treatment of primary and secondary orgasmic dysfunction: A methodological review of the literature since 1970. *Journal of Sex and Marital Therapy*, 1978, 4, 155–176.

Kinsey, A. C., Pomeroy, W. B., Martin, C. E., & Gebhard, P. H. *Sexual behavior in the human female*. Philadelphia: Saunders, 1953.

Kroger, W. S., & Fezler, W. D. *Hypnosis and behavior modification: Imagery conditioning*. Philadelphia: Lippincott, 1976.

Lamont, H. Vaginismus. In R. Gemme & C. Wheeler (Eds.), *Progress in sexology*. New York: Plenum, 1976.

Lazarus, A.A. The treatment of chronic frigidity by systematic desensitization. *Journal of Nervous and Mental Disease*, 1963, 136, 272–278.

Leiblum, S. R. & Pervin, L. A. Introduction: The development of sex therapy from a sociocultural perspective. In S. R. Leiblum & L. A. Pervin (Eds.), *Principles and practice of sex therapy*. New York: Guilford, 1980.

Levine, S. B. *Conceptual suggestions for outcome research in sex therapy*. Paper presented at the meeting of the Eastern Association for Sex Therapy, Philadelphia, March 1979.

Lief, H., & Karlen, A. (Eds.). *Sex education in medicine: A monograph*. New York: Spectrum, 1976. (Distributed by Halsted Press, division of Wiley.)

Lobitz, W. C., & Lobitz, G. K. Clinical assessment in the treatment of sexual dysfunctions. In J. LoPiccolo & L. LoPiccolo (Eds.), *Handbook of sex therapy.* New York: Plenum, 1978.

Lobitz, W., & LoPiccolo, J. New methods in the behavioral treatment of sexual dysfunction. *Journal of Behavior Therapy and Experimental Psychiatry,* 1972, *3,* 265–271.

Locke, H. J., & Wallace, R. Short marital adjustment and prediction test: Their reliability and prediction. *Marriage and Family Living,* 1959, *21,* 251–255.

LoPiccolo, J. *Methodological issues in research on treatment of sexual dysfunctioning.* Paper prepared for NIMH conference on Methodology in Research on Human Sexuality, Washington, D.C., November 1977.

LoPiccolo, J., & Lobitz, W. The role of masturbation in the treatment of orgasmic dysfunction. *Archives of Sexual Behavior,* 1972, *2,* 162–171.

LoPiccolo, J., & Steger, J. C. The sexual interaction inventory: A new instrument of assessment of sexual dysfunction. *Archives of Sexual Behavior,* 1974, *3,* 585–595.

LoPiccolo, L. Low sexual desire. In S. R. Leiblum & L. A. Pervin (Eds.), *Principles and practice of sex therapy.* New York: Guilford, 1980.

LoPiccolo, L., & Nowinski, J. Sex therapy. In C. Golden (Ed.), *Handbook of medical psychology and behavioral medicine.* New York: Grune & Stratton, 1981.

Masters, W. H., & Johnson, V. E. *Human sexual response.* Boston: Little, Brown, 1966.

Masters, W. H., & Johnson, V. E. *Human sexual inadequacy.* Boston: Little, Brown, 1970.

Masur, F. *Psychological techniques in primary care: A problem management handbook for the health professional.* New York: Plenum, in press.

McGovern, K. B., Stewart, R., & LoPiccolo, J. Secondary orgasmic dysfunction: I. Analysis and strategies for treatment. *Archives of Sexual Behavior,* 1975, *4,* 265–275.

Miller, W. R., & Lief, H. I. The sex knowledge and attitude test (SKAT). *Journal of Sex and Marital Therapy,* 1979, *5,* 282–287.

Morokoff, P. J., & Heiman, J. R. Effects of erotic stimuli on sexually functional and dysfunctional women: Multiple measures before and after sex therapy. *Behaviour Research and Therapy,* 1980, *18,* 127–137.

Mountjoy, P. Some early attempts to modify penile erection in horse and human: An historical analysis. *Psychological Record,* 1974, *24,* 291–308.

Munjack, D., & Oziel, L. *Sexual medicine and counseling in office practice.* Boston: Little, Brown, 1980.

Oziel, L. Inconsistency of coital orgasm in women. *Medical Aspects of Human Sexuality,* September 1978, pp. 16–28.

Paul, G. L. Strategy of outcome research in psychotherapy. *Journal of Consulting Psychology,* 1967, *31,* 109–118.

Peterson, G. B., & Peterson, L. R. Sexism in the treatment of sexual dysfunction. *The Family Coordinator,* 1973, *22,* 397–404.

Reiss, I. L. *The social context of premarital sexual permissiveness.* New York: Holt, Rinehart & Winston, 1967.

Rook, K. S., & Hammen, C. L. A cognitive perspective on the experience of sexual arousal. *Journal of Social Issues,* 1977, *33,* 7–29.

Rosenbaum, S. Pretended orgasm. *Medical Aspects of Human Sexuality,* April 1970, pp. 84–96.

Schiavi, R. C., Derogatis, L. R., Kuriansky, J., O'Connor, D., & Sharpe, L. The assessment of sexual function and marital interaction. *Journal of Sex and Marital Therapy,* 1979, *5,* 169–224.

Serber, M. Videotape feedback in the treatment of couples with sexual dysfunction. *Archives of Sexual Behavior,* 1974, *3,* 377–380.

Sintchak, G., & Geer, J. A vaginal plethysmograph system. *Psychophysiology*, 1975, *12*, 113–115.

Snyder, A., LoPiccolo, L., & LoPiccolo, J. Secondary orgasmic dysfunction: A case study. In J. Fischer & H. L. Gochros (Eds.), *Handbook of behavior therapy with sexual problems* (Vol. 2). New York: Pergamon, 1977.

Sorg, D. A. Relationship factors in female unresponsiveness. *Medical Aspects of Human Sexuality*, April 1978, pp. 49–50.

Sotile, W. M., Kilmann, P. R., & Scovern, A. Definitions and classifications of psychogenic female sexual dysfunction. *Journal of Sex and Marital Therapy*, 1977, *3*, 21–27.

Spanier, G. B. Measuring dyadic adjustment: New scales for assessing the quality of marriage and similar dyads. *Journal of Marriage and the Family*, 1976, *38*, 15–28.

Sultan, F. *The relationship of pubococcygeal condition to female sexual responsiveness in a normal population.* Paper presented at the 14th Annual Convention of the Association for Advancement of Behavior Therapy, New York, 1980.

Tavris, C., & Sadd, S. *The Redbook report on female sexuality.* New York: Dell, 1977.

Tollison, C.D., & Adams, H. C. *Sexual disorders: Treatment, theory, and research.* New York: Gardner, 1979.

Ullmann, L., & Krasner, L. *A psychological approach to abnormal behavior.* Englewood Cliffs, N.J.: Prentice-Hall, 1969.

Wincze, J. P. Sexual dysfunction (distress and dissatisfaction). In S. M. Turner, K. S. Calhoun, & H. E. Adams (Eds.), *Handbook of clinical behavior therapy.* New York: Wiley, 1981.

Wincze, J. P., Hoon, E. F., & Hoon, P. W. Physiological responsivity of normal and sexually dysfunctional women during erotic stimulus exposure. *Journal of Psychosomatic Research*, 1976, *20*, 445–451.

Wincze, J. P., Hoon, E. F., & Hoon, P. W. Multiple measure analysis of women experiencing low sexual arousal. *Behaviour Research and Therapy*, 1978, *16*, 43–49.

Zeiss, A. M., Rosen, G. M., & Zeiss, R. A. Orgasm during intercourse: A treatment strategy for women. *Journal of Consulting and Clinical Psychology*, 1977, *45*, 891–895.

Zilbergeld, B., & Evans, M. The inadequacy of Masters and Johnson. *Psychology Today*, August 1980, pp. 29–43.

Zussman, L., & Zussman, S. *Getting together: A guide to sexual enrichment for couples.* New York: Morrow, 1979.

6

INTERPERSONAL EFFECTIVENESS IN ASSERTIVE SITUATIONS

MARSHA M. LINEHAN

OVERVIEW

The primary focus of the present chapter is on the development of assertive and social influence skills. Theoretical and empirical papers on assertion have typically defined assertive behavior in terms of the class or topography of the response. Self-expressiveness, standing up for one's rights (class definitions), eye contact, and firm voice tone (topography) have been included in assertion definitions. In contrast, this chapter employs a definition of assertion which stresses effectiveness in social influence situations. Although the discussion will center on therapy with women, a fundamental assumption is that attention to the concerns and problems of women can be of benefit in the development of better treatment for men.

Therapists who aim to transmit assertive skills must address three questions: (1) What skills should be taught? (2) How should skills be measured? (3) What methods of treatment should be used. These issues will be addressed after a discussion of the relevance of assertive behavior and social skill to current concerns about women's mental health. To set the topic of assertion within the general framework of social skills and interpersonal effectiveness, definitions of assertion, social skills, and effective social behavior are provided. I will then move into a rather extensive discussion of what skills should be included in a comprehensive assertion training package. The organization of the chapter reflects my bias in favor of theory. Without an adequate understanding of the

Marsha M. Linehan. Department of Psychology, University of Washington, Seattle, Washington.

behaviors to be modified, and skills to be increased, it would seem impossible to organize an efficient and effective therapy program. In addition, an enormous amount has already been written on how to conduct effective assertiveness programs and how to assess social skills. A detailed reexamination of these methods here would be redundant.

BACKGROUND

Social skills training is often viewed as a major achievement of the behavioral approach to mental health treatments (Bellack & Hersen, 1979). Methods of teaching people to behave in a forthright, assertive manner, may be the most common form of social skills training. The popularity of assertion training is attested to by the burgeoning number of books on the topic (Alberti & Emmons, 1978; Baer, 1976; Bloom, Coburn, & Pearlman, 1975; Bower & Bower, 1976; Butler, 1976; Cheek, 1976; Galassi & Galassi, 1977; Gambrill & Richey, 1976; Jakubowski & Lange, 1978; Lange & Jakubowski, 1976; Liberman, King, DeRisi, & McCann, 1975; Osborn & Harris, 1975; Phelps & Austin, 1975), countless magazine articles, newspaper stories, workshops, training programs, and classes.

Attention to assertive behavior in the psychological literature has grown along with the movement for women's rights of the 1970s and 1980s. The rights of the individual are a common focus of both the assertiveness literature, which considers how to teach unassertive individuals to express their desires, and the women's movement, which considers how to advance women's economic, social, and political power. Between 1971 and 1981, almost every women's magazine in the United States has published at least one article on assertion, and several books have been directed specifically at helping women improve their own assertion skills (Baer, 1976; Bloom et al., 1975; Butler, 1976; Osborn & Harris, 1975). As Fodor and Epstein (in press) noted: "In many ways, the movement represents more of an educational remediation enterprise with public relations overtones than a clinical therapeutic endeavor."

Despite its popularity, assertion training is firmly rooted in the clinical, experimental, and theoretical behavior therapy literature. To date, at least 900 scholarly papers on the topic have been written and over 20 different assertion scales have been developed (Moore, 1981). It would be a rare textbook on behavior modification that did not discuss assertion training (e.g., Bellack & Hersen, 1977; Craighead, Kazdin, & Mahoney, 1976; Gambrill, 1978; Goldfried & Davison, 1976; Lanyon & Lanyon,

1978; Rimm & Masters, 1979). As with the popular attention to assertion training, much of the academic attention has also been focused on assertion training for women. Women have been the primary subjects in clinical research on assertion training (Linehan & Egan, 1979). Although the development and popularization of assertion training was the pioneering work of three men—Andrew Salter (1949), Joseph Wolfe (1958), and Arnold Lazarus (1966)—women behavior therapists (e.g., Jakubowski-Spector, 1973; Linehan & Egan, 1979; MacDonald, 1974; Osborn & Harris, 1975; Wolfe & Fodor, 1978) have developed and disseminated methods of assertion training and assessment aimed at the problems of women.

INTERPERSONAL BEHAVIOR, PSYCHOPATHOLOGY, AND WOMEN

A link between social inadequacy and other psychological disturbances has often been documented (Kazdin, 1979; Bellack & Hersen, 1979). Social inadequacy, including social withdrawal, poor interpersonal problem solving, and social insensitivity, has been related to both the diagnosis and prognosis of neurotic and psychotic adult behavior (Argyle, Alkema, & Gilmour, 1971; Curran, Miller, Zwick, Monti, & Stout, 1980; Jenkins & Gurel, 1959; Platt, Siegel, & Spivack, 1975). Social isolation among children has been related to later identification as a delinquent (Roff, Sells, & Golden, 1972), school dropouts (Hartup, 1970), and low academic performance (Strain, Shores, & Kerr, 1976). Degree of high school social activity is predictive of later diagnosis of neurosis and psychosis (Barthell & Holmes, 1968). Rinn and Markle (1979) report that of children referred to a mental health clinic, 87% experience problems with one or more components of social skills. Insufficient assertive behavior has been demonstrated by clients presenting problems of depression (Libet & Lewinsohn, 1973), alcoholism (Miller & Eisler, 1977; O'Leary, O'Leary, & Donovan, 1976), drug addiction (Callner & Ross, 1976), and hysterical neurosis (Blanchard & Hersen, 1976). Prior day nonassertion is related to next day depression (Sanchez & Lewinsohn, 1980). Although these findings do not allow the conclusion that social inadequacy causes psychological disturbance, they do suggest that attention to the client's interpersonal functioning may be a critical factor in the treatment of many behavior disorders.

Psychological disturbance among women may be objectively worse than among men (Gove & Tudor, 1973). Women are the majority of recipients of mental health services (*Report of the President's Commission on Mental Health*, 1978). Alcohol problems of women are increasing in frequency and severity (McCrady, 1979). Jones (1977) concluded from a survey of parasuicide in England that if current trends continued, by 1984 every emergency bed in the country will be filled with women who have poisoned themselves.

Given the relationship between interpersonal difficulties, behavioral problems, and emotional distress, and the findings that women more often than men have mental health problems, it is interesting to examine evidence about sex differences in social skills. Maccoby and Jacklin (1974) exhaustively reviewed research on sex differences in social behavior and concluded that males and females do not differ in sociability. They found no consistent sex differences in diverse social behaviors, including attraction, empathy, interpersonal sensitivity, social dependency, nurturance, and helpgiving. However, they based their conclusion on many studies with children and a few studies of young adults. Thus, they could not determine whether older women and men differ in social behavior.

An absence of clear-cut sex differences during early childhood and adolescence on most measures of sociability and positive interpersonal behaviors does not by itself rule out the hypothesis that more women than men have inadequate social behavior repertoires. Blechman (1980, 1981) persuasively argued that women and men inhabit different social environments during the adolescent and adult years; these environmental differences obstruct competent task and social functioning in women. It is plausible that sex differences in interpersonal repertoires may not be a function of early childhood experiences. Instead, the critical developmental period for a girl may begin with the onset of physical maturity and the attendant pressures to marry and raise children.

It is also possible that interpersonal difficulties closely related to women's problems in living are situation specific. Converging lines of research suggest that males and females may differ in the types of social situations in which they feel comfortable and function well. Eagly (1978), in her review of the literature on sex differences in susceptibility to influence, concluded that females are not consistently more susceptible than men, but women are more susceptible in group pressure situations. Many studies have shown that males prefer large-group activities, whereas females prefer close friendships and dyadic relationships (Maccoby & Jacklin, 1974). As Maccoby and Jacklin noted, this sex difference in preferred group size may affect achievement of major life goals.

Women may be at a disadvantage relative to men if they avoid large-group interaction and do not develop the skills needed in those settings. Additionally, most well-established groups have dominance hierarchies. Thus, women who avoid large groups may be uncomfortable and unskilled in settings where power and dominance are unequally distributed.

In both small and large groups, women may be less skilled at exerting social influence than men. Women are consistently found to be less aggressive and less dominant than men across situations and tasks (Bandura, 1977; Maccoby & Jacklin, 1974). Women's social behavior is often less involved with the group task, whether problem solving or persuasion, and more focused on facilitating others' communication (Hall, 1972; Barron, 1971); men's behavior is more often oriented toward personal gain (Eagly, 1978). Men talk more in groups than women, expressing and supporting their own ideas, while women make fewer contributions directly related to the problem to be solved (Aries, 1977; Bernard, 1972; Hall, 1972; Hilpert, Kramer, & Clark, 1975; Swacker, 1972). In a particularly interesting study, Zimmerman and West (1975) taped conversations of same-sex and mixed-sex pairs in a natural setting. They found men more often than women took control of the conversation; 98% of the interruptions and 100% of the overlaps in conversation which occurred when two people talked at once were made by men.

Women's self-reported goals in social interactions may also differ from men's; consistent with their behavior, women may favor interpersonal goals over task completion. Data supporting this point of view were reported by Block (1973) in a cross-cultural study of six countries (the United States, England, Finland, Norway, Sweden, and Denmark). Women stated they would like to be loving, affectionate, sympathetic, and generous people. Men preferred to be assertive, dominating, competitive, and critical. The hypothesis of sex differences in social goals fits traditional, cultural stereotypes of women's proper role in social groups. The traditional feminine sex role dictates that the ideal woman act in a nonassertive or passive manner. A woman who fits the feminine stereotype is oriented toward other people, seeking to nurture them and to receive her satisfactions through their accomplishments (Linehan & Egan, 1979).

Many women view assertion training as a way to achieve an expanded role definition, one which makes the exercise of social influence feminine. In the past, women relied on men to exercise influence for them, and used their attractiveness to motivate men. This "behind the throne," indirect mode of influence, however, was often ineffectual. With rising divorce rates, later marriages, and longer life spans for women than for men, a woman can no longer expect that a man will be available to look out for her welfare. Even the lives of women who prefer the traditional feminine role of dependency and nonassertiveness are disrupted by rapid social change. As women's roles within marriage and families change, and as their aspirations in the work environment increase, their need for diverse social skills becomes more apparent. If they are to be successful in traditional and novel settings, if they are to occupy anything other than the lowest status and power positions, women must learn to exert influence and leadership.

ASSERTIVE BEHAVIOR: THE TOPOGRAPHICAL VIEW

Assertive behavior has most often been defined in terms of its topographical characteristics rather than in terms of its effectiveness. Thus, the focus has been on a description of specific behaviors rather than on analysis of the function of the behavior in specific situations. Wolfe (1973) defined assertion as "expressing emotions other than anxiety" (p. 89); others included the expression of personal rights, preferences, and opinions in their definitions (Galassi & Galassi, 1977; Lange & Jakubowski, 1976; MacDonald, 1974; Rich & Schroeder, 1976). Topographical definitions of the assertive response have included these components: (1) self-expression, a statement of one's rights; (2) a style of speech which is direct and open, verbally fluent, with good eye contact, moderate speech volume, and appropriate response latency; (3) little anxiety or fear; and (4) little coercion or aggression (Linehan & Egan, 1979). Note that classification of responses into these categories is typically based on observer ratings of behavior without reference to the function or effects of the behavior in a particular situation.

Of special relevance to the treatment of women is information about sex differences in the effectiveness of behaviors which have been topographically defined as assertive. To date, information has only been gathered about differences in observer evaluations of assertive males and females, and the results are equivocal. Several studies found that assertive females were evaluated more negatively than assertive males. Observers have rated assertive behavior by women more negatively than identical behavior by men (Kelly, Kern, Kirkley, Patterson, & Keane, 1980). When both sexes exhibit the same assertive behaviors, females are rated as more aggressive (Rose & Tryon, 1979), as more undesirable and ineffective (Connor, Serbin, & Ender, 1978), and as less intelligent and likeable (Lao, Upchurch, Corwin, & Grossnickle, 1975).

Many other studies have found no differences in observer ratings of men's and women's assertive responses. Linehan and Seifert (in press) asked male and female observers to rate global, one-line descriptions of male and female assertive responses. The descriptions did not portray details of the response. Both men and women expected worse ratings from the opposite sex than from the same sex. In fact, neither judges' sex nor assertive actors' sex influenced the ratings. In two studies, observers evaluated assertive actors on several interpersonal variables after reading lengthy descriptions of assertive interactions, which varied situation type and response style. Neither sex of subject nor sex of assertive actor affected the ratings (Epstein, 1980; Linehan, Brown, Nielsen, Olney, & McFall, 1980). Judges who heard audiotapes of assertive actors did not differ in their evaluations of men's and women's behavior (Hess, Bridgwater, Bornstein, & Sweeney, 1980). Studies of bias in the ratings of assertive behavior, have generally presented observers with identical spoken or written verbal scripts. Inconsistent findings may have emerged because actors' nonverbal behavior was equated in some studies and not in others. Yet nonverbal behavior may have a profound influence on the observer's opinion (Romano & Bellack, 1980).

ASSERTIVE BEHAVIOR: A FUNCTIONAL VIEW

Assertive behavioral skills can be considered a subset of more general social skills. Thus, it is instructive to examine how the concept of general social skill is defined. The most commonly cited definition of social skill was proposed by Libet and Lewinsohn (1973): "the complex ability both to emit behaviors which are positively or negatively reinforced and not to emit behaviors that are punished or extinguished by others." Rimm and Masters (1979) added the notion of "miminal effective response," the ability to obtain reinforcement (and presumably to avoid punishment and extinction) with a minimum of effort and negative emotion. Combining the two concepts Gambrill (1978) suggested that the socially skilled person efficiently secures high levels of social reinforcement, by performing few behaviors that are ignored or punished.

Social skill might also be defined as the ability to emit effective responses in interpersonal situations. Effective responses maximize short-term and long-term positive results and minimize short-term and long-term negative results (Goldfried & D'Zurilla, 1969). Effective behavior produces *the intended or expected* result (*New Webster's Dictionary*, 1980). Thus, socially skilled, behavior should be defined in terms of its effective function in a situation, rather than in terms of its topography. Behavior with the same topographical characteristics may be effective, or skilled, in one setting but ineffective in another. In Chapter 13 of this volume, Padawer and Goldfried point out that effective social behavior is incompatible with interpersonal anxiety.

Although most definitions of assertiveness emphasize response topography, the concept of effectiveness is implicit in many others. Phrases such as "expressions which cause others to take them into account" (MacDonald, 1974); "actions in one's own best interests" (Alberti & Emmons, 1978); "effective social problem solving" (Heimberg, Montgomery, Madsen, & Heimberg, 1977); and "skill of maintaining and enhancing reinforcement" (Rich & Schroeder, 1976) have appeared in discussions of assertive responses. An emphasis in the literature on social appropriateness of the response (e.g., Wolfe, 1973), however, suggests that at times, the adherence to social norms may be considered more important than the effectiveness of the response in achieving one's aims.

There is good reason to define assertive behavior in terms of the actor's goals in a particular situation. Reconsidering the notion of social skill as the ability to effect reinforcing consequences while avoiding negative ones, assertive behavior can be functionally defined in terms of the specific types of reinforcing consequences sought and achieved by the individual. Three types of consequences can be differentiated: (1) effectiveness in achieving the objectives of the response (objectives effectiveness); (2) effectiveness in maintaining or enhancing the relationship with the other person in the interaction (relationship effectiveness); and, finally, (3) effectiveness in maintaining the self-esteem of the assertive person (self-respect effectiveness) (Linehan, 1977a; Linehan & Egan; 1979, in press).

The value of these goals varies across time, situations, and actors. When a customer attempts to return faulty merchandise to a store, objectives effectiveness (getting the item exchanged or a refund) may be more important than relationship effectiveness (maintaining a positive relationship with the store manager). In trying to get one's best friend to go to a particular movie, relationship effectiveness (maintaining the close relationship) may be more important than the objective (getting the friend to go to the movie). Note that the methods and the intensity of persuasion attempts may be more restricted in the second example than they were in the first example. The importance of maintaining self-esteem can also vary across individuals and situations. For example, a woman may be willing to act helpless in the evening to please her date (where the relationship is very important), but may resist similar behaviors to make her male co-workers feel less threatened (where principles are very important).

This analysis implies that effective assertive behavior is congruent with personal goals. Therefore assertion training must teach the behavior required for different situations and for different goals, and how to select responses congruent with situation-specific values. The therapist must emphasize content as much as method of assertion.

OBJECTIVES EFFECTIVENESS

MacDonald (1974), in a study of the assertion concept, distinguished four situations in which assertive behavior is expected: (1) those in which the outcome of the situation is unclear; someone is attempting to get the person to give in to a demand contrary to the person's preference, or someone could do something the person would like, but only at the person's initiation; (2) those in which the person is asked to do someone a favor involving some effect or cost; (3) those in which the person has been insulted; and (4) those in which another is or has been inconsiderate to the person. As can be seen, in each situation, the assertive actor exerts social influence, changing the other person's behavior, or resisting others' unwanted influence.

Reexamination of the topographical definitions of assertion discussed earlier reveals that the implicit goal of each assertion category is to exert or resist influence. For example, standing up for one's rights is generally intended to change one's environment such that current and/or future rights are not jeopardized; expressions of preference are attempts to resist influence, to influence events in accord with one's own preferences, or simply to communicate to another where one stands or how one feels. The objectives of the assertive interaction, therefore, are to influence or resist influence in interpersonal situations; objectives effectiveness asesses to what extent the behavior is successful in achieving these aims. The focus of objectives effectiveness is on small-group, face-to-face interaction, rather than on social influence attempts in larger, less personal groups (e.g., political organizations, the media).

RELATIONSHIP EFFECTIVENESS

By definition, interpersonal encounters require a relationship, however transitory, with another person. The relationship effectiveness of the assertive response refers to how well it serves to maintain or enhance the alliance or bond with the other individual or group of individuals. The important point to be made here is that every assertive response can be evaluated in terms of its relationship effectiveness. Although the effectiveness of a response in terms of the relationship is not wholly independent from obtaining the objectives of the interaction, it seems clear that a response could be high in objectives effectiveness but low in relationship effectiveness. Commanding a subordinate to do one's bidding or sharply refusing a request while giving no reason, may be productive but not endearing. In contrast, a response can also be so effective in maintaining good will that it loses much of its force in obtaining the objective. For example, asking friends how they like the play they went to last week may engender good feelings but it may not be very effective in getting them to pay back the money you loaned them to buy the tickets. (On the other hand, we should note that with some people, this may be very effective.) With other people, any attempt, direct or otherwise, to exert influence or act independently may jeopardize the relationship.

SELF-RESPECT EFFECTIVENESS

In most definitions of assertion, objectives effectiveness is implicit; in most studies on the effects of assertion, measures of relationship effectiveness are included. Little attention, however, has been given to the effect of an assertive response on the individual's self-respect. Self-respect effectiveness refers to how well the assertive response serves to maintain or enhance the individual's sense of integrity. Self-respect is not a term generally studied or defined in psychological literature. As used here it refers to a broad set of self-referents, including one's sense of integrity, morality, mastery, and self-esteem. Within behavioral theory, it most closely resembles Bandura's use of the term self-efficacy (1977), although the term is broader in scope than self-efficacy.

It is possible for a particular behavior–situation interaction to have high objectives and relationship effectiveness while at the same time having low self-respect effectiveness. Consider the woman who loses the tennis game to get a date, who bribes an employee to get a kickback, or who keeps her mouth shut on an important issue to keep the peace. Maintenance of self-respect effectiveness can at times involve high cost or risk. Consider the woman who is expected to participate in sexual activities with her employer in order to keep his good will and her job.

MAXIMIZING EFFECTIVENESS: ASSERTIVE SKILL

The dilemma posed by the assertive situation is how to maximize effectiveness across all three content areas. The best response will suit the individual's short- and long-range goals and the details of the particular situation. The goal of assertion training should be to teach clients how to achieve these ends. Thus assertive skill can be defined as the complex capability to emit behaviors or patterns of responses that maximize interpersonal influence and the resistance of unwanted social influence (objectives effectiveness) while at the same time maximizing gains and minimizing losses in the relationship with the other person (relationship effectiveness) and maintaining one's own integrity and sense of mastery (self-respect effectiveness).

JUGGLING GOALS

Issues of relationship and self-respect effectiveness are particularly relevant for women. As was pointed out earlier, many women, at least traditionally, value interpersonal relationships to a greater extent than men, whereas men often appear more oriented to goal attainment. Teaching or encouraging women to emit behaviors which are low in relationship effectiveness, therefore, would appear to contradict the values orientation of many women. The importance of self-respect effectiveness is also particularly relevant to women. One of the major goals of the women's movement and of much of our therapy with women is oriented at increasing their sense of mastery or competence, self-respect, and general integrity. To the extent that we teach them behaviors which are low in self-respect effectiveness we are jeopardizing these aims.

Increasing their own objectives effectiveness, however, is becoming increasingly important for women and critical for their welfare as they respond to the changing social forces and demands of our times. To the extent that one's goals in life require influencing others, the lack of objectives effectiveness can seriously compromise one's ability to interact in a competent manner. As we have noted, an interest in objectives effectiveness has traditionally been more characteristic of men. The challenge of assertive training for women involves teaching women how to maximize their effectiveness in these areas, those of social influence, while at the same time respecting women's concerns about positive relationships and self-respect.

TIME PERSPECTIVE

Most of the examples given so far focus on the immediate effects of assertive behaviors. In considering an overall treatment strategy, however, both the client and therapist must use a long-range time perspective, and consider both immediate and permanent effects. For example, although a particular woman might be able to satisfactorily sacrifice self-respect for a relationship over a short period of time, it must be questioned whether this strategy would work over time. Or, will the woman who disregards the effects of her behaviors on relationships to get "ahead," to get "equality now," or to achieve some other objective, be happy with the results at a later point. Often the woman seeking assertion training has already become aware of the long-term consequences of sacrificing both objectives and self-respect in order to keep others happy.

THE CONTENT OF ASSERTIVE TRAINING PROGRAMS

Assertive training programs should be designed to transmit sets of specific skills. Common sense, as well as research data (e.g., Epstein, 1980; Linehan & Seifert, in press; Linehan et al., 1980), indicate that the assertive effectiveness of any response varies with the situation. Since the type of effectiveness sought will also vary with the individual's values, a complete training program must provide an array of cognitive, emotional, and overt verbal and nonverbal skills (Linehan, 1979). In what follows, I will outline and discuss the types of skills needed.

COGNITIVE SKILLS

Cognitive factors in social and assertive skills are receiving increased attention in the psychological literature. For example, Meichenbaum, Butler, and Gruson (1981) include cognitive process and cognitive structure (as well as overt behaviors) in their conceptual model of social competence. Trower's (1979) model of social skill includes perceptual processes, such as problem solving and sequencing. Bruch (1981) compared the cognitive characteristics of high- and low-assertive individuals, and found that highly assertive individuals had more assertive content knowledge, made more positive self-statements, and processed information in a more abstract style.

An emphasis on teaching cognitive skills needed to select effective responses rather than on teaching overt, motor behaviors, selected on some a priori basis as effective in assertive situations, is relevant for women on at least two accounts. First, as appropriate social interaction patterns change to reflect greater equality of the sexes, the overt behaviors needed in a particular situation will change. The woman who cannot modulate her behavior to fit the circumstances, sensitivities of others in the situations, and the times has little change of remaining effective in influencing others. Secondly, teaching women to evaluate situations accurately and construct their own response to fit the circumstances places more responsibility on the individual client and less on the therapist. This is particularly important when the therapist's own skills in the relevant situations are less than required or when the attitudes of the therapist on women's issues might get in the way of recommending the most effective strategies. This latter concern seems as appropriate to the "liberated" therapist as to the "unliberated" one. What good is it to actively encourage a reluctant single mother to openly demand her due rights in a work situation if she thereby loses her job or jeopardizes her chances for a promotion?

Social Sensitivity

Experimental studies have demonstrated that the skills which comprise social sensitivity can be separated from the decision making, or action–choice skills, involved in social judgment (Welford, 1976). Social sensitivity consists of a set of cognitive skills which involve the discrimination and selective coding of the vast array of information that one is confronted with in social interactions, and the linking of these pieces of new information to other information and knowledge to give them context and meaning. Research in cognitive psychology, as well as recent theoretical formulations of general social skills and competence, indicate that the processes of *discrimination, coding* (or labeling), and interpersonal *attributions* play a critical role in successful social performance (Trower, 1979; Meichenbaum & Asarnow, 1979; Meichenbaum *et al.*, 1981; Linehan & Egan, in press). Research on social sensitivity and assertion, however, is just beginning in the behavioral literature (e.g., Morrison & Bellack, 1981); most studies to date have focused on the evaluations of assertive behaviors by *others* rather than on the attainment and use of information by the assertive actors themselves (e.g., Romano & Bellack, 1980).

Social Judgment

Social sensitivity alone is insufficient for effective social interaction. Social judgment is also required; its interdependent cognitive skill components involve the choice of a set of behaviors which will achieve selected goals in a particular situation. The first step in social judgment is to identify (or cognitively generate) potentially effective responses. These responses are generated automatically in familiar situations (see Langer, 1978, for a review of automatic behavior); novel situations require the invention of new responses. The second step is to evaluate potential responses in light of capabilities and situation-specific goals. The third step is to estimate the probable effect on others of potential responses. The three steps represent skill components of social judgment: (1) *behavior generation,* (2) *self-prediction,* and (3) *outcome prediction* (see Mischel, 1973, for a fuller description of each of these capabilities).

     The social judgment skills listed here are similar to those defined as social problem solving (Trower, 1979; Spivack, Platt, & Shure, 1976). The results of faulty self-predictions and outcome predictions are most often referred to in the cognitive–behavioral literature as irrational beliefs or maladaptive self-statements (e.g. Ellis, 1962, Meichenbaum, 1977; Mahoney, 1974). Fiedler and Beach (1978) showed that cognition (in the form of social judgment) does affect assertion. They found that the difference between those who decide to act assertively and those who do not, lies in the latter's assessments of the probabilities that bad consequences will follow assertion and good consequences will not. Evaluations of how bad or how good those consequences would be did not affect the decision for assertion. Other research has confirmed the role of social judgment in assertive behavior (e.g., Schwartz & Gottman, 1976; Bruch, 1981).

Self-Regulation Skills

Self-regulation uses feedback from the environment to monitor and change behavior to fit circumstances. Theories of self-regulation are prominent in the behavior modification literature and various "self-control" therapies have been developed (see Kanfer, 1980, for reviews). An application of self-regulation theory to assertion would suggest that ineffective behavior in social influence situations may be due to the person's inability to regulate and change responses as situations develop. For example, either excessive rigidity or impulsivity in such settings would be an impediment to successful assertive behavior.

PHYSIOLOGICAL AROUSAL AND EMOTIONAL SKILLS

Investigations of the relationship between autonomic functioning and effective assertive behavior have yielded inconsistent results (Hersen, Bellack, & Turner, 1978; McFall & Marston, 1970; Schwartz & Gottman, 1976; Twentyman & McFall, 1975). The hypothesis that autonomic arousal interferes with overt assertive behavior has received only limited support. To account for these inconsistencies, Eisler (1976) and Bellack and Hersen (1978) proposed that arousal and social skill are unrelated; some individuals function effectively with high arousal while others are effective with little arousal. At the same time, it is clear that extreme emotional arousal, incapacitating fear, or uncontrollable anger impede effective assertion. Thus, the ability to manage extreme emotional states may be a prerequisite of effective functioning.

In analyzing assertive problems, it seems that an additional emotional skill might be useful. This skill involves the ability to experience or generate a range of emotional responses. Although emotional arousal within a particular situation may or may not be critical to success, it seems clear that strong emotions, such as love or hate, may have an effect on how long an individual is willing to persist in an assertive pursuit.

OVERT BEHAVIORAL SKILLS

A large number of books have been written describing effective, overt social and assertive behaviors. The interested reader is referred to Linehan and Egan (1979), Bower and Bower (1976), and Jakubowski and Lange (1978) for general books on assertion and effective, overt behaviors. Most of the self-help books on assertion can also be used by the therapist to help the client formulate overt assertive strategies which might be effective (e.g., Alberti & Emmons, 1978; Galassi & Galassi, 1977; Gambrill & Richey, 1976). As noted previously, a number have been written specifically for women (e.g., Baer, 1976; Bloom et al., 1975; Butler, 1976; Phelps & Austin, 1975; Osborn & Harris, 1975). In addition, the reader is referred to Argyle (1975) and Knapp (1978) for comprehensive reviews of nonverbal interactions, to Clark and Clark (1977) for verbal behavior, and to Worchel and Cooper (1979) for a good overview of social psychology.

The necessary, empirical behavior therapy research relating specific behavioral patterns to particular outcomes in designated social settings has just begun (Hess et al., 1980). A large body of social psychological research on interpersonal interactions exists; however, very little of it has focused on the modification of individual interpersonal effectiveness. Bridges between existing research on social influence and assertiveness training programs are needed. To date, most of the literature has divided overt performance variables into verbal and nonverbal categories. Generally, the verbal category includes the actual content of the message as well as the sequence of words (Trower, 1979). The nonverbal category includes facial expression, gaze, posture, gesture, spatial behavior, bodily contact, physical appearance, and tone, speed, and pitch of speech. A number of studies have correlated specific nonverbal and verbal components with other measures of assertion, in order to describe behavioral characteristics of high-assertive individuals (Romano & Bellack, 1980; Eisler, Miller, & Hersen, 1973). There is a critical need for research relating each of these components to actual effectiveness.

ASSESSMENT OF ASSERTION SKILL

Appropriate assertion therapy, as does any therapy, depends on an accurate assessment of the individual case. An adequate assessment must address four questions:

1. What skills and performance areas should be targeted?

2. What are the situational and behavioral variables controlling the ineffective behavior? Since assertive behaviors may be situationally specific (Eisler, Hersen, Miller, & Blanchard, 1975), an adequate assessment must discover in which situations the individual is skilled and behaves effectively and in those which she does not. Assertive performance is also related to person variables, such as the individual's short- and long-range goals. Thus, assessment of these variables is needed to determine their influence on the individual's behavior in relevant areas.

3. What are the personal and environmental characteristics which will influence treatment outcome? A woman's overly high standards, for example, may interfere with any self-control program since she may punish herself for less than perfect performance and fail to reward herself sufficiently to maintain progress. A skilled friend may provide a useful model. Asking the client to speculate about possible hindrances to treatment success, or to recall prior successes at self-change, may point out useful techniques.

4. Is therapy effective at producing desired outcome? Assessment conducted throughout treatment will insure that the treatment plan can be modified to maximize process. The interested reader is referred to Goldfried and Davison (1976) and Linehan (1977b) for further discussion of these assessment issues in the clinical setting.

Assessment methodologies have focused on the assertive response, rather than on the assertive situation (Kolotkin, 1980; Kazdin 1979; MacDonald, 1978). Even though available measurement procedures sample widely from a cross-section of situations, scores on the assessment instruments are generally calculated by summing scores across items in the inventories and over situations in role play and *in vivo* assessments. However, the fact that this practice is used in research is no reason why the individual clinican has to do likewise. Instead, important information can be gained by examining responses to each individual item on the assessment device used. For example, a three-step strategy based on this approach might include: (1) giving the woman client a self-report assertion inventory; (2) selecting items where she indicates difficulty and conducting a role-play assessment in the therapy session, based on those situations; and then (3) asking the woman to carefully observe and record her behavior in those situations *in vivo* during the coming weeks. (If the situations are not common, the client can be asked to seek out the situations.)

The critical problem in the assessment task is selection of the target for behavior change. The target for change might be cognitive, emotional, or performance skills, an aspect of modifying the environment, or some combination thereof. The focus of treatment must be tied to the assessment process. Generally, the first target of change is either the most severe behavioral deficit or the deficit which is easiest to change. If the deficits are large in all areas, however, a focus on the target behaviors as an integrated system is probably called for. Even if the initial assessment doesn't give a clear-cut indication of the most appropriate target, continuing assessment as treatment progresses will provide information on the efficacy of modifying the targets which are selected. If the targeted behaviors are changing, but assertive effectiveness is not improving, then different target behaviors should probably be selected. On the other hand, if the target behaviors themselves are not changing, then a different treatment method may be needed.

The most common methods of clinical assessment are the behavioral interview, paper-and-pencil questionnaires, self-monitoring, role plays, and *in vivo* observation. The targets of most methodologies have been overt performance and performance capability (mainly by paper-and-pencil questionnaires and role-play tests); however, cognitive variables are gaining increasing attention. The reader interested in pursuing the topic is referred to Curran and Wessberg (1981), Hersen and Bellack (1977), Bellack (1979), and MacDonald (1978) for excellent overviews of the available methodologies. In addition, since role-play assessment has become so closely identified with the assessment of assertive behavior, the reader is referred to a series of articles by Bellack and Hersen and their associates on the validity of the role-play test as a measure of *in vivo* performance (Bellack, Hersen, & Turner, 1978, 1979; Van Hasselt, Hersen, & Bellack, 1981; Curran, 1978).

INTERVENTION STRATEGIES

Over the last ten years, there have been an enormous number of studies examining various treatment components and combinations thereof. Many studies have included only women clients (Linehan *et al.*, 1979;

Wolfe & Fodor, 1978) or only men (Eisler, Hersen, & Miller, 1973; Finch & Wallace, 1977). With one exception (Friedman, 1968), studies including both sexes did not break down their results by sex (Galassi, Galassi, & Litz, 1974; Schinke & Rose, 1976). At this point, therefore, without data to the contrary, it seems reasonable to suppose that the same *methods* of intervention should be used with both males and females.

When used precisely, the term "assertion training" refers to the *goal* of treatment and could, theoretically, involve any treatment modality. In practice, however, the term usually refers to a set of treatment procedures commonly used by behavior therapists for assertive training. The techniques most often referred to include instructions, in-session response practice, modeling, coaching and feedback, and *in vivo* response practice. The reader may be wondering, at this point, just how to apply these techniques of instructions, response practice, feedback and coaching, and *in vivo* practice. What instructions should one give? What are good ideas for homework assignments? What sorts of coaching guidelines should be used? In general, research articles assume that the reader knows how to apply the procedures. For the interested reader, there are several good sources of information. The first source is textbooks designed to teach behavior modifications skills (Gambrill, 1978; Goldfried & Davison, 1976; Kanfer & Goldstein, 1980; Rimm & Masters, 1979). A second source is authors of assertion articles. Often, in order to conduct the treatment and train therapists, these authors have written treatment manuals. These vary in specificity and clinical content but may present step-by-step guidelines on how to conduct the research therapies. The ambitious reader, for example, could simply turn to the reference section of the article and write the first authors of each treatment study asking for the manual used in the article. At times the authors will ask for a small fee to cover mailing and copying. This same strategy would also be effective in obtaining the assessment materials, including role-play tests and scoring manuals, used by those researchers. A third source is workshops, offered at professional conventions, or in the community. Finally, if other sources are not readily available (or in addition to other input) clinicians in the area, skilled in social skills training, are often available for professional supervision (usually for a fee).

Most empirical investigations of assertion training procedures fall into one of three categories: (1) comparisons between complex treatment packages; (2) comparisons of the components within treatment packages; and (3) comparisons of treatments with different targets. Complex treatment packages (Rathus, 1973; Galassi et al., 1974; Schinke & Rose, 1976; Rimm, Hill, Brown, & Stuart, 1974; Finch & Wallace, 1977; Linehan, Walker, Bronheim, Haynes, & Yevzeroff, 1979) combining several or all of the components listed above have been shown to be effective with a variety of treatment populations. Studies focusing on treatment components have shown that overt and imaginal response practice, modeling, and coaching increase targeted assertive behavior (McFall & Lillesand, 1971; McFall & Marston, 1970; McFall & Twentyman, 1973; Hersen, Eisler, Miller, Johnson, & Pinkston, 1973; Friedman, 1968; Kazdin, 1974, 1976).

Kazdin (1974, 1976) has pioneered investigations of the effects of reinforcement on the development and maintenance of assertive responding, and showed that the addition of reinforcement to covert modeling increases treatment effectiveness. Explorations of reinforcement parameters are relevant to the feminist contention that women are often punished or ignored when assertive. Kazdin's findings imply that the therapist must model assertive behavior during therapy sessions and that the woman client must be exposed to competent models who are rewarded for assertive behavior. If women are taught effective responses, rather than topographically selected repertoires, they will be reinforced directly.

Comparisons of treatments with different response targets have contrasted approaches focused on overt behaviors with strategies focused on direct anxiety reduction (Thorpe, 1975; Trower, Yardley, Bryant, & Shaw, 1978; Weinman, Gelbart, Wallace, & Post, 1972) and on modification of cognitive behaviors (Thorpe, 1975; Linehan et al., 1979; Wolfe & Fodor, 1978). Results have been inconclusive in demonstrating superiority of one method over the others, although treatments employing some emphasis on overt behavior rehearsal seem more effective than those missing this focus (Linehan et al., 1979). Because these studies randomly assign clients to treatments, the treatments probably interact with the individual differences in each of the three response systems. Yet this problem is rarely anticipated in study design or included in post hoc data analysis.

CONCLUSIONS AND RECOMMENDATIONS

The field of behavior modification has produced treatment methods which transmit affective, cognitive, and overt motor skills and increase effectiveness in assertive situations. Still needed are rules for fitting treatment methods to individual clients and for selecting target behavior systems. Social skills training is an art form, which requires clinician insight and intuition.

This chapter contends that assertion training research should move away from topographically "assertive" repertoires and toward the teaching of skills which are effective in assertive situations. In determining effectiveness, three goals should be considered: objectives effectiveness, relationship effectiveness, and self-respect effectiveness. The specific emphasis on one type of effectiveness must depend on the individual woman's goals and values. In sum, this chapter recommends an idiographic approach to assertiveness training with women.

Several recommendations for the clinical use of assertiveness training follow from the conclusions of this chapter.

1. Clarification of client values is the necessary first step in planning for assertiveness training.

2. Whatever method of assertiveness training the clinician employs, the goals should be to enhance client acquisition of responses. Effective responses achieve goals valued by the client in situations that formerly were problematic.

3. Assertiveness training methods must enhance a woman's effectiveness in goal attainment, in personal relationships, and encourage self-respect.

4. Assertiveness strategies should be selected with short- and long-range consequences in mind.

5. Training in setting priorities consistent with personal values is a necessary component of assertiveness training for women.

6. Complete assertiveness training will transmit new cognitive, emotional, and action skills. The ability to decide how to act in a given situation is a necessary skill, as is the ability to evaluate one's own performance, and regulate future performances accordingly.

7. Assessment conducted throughout treatment and follow-up insures that divergent goals are considered.

8. Instructions, rehearsal, modeling, coaching and feedback, and reinforcement can be used singly or together to transmit target assertive behaviors.

REFERENCES

Alberti, R. E., & Emmons, M. L. *Your perfect right* (3rd ed.). San Luis Obispo, Calif.: Impact, 1978.
Argyle, M. *Bodily communication*. London: Methuen, 1975.
Argyle, M., Alkema, F., & Gilmour, R. The communication of friendly and hostile atti-

tudes. *British Journal of Social and Clinical Psychology,* 1971, *20,* 386–401.

Aries, E. Male–female interpersonal styles in all male, all female and mixed groups. In A. G. Sargent (Ed.), *Beyond sex roles.* St. Paul: West, 1977.

Baer, J. *How to be an assertive (not aggressive) woman in life, in love, and on the job: A total guide to self-assertiveness.* New York: Signet, 1976.

Bandura, A. Self-efficacy: Toward a unifying theory of behavioral change. *Psychological Review,* 1977, *84,* 191–215.

Barron, N. Sex-typed language: The production of grammatical cases. *Acta Sociologica,* 1971, *14,* 24–72.

Barthell, C. N., & Holmes, D. S. High school yearbooks: A nonreactive measure of social isolation in graduates who later became schizophrenic. *Journal of Abnormal Psychology,* 1968, *73,* 313–316.

Bellack, A. S. Behavioral assessment of social skills. In A. S. Bellack & M. Hersen (Eds.), *Research and practice in social skills training.* New York: Plenum, 1979.

Bellack, A. S., & Hersen, M. *Behavior modification: An introductory textbook.* Baltimore: Williams & Wilkin, 1977.

Bellack, A. S., & Hersen, M. Chronic psychiatric patients: Social skills training. In M. Hersen & A. S. Bellack (Eds.), *Behavior therapy in the psychiatric setting.* Baltimore: Williams & Wilkins, 1978.

Bellack, A. S., & Hersen, M. *Research and practice in social skills training.* New York: Plenum, 1979.

Bellack, A. S., Hersen, M., & Turner, S. M. Role-play tests for assessing social skills: Are they valid? *Behavior Therapy,* 1978, *9,* 448–461.

Bellack, A. S., Hersen, M., & Turner, S. M. Relationship of role playing and knowledge of appropriate behavior to assertion in the natural environment. *Journal of Consulting and Clinical Psychology,* 1979, *47,* 670–678.

Bem, S. The measurement of psychological androgyny. *Journal of Consulting and Clinical Psychology,* 1974, *42,* 155–162.

Bernard, J. *The sex game.* New York: Atheneum, 1972.

Blanchard, E. B., & Hersen, M. Behavioral treatment of hysterical neurosis: Symptom substitution and symptom return reconsidered. *Psychiatry,* 1976, *39,* 118–129.

Blechman, E. A. Ecological sources of dysfunction in women: Issues and implications for clinical behavior therapy. *Clinical Behavior Therapy Review,* 1980, *2,* 1–16.

Blechman, E. A. Competence, depression and behavior modification with women. In M. Hersen (Ed.), *Progress in behavior modification* (Vol. 12). New York: Academic, 1981.

Block, J. H. Conceptions of sex role: Some cross cultural and longitudinal perspectives. *American Psychologist,* 1973, *28,* 512–526.

Bloom, L. Z., Coburn, K., & Pearlman, J. *The new assertive woman.* New York: Del, 1975.

Bower, S. A., & Bower, G. H. *Asserting yourself: A practical guide for positive change.* Reading, Mass.: Addison-Welsey, 1976.

Bruch, M. A. A task analysis of assertive behavior revisited: Replication and extension. *Behavior Therapy,* 1981, *12,* 217–230.

Butler, P. E. *Self-assertion for women.* San Francisco: Canfield, 1976.

Callner, D. A., & Ross, S. M. The reliability and validity of three measures of assertion in a drug addict population. *Behavior Therapy,* 1976, *7,* 659–667.

Cheek, D. K., *Assertive black. . .puzzled white.* San Luis Obispo, Calif.: Impact, 1976.

Clark, H. H., & Clark, E. V. *Psychology and language.* New York: Harcourt, Brace, Jovanovich, 1977.

Connor, J. M., Serbin, L. A., & Ender, R. A. Responses of boys and girls to aggressive, assertive, and passive behaviors of male and female characters. *Journal of Genetic Psychology,* 1978, *133,* 59–69.

Craighead, W. E., Kazdin, A. E., & Mahoney, M. J. *Behavior modification: Principles, issues and applications.* Boston: Houghton Mifflin, 1976.

Curran, J. P. Comments on Bellack, Hersen, and Turner's paper on the validity of role-play test. *Behavior Therapy*, 1978, *9*, 462–468.

Curran, J. P., Miller, I. V., Zwick, W. R., Monti, P. M., & Stout, R. L. The socially inadequate patient: Incidence rate, demographic and clinical features, and hospital and posthospital functioning. *Journal of Consulting and Clinical Psychology*, 1980, *48*, 375–382.

Curran, J. P., & Wessberg, H. W. Assessment of social inadequacy. In D. H. Barlow (Ed.), *Behavioral assessment of adult disorders.* New York: Guilford, 1981.

Eagly, A. H. Sex differences in influenceability. *Psychological Bulletin*, 1978, *1*, 86–116.

Eisler, R. M. The behavioral assessment of social skills. In M. Hersen & A. S. Bellack (Eds.), *Behavioral assessment: A practical handbook.* New York: Pergamon, 1976.

Eisler, R. M., Hersen, M., & Miller, P. M. Effects of modeling on components of assrtive behavior. *Journal of Behavior Therapy and Experimental Psychiatry*, 1973, *4*, 1–6.

Eisler, R. M. Hersen, M. Miller, P. M., & Blanchard, E. B. Situational determinants of assertive behaviors. *Journal of Consulting and Clinical Psychology*, 1975, *43*, 330–340.

Eisler, R. M., Miller, P. M., & Hersen, M. Components of assertive behavior. *Journal of Clinical Psychology*, 1973, *29*, 295–299.

Ellis, A. *Reason and emotion in psychotherapy.* New York: Lyle Stuart, 1962.

Epstein, N. Social consequences of assertion, aggression, passive aggression, and submission: Situational and dispositional determinants. *Behavior Therapy*, 1980, *22*, 662–669.

Fiedler, D., & Beach, L. R. On the decision to be assertive. *Journal of Consulting and Clinical Psychology*, 1978, *46*, 537–546.

Finch, B. E., & Wallace, C. J. Successful interpersonal skills training with schizophrenic inpatients. *Journal of Consulting and Clinical Psychology*, 1977, *45*, 885–890.

Fodor, I. G., & Epstein, R. C. Assertiveness training for women: Where are we failing? In E. Foa & P. Emmelkamp (Eds.), *Failures in bheavior therapy*, New York: Wiley, in press.

Friedman, P. H. *The effects of modeling and role playing on assertive behavior.* Unpublished doctoral dissertation, University of Wisconsin, 1968.

Galassi, M. D., & Galassi, J. P. *Assert yourself! How to be your own person.* New York: Human Sciences, 1977.

Galassi, M. D., Galassi, J. P., & Litz, M. C. Assertive training in groups using video feedback. *Journal of Counseling Psychology*, 1974, *21*, 390–394.

Gambrill, E. D. *Behavior modification: A handbook of assessment, intervention, and evaluation.* San Francisco: Jossey-Bass, 1978.

Gambrill, E. D., & Richey, C. A. *It's up to you: Developing assertive social skills.* Millbrae, Calif.: Les Femmes, 1976.

Goldfried, M. R., & Davison, G. C. *Clinical behavior therapy.* New York: Holt, Rinehart & Winston, 1976.

Goldfried, M. R., & D'Zurilla, T. J. A behavioral–analytic model for assessing competence. In C. D. Spielberger (Ed.), *Current topics in clinical and community psychology.* New York: Academic, 1969.

Gove, W. R., & Tudor, J. F. Adult sex roles and mental illness. *American Journal of Sociology*, 1973, *78*, 812–835.

Hall, K. *Sex differences in initiation and influence in decision-aming groups of perspective teachers.* Unpublished dissertation, Stanford University, 1972.

Hartup, W. W. Peer interaction and social organization. In P. Mussen (Ed.), *Carmichael's manual of child psychology* (Vol. 2). New York: Wiley, 1970.

Heimberg, R. G., Mongomery, D., Madsen, C. H., & Heimberg, J. S. Assertion training: A review of the literature. *Behavior Therapy*, 1977, *8*, 953–971.

Hersen, M., & Bellack, A. S. Assessment of social skills. In A. R. Ciminero, K. S. Calhoun, & H. E. Adams (Eds.), *Handbook of behavioral assessment*. New York: Wiley, 1977.

Hersen, M., Bellack, A. S., & Turner, S. M. Assessment of assertiveness in female psychiatric patients: Motor and autonomic measures. *Journal of Behavior Therapy and Experimental Psychiatry*, 1978, 9, 11–16.

Hersen, M., Eisler, R., Miller, P., Johnson, M., & Pinkston, S. Effects of practice, instructions, and modeling on components of assertive behavior. *Behaviour Research Therapy*, 1973, 11, 443–451.

Hess, E. P., Bridgwater, C. A., Bornstein, P. H., & Sweeney, T. M. Situational determinants in the perception of assertiveness: Gender-related influences. *Behavior Therapy*, 1980, 22, 49–58.

Hilpert, F., Kramer, C., & Clark, R. A. Participants' perceptions of self and partner in mixed sex dyads. *Central States Speech Journal*, Spring, 1975, 26, 52–56.

Jakubowski, P., & Lange, A. J. *The assertive option: Your rights and responsibilities*. Champaign, Ill.: Research, 1978.

Jakubowski-Spector, P. Facilitating the growth of women through assertive training. *The Counseling Psychologist*, 1973, 4, 76–86.

Jenkins, R. L., & Gurel, L. Predictive factors in early release. *Mental Hospital*, 1959, 10, 11–14.

Jones, D. I. R. Self-poisoning with drugs: The past twenty years in Sheffield. *British Medical Journal*, 1977, 1, 28–29.

Kanfer, F. H. Self-management methods. In F. H. Kanfer & A. P. Goldstein (Eds.), *Helping people change: A textbook of methods* (2nd ed.). New York: Pergamon, 1980.

Kanfer, F. H., & Goldstein, A. P. (Eds.). *Helping people change: A textbook of methods* (2nd ed.). New York: Pergamon, 1980.

Kazdin, A. E. Effects of covert modeling and model reinforcement on assertive behavior. *Journal of Abnormal Psychology*, 1974, 83, 240–252.

Kazdin, A. E. Effects of covert modeling, multiple models, and model reinforcement on assertive behavior. *Behavior Therapy*, 1976, 7, 211–222.

Kazdin, A. E. Socipsychological factors in psychopathology. In A. S. Bellack & M. Hersen, (Eds.), *Research and practice in social skills training*. New York: Plenum, 1979.

Kelly, J. A., Kern, J. M., Kirkley, B. G., Patterson, J. N., & Keane, T. M. Reactions to assertive versus unassertive behavior: Differential effects for males and females and implications for assertiveness training. *Behavior Therapy*, 1980, 11, 670–682.

Knapp, M. L. *Nonverbal communication in human interaction*. New York: Holt, Rinehart & Winston, 1978.

Kolotkin, R. A. Situation specificity in the assessment of assertion: Considerations for the measurement of training and transfer. *Behavior Therapy*, 1980, 2, 651–661.

Lange, A. J., & Jakubowski, P. *Responsible assertive behavior: Cognitive/behavioral procedures for trainers*. Champaign, Ill.: Research, 1976.

Langer, E. Rethinking the role of thought in social interaction. In J. Harvey, W. Ickes, & R. Kidd (Eds.), *New directions in attribution research* (Vol. 2). Hillsdale, N.J.: Erlbaum, 1978.

Lanyon, R. I., & Lanyon, B. P. *Behavior therapy: A clinical introduction*. Reading, Mass.: Addison-Wesley, 1978.

Lao, R. C., Upchurch, W. H., Corwin, B. J., & Grossnickle, W. F. Biased attitudes toward females as indicated by ratings of intelligence and likeability. *Psychological Reports*, 1975, 37, 1315–1320.

Lazarus, A. A. Behaviour rehearsal vs. non-directive therapy vs. advice in effective behaviour change. *Behaviour Research and Therapy*, 1966, 4, 209–212.

Liberman, R. P., King, L. W., DeRisi, W. J., & McCann, M. *Personal effectiveness: Guiding people to assert themselves and improve their social skills*. Champaign, Ill.: Research, 1975.

Libet, J. M., & Lewinsohn, P. H. The concept of social skill with special reference to the behavior of depressed persons. *Journal of Consulting and Clinical Psychology*, 1973, *40*, 304–312.

Linehan, M. M. Book review: *Asserting yourself: A practical guide for positive change* by S. A. Bower and G. H. Bower. *Behavior Modification*, 1977, *1*, 567–570.(a)

Linehan, M. M. Issues in behavioral interviewing. In J. D. Cone & R. P. Hawkins (Eds.), *Behavioral assessment: New directions in clinical psychology*. New York: Brunner/Mazel, 1977.(b)

Linehan, M. M. A structured cognitive behavioral approach to assertion training. In P. C. Kendall & S. D. Hollon (Eds.), *Cognitive–behavioral interventions: Theory, research, and procedures*. New York: Academic, 1979.

Linehan, M. M., Brown, S. H., Nielsen, S. L., Olney, K., & McFall, R. M. *The effectiveness of three styles of assertion*. Paper presented at Association for the Advancement of Behavior Therapy, New York, 1980.

Linehan, M. M., & Egan, K. J. Assertion training for women. In A. S. Bellack & M. Hersen (Eds.), *Research and practice in social skills training*. New York: Plenum, 1979.

Linehan, M. M., & Egan, K. J. *Succeeding socially*. London: Lifecycle, in press.

Linehan, M. M., Goldfried, M. R., & Goldfried, A. P. Assertion therapy: Skill training or cognitive restructuring. *Behavior Therapy*, 1979, *10*, 372–388.

Linehan, M. M., & Seifert, R. Sex and contextual differences in the appropriateness of assertive behavior: Fact or myth? *Psychology of Women Quarterly*, in press.

Linehan, M. M., Walker, R. O., Bronheim, S., Haynes, K. F., & Yevzeroff, H. Group vs. individual assertion training. *Journal of Consulting and Clinical Psychology*, 1979, *47*, 1000–1002.

Maccoby, E. E., & Jacklin, C. N. *The psychology of sex differences*. Stanford, Calif.: Stanford University Press, 1974.

MacDonald, M. L. *A behavioral assessment methodology applied to the measurement of assertion*. Unpublished doctoral dissertation, University of Illinois at Urbana, 1974.

MacDonald, M. L. Measuring assertion: A model and a method. *Behavior Therapy*, 1978, *9*, 889–899.

Mahoney, M. J. *Cognition and behavior modification*. Cambridge, Mass.: Ballinger, 1974.

McCrady, B. S. *Behavior therapy and the female alcoholic*. Paper presented at the Association for Advancement of Behavior Therapy Meeting, San Francisco, 1979.

McFall, R. M., & Lillesand, D. B. Behavior rehearsal with modeling and coaching in assertion training. *Journal of Abnormal Psychology*, 1971, *7*, 313–323.

McFall, R. M., & Marston, A. An experimental investigation of behavioral rehearsal in assertive training. *Journal of Abnormal Psychology*, 1970, *76*, 295–303.

McFall, R. M., & Twentyman, C. T. Four experiments on the relative contributions of rehearsal, modeling, and coaching assertin training. *Journal of Abnormal Psychology*, 1973, *81*, 199–218.

Meichenbaum, D. H. *Cognitive behavior modification*. New York: Plenum, 1977.

Meichenbaum, D. H., & Asarnow, J. Cognitive-behavior modification and metacognitive development: Implications for the classroom. In P. Kendall & S. Hollon (Eds.), *Cognitive–behavioral interventions: Theory research and procedures*. New York: Academic, 1979.

Meichenbaum, D. H., Butler, L., & Gruson, L. Toward a conceptual model of social competence. In J. D. Wine & M. D. Smye (Eds.), *Social competence*. New York: Guilford, 1981.

Miller, P. M., & Eisler, R. M. Assertive behavior of alcoholics: A descriptive analysis. *Behavior Therapy*, 1977, *8*, 146–149.

Mischel, W. Toward a cognitive social learning reconceptualization of personality. *Psychological Review*, 1973, *80*, 50–83.

Moore, D. *Annotated bibliography update*. San Luis Obispo, Calif.: Impact, 1981. Cited in I.

G. Fodor & R. C. Epstein, Assertiveness training for women: Where are we failing? In E. Foa & P. Emmelkamp (Eds.), *Failures in behavior therapy*. New York: Wiley, in press.

Morrison, R. L., & Bellack, A. S. The role of social perception in social skill. *Behavior Therapy*, 1981, *12*, 69–79.

New Webster's dictionary of the English language, New York: Delair, 1980.

O'Leary, D. E., O'Leary, M. R., & Donovan, D. M. Social skill acquisition and psychological development of alcoholics: A review. *Addictive Behaviors*, 1976, *1*, 111–120.

Osborn, S. M., & Harris, G. G. *Assertive training for women*. Springfield, Ill.: Thomas, 1975.

Phelps, S., & Austin, N. *The assertive woman*. Fredericksburg, Va.: Book Crafters, 1975.

Platt, J. J., Siegel, J. M., & Spivack, G. Do psychiatric patients and normals see the same solutions as effective in solving interpersonal problems? *Journal of Consulting and Clinical Psychology*, 1975, *43*, 279.

Report of the President's Commission on Mental Health. Washington, D.C.: U.S. Government Printing Office, 1978.

Rathus, S. A. Instigation of assertive behavior through videotape-mediated assertive models and directed practice. *Behaviour Research and Therapy*, 1973, *11*, 57–65.

Rich, A. R., & Schroeder, H. W. Research issues in assertiveness training. *Psychological Bulletin*, 1976, *83*, 1081–1096.

Rimm, D., Hill, G., Brown, N., & Stuart, J. Group-assertive training in treatment of expression of inappropriate anger. *Psychological Reports*, 1974, *34*, 791–798.

Rimm, D. C., & Masters, J. C. *Behavior therapy: Techniques and empirical findings* (2nd ed.). New York: Academic, 1979.

Rinn, R. C., & Markle, A. Social skill deficits in children. In A. S. Bellack & M. Hersen (Eds.), *Research and practice in social skills training*. New York: Plenum, 1979.

Roff, M., Sells, S. B., & Golden, M. M. *Social adjustment and personality development in children*. Minneapolis: University of Minnesota Press, 1972.

Romano, J. M., & Bellack, A. S. Social validation of a component model of assertive behavior. *Journal of Consulting and Clinical Psychology*, 1980, *48*, 478–490.

Rose, Y., & Tryon, W. Judgments of assertive behavior as a function of speech loudness, latency, content, gestures, inflection and sex. *Behavior Modification*, 1979, *3*, 112–123.

Salter, A. *Conditioned reflex therapy*. New York: Creative Age, 1949.

Sanchez, V., & Lewinsohn, P. M. Assertive behavior and depression. *Journal of Consulting and Clinical Psychology*, 1980, *48*, 119–120.

Schinke, S. P., & Rose, S. D. Interpersonal skill training in groups. *Journal of Counseling Psychology*, 1976, *23*, 442–448.

Schwartz, R. M., & Gottman, J. M. Toward a task analysis of assertive behavior. *Journal of Consulting and Clinical Psychology*, 1976, *44*, 910–920.

Spivack, G., Platt, J. J., & Shure, M. B. *The problem solving approach to adjustment: A guide to research and intervention*. San Francisco: Jossey-Bass, 1976.

Strain, P., Shores, R. E., & Kerr, M. A., An experimental analysis of "spillover" effects on the social interactions of behaviorally handicapped preschool children. *Journal of Applied Behavior Analysis*, 1976, *9*, 31–40.

Swacker, M. The sex of the speaker as a sociolinguistic variable. In B. Thorne & N. Henley (Eds.), *Language and sex: Difference and dominance*. Rowley, Mass.: Newbury House, 1972.

Thorpe, G. L. Desensitization, behavioral rehearsal, self-instructional training, and placebo effects on assertive-refusal behavior. *European Journal of Behavioral Analysis and Modification*, 1975, *1*, 30–44.

Trower, P. Fundamentals of interpersonal behavior: A social-psychological perspective. In A. S. Bellack & M. Hersen (Eds.), *Research and practice in social skills training*. New York: Plenum, 1979.

Tower, P., Yardley, K., Bryant, B. M., & Shaw, P. The treatment of social failure: A comparison of anxiety-reduction and skill-acquisition procedures on two social problems. *Behavior Modification*, 1978, *2*, 41–60.

Twentyman, C. T., & McFall, R. M. Behavioral training of social skills in shy males. *Journal of Consulting and Clinical Psychology*, 1975, *43*, 384–395.

Van Hasselt, V. B., Hersen, M., & Bellack, A. S. The validity of role play tests for assessing social skills in children. *Behavior Therapy*, 1981, *12*, 202–216.

Weinman, B., Gelbart, P., Wallace, M., & Post, M. Inducing assertive behavior in chronic schizophrenics: A comparison of socioenvironmental, desensitization, and relaxation therapies. *Journal of Consulting and Clinical Psychology*, 1972, *39*, 246–253.

Welford, A. T., *Skilled performance: Perceptual and motor skills.* Glenview, Ill.: Scott, Foresman, 1976.

Witkin, H. A. *Personality through perception: An experimental and clinical study.* New York: Harper, 1954.

Wolfe, J. L., & Fodor, I. G. A comparison of three approaches to modifying assertive behavior in women: Modeling-plus-behavior rehearsal, modeling-plus-behavior rehearsal-plus-rational therapy, and conscious-raising. *Behavior Therapy*, 1978, *8*, 567–574.

Wolfe, J. *Psychotherapy by reciprocal inhibition.* Stanford, Calif.: Stanford University Press, 1958.

Wolfe, J. *The practice of behavior therapy.* New York: Pergamon, 1973.

Worchel, S., & Cooper, J. *Understanding social psychology.* Homewood, Ill.: Dorsey, 1979.

Zimmerman, D. H., & West, C. Sex roles, interruptions and silences in conversation. In B. Thorne & N. Henley (Eds.), *Language and sex: Diverence and dominance.* Rowley, Mass.: Newbury House, 1975.

7

MARRIAGE AND THE FAMILY: AN UNCONSCIOUS MALE BIAS IN BEHAVIORAL TREATMENT?

ALAN S. GURMAN
MARJORIE H. KLEIN

OVERVIEW AND BACKGROUND

While the outcomes of the various psychotherapies have received increasingly careful scrutiny over the last two decades (e.g., Bergin & Garfield, 1971; Garfield & Bergin, 1978; Gurman & Razin, 1977; Meltzoff & Kornreich, 1970), the impact of the social values implicit in these treatment models and in their outcome criteria has received a good deal less attention. In particular, the impact of these therapeutic models and methods on the lives of women, as wives and mothers, has received little empirical study (Brodsky & Hare-Mustin, 1980).

Of all the areas of one's life that reflect and influence each person's awareness of gender roles, certainly none is as powerful as that of marriage and the family. It is here that the consequences for women of traditional socialization are most obvious, pervasive, and self-perpetuating. The marriage and family therapist, then, perhaps more than any other psychotherapist, is in the position of having profound opportunities to influence gender role attitudes.

The influence of gender-role stereotyping on the practice of family therapy in general has been considered elsewhere in discussions of alternatives to current practices (APA Task Force, 1975, 1978; Hare-Mustin, 1978, 1979; Rice & Rice, 1977), and in the context of treatment outcome evaluation (Gurman & Klein, 1980; Klein, 1976). To date, however, all such discussions, and the few existing empirical investigations in the

Alan S. Gurman and Marjorie H. Klein. Department of Psychiatry, University of Wisconsin Medical School, Madison, Wisconsin.

area (e.g., Abramowitz, 1977; Magnus, 1975), have discussed gender-role stereotyping within particular family therapy approaches only to illustrate the existence of the phenomenon. No published reports have yet examined in detail the role of gender bias within a particular family treatment approach. While any of the major models of family therapy (Gurman & Kniskern, 1981a) could be examined usefully in the light of feminist concerns, it is important that behavioral marriage and family therapy (BMFT) be considered in such a framework for three reasons. First, BMFT is among the most widely used approaches in marriage and family therapy (Gurman, 1978; Gurman & Kniskern, 1978a, 1981a; Gurman & Knudson, 1978). Second, no method of marital–family therapy has received as much empirical attention as BMFT (Barton & Alexander, 1981; Gordon & Davidson, 1981; Gurman & Kniskern, 1978a, 1978b, 1981b; Jacobson, 1978, 1979b). Finally, behavior therapy in general often has been proposed to be inherently compatible with feminist values and with the achievement of feminist aims (Blechman, 1980; Fodor, 1974; Lazarus, 1974; Tennov, 1975).

In this chapter, three domains central to any psychotherapeutic method will be examined in light of feminist concerns. First, common behavioral views of marital–family dysfunction will be considered. This will be followed by a discussion of some of the ways in which these views influence the actual practice of BMFT, especially in terms of assessment, treatment planning, and the choice of treatment goals. Finally, the nature of the outcome criteria used to evaluate the efficacy of BMFT will be addressed.

In all three domains, it will be argued that while BMFT does not manifestly depend in any way on prevailing gender biases, there are salient trends in BMFT research and practice that may reflect, and even "reinforce," traditional sexist values and thus obscure significant issues in the delivery of marital and family therapy services to women. The position taken in this chapter will be that these trends appear to constitute what Bem and Bem (1970) call a "nonconscious ideology," that is, a "set of beliefs and attitudes which [are accepted] implicitly but which remains outside . . . awareness because alternative conceptions of the world remain unimagined." (p. 89)

BEHAVIORAL VIEWS OF MARITAL AND FAMILY DYSFUNCTION

For meaningful assessment of treatment outcomes, there must be some standard against which clinical changes can be compared. From a feminist perspective, certain models of psychological functioning, especially psychoanalytic models, contain explicit biases against women, and endorse different standards of psychological health for women and for men (Chesler, 1972). Behavior therapy in general, and BMFT in particular, seems, at first blush, to have avoided, or even transcended, such gender biases by virtue of its explicit disavowal of attempts to define "ideal" states or forms of psychological functioning. For example, Weiss (1978) has taken the position that "behavior modification is not a theory of human interactions; it is better described as a technology derived from learning principles, which are quite frankly mute on the issue of a theory of adult intimacy in a long-term committed relationship" (p. 173).

To deal with the lack of a comprehensive theory of healthy marital and family relationships, behaviorists have adopted a highly pragmatic approach to identifying the criteria for "successful" and "unsuccessful" intimate relationships. This approach is called the "Matching-to-Sample" philosophy (Alexander & Barton, 1976; Barton & Alexander, 1981; Parsons & Alexander, 1973). Rather than offering theoretical propositions about the nature of healthy marital and family relationships, the approach is firmly grounded in empirical investigation. As Barton and Alexander (1981) state unambiguously, "This philosophy asserts that there is not necessarily a theoretically-derived ideal form of family process, but rather that remediating family problems might best be accomplished by helping disturbed families attain the same patterns of family interaction that are characteristic of nondistressed families" (p. 415). As described by Gottman (1979) in the context of marriage, this approach involves finding the "process dimensions that distinguish marriages that are believed by the spouses to be functioning well from marriages that are believed by the spouses to be functioning badly" (p. 263). This approach typically involves the comparative study of clinic versus nonclinic couples and families.

Such a stance seems to extol objectivity and, in so doing, to be free of gender bias. However, hidden within this approach are two subtle, yet pervasive, assumptions: first, that the absence of felt distress is a reasonable criterion by which to judge the quality of marital and family relationships and, second, that what is typical or modal in family relationships offers a suitable standard of comparison for assessing the quality of a given marriage or family. Indeed, it is these two assumptions that are at the core of feminist critiques of traditional family interaction and socialization patterns (Bernard, 1973; Chesler, 1972; Firestone, 1970; Rich, 1976). Thus, this apprently "neutral" approach to distinguishing between desirable and undesirable marital and family relationship patterns unwittingly and, therefore, covertly, continues the long-standing tradition in research on the family, of reflecting the dominant cultural conceptions of intimate relationships (Hicks & Platt, 1970; Laws, 1971). These common standards of marital and family happiness often include such antifeminist principles as the following: (1) that a "happy" marriage requires a value system shared by the couple, often requiring a wife's conformity, accommodation, and submission to her husband's values and needs (Barry, 1970; Fineberg & Lowman, 1975); (2) that the family division of labor should involve task specialization along gender role lines; and (3) that psychological functions, such as rationality and nurturance, should also be distributed in terms of gender. Related to this last assumption is the belief that childbearing and childrearing should be uniformly pleasing experiences for a woman, indeed, her peak experiences in life.

If, in fostering the Matching-to-Sample philosophy, BMF therapists would be comprehensive in their use of empirical data on the normative psychological experiences of women, they could not, but for their culturally determined blind spots, escape the clinical implications of such replicated findings as the following: (1) that, in their traditional familial role as the primary caretaker of children, women experience a great deal of role strain (e.g., Blood & Wolfe, 1960; Paris & Luckey, 1966; Perlin & Johnson, 1977; Radloff, 1975); (2) that married but not single women show a higher incidence of mental illness than men (e.g., Gove, 1976; Gove & Tudor, 1973), especially depression (e.g., Radloff, 1975; Weissman & Klerman, 1977); and (3) that some debilitating psychological disorders, such as agoraphobia, are disproportionately common among married women (Goldstein & Chambless, 1978) and seem to reflect directly women's traditionally dependent role in marriage (Chambless & Goldstein, 1980). Thus, the absence of felt distress put forth by the Matching-to-Sample philosophy as a useful criterion of the level of marital or family functioning may be grossly misleading and harmful to women, if adopted widely. As Klein (1976) has emphasized, "Pain in response to a bad situation is adaptive, not pathological. . . . The depression, and later the anger, of the woman trapped in an unsatisfying role [e.g., marital] . . . may be healthy steps in recognizing and doing something about a dehumanizing situation" (p. 90).

In summary, there is absolutely no evidence that BMFT explicitly advocates criteria for "ideal" marital and family life that are antagonistic to feminist values and women's growth. Ironically, on the other hand,

BMFT's systematic effort to eschew such theoretically based value positions has created a situation in which there is a real risk of de facto endorsement and reinforcement of values about female participation in marriages and families that are harmful to women's psychological welfare. While explanations of this curious irony are open to speculation, the major culprit may be the undue emphasis within BMFT on viewing behavior at face value. With rare exceptions (e.g., Barton & Alexander, 1980), BMF therapists, unlike most other family therapists (cf. Gurman & Kniskern, 1981a), do not accept the idea that overt behavior has important relationship-defining functions. Rather, BMF therapists generally assert (e.g., Jacobson & Margolin, 1979; Jacobson & Weiss, 1978) that the topography of particular target behaviors is best viewed literally rather than symbolically. From a feminist perspective, the myth that "Behavior Is Behavior Is Behavior" (cf. Gurman & Knudson, 1978; Gurman, Knudson, & Kniskern, 1978; Knudson, Gurman, & Kniskern, 1980), that is, that behavior counts are all that count, may be especially insidious.

BEHAVIORAL MARRIAGE AND FAMILY THERAPY IN PRACTICE

In clinical practice, the overwhelming tendency within BMFT to view behavior literally, and to ignore and implicit relationship defining nature of overt behavior, leads to what Hines and Hare-Mustin (1978) have called "the myth of valueless thinking," that is, the myth that "the technology of behavior modification is neutral with respect to social values" (Blechman, 1980). It is doubtful that technology per se may be neutral. As Bergin (1980a) has stated the matter bluntly, "Techniques are . . . a means for mediating the value influence intended by the therapist. It is inevitable that the therapist be such a moral agent" (p. 97). While behaviorism has attempted to rid psychology of the concept of intention (cf. Jacobson, 1977; Knudson et al., 1980), and while certainly few BMF therapists would assert antifeminist values, behavioral family therapists must be willing to assume responsibility for all the effects of their interventions, whether consciously intended or not. Let us now consider some of the most prominent ways in which failure to anticipate second-order effects of standard BMFT intervention may produce negative results for women, even in the face of apparently successful first-order clinical change.

The unintended gender bias that may occur in BMFT is directly attributable to what we see as two fundamental clinical errors, to wit: (1) the clinical implementation of normative relationship standards based on the Matching-to-Sample philosophy discussed earlier; and (2) the tendency of BMF therapists not to challenge their patients' problem definitions and self-presentations.

"MATCHING-TO-SAMPLE" IN ACTION

The first step in Matching-to-Sample, described earlier, is to identify the process dimensions that distinguish "functional" and "dysfunctional" (usually clinic vs. nonclinic) couples and families. The second step is to "design an intervention program that teaches [couples] who believe their [marriages] are functioning badly to interact . . . as do [couples] who believe their [marriages] are functioning well" (Gottman, 1979, p. 263). The same logic is also applied to families, of course (Barton & Alexander, 1981). As already noted, "well-functioning" marriages and families in our culture are often dangerous to the psychological health of women.

To make more concrete the way in which such normative standards may receive considerable de facto endorsement in BMFT, let us consider, for illustrative purposes, the impact of a widely used assessment device in behavioral marriage therapy (BMT) (Jacobson, 1979a, 1979b, 1981; Weiss & Margolin, 1978), the Spouse Observation Checklist (SOC) (Weiss, 1975). The SOC is a "rather comprehensive list of events and behaviors that can occur in a marital relationship" (Jacobson & Weiss, 1978, p. 515). This checklist of about 400 spouse behaviors is grouped into 12 categories, for example, Companionship, Affection, Household Responsibilities. Most of these categories are further divided into two lists of pleasing (P) and Displeasing (D) behaviors, which, as Weiss and Margolin (1978) note, have been "categorized *a priori* as pleasing and displeasing" (p. 577; emphasis added).[1] These a priori categorizations

---

[1] Quite recently, there has been experimentation with various formats for presenting SOC items to couples, including the removal of the headings, "Pleases" and "Displeases." Such attempts to avoid biasing couples as to the "correct" valence of each item do little to resolve the problem we are raising. Even when the lists are presented "neutrally," implicit therapist endorsement of gender biased behavior is still a high risk, since, as we will discuss in the next section, BMFT therapists rarely challenge the validity of their clients' complaints. Moreover, the summary codes of the *"most influential attempt* thus far to measure marital behavior within a social learning framework" (Jacobson, 1981), that is, the Marital Interaction Coding System, still retain the descriptors, "positive" (e.g., agree, compromise, comply) and "negative" (e.g., criticize, interrupt, disagree) (Jacobson, 1981).

serve as a bench mark for differentiating "successful" from "unsuccessful" marriages. Behaviors reflective of "reciprocity," the desirable
approach to interpersonal influence from a social learning perspective
(Jacobson, 1981), predominate among the P's, and behaviors reflective
of "coercion," the undesirable approach, predominate among the D's.
This classification of items in the SOC may be quite antithetical to a
woman's growth. For example, items such as, "Spouse offered unsoli-
cited advice," "Spouse interrupted me," "Spouse disapproved of something I did," and "Spouse disagreed harshly with something I said,"
are considered D's. To list such items as "D's" is to assert *implicitly* that
such behaviors should either be eliminated from a marriage, or, at least,
maintained at minimal frequencies (Gurman & Knudson, 1978). Translation of such items into the possible checklist responses of a traditional
role-oriented husband, then, might yield a composite list such as, "My
wife should not complain, criticize, interrupt, disagree harshly," etc. To
borrow a phrase from the television show *All in the Family*, "Stifle!" As
one of us has argued elsewhere (Gurman & Knudson, 1978; Gurman *et
al.*, 1978; Knudson *et al.*, 1980), identifying such marital behaviors as a
priori D's, simply because of "the way particular events are *often* experienced by couples" (Jacobson & Weiss, 1978, p. 151), can produce a
decidedly repressive tone in marriage, and one that fosters women's
submission, accommodation, and dependency. It could be argued that
the SOC is not gender biased, in that the categorization of its items
would exert the "same" effect on husbands. Still, we think that, if not
used carefully, the SOC will tend to be used in husband's favor, since
women, of course, often believe in the same gender-stereotyped views
of women as do men, and since most marriage therapists are also men.
Note also the similarity between the expectations of women that may
be reinforced unwittingly within BMT, and two of the major themes
identified by the American Psychological Association's task force on sex
bias in psychotherapy: (1) "Theme: The therapist . . . denies the adaptive and self-actualizing potential of assertiveness for female clients and
fosters concepts of women as passive and dependent" (APA, 1975, p.
1172); (2) "The therapist assumes that problem resolution and self-ac-
tualization for women comes from marriage or perfecting the role of
wife" (APA, 1975, p. 1171). Moreover, as Christenson and Nies (1980)
recently noted, all 100 "we" items on the SOC are P's, implying that
"we-ness" is always good, desirable, and the like. Women's autonomy
is not well served by such a message.

As hard as BM therapists may try to present these P/D lists as "neutral," common marital behaviors (e.g., Jacobson & Weiss, 1978), the likely impact of an expert psychotherapist's presentation of these items is that the modal patient will equate P's with "goodness," and D's with "badness." Efforts to deny such metalevel implications (e.g., Jacobson & Weiss, 1978) appear to us naive and self-deceptive. Moreover, such efforts at denial are not at all consistent with the dominant views within behaviorism regarding the equation of "goodness" with reinforcement. For example, Skinner (1971) states that "good things are positive reinforcers" (p. 103), and Krasner (1977) echoes this view: "That which leads to positive reinforcement for the individual is good; that which leads to aversive consequences is bad" (p. 631). At least two leading BM therapists have acknowledged this danger: "While most therapists strive to not have their values unduly influence their clients, it seems clear that influence occurs by the questions asked . . . and the therapeutic targets the clients are helped to establish . . . often a bias left unsaid may result in a more subtle or insidious influence process which would be counterproductive" (O'Leary & Turkewitz, 1978, pp. 263–264).

PROBLEM DEFINITION AND TREATMENT GOALS IN BEHAVIORAL MARRIAGE AND FAMILY THERAPY

O'Leary and Turkewitz's (1978) observation leads our discussion directly to the area of treatment planning and the establishment of clinical treatment goals. Given the mythical premise that behavioral *technology* is neutral with regard to social values, it follows logically that BMF *therapists* can and should remain nonjudgmental about the desirability of the behavior change objectives expressed by their clients. For example, Jacobson (1981), one of the most influential BM therapists, takes the position that the problem definition phase of BMT should "remain uncontaminated by attempts [by a spouse] to deny the validity of a complaint . . . when a behavior is upsetting to a spouse, it is a priori valid" (p. 569). Thus, it is not the place of either spouse *or* of the therapist to question or challenge either spouse's behavior change goals. Such an apparently benign, even benificent, consumer-oriented attitude is fraught with dangers to women as individuals, and as wives and mothers. For example, consider the following illustration of the results and obvious value-laden implications of one BM therapist's adoption of the "neutral," uninvolved bystander model for therapist behavior advocated by BMFT:

"The husband was more interested in sex than his wife. The husband wanted to have fellatio. The wife's interests ran in the direction of having an ideally furnished apartment; French Provincial furniture was more to her taste. A contract was then negotiated whereby the husband got fellatio fives times a week and the wife . . . got her French Provincial furniture" (Koch & Koch, 1976, p. 40). While such oppressive and sexist behavioral exchanges are rarely implemented under the direction of a truly skilled BM therapist, this unfortunate instance demonstrates the extent to which a "hands-off" stance regarding personal values about intimate relationships on the part of a BM therapist can implicitly perpetuate exceedingly damaging and demeaning notions about how women "ought" to behave, and what they "ought" to do, to gain power and influence in marriage. Although it could be argued that the error in this case was a "human" one, attributable to the insensitivity of *one* particular therapist, to do so would be to deny fundamentally the dangers of self-delusional attempts by psychotherapists to remain value-free.

But we do not need to limit our discussion of misguided attempts at neutrality on feminist value issues to such dramatically offensive instances. More prosaic evidence of such outcomes can be found even in the mainstream of the behavior therapy literature. For example, Jacobson (1979b) recently published a report of a series of six separate single-subject, multiple-baseline marital therapy cases. The behavior change objectives desired by the husbands of their wives in these cases (and achieved in all instances) included behaviors such as increasing the wives' household accomplishments (three cases), and decreasing the wives' verbal criticism (two cases) of their husbands. According to the published report, it appeared unlikely that the therapist ever bothered to inquire whether the wives' behaviors of concern to their husband represented more fundamental gender role attitudes. Without such a clinical inquiry, of course, the possibility of attempting to change such views is quite limited.

This typical acceptance by the BMF therapist of initially stated behavior change objectives may run into difficulty on another score, that is, the assumption that behaviors coded as "positive" and "negative" by behavioral interaction coding schemes such as the Marital Interaction Coding System (Hops, Wills, Patterson, & Weiss, 1976; Weiss & Margolin, 1978), reliably indicate the actual relationship value and meaning of the behaviors. For example, a formerly nonassertive wife may show increased autonomy and the use of overt power through marital therapy, and greatly increase her frequency of verbal disagreement, criticism, and complaints. Such an acceleration of "negative" behaviors may, indeed, betoken her profound efforts to redefine the marital relationship as egalitarian, and as one in which accommodation to her husband's needs and desires has been replaced by a willingness to engage openly in conflict. Nonetheless, failure to attach the clinically appropriate meaning to the appearance of these "negative" behaviors may obscure the *positive* value of purportedly negative verbal behaviors, and the *negative* value of purportedly "positive" behaviors, such as "agree" and "compromise." Conversely, when such "negative" verbal behaviors occur at high rates early in therapy, a significant reduction in their frequency during therapy, as may be requested by a traditionally oriented husband, *may* imply the wife's regression to passive, dependent means of obtaining reinforcement from her husband.

It is also not clear how these measures take account of differences of initial values, or baseline levels, that, in turn, affect the direction of change desired. For example, increases in the frequency of assertive behavior are probably desirable for women with low initial levels of such behavior, whereas no increase in assertiveness may be appropriate for women with high base rates.

It must be noted, however, that methods of marital therapy (e.g., Gurman, 1981) which aim at improving a woman's self-esteem and social competence (Blechman, 1981) necessarily run a higher risk of leading to marital dissolution than do more complacent approaches. As many authors have suggested, and as some recent research also corroborates, however, dissolution of a marriage does not necessarily represent a less than optimal outcome (Cookerly, 1980). It is incumbent on the marital therapist of any theoretical persuasion to acknowledge to his or her patients the real possibility that what may emerge as a successful course of treatment for one spouse may be "unsuccessful" for the dyad qua dyad in terms of the stability of their relationship.

Finally, despite obvious behavioral proclivities to emphasize change in overt behavior, doing so runs the risk of achieving only pseudo-change. For example, at his wife's request, a husband may increase his public involvement in washing the dishes and changing the diapers, yet his private attitude of how he "helps out his wife with *her* tasks" may belie the apparent meaning of hiw newly acquired household behavior. Indeed, the wife of this man may, herself, foster the collusive delusion that her husband has changed his behavior by having come to emphasize genuinely with his wife's "former" dehumanized position in the family.

The husband's motivation for making these behavior changes *may* derive from anticipated negative reinforcement, that is, "I'll do this stuff to get her off my back." However, BMF therapists are warned adamantly about the dangers of attributing intentionality to behavior (e.g., Jacobson, 1977), and such dissimulation is likely to go unnoticed. BM therapists would counter that if there are continuing dissatisfactions, further assessment would be indicated. Unfortunately, if the wife is now satisfied because of her husband's increased household activity, she may believe falsely that "he has really changed." Yet, from a feminist perspective, nothing substantial has changed. In the end, the *appearance* of egalitarianism, without congruent attidues *and* intentions may be worse than straightforward sexism which, at least, can be straightforwardly challenged.

FAMILY INVOLVEMENT IN THE THERAPEUTIC CHANGE PROCESS

In addition to these conceptual and technical aspects of BMFT, there is a structural component of behavioral *family* therapy that often adds fuel to this gender biased fire. Gordon and Davidson (1981), reviewing the literature on behavioral parent training, note that "in almost all reports, mothers are the primary recipients of parent training, with fathers being involved in only a few cases" (p. 531). Gordon and Davidson also note that this impression gleaned from the published literature is representative of everday clinical practice, in which fathers are also much less likely than mothers to participate in behavioral treatment. Their impression of the disproportionate involvement of mothers in parent training has also been documented independently by Patterson and Fleischman (1979) and Gurman and Kniskern (1978a). On empirical grounds alone this practice can be questioned, since there is good reason to expect that, in general, treatment outcomes are enhanced by fathers' participation (Gordon & Davidson, 1980; Gurman & Kniskern, 1978a, 1981b).

Just as offering individual therapy for marital problems to a woman is likely to reinforce a woman's sense of socialized guilt for marital disharmony (Gurman & Klein, 1980), offering parent training to mothers alone implicitly places the responsibility for the major burden of change on her shoulders. In doing so, such behavioral intervention runs the risk of conveying two unintended, yet very damaging, messages: first, as Hare-Mustin (1979) has put it, that the man (husband) is "the doer and woman the nurturer, assuming that traditional roles are necessary for healthy family functioning" (p. 31). Note how such an implication directly parallels one of the major themes put forth by the American Psychological Association's (1975) task force on sex bias in psychotherapy regarding the fostering of traditional sex roles: "Theme: In family therapy or treatment of children, the therapist supports the idea that child rearing and thus the child's problems are solely the responsibility of the mother" (p. 1171).

The second implicit message in such a practice is that the mother alone is not only responsible for effecting change in her child's behavior, but also that she is the *cause* of parent–child conflict or of deviant child behavior. While BMF therapists have never asserted, nor do they believe, that mothers are the primary inducers of childhood psychopathology, the widespread practice of treating the family in the father's absence comes dangerously close to paralleling such historically influential gender-biased notions as that of the so-called "schizophrenogenic" mother (e.g., Jackson, Block, Block, & Patterson, 1958).

Thus, even when an apparently positive treatment outcome may occur in behavioral parent training, that is, in the behavior of the targeted child, this may be achieved at a substantial, though subtle, psychological cost to the mother. In this context, it is interesting to note Patterson and Fleischman's (1979) comment that "one would expect that effective training in child management skills would also increase the mother's self-esteem" (p. 171). To date, no empirical study of behavioral family intervention has included such an outcome measure (cf. Gordon & Davidson, 1981; Gurman & Kniskern, 1978a). Moreover, were such a side-effect outcome to be documented, it could still be argued that the fundamental implicit bias of the necessity of mothers' (and, hence, of fathers') fulfillment of traditional family roles had gone unnoticed and, hence, unchallenged. On the contrary, it is possible, and empirically testable, that by helping mothers whose children show behavior disorders to achieve increased self-esteem by other routes, the child's behavior may change as a consequence, without formal parent training.

ASSESSING THE OUTCOMES OF BEHAVIORAL MARRIAGE AND FAMILY THERAPY

The foregoing discussion is not of solely clinical interest but, indeed, has a direct bearing on the nature of the outcome criteria that typically have been used, and those that should be used, in assessing the outcomes of BMFT. Elsewhere, one of us has presented guidelines for the conduct of family therapy outcome research in general (Gurman & Kniskern, 1978a, 1978b, 1978c, 1981b), and we have offered some recommendations for the evaluation of marital–family therapy outcomes from a feminist perspective (Gurman & Klein, 1980). Here, we will briefly identify the major implications for the choice of outcome criteria that follow from a woman's perspective on the Matching-to-Sample clinical research philosophy, and the application of this approach in BMFT. These implications fall under three related, yet separable, major headings: the use of normative criteria to assess therapeutic outcomes; the meaning and effects of symptom removal; and the levels and sequences of treatment goals.

THE USE OF NORMATIVE CRITERIA TO ASSESS CLINICAL CHANGE

Kazdin and Wilson (1978a, 1978b) have argued that a patient's achievement of "normative levels of behavior after treatment" (Kazdin & Wilson, 1978a, p. 408) is a major criterion on which the importance of therapeutic effects can be based. While acknowledging that for certain populations (e.g., the mentally retarded), normative standards may not be an appropriate criterion, Kazdin and Wilson (1978a) assert that "the limitations of normative data as a universal criterion need not detract from the problem areas where individuals can be *returned to normative levels* of functioning" (p. 408; emphasis added). It is clear that the use of such normative criteria of change, which of course is required by the Matching-to-Sample philosophy, is a risky strategy when attempting to assess marital–family therapy outcome in ways that are sensitive to women's roles. This is especially dangerous in cases where changes in one spouse's attitudes and exvectations (e.g., woman becoming more liberated) is a source of the conflict. Implicit endorsement of change criteria which are likely to be biased against the psychological welfare of women has occurred frequently in the BMFT literature through the use of three particular types of normatively based outcome measures.

First, as suggested earlier, the use of "positive" and "negative" *verbal behaviors* as criteria for assessing BMFT outcomes has the potential for reinforcing stereotypic feminine passivity and nonassertiveness. While there is substantial evidence (e.g., Jacobson, 1979a) that the relative rates of "positive" and "negative" verbal behaviors discriminate between distressed and nondistressed couples, the failure of researchers to attend to the idiosyncratic and contextually personalized meaning of such behaviors *within* particular dyads may obscure the actual relationship implications of such behavior. Thus, there is a need to modify or supplement available behavioral interaction coding systems in order to reflect accurately the clinical and real-life significance of such changes of verbal behavior.

Second, scores on paper-and-pencil *inventories of marital satisfaction* (e.g., Locke & Wallace, 1959), in wide use by BMT researchers (e.g., Jacobson, 1979b), reveal nothing about the sources of satisfaction/ dissatisfaction in the relationship, and the item composition of such inventories often define "successful" marriages in ways that reinforce sex-stereotyped marital standards. Since women are expected to accommodate to their mates' needs more than men (Barry, 1970) to "insure" marital stability, such inventories are problematic from a feminist view. Still, since such inventories do have discriminant validity, they could continue to be used if they are supplemented by independent evidence that, for women, high posttherapy "adjustment" scores are not the result of excessive, personally stultifying accommodation to societally sanctioned relationship styles.

Finally, measures of *family functioning,* in common use in BFT research (Gurman & Kniskern, 1978a), say little about the operative components in a family's transactional style, and even less about how psychological costs and benefits are allocated in the family. Families which are functional (e.g., can provide nurturance, companionship, and socialization for children and can assure internal harmony) by conventional standards may run into great difficulty when confronted with women's emerging demands for alternative family structures, which include altered role responsibilities in areas such as child care, health maintenance, and job involvement. Thus, it is important that behavioral measurement strategies address both the present level of family functioning *and* the relative costs and benefits of such functioning for women. In a word, what is functional for the family *may* be deleterious for women.

As Bergin (1980b) has stated unambiguously, "the goals of therapy are only derivable from value judgments" (p. 12). Behavioral therapists' assertions of the value-free nature of "objective" data notwithstanding, the present analysis leads us to the conclusion that *the use of normative change criteria to assess the efficacy of BMFT, when unsupplemented by other evidence of the clinical significance of therapeutic change, should be viewed with caution, if not outright suspicion.*

THE EFFECTS OF SYMPTOM REMOVAL IN BEHAVIORAL MARRIAGE AND FAMILY THERAPY

As suggested earlier, when a woman is *not* the identified patient (IP) in BFT (as in all cases of childhood behavior as the presenting complaints), the effects, even positive effects, of changes in other family members (e.g., children) must be considered in the light of the secondary consequences of such changes for the woman. When a woman *is* the IP (e.g., as in depression), her symptomatic change is not in itself a sufficient index of a genuinely positive therapeutic outcome. When a woman is *an* IP, but not the only IP (as in cases of marital conflict), measurement of pre- to posttreatment change in targeted overt behavioral "excesses" and "deficits" is similarly insufficient.

LEVELS AND SEQUENCES OF TREATMENT GOALS

In general, BMFT research generally has failed to keep clear the distinction between *mediating* and *ultimate* treatment goals:

> Mediating goals are those which reflect the clinican's assumptions regarding the necessary steps and stages through which a patient must progress if the treatment is to be effective. These goals represent the postulated enabling or intermediate conditions which will permit the attainment of the ultimate goals. The ultimate goals of psychotherapy must, however, go beyond such hypothesized mediating variables as inferences regarding the resolution of neurotic conflicts, growth, . . . etc. (Parloff, 1976, p. 317)

Mediating and ultimate goals in BMFT, as in family therapy in general (Gurman & Klein, 1980), are often confused. For example, improved communication skill may be equated with increased intimacy when it represents only a more efficient, and cautious, style of verbal expression. A redistributed division of household labor may be confused with role flexibility, when it really represents avoidance of fundamental problems of gender role definition.

Gurman and Kniskern (1981b) also consider the temporal aspects of goal selection, and draw a distinction between *initial goals*, that is, those reflecting changes explicitly desired by members or subunits of the family early in treatment, and *emergent goals*, that is, those not explicitly stated at the outset of therapy, but which emerge during the process of treatment. BMFT research, of course, has emphasized exclusively the cinical outcomes of initial goals. Women often present themselves as unduly responsible for marital and family relationship difficulties, often suffer from perceptible social skill deficits such as assertiveness, and often fear that they may ask for "too much" family change, or ask for change "too quickly." Often, it is only after some weeks or months of therapy that such women begin to challenge traditional role allocations and responsibilities. Thus, it is essential that BMFT outcome studies incorporate into their research protocols methods for assessing change involving emergent goals as well as those involving initial goals.

CONCLUSIONS AND RECOMMENDATIONS

In this chapter, it has been argued that behavioral marriage and family therapy unwittingly runs the risk of reinforcing stereotyped views of male and female roles in the family because of an emphasis on normative relationship standards and because of common clinical practices. In this way, BMFT, like behavior therapy in general (cf. Kitchener, 1980), with its emphasis on clinical pragmatism, "consists of straightforward implementation of the values of the dominant social system. In other words, the clinical operation functions within the system. It does not ordinarily question the system but tries to make the system work" (Bergin, 1980a, p. 101).

It is inevitable for the premises and the practice of any psychotherapy to be value laden. This in itself does not constitute an ethical danger. Rather, the danger derives from the possibility that, because of their assertions of objective, data-based neutrality, BMF therapists will ignore the gender-biased premises of important parts of their work. This, in turn, would constrain BMF therapists from responsibly informing clients of values implicit in their treatment methods. While the focus of this discussion has been on marriage and family therapy from a behavioral perspective, it must be emphasized that BMFT hardly stands alone in risking implicit endorsement of family relationship values which may conflict with the overt and best psychological interests of women. Elsewhere, we have elaborated how such endorsements may unwittingly influence the practice of marital therapy from psychodynamic and systems theory perspectives (Foster & Gurman, in press).

Marriage and family therapists should not impose their own personal gender-role values on their clients, whatever these values may be, and no matter how convinced they may be of the moral or psychological goodness of their views. But, as Berger (1979) points out, in order to act responsibly, family therapists must first clarify their own personal values and, second, be willing to acknowledge these values to their clients, so that they do not limit their clients' choices. Indeed, it may not be sufficient for therapists merely to take the initiative in defining their own values, but may also be necessary and even promoting of personal authority and autonomy to explicitly invite patients to define their own marital and family values, and even to inquire about, and at times, challenge, their therapists' values. Moreover, family therapists as a group must be willing to acknowledge the sex-role biases contained in their *professional* views of marriage and family relationships, and in the clinical practices which follow from these views.

ACKNOWLEDGMENTS

The authors are grateful to Laura Giat, Sharon Foster, David Rice, and Dorothea Torstenson for their helpful comments on an earlier draft of this chapter.

REFERENCES

Abramowitz, C. V. Blaming the mother: An experimental investigation of sex-role bias in countertransference. *Psychology of Women Quarterly*, 1977, 2, 24–34.

Alexander, J. F., & Barton, C. Behavioral systems therapy for families. In D. H. L. Olson (Ed.), *Treating relationships*. Lake Mills, Iowa: Graphic, 1976.

American Psychological Association Task Force. Report of the task force on sex bias and sex-role stereotyping in psychotherapeutic practice. *American Psychologist*, 1975, 30, 1169–1175.

American Psychological Association Task Force. Guidelines for therapy with women. *American Psychologist*, 1978, 33, 1122–1123.

Barry, W. A. Marriage research and conflict: An integrative review. *Psychological Bulletin*, 1970, 73, 41–54.

Barton, C., & Alexander, J. F. Functional family therapy. In A. S. Gurman & D. P. Kniskern (Eds.), *Handbook of family therapy*. New York: Brunner/Mazel, 1981.

Bem, S. L., & Bem, D. J. Case study of a nonconscious ideology: Training the woman to know her place. In D. J. Bem, *Beliefs, attitudes and human affairs*. Belmont, Calif.: Brooks/Cole, 1970.

Berger, M. Men's new family roles—Some implications for therapists. *The Family Coordinator*, 1979, 28, 638–646.

Bergin, A. E. Psychotherapy and religious values. *Journal of Consulting and Clinical Psychology*, 1980, 48, 95–105. (a)

Bergin, A. E. Behavior therapy and ethical relativism: Time for clarity. *Journal of Consulting and Clinical Psychology*, 1980, 48, 11–13. (b)

Bergin, A. E., & Garfield, S. L. (Eds.). *Handbook of psychotherapy and behavior change: An empirical analysis*. New York: Wiley, 1971.

Bernard, J. *The future of marriage*. New York: Bantam, 1973.

Blechman, E. Behavior therapies. In A. M. Brodsky & R. T. Hare-Mustin (Eds.), *Women and psychotherapy*. New York: Guilford, 1980.

Blechman, E. A. Competence, depression and behavior modification with women. In M. Hersen, R. Eisler & P. Miller (Eds.), *Progress in behavior modification* (Vol. 12). New York: Academic, 1981.

Blood, R. O., & Wolfe, D. M. *Husbands and wives: The dynamics of married living*. Glencoe, Ill.: Free Press, 1960.

Brodsky, A. M., & Hare-Mustin, R. T. (Eds.). *Women and psychotherapy*. New York: Guilford, 1980.

Chambless, D. L., & Goldstein, A. J. Anxieties: Agoraphobia and hysteria. In A. M. Brodsky & R.T. Hare-Mustin (Eds.), *Women and psychotherapy*. New York: Guilford, 1980.

Chesler, P. *Women and madness*. Garden City, N.Y.: Doubleday, 1972.

Christenson, A., & Nies, D. C. The Spouse Observation Checklist: Empirical analysis and critique. *American Journal of Family Therapy*, 1980, *8*, 69–79.

Cookerly, J. R. Does marital therapy do any lasting good? *Journal of Marital and Family Therapy*, 1980, *6*, 393–397.

Fineberg, B. L., & Lowman, J. Affect and status dimensions of marital adjustment. *Journal of Marriage and the Family*, 1975, *37*, 155–160.

Firestone, S. *The dialectic of sex: The case for feminist revolution*. New York: Morrow, 1970.

Fodor, I. G. The phobic syndrome in women: Implications for treatment. In V. Franks & V. Burtle (Eds.), *Women in therapy*. New York: Brunner/Mazel, 1974.

Foster, S. W., & Gurman, A. S. Social change and couples therapy: A troubled marriage. In C. Nadelson & D. Polonsky (Eds.), *Marriage and divorce: A contemporary perspective*. New York: Guilford, in press.

Garfield, S. L., & Bergin, A. E. (Eds.). *Handbook of psychotherapy and behavior change: An empirical analysis* (2nd ed.). New York: Wiley, 1978.

Goldstein, A. J., & Chambless, D. L. A reanalysis of agoraphobia. *Behavior Therapy*, 1978, *9*, 47–59.

Gordon, S., & Davidson, N. Behavioral parent training. In A. S. Gurman & D. P. Kniskern (Eds.), *Handbook of family therapy*. New York: Brunner/Mazel, 1981.

Gottman, J. M. *Marital interaction:* Experimental investigations. New York: Academic, 1979.

Gove, W. R. The relationship between sex roles, marital status, and mental illness. In A. Kaplan & J. P. Bean (Eds.), *Beyond sex role stereotypes: Readings toward a psychology of androgyny*. Boston: Little, Brown, 1976.

Gove, W., & Tudor, J. Adult sex roles and mental illness. *American Journal of Sociology*, 1973, *78*, 812–835.

Gurman, A. S. Contemporary marital therapies: A critique and comparative analysis of psychoanalytic, behavioral and systems theory approaches. In T. Paolino & B. McCrady (Eds.), *Marriage and marital therapy*. New York: Brunner/Mazel, 1978.

Gurman, A. S. Integrative marital therapy: Toward the development of an interpersonal approach. In S. H. Budman (Ed.), *Forms of brief therapy*. New York: Guilford, 1981.

Gurman, A. S., & Klein, M. H. Marital and family conflicts. In A. M. Brodsky & R. T. Hare-Mustin (Eds.), *Women and psychotherapy*. New York: Guilford, 1980.

Gurman, A. S., & Kniskern, D. P. Research on marital and family therapy: Progress, perspective and prospect. In S. Garfield & A. Bergin (Eds.), *Handbook of psychotherapy and behavior change* (2nd ed.). New York: Wiley, 1978. (a)

Gurman, A. S., & Kniskern, D. P. Behavioral marriage therapy: II. Empirical perspective. *Family Process*, 1978, *12*, 139–148. (b)

Gurman, A. S., & Kniskern, D. P. Deterioration in marriage and family therapy: Empirical, clinical and conceptual issues. *Family Process*, 1978, *17*, 3–20. (c)

Gurman, A. S., & Kniskern, D. P. (Eds.). *Handbook of family therapy*. New York: Brunner/Mazel, 1981. (a)

Gurman, A. S., & Kniskern, D. P. Family therapy outcome research: Knowns and unknowns. In A. S. Gurman & D. P. Kniskern (Eds.), *Handbook of family therapy*. New York: Brunner/Mazel, 1981. (b)

Gurman, A. S., & Knudson, R. M. Behavioral marriage therapy: I. A psychodynamic-systems analysis and critique. *Family Process*, 1978, *17*, 121–138.

Gurman, A. S., Knudson, R. M., & Kniskern, D. P. Behavioral marriage therapy: IV. Take two aspirin and call us in the morning. *Family Process*, 1978, *17*, 165–180.

Gurman, A. S., & Razin, A. M. *Effective psychotherapy: A handbook of research*. New York: Pergamon, 1977.

Hare-Mustin, R. T. A feminist approach to family therapy. *Family Process*, 1978, *17*, 181–194.

Hare-Mustin, R. T. Family therapy and sex role stereotypes. *The Counseling Psychologist*, 1979, *8*, 31–32.

Hicks, M. W., & Platt, M. Marital happiness and stability: A review of the research in the sixties. *Journal of Marriage and the Family*, 1970, *32*, 59–78.

Hines, P. M., & Hare-Mustin, R. T. Ethical concerns in family therapy. *Professional Psychology*, 1978, *9*, 165–171.

Hops, H., Wills, T., Patterson, G., & Weiss, R. *Marital Interaction Coding System*. Unpublished manuscript, University of Oregon, 1976.

Jackson, D. D., Block, J., Block, J. E., & Patterson, V. Psychiatric conceptions of the schizophrenic patient. *AMA Archives of Neurology and Psychiatry*, 1958, *79*, 448–459.

Jacobson, N. S. Training couples to solve their marital problems: A behavioral approach to relationship discord: Part I. Problem-solving skills. *International Journal of Family Counseling*, 1977, *4*, 22–31.

Jacobson, N. S. A review of the research on the effectiveness of marital therapy. In T. Paolino & B. McCrady (Eds.), *Marriage and marital therapy*. New York: Brunner/Mazel, 1978.

Jacobson, N. S. Increasing positive behavior in severely distressed marital relationships: The effects of problem-solving training. *Behavior Therapy*, 1979, *10*, 311–326. (a)

Jacobson, N. S. Behavioral treatments for marital discord: A critical appraisal. In M. Hersen, R. Eisler, & P. Miller (Eds.), *Progress in behavior modification* (Vol. 7). New York: Academic, 1979. (b)

Jacobson, N. S. Behavioral marital therapy. In A. S. Gurman & D. P. Kniskern (Eds.), *Handbook of family therapy*. New York: Brunner/Mazel, 1981.

Jacobson, N. S., & Margolin, G. *Marital therapy: Strategies based on social learning and behavior exchange principles*. New York: Brunner/Mazel, 1979.

Jacobson, N. S., & Weiss, R. L. Behavioral marriage therapy: III. The contents of Gurman et al. may be hazardous to our health. *Family Process*, 1978, *17*, 149–163.

Kazdin, A., & Wilson, G. T. Criteria for evaluating psychotherapy. *Archives of General Psychiatry*, 1978, *35*, 407–416. (a)

Kazdin, A., & Wilson, G. T. *Evaluation of behavior therapy: Issues, evidence and research strategies*. Cambridge, Mass.: Ballinger, 1978. (b)

Kitchener, R. F. Ethical relativism and behavior therapy. *Journal of Consulting and Clinical Psychology*, 1980, *48*, 1–7.

Klein, M. H. Feminist concepts of therapy outcome. *Psychotherapy: Theory, Research and Practice*, 1976, *13*, 89–95.

Knudson, R. M., Gurman, A. S., & Kniskern, D. P. Behavioral marriage therapy: A treatment in transition. In C. M. Franks & G. T. Wilson (Eds.), *Annual review of behavior therapy: Theory and practice* (Vol. 7). New York: Brunner/Mazel, 1980.

Koch, J., & Koch, L. *The marriage savers*. New York: Coward, McCann & Geoghegan, 1976.

Krasner, L. Behavior modification: Ethical issues and future trends. In H. Leitenberg (Ed.), *Handbook of behavior modification*. Englewood Cliffs, N.J.: Prentice-Hall, 1977.

Laws, J. L. A feminist review of marital adjustment literature: The rape of the Locke. *Journal of Marriage and the Family*, 1971, *33*, 483–516.

Lazarus, A. A. Women in behavior therapy. In V. Franks & V. Burtle (Eds.), *Women in therapy*. New York: Brunner/Mazel, 1974.

Locke, H. J., & Wallace, K. M. Short marital adjustment and prediction tests: Their reliability and validity. *Marriage and Family Living*, 1959, *21*, 251–255.

Magnus, E. C. *Measurement of counselor bias (sex-role stereotyping) in assessment of marital couples with traditional and non-traditional interaction patterns* (Doctoral dissertation, University of Georgia, 1975). *Dissertion Abstracts International*, 1975, *36*, 4026–4027A.

Meltzoff, J., & Kornreich, M. *Research in psychotherapy*. Chicago: Atherton, 1970.

O'Leary, K. D., & Turkewitz, H. Treatment of marital disorders from a behavioral perspective. In T. Paolino & B. McCrady (Eds.), *Marriage and marital therapy*. New York: Brunner/Mazel, 1978.

Paris, B. L., & Luckey, E. B. A longitudinal study in marital satisfaction. *Sociological and Social Research*, 1966, *50*, 212–222.

Parloff, M. B. The narcissism of small differences—and some big ones. *International Journal of Group Psychotherapy*, 1976, *26*, 311–319.

Parsons, B. & Alexander, J. F. Short-term family intervention: A therapy outcome study. *Journal of Consulting and Clinical Psychology*, 1973, *41*, 195–201.

Patterson, G. R. & Fleischman, M. J. Maintenance of treatment effects: Some considerations concerning family systems and follow-up data. *Behavior Therapy*, 1979, *10*, 168–185.

Perlin, L. I. & Johnson, J. S. Marital status, life-strains and depression. *American Sociological Review*, 1977, *42*, 704–715.

Radloff, L. S. Sex differences in depression: The effects of occupation and marital status. *Sex Roles*, 1975, *1*, 249–265.

Rice, D. G., & Rice, J. K. Non-sexist "marital" therapy. *Journal of Marriage and Family Counseling*, 1977, *3*, 3–9.

Rich, A. *Of woman born*. New York: Norton, 1976.

Skinner, B. F. *Beyond freedom and dignity*. New York: Knopf, 1971.

Tennov, D. *Psychotherapy: The hazardous cure*. New York: Abelard-Schuman, 1975.

Weiss, R. L. *Spouse Observation Checklist*. Unpublished manuscript, University of Oregon, 1975.

Weiss, R. L. The conceptualization of marriage and marriage disorders from a behavioral perspective. In T. Paolino & B. McCrady (Eds.), *Marriage and marital therapy*. New York: Brunner/Mazel, 1978.

Weiss, R. L., & Margolin, G. Marital conflict and accord. In A. R. Ciminero, M. S. Calhoun, & H. E. Adams (Eds.), *Handbook of behavioral assessment*. New York: Wiley, 1978.

Weissman, M., & Klerman, G. L. Sex differences and the epidemiology of depression. *Archives of General Psychiatry*, 1977, *34*, 98–111.

8

PARENTING: TRAINING MOTHERS AS BEHAVIOR THERAPISTS FOR THEIR CHILDREN

CYD C. STRAUSS
BEVERLY M. ATKESON

OVERVIEW

Over the past 15 to 20 years the role of the behavioral psychologist working with children has gradually changed from that of direct change agent to consultant (Tharp & Wetzel, 1969). Instead of treating the child directly, the child behavior therapist most often works with the child's parents to teach them effective skills and techniques to apply to their child's problems. A relatively large research literature now exists under the heading "parents as behavior therapists" (Graziano, 1977; Lutzker, 1980; O'Dell, 1974).

The term "parents" is a misnomer, however. Parent training often involves just mothers and their children (Berkowitz & Graziano, 1972; Hughes & Haynes, 1978; Lutzker, 1980). Fathers have been included in only a few studies (Azrin & Thienes, 1978; Eyberg & Johnson, 1974; Wahler, 1969). Despite the change in work patterns and the shifting role of women in our society, mothers still have primary responsibility for child rearing and for assistance in the treatment of troubled children (Graziano, 1977).

This chapter first reviews the parent training literature with special emphasis on target behaviors, populations, skills, and training techniques. Second, the chapter focuses on assessment and treatment issues of special concern to child behavior therapists—issues that may have

Cyd C. Strauss and Beverly M. Atkeson. Department of Psychology, University of Georgia, Athens, Georgia.

impact on the outcome of parent training. In addition, the causes of child behavior problems are discussed. Finally, recommendations concerning the treatment of mothers and their children are made.

BACKGROUND

Parent training methods have been applied to a variety of child behavior problems. Characteristics of the children targeted for treatment, and to a lesser extent, characteristics of their mothers, have varied also. Most frequently, therapists have used a combination of training strategies to teach mothers to improve the way in which they consequate child behaviors.

PROBLEM BEHAVIORS

Parent training techniques have been applied most often to child behaviors that can generally be described as "out of control." Mothers have been taught to reduce their children's aggressiveness toward others (hitting, kicking, fighting), physical destructiveness, disobedience, temper tantrums, high-rate annoying behaviors (yelling, whining, high activity level), and community rule violations such as stealing and fire setting (Bernal, Duryee, Pruett, & Burns, 1968; Patterson, 1974; Peed, Roberts, & Forehand, 1977). These problem behaviors have been labeled noncompliance (Forehand & McMahon, 1981), aggression (Patterson, 1976), and oppositional behavior (Wahler, 1969, 1980).

Mothers have also been trained as change agents for school-related problems. They have been taught to decrease their children's disruptive behaviors in the classroom (Ayllon, Garber, & Pisor, 1975) and to increase their children's academic behaviors in school (Bailey, Wolf, & Phillips, 1970; Schumaker, Hovell, & Sherman, 1977) and at home (Hall, Cristler, Cranston, & Tucker, 1970; Ryback & Staats, 1970). They have also been included in the treatment of school phobias (Ayllon, Smith, & Rogers, 1970; Hersen, 1970; Tahmisian & McReynolds, 1971) and truancy (MacDonald, Gallimore, & MacDonald, 1970; Thorne, Tharp, & Wetzel, 1967). In treatment of most school-related problems mothers have worked with teachers as change agents and provided home-based reinforcement (Atkeson & Forehand, 1979).

In addition, mothers have used *in vivo* desensitization procedures to reduce the fear of riding a bus (Luiselli, 1978), of loud noises (Stableford, 1979; Tasto, 1969), and of water (Bentler, 1962). They have eliminated daytime and bedtime thumb-sucking (Knight & McKenzie, 1974; Ross, 1975), enuresis (Azrin & Thienes, 1978), encopresis (Crowley & Armstrong, 1977), and constipation (Wright & Bunch, 1977). Mothers of normal children have been taught to reduce less deviant, annoying child behavior during shopping trips (Barnard, Christopherson, & Wolf, 1977), to improve mealtime conversations (Jewett & Clark, 1978), and to keep children in automobile safety seats (Christophersen, 1977).

SAMPLE CHARACTERISTICS

Children treated have ranged in age from preschool (Reisinger & Ora, 1977) to adolescent (Weathers & Liberman, 1975), and have included mentally retarded (Arnold, Sturgis, & Forehand, 1977), learning disabled (Doleys, Doster, & Cartelli, 1976), autistic (Luiselli, 1978), delinquent (Alexander & Parsons, 1973), and hyperactive (Crozier & Katz, 1979) children. Most have been males, although females also have been treated.

Although mothers' demographic and behavioral characteristics are often not documented, the majority of mothers trained have been White and middle-class (Hargis & Blechman, 1979). Psychotic or severely maladjusted mothers have typically been excluded from parent training; however, abusive parents have recently received some attention from behavioral researchers (Reid, Taplin, & Lorber, 1980). Investigators are now beginning to study the influence of maternal adjustment on initial treatment contact, treatment outcome, and maintenance of treatment gains (Griest & Forehand, in press).

PARENTING SKILLS

Parent training programs have generally focused on differential reinforcement of appropriate behaviors and punishment or extinction of inappropriate behaviors. For example, Hall, Axelrod, Tyler, Grief, Jones, and Robertson (1972) had one mother given her child money each time he wore an orthodontic device, which resulted in the desired outcome.

Other mothers have learned to reward compliance (Jason, 1977), non-aggressive behavior (Zeilberger, Sampen, & Sloane, 1968), and appropriate sibling interactions (Lavigueur, 1976).

Differential positive reinforcement generally is not effective in modifying the behavior of problem children unless used in combination with some form of punishment (Forehand & Atkeson, 1977). Time out is the most frequently employed punishment procedure in parent training (Nay, 1979; O'Dell, Krug, O'Quin, & Kasnetz, 1980; Zeilberger *et al.*, 1968). In time out the mother takes the child from the site where the inappropriate behavior occurred and places the child in a chair or other location so that the child is away from parental attention or other positive sources of reward for a fixed period of time. Time out is generally effective, avoids physical harm to the child, and produces few side effects (Powers & Osborne, 1976).

Token reinforcement systems have also been combined with differential reinforcement. Bucher and Raume (1979) arranged a token system in which parents gave points to their 8-year-old daughter when she picked up her toys. The points were later exchanged for concrete rewards. Not only was there an increase in frequency of the targeted behavior but also in three related behaviors (e.g., picking up clothing). Parents have used token systems to increase compliance with a drug regimen for a child with phenylketonuria (Fox & Roseen, 1977), to decrease hair pulling (Gray, 1979), to increase completion of chores (Hall *et al.*, 1972), and to decrease eating time during meals (Sanok & Ascione, 1978).

Most parent training programs have focused on consequating appropriate and inappropriate child behaviors. Relatively little attention has been given to antecedents to child behavior (Forehand, King, Peed, & Yoder, 1975; Patterson, 1976, 1977). However, some parent trainers have instructed parents in the use of appropriate commands with children (Forehand & Peed, 1979).

In the treatment of families with older children and adolescents, both the parents and the child acquire new skills. In most interventions families learn to negotiate contingency contracts in which the rights and responsibilities of each family member are clearly specified (Alexander & Parsons, 1973; Stuart, 1971; Weathers & Liberman, 1975). Frequently families are also trained in problem-solving and communication skills (Alexander & Parsons, 1973; Blechman, 1980; Robin, Kent, O'Leary, Foster, & Prinz, 1977).

INTERVENTION STRATEGIES

Combinations of several intervention strategies are usually used to teach behavioral skills and principles to mothers (McMahon & Forehand, 1978). In most cases, didactic instruction is combined with skill practice. Verbal instruction is widely used; manuals also have been developed to teach the use of time out (Johnson, Whitman, & Barloon-Noble, 1978), differential reinforcement (McMahon & Forehand, 1978), and shaping of desired behavior (Kelley, Embry, & Baer, 1979). Perhaps the most widely used programmed written manuals are Patterson and Gullion's (1968) *Living with Children* and Becker's (1971) *Parents Are Teachers*. Videotapes, audiotapes, and *in vivo* demonstrations of parenting skills have all been used to augment instructions. Combinations of behavior rehearsal, corrective feedback, and positive reinforcement of successive approximations of the desired parent behavior have also gained widespread use (Crozier & Katz, 1979; Forehand & McMahon, 1981; Robin et al., 1977). Therapists have cued and reinforced mothers during behavior rehearsal over a miniature radio transmitter a mother wears in her ear (Forehand & King, 1977) and with hand and light signals (Lavigueur, 1976; Wahler, Winkel, Peterson, & Morrison, 1965; Weathers & Liberman, 1975).

In order to insure treatment completion, some investigators have made therapy sessions contingent on parental attendance and homework completion (Eyberg & Johnson, 1974; Mira, 1970). Others have provided contingent payment or fee reduction (O'Dell, Blackwell, Larcen, & Hogan, 1977). McMahon and Forehand (1978) and O'Dell, Blackwell, Larcen, and Hogan (1977) have made advancement through steps in the therapy program contingent on parental skill acquisition. Therapist attention and family members' approval have been used to promote continued application of newly acquired problem-solving and parenting skills (Blechman, 1980; Kelley et al., 1979).

Despite its critical importance, maintenance of parental behavior changes has received less attention than initial acquisition of skills (Conway & Bucher, 1976; Stokes & Baer, 1977). Instruction in self-control, instruction in social learning principles, and intermittent contact following treatment have all been used in efforts to facilitate maintenance of parenting skills. For example, Wells, Griest, and Forehand (1980) compared parent training alone with parent training plus parent self-control training. In self-control training, mothers monitored and rewarded themselves for using their new skills during the 2-month follow-up. At posttreatment, the two conditions did not differ but, 2 months later, children whose mothers received parent and self-control training were less deviant and more compliant. It is not clear how this result came about since the skills of the two groups of parents did not differ at follow-up.

Instruction of parents in social learning principles has been added to parent training programs to enhance maintenance of treatment gains. McMahon, Forehand, and Griest (1981) found parent satisfaction, parent knowledge of social learning principles, parent perceptions of child adjustment, and targeted parent and child behaviors to be superior at a 2-month follow-up when mothers received additional training in social learning principles. Since mothers who were taught social learning principles and parenting skills received extra therapy time, it is unclear whether additional training in parenting skills also would have led to the same outcome. In a smaller study, Glogower and Sloop (1976) also found that instruction in general behavioral principles facilitated parent training. They equated the number of treatment sessions in the groups that received parent training alone and parent training plus behavioral principles. This eliminated differences in therapeutic time as an alternative explanation of the findings.

Regular contacts have also been used to enhance maintenance (Patterson, Cobb, & Ray, 1973; Worland, Carney, Milich, & Grame, 1980). Worland et al. (1980) used telephone calls to obtain daily reports of child behavior during training and to promote the use of new skills. Patterson et al. (1973) maintained telephone contact with parents after treatment and provided periodic retraining to help sustain behavior changes. Wahler (1975) also found it necessary to "fade out" therapy with posttreatment "booster" sessions.

Training techniques that promote acquisition and maintenance of parenting skills have been combined to form standardized training programs. Treatment programs developed by Gerald Patterson and his colleagues, Rex Forehand and his associates, and Robert Wahler and his co-workers have received widespread interest from researchers and clinicians.

Patterson's program was developed for young, aggressive children. A description of the treatment procedures has been provided by Patterson (1974, p. 473). This treatment package has been evaluated extensively by Patterson and his co-workers (Arnold, Levine, & Patterson,

1975; Fleischman & Szykula, 1981; Patterson, 1974; Patterson & Reid, 1973; Taplin & Reid, 1977; Weinrott, Bauske, & Patterson, 1979).

Another standardized parent training program was designed by Hanf (Hanf & Kling, 1973). Forehand and his associates have modified Hanf's program for use with 3- to 8-year-old children and have provided evidence of short- and long-term effects on mother and child behavior (Forehand & King, 1977; Forehand, Sturgis, McMahon, Aguar, Green, Wells, & Breiner, 1979; Forehand, Wells, & Griest, 1980; Peed et al., 1977). Forehand's modification of the Hanf program incorporates written and verbal instructions, modeling, role playing with the therapist and with the child, prompting and feedback, and use of a bug-in-the-ear device. McMahon, Forehand, and Griest (1981) have provided a detailed summary of this treatment program.

Wahler's (1980) treatment program incorporates instruction, modeling, prompting, behavioral rehearsal and feedback, and fading of the treatment procedures. The program follows a baseline period of 4 to 6 weeks, during which child opposition, specific aspects of the mother's behaviors (e.g., yelling and scolding), and social interactions are observed. Wahler's parent training program has been shown to produce short-term reductions in children's oppositional behavior, as well as reductions in mother's excessive use of yelling and scolding. Unfortunately, as is typical of many parent training programs, treatment changes were not maintained over an 8-month to 1-year follow-up period (Wahler, 1980).

Although several researchers have worked with parents and their adolescent children in training them to use contingency contracting, problem solving skills, and communications skills, only a few standardized treatment programs have been presented in the literature. Blechman (1980) has designed board games which guide families through the negotiation of contingency contracts. At the same time, families acquire problem-solving strategies which can later be applied to novel problems. Alexander and Parsons (1973; Parsons & Alexander, 1973) have developed a family intervention program designed to increase family reciprocity, clarity of communication, and contingency contracting. Martin (1977) and Robin et al. (1977) have shifted the focus away from contingent refinforcement of target behavior to the acquisition of sets of communication, problem-solving, and self-expression skills. Various strategies have been incorporated into adolescent treatment programs: modeling, behavioral rehearsal, phone monitoring, prompting, praise, and training manuals.

CAUSAL FACTORS

The selection of mothers as therapists for their children is predicated on the assumption that the environment is influential in controlling child behavior. To produce lasting changes in problem behaviors, behavior therapists attempt to modify the environment—primarily the mother's behavior. A possible deduction from the above is that the mother has in some way caused her child's behavior problems or is, at the least, maintaining these problems.

Evidence supporting this deduction comes from studies that compare the behavior of mothers of clinic and nonclinic child populations. Some of these studies suggest that mothers of clinic-referred children contribute to their children's behavior problems. For example, Cunningham and Barkley (1979) observed mothers while interacting with normal and hyperactive sons during free play and structured tasks prior to implementation of treatment. They found that mothers of hyperactive boys provided less positive attention contingent on their children's social, play, and compliant on-task behaviors than mothers of normal boys. Mothers of hyperactive children were more controlling and provided more structure during play, task-related activities, and social interactions than mothers of nonhyperactive children. Campbell (1975) also found that mothers of hyperactive children were more controlling and involved in their children's attempts to complete tasks than mothers of normal children. Forehand *et al.* (1975) compared mother–child interactions of clinic and nonclinic families during free play and found that clinic mothers issued significantly more commands to their children than nonclinic mothers.

A number of other studies, however, have failed to find differences in the parenting behavior of mothers of clinic and of nonclinic children. Forehand *et al.* (1980) compared mothers of noncompliant children and of nonproblem children and found no pretreatment differences in their behavior toward their children. Griest, Forehand, Wells, and McMahon (1980) and Lobitz and Johnson (1975) also found no differences between families referred for treatment and nonclinic families.

Even when differences are found in maternal behavior between normal and clinical populations, it is not clear that the behavior of the mother has produced the maladaptive behavior of the child. Bell (1968) has argued that just the opposite may be true; that is, differences in maternal behavior may be caused by differences in child behavior. Evidence supporting this view has been reported by Barkley and Cunningham (1979). They found that mothers of hyperactive children reduced their use of directiveness and increased their use of positive attention contingent on compliance when their children showed increased compliance after being treated with the drug methylphenidate (Ritalin). Further, Whalen, Henker, and Dotemoto (1980) showed that teachers exhibited more intense and controlling modes of interacting with hyperactive children who were given placebos than with either hyperactive children who received methylphenidate or normal comparison children. When hyperactive children behaved more "normally" in these studies as a result of drug treatment, their mothers and teachers behaved more "normally" toward them. This supports Bell's contention that the parenting strategies used by mothers are a reaction to their child's misbehavior rather than a cause of it.

It is not necessary to accept either the position that the behavior of parents causes the behavior of their children or vice versa. In fact, it is more appropriate to assume that the behavior of the child and parent reciprocally affect each other. Bandura (1977) has suggested that most psychological factors that are causally related exert their influence in a bidirectional manner.

Patterson (1976) has proposed a behavioral formulation for the development and maintenance of aggressive behaviors in children which emphasizes the reciprocity between mother and child behaviors. According to his "coercion hypothesis," rudimentary aversive behaviors (e.g., crying) may be instinctual in the newborn infant. Such behaviors shape the mother in the skills necessary for the infant's survival. As most infants develop, prosocial verbal and social skills replace rudimentary coercive behaviors. However, some children continue to use aversive behaviors to control their environment. Patterson and Reid (1973) have proposed that negative reinforcement may escalate and maintain coercive behaviors. In the negative reinforcement model, coercive behavior on the part of one family member is reinforced when it results in the termination of aversive behavior by another family member. The following sequence illustrates negative reinforcement of coercive behavior: (1) The mother issues a command; which leads to (2) whining and crying by the child; which causes (3) the mother to withdraw the command to stop her child's continued crying. In this manner, the child's aversive behavior (whining and crying) is negatively reinforced by the removal of the original command. Escalation of coercive behavior occurs in the next sequence: (1) The mother gives a command; (2) the child whines and cries again; (3) the mother raises her voice and reissues the command; (4) the child cries even louder; (5) yelling, the mother repeats the command; and (6) the child finally complies. The mother's aversive behavior is thus reinforced by the child's eventual compliance. In both examples, negative reinforcement increases the future probability of coercion by mother and child. Furthermore, if this style of interacting continues over long periods of time, significant increases in the rate and intensity of coercive behaviors would occur as family members are reinforced for engaging in aggressive behaviors.

In sum, research examining causal factors in child behavior problems supports a bidirectional model in which mother–child interactions produce maladaptive behaviors in both the mother and the child. Therapists working with mothers to modify their children's behavior problems should be sensitive to this issue. Because mothers have the major responsibility for child rearing in our society, they are also frequently blamed for their children's problems. Within a behavioral framework, neither family member is at fault although the goal of therapy is the modification of mother–child interactions. Even this model is not without limitations in that it ignores the possibility that other factors may be contributing to either the mother's or the child's problem behaviors. Careful pretreatment assessment is always needed to insure that mother–child interactions are the appropriate targets for modification.

MAINTENANCE AND GENERALITY OF TREATMENT EFFECTS

Behavior therapists have developed numerous procedures to train mothers as direct change agents for children's problem behaviors. Early clinical and research efforts were aimed for immediate improvements. With time, behavior therapists have come to realize that this goal is inadequate. Attention has now focused on the maintenance and generality of treatment effects, the cost effectiveness of different treatment procedures, and the importance of client variables to treatment referral and outcome.

Four types of generalization of treatment effects are distinguished in the literature (Forehand & Atkeson, 1977). Temporal generality or maintenance refers to the durability of mother and child behavior changes over time. Setting generality concerns the occurrence of behavior changes outside of the therapy setting, (e.g., home, school, car, supermarket). Behavioral generality refers to changes in child behaviors other than those targeted for treatment. Sibling generality refers to changes in the treated child's siblings.

Various strategies have been used to enhance maintenance of treatment effects. Researchers have made reduced fees and therapy sessions contingent upon completed homework assignments and regular therapy attendance (Eyberg & Johnson, 1974; O'Dell, Blackwell, Larcen, & Hogan, 1977). Another approach used to improve temporal generality is instruction of parents in the behavioral principles that underlie treatment techniques (Glogower & Sloop, 1976; McMahon, Forehand, & Griest, 1981). Wahler (1975) and Patterson (1974) maintained contact following treatment termination and provided "booster" sessions to facilitate maintenance of parent and child behavior changes. Instruction in self-control has been reported to improve maintenance of treatment effects (Wells et al., 1980). A final approach involves the gradual fading of treatment (Hall et al., 1972; Herbert & Baer, 1972). When studies do not include procedures designed to enhance temporal generality, conflicting results are obtained. Some report that treatment changes are maintained at follow-up (Forehand et al., 1979; Patterson, 1974) while others do not (Wahler, 1980).

Because most parent training occurs in the clinic, generality of treatment effects to other settings is essential. Few studies have determined empirically which procedures facilitate setting generality. Glogower and Sloop (1976) and O'Dell, Flynn, and Benlolo (1977) both presented lectures on behavioral principles to parents. Glogower and Sloop (1976) found that teaching behavioral principles led to more positive outcomes in the home, while O'Dell, Flynn, and Benlolo (1977) did not. Blechman (1980) showed that problem-solving skills transferred from the clinic to the home when praise was provided for successes during therapy but not when praise and a monetary payment was used. Other techniques which may enhance setting generality are discussion of this topic with mothers during treatment (Forehand & McMahon, 1981; Mash, Lazere, Terdal, & Garner, 1973), homework assignments (Bernal et al., 1968; Forehand & McMahon, 1981), and use of a simulated home environment for clinic treatment (Hanf & Kling, 1973).

Behavioral generality should reduce the number of child behaviors targeted for treatment and prevent future behavior problems. Patterson and his colleagues (Patterson, 1974; Patterson & Reid, 1973; Wiltz & Patterson, 1974) have assessed the effects of intervention on both target and nontarget behaviors. They found significant decreases in target but not in nontarget behaviors. Other investigators have obtained similar results (Moore & Bailey, 1973; Resick, Forehand, & McWhorter, 1976). Since just a few studies have found spontaneous behavioral generality resulting from parent training (Sajwaj & Hedges, 1971; Zeilberger et al., 1968), researchers have begun to design procedures to enhance change in nontarget behaviors. The effects of providing information about behavior management principles have been inconsistent: One study found that behavioral generality was enhanced by information (Glogower & Sloop, 1976) while the other study did not (O'Dell, Flynn, & Benlolo, 1977).

Sibling generality, according to Lavigueur, Peterson, Sheese, and Peterson (1973), may result from any of the following: The parents apply skills to siblings of the treated child and change sibling behavior, the sibling observes and imitates the target child's appropriate behavior, and the sibling receives less attention from parents for deviant behavior. In a case study, Lavigueur et al. (1973) reported that an untreated sibling's behavior improved when parent training focused on another child in the family; the mother provided less attention for the sibling's undesirable behavior, with consequent reductions in inappropriate behavior. In a group-comparison study of parent training (Humphreys, Forehand, McMahon, & Roberts, 1978), parenting behaviors and the untreated sibling's behavior improved. Lavigueur (1976) used parents and siblings in two families as behavior modifiers with positive effects on siblings' behavior. Siblings improved on the specific behavior that was treated in the target child and reduced their general output of inappropriate behavior. In these and other studies (Arnold et al., 1975; Resick et al., 1976), parent training appeared to benefit sibling behavior; however, these studies have had small samples and sometimes have treated the sibling directly.

To summarize, parent training has been effective in producing short-term behavior changes in both parents and children. Maintenance of these behavior changes has been more problematic. Generalization to nontarget behaviors, siblings of the treated child, and to new settings has not been consistently demonstrated. Additional investigations of appropriate methods for promoting maintenance and generalization are needed.

COST EFFECTIVENESS OF TREATMENT

Presentation of parenting skills via written materials is the least expensive means of teaching behavioral methods to mothers, since it involves little therapist time. The low cost of written presentation must be weighed against the efficacy of this approach. Johnson and Green (1978) found that written instruction produced durable effects when teaching one mother to use time-out procedures, but found auditory cues as well as written instruction were needed when teaching a second mother to use differential reinforcement and time out. In a report of three case studies, Green, Budd, Johnson, Lang, Pinkston, and Rudd (1974) compared three techniques for teaching the use of time out: written and verbal instructions, written and verbal instructions plus an auditory signal indicating when to use time out, and modeling. Although all three techniques produced positive outcomes, the authors preferred written and verbal instructions alone because of their low cost. McMahon and Forehand (1978) used a multiple-baseline design to examine the effect of written materials on the frequency of inappropriate mealtime behaviors in three children. The written manual provided a rationale for using the recommended time out and differential reinforcement procedures, instructions in appropriate use of these two techniques, and illustrations of how time out and differential reinforcement can be used at mealtime. Therapist contact with the three mothers was confined to provision of the written materials and explanation of the treatment program. This procedure substantially reduced rates of inappropriate mealtime behaviors and improved parenting behaviors, with maintenance at a 6-week follow-up. These results suggest that written instructions alone can produce favorable outcomes in certain targeted behaviors.

O'Dell (1978) and his colleagues have evaluated various training techniques with inconsistent results. A study which compared a written manual alone, a film plus a written manual, and a no-treatment condition found no differences in parents' acquisition of time-out skills (O'Dell, Krug, Patterson, & Faustman, 1980). However, the three treatment groups performed better than the no-treatment group on a multiple-choice exam and an in-home assessment of parents' use of time-out skills with a child actor. In contrast, O'Dell, Mahoney, Horton, and Turner (1979) found that mothers who received a film plus individual rehearsal and "check out" of understanding of methods did better than mothers who received no treatment, exposure to a written manual alone, or individual modeling and rehearsal alone, on the Time-Out Situation Test of skill acquisition. There were no significant differences among treatment groups in reported satisfaction with training, comprehension and memory of the material, or parents' use of time out. Nay (1975) also found that parents learned time-out skills better from modeling and modeling-plus-role-playing than from written instructions and lecture.

In a third study, O'Dell and co-workers (O'Dell, Krug, O'Quin, & Kasnetz, 1980) found no differences in mothers' abilities to implement time out when the following parent training methods were compared: written manual alone, written manual and individual check out, audiotape alone, audiotape plus individual check out, and modeling and behavioral rehearsal. Finally, O'Dell and his colleagues (O'Dell, O'Quin, Alford, O'Briant, Bradlyn, & Giebenhain, 1980) contrasted four different techniques for teaching parents to dispense positive reinforcement: a written manual, an audiotape containing the same material as the manual, videotaped modeling, and live modeling and rehearsal with the child. When compared with no training, all of the training procedures led to better performances on a home assessment. Of the four training techniques, the least effective was the audiotape.

Although group parent training has been found effective (Diament & Coletti, 1978; Ferber, Keeley, & Shemberg, 1974; Glogower & Sloop, 1976), the cost effectiveness of group versus individual parent training is unclear. Grief (1978) found that group training was more efficient, while Mira (1970) found that individual training was superior. Worland et al. (1980) showed that no additional benefits resulted when individual training was added to group training with "hard-to-manage" children.

In summary, no technique has consistently been found to be superior in changing both mother and child behaviors. Equivocal results may be due to several factors. First, the effectiveness of treatment methods may vary with mothers' educational and intellectual levels. O'Dell, O'Quin, Alford, O'Briant, Bradlyn, and Giebenhain (1980) found that only the videotape technique was equally effective at all levels of socioeconomic status, educational attainment, and reading competence. Instruction via written manual, audiotape, and live modeling and rehearsal was most effective with educated clients. Second, effectiveness may depend upon the skills taught and the behaviors targeted for change. The studies reviewed trained mothers in the use of time out, differential reinforcement, or both. In some studies the use of these skills was confined to a single behavior; in others, a variety of child behaviors was targeted. Finally, equivocal results may reflect the use of different outcome measures both within and across studies. To date, most research has focused on short-term cost effectiveness; little is known about long-term cost effectiveness.

FAMILY VARIABLES' INFLUENCE ON TREATMENT

Not all studies have found positive effects with parent training for child behavior problems (Ferber *et al.*, 1974; Sajwaj, 1973; Wahler, 1969). One promising explanatory hypothesis focuses on family functioning (Griest & Forehand, in press), including maternal adjustment, marital adjustment, divorce, and extrafamilial adjustment.

MATERNAL ADJUSTMENT

Several studies have found an association between the psychological adjustment of mothers and the behavior problems of children (Rickard, Forehand, Wells, Griest, & McMahon, 1981; Weissman, Paykel, & Klerman, 1972). Rutter (1966) found that depression was more common in parents of behavior problem children than in parents of nonbehavior problem children. Griest *et al.* (1980) reported that mothers of clinic-referred children were significantly more depressed and anxious than mothers of nonclinic children.

Recent research also has shown an association between maternal adjustment and the child's referral for treatment. Ross (1974) suggested that depression may reduce a mother's threshold for child misbehavior. When the children of depressed mothers misbehave at a rate comparable to that of other normal children, depressed mothers may perceive the behavior as deviant and seek professional help for child problems. In support of Ross's hypothesis, mothers of clinic-referred children often perceive their offspring as significantly more deviant than mothers of nonclinic children (Forehand *et al.*, 1975; Lobitz & Johnson, 1975; Rickard *et al.*, 1981); however, mothers' perceptions are not always accurate (Lobitz & Johnson, 1975; Rickard *et al.*, 1981). Maternal depression alone or maternal depression in combination with actual child deviance predicted maternal perceptions of child behavior (Griest *et al.*, 1980; Griest, Wells, & Forehand, 1979); and maternal perceptions of child behavior, rather than actual child behavior, discriminated best between clinic and nonclinic children (Griest *et al.*, 1980; Lobitz & Johnson, 1975).

Rickard *et al.* (1981) divided clinic-referred children into a clinic deviant group (who exhibited significantly higher rates of problem behavior than nonclinic children) and a clinic nondeviant group (whose behavior was not different from that of nonclinic children). Mothers of both clinic deviant and clinic nondeviant children regarded their children's behavior as significantly more deviant than did mothers of nonclinic children, despite the absence of actual differences between nondeviant clinic and nonclinic children. Mothers of nondeviant clinic children were significantly more depressed than mothers in the other two groups, and mothers of deviant clinic children displayed more deficits in parenting skills than mothers in the clinic nondeviant group.

Investigators of the relationship between maternal adjustment and the outcome of parent training have reported that depressed mothers were more likely to drop out of treatment (McMahon, Forehand, Griest, & Wells, 1981) and less likely to participate in follow-up assessments (Griest, Forehand, & Wells, 1981). However, participation in parent training programs may benefit maternal adjustment. Forehand et al. (1980) found that mothers were significantly less depressed following completion of their parent training program. Patterson and Fleischman (1979) also reported that, following parent training, mothers had fewer somatic complaints and were less anxious, fatigued, angry, and confused.

MARITAL ADJUSTMENT

Most investigators have found a correlation between deviant child behavior and parents' marital difficulties (Ferguson & Allen, 1978; Johnson & Lobitz, 1974; Oltmanns, Broderick, & O'Leary, 1977). However, Griest and co-workers (1981) found no differences in self-reported marital satisfaction between the parents of clinic-referred, noncompliant children and the parents of nonclinic children.

The impact of marital discord on the effectiveness of parent training is unclear. Forehand, Griest, Wells, and McMahon (1982) and Oltmanns and colleagues (1977) found no relationship between marital satisfaction and treatment outcome. In contrast, Reisinger, Frangia, and Hoffman (1976) reported that mothers with marital difficulties were least likely to maintain parenting skills and to generalize them to the home.

Researchers have also asked whether parent training improves marital satisfaction. Although Oltmanns and co-workers (1977) found that parent training did not change marital satisfaction, in another study, increases in marital satisfaction followed changes in child behavior (Scovern, Bukstel, Kilmann, Laval, Busemeyer, & Smith, 1980), and were maintained 6 months following treatment. Forehand *et al.* (1982) divided mothers into three groups based on pretreatment levels of reported marital satisfaction. Mothers in the low-marital-satisfaction group reported improvement in marital satisfaction at treatment termination but not at a 2-month follow-up assessment. No changes in marital satisfaction were reported by mothers in the medium- or high-satisfaction groups. Child behavior problems were reduced at the posttreatment and 2-month follow-up assessments for all levels of marital satisfaction.

The failure to produce lasting improvement in the low-marital-satisfaction group may be best explained by contrasting the methods employed in this study with those implemented by Scovern *et al.* (1980). Scovern and co-workers may have effected positive and durable results because they included both parents in parent training (vs. inclusion of mothers only in the Forehand *et al.* study) and because their parent training involved skills aimed at improving communication between parents and their older children (vs. contingency management skills for younger children in the Forehand study). The acquisition of communication skills may be more relevant to adjustment problems between married partners than are the parenting skills typically taught for younger children. Changes in marital satisfaction probably have to be approached directly (e.g., by supplementing parent training with marital therapy), since they may not automatically result from parent training alone.

DIVORCE

Most parent–child relations undergo a process of disequilibrium characterized by conflict in the period surrounding the separation and divorce (Hetherington, 1979). To date, Hetherington, Cox, and Cox (1978) have provided the most systematic examination of parent–child interactions during the 2-year period following divorce. However, their data are limited to middle-class parents with preschool children. When compared with married people, divorced people exhibited more difficulty in the parent role as measured by diary records, interviews, and laboratory observations. In interactions with their preschool children, the divorced were found to make fewer maturity demands, show less affection, communicate less well, give more commands, and discipline more inconsistently than married persons. The divorced mother communicated less, was less consistent, and used fewer positive behaviors and more negative behaviors in interactions with sons than in interactions with daughters. These difficulties in parenting with preschool children were greatest during the first year following divorce. By the end of the second year, the parent–child interactions had improved but still differed from those of married persons (Hetherington et al., 1978).

Hetherington and co-workers (1978) also found differences in child behavior associated with divorce. Preschool children in divorced families exhibited more negative behavior: they obeyed less, made more dependency demands, and ignored their parents more than children in married families. Children in divorced families, especially boys, exhibited more negative behavior toward their mothers than their fathers. The preschool children's negative behavior appeared to peak at 1 year following divorce and to show improvement by 2 years post divorce (Hetherington et al., 1978).

In attempting to explain difficulties in parenting following divorce, Wallerstein and Kelly (1975; Kelly & Wallerstein, 1977) postulate that personal problems (precipitated or exacerbated by the divorce) are the major influence on parents' functioning. Hetherington and colleagues (1978), however, adopt the interactional position that divorced persons are more dysfunctional in parenting and that divorced children are more deviant with their parents. Factors outside the family also may affect parent–child functioning. Following divorce, most families experience considerable loss in economic status (Bane, 1976; Bloom, Asher, & White, 1978; Espenshade, 1979) and extrafamilial support (Anspach, 1976; Longfellow, 1979). Changes in residence and occupational status may also occur (Hetherington, 1980; Wallerstein & Kelly, 1980).

Research examining the structure and functioning of single-parent families after they have restabilized following divorce is extensive and controversial. Concerning the effects of growing up in a single-parent home, some find deterimental effects (Biller, 1976; Hetherington & Deur, 1971; Shinn, 1978); others conclude that methodological limitations invalidate or severely restrict the findings (Blechman, 1982; Herzog & Sudia, 1973). However, all qualify the relationship between marital status and family functioning by pointing out the importance of possible mediating factors (e.g., socioeconomic status).

Hetherington (Hetherington et al., 1978) reported that parent training following divorce not only facilitated parent–child interactions, but also improved mothers' personal adjustment. These results, however, are based on a relatively small sample of divorced mothers who elected to participate in parent training during the 2 years following their divorce. On a more pessimistic note, Strain, Young, and Horowitz (1981) reported that single parents were less likely than married parents to complete parent training programs and if they did finish treatment they were less inclined to maintain treatment gains. However, Blechman (in press) found no differences between one- and two-parent families in treatment acceptance, attendance, and outcome.

EXTRAFAMILIAL ADJUSTMENT

Wahler and his co-workers (Wahler, 1980; Wahler & Afton, 1980) have suggested that aversive extrafamilial relations, coercive parent–child interactions, and failure to maintain treatment gains are interrelated. The social contacts of insular mothers are primarily aversive exchanges with kinfolk and helping agency representatives. Noninsular mothers maintain regular, nonaversive contact with friends. Immediately following treatment insular and noninsular mothers demonstrated the same level of competence. However, only noninsular mothers and their children maintained behavior changes at follow-up (Wahler, 1980; Wahler & Afton, 1980). The relationship between insularity and parent–child interactions is supported further by the finding that insular mothers had fewer problems with their children on days when they had positive extrafamilial contacts.

In conclusion, variables outside the parent–child relationship may influence who enters treatment, who stays in treatment, and who maintains improvement following treatment. Parental personal adjustment, marital relations, divorce, and community contacts need to be considered in the design of parent training treatment packages. Recently, Blechman (1981) has devised an algorithm to guide therapists in selecting appropriate behavioral interventions for families with varying needs.

ASSESSMENT ISSUES

Assessment of child behavior problems is required for selection of intervention strategies and evaluation of short- and long-term treatment effects. An ideal baseline assessment involves functional analysis of child behavior problems which identifies the antecedents and consequences of target behaviors in intrafamilial and extrafamilial relationships. Although behavioral assessment procedures are useful in identifying behaviors to be targeted in treatment, they provide little help in the selection of effective treatment strategies (Ciminero & Drabman, 1977). Assessment of short- and long-term treatment effects is complex, because different outcome measures may yield different conclusions regarding the effectiveness of parent training (Atkeson & Forehand, 1978). At the same time, multiple dimensions must be evaluated (e.g., child behavior, parent perceptions, parent behavior, parent adjustment) because no single measure accurately reflects treatment outcome (Atkeson & Forehand, 1981).

Parent training effects have been assessed by independent observers, parent observers, and parent ratings of child behavior. Teacher ratings of children's school behavior, academic grades, school attendance, and police contacts have been used less frequently to assess outcome. Direct observations of behavior have been collected in the laboratory (Forehand et al., 1980; Glogower & Sloop, 1976; Grief, 1978) and the home (Eyberg & Johnson, 1974; Forehand et al., 1980; Wahler, 1980). Until recently, most investigators have collected observational data only on child behaviors (Bernal et al., 1968) or collected observational data on both mother and child behaviors, but reported only child data (Patterson, 1974). Studies assessing and reporting changes in both mother and child behaviors via observational data include Forehand et al. (1980), Taplin and Reid (1977), and Wahler (1975). Recognizing the expense of direct observations, several investigators (Bernal, Gibson, Williams, & Pesses, 1971; Johnson & Bolstad, 1975; Johnson, Christensen, & Bellamy, 1976) have replaced human observers with audio recording equipment. Although direct observations provide a reliable and valid description of treatment outcome, they are not without problems. Limitations include: (1) loss of information with the use of a coding system; (2) bias in assessing and calculating interobserver agreement; (3) lack of stability in baseline data; (4) observer error; (5) subject reactivity to being observed; and (6) effect of setting instructions (Atkeson & Forehand, 1981; Hughes & Haynes, 1978).

Parent observers have collected data on the occurrence/nonoccurrence of child behaviors (Barnard et al., 1977; Walter & Gilmore, 1973), on the frequency of child behaviors (Karoly & Rosenthal, 1977; Worland et al., 1980), and on the duration of certain low-rate child behaviors (Eyberg

& Johnson, 1974; Johnson, Bolstad, & Lobitz, 1976) in order to assess parent training outcome. In addition to the problems found with independent observer data, demand characteristics and impression management may affect parent-collected data (Atkeson & Forehand, 1978).

Assessment of parent training has also included parent ratings to evaluate changes in parent perceptions of child behavior (Eyberg & Johnson, 1974; Forehand et al., 1980). Parent-completed questionnaires have several advantages: (1) They are self-administered; (2) they require relatively little time to administer, score, and interpret; and (3) they yield quantitative data (Haynes, 1978). However, because of frequent problems with test–retest reliabilities, their value as outcome measures is somewhat limited.

In addition to direct observation data, changes in mother behavior have been inferred from analogue observations of mothers with child actors (O'Dell, Krug, Patterson, & Faustman, 1980). Measures have also been devised to test mothers' knowledge of behavior principles (Baker, Heifetz, & Murphy, 1980), personal adjustment (Forehand et al., 1980), marital satisfaction (Scovern et al., 1980; Forehand et al., 1982), extrafamilial adjustment (Wahler, 1980; Wahler & Afton, 1980), and treatment satisfaction (Forehand et al., 1980; O'Dell et al., 1977).

More recently, it has been suggested that assessment procedures be expanded to include social validation of behavioral interventions (Kazdin, 1977; Wolf, 1978). Three types of social validity have been delineated (Wolf, 1978): (1) The goals of parent training should be socially acceptable; (2) the procedures used in parent training should be socially appropriate and acceptable to the child and caregivers; and (3) the effects and side effects of the treatment procedure should be satisfactory to the consumers. Socially valid treatment goals might be selected by observing nonclinic populations and by obtaining expert opinions about appropriate child and parent behavior. Socially valid treatment procedures might be obtained by involving the child and parents in the selection of intervention strategies. Finally, the social validity of treatment effects might be evaluated by comparison of the behaviors of treated families with nonclinic families (the matching-to-sample approach), or by the consumers' subjective evaluation of the treatment outcome through interviews and questionnaires. Gurman and Klein (Chapter 7, this volume) have explained their criticisms of the matching-to-sample approach, while Warburton and Alexander (Chapter 15) have defended this approach.

Several researchers have examined the social validity of parent training outcomes (Patterson, 1974; Patterson & Reid, 1973). Forehand *et al.*
(1980) obtained home observations of mothers and children and mother
ratings of children before treatment, immediately after treatment, and
2 months after treatment. Mothers also rated their satisfaction with treatment at termination. The observed behaviors of clinic-referred children
were significantly less appropriate than those of their nonclinic peers
prior to treatment, but were not different following treatment. Before
and immediately after treatment, clinic mothers rated their children as
significantly more deviant than did nonclinic mothers, but ratings by
the two groups of mothers did not differ at follow-up. Mothers of clinic-
referred children also reported satisfaction with the outcomes of therapy.

CONCLUSIONS AND RECOMMENDATIONS

The training of mothers as behavior therapists for their children has
generally been effective in producing immediate change in both mother
and child behaviors. Mothers have been trained successfully to modify
a wide range of problematic behaviors in their younger children and to
improve communication with older children. With substantial experimental evidence that mothers can function as behavior therapists, new
issues concerning etiology, assessment, and treatment have emerged.
In addition, significant social changes in the last decade present new
challenges for the parent trainer. The women's movement and women's
increased participation in the labor force have and will continue to produce profound changes in the family as a social institution (Conger,
1981). Parent trainers must be sensitive to changing roles and role relationships within families. Assessment of family roles and role expectations should always be included. Treatment packages which address
the increased stresses on today's families are needed. Examination of
the research literature also reveals additional neglected areas.

1. Studies which provide relevant data suggest that most recipients
of parent training have been White, middle-class mothers and their
children. Demographic data should always be reported. Evaluation of
treatment effectiveness with non-White, non-middle-class families is
needed.

2. Parent training programs generally focus on consequating child
behaviors. Research is needed delineating antecedents to appropriate

and inappropriate child behaviors so that modification of antecedents can be included in the skills acquired by mothers.

3. Techniques to enhance maintenance and generality of treatment effects are needed.

4. Evaluations of the cost effectiveness of various intervention strategies are needed.

5. Although not specifically addressed, except to note their absence, the advantages and limitations of including fathers in parent training programs should be examined. Parent training that fails to include fathers may adversely affect the functioning of the family unit; as a result of mother's increased skills, father may feel more inept and assume less responsibility for parenting.

6. Although tentative evidence links the success of parent training to the mother's personal adjustment, marital satisfaction, and extrafamilial contact, more research is needed to explore these variables. Treatment packages which address the needs of mothers as adult women, in addition to their needs as parents, need to be developed and evaluated.

7. With increased national attention on divorced and other single parents, research on the relationship of family variables to clinic status and treatment outcome has also increased. However, few studies have examined the specific treatment needs of single mothers and divorced families. Treatment packages for this special population should be developed and evaluated.

8. Pretreatment and posttreatment assessments focus mainly on child behaviors. More attention should be directed to maternal attitudes and skills.

9. Assessment procedures which will aid in treatment selection must be developed.

10. Information about the parenting skills, attitudes, and behavior of well-functioning families should be given more importance in determining goals for parent training. Parents and children, as consumers, should have input into the selection of treatment interventions and the evaluation of treatment outcome.

ACKNOWLEDGMENTS

The authors would like to express appreciation to Rex L. Forehand and Marc N. Branch for their critical comments during preparation of this chapter.

Preparation of this chapter was supported in part by NIMH Grant MH-28859.

REFERENCES

Alexander, J., & Parsons, B. Short-term behavioral intervention with delinquent families: Impact on family process and recidivism. *Journal of Abnormal Psychology*, 1973, *81*, 219–225.

Anspach, D. F. Kinship and divorce. *Journal of Marriage and the Family*, 1976, *38*, 323–330.

Arnold, J. E., Levine, A. G., & Patterson, G. R. Changes in sibling behavior following family intervention. *Journal of Consulting and Clinical Psychology*, 1975, *43*, 683–688.

Arnold, S., Sturgis, E., & Forehand, R. L. Training a parent to teach communication skills: A case study. *Behavior Modification*, 1977, *1*, 257–276.

Atkeson, B., & Forehand, R. L. Parent behavioral training for problem children: An examination of studies using multiple outcome measures. *Journal of Abnormal Child Psychology*, 1978, *6*, 449–460.

Atkeson, B. M., & Forehand, R. L. Home-based reinforcement programs designed to modify classroom behaviors: A review and methodological evaluation. *Psychological Bulletin*, 1979, *86*, 1298–1308.

Atkeson, B. M., & Forehand, R. L. Conduct disorders. In E. J. Mash & L. G. Terdal (Eds.), *Behavioral assessment of childhood disorders*. New York: Guilford, 1981.

Ayllon, T., Garber, S., & Pisor, K. The elimination of discipline problems through a combined school–home motivational system. *Behavior Therapy*, 1975, *6*, 616–626.

Ayllon, T., Smith, D., & Rogers, M. Behavioral management of school phobia. *Journal of Behavior Therapy and Experimental Psychiatry*, 1970, *1*, 125–138.

Azrin, N. H., & Thienes, P. M. Rapid elimination of enuresis by intensive learning without a conditioning apparatus. *Behavior Therapy*, 1978, *9*, 342–354.

Bailey, J. S., Wolf, M. M., & Phillips, E. L. Home-based reinforcement and the modification of pre-delinquents' classroom behavior. *Journal of Applied Behavior Analysis*, 1970, *3*, 223–233.

Baker, B. L., Heifetz, L. J., & Murphy, D. M. Behavioral training for parents of mentally retarded children: One-year follow-up. *American Journal of Mental Deficiency*, 1980, *85*, 31–38.

Bandura, A. *Social learning theory*. Englewood Cliffs, N.J.: Prentice-Hall, 1977.

Bane, M. J. Marital disruption and the lives of children. *Journal of Social Issues*, 1976, *32*, 103–117.

Barkley, R., & Cunningham, C. E. The effects of methylphenidate on the mother–child interactions of hyperactive children. *Archives of General Psychiatry*, 1979, *36*, 201–208.

Barnard, J. C., Christophersen, E. R., & Wolf, M. M. Teaching children appropriate shopping behavior through parent training in the supermarket setting. *Journal of Applied Behavior Analysis*, 1977, *10*, 49–59.

Becker, W. C. *Parents are teachers*. Champaign, Ill.: Research, 1971.

Bell, R. A reinterpretation of direction of effects in studies of socialization. *Psychological Review*, 1968, *75*, 81–95.

Bentler, P. M. An infant's phobia treated with reciprocal inhibition therapy. *Journal of Child Psychology and Psychiatry*, 1962, *3*, 185–189.

Berkowitz, B. P., & Graziano, A. M. Training parents as behavior therapists: A review. *Behaviour Research and Therapy*, 1972, *10*, 297–317.

Bernal, M. E., Duryee, J. S., Pruett, H. L., & Burns, B. J. Behavior modification and the brat syndrome. *Journal of Consulting and Clinical Psychology*, 1968, *32*, 447–455.

Bernal, M. E., Gibson, D. M., Williams, D. E., & Pesses, D. I. A device for automatic audiotape recording. *Journal of Applied Behavior Analysis*, 1971, *4*, 151–156.

Biller, H. B. The father and personality development: Parental deprivation and sex-role development. In M. E. Lamb (Ed.), *The role of the father in child development*. New York: Wiley, 1976.

Blechman, E. A. Family problem-solving training. *American Journal of Family Therapy*, 1980, *8*, 3–22.

Blechman, E. A. Toward comprehensive behavioral family intervention: An algorithm for matching families and interventions. *Behavior Modification*, 1981, *5*, 221–236.

Blechman, E. A. Are children with one parent at psychological risk? A methodological review. *Journal of Marriage and the Family*, 1982, *44*, 179–195.

Blechman, E. A. Early intervention with high-risk children from one- and two-parent families. In L. A. Hamerlynck (Ed.), *Essentials of behavioral treatment for families*. New York: Brunner/Mazel, in press.

Bloom, B. L., Asher, S. J., & White, S. W. Marital disruption as a stressor: A review and analysis. *Psychological Bulletin*, 1978, *85*, 867–894.

Bucher, B., & Raume, J. Generalization of reinforcement effects in a token program in the home. *Behavior Modification*, 1979, *3*, 63–72.

Campbell, S. Mother–child interaction: A comparison of hyperactive, learning disabled, and normal boys. *American Journal of Orthopsychiatry*, 1975, *45*, 51–57.

Christophersen, E. R. Children's behavior during automobile rides: Do car seats make a difference? *Pediatrics*, 1977, *60*, 69–74.

Ciminero, A. R., & Drabman, R. S. Current trends in the behavioral assessment of children. In B. B. Lahey & A. E. Kazdin (Eds.), *Advances in clinical child psychology* (Vol. 1). New York: Plenum, 1977.

Conger, J. J. Freedom and commitment: Families, youth, and social change. *American Psychologist*, 1981, *36*, 1475–1484.

Conway, J. B., & Bucher, B. D. Transfer and maintenance of behavior change in children: A review and suggestions. In E. J. Mash, L. A. Hamerlynck, & L. C. Handy (Eds.), *Behavior modification and families*. New York: Brunner/Mazel, 1976.

Crowley, C. P., & Armstrong, P. M. Positive practice, overcorrection and behavior rehearsal in the treatment of three cases of encopresis. *Journal of Behavior Therapy and Experimental Psychiatry*, 1977, *8*, 411–416.

Crozier, J., & Katz, R. C. Social learning treatment of child abuse. *Journal of Behavior Therapy and Experimental Psychiatry*, 1979, *10*, 213–220.

Cunningham, C. E., & Barkley, R. A. The interactions of normal and hyperactive children with their mothers in free play and structured tasks. *Child Development*, 1979, *50*, 217–224.

Diament, C., & Colletti, G. Evaluation of behavioral group counseling for parents of learning-disabled children. *Journal of Abnormal Psychology*, 1978, *6*, 385–400.

Doleys, D., Doster, J., & Cartelli, L. Parent-training techniques: Effects of lecture-role playing followed by feedback and self-recording. *Journal of Behavior Therapy and Experimental Psychiatry*, 1976, *7*, 359–362.

Espenshade, T. J. The economic consequences of divorce. *Journal of Marriage and the Family*, 1979, *41*, 615–625.

Eyberg, S. M., & Johnson, S. M. Multiple assessment of behavior modification with families: Effects of contingency contracting and order of treated problems. *Journal of Consulting and Clinical Psychology*, 1974, *42*, 594–606.

Ferber, H., Keeley, S. M., & Shemberg, K. M. Training parents in behavior modification: Outcome of and problems encountered in a program after Patterson's work. *Behavior Therapy*, 1974, *5*, 415–419.

Ferguson, L. R., & Allen, D. R. Congruence of parental perceptions, marital satisfaction, and child adjustment. *Journal of Consulting and Clinical Psychology*, 1978, *46*, 345–346.

Fleischman, M. J., & Szykula, S. A. A community setting replication of a social learning treatment for aggressive children. *Behavior Therapy*, 1981, *12*, 115–122.

Forehand, R. L., & Atkeson, B. M. Generality of treatment effects with parents as therapists: A review of assessment and implementation procedures. *Behavior Therapy*, 1977, *8*, 575–593.

Forehand, R. L., Cheney, T., & Yoder, P. Parent behavior training: Effects on the noncompliance of a deaf child. *Journal of Behavior Therapy and Experimental Psychiatry*, 1974, *5*, 281–283.

Forehand, R. L., Griest, D., Wells, K. C., & McMahon, R. Side effects of parent counseling on marital satisfaction. *Journal of Counseling Psychology*, 1982, *29*, 104–107.

Forehand, R. L., & King, H. E. Noncompliant children: Effects of parent training on behavior and attitude change. *Behavior Modification*, 1977, *1*, 93–108.

Forehand, R. L., King, H. E., Peed, S., & Yoder, R. Mother–child interactions: A comparison of a non-compliant clinic group and a non-clinic group. *Behaviour Research and Therapy*, 1975, *13*, 79–84.

Forehand, R. L., & McMahon, R. J. *Helping the noncompliant child: A clinician's guide to parent training*. New York: Guilford, 1981.

Forehand, R. L., & Peed, S. Training parents to modify noncompliant behavior of their children. In A. J. Finch, Jr. & P. C. Kendall (Eds.), *Treatment and research in child psychopathology*. New York: Spectrum, 1979.

Forehand, R. L., Sturgis, E., McMahon, R., Aguar, D., Green, K., Wells, K., & Breiner, J. Parent behavioral training to modify child non-compliance: Treatment generalization across time and from home to school. *Behavior Modification*, 1979, *3*, 3–26.

Forehand, R. L., Wells, K. C., & Griest, D. L. An examination of the social validity of a parent training program. *Behavior Therapy*, 1980, *22*, 488–502.

Fox, R. A., & Roseen, D. L. A parent administered token program for dietary regulation of phenylketonuria. *Journal of Behavior Therapy and Experimental Psychiatry*, 1977, *8*, 441–443.

Glogower, F., & Sloop, E. W. Two strategies of group training. *Behavior Therapy*, 1976, *7*, 177–184.

Gray, J. Positive reinforcement and punishment in the treatment of childhood trichotillomania. *Journal of Behavior Therapy and Experimental Psychiatry*, 1979, *10*, 125–129.

Graziano, A. M. Parents as behavior therapists. In M. Hersen, R. M. Eisler, & P. M. Miller (Eds.), *Progress in behavior modification* (Vol. 4). New York: Academic, 1977.

Green, D. R., Budd, K., Johnson, M., Lang, S., Pinkston, E., & Rudd, S. Training parents to modify problem child behaviors. In E. J. Mash, L. C. Handy, & L. A. Hamerlynck (Eds.), *Behavior modification approaches to parenting*. New York: Brunner/Mazel, 1974.

Grief, E. F. *A comparison of individual and group parent–child interaction training*. Unpublished manuscript, Arizona State University, 1978.

Griest, D. L., & Forehand, R. L. "How can I get any parent training done with all these other problems going on?": The role of family variables in child behavior therapy. *Child Behavior Therapy*, in press.

Griest, D. L., Forehand, R. L., & Wells, K. C. Follow-up assessment of parent behavior training: An analysis of who will participate. *Child Study Journal*, 1981, *11*, 221–229.

Griest, D. L., Forehand, R. L., Wells, K. C., & McMahon, R. J. An examination of differences between nonclinic and behavior problem clinic-referred children and their mothers. *Journal of Abnormal Psychology*, 1980, *89*, 497–500.

Griest, D., & Wells, K. C., & Forehand, R. L. An examination of maternal perceptions of maladjustment in clinic-referred children. *Journal of Abnormal Psychology*, 1979, *88*, 277–281.

Hall, R. V., Axelrod, S., Tyler, L., Grief, E., Jones, F. C., & Robertson, R. Modification of behavior problems in the home with a parent as observer and experimenter. *Journal of Applied Behavior Analysis*, 1972, *5*, 53–64.

Hall, R. V., Cristler, C., Cranston, S. S., & Tucker, B. Teachers and parents as researchers using multiple baseline designs. *Journal of Applied Behavior Analysis*, 1970, 3, 247–255.

Hanf, C., & Kling, F. *Facilitating parent–child interactions: A two-stage training model*. Unpublished manuscript, University of Oregon Medical School, 1973.

Hargis, K., & Blechman, E. A. Social class and training of parents as behavior change agents. *Child Behavior Therapy*, 1979, 1, 69–74.

Haynes, S. N. *Principles of behavioral assessment*. New York: Gardner, 1978.

Herbert, E., & Baer, D. Training parents as behavior modifiers: Self-recording of contingent attention. *Journal of Applied Behavior Analysis*, 1972, 5, 139–149.

Hersen, M. Behavior modification approach to a school phobia case. *Journal of Clinical Psychology*, 1970, 26, 128–132.

Herzog, E., & Sudia, C. Children in fatherless families. In B. M. Caldwell & H. N. Ricciuti (Eds.), *Review of child development research* (Vol. III). Chicago: University of Chicago Press, 1973.

Hetherington, E. M. Divorce: A child's perspective. *American Psychologist*, 1979, 34, 851–858.

Hetherington, E. M. Children and divorce. In R. Henderson (Ed.), *Parent–child interaction: Theory, research, and prospect*. New York: Academic, 1980.

Hetherington, E. M., Cox, M., & Cox, R. The aftermath of divorce. In J. H. Stephens & M. Mathews (Eds.), *Mother–child, father–child relations*. Washington, D. C.: National Association for the Education of Young Children, 1978.

Hetherington, E. M., & Deur, J. L. The effects of father absence on child development. *Young Children*, 1971, 26, 233–248.

Hughes, H. M., & Haynes, S. N. Structured laboratory observation in the behavioral assessment of parent–child interactions: A methodological critique. *Behavior Therapy*, 1978, 9, 428–447.

Humphreys, L., Forehand, R., McMahon, R., & Roberts, M. Parent behavioral training to modify child noncompliance: Effects on untreated siblings. *Journal of Behavior Therapy and Experimental Psychiatry*, 1978, 9, 235–238.

Jason, L. A. Modifying parent–child interactions in a disadvantaged family. *Journal of Clinical Child Psychology*, 1977, 6, 38–40.

Jewett, J., & Clark, H. B. *Training preschoolers to use appropriate dinnertime conversation: An analysis of generalization from school to home*. Unpublished manuscript, Children's Services, Las Vegas, Nev., 1978.

Johnson, M. R., & Green, D. R. *Effectiveness and durability of written instructions: Parental application of differential attention and time out for undesirable behaviors in children*. Unpublished manuscript, University of Notre Dame, 1978.

Johnson, M. R., Whitman, T. L., & Barloon-Noble, R. A home-based program for a preschool behaviorally disturbed child with parents as therapists. *Journal of Behavior Therapy and Experimental Psychiatry*, 1978, 9, 65–70.

Johnson, S. M., & Bolstad, O. D. Reactivity to home observations: A comparison of audio recorded behaviors with observers present or absent. *Journal of Applied Behavior Analysis*, 1975, 8, 181–185.

Johnson, S. M., Bolstad, O. D., & Lobitz, G. K. Generalization and contrast phenomena in behavior modification with children. In E. J. Mash, L. A. Hamerlynck, & L. C. Handy (Eds.), *Behavior modification with families*. New York: Brunner/Mazel, 1976.

Johnson, S. M., & Christensen, A., & Bellamy, G. T. Evaluation of family intervention through unobtrusive audio recordings: Experience in "bugging" children. *Journal of Applied Behavior Analysis*, 1976, 9, 213–219.

Johnson, S. M., & Lobitz, G. K. The personal and marital adjustment of parents as related to observed child deviance and parenting behaviors. *Journal of Abnormal Child Psychology*, 1974, 2, 192–207.

Karoly, P., & Rosenthal, M. Training parents in behavior modification: Effects on perceptions of family interaction and deviant child behavior. *Behavior Therapy*, 1977, *8*, 406–410.

Kazdin, A. E. *The token economy: A review and evaluation*. New York: Plenum, 1977.

Kelley, M. L., Embry, L. H., & Baer, D. M. Skills for child management and family support: Training parents for maintenance. *Behavior Modification*, 1979, *3*, 373–396.

Kelly, J. B., & Wallerstein, J. S. Brief interventions with children in divorcing families. *American Journal of Orthopsychiatry*, 1977, *47*, 23–39.

Knight, M. R., & McKenzie, H. S. Elimination of bedtime thumb-sucking in home settings through contingent reading. *Journal of Applied Behavior Analysis*, 1974, *1*, 33–38.

Lavigueur, H. The use of siblings as an adjunct to the behavioral treatment of children in the home with parents as therapists. *Behavior Therapy*, 1976, *7*, 602–613.

Lavigueur, H., Peterson, R. F., Sheese, G., & Peterson, L. W. Behavioral treatment in the home: Effects on an untreated sibling and long-term follow-up. *Behavior Therapy*, 1973, *4*, 431–441.

Lobitz, G. K., & Johnson, S. M. Normal versus deviant children: A multimethod comparison. *Journal of Abnormal Child Psychology*, 1975, *3*, 353–374.

Longfellow, C. Divorce in context: Its impact on children. In G. Levinger & O. C. Moles (Eds.), *Divorce and separation: Context, causes, and consequences*. New York: Basic Books, 1979.

Luiselli, J. K. Treatment of an autistic child's fear of riding a school bus through exposure and reinforcement. *Journal of Behavior Therapy and Experimental Psychiatry*, 1978, *9*, 169–172.

Lutzker, J. R. Deviant family systems. In B. B. Lahey & A. Kazdin (Eds.), *Advances in clinical child psychology* (Vol. 3). New York: Plenum, 1980.

MacDonald, W. S., Gallimore, R., & MacDonald, G. Contingency counseling by school personnel: An economical model of intervention. *Journal of Applied Behavior Analysis*, 1970, *3*, 175–182.

Martin, B. Brief family interventions: Effectiveness and the importance of including father, *Journal of Consulting and Clinical Psychology*, 1977, *45*, 1002–1010.

Mash, E. J., Lazere, R., Terdal, L., & Garner, A. Modification of mother–child interactions; A modeling approach for groups. *Child Study Journal*, 1973, *3*, 131–143.

McMahon, R. J., & Forehand, R. L. Nonprescriptive behavior therapy: Effectiveness of a brochure in teaching mothers to correct their children's inappropriate mealtime behavior. *Behavior Therapy*, 1978, *9*, 814–820.

McMahon, R. J., Forehand, R. L., & Griest, D. L. Effects of knowledge of social learning principles on enhancing treatment outcome generalization in a parent training program. *Journal of Consulting and Clinical Psychology*, 1981, *49*, 526–532.

McMahon, R. J., Forehand, R. L., Griest, D. L., & Wells, K. C. Who drops out of treatment during parent behavioral training? *Behavioral Counseling Quarterly*, 1981, *2*, 79–85.

Mira, M. Results of a behavior modification training program for parents and teachers. *Behaviour Research and Therapy*, 1970, *8*, 309–311.

Moore, B. L., & Bailey, J. S. Social punishment in the modification of a preschool child's "autistic-like" behavior with a mother as therapist. *Journal of Applied Behavior Analysis*, 1973, *6*, 497–507.

Nay, W. R. A systematic comparison of instructional techniques for parents. *Behavior Therapy*, 1975, *6*, 14–21.

Nay, W. R. Parents as real life reinforcers: The enhancement of parent-training effects across conditions other than training. In A. P. Goldstein & F. H. Kanfer (Eds.), *Maximizing treatment gains: Transfer enhancement in psychotherapy*. New York: Academic, 1979.

O'Dell, S. L. Training parents in behavior modification: A review. *Psychological Bulletin*, 1974, *81*, 418–433.

O'Dell, S. L. *A comparison and evaluation of methods for producing behavior change in parents.* Paper presented at the meeting of the Association for Advancement of Behavior Therapy, Chicago, 1978.

O'Dell, S. L., Blackwell, L. J., Larcen, S. W., & Hogan, J. L. Competency based training for severely behaviorally handicapped children and their parents. *Journal of Autism and Childhood Schizophrenia*, 1977, *7*, 231–242.

O'Dell, S. L., Flynn, J., & Benlolo, L. A comparison of parent training techniques in child behavior modification. *Journal of Behavior Therapy and Experimental Psychiatry*, 1977, *8*, 261–268.

O'Dell, S. L., Krug, W. W., O'Quin, J. A., & Kasnetz, M. Media-assisted parent training—a further analysis. *Behavior Therapist*, 1980, *3*, 19–21.

O'Dell, S. L., Krug, W. W., Patterson, J. N., & Faustman, W. O. An assessment of methods for training parents in the use of time-out. *Journal of Behavior Therapy and Experimental Psychiatry*, 1980, *22*, 21–25.

O'Dell, S. L., Mahoney, N. D., Horton, W. G., & Turner, P. E. Media-assisted parent training: Alternative models. *Behavior Therapy*, 1979, *10*, 103–110.

O'Dell, S. L., O'Quin, J. A., Alford, B. A., O'Briant, A. L., Bradlyn, A. S., & Giebenhain, J. E. *Predicting the acquisition of parenting skills via four training methods.* Unpublished manuscript, University of Mississippi, 1980.

O'Leary, K. D., Turkewitz, H., & Taffel, S. J. Parent and therapist evaluation of behavior therapy in a child psychological clinic. *Journal of Consulting and Clinical Psychology*, 1973, *41*, 279–283.

Oltmanns, T., Broderick, J., & O'Leary, K. D. Marital adjustment and the efficacy of behavior therapy with children. *Journal of Consulting and Clinical Psychology*, 1977, *45*, 724–729.

Parsons, B. V., & Alexander, J. F. Short-term family intervention: A therapy outcome study. *Journal of Consulting and Clinical Psychology*, 1973, *41*, 195–201.

Patterson, G. R. Interventions for boys with conduct problems: Multiple settings, treatments, and criteria. *Journal of Consulting and Clinical Psychology*, 1974, *42*, 471–481.

Patterson, G. R. The aggressive child: Victim or architect of a coercive system. In L. A. Hamerlynck, L. C. Handy, & E. J. Mash (Eds.), *Behavior modification and families* (Vol. I: *Theory and research*). New York: Brunner/Mazel, 1976.

Patterson, G. R. Accelerating stimuli for two classes of coercive behaviors. *Journal of Abnormal Psychology*, 1977, *5*, 335–350.

Patterson, G. R., Cobb, J. A., & Ray, R. S. A social engineering technology for retraining the families of aggressive boys. In H. E. Adams & I. P. Unikel (Eds.), *Issues and trends in behavior therapy*. Springfield, Ill.: Thomas, 1973.

Patterson, G. R., & Fleischman, M. J. Maintenance of treatment effects: Some considerations concerning family systems and follow-up data. *Behavior Therapy*, 1979, *10*, 168–185.

Patterson, G. R., & Gullion, E. *Living with children: New methods for parents and teachers.* Champaign, Ill.: Research, 1968.

Patterson, G. R., & Reid, J. B. Intervention for families of aggressive boys: A replication study. *Behaviour Research and Therapy*, 1973, *11*, 383–394.

Peed, S., Roberts, M., & Forehand, R. Evaluation of the effectiveness of a standardized parent training program in altering the interaction of mothers and their noncompliant children. *Behavior Modification*, 1977, *1*, 323–350.

Powers, R. B., & Osborne, J. G. *Fundamentals of behavior.* St. Paul, Minn.: West, 1976.

Reid, J. B., Taplin, P. F., & Lorber, R. *A social interactional approach to the treatment of abusive families*. Paper presented at the 11th Banff International Conference on Behavior Modification, Banff, Canada, 1980.

Reisinger, J. J., Frangia, G. W., & Hoffman, E. G. Toddler management training: Generalization and marital status, *Journal of Behavior Therapy and Experimental Psychiatry*, 1976, *7*, 335–340.

Reisinger, J. J., & Ora, J. P. Parent–child clinic and home interaction during toddler management training. *Behavior Therapy*, 1977, *8*, 771–786.

Resick, P. A., Forehand, R., & McWhorter, A. The effect of parent treatment with one child on an untreated sibling. *Behavior Therapy*, 1976, *7*, 544–548.

Rickard, K. M., Forehand, R., Wells, K. C., Griest, D. L., & McMahon, R. J. Factors in the referral of children for behavioral treatment: A comparison of mothers of clinic-referred deviant, clinic-referred nondeviant, and nonclinic children. *Behaviour Research and Therapy*, 1981, 19, 201–205.

Robin, A. L., Kent, R., O'Leary, K. D., Foster, S., & Prinz, R. An approach to teaching parents and adolescents problem-solving communication skills. *Behavior Therapy*, 1977, *8*, 639–643.

Ross, A. O. *Psychological disorders of children: A behavioral approach to theory, research, and therapy*. New York: McGraw-Hill, 1974.

Ross, J. Parents modify thumbsucking; A case study. *Journal of Behavior Therapy and Experimental Psychiatry*, 1975, *6*, 248–249.

Rutter, M. *Children of sick patients: An environmental and psychiatric study* (Institute of Psychiatry, Maudsley Monographs, No. 16). London: Oxford University Press, 1966.

Ryback, D., & Staats, A. W. Parents as behavior therapy technicians in treating reading deficits (dyslexia). *Journal of Behavior Therapy and Experimental Psychiatry*, 1970, *1*, 109–119.

Sajwaj, T. Difficulties in the use of behavioral techniques by parents in changing child behavior: Guides to success. *Journal of Nervous and Mental Disease*, 1973, *156*, 395–403.

Sajwaj, T., & Hedges, D. *Side-effects of a procedure in an oppositional retarded child*. Paper presented at the meeting of the Western Psychological Association, San Francisco, 1971.

Sanok, R. L., & Ascione, R. F. The effects of reduced time limits on prolonged eating behavior. *Journal of Behavior Therapy and Experimental Psychiatry*, 1978, *9*, 177–179.

Schumaker, J. B., Hovell, M. F., & Sherman, J. A. An analysis of daily report cards and parent managed privileges in the improvement of adolescents' classroom performance. *Journal of Applied Behavior Analysis*, 1977, *10*, 449–464.

Scovern, A. W., Bukstel, L. H., Kilmann, P. R., Laval, R. A., Busemeyer, J., & Smith, V. Effects of parent counseling on the family system. *Journal of Counseling Psychology*, 1980, *27*, 268–275.

Shinn, M. Father absence and children's cognitive development. *Psychological Bulletin*, 1978, *85*, 295–324.

Stableford, W. Parental treatment of a child's noise phobia. *Journal of Behavior Therapy and Experimental Psychiatry*, 1979, *10*, 159–160.

Stokes, T. F., & Baer, D. M. An implicit technology of generalization. *Journal of Applied Behavior Analysis*, 1977, *10*, 349–367.

Strain, P., Young, C. C., & Horowitz, J. An examination of child and family demographic variables related to generalized behavior change during oppositional child training. *Behavior Modification*, 1981, *5*, 15–26.

Stuart, R. B. Behavioral contracting with the families of delinquents. *Journal of Behavior Therapy and Experimental Psychiatry*, 1971, *2*, 1–11.

Tahmisian, J., & McReynolds, W. Use of parents as behavioral engineers in the treatment of a school-phobic girl. *Journal of Consulting Psychology*, 1971, *18*, 225–228.

Taplin, P., & Reid, J. B. Changes in parent consequation as a function of family intervention. *Journal of Consulting and Clinical Psychology*, 1977, *4*, 973–981.

Tasto, D. L. Systematic desensitization, muscle relaxation and visual imagery in the counterconditioning of a four-year-old phobic child. *Behaviour Research and Therapy*, 1969, *7*, 409–411.

Tharp, R. G., & Wetzel, R. J. *Behavior modification in the natural environment*. New York: Academic, 1969.

Thorne, G. L., Tharp, R. G., & Wetzel, R. J. Behavior modification techniques: New tools for probation officers. *Federal Probation*, 1967, *31*, 21–26.

Wahler, R. G. Setting generality: Some specific and general effects of child behavior therapy. *Journal of Applied Behavior Analysis*, 1969, *2*, 239–246.

Wahler, R. G. Some structural aspects of deviant child behavior. *Journal of Applied Behavior Analysis*, 1975, *8*, 27–42.

Wahler, R. G. The insular mother: Her problems in parent–child treatment. *Journal of Applied Behavior Analysis*, 1980, *13*, 207–219.

Wahler, R. G., & Afton, A. D. Attentional processes in insular and noninsular mothers: Some differences in their summary reports about child problem behaviors. *Child Behavior Therapy*, 1980, *2*, 25–41.

Wahler, R. G., Winkel, G. H., Peterson, R. F., & Morrison, D. C. Mothers as behavior therapists for their own children. *Behaviour Research and Therapy*, 1965, *3*, 113–124.

Wallerstein, J. S., & Kelly, J. B. The effects of parental divorce: Experiences of the preschool child. *Journal of the American Academy of Child Psychiatry*, 1975, *14*, 600–616.

Wallerstein, J. S., & Kelly, J. B. California's children of divorce. *Psychology Today*, 1980, *1*, 67–76.

Walter, H., & Gilmore, S. Placebo versus social learning effects in parent training procedure to alter the behavior of aggressive boys. *Behavior Therapy*, 1973, *4*, 361–377.

Weathers, L., & Liberman, R. Contingency contracting with families of delinquent adolescents. *Behavior Therapy*, 1975, *6*, 356–366.

Weinrott, M., Bauske, B., & Patterson, G. R. Systematic replication of a social learning approach to parent training. In P. O. Sjoden (Ed.), *Trends in behavior therapy*. New York: Academic, 1979.

Weissman, M. M., Paykel, E. S., & Klerman, G. L. The depressed woman as mother. *Social Psychiatry*, 1972, *7*, 98–108.

Wells, K. C., Griest, D. L., & Forehand, R. The use of a self-control package to enhance temporal generality of a parent training program. *Behaviour Research and Therapy*, 1980, *18*, 347–353.

Whalen, C. K., Henker, B., & Dotemoto, S. Methylphenidate and hyperactivity: Effects on teacher behaviors. *Science*, 1980, *208*, 1280–1282.

Wiltz, N. A., & Patterson, G. R. An evaluation of parent training procedures designed to alter inappropriate aggressive behavior of boys. *Behavior Therapy*, 1974, *5*, 215–221.

Wolf, M. M. Social validity: The case for subjective measurement or how applied behavior analysis is finding its heart. *Journal of Applied Behavior Analysis*, 1978, *11*, 203–214.

Worland, J., Carney, R., Milich, R., & Grame, C. Does in-home training add to the effectiveness of operant group parent training? A two-year evaluation. *Child Behavior Therapy*, 1980, *2*, 11–24.

Wright, D. F., & Bunch, G. Parental intervention in the treatment of chronic constipation. *Journal of Behavior Therapy and Experimental Psychiatry*, 1977, *8*, 93–95.

Zeilberger, J., Sampen, S. E., & Sloane, H. N. Modification of a child's problem behaviors in the home with the mother as therapist. *Journal of Applied Behavior Analysis*, 1968, *1*, 47–53.

9

HEALTH MAINTENANCE: EXERCISE AND NUTRITION

JOHN P. FOREYT

G. KEN GOODRICK

OVERVIEW

The purpose of this chapter is to describe behavioral strategies to increase women's exercise level and to improve the quality of their diets. The suggested procedures are suitable for normal, reasonably well-functioning women who are not under psychological or psychiatric treatment for serious psychopathology. Treatment of women who have psychological problems linked to obesity will require treatment such as that described by Fodor and Thal (Chapter 14, this volume). The emphasis in this chapter is on prevention. A central concept is that women need to actively improve their psychological as well as physical health, rather than passively relying on palliative medications. A package of the suggested procedures can be provided to groups of 8–10 women, weekly for 10 weeks, then once or twice monthly for the remainder of 1 year. Continued contact would be needed for maintenance of therapeutic gains.

BACKGROUND

Our life-styles have changed dramatically during the last 60 years. We eat too many calories, too much salt and sugar, and too much fat. At the beginning of this century, almost 40% of our calories came from grain products, vegetables, and fruits. Currently, only about 20% of

John P. Foreyt and G. Ken Goodrick. Baylor College of Medicine, Houston, Texas.

calories come from these three sources. Intake of fats and refined and processed sugars now make up almost 60% of total caloric intake. On the average, every person in the United States consumes 100 pounds of sugar and 125 pounds of fat each year. Several of the leading causes of death in the United States, including heart disease, stroke, hypertension, diabetes, cirrhosis of the liver, and a number of cancers have been linked in some form to our diet. One in six women will die of heart disease or stroke before age 60 (Select Committee on Nutrition and Human Needs, U.S. Senate, 1977). Our rate of physical activity has also changed significantly. Recent polls (Harris & Associates, 1978; Yankelovich, Skelly, & White, 1979) indicate that only about 35% of American women are involved in some sort of regular exercise. The percentage of men who do so is slightly higher, 41%. Most of those who reported not exercising said they lacked the time or the willpower to begin an exercise habit.

The overconsumption of food along with our sedentary life-style has become a significant health problem. Inactivity and improper diet also contribute to psychological problems such as depression. The high incidence of psychophysiological disorders including insomnia and tension headaches in women may reflect a lack of sufficient exercise and an overutilization of caffeine. If women can be persuaded to become physically fit and to eat appropriate diets, then they may become more aware of health problems associated with muscle tension and dietary stress. Since about 65% of American women do not exercise regularly, and almost half of them are overweight, the majority of women would benefit from behavior modification programs designed to increase activity levels and to change their diets. While the number of women taking up aerobic exercise is increasing (Harris & Associates, 1979), and most women have had experience dieting, for the indefinite future there will be a large number who will need behavioral intervention, especially in the *maintenance* of newly acquired exercise and dietary habits.

EXERCISE AND WOMEN'S HEALTH

Aerobic exercises, such as jogging or swimming, involve sustained use of large muscle groups and increased respiration (Cooper, 1970). It cannot be overemphasized how important regular aerobic exercises can be for women. They can improve cardiovascular disease risk factors, which are of increasing importance for women as they enter into occupations characterized by low activity and high stress. They can be beneficial in depression and in coping with boredom; they can increase energy and help to control excess body fat. Regular exercisers also report better sleep, more enjoyment of food, feeling and looking younger, and decreased dysmenorrhea (menstrual pain). However, less than 10% of American adult women perform enough regular vigorous exercise to experience these beneficial effects (Harris & Associates, 1979). While the fitness craze continues to grow in this country, the vast majority adopt sedentary life-styles. About 40% of American females are obese; obesity is highly related to inactivity (Rogers, Mahoney, Mahoney, Straw, & Kenigsberg, 1980).

The person who attempts to modify exercise behavior in women should be aware of the cultural factors that lead to inactivity in adult females (Foreyt & Goodrick, 1982). When a girl reaches puberty, activity level from play decreases. The aerobic fitness level (Cooper, 1970) for most females reaches a peak at about 12 years of age and then drops to a low level (Bailey, 1973). This is probably due to the fact that it is less fashionable for young teenage females to involve themselves in aerobic activities. While female adolescents may participate in sports during physical education classes, they are less likely to engage in after-school activities such as football or basketball, than are males. In addition, most physical education programs do not require aerobic exercise in the last years of high school, nor do they teach students how to develop lasting aerobic exercise habits (Goodrick & Iammarino, 1982).

Mothers and older peers often emphasize "ladylike" behavior. Many are preoccupied with preparing the young girl for adult life by improving her appearance. As Fodor and Thal point out in their chapter on obesity, the cultural milieu for women is reflected in the content of popular women's magazines. These emphasize pop psychology, food preparation, make-up and hair-styling techniques, as well as fad diets for weight reduction and untested exercise regimens. The exercise suggestions tend to be variations on calisthenics routines for cosmetic rather than psychophysiological improvement. It is likely that such exercise routines are adopted initially with high hopes, but are discontinued after a few weeks, yielding the same behavioral pattern seen in dieting (Stunkard, 1957).

Teenage females become sensitive to their body image. Virtually all teenage girls feel at some time that they are too fat. The figure ideals of today are provided by very thin adolescents and prepubescents. Very small increases in weight, from fat deposition or fluid retention, can

propel a young woman into serious dieting. This voluntary calorie restriction will reduce the perceived energy for activity, thus decreasing
the probability of exercise. Dieting and inactivity can lead to a greater
propensity to deposit fat, causing more dieting, and completing a vicious
cycle which leads to normal or obese weight, chronic dieting, and low
activity levels (Foreyt & Goodrick, 1981).

One hundred years ago the typical farmer's wife may have ex-
pended up to 7500 calories each week in household chores. Today, the
typical homemaker or working woman expends only a small fraction of
this figure in the activities required for normal functioning. Less than
15% of all Americans (Harris & Associates, 1979) meet a minimum criterion for aerobic activities (Cooper, 1970). About half of the population
lives a sedentary existence, while the remaining 35% engage in non-
aerobic leisure activities such as bowling.

The goal of group leaders working to modify activity levels in
women is to help their clients develop and maintain regular aerobic
exercise habits, including stretching for flexibility and exercises for
strengthening the abdominal and back muscles. Aerobic exercise fundamentals are covered adequately elsewhere (e.g., Cooper, 1970). Flexibility and strengthening exercises such as those suggested by Simmons
(1980) are also appropriate. Back and abdominal strengthening are particularly important since about 80% of adult Americans will suffer serious
back trouble sometime in their lives unless they perform preventive
exercise (Kraus, 1970). Pregnancy increases the need for a strong, flexible
back and stomach. Abdominal strengthening, in addition to being critical
for a healthy back, may help in maintaining a flatter stomach. Strong
abdominal muscles may also play a role in proprioceptive feedback of
fullness sensations to regulate eating.

In order to help women achieve these goals, the group leader must
properly motivate the client to begin exercise. This involves:

    1. Ascertaining if the client harbors any reservations about ex-
ercise or any misconceptions about the costs and benefits involved.
    2. Teaching the client about the potential physiological and
psychological benefits of regular aerobic exercise.

The group leader must then carefully guide the client into and through
a program which will result in the establishment of an enduring exercise
habit. This will involve:

    1. Using principles of self-regulation to determine exercise in-

tensity, to maximize benefits, and to minimize aversive consequences.

2. Using behavioral self-management principles to help in habit development.

3. Helping the client solve problems as she attempts to integrate exercise into her life-style.

CORRECTING MISCONCEPTIONS AND RESERVATIONS ABOUT EXERCISE

Even though a woman may be eager to commence an exercise program, it is important that her expectations be realistic. For those women who appear reluctant to exercise, the cognitive restructuring suggested in this section may be helpful in persuading them to get started. The following cognitions regarding exercise are listed, along with strategies for changing them.

"Exercise is too boring." Most women who feel this way probably have never exercised to the point where psychological benefits are maximized. Virtually all persons who *regularly* perform aerobic exercise seem to enjoy it most of the time. If not, they can exercise on a stationary bicycle in front of a television or while reading a book. They can exercise with friends to make it a social event. There are books which help one to experience walking (e.g., Kuntzleman, 1979; Sussman, 1967) or jogging (e.g., Glasser, 1976; Kostrubala, 1976) as enjoyable activities.

"Exercise is too painful." Exercise can be painful if begun too intensively. Using self-regulation techniques, overexertion is minimized and muscle soreness should occur only in the first week or so. After several weeks the exercises can be experienced as a pleasure.

"I don't have enough time." Regular aerobic exercise can take as little as 5% of one's total waking hours. The group leader can work with the client on time management.

"I have children; I can't leave home." About one fifth of women who are not getting sufficient exercise say that family obligations prevent them from being more active (Harris & Associates, 1979). If at-home exercise is impractical for a mother, the group leader can help the client organize "exercise klatches" in which the client joins her neighbors for exercise, with one staying home to care for young children.

"Exercise will make me too masculine in appearance." It should be pointed out to the client that aerobic exercise does not increase muscular bulk,

but will tone muscle and reduce excess fat. Top fashion models perfoim extensive exercises to maintain their visual appeal. While physical "masculinity" in females may promote participation in sports, the reverse is not true.

"Exercise is too dangerous." From a physical standpoint, the potential injuries from exercises such as jogging can be minimized through preventive stretching exercises and by gradually increasing intensity through self-regulation. There is the danger of attack by males when exercising in public. Exercising in groups or at parks where other exercisers are present could decrease the probability of this sort of problem. If the urban atmosphere is polluted, an indoor, stationary bicycle or jogging trampoline could be used.

"Exercise makes me too tired." The fact is that regular aerobic exercise will increase physical work capacity, so that the physically fit person will feel *less* tired than the unfit person, given equal daily work demands.

"I don't have enough energy to exercise in the morning/after work." It is the general experience of regular exercisers that they feel more energetic after exercising than before. If one exercises at an intensity that is self-regulated by perceived exertion, then perceptions of overexertion will be minimized. The inexperienced exerciser needs to be encouraged to get through the first few minutes of exercise which may seem unpleasant.

"I get asthma when I exercise." The person who suffers from exercise-induced asthma should be referred to a physician who may prescribe inhalation of disodium cromoglycate before exercise (Anderson, 1981).

"I'm too fat to do vigorous exercise." Unless physically unable to walk, even very obese persons can participate in aerobic exercises such as walking or aquatics. Recent research shows that aerobic exercise increases the chances for success in weight-loss therapy (Brownell & Stunkard, 1980). Women with cardiac disorders or other problems which contraindicate a normal exercise program may still be able to achieve an improvement in fitness through referral to a cardiac rehabilitation program at a local hospital.

COGNITIONS ABOUT AEROBIC EXERCISES

Recognizing that client cognitions affect the acquisition and maintenance of new skills, various behavioral treatment programs aim to transmit new information and change maladaptive attitudes. Many of the chapters in this book describe cognitive treatment components in detail—for example, Padawer and Goldfried on anxiety (Chapter 13); Norman, Johnson, and Miller on depression (Chapter 11); Fodor and Thal on obesity (Chapter 14); Warburton and Alexander on delinquency (Chapter 15). Cognitions make equally important contributions to preventive programs. The more reasons a client has for exercising, the more likely she is to persevere in the face of real and perceived barriers to exercise. To this end the female client entering an exercise program should be acquainted with the numerous, potential benefits of exercise.

PHYSIOLOGICAL BENEFITS

Regular aerobic exercise can help reduce excess fat. There is a high negative correlation between percentage body fat and aerobic fitness (Rogers, Mahoney, Mahoney, Straw, & Kenigsberg, 1980). Obese women who walked for 1 to 2 hours daily lost more pounds and felt much better than they had with dieting alone (Gwinup, 1975). Aerobic exercise may increase metabolic rate so that more calories are burned up even during nonexercise periods (Brownell & Stunkard, 1980). Control of appetite may be better if a minimum of aerobic exercise is done (Mayer, 1968; Blair, Ellsworth, Haskell, Stern, Farquhar, & Wood, 1981). Sedentary persons tend to eat *less* when they increase their exercise levels. Increasing levels of exercise result in proportional increases in appetite so that excess calories are not ingested.

Many normal-weight, sedentary women may have a higher than desirable amount of body fat. Because of their susceptibility to gain weight easily, they may become chronic dieters. Regular aerobic exercise can firm up their bodies and allow them to stop dieting and to enjoy food.

Regular aerobic exercise reduces cardiovascular disease risk by:

1. Increasing the high-density-lipoprotein cholesterol ratio.
2. Reducing triglycerides and plasma free fatty acids.
3. Improving glucose tolerance.
4. Decreasing insulin values independent of changes in blood glucose.
5. Reducing heart rate and blood pressure at submaximal work loads.
6. Increasing stroke volume and arteriovenous oxygen delivery through a decrease in oxyhemoglobin affinity.
7. Increasing myocardial vascularity.

8. Reducing frequency of ectopic ventricular activity.

9. Changing platelet adhesiveness, fibronolysis, and thyroid hormone metabolism favoring reduced cardiovascular disease.

10. Reducing adrenergic response to stress, with decreased catecholamine production (Oberman, 1980).

Regular aerobic exercise can slow the effects of aging by:

1. Reducing the effect of aging on reaction and decision time (Sherwood & Selder, 1979).

2. Preventing osteoporosis, or demineralizing of bones, which causes greater fracturability (Smith & Reddan, 1976).

3. Preventing or forestalling the decline in physical working capacity which normally occurs with aging (Kasch & Wallace, 1976).

4. Preventing or forestalling the loss of muscle strength and the gain of fat normally associated with aging (Kasch & Wallace, 1976.)

PSYCHOLOGICAL BENEFITS

There are many psychological benefits of regular aerobic exercise, some of which may be of particular importance to women:

1. The elevation of endorphin levels which produce the elative feeling known as the exercisers' "high" (Appenzeller, 1981).

2. Reduction in depression (Greist, Eischens, Klein, & Faris, 1979). Women are more prone to depression in our society; exercise can be as effective for mild depression as psychotherapy.

3. Reduction in anxiety (Morgan, 1979).

4. Improved quality of sleep (Heinzelman & Bagley, 1970).

5. Increased sense of well-being and energy (Heinzelman & Bagley, 1970; Riddle, 1980).

6. Improved self-image (Heinzelman & Bagley, 1970). Whereas many avenues for achievement are still closed to women, becoming physically fit can help improve self-concept since even few men are fit. Becoming fit provides a definite and concrete success experience which can build self-confidence and provide the physical energy to persevere in self-improvement efforts (Goodrick, 1978).

7. Reported improvement in concentration, assertiveness, and creative thinking (Harris & Associates, 1979).

8. Many female joggers report that the overall relaxing effect of regular aerobic exercise tends to reduce the severity of muscular dystonia during menstruation.

9. Improvement in physical fitness through exercise is congruent with the feminist approach to self-improvement (Sturdivant,

1980), which is concerned with helping women overcome feelings of shame and weakness regarding the female body. Both the emphasis in our society on the unclean nature of menstruation and the perceived need for elaborate cosmetic modifications tend to give some females a negative body image. The development of "physical culture" through becoming physically fit can help improve body image.

ESTABLISHING THE EXERCISE HABIT

After misconceptions have been addressed, and psychophysiological benefits have been explained, the group leader will need to guide the client into her initial experiences with aerobic exercise. This may occur in a formal group treatment context. However, assuming that attendance at an exercise group cannot continue indefinitely, the suggestions given here will apply mainly to the development of exercise habits which are independent of any particular exercise facility or group.

SOCIAL INFLUENCES

The client needs to consider who may support or hinder her aerobic activities. The group leader can urge the client to convince significant others of the importance of her fitness program (thereby also helping the client to convince herself). The group leader should discuss the possible changes in relationships which might occur if the client were to spend 5 hours a week exercising. Women who desire to exercise may need to coordinate their activity with that of their husbands. While exercising together might be highly desirable for safety and camaraderie, only about one third of husbands and wives reported being in agreement regarding performing exercise as their leisure-time activity (Yankelovich, Skelly, & White, 1979). The sedentary life-style of a homemaker, for example, may be highly rewarding to her husband. Behavioral treatment programs for obesity have used techniques to improve spousal support (Brownell, Heckerman, Westlake, Hayes, & Monti, 1978). Similar techniques might be useful to motivate husbands to support and share the exercise experiences of their wives. The client may need assertiveness training and/or marriage counseling to get family and friends to accept her new life-style.

PREVIOUS FAILURE ANALYSIS

The client may have attempted other exercise programs without being able to maintain a regular habit. The reasons for previous relapses to inactivity need to be discussed.

TREATMENT SCHEDULE

It may take up to 10 weeks of regular activity to ensure that all clients have a chance to achieve a level of fitness at which exercise is perceived as enjoyable. During this period the group leader or her associate should exercise with the client groups to get and give feedback during exercise. During the first 5 weeks, clients should attend at least three sessions per week. Preferably each exercise session should last about 45 minutes. Appreciable loss of excess body fat does not occur unless exercise periods last more than 30 minutes (Franklin & Rubenfire, 1980). The antidepressant benefits and "exercise high" are maximized if exercise periods last at least 45 minutes (Kostrubala, 1976). During the last 5 weeks, one or two of the exercise sessions each week should be "homework" assignments, with the clients exercising on their own. The group sessions can then include a problem-solving discussion to help clients overcome real and perceived barriers to their exercise. During this time, the group leader can help the clients find exercise facilities in the community as well as potential exercise partners.

FEEDBACK

In order that women in the process of improving cardiovascular, aerobic fitness can get quantitative feedback of their progress, they should be tested on a bicycle ergometer (Astrand, 1960) or with the 12-minute run test (Cooper, 1970). This will enable categorization of fitness level according to Cooper's (1970) criteria, and will provide objective evidence of improvement in cardiovascular health. Fitness tests should be given at the beginning and end of the 10-week training phase for motivational feedback. After the 10-week training phase ends, a maintenance program should be available for up to a year which provides some form of regular client–group leader contact and a procedure for reintervention in case of relapse.

AEROBIC EXERCISE PACING

To minimize discomfort for the client, exercise intensity should be based on how she feels while exercising and on her perceived effort. Perceived effort, as assessed on a scale developed by Borg (1973), may be independent of feeling state during exercise. Exercise intensity needs to be low enough so that the client reports feeling good during the exercise, yet high enough to optimize cardiovascular fitness. Burke (1979) has determined the levels of perceived effort on Borg's scale that correspond to optimal intensities of exercise. If careful attention is paid to how the client experiences her exercise, the likelihood that she will experience aerobic exercise as painful or exhausting should be minimized. In programs that emphasize aerobic points, heart rate, or speed, clients sometimes find themselves satisfying their exercise quotas but feeling terrible while exercising. No one can be expected to develop an exercise habit under such conditions.

It is well documented that many regular aerobic exercisers find their exercise to be a pleasurable leisure-time activity (Glasser, 1976; Kostrubala, 1976). The aerobics program developed by Greist and his associates for the treatment of depression (Greist & Eischens, 1979) is especially suitable for aerobics training for women who have a negative attitude toward exercise. This approach involves self-regulation of exercise intensity based on feeling states and perceived breathing effort. Greist and Eischens (1979) have described the sequencing of activities and the associated qualitative aspects of each exercise experience. The basic principles of exercise regulated by level of self-perceived exertion and breathing can be adapted to any aerobic exercise.

BEHAVIORAL TECHNIQUES TO DEVELOP EXERCISE HABITS

Some have used behavioral self-management techniques to increase aerobic exercise behavior (Epstein, Thompson, & Wing, 1980; Keefe & Blumenthal, 1980; Turner, Polly, & Sherman, 1976; Wysocki, Hall, Iwata, & Riordan, 1979). These techniques generally involve self-monitoring, stimulus control, and contingency management, as well as structuring social influence. These techniques can be used during the initial training period to help clients develop an aerobic life-style. The clients should regard the techniques as useful tools for habit formation until they reach the point where exercise can be self-reinforcing.

SELF-MONITORING

Self-monitoring involves the recording of exercises, along with feeling state and perceived effort during exercise. Perceived positive or negative consequences of exercise are recorded. An explanation for missed exercise periods, as well as suggestions for solving the problems that interfere with regular exercise, should be recorded daily on forms provided to the client (Figures 9-1 and 9-2). The exercise recording form (Figure 9-1) should be taped on a wall or door at home where it will be seen daily. This form and the problem analysis form (Figure 9-2) can be used for discussion during the training period.

During the maintenance period, exercise records should be sent in weekly. Clients can be provided with a stack of self-addressed postcards or forms. Continued contact with the therapist may be important for maintenance of exercise (Wright, 1980). Failure to return the forms would automatically initiate a telephone follow-up to set up a relapse prevention strategy, if needed.

STIMULUS CONTROL

Through a history of differential reinforcement with various external conditions, a person may come to associate specific stimuli with certain behaviors. Stimulus control of behavior involves eliminating the stimuli

FIGURE 9-1. Exercise self-monitoring form.

NAME	Susan Wilson					
Date	Time	Activity	Duration	Perceived exertion	How I felt	Comments
9/26	7 A.M.	Jog	50 min	5	4	Raining
9/27	Didn't exercise				2	Got a cold

Perceived exertion scale	How I felt
1—Very, very light	1—Terrible
2—Very light	2—Bad
3—Fairly light	3—So-so
4—Somewhat hard	4—Good
5—Hard	5—Fantastic
6—Very hard	
7—Very, very hard	

NAME Susan Wilson	
Date Reason for not exercising	How I could overcome this barrier to exercise
9/28 Felt tired when I woke up. Decided to stay in bed a little longer instead of riding exercise bicycle.	Don't decide not to exercise while in bed. After I got up and got moving, I felt O.K.

FIGURE 9-2. Problem analysis form.

which elicit maladaptive behavior, or, conversely, arranging the environment so that there are stimuli conducive to adaptive behavior (Mahoney & Arnkoff, 1979). Linking exercise to a particular time through scheduling is one example of stimulus control. Preparing exercise clothing and equipment and leaving them out at night may promote exercise the next morning. If feelings of tiredness become associated with deciding not to exercise in the morning, such a decision should not be made until one has allowed a cup of coffee to take effect. These techniques minimize "giving up" prematurely. For stretching exercises, and for stationary bicycles, a special place in the home should be arranged, to obviate the need to prepare a space every time exercise is done.

CONTRACTING

Several studies have used contracting techniques to increase exercise behavior (Epstein, Thompson, & Wing, 1980; Keefe & Blumenthal, 1980; Wysocki, Hall, Iwata, & Riordan, 1979; Turner, Polly, & Sherman, 1976). A written agreement makes valued outcomes contingent upon attendance or performance in exercise class. One technique requires clients to give a deposit at the beginning of the training period. This is refunded contingent upon attendance and return of self-monitoring forms. Forfeited deposits are given to disliked organizations. It is best not to base refunds on performance, since each woman's goals and rates of achievement will be different. An appropriate criterion for the reward is regular exercise for 45–60 minutes per day, three to four times a week. Symbolic reinforcers (certificates, T-shirts, etc.) can also be used with contracts. Contracts should be written for periods not shorter than 6 months, to emphasize that exercising for fitness should be a lifetime behavior. Contracts should also require gradual improvement. A strong achievement orientation at the beginning may cause overexercise or excessive fear of failure. Since contracting requires the scrutiny of others, the motivational effects may wear off after the client leaves an exercise program. Therefore, even when contracts are used at the beginning of a program, clients should be guided in self-motivational techniques such as stimulus control and attention to the psychological rewards of exercise.

RUNNING ANOREXIA

The group leader's effort to get the female client to exercise may be so successful that excessive exercise results. This can cause problems in relationships due to the time involved. In addition, physical symptoms such as extreme thinness and amenorrhea may occur, with or without the obsessiveness regarding perceived body fat seen in anorexia nervosa (Norval, 1980).

NUTRITION AND WOMEN'S HEALTH

The most common nutritional problem for women is obesity. Special problems in the treatment of obesity in females have been covered elsewhere (Foreyt & Goodrick, 1982; Fodor & Thal, Chapter 14, this volume). Other nutritional problems interfere with women's optimal health and functioning. Some of these nutritional problems affect perceived energy level and tendency to exercise; use of caffeine and simple carbohydrates are examples.

Although younger females generally have a lower risk for cardiovascular disease, the incidence rises sharply after menopause (American Heart Association, 1979). Working women, regardless of employment status, report significantly more symptoms of emotional distress than men (Haynes & Feinleib, 1980). Coronary heart disease rates are almost twice as great among women holding clerical jobs, currently over one third of female workers in the United States, as compared to housewives. The most significant predictors of coronary heart disease among clerical workers include suppressed hostility, having a nonsupportive boss, and decreased job mobility (Haynes & Feinleib, 1980). Coronary heart disease rates are higher among women who have married, especially among those who have raised three or more children. Apparently the added stress of employment plus raising a family places excessive demands on working women. For these reasons, women should be aware of their blood lipids and take appropriate nutritional action should these lipids become abnormally high. Finally, the average American diet contains too much fat, protein, and simple carbohydrates, and not enough complex carbohydrates and fiber. The dietary recommendations of the Pritikin program (Pritikin, 1979), the American Heart Association (Eshleman & Winston, 1979), or the Living Heart Diet (Gotto, DeBakey, Scott, & Foreyt, in press) all have these as goals.

ENERGY LEVEL: CAFFEINISM

A common complaint of sedentary homemakers and office personnel is a feeling of fatigue that recurs throughout the day. Paradoxically, sometimes this is linked with insomnia. An aerobic life-style may boost energy during the day and promote better sleep. However, the standard remedy for fatigue is caffeine, either in coffee or in soft drinks. Even a small amount can disrupt normal sleep patterns. More than four cups of coffee a day can lead to caffeinism, or psychological addiction to caffeine. Often, when attempting to withdraw suddenly from coffee, patients will get headaches from cerebral vasodilation (Greden, Victor, Fontaine, & Lubetsky, 1980). A behavioral shaping program to reduce caffeine intake gradually can avoid headaches and ease the psychological transition. In a shaping program (Foxx & Rubinoff, 1979) the client self-records coffee intake, and plots daily intake of coffee on a graph. Monetary incentives reward intake less than daily caffeine limits; clients lose $2.50 of a $20 deposit on any day they exceed their limits. A substantial reduction in coffee drinking, from nine to three cups a day, can be achieved over about seven weeks.

ENERGY LEVEL: REDUCING INTAKE OF SIMPLE CARBOHYDRATES

Another factor which may affect perceived energy levels during the day is the intake of simple carbohydrates, or sugars. Many females are involved in diets, and dietary restriction can increase cravings for sugars (Wooley, Wooley, & Dyrenforth, 1979). When sugars are ingested in large quantities, such as in sweet rolls, the blood sugar level soon peaks. The insulin reaction to this increase in sugar level works to keep the level down. However, the insulin response lasts longer than the available sugar entering the blood. The end result is a blood sugar level that is abnormally low, and this can cause feelings of tiredness. Since insulin levels are highest between 4 A.M. and 10 A.M., it is especially important to avoid consumption of simple carbohydrates for breakfast. The caffeine in coffee also tends to raise blood sugar levels temporarily, making the situation worse. A behavioral approach to this problem would involve hourly self-recording of sugar intake, perceived energy level, and mood.

MAKING QUALITATIVE CHANGES IN THE DIET

After nutrition education and counseling from a dietitian, the first step in helping to change diet is self-monitoring. Everything eaten or drunk needs to be recorded, including quantity and caloric content. Self-monitoring increases awareness of eating, and helps the client learn caloric values. Self-monitoring may result in some immediate changes in diet, but the reactive effect wears thin over time (Bellack, Rozensky, & Schwartz, 1974). Clients may also resist the instruction to keep complete records, complaining that they take too much time, that they are too complicated, or that the technique won't work for them. The group leader needs to anticipate these problems by pointing out how easy recording is, and how the technique will work if done conscientiously over a long time. In order to encourage good record keeping, portions of a deposit could be returned contingent on appropriate records. For educational purposes, the recording form could have a column for labeling foods, using letter codes such as "S" for sugar, "F" for high fat, "C" for high cholesterol, etc. A recording form is shown in Figure 9-3.

FIGURE 9-3. Self-monitoring form for dietary intake.

NAME Susan Wilson

DATE 9/29

Time	Where	With whom	What	How much	× Calories	=	Total calories	Too much: S = Sugar F = Fat C = Cholesterol
8 A.M.	Kitchen	Husband	Eggs	3	80		240	C
			Butter	1 T.	100		100	F,C
			Toast	3 oz.	80		240	
			Coffee	12 oz.	—		—	
			Sugar	4 t.	16		64	S
							644	

Although faking occurs at times by some clients, it has been our clinical experience that most clients make a conscientious effort to keep records. Spot checks, such as blood tests analyzed for lipids, and regular weighing help reduce the number of inaccurate recordings.

BEHAVIORAL SELF-MANAGEMENT OF DIET

In addition to self-monitoring, other behavioral techniques for changing the quality of the diet have been used to help the client develop self-management skills. These techniques are applicable to achieve any desired dietary changes.

PROBLEM SOLVING

A problem-solving strategy is important if a client is to select solutions for her personal problems. One helpful problem-solving approach is Mahoney's (1977) "Personal Science" procedure. Using the mnemonic "SCIENCE," seven subskills needed for successful adjustment are taught: (1) Specify general problem. (2) Collect information. (3) Identify causes or patterns. (4) Examine options. (5) Narrow options and experiment. (b) Compare data. (7) Extend, revise, or replace. Personal problems are viewed as amenable to scientific reasoning, and the skills taught parallel scientific research skills. Patients should be able to use the personal science model to help them solve any dietary problems which might arise after the formal treatment program has ended. The problem-solving approach is especially useful with bright, motivated women. We have not found it helpful with semiliterate, poorly educated clients. With those, we have relied on the basic behavioral principles, assigning simple food diaries, standard stimulus control procedures (eat in one place, eliminate the distraction of television while eating, etc.), and short-term contracts with immediate rewards.

COGNITIVE TECHNIQUES

Cognitions play an important role in maintaining poor nutrition. A number of strategies help clients identify and alter cognitive self-statements that interfere with a lasting, healthful diet. For example, the repetition of counter statements several times a day may weaken a pessimistic belief. A woman who has said to herself, "I've been on hundreds of diets before; I'll never be able to stay on this one," may be asked to repeat a counterstatement such as: "This program has taught me some wonderful new strategies to help me stay on my diet this time. There is a first time for everything." Even if she doesn't completely believe the counterstatements at first, the repetition several times a day may still be useful.

A client may also be asked to keep a "thoughts diary" in which she records her thoughts concerning food over a week. She then goes over her diary with the group leader, discussing each of the past week's food-related thoughts. She can be taught a three-step strategy as a method for gradually learning to improve poor thought patterns. This strategy involves:

    1. "Tuning in" to negative thought patterns.
    2. Evaluating whether these thought patterns are unreasonable, self-defeating, or discouraging.
    3. Deliberately changing these poor thought patterns to more encouraging, positive self-talk.

A number of other strategies have been developed for helping individuals change negative thought patterns (Emery, Hollon, & Bedrosian, 1981).

URGE CONTROL

Some clients may experience uncontrollable urges to eat inappropiately. For example, cravings for sweets may lead to an ice-cream binge. Preliminary findings about urge control for the overweight seem favorable, and might be worthwhile using on an experimental basis to help clients cope with undesired eating (Rosen, 1981; Youdin & Hemmes, 1978). Urge control techniques encourage self-confrontation. In one method (Rosen, 1981), the client is instructed to pause before eating the inappropriate food, and to ask herself if she really wants to eat it more than she wants to stick to a healthful diet. If the decision to eat is made, she must watch herself eat in a mirror. The client must also record everything she eats, on the self-monitoring form. In another method, the client records inappropriate urges to eat on a wrist counter (Youdin & Hemmes, 1978). Every time an urge occurs, the client must answer questions about the urge on a 3 × 5 card. Both methods can be applied to urges for high-sodium or high-cholesterol foods as well as to urges for high-calorie items.

STIMULUS CONTROL

Food diaries reveal a number of patterns of inappropriate eating. Strategies for modifying these patterns need to be devised by client and group leader together. Typical stimulus control strategies require that the client confine all eating behavior to the dining room table, shut off the radio or television during a meal, use smaller plates or silverware, store problem foods out of sight, go grocery shopping with a complete list of needed foods, and hang helpful reminder signs and pictures throughout the home (Stuart & Davis, 1972).

CONTINGENCY MANAGEMENT

Formal reward systems can increase motivation to stay on a dietary regimen (Foreyt, 1977). Clients can be taught to give themselves points for carrying out specific behavioral prescriptions, such as regularly weighing themselves, for faithfully recording all of their food consumption, or for making particular changes in their eating patterns. After patients receive a certain number of points, they then reward themselves with some predetermined reinforcer. Formal contracts are frequently written to help ensure compliance with the behavioral assignments.

STRESS MANAGEMENT

Stress management techniques are particularly useful for those who tend to lose control over their diet when feeling anxious or tense. Some form of relaxation training is frequently helpful. All of the relaxation techniques require some practice, but most individuals can learn the skill in about 3 weeks if they practice regularly. Progressive relaxation is a widely used technique because it is fairly easy to learn in a short period of time. Most people who practice relaxing twice a day, for 15 minutes a session, for about 3 weeks, can relax quickly. In particular, they can relax when they find themselves thinking about food at inappropriate times. For example, when a woman watches a television commercial about a par-

ticularly attractive food, she can let herself fall into the relaxation response. The deep-muscle relaxation will frequently diminish psychological
cravings.

MODELING

A number of dietary change programs use as therapists people who
have previously completed the program successfully (Stuart, 1977).
Weight Watchers, for example, employs individuals who have been
successful in their program and who now serve as models to new participants, explaining how they used particular strategies to modify their
own life-styles.

MAINTAINING GOOD NUTRITIONAL HABITS

To be totally successful, clients must be motivated to maintain the good
nutritional habits taught them during the treatment phase. There are
several ways of doing this. Since changes do occur for most clients
during a formal treatment period, treatment should be extended until
the new behaviors have been tried for a long enough period that they
are comfortable in carrying them out. Continued periodic contact with
the group leader will increase the chances that clients will successfully
continue in their change programs. Increasing activity levels through
aerobic exercise may become self-reinforcing and habitual for some people. Qualitative changes in diet often occur as the client begins to think
of herself as a regular exerciser. Attention to the cognitions which make
staying on a diet difficult, and alteration of these thought patterns, also
make maintenance easier.

CONCLUSIONS AND RECOMMENDATIONS

The strategies described in this chapter are designed to help women
change their exercise and eating behaviors. The ultimate goal is to transmit self-control by showing participants how to manipulate the antecedents and consequences of target behaviors.

   1. The program we recommend includes 10 weekly meetings, with

one or two meetings per month over the following year. Continued group leader contact may be necessary to ensure that life-style changes persist. In the course of a year, many clients will experience and learn to overcome various real and perceived barriers.

2. Each time a barrier to exercise or appropriate eating arises, the client needs to adopt a problem-solving approach. Cognitively unprepared clients will use the smallest of barriers as an excuse to relapse. The teaching of cognitive skills to prevent relapse (Marlatt & Gordon, 1980) is an important part of health life-style modification. One skill needed by many women is to regard setbacks as learning experiences rather than as excuses to give up. Preparing women for the fact that they will fail to exercise or to eat appropriately from time to time, and providing them with constructive cognitive scenarios may help inoculate them against the deleterious effects of short-term failure on self-esteem and perseverance. An emphasis on cognitive training, together with extended group leader contact, affects the way women feel about themselves while helping them to improve health behaviors.

3. Clients who consider themselves as victims of uncontrollable circumstances easily justify quitting a new regimen, without self-blame or guilt. Since martyrdom cognitions signal both positive and negative reinforcement, they will persist until the client herself confronts them. Women clients need to recognize that most reasons for giving up healthful regimens involve self-deception. Some clients who claim that they have no time to exercise have tight schedules which need to be modified, since no leisure time or exercise predict psychological and physiological disaster. When time management analysis shows how time can be made available for exercise, busy clients must reanalyze their motivations for exercise. With the exception of valid medical reasons, any relapse to former inactive levels or old eating habits will be due to the client's failure to persevere, not to uncontrollable external constraints.

4. When clients fail to take responsibility for their actions, the group leader must point this out without chastising the client. The role of the group leader is to encourage performance of the self-management procedures which bring about a healthier life-style.

Some (Fodor & Thal, Chapter 14, this volume) maintain that behavior modification causes more psychological problems in women than it cures, by stressing will power or self-control. Failures are regarded as indications that will power or self-control is lacking as a personality attribute. Socialization processes lead women to believe that they have less self-control than men. This damages self-esteem and may lead to a self-fulfilling prophecy—feelings of inadequacy lead to poor performance and actual inadequacy.

The behavioral self-management approach described here does not regard self-control as a personality attribute, but as a deficit in a variety of learned behaviors. Deficits in learned behavior are caused by sex-biased environments, not by flaws characteristic of women. Cognitive analyses of women's efforts to change reveal that they are more likely to expect failure, and a history of repeated failures tends to make them premature quitters. Therefore, intervention with women must arrange for gradual improvement while minimizing failure episodes.

ACKNOWLEDGMENTS

This work was supported by the National Heart, Lung, and Blood Institute, National Institutes of Health, Grant No. HL 17269.

REFERENCES

American Heart Association. *Heart facts, 1980*. Dallas, Tex.: American Heart Association, 1979.

Anderson, S. D. Drugs affecting the respiratory system with particular reference to asthma. *Medicine and Science in Sports and Exericse*, 1981, *13*, 259–265.

Appenzeller, O. What makes us run? *New England Journal of Medicine*, 1981, *305*, 578–580.

Astrand, I. Aerobic work capacity in men and women with special reference to age. *Acta Physiologica Scandinavica*, 1960, *49*, Suppl. 169.

Bailey, D. A. Exercise, fitness and physical education for the growing child—a concern. *Canadian Journal of Public Health*, 1973, *64*, 421–430.

Bellack, A. S., Rozensky, R., & Schwartz, J. A comparison of two forms of self monitoring in a behavioral weight reduction program. *Behavior Therapy*, 1974, *5*, 523–530.

Blair, S. N., Ellsworth, N. M., Haskell, W. L., Stern, M. P., Farquhar, J. W., & Wood, P. D. Comparison of nutrient intake in middle-aged men and women runners and controls. *Medicine and Science in Sports and Exercise*, 1981, *13*, 310–315.

Borg, G. A. V. Perceived exertion: A note on "history" and methods. *Medicine and Science in Sports*, 1973, *5*, 90–93.

Brownell, K. D., Heckerman, C. L., Westlake, R. J., Hayes, S. C., & Monti, P. M. The effect of couples training and partner co-operativeness in the behavioral treatment of obesity. *Behaviour Research and Therapy*, 1978, *16*, 323–333.

Brownell, K. D., & Stunkard, A. J. Physical activity in the development and control of obesity. In A. J. Stunkard (Ed.), *Obesity*. Philadelphia: Saunders, 1980.

Burke, E. J. Individualized fitness program: Using perceived exertion for the prescription of healthy adults. *Journal of Physical Education and Recreation*, 1979, *50*, 35–37.

Cooper, K. B. *The new aerobics*. New York: Evans, 1970.

Emery, G., Hollon, S. D., & Bedrosian, R. C. (Eds.). *New directions in cognitive therapy: A casebook*. New York: Guilford, 1981.

Epstein, L. H., Thompson, J. K., & Wing, R. R. The effects of contract and lottery procedures on attendance and fitness in aerobics exercise. *Behavior Modification*, 1980, *4*, 465–479.

Eshleman, R., & Winston, M. *The American Heart Association cookbook* (3rd ed.). New York: McKay, 1979.

Foreyt, J. P. (Ed.). *Behavioral treatments of obesity*. New York: Pergamon, 1977.

Foreyt, J. P., & Goodrick, G. K. Weight disorders. In C.J. Golden, S.S. Alcaparras, F. D. Strider, & B. Graber (Eds.), *Applied techniques in behavioral medicine*. New York: Grune & Stratton, 1981.

Foreyt, J. P., & Goodrick, G. K. Gender and obesity. In I. Al-Issa (Ed.), *Gender and psychopathology*. New York: Academic, 1982.

Foxx, R. M., & Rubinoff, A. Behavioral treatment of caffeinism: Reducing excessive coffee drinking. *Journal of Applied Behavior Analysis*, 1979, *12*, 335–344.

Franklin, B. A., & Rubenfire, M. Losing weight through exercise. *Journal of the American Medical Association*, 1980, *244*, 377–379.

Glasser, W. *Positive addiction*. New York: Harper & Row, 1976.

Goodrick, G. K. An alternative approach to risk reduction. *Health Values*, 1978, *2*, 297–300.

Goodrick, G. K., & Iammarino, N. K. Teaching aerobic lifestyles: New perspectives. *Journal of Physical Education, Recreation and Dance*, 1982, *53*, 48–50.

Gotto, A. M., DeBakey, M. E., Scott, L. W., & Foreyt, J. P. *The living heart diet*. New York: Raven, in press.

Greden, J. F., Victor, B. S., Fontaine, P., & Lubetsky, M. Caffeine-withdrawal headache: A clinical profile. *Psychosomatics*, 1980, *21*, 411–418.

Greist, J. H., & Eischens, R. R. *Antidepressant running*. Unpublished manuscript, University of Wisconsin, Psychiatry Department, 1979.

Greist, J. H., Eischens, R. R., Klein, M. H., & Faris, J. W. Antidepressant running. *Psychiatric Annals*, 1979, *9*, 134–140.

Gwinup, G. Effect of exercise alone on the weight of obese women. *Archives of Internal Medicine*, 1975, *135*, 676–680.

Harris, L., & Associates. *Health maintenance*. Newport, Calif.: Pacific Mutual Life Insurance Co., 1978.

Harris, L., & Associates. *The Perrier study: Fitness in America*. New York: Perrier–Great Waters of France, 1979.

Haynes, S. G., & Feinleib, M. Women, work and coronary heart disease: Prospective findings from the Framingham heart study. *American Journal of Public Health*, 1980, *70*, 133–141.

Heinzelman, F., & Bagley, R. W. Response to physical activity programs and their effects on health behavior. *Public Health Reports*, 1970, *85*, 905–911.

Kasch, F. W., & Wallace, J. P. Physiological variables during 10 years of endurance exercise. *Medicine and Science in Sports*, 1976, *8*, 5–8.

Keefe, F. J., & Blumenthal, J. A. The life fitness program: A behavioral approach to making exercise a habit. *Journal of Behavior Therapy and Experimental Psychiatry*, 1980, *22*, 31–34.

Kostrubala, T. *The joy of running*. Philadelphia: Lippincott, 1976.

Kraus, H. *Clinical treatment of back and neck pain*. New York: McGraw-Hill, 1970.

Kuntzleman, C. T. *The complete book of walking: Total fitness step-by-step*. New York: Simon & Schuster, 1979.

Mahoney, M. J. Personal science: A cognitive learning therapy. In A. Ellis & R. Grieger (Eds.), *Handbook of rational–emotive therapy*. New York: Springer, 1977.

Mahoney, M. J., & Arnkoff, D. B. Self management. In O. F. Pomerleau & J. P. Brady (Eds.), *Behavioral medicine: Theory and practice*. Baltimore: Williams & Wilkins 1979.

Marlatt, G. A., & Gordon, J. R. Determinants of relapse: Implications for the maintenance of behavior change. In P. O. Davidson & S. M. Davidson (Eds.), *Behavioral medicine: Changing health lifestyles*. New York: Brunner/Mazel, 1980.

Mayer, J. *Overweight: Causes, cost and control*. Englewood Cliffs, N.J.: Prentice-Hall, 1968.

Morgan, W. P. Psychological effects of physical activity. In F. J. Nagle & H. J. Montoye (Eds.), *Exercise, health and disease*. Springfield, Ill.: Thomas, 1979.

Norval, J. D. Running anorexia. *South African Medical Journal*, 1980, *58*, 1024.

Oberman, A. The role of exercise in preventing coronary heart disease. In E. Rapaport (Ed.), *Current controversies in cardiovascular disease*. Philadelphia: Saunders, 1980.

Pritikin, N. *The Pritikin program for diet and exercise*. New York: Grosset & Dunlap, 1979.

Riddle, P. K. Attitudes, beliefs, behavioral intentions, and behaviors of women and men toward regular jogging. *Research Quarterly for Exercise and Sport*, 1980, *51*, 663–674.

Rogers, T., Mahoney, M. J., Mahoney, B. K., Straw, M. K., & Kenigsberg, M. I. Clinical assessment of obesity: An empirical evaluation of diverse techniques. *Behavioral Assessment*, 1980, *2*, 161–181.

Rosen, L. W. Self-control program in the treatment of obesity. *Journal of Behavior Therapy and Experimental Psychiatry*, 1981, *12*, 163–166.

Select Committee on Nutrition and Human Needs, United States Senate. *Dietary goals for the United States* (2nd ed.). Washington, D.C.: U.S. Government Printing Office, 1977.

Sherwood, D. E., & Selder, D. J., Cardiorespiratory health, reaction time, and aging. *Medicine and Science in Sports*, 1979, *11*, 186–189.

Simmons, R. *Never-say-diet book*. New York: Warner, 1980.

Smith, E. L., & Reddan, W. Physical activity—A modality for bone accretion in the aged. *American Journal of Roentgenology*, 1976, *126*, 1297.

Stuart, R. B. Self-help approach to self-management. In R. B. Stuart (Ed.), *Behavioral self-management: Strategies, techniques and outcome*. New York: Brunner/Mazel, 1977.

Stuart, R. B., & Davis, B. *Slim chance in a fat world: Behavioral control of obesity*. Champaign, Ill.: Research, 1972.

Stunkard, A. J. The dieting depression: Incidence and clinical characteristics of untoward responses to weight reduction regimens. *American Journal of Medicine*, 1957, *23*, 77–86.

Sturdivant, S. *Therapy with women: A feminist philosophy of treatment*. New York: Springer, 1980.

Sussman, A. *The magic of walking*. New York: Simon & Schuster, 1967.

Turner, R. D., Polly, S., & Sherman, A. R. A behavioral approach to individualized exercise programming. In J. D. Krumboltz & C. E. Thoresen (Eds.), *Counseling methods*. New York: Holt, Rinehart & Winston, 1976.

Wooley, S. C., Wooley, O. W., & Dyrenforth, S. R. Theoretical, practical and social issues in behavioral treatments of obesity. *Journal of Applied Behavior Analysis*, 1979, *12*, 3–25.

Wright, L. The standardization of compliance procedures, or the mass production of ugly ducklings. *American Psychologist*, 1980, *35*, 119–122.

Wysocki, T., Hall, G., Iwata, B., & Riordan, M. Behavioral management of exercise: Contracting for aerobic points. *Journal of Applied Behavior Analysis*, 1979, *12*, 55–64.

Yankelovich, Skelly, & White, Inc. *Family health in an era of stress*. Minneapolis: General Mills, 1979.

Youdin, R., & Hemmes, N. S. The urge to overeat—the initial link. *Journal of Behavior Therapy and Experimental Psychiatry*, 1978, *9*, 227–233.

10

PHYSICAL AGGRESSION: TREATING THE VICTIMS

ELLEN FRANK
BARBARA DUFFY STEWART

OVERVIEW

Two painful, and until recently, hidden problems in the lives of women have resulted from physical aggression against women. Rape victimization and wife abuse were rarely discussed prior to the early 1970s. With the advent of the women's movement and a greater freedom to speak about sexuality and aggression, came a willingness to acknowledge and to formulate responses to these two problems. In most cases the initial responses to both rape and wife abuse took the form of grassroots support centers providing crisis intervention and, in the case of wife abuse, shelter for victims. Systematic attempts to understand the nature of the psychological trauma experienced by victims did not come for several years. Well-defined approaches to treatment of these problems are only now beginning to emerge. In the case of rape victims, behavioral interventions have been the most common of the approaches investigated. Studies of treatment for the problem of wife abuse are in their infancy and few have emerged in the area of behavior modification. While there are a number of common threads in the exploration of these two problems of living for women, some of which will be addressed in our conclusions, it seems preferable to address them separately in the body of this chapter. Accordingly, the chapter will focus first on behavioral interventions with victims of rape and second, on interventions with victims of wife abuse.

Ellen Frank and Barbara Duffy Stewart. Western Psychiatric Institute and Clinic, Department of Psychiatry, University of Pittsburgh School of Medicine, Pittsburgh, Pennsylvania.

BACKGROUND OF THE PROBLEM OF RAPE VICTIMIZATION

Although interest in the crime of rape goes back at least as far as the biblical story of Dinah, active concern about the effect of rape on victims of this crime and strategies for its prevention did not emerge until the early 1970s. Concurrent with the liberalization of sexual attitudes and the emergence of the feminist movement, agencies, institutions, and groups of concerned individuals sought to improve the manner in which rape victims were treated.

During the late 1960s rape was the fastest rising crime in the United States (U.S. Department of Justice, Federal Bureau of Investigation, 1967), and it was during this period that the feminist movement became actively concerned with the problem of rape and the difficulties faced by rape victims (Wood, 1973). Because of the climate surrounding this crime, many women did not report it. Those who did, frequently found themselves subjected to harassment and questions concerning their own behavior and morals (Queen's Bench Foundation, 1975). Although the broad-based feminist action against rape has done little to affect the incidence of the crime (U.S. Department of Justice, Federal Bureau of Investigation, 1979), attitudes about the rape victim are finally beginning to change. This change is reflected in new legislation (Wolfe, 1974), in changing attitudes on the part of police and emergency-room personnel, and in the increasing numbers of rape crisis centers across the country (Hilberman, 1976).

Whereas at one time the rape victim's character was called into question as much as her assailant's, now most states prohibit questioning about the victim's prior sexual experience or reputation. Corroboration requirements which made conviction of the rapist virtually impossible in most situations have been revoked in almost all the states where such laws once existed. In addition, several states have broadened their rape laws to include sodomy and other offenses not involving vaginal penetration with the penis (Wolfe, 1974). Policemen, policewomen, doctors, and nurses who were once skeptical of the rape victim's innocence and insensitive to her trauma are becoming more tactful in their handling of women who have been sexually assaulted (Hilberman, 1976).

Today, in almost any major city, a rape victim can find someone to help her meet the specific needs (legal advice, medical attention, a sympathetic ear) she experiences during the first 24 to 48 hours following the assault. It is more difficult however, to find someone expert in the treatment of the fear, anxiety, depression, and sexual and social dysfunction which often emerge subsequent to the initial trauma. The most recent estimates suggest that 1 in 10 women will experience a sexual assault at some time during her life. The FBI *Uniform Crime Reports for the United States, 1979* (U.S. Department of Justice, Federal Bureau of Investigation, 1980), indicate that there were 75,989 reported rapes during that year. The city of Pittsburgh and surrounding Allegheny County had 582 rapes during 1979, a low incidence for a metropolitan area of over 2¼ million inhabitants.

EPIDEMIOLOGIC DATA

Data on the epidemiology of rape and other crimes which stigmatize the victim are susceptible to bias. In *Understanding the Rape Victim: A Synthesis of Research Findings*, Katz and Mazur (1979) kept this bias in mind when they summarized the findings of studies from a variety of disciplines. The mean age of rape victims in all studies fell between 18 and 25, and little difference was observed between those subjects selected from a hospital emergency room (mean = 22.2 years) and those who reported to the police (mean = 21.4 years). Katz and Mazur noted that the Black woman appears far more vulnerable to rape than the White woman. Single women also tend to be greatly overrepresented. In studies that included both intrafamilial and extrafamilial sexual assault victims of all ages (e.g., Amir, 1971; MacDonald, 1971), the percentage of unmarried victims was approximately 75%. However, Burgess and Holmstrom (1974a), who excluded children aged 16 and under, found that 62% of victims were single. Educational data suggest that women with little education are a greater risk for sexual assault. However, many victims are in the process of completing their education. Katz and Mazur (1979) concluded that high school and college students, are at particularly high risk for sexual victimization. At least two speculative explanations deserve further consideration. Marriage may shelter women from rape, in some unknown fashion. A second possibility is that students may more often enter intimate or semi-intimate situations with strangers, thereby increasing the likelihood of acquaintance rape.

Of those women who experience a sexual assault, most will not report the crime to the police and probably less than half will seek help from a hospital or crisis or counseling center (Katz & Mazur, 1979). Last year, over 400 rape victims sought help from Pittsburgh's two rape crisis centers. Among recent victims who sought help, were many who simply requested information about how the criminal justice system operates or where to find appropriate medical treatment. About half of this help-seeking group, however, was willing to speak to a therapist. Our experience suggests that three quarters of those who agree to speak to a therapist feel the need for ongoing counseling or therapy in order to return to normal functioning. Of those women willing to confer with a therapist, 25 to 35% return to their normal level of functioning within a few weeks after the rape.

PSYCHOLOGICAL DISTRESS

Although the literature on the crime of rape is extensive, almost none of it has been concerned with the victim's emotional response or subsequent psychological problems. Probably the largest, most detailed study of the crime (Amir, 1971) never mentions the victim's emotional or psychological reaction to the assault. Only within the last 10 years have researchers and clinicians begun to consider psychological response to rape, and its treatment. The first modern discussion of the psychological response to rape was in an article on the medical management of victims (Halleck, 1962). Since then authoritative studies of rape victims have emphasized fear and anxiety as the predominant psychological sequelae of sexual assault. Although Sutherland and Scherl (1970), Burgess and Holmstrom (1974a), The Queen's Bench Foundation (1975), and Notman and Nadelson (1976) studied victims under different circumstances, all found symptoms of fear and anxiety in their populations.

In the first systematic study of the response to rape, a full array of self-report instruments was used to assess 46 recent sexual assault victims and 35 controls matched for age, race, and neighborhood (Kilpatrick, Veronen, & Resick, 1979). Victims and controls described their levels of fear, psychological symptoms, subjective mood states, and both current and general anxiety level. At the first assessment, victims reported significantly more fear, anxiety, mood disturbance, and symptom disturbance than nonvictims. The picture was the same 1 month later. By the 3-month assessment, victims differed from nonvictims only on symptom inventory scores of interpersonal sensitivity, trait anxiety, phobic anxiety, paranoid ideation, and psychoticism; there were no differences on state anxiety, somatization, obsessive–compulsive behavior, depression, hostility, or mood-state scales. Kilpatrick et al. (1979) reported that by the 6-month assessment, victims differed from nonvictims on only 7 out of 28 measures of distress and all of these were measures of fear and anxiety; however, no data are provided regarding differential dropout of distressed victims. Repeated-measures analyses of data from the 19 victims and 20 controls who completed all four assessments, also revealed anxiety, fear, mood disturbance, and symptom disturbances as time elapsed following rape. From their data, Kilpatrick and colleagues argued that the long-term impact of sexual assault is elevated anxiety and fear. Only two of the studies published before 1979 (Sutherland & Scherl, 1970; Peters, 1975a, 1975b) mentioned depression as a feature of the normative response to rape. Burgess and Holmstrom (1974a) observed depression only in victims with a previous history of physical or psychiatric problems.

Our research group (Frank, Turner, & Duffy, 1979), on the other hand, has been impressed with the extent to which female rape victims report depressive symptoms. Furthermore, our research (Frank & Stewart, 1982) along with that of Calhoun and Atkeson (1980), Miller, Williams, and Bernstein (1979), and Shore (1980) has encountered disrupted familial and social relationships in the aftermath of a sexual assault. In one of our studies (Frank, Turner, & Duffy, 1979), recent victims (a few days to 4 weeks postrape) were assessed for depressive symptomatology using a well-validated, self-report inventory (Beck Depression Inventory) in combination with a formal psychiatric evaluation. A psychiatrist whose sole task in the study was preliminary assessment, determined which subjects met Research Diagnostic Criteria for depressive disorders (Spitzer, Endicott, & Robins, 1978) basing his judgment on subject responses to the Beck Depression Inventory (Beck, Ward, Mendelson, Mock, & Erbaugh, 1961) and on therapists' observations of depressive symptoms. When assessed within 1 month following the assault, 53% of the women who scored above 16 on the Beck Depression Inventory (24% of the total group) met diagnostic criteria for a major depressive disorder.

In a longitudinal study focused primarily on depression, Atkeson, Calhoun, Resick, and Ellis (1982) examined the course of recovery in 115 recent victims of sexual assault who received no treatment. They also assessed 87 matched controls at the same six points in time. Assessments were carried out 2 weeks, 1 month, 2 months, 4 months, 8 months, and 1 year after the assault. On a self-report measure of depression, the Beck Depression Inventory (Beck et al. 1961), 75% of the victimized subjects reported mild to severe depressive symptomatology at the 2-week assessment. By 12 months postassault, only 26% of the victims continued to be symptomatic. When the Beck Depression Inventory was used to compare victims with nonvictims, Atkeson *et al.*'s (1982) victimized subjects were significantly different at 2 weeks, 1 month, and 2 months postassault, but not at the three subsequent assessments. The same was true when depression was measured by the clinician-rated Hamilton Psychiatric Rating Scale for Depression (Hamilton, 1960), suggesting that while it may take up to 4 months for depressive symptomatology to remit significantly, recovery can occur in the absence of treatment.

GENERALIZABILITY OF FINDINGS

A problem which plagues all relevant research projects is the extent to which the samples are representative of the universe of rape victims. Although neither we, nor Kilpatrick *et al.* (1979), nor Calhoun and Atkeson (1980) were able to observe any differences between those rape victims who became project participants and nonparticipants in terms of demographic characteristics or factors in the rape situation, we unfortunately have no information about the psychological condition of those victims who choose not to participate at all. What we can say about the women in our study is that they are representative of victims who seek psychological counseling postrape, and by this very fact, represent an appropriate group for study.

THERAPEUTIC VALUE OF REPEATED ASSESSMENT

Both Kilpatrick *et al.* (1979) and Calhoun, Atkeson, and Resick (1979), commenting on the spontaneous improvement in their populations, suggested that repeated assessment by empathic clinicians may in itself be therapeutic. Since Shore (1980) gathered data less often than Kilpatrick or Calhoun, her findings are relevant to the presumption that frequent assessment is therapeutic. Shore interviewed 127 sexual assault victims, anytime from a few days to 37 months after the assault. She repeated the interview 6 months later with 77 women (61% of the initial sample). At the 6-month interview most women had returned to their preassault levels of employment and religious activities; involvement in education and training, unaffected at the time of the first interview, remained stable. Scores for problems, fears, and avoidant behavior, which were high just after the incident but had subsided by the first interview, increased markedly by the time of the 6-month interview. Self-image, which was significantly impaired after the assault, remained poor 6 months later. In sum, Shore found considerable impairment 6 months after assault, among women who had received infrequent assessments. Like Kilpatrick, Shore suggested that fears and avoidance behaviors persist in an untreated population of rape victims. A recent study by Resick, Calhoun, Atkeson, and Ellis (1981) sheds additional light on the assumption that frequent assessment is therapeutic. Social adjustment of a group of victims assessed at six time points was compared with a group tested one time, 2, 4, or 8 months postassault. Single-testing victims showed significantly more impairment in total social adjustment than did those who were given multiple assessments.

BEHAVIORAL TREATMENT OF RAPE VICTIMS

Although rape could cause a series of medical sequelae that need to be considered during the course of psychological treatment, this rarely happens when the victim gets adequate emergency care, including a test for venereal disease. The rape victim must take responsibility for obtaining test results and seeking appropriate medical treatment. Despite popular fantasies, pregnancy rarely follows rape. During the 3½ years of our study, less than 3% of our subjects have become pregnant as a result of the rape—a statistic that conforms to estimates cited by other investigators in the field (Katz & Mazur, 1979)—and only one subject has been treated on an inpatient basis because of medical complications resulting from the rape.

It is our belief that anyone requesting treatment, whether or not her experience would meet the legal definition of rape, is entitled to our help. Therefore, in our study, all subjects who request psychological treatment are randomly assigned to one or two behavioral treatments. Both treatment protocols are carried out by female therapists with Master's degrees in either social work, counseling, or clinical psychology. The 42 women are predominantly young, White, and single. Their ages range from 14–52 years, with a mean of 24.5; 78% are White; 68% have religious affiliations other than Catholic; 51.2% have training beyond high school; 85.4% are single and 82.9% live with other people. Thus far, 17 women have completed a course of 14 1-hour sessions of systematic desensitization and 25 women have completed 14 1-hour sessions of cognitive therapy. There are no statistically significant differences in the demographic makeup of the two treatment groups.

SYSTEMATIC DESENSITIZATION

If the predominant and most long-lasting effects of rape victimization are fear and anxiety, then treatment designed to eliminate these symptoms should provide the greatest immediate relief and the most enduring treatment gains. Systematic desensitization, a procedure designed to reduce or eliminate maladaptive anxiety and its behavioral correlates, would appear to be an optimal treatment for the fears which develop subsequent to a rape experience. Since this treatment was formally introduced by Wolpe (1958) it has been subjected to extensive experimentation and the literature concerning its efficacy is voluminous (Paul, 1969; Rimm & Masters, 1979). Although systematic desensitization has been found to be an effective treatment for many behavioral disorders, it applies best to those complaints in which the cues for fear or anxiety are easily pinpointed.

Once a client's specific fears or avoidance behaviors are identified through the Target Complaints Assessment,[1] she is taught progressive muscle relaxation (Jacobson, 1938, 1970). In relaxation training, the client learns to alternately tense and relax various muscle groups until she achieves a state of relaxation or calm. During the first three sessions, the client lies on a couch, closes her eyes, and assumes a comfortable position. She is then instructed to allow her thoughts to ramble. After 3 minutes, the therapist begins the relaxation exercises, and instructs the client about how to tense and relax each muscle group while suggesting that the client feel serene. Clients are to practice the exercises at home in the morning and at night. If the client has difficulty becoming relaxed, variations on the training procedure are introduced. For example, a client may be asked to envision herself in a particularly soothing environment such as an empty beach, a field of grass, or a warm tub, as an aid to relaxation. Or, she may be asked to recall a time in her life when she felt especially comfortable and to imagine herself in a specific situation during that time. Usually at the fourth visit, the client is asked to turn her attention again to her list of three target complaints which resulted from the rape. Table 10-1 provides a list of the most frequently cited target complaints. These target complaints are each broken down into specific scenes or examples of the problems and the woman rates the scenes on a scale ranging from 0 (no anxiety) to 10 (intense anxiety).

---

[1] The Target Complaints Assessment, designed for use in this protocol, can be obtained by writing Ellen Frank, Western Psychiatric Institute, Pittsburgh, Pa. 15261.

TABLE 10-1. Frequently Cited Target Complaints of Rape Victims

	Percentage of total complaints cited
Fear of being alone/staying alone/being outside	18.3
Feeling different since assault—people's reaction/look different/shame/insecure	15.7
Fear of/distrust/discomfort with men	13.1
Difficulty sleeping	9.2
Fear of a specific place (e.g., street, car, room)	9.2
Discomfort in social situations	7.8
Fear of seeing rapist or recurrent rape	3.9
Difficulty eating or eating too much	2.6
Fear of or difficulty with sexual expression	2.6
Fear of trial/prosecuting/legal system	2.6
Other	14.5

Note. Thirty systematic desensitization clients cited a total of 76 target complaints.

The component scenes of each problem are then arranged in a hierarchy, from the least anxiety-provoking event to the most anxiety-provoking event. This method of hierarchy construction individualizes the treatment process and conforms to the early recommendations of Wolpe (1969). If, after therapy begins, a woman feels differently about a scene · than she did before, the hierarchy is rearranged.

Sample hierarchies are displayed in Table 10-2 and a set of sample scenes appears in Table 10-3. During treatment, the client imagines each scene in each hierarchy while relaxed, beginning with the least distressing scenes. The client signals when she experiences anxiety, and stops imagining the scene. Each scene is presented twice, and no more than three scenes are presented per session, until the client has imagined each item in the hierarchy without anxiety. If a client has several hierarchies, one scene from each hierarchy is presented during a session. At the end of each session, the client discusses unreported anxiety, problems imagining the scene and other difficulties. In order that all sessions end on a positive note, no session ends on a scene that elicited anxiety. If necessary, less distressing scenes are presented to accomplish this goal.

Although our subjects were never told that they should attempt in real life the activities described in the scenes, approximately 75% of the women we have studied developed a pattern of following each treatment session with *in vivo* exposure to the stimuli described in that session. These efforts were reported spontaneously, usually with great pride on the subject's part. Occasionally, subjects anticipated steps in the hierarchy or unintentionally found themselves exposed *in vivo* to items not yet dealt with in treatment. When *in vivo* exposure to such stimuli produced little or no anxiety, hierarchies were rearranged accordingly.

TABLE 10-2. Two Sample Hierarchies

Fear of going out alone

---

1. Go out with mother to the shopping mall
2. Going ice skating
3. Jogging with friends
4. Going to neighborhood store
5. Going to movies downtown
6. Walking to school
7. Go for evening swim at school
8. Jogging alone
9. Going to playground at night alone

Fear of men

---

1. At home on Sunday afternoon with father and brothers (watching football game)
2. With father and brothers in car, at night, driving to mall
3. With father and brothers in mall (crowds pushing and shoving)
4. In mall, separated from dad and brothers (can see them)
5. With old friend Sam (who knows about assault)
6. Male cousins over (alone with them—they ask questions)
7. While separated from dad and brothers in mall (jostled by man)
8. Daytime—leaving appointment (man in elevator looks)
9. Walking alone on campus—daylight (walk by group of guys)
10. Talking to friend of roommate's boyfriend—roommate leaves for moment (you keep talking to friend)
11. Going to party with female friends
12. In bar with roommate—few women in bar (men crowd around)
13. In bar with roommate (guy asks for a dance)
14. At night—walking to dorm with roommate (men's voices coming toward you)
15. Blind date—set up by friend (going with another couple)
16. Date—have been out once before (movie and dinner)

TABLE 10-3. Two Sample Hierarchy Narratives

Hierarchy 1, Item 3

Jogging at oval with friends

You and Karen and Georgia and MaryAnn are walking to the Oval. It's a beautiful cool sunny day and you love the feeling of the cool air on your face. You and your friends start to jog together, but soon you break off and you're running ahead of the rest of the girls. When you're done, you stand against a tree and wait and watch the rest of them finish.

Hierarchy 2, Item 9

Walking on campus

Bright spring day. The trees are budding and the sun is warm. You are walking to a 10 o'clock class. You have your books under your arm, walking very slowly enjoying the sun and the spring smells and looking at the flowers. In the distance, you hear the sounds of men's voices and see a group of guys coming toward you. You don't know them. They come toward you—they are talking and laughing. They look at you as you walk by and you keep walking slowly to class as you hear their voices fade.

COGNITIVE THERAPY

In choosing a second treatment approach which could be expected to be effective with sexual assault victims evidencing depressive symptoms, we considered a number of factors. It seemed important to choose a treatment consistent with our belief that most of the responses observed within out population were normal. To avoid the implication that rape victims are psychiatric cases, we sought a treatment which could be conducted by individuals without medical training and which did not require pharmacologic adjuncts to treatment. We wanted an intervention which, like systematic desensitization, has a brief, intensive format, enabling a rapid return to preassault social functioning. Finally, we sought a treatment in which the mechanisms of expected change are made explicit and the client feels in control of the treatment process. Beck's cognitive therapy (Beck, 1972), discussed in detail in Norman, Johnson, and Miller's chapter on depression (Chapter 11, this volume), appeared to meet these requirements. Cognitive therapy is a directive, time-limited approach which has been demonstrated to be at least as effective as tricyclic antidepressant in treating serious depression (Rush,

Beck, Kovacs, & Hollon, 1977). A skilled therapist from any of the helping professions (psychiatry, psychology, social work, or nursing) can be
trained to conduct cognitive therapy. Its mechanisms of change are made
explicit from the outset of treatment, and each treatment session is intended to reinforce the patient's understanding of how the treatment
works. Finally, the essence of the change sought as a result of cognitive
therapy is increased control (in particular, of cognitive processes), a goal
entirely consistent with our perception of the needs of recent rape victims.

Cognitive therapy aims to change maladaptive habits by encouraging the individual to recognize the "silent assumptions" governing
behaviors. An individual's cognitions (verbal or imagined events in the
stream of consciousness) filter past, present, and future experience
through preexisting assumptions about the world. For example, a rape
victim is likely to focus on exaggerated perceptions of her inadequacy,
powerlessness, and incompetence, and on thoughts such as: "Being
raped was my own fault," or "I am worthless now that I've been raped."
Cognitive therapy techniques are designed to help clients identify and
test the reality of distorted and dysfunctional beliefs, referred to as
"automatic negative thoughts" by Beck. The three phases of treatment
progress from concrete to abstract interpretations of the problem. Group
I cognitive techniques challenge maladaptive thinking with homework
tasks which change behavior, and encourage novel thinking about specific situations and behaviors. Homework includes (1) a weekly activity
schedule—the client rates the amount of mastery or pleasure she got
from the activities listed in her log; (2) graded task assignments—the
client undertakes a series of tasks to reach a goal she considers difficult
or impossible (e.g., going out alone).

Beck (Beck, Rush, Shaw, & Emery, 1979) argues that experiences
which give a distressed individual a sense of mastery or pleasure, reduce
discomfort and automatic negative thoughts. Guided by responses to
the activity schedule, graded task assignments may also be designed to
increase the sheer level of activity, to upgrade the quality of activity or
to enable gradual approach to situations or tasks avoided since the assault. Early in treatment, the weekly activity schedule is also used to
identify situations which elicit automatic negative thoughts. This is helpful when clients have difficulty identifying and recording automatic negative thoughts. Both during the explanation of the rationale for cognitive
therapy and during the early treatment sessions, the therapist listens
carefully for statements which have the characteristics of an automatic

negative thought. These statements typically include an absolute such as "always," "never," "only," or "none," and are usually statements about the client herself, her world, or her future, "My parents will never trust me again," would be a classic example. The therapist labels these statements as automatic thoughts, and explains how the client can record when they occur, along with the situations which elicited them, and the feelings which result, on the daily record of automatic negative thoughts. In the second (Group II) phase of treatment, therapist and client work together to identify the cognitive distortion that gave rise to the auto-matic thought and to construct a rational, adaptive response. For ex-ample, Susan, a recent rape victim, found herself talking with a boy in her class whom she believed knew about the assault. She immediately thought, "Kenny is disappointed and upset with me. He will never think good of me again." The feelings she recorded in association with that thought were "anger" and "depression." In the therapy session, the therapist might ask Susan to examine the evidence that (1) Kenny is disappointed or upset *now*, and (2) even if he is upset at present, that this necessarily means that he will *never* alter that view. If Susan pointed to a look on Kenny's face as evidence of his disappointment, the therapist would question the meaning of the evidence, asking the client to offer alternative explanations such as "He was having a bad day," "He was worried about an exam." If Kenny was clearly disappointed with Susan, the therapist would question the stability of his current mood, by asking the client to recall times when Kenny or other people were upset with her and got over it. The therapist would then ask Susan to formulate an adaptive response to this particular situation such as: "Kenny is obviously upset about something. It's probably the math test he just got back," or "Kenny is disappointed that I got into the situation I did last weekend, but I know he'll get over it in a few days. He always does." Susan will then be asked to reevaluate her depressed and angry feelings about Kenny in light of her new view of the situation. Invariably, reev-aluation produces positive feelings to the formerly distressing situation. A client, in formulating adaptive responses, is asked to explore a variety of *rational* views of a situation and choose that view which promotes the best feelings for her. Clients are not encouraged to formulate belief systems based on lies. A belief whose accuracy cannot be proven is retained as long as it can be considered a *reasonable* possibility.

Some clients eventually go on to the third (Group III) phase of treatment, in which the client explores her basic assumptions about the world. Beck (Beck *et al.*, 1979) argued that certain beliefs predispose

individuals to depression and anxiety. Basic assumptions are common
themes which unify a client's automatic negative thoughts. Basic assumptions are resistant to change perhaps because each one is supported
by numerous automatic thoughts. In our study population, women have
reported assumptions such as, "I can't live without love"; "If someone
disagrees with me it means he doesn't like me"; and "My value as a
person depends on what others think of me." When basic assumptions
are replaced with realistic attitudes (e.g., "It is more pleasant to be loved,
but I can live without love," or "If people disagree with me it means
simply they have a different view of the topic or situation; it says nothing
about what they think of me as a person"), an improved view of the
self, the world, and the future facilitates positive thought and action in
a variety of circumstances. In our project, subjects who had a prior
history of difficulties with depression and were in need of exploring
their basic belief systems accounted for only 20% of the cognitive therapy
subjects. Most sexual assault victims progressed so rapidly in symptom
reduction that they ended treatment before they explored their basic
assumptions.

EFFICACY OF SYSTEMATIC DESENSITIZATION AND COGNITIVE THERAPY WITH RAPE VICTIMS

For preliminary outcome analysis, paired t-tests compared the pre- and
posttreatment scores of 17 women who received systematic desensitization. As Table 10-4 shows there was significant improvement on all
five self-report measures and on three of five Social Adjustment Scale–II
scores: work/school, social/leisure, and general social. Systematic desensitization's effectiveness is reflected in the self-report inventories, interviews, and in significant improvement on the target complaints' ratings.
Improvement in depression, self-esteem, and general social functioning
was unexpected and suggests that desensitization did more than just
reduce anxiety. It is unclear whether these changes reflect the natural
recovery process, so that similar improvement might have occurred
without intervention. Preliminary analysis of cognitive therapy's effects
shown in Table 10-5 found that the 25 cognitive therapy subjects made
significant ($p < .001$) improvement in depression, fear, anxiety, and self-
esteem. Trait anxiety would not be expected to change between pre-
and posttreatment assessment; yet it also decreased significantly. Per-

TABLE 10-4. Systematic Desensitization Subjects: Summary of Self-Report and Social Adjustment Scale Data at Pre- and Posttreatment Assessment

Instrument	Pretreatment	Posttreatment	t
Self-report instruments[a]			
Beck Depression Inventory	16.5 ± 7.2	7.1 ± 6.4	6.48***
State Anxiety Inventory	49.6 ± 14.9	32.9 ± 8.9	4.07***
Trait Anxiety Inventory	43.9 ± 10.6	36.0 ± 9.9	3.57**
Fear Survey Schedule	298.8 ± 80.7	225.2 ± 46.2	3.67**
Janis–Field Scale	68.8 ± 11.6	79.5 ± 9.7	4.41***
Social Adjustment Scale			
Work/school[b]	2.1 ± .92	1.3 ± .80	2.69*
Household[c]	1.8 ± 1.1	1.3 ± .99	1.99
External family[c]	1.5 ± 1.1	.93 ± .92	1.96
Social/leisure[d]	2.7 ± 1.2	1.8 ± 1.3	2.91**
General[d]	2.3 ± .68	1.6 ± .72	2.82**

[a]$n = 17.$ [c]$n = 14.$ *$p = .05.$
[b]$n = 15.$ [d]$n = 16.$ **$p < .01.$
                         ***$p < .001.$

TABLE 10-5. Cognitive Therapy Subjects: Summary of Self-Report and Social Adjustment Scale Data at Pre- and Posttreatment Assessment

Instrument	Pretreatment	Posttreatment	t
Self-report instruments[a]			
Beck Depression Inventory	20.2 ± 10.5	7.0 ± 6.6	8.22***
State Anxiety Inventory	56.9 ± 16.0	39.1 ± 12.3	5.52***
Trait Anxiety Inventory	47.5 ± 12.9	38.7 ± 10.5	3.65***
Fear Survey Schedule[b]	311.5 ± 86.0	233.4 ± 69.5	8.13***
Janis–Field Scale	60.4 ± 16.8	70.7 ± 15.4	4.43***
Social Adjustment Scale			
Work/school[c]	2.4 ± 1.3	1.0 ± .97	3.15**
Household[d]	2.1 ± 1.1	1.3 ± 1.0	2.45*
External family[e]	2.2 ± 1.1	1.3 ± .95	3.39**
Social/leisure[f]	2.4 ± 1.1	1.6 ± .98	3.18**
General[f]	2.5 ± .93	1.6 ± .87	4.17***

[a]$n = 25.$ [c]$n = 16.$ [e]$n = 19.$ *$p < .05.$
[b]$n = 24.$ [d]$n = 15.$ [f]$n = 21.$ **$p < .01.$
                                      ***$p < .001.$

haps both systematic desensitization and cognitive therapy affect not only the victim's current level of anxiety, but also her perception of her general anxiety level.[2] Subjects made dramatic, and significant improvements in SAS-II social adjustment scores for work, household, family life, leisure activity, and general adjustment; they also reported less discomfort from their target complaints. Cognitive therapy seems to be particularly suited to the treatment of rape victims since it can focus both on symptoms of depression and of anxiety. This gives the therapist one consistent way of working with the rape victim on all her problems. Moreover, the process of cognitive therapy appears to provide the woman with confidence that she can control her thoughts and, through them, her feelings and actions. It is our experience that the acquisition of a sense of control over their own lives and feelings has a powerful therapeutic effect on sexual assault victims since a sense of control is precisely what they feel they have lost.

Information about the best treatment for rape victims will only result from systematic comparisons between untreated and treated subjects. The course of recovery of untreated subjects in the Calhoun et al. (1979) and Kilpatrick et al. (1979) studies could be compared with the recovery of treated subjects in our study; yet, such a comparison would yield questionable findings. Initial levels of depression, fear, and anxiety appear similar in the treated and untreated groups, but there are substantial differences in the racial demographics of the two samples which reflect local populations. In our project, subjects who had a prior history of difficulties with depression and were in need of exploring their basic belief systems accounted for only 20% of the cognitive therapy subjects. There are several ways in which an untreated control group could be constituted, but most of them raise ethical questions. A majority of victims would adjust well if assigned simply to medical examination and treatment, yet a minority would remain sufficiently symptomatic to cause the ethical researcher serious concern. Another option is the treatment-on-demand model (Weissman, Prusoff, DiMascio, Neu, Goklaney, & Klerman, 1979). This is a model which we have recently begun to employ. The control group receives treatment when they request it rather than no treatment, reducing ethical concerns about withholding treatment.

---

[2] *Editor's note.* It will be interesting to learn how these two treatments fare when subjected to a repeated-measures, multivariate analysis of variance.

BRIEF BEHAVIORAL INTERVENTION PROCEDURE

Kilpatrick, Veronen, and Resick (1980) in Charleston, South Carolina, are also studying behavioral treatment of sexual assault victims. They have begun to offer a Brief Behavioral Intervention Procedure (BBIP) to recent rape victims. Evidence that participation in an assessment procedure alone had therapeutic value (Kilpatrick *et al.*, 1979), coupled with a belief that sustained treatment was not feasible for all recent victims, prompted them to develop the brief treatment program. The BBIP is conducted by peer counselors and lasts approximately 4–6 hours. It includes an induced affect interview in which victims are asked to describe the assault in detail, and an educational component in which the counselor describes typical fear and anxiety reactions and the ways in which victim-blame myths contribute to self-blame. Finally, three specific coping skills are taught, including relaxation techniques (deep-muscle relaxation and deep breathing), guided self-dialogue, and strategies for avoiding avoidance. Fifteen women were randomly assigned to one of three conditions: the BBIP, repeated assessment, or delayed assessment. Treatment effects were assessed by these dependent measures: the Bown Self-Report Inventory, Derogatis Symptom Checklist, Profile of Mood States Scale, State–Trait Anxiety Inventory, and the Veronen–Kilpatrick Modified Fear Survey Schedule. In preliminary data analysis, the BBIP proved no more effective than repeated or delayed assessment. Repeated assessment, even though it was infrequent, had the greatest therapeutic effect.

TREATMENT OF SEXUAL PROBLEMS

In New York City, Becker (1981) and Abel have recruited victims of rape and incest through ads, newspaper stories, and contacts at mental health centers. To be included in the study, a woman must be at least 2 months postassault. Forty-seven percent of the sample were assaulted more than 3 years earlier, 37% between 1 and 3 years earlier, 14% between 3 and 12 months earlier, and 2% between 2 and 3 months earlier. The first subjects recruited included 40 women who were victims of rape alone, 30 women who were victims of incest alone, and 30 women who experienced both incest and rape. The mean number of sexual victimization experiences per subject was 2.1. The mean age of the group was 29.5 years, with a median of 28 years. The sample consisted of 7% Hispanics,

21% Blacks, and 72% Whites. Compared with samples of rape victims described thus far, this group appears to have a somewhat higher socioeconomic status. It is a well-educated group, in which 60% have some college education. The first hundred subjects, reported these dysfunctions: general avoidance and/or fear of sex, 57.5%; desire-phase disorder, 46.8%; arousal-phase disorder, 48.9%; primary orgasmic disorder, 2.1%; secondary orgasmic disorder, 10%; dyspareunia, 4%.

Becker and Abel randomly assign women to one of four treatment conditions: immediate group therapy, delayed group therapy, immediate individual therapy, or delayed individual therapy. Both delayed treatments involve a 10-week waiting period. Each condition provides 10 50-minute treatment sessions over 10 weeks, and permits the subject to choose a male or female therapist. Approximately 66% of the subjects have chosen a female therapist, 23% have no preference, and only 7% preferred a male therapist. Some subjects have changed their work schedules in order to meet with a female therapist. The content of all treatment conditions is identical. In every treatment condition, the first session establishes specific, behavioral goals. Since many women first select a vague goal such as, "being able to trust men again," they are encouraged to restate their goals as observable behaviors, for example, "being able to go out on a date," "being able to permit a man to touch me," "being able to engage in sexual intercourse." The next two to three sessions focus on body image and awareness training with the aim of returning a sense of control over her body to the woman. Women are encouraged to become acquainted with their bodies and to experience pleasure from viewing and touching their bodies. For women with orgasmic dysfunction, body awareness training is extended to full masturbatory training with orgasm as a goal. During these initial sessions, many women who gained weight after the rape start diets and lose the excess weight, which they then view as a protective covering from future assault. With more control of their own bodies, they feel more comfortable as attractive women. The fourth and fifth sessions establish cognitive changes through fantasy training in which subjects read sexual fantasies written by other women and then create their own fantasies. Many women stop fantasizing after an assault; permission to fantasize provides great relief. In the remaining treatment sessions, assertiveness training combined with sensate focus and pleasuring exercises teaches women to be effective when they ask their sexual partners to do things they like and to stop doing things they dislike. In the final session, women review treatment gains and speculate about their future sexual experience.

To date, Becker and Abel have treated 35 women. Preliminary inspection of results suggests that about 80% made progress toward their behavioral goals, and that the victims of incest made the least progress. Group treatment appears more effective than individual treatment, and delayed treatment seems to dilute motivation for change. About half the women in the delayed treatments dropped out during the waiting period, suggesting that there is a critical period during which decisions for change must be made and pursued.

OTHER BEHAVIORAL STRATEGIES

Strategies which have effectively reduced other types of anxiety could be applied and evaluated as methods of treating rape victims. Anxiety-reduction strategies are discussed in detail by Padawer and Goldfried (Chapter 13, this volume). *In vivo* exposure, either in a graded hierarchy or in an implosive format, seems to be an appropriate intervention for rape victims (Bandura, 1969; Marks, Boulougouris, & Marset, 1971; Stampfl & Levis, 1967). Burgess and Holmstrom (1974b) described a rape victim who was able to rid herself of her fear of the locale where she was raped. At first, she found herself "sneaking up" on the alley in which the incident occurred and quickly running past it. On subsequent occasions, she was able to walk past the alley without experiencing fear. This victim seems to have rid herself of fear through implosive exposure to the aversive stimulus. There is good reason to believe that exposure to the feared stimulus is necessary. The choice of systematic desensitization (in which the client approaches the feared situation in graded, manageable steps) or of implosion (in which the client is presented with all aspects of the feared situation at once) must be made carefully. The victim's own estimate of her preparedness should determine the manner in which exposure takes place. Our experience with over 100 recent rape victims leads us to believe that victims know when they are ready to try new behavior. The greatest distress occurs among victims who are not ready but are pushed into change by family members or friends, and among victims who are ready for change and are hindered by well-intentioned but overprotective friends and relatives.

Behavior rehearsal may also help rape victims (Lazarus, 1966;

Wolpe, 1958, 1969), by facilitating the extinction of anxiety and improving self-confidence. We have used behavior rehearsal since it enables the victim to develop a comfortable plan of action. With the counselor playing the role of a family member or a friend, the victim rehearses confronting significant others and telling them about the rape event. Behavioral rehearsal familiarizes the victim with interviews with the police, and prepares the victim for social interactions with peers, especially males. Most important, behavior rehearsal prepares women for anxiety provoking courtroom proceedings.

The rape victim's fear, anxiety, and depression have received some attention from clinicians, but disgust, guilt, and shame also influence the victim's interaction, and impede movement toward normalization. Treatment of specific symptoms and discussion of the victim's experience and feelings rarely alleviate these emotions, which are manifested by a series of intensely negative thoughts. Either alone, or as an adjunct to the therapiest discussed earlier, thought-stopping (Wolpe, 1958, 1973) may prove useful, since it is designed to transmit control over persistent, upsetting thoughts. The client learns to shift attention from troublesome thoughts to pleasant ones. This is accomplished by teaching the client to say "Stop!" either aloud or under her breath as soon as she is aware of having a distressing thought. She immediately substitutes a pre-established image of a pleasant situation, such as relaxing on a beach, and concentrates on that image for as long as is necessary to keep the distressing thought from returning. The efficacy of the procedure can be enhanced by instructing the client to wear a rubber band around her wrist and to snap it when she says the word "Stop!" This adds a punishment component which tends to decrease the frequency of the distressing thought at a more rapid rate. Once thought-stopping is successful, the therapist may choose to confront the client's feelings of guilt or shame by challenging the basic assumptions relevant to the troublesome thought.

Most rape prevention programs, provided by rape crisis centers, attempt to increase community awareness of the crime of rape and to teach self-defense skills to women. Behavioral strategies have yet to be applied to rape prevention. Bart (1981) suggested that a distinguishing feature of victims of attempted (as opposed to completed) rapes is their assertive, yet nonaggressive behavior. Therefore, social skills training with particular emphasis on assertive responses may prove to have value in rape prevention.

BACKGROUND OF THE PROBLEM OF WIFE ABUSE

Our understanding of the nature and consequences of wife abuse is currently at the level which our understanding of rape victimization reached with the publication of Burgess and Holmstrom's paper, "Rape Trauma Syndrome," in 1974. The incidence and prevalence of the problem of wife abuse has been established (Gelles, 1974; Rounsaville & Weissman, 1977–1978). Good descriptions of the nature of abusive relationships have appeared in the literature (Davidson, 1978; Gelles, 1974; Walker, 1979) and the association between wife abuse and other problems such as alcoholism and child abuse has been established (Gayford, 1975; Gelles, 1974; Hilberman & Munson, 1977–1978; Scott, 1974; Walker, 1979; Wolfgang, 1976). Descriptions of the nature of the psychological response to abuse have begun to appear (Rounsaville, Lifton, & Bieber, 1979); however, there have been no systematic assessments of psychological consequences of abuse. Treatment of abused women is in its infancy and only descriptive reports of treatment programs have appeared (Lieberknecht, 1978; Rounsaville, Lifton, & Bieber, 1979). Systematic studies of treatment efficacy are only now getting under way. For these reasons, our discussion of wife abuse and the treatment of its victims must be brief and speculative. While it is believed (Davidson, 1977) that the problem of wife abuse has been plaguing Western society for centuries it was not until early in the last decade that information regarding the incidence and consequences of spouse abuse emerged. The outrage of the women's movement encouraged serious inquiry into the problem by researchers, service providers, and legislators (Roy, 1977). Wife abuse is also called "wife beating" and "wife battery." "Battered wife" is the most common description of the victim; however, the term does not imply that the victim is legally married to the batterer, but simply that the batterer represents the male partner in a couple.

Violence may be the norm in as many as 50% of all American families. Gelles (1974) estimated conservatively that in more than one sixth of all households, a man strikes a woman at least once a year. To explain the frequently violent behavior of American families, Wolfgang (1976) observed that "violence in the family is partly a reflection of violent expression in the culture generally" (p. 325). Wife battery appears to occur as frequently in middle- and upper-income families as in lower-income families, even though police records show more violence in the latter families. Hilberman (1980) argues that the beating of lower-income women more often comes to the attention of public agencies and police, whereas the more affluent woman seeks aid from private physicians and attorneys who protect the family's privacy. Confirmation of this suspicion comes from Pennsylvania where the Protection from Abuse Act allows an abused woman to bar her husband from the home. Frieze (1981) searched court records and found that a large percentage of women claiming abuse came from middle- and upper-income levels. To emphasize that wife and child battery is not a crime exclusively limited to the impoverished slum dweller, Davidson (1978) reported that her father, a minister, psychologically and physically terrorized her mother, herself, and her siblings.

Although the causes are not clear, spouse abuse seems to be correlated with a history of abuse in the family of origin, alcoholism, jealousy, and child abuse. A surprising number of abused wives report parental violence in their own as well as in their husbands' families of origin (Hilberman & Munson, 1977–1978; Scott, 1974). Among 100 abused wives, 23% of the victims and 50% of the batterers had a generational history of familial violence (Gayford, 1975). An association between alcoholism and wife abuse has often been reported (Gayford, 1975; Gelles, 1974; Hilberman & Munson, 1977–1978; Scott, 1974; Walker, 1979). In Gayford's (1974) sample, 74% of batterers were intoxicated occasionally or regularly. In Hilberman and Munson's (1977–1978) sample, 93% of batterers drank before or during violence. According to Walker (1979) the batterer drinks to cope with severe life stress; however, drinking exacerbates the tension and encourages aggression. The display of physical and sexual aggression is thought to enhance the batterer's sense of self-esteem (Frieze, 1981).

Husbands' jealousy about real or imagined infidelity also contributes to wife battering (Gayford, 1975; Gelles, 1974; Hilberman & Munson, 1977–1978; Walker, 1979). The husband's badgering of his wife about suspected infidelity, at times leads the wife to admit to a nonexistent extramarital relationship to end the argument. Hilberman and Munson (1977–1978) reported that jealousy or possessiveness was present in 95% of their sample's abusive marriages. Two patterns of child abuse are associated with wife beating. Hilberman and Munson (1977–1978), who observed either physical or sexual abuse of children in one third of their sample, found that some husbands beat both wives and children, and other husbands beat wives who, in turn, abuse the children. In Gayford's sample of abusive couples (1975), 37% of the women and 54% of the men beat children. The children suffer as witnesses and targets of violence, and are vulnerable to somatic, psychological, and behavioral dysfunctions (Hilberman, 1980).

Reports of the psychological status of abused women first appeared in 1978 when Rounsaville and Weissman (1977–1978) described the psychiatric status of 31 abused women. On a self-report depression scale (CES-D), 80% reported moderate to severe depression. Diagnostic interviews identified symptoms of depression in 52%, symptoms of schizophrenia in 12%, and drug abuse in 6%. Using DSM-II criteria (*Diagnostic and Statistical Manual of Mental Disorders*, 2nd ed., 1968), only 29% were free from conditions warranting psychiatric diagnostic labels. Unlike Rounsaville and Weissman, who emphasized depression as the outcome of abuse, Hilberman (Hilberman & Munson, 1977–1978) considered fear and anxiety to be the primary symptoms of abuse women. Abused women experience unending stress due to ever present threat. They are hyperalert and vigilant, unable to relax or sleep. They experience fatigue, hopelessness, despair, guilt, and shame. They rarely describe themselves as angry at people other than themselves.

CURRENT APPROACHES TO TREATMENT OF ABUSE

Violence directed at a woman is wife abuse when it is a chronic occurrence in an enduring, heterosexual relationship. Since termination of abusive behavior is a reasonable goal, treatment inevitably focuses on the dyad, and involves individual, group, and marital therapy. Some men refuse treatment and some abused women leave the abusive relationship. Treatments are needed for these women and for women whose husbands have merely ceased their abuse. Hilberman (1980) identified three issues in the treatment of battered women: impaired self-esteem, emotional isolation, and lack of trust. As a clinician, Hilberman challenges the mythology about wife abuse which supports the battered woman's belief system. The battered woman believes that violence is normal; that her husband's violence is a logical result of his illness, intoxication, unemployment, or stress; that the violence is justified by her bad behavior and, that she can control violence by being good. This belief system enables the battered woman to control her rage. When therapy increases her awareness of anger and her assertiveness, and leads to plans for education, employment, or divorce, violence at home may increase. For this reason, the woman must determine how fast to change, and judge what changes will be safe for her and for her children.

Lieberknecht (1978) follows these steps when treating abused women. She begins by encouraging grief about the loss of a love relationship which provided self-respect, security, physical well-being, and trust. In the second step, the client becomes aware of feelings of loss and anger, and learns to trust her own self-protectiveness responses. In the third step, the client sets goals, accomplishes relevant daily tasks, and rehearses problem-solving skills. The goal of treatment is to enhance self-sufficiency by making use of the woman's new skills and the social and economic resources of the local community.

Rounsaville, Lifton, and Bieber (1979) noticed the social isolation and feelings of stigmatization of battered women, and decided that group treatment would foster independence, and raise awareness about women's issues. Potential group participants were referrals from a hospital emergency room and a mental health center with a history of recent physical abuse by a partner. Of the 75 identified patients, only 31 came for follow-up evaluation, and only 10 of these women became involved in treatment. Most group members were under 30, and from lower socioeconomic classes IV and V. Blacks and Catholics were overrepresented. The group was led by a male and a female therapist for 20 90-minute weekly sessions. Attendance was a constant and serious problem, with only four members attending throughout. Of those who did attend, all had a significant level of depression, and all but one had had more than 3 months of previous psychotherapy. Women who left their husbands attended fewer sessions than the others. In the first two sessions, women focused on their abusive relationships; in the next four sessions, group members became more interested in one another's problems and confronted each other's inconsistent thinking. After eight sessions, many group members made significant changes. Some left abusive relationships; others returned to a formerly abusive relationship. All the women vacillated about their abusive partners. After 15 sessions, all the women reported treatment gains and more stable living arrangements; however no follow-up data are available to verify these claims. The therapist's interventions were informative and supportive at first, confrontational and interpretive later on. The authors state that dependency and defenses against dependency were the principal themes of the group. Treatment was particularly helpful to those who attended regularly, but it did not appeal to the majority of those identified (86.7%) or of those screened (67.8%). Individual therapy may be required for women who cannot tolerate self-disclosure in a group.

POTENTIAL USES FOR BEHAVIOR THERAPY IN THE TREATMENT OF
BATTERED WOMEN

Behavioral approaches to the treatment of battered women have yet to
be described in the literature. While assertiveness and social skills training could be provided, cognitive-behavior therapy, with its emphasis on
the correction of maladaptive thinking, seems most appropriate. The
thinking of abused women apparently involves maladaptive basic assumptions that violence in families is the norm, that they are worthless
and deserve abuse, and that the violence will cease if they are "better"
wives. It seems likely that these assumptions are accompanied by feelings of depression, worthlessness, and helplessness. These assumptions
encourage women to believe they should tolerate repeated abuse and
prevent them from exploring alternatives.

CONCLUSIONS AND RECOMMENDATIONS

Advances have been made in the empirical study of behavioral interventions for rape victims; strategies for treating victims of household
violence have yet to be tested. With growing public concern about the
victims of wife abuse, more efforts will probably be made to develop
and test behavioral interventions with battered women. Enough case
studies and descriptive reports have appeared. Systematic research is
needed on the impact of aggression against women and on the efficacy
of treatment strategies.

Research and dissemination of information about rape and wife
abuse present special problems. Concern about these women began, not
in academic departments of psychology or psychiatry, or among mental
health professionals, but with people who established rape crisis centers
and domestic violence shelters as alternatives to existing mental health
facilities. The staffs of these centers are self-taught experts in crisis intervention. They are reluctant to participate in research conducted by
professionals and to use interventions associated with psychology or
psychiatry. In the Pittsburgh Project we found that these difficulties can
be overcome by establishing mutually supportive relationships between
crisis center staff and researchers.

Primary prevention of rape and wife abuse requires sweeping
changes in gender role definitions, in the socialization of women, and

in our tolerance for violent behavior. Secondary prevention efforts might focus on the youngest targets of aggression, since the victims of rape and wife abuse appear to have been brutalized during childhood. Unfortunately, this pattern of repeated abuse is sometimes misinterpreted as evidence that women "ask for" abuse, rather than as evidence that men are in the habit of abusing powerless family members. Data presented by Miller, Moeller, Kaufman, Divasto, Pathak, and Christy (1978) and by Becker (1981) substantiate clinical impressions of increased childhood victimization in rape victims and battered women. We believe that these childhood victims should be the targets of secondary prevention efforts. Little girls learn from the experience of incest that to survive in a hostile world, they must tolerate abuse, since they have no other options. It is little wonder that as adolescents they become rape victims and as adults they participate in abusive heterosexual relationships. Intervention with incest victims may prevent only a small but socially significant portion of acts of physical aggression against women.

Finally, the following treatment recommendations apply to victims of both rape and wife abuse:

1. Reassure the client that many of her reactions and feelings are normal responses to her current situation.
2. Help her to clarify questions of self-blame.
3. If treatment is indicated, choose treatment strategies which help the client regain a sense of control.

REFERENCES

Amir, M. *Patterns of forcible rape.* Chicago: University of Chicago Press, 1971.

Atkeson, B. M., Calhoun, K. S., Resick, P. A., & Ellis, E. M. Victims of rape: Repeated assessment of depressive symptoms. *Journal of Consulting and Clinical Psychology,* 1982, *50,* 96–102.

Bandura, A. *Principles of behavior modification.* New York: Holt, Rinehart & Winston, 1969.

Bart, P. B. A study of women who both were raped and avoided rape. *Journal of Social Issues,* 1981, *4,* 123–137.

Beck, A. T. *Depression: Causes and treatment.* Philadelphia: University of Pennsylvania Press, 1972.

Beck, A. T., Rush, A. J., Shaw, B. F., & Emery, G. *Cognitive therapy of depression.* New York: Guilford, 1979.

Beck A. T., Ward, C. H., Mendelson, M., Mock, J., & Erbaugh, J. An inventory for measuring depression. *Archives of General Psychiatry,* 1961, *4,* 561–571.

Becker, J. Personal communication, April 13, 1981.

Burgess, A. W., & Holmstrom, L. L. Rape trauma syndrome. *American Journal of Psychiatry,* 1974, *131,* 981–986. (a)

Burgess, A. W., & Holmstrom, L. L. *Rape: Victims of crisis.* Bowie, Md.: Brady, 1974. (b)

Calhoun, K. S., & Atkeson, B. M. Personal communication, April 18, 1980.

Calhoun, K. S., Atkeson, B. M., & Resick, P. A. *Incidence and patterns of depression in rape victims.* Paper presented at the meeting of the Association for Advancement of Behavior Therapy, San Francisco, December 1979.

Davidson, T. Wife beating: A recurring phenomenon throughout history. In M. Roy (Ed.), *Battered women: A psychological study of domestic violence,* New York: Van Nostrand, 1977.

Davidson, T. *Conjugal crime: Understanding and changing the wife-beating pattern.* New York: Hawthorne, 1978.

Diagnostic and statistical manual of mental disorders (2nd ed.). Washington, D.C.: American Psychiatric Association, 1968.

Frank, E., & Stewart, B. D. The treatment of depressed rape victims: An approach to stress-induced symptomatology. In P. Clayton (Ed.), *Treatment of depression: Old controversies, new approaches.* Raven, 1982.

Frank, E., Turner, S. M., & Duffy, B. Depressive symptoms in rape victims. *Journal of Affective Disorders,* 1979, *1*, 269–277.

Frieze, I. H. *Marital rape.* Paper presented at University of Pittsburgh, Women's Studies Department Symposium on Rape, April 7, 1981.

Gayford, J. J. Wife-battering: A preliminary survey of 100 cases. *British Medical Journal,* 1975, *1*, 194–197.

Gelles, R. J. *The violent home: A study of physical aggression between husbands and wives.* Beverly Hills, Calif.: Sage, 1974.

Halleck, S. L. The physician's role in management of victims of sex offenders. *Journal of the American Medical Association,* 1962, *180*, 273–278.

Hamilton, M. A rating scale for depression. *Journal of Neurology, Neurosurgery, and Psychiatry,* 1960, *23*, 56–62.

Hilberman, E. *The rape victim.* Washington, D.C.: American Psychiatric Association, 1976.

Hilberman, E. Overview: The "wife-beater's wife" reconsidered. *American Journal of Psychiatry,* 1980, *137*, 1336–1347.

Hilberman, E., & Munson, M. Sixty battered women. *Victimology,* 1977–1978, *2*, 460–471.

Jacobson, E. *Progressive relaxation.* Chicago: University of Chicago Press, 1938.

Jacobson, E. *Modern treatment of tense patients.* Springfield, Ill.: Thomas, 1970.

Katz, S., & Mazur, M. A. *Understanding the rape victim: A synthesis of research findings.* New York: Wiley, 1979.

Kilpatrick, D. G., Veronen, L. J., & Resick, P. A. The aftermath of rape: Recent empirical findings. *American Journal of Orthopsychiatry,* 1979, *49*(4), 658–669.

Kilpatrick, D. G., Veronen, L. J., & Resick, P. A. *The brief behavior intervention procedure: A new treatment for recent rape victims.* Poster session presented at the 14th Annual Convention of the Association for Advancement of Behavior Therapy, New York City, November 21–23, 1980.

Lazarus, A. A. Behavior rehearsal vs. non-directive therapy vs. advice in effecting behavior change. *Behaviour Research and Therapy,* 1966, *4*, 209–212.

Lieberknecht, K. Helping the battered wife. *American Journal of Nursing,* 1978, 654–656.

MacDonald, J. M. *Rape offenders and their victims.* Springfield, Ill.: 1978, 654–656.

Marks, I., Boulougouris, J., & Marset, P. Flooding versus desensitization in the treatment of phobic patients: A cross-over study. *British Journal of Psychiatry,* 1971, *119*, 353–375.

Miller, J., Moeller, D., Kaufman, A., Divasto, P., Pathak, D., & Christy, J. Recidivism among sex assault victims. *American Journal of Psychiatry,* 1978, *135*(9), 1103–1104.

Miller, W. R., Williams, A. M., & Bernstein, M. H. *The effects of rape on marital and sexual adjustment.* Paper presented at the meeting of the Eastern Association for Sex Therapy, Philadelphia, March, 1979.

Notman, M. T., & Nadelson, C. C. The rape victim: Psychodynamic considerations. *American Journal of Psychiatry,* 1976, *133,* 408–413.

Paul, G. L. Outcome of systematic desensitization: II. Controlled investigations of individual treatment, technique variations, and current status. In C. M. Franks (Ed.), *Behavior therapy: Appraisal and status,* New York: McGraw-Hill, 1969.

Peters, J. J. Social, legal, and psychological effects of rape on the victim. *Pennsylvania Medicine,* 1975, *78*(2), 34–36. (a)

Peters, J. J. Social psychiatric study of victims reporting rape. *Scientific Proceedings of the 128th Annual Meeting of the American Psychiatric Association,* Washington, D.C., 1975, pp. 111–112. (b)

Queen's Bench Foundation. *Rape victimization study.* San Francisco: Queen's Bench Foundation, 1975.

Resick, P. A., Calhoun, K. S., Atkeson, B. M., & Ellis, E. M. Social adjustment in victims of sexual assault. *Journal of Consulting and Clinical Psychology,* 1981, *49,* 705–712.

Rimm, D. C., & Masters, J. C. *Behavior therapy: Techniques and empirical findings* (2nd ed.). New York: Academic, 1979.

Rounsaville, B., Lifton, N., & Bieber, M. The natural history of a psychotherapy group for battered women. *Psychiatry,* 1979, *42,* 63–78.

Rounsaville, B., & Weissman, M. M. Battered women: A medical problem requiring detection. *International Journal of Psychiatry in Medicine,* 1977–1978, *8,* 191–202.

Roy, M. (Ed.). *Battered women: A psychosociological study of domestic violence.* New York: Van Nostrand, 1977.

Rush, A. J., Beck, A. T., Kovacs, M., & Hollon, S. Comparative efficacy of cognitive therapy and pharmacotherapy in the treatment of depressed out-patients. *Cognitive Therapy and Research,* 1977, *1,* 17–37.

Scott, P. D. Battered wives. *British Journal of Psychiatry,* 1974. *125,* 433–441.

Shore, B. *An examination of critical process and outcome factors in rape.* NIMH Grant No. 171-14-8194. Report to the Public, 1979; Final Report, 1980.

Spitzer, R., Endicott, J., & Robins, E. Research diagnostic criteria: Rationale and reliability. *Archives of General Psychiatry,* 1978, *35,* 773–782.

Stampfl, T., & Levis, D. Essentials of implosive therapy: A learning theory based psychodynamic behavioral therapy. *Journal of Abnormal Psychology,* 1967, *72,* 496–503.

Sutherland, S., & Scherl, D. J. Patterns of response among victims of rape. *American Journal of Orthopsychiatry,* 1970, *40,* 503–511.

United States Department of Justice, Federal Bureau of Investigation. *Uniform crime reports for the United States.* Washington, D.C.: U.S. Government Printing Office, 1967.

United States Department of Justice, Federal Bureau of Investigation. *Uniform crime reports for the United States.* Washington, D.C.: U.S. Government Printing Office, 1980.

Walker, L. E. *The battered woman.* New York: Harper & Row, 1979.

Weissman, M. M., Prusoff, B. A., DiMascio, A., Neu, C. Goklaney, M., & Klerman, G. L. The efficacy of drugs and psychotherapy in the treatment of acute depressive episodes. *American Journal of Psychiatry,* 1979, *136,* 555–558.

Wolfe, L. New rape laws ending the anti-victim bias. *The New York Times,* December 1, 1974, p. 47.

Wolfgang, M. E. Family violence and criminal behavior. *Bulletin of the American Academy of Psychiatry and the Law,* 1976, *4,* 316–327.

Wolpe, J. *Psychotherapy by reciprocal inhibition.* Stanford, Calif.: Stanford University Press, 1958.

Wolpe, J. *The practice of behavior therapy* (1st ed.). New York: Pergamon, 1969.

Wolpe, J. *The practice of behavior therapy* (2nd ed.). New York: Pergamon, 1973.

Wood, P. L. The victim in a forcible rape case: A feminist view. *American Criminal Law Review,* 1973, *22,* 335–354.

III

DISORDERS COMMON
AMONG WOMEN

Among adolescent and adult women, the incidence and prevalence of depression, physiological, and reproductive disorders, excessive anxiety and related behavioral deficits, and disturbances in eating, are disproportionately high. The four chapters in this part of the book review and critique evidence about etiology, behavioral assessment, and treatment of disorders common among women.

Depression is a core phenomenon in behavior modification with women. Recent recognition of the disproportionate incidence and prevalence of depression among women has already influenced epidemiologic research, basic inquiries into depression, and design of intervention strategies. In Chapter 11 Norman, Johnson, and Miller provide a thorough, scholarly review of the developments in these fields. Their chapter also sets forth an integrated behavioral–cognitive approach to depression which recognizes the circumstances that contribute to depression in women and impede its treatment. Given the heterogeneity of depression, Norman, Johnson, and Miller favor intensive, multimodal, pretreatment assessment, and treatment tailored to suit the results of baseline evaluation.

As Calhoun and Sturgis point out in Chapter 12, physiological and reproductive disorders prevalent among women have long been attributed either to a neurotic feminine temperament, or to poor self-control. As a result, basic psychological and physiological mechanisms have not been studied with scientific rigor, and rational treatments have not been developed. The breakthroughs in prostaglandin research are exceptions which hold promise for the understanding of other forms of undiagnosable pain in women. The medical and psychological complaints most often brought to general practitioners by women are described in Calhoun and Sturgis's chapter, which introduces an important new subspecialty in behavioral medicine—behavioral gynecology.

No behavioral procedures are more widely disseminated to women than methods of treating anxiety. Padawer and Goldfried (Chapter 13) reconcile these technical advances in the treatment of women with cognitive–social psychology's findings about sex-role attitudes and behavior. Readers with a special interest in sex-role constructs will appreciate the different ways in which this chapter and Beck and Barlow's (Chapter 2) approach the same intellectual problem. Padawer and Goldfried depict in detail how the social environs of adolescent and adult women encourage maladaptive, albeit rational fear. The difficulties that women encounter in assertion and achievement, and the anxiety that results even when women succeed, are described along with detailed information about relevant treatments. Padawer and Goldfried portray a rich sample of the complicated family and work problems that modern women confront, problems that create anxiety because they lend themselves to few totally satisfactory solutions.

While Foreyt and Goodrick in Chapter 9 considered weight loss in the context of a preventive program of health maintenance, Fodor and Thal (Chapter 14) focus on weight disorders of clinical severity. After describing clinical weight disorders, Fodor and Thal address American women's preoccupation with slenderness. They argue that this preoccupation causes a variety of weight disorders, and that behaviorists' unquestioning acceptance of this preoccupation imperils the efficacy of standard behavioral weight-loss programs. A cognitive–behavioral approach, which challenges cultural assumptions about the ideal female body, is described along with illustrative case study data. Frank and Stewart (Chapter 10) urged designers of behavioral treatments for physically victimized women to draw upon advances made by women's self-help groups. Similarly, Fodor and Thal urge behaviorists to learn from the women's movement how to promote self-acceptance on the part of self-derogatory women, who regard attractiveness as their most important personal characteristic.

11

DEPRESSION:
A BEHAVIORAL–COGNITIVE APPROACH

WILLIAM H. NORMAN
BELINDA A. JOHNSON
IVAN W. MILLER, III

OVERVIEW

Amidst increasing awareness of the personal and social impact of depression (Schuyler & Katz, 1974; Becker, 1974; Friedman & Katz, 1974), theoretical explanations and empirical investigations have proliferated. Although behavior therapists have only begun to focus on depression, the application of behavioral techniques has increased significantly during recent years. This increase may be attributed to claims of efficacy for behavior therapy, and to the sophistication of behavioral–cognitive conceptual formulations and measurement procedures for depression.

This chapter conceptualizes depressive disorders in a social learning framework. The discussion focuses on the behavioral–cognitive formulations of depression and issues relevant to assessment and treatment of depression, with special attention given to women. The chapter is divided into several major sections: (1) definitions and clinical features of depression; (2) prevalence of depression among women; (3) integration of behavioral assessment and traditional diagnosis; and (4) behavioral–cognitive formulations of depression and treatment strategies.

William H. Norman. Section of Psychiatry and Human Behavior, Brown University–Butler Hospital, Providence, Rhode Island.

Belinda A. Johnson. Brown University Health Services, Providence, Rhode Island.

Ivan W. Miller, III. Section of Psychiatry and Human Behavior, Brown University–Butler Hospital, Providence, Rhode Island.

BACKGROUND

DEFINITION AND CLINICAL FEATURES OF DEPRESSION

A definition of depression is difficult because of its multiple meanings in clinical work, research, and everyday usage. Depression has been conceptualized from many points of view (e.g., behavioral, dynamic, cognitive), and definitions vary according to theoretical orientation and discipline (e.g., neurophysiology, pharmacology, psychology, psychiatry). The problem of defining depression is further complicated by the multiple etiological factors in depression (e.g., genetic, biochemical, environmental), the heterogeneity of clinical manifestations within depressive disorders, and variations in the acquisition and maintenance of dysfunctional depressive symptoms and behaviors. A related difficulty is that the term has been used to refer to a mood, a symptom, and a syndrome (Beck, 1967). As a mood, depression is part of the fabric of everyday life and a universal adaptive response to stress, frustrations, and loss. Most people are subject to occasional episodes of sadness as well as variations in the intensity and frequency of the sadness experience (Wessman & Ricks, 1966). While the distinction between normal sadness and severe clinical depression is easily judged, therapists do not always agree on the criteria for distinguishing when an individual has crossed the boundary between normal depression and clinical depression. For instance, severe depression is considered normal in the context of certain environmental events such as the loss of a significant loved one. An acute grief reaction may be regarded as adaptive even though there is no qualitative difference in the symptomatology between grief and clinical depression. However, when the symptoms suggestive of depression continue several months subsequent to the loss, professional intervention is usually thought to be warranted. This example illustrates the utility of operationalized criteria for the diagnosis of depression.

Depression as a clinical syndrome is our concern for this discussion. The depressive syndrome refers to the covariance of a cluster of behaviors that generally contribute to a diagnosis of depression. Although there is no one depressive syndrome, there is considerable agreement across studies (e.g., Grinker, Miller, Sabshin, Nunn, & Nunnally, 1961) as to the constituents of the depression syndrome. These symptoms are often conceptually divided into behavioral, cognitive, somatic, and affective clusters (Beck, 1967). Table 11-1 summarizes behaviors and symp-

TABLE 11-1. Symptoms of Depression

Affective	Behavioral	Cognitive	Somatic
Mood characterized by reports of feeling sad, blue, despondent, gloomy, etc.	Psychomotor retardation and/or psychomotor agitation	Low self-evaluation characterized by reports of inadequacy, failure, worthlessness, helplessness, powerlessness	Sleep disturbance, usually initial and/or terminal insomnia
Decreased capacity to experience gratification and pleasure	Neglect of personal appearance and grooming	Self-blame and self-criticism	Loss of libido
Feelings of guilt	Crying	Negative expectations and pessimistic about future	Loss of energy: fatigue, lethargy
Feelings of anxiety	Speech slow	Diminished ability to concentrate with complaints of "slowed thinking," or "mixed-up thoughts"	Gastrointestinal—indigestion, constipation, weight loss
Diurnal variation	Volume of speech decreased	Thoughts of suicide	Headaches
	Decreased capacity to do ordinary work		Dizzy spells
	Decreased sexual activity		Generalized pain
	Social withdrawal—sits alone quietly, stays in bed much of time, does not enter into activities with others		
	Suicide attempts		

Note. Adapted by permission from "Behavioral Treatment of Depression" by P. M. Lewinsohn, A. Biglan, and A. M. Zeiss, in P. O. Davidson (Ed.), *The Behavioral Management of Anxiety, Depression and Pain*, New York: Brunner/Mazel, 1976.

toms that, in varying combinations, commonly constitute the depressive syndrome. Very rarely do depressed individuals experience only one of the many symptoms listed; most often the depressed individual experiences a pervasive disturbance of mood plus a combination of the behaviors listed in Table 11-1. Consequently, individuals who are labeled depressed are quite heterogeneous.

Given the problems in definition, it is especially important that the criteria which are used to diagnose the person as depressed are made explicit. The Research Diagnostic Criteria (Spitzer, Endicott, & Robins, 1978) and the DSM-III (the American Psychiatric Association's third edition of the *Diagnostic and Statistical Manual of Mental Disorders,* 1980) are two examples of systems providing operational criteria for disordered behaviors which must be observed in order to justify the diagnosis of depression. From a behavioral viewpoint, a detailed behavioral description is equally as important as explicit criteria for diagnosis, since it facilitates the identification of specific events and behavioral patterns which interfere with the person's social and interpersonal functioning. Thus, a depressive disorder is presumed when depression is judged to be of extreme intensity, frequency, and/or duration relative to the environmental context. The integration of operationalized diagnostic criteria and the behavioral analysis of depression will be discussed in more detail later in the chapter.

PREVALENCE OF DEPRESSION AMONG WOMEN

Depression represents a significant mental health problem which affects a substantial proportion of the population. Of all psychiatric hospital admissions 15 to 25% are for depression (Schuyler, 1974; Turns, 1978). In addition, epidemiological surveys have estimated that 2 to 4% of the population is depressed to the extent that treatment intervention is warranted (e.g., Turns, 1978; Levitt & Lubin, 1975), and that 10 to 20% of the population will experience a clinical depression in their lifetime (Schuyler, 1974; Ripley, 1977; Weissman & Myers, 1978).

It is a well-documented epidemiological finding that the prevalence of depression is greater among women than men. In a review of studies of diagnosed and treated depressed patients, as well as community surveys including both treated and untreated cases, Weissman and Klerman (1977) found that in every age group the rates of depression for women were higher than those for men. Differences are conceptually as well as statistically significant; in community surveys, for instance, sex ratios were 2 or 3 to 1. This finding has stimulated reflection on and investigation of possible biological and psychosocial sex differences that might account for the differential rates. The variety of hypotheses that have been proposed is of interest here because of their differing treatment implications. While some proportion of higher female incidence may be explained endocrinologically (e.g., in postpartum and premenstrual depression and the side effects of birth-control pills), this factor affects only a small number of women and is not sufficient in itself to account for the large sex differences that have been found (Weissman & Klerman, 1977). Although advances in the biochemistry and physiology of depression eventually may identify biological reasons for the higher prevalence of depression among women, no definitive evidence is currently available. Thus, there has been an increasing focus on socialization and cultural factors.

One line of inquiry has focused on the relationship between depression and stress (e.g., Brown & Harris, 1978; Paykel, 1979). The experience of high levels of stress is said to be one precipitant of depression. Paykel, Myers, Diendelt, Klerman, Lindenthal, and Pepper (1969), for example, categorized the life-stress events experienced by 185 depressed clients in the 6 months immediately prior to onset of their depressive symptoms and found three times more stressful events than among matched nondepressed controls. Typically, studies of stress have not addressed the question of sex differences, and the limited available data are inconclusive. This may be due to the fact that the majority of life-event measures used to assess stress exclude more events relevant to women than to men, and ignore the possibility that women may experience greater stress than men when exposed to the same stressors (Makosky, 1980). Another possibility is that depression is one of several possible responses to life stress, and that this response is mediated by life-style. In a study of 33-year-old, normal female college graduates, Stewart and Salt (1981) found that stressors centering around the family were associated with depression, particularly among housewives, while job-related stresses were associated with physical illness, particularly among work-centered (i.e., unmarried) women.

Gove (1979, 1980; Gove & Tudor, 1977) has taken a different approach, arguing that several aspects of married women's sex role expose them to greater stress than men or unmarried women. Among these he includes: (1) restriction to the single societal role of housewife which limits their flexibility in obtaining gratification, as opposed to men, who have both work and family roles; (2) the frustrating nature, for many women, of their major instrumental activity (i.e., raising children and keeping house); (3) the relatively unstructured quality of the housewife role, which allows time for brooding in a way that most jobs outside the home do not; (4) unclear and diffuse expectations, together with a lack of direct control over their futures; and (5) for working women, lower income and status occupations than for men, a societal orientation for their careers that takes them less seriously than men's, and the added strain of doing most of the housework. Assuming that greater stress results in higher rates of mental illness, his argument is supported by evidence that the greatest female predominance in mental illness is among the married; unmarried males have higher rates of mental disorders than unmarried females (Gove, 1972; Radloff, 1975; Goldman & Ravid, 1980).

Regardless of whether or not women experience more stress than men in this society, the reality is that in regard to education, occupational advancement, and earnings, women as a class are at a disadvantage. Women are clustered in the lowest-paying occupations and are disproportionately represented below the poverty line. "Discrimination against women continues in all the major institutions of society" (*President's Commission on Mental Health, Special Population Subpanel on Mental Health in Women*, 1978, p. 298). That these environmental disadvantages may have some implications for depression is reflected in epidemiological findings that for both sexes, low income, low education, and low-status employment are associated with a high incidence of depression (Radloff, 1980). Poverty may be particularly important. In an outcome study of the treatment of depression in women of low socioeconomic status, Padfield (1976) found that an income level below the poverty line was a deterrent to improvement; regardless of treatment condition, those whose monthly income was above $400 improved more than those whose income was less.

Weissman and Klerman (1977) have summarized two hypothesized pathways to depression coming out of the literature on the effect of women's disadvantaged social status. In what they named the "social status hypothesis," social discrimination and resulting inequities make it difficult for women to achieve their goals by direct action. Thus, they find themselves in comparatively helpless positions, with feelings of low self-esteem, and ultimately, clinical depression. The alternative analyses, which they name the "learned helplessness hypotheses," focus on women's socialization experiences and cultural stereotypes of femininity which include a negative valence for assertiveness and a positive valence for helplessness. Thus, women have limited response repertoires for coping with stress, feel powerless to exert control in their lives, and in ways that will be developed more fully later in the chapter, their learned helplessness may result in depression. Although we shall return to further discussion of the assessment and treatment implications of social–cultural factors in the depression of women, for the present discussion it is important to note that, depending upon the values of the client and therapist and the specifics of the situation, the behaviors targeted for change can be quite diverse, and therefore an adequate assessment, and specifically a behavior analysis, is essential.

ASSESSMENT OF DEPRESSION

Given the multiple etiological factors of depression, the heterogeneity of clinical manifestations within the depression syndrome, and variations in the course of dysfunctional depressive behaviors, the clinical assessment of the depressed client should be multidimensional and include: (1) comprehensive physical examination; (2) differential diagnosis, including description of past and present symptomatology; (3) assessment of severity; and (4) behavioral analysis of specific problematic factors, and their response to treatment intervention. The remainder of this section will discuss each component of the assessment process.

PHYSICAL EXAMINATION

A comprehensive physical examination is necessary to investigate possible medical causes of depression. A number of medications may cause depressive symptomatology (reserpine, α-methyldopa, propranolol, steroids, etc.). Of special significance for the treatment of depressed women is the finding that for some women birth-control pills may produce depressive symptoms (Adams, Rose, & Folkard, 1973; Weissman & Slaby, 1973; Winston, 1973). In addition, depressive symptoms may result from or covary with various medical disorders including thyroid disease, pernicious anemia, rheumatoid arthritis, and cancer. In order to rule out these potential causes, a complete physical examination and medical history should be obtained prior to initiating treatment.

DIFFERENTIAL DIAGNOSIS—PAST AND PRESENT SYMPTOMATOLOGY

There are several reasons for including this component in the assessment process. Unlike previous diagnostic systems (e.g., the *Diagnostic and Statistical Manual of Mental Disorders*, 2nd ed. [DSM-II], 1968) the development of the Research Diagnostic Criteria (Spitzer *et al.*, 1978) and the DSM-III (1980) provide operational criteria for disordered behaviors and have adequate reliability. When used in conjunction with recently developed interview schedules such as the Schedule for Affective Disorders and Schizophrenia (Endicott & Spitzer, 1978), Present State Examination (Wing *et al.*, 1974), and Diagnostic Interview Schedule (Robins, Helzer, Croughan, & Ratcliffe, 1981), which also have adequate reliability, these procedures offer a comprehensive assessment of present symptomatology, premorbid history, and operational criteria for differential diagnosis.

Diagnostic information is relevant to the treatment decision-making process. Since depression often accompanies other disorders (e.g., alcohol abuse, schizophrenia, anxiety disorders), it is important to establish the entire pattern for a given client. The presence of another concurrent disorder may have important treatment implications. Furthermore, diagnostic distinctions among types of depressive disorders may suggest particular types of treatment. For example, a client who is currently depressed but reports a history of symptoms and experiences consistent with a diagnosis of bipolar affective disorders (e.g., manic and depressive episodes) may respond more favorably to a drug regime (e.g., lithium carbonate, tricyclic antidepressants) than other forms of treatment intervention (Depue & Monroe, 1978, 1979). While it is not the purpose of this chapter to review the various predictors of effectiveness of antidepressant medication, depressed patients who show severe depression with somatic symptoms, including disorders of sleep, appetite, sexual functioning, activity level, and concentration should be evaluated for antidepressant medication. In addition, the following variables indicate that a favorable response to medication is likely: (1) history of the client's favorable response to medication; (2) history of manic episodes (e.g., bipolar affective disorder); (3) the presence of delusions or hallucinations; and (4) familial history of bipolar affective disorder.

SEVERITY OF DEPRESSION

The severity or level of depression can be assessed from a variety of data sources, including: self-report, interviewer report, and behavioral observation (for a comprehensive review of assessment of severity see chapters by Lewinsohn & Lee, 1981; Rehm, 1976). Self-report scales such as the Beck Depression Inventory (Beck, 1967); Zung Depression Scale (Zung, 1965); Depressive Adjective Checklist (Levitt & Lubin, 1975); and the MMPI D-scale have been shown to have adequate reliability and validity for clinical usage. Interview rating scales such as the Hamilton Rating Scale (Hamilton, 1960); the Feelings and Concerns Checklist (Grinker, Miller, Sabshin, Nunn, & Nunnally, 1961); and the Raskin Depression Scale (Raskin, Schulterbrandt, Reatig, Crook, & Odle, 1974) appear to be valid instruments for assessment of severity of depression. Finally, a few attempts to assess overt behavior of depressed inpatients (Williams, Barlow, & Agras, 1972; Norman & Nelson, 1978) have suggested that behavioral ratings may assess a dimension of depression different from self-report or interviewer ratings. In general these measures are often combined and provide a more comprehensive measure of depression and its severity. In addition, the therapist should assess the suicide potential of the depressed client. While demographic variables such as age, sex, marital status, and arrest record predict an increased risk for suicide (Burglass & Horton, 1974; Lettieri, 1974), idiographic variables such as level of hopelessness (Beck, Kovacs, & Weissman, 1975; Beck, Weissman, Lester, & Trexler, 1974), history of previous suicide attempts, and absence of social support may increase the therapist's predictive power.

Sex differences have not been systematically investigated for most of these instruments, which have been normed on undifferentiated samples of males and females. While women in the general population score higher on measures of depression, this does not appear to be due to measurement bias, but rather to the high percentage of women who meet research criteria for a depressive disorder (Weissman & Klerman, 1977). Depressed women do not differ in severity from depressed men (Clancy & Gove, 1974; Amenson & Lewinsohn, 1981). However, Hammen and Padesky (1977) report that females do show a different pattern of depressive symptomatology than do males. Females tend to report greater indecisiveness and self-dislike, while males report greater inability to cry, decreased social interest, sense of failure, and somatic symptoms.

INTEGRATION OF BEHAVIORAL ANALYSIS AND TRADITIONAL DIAGNOSIS: BEHAVIORAL ANALYSIS OF DEPRESSION

While most therapists evaluate medical factors, premorbid history, depressive symptomatology, and severity of depression, and formulate a diagnosis, these data may not suffice to select effective treatment. For example, knowledge of a client's severe depression, diagnosis of unipolar depression, and lack of medical complications is insufficient to predict whether social skills training, cognitive therapy, antidepressant medication, or some combination of these interventions will be effective. This example illustrates one disadvantage of total reliance on diagnostic formulations. In accordance with Nathan's (1981) point of view, the utility of traditional diagnostic formulations is greater with those disorders for which drug treatment is the treatment of choice (e.g., lithium carbonate for bipolar affective disorder). When a preferred treatment does not exist, a behavioral analysis may provide direction for intervention.

Behavioral analysis, the cornerstone of the behavioral treatment of the depressed individual, involves: (1) identification of specific target behaviors that disrupt functioning (e.g., impaired social relations, low self-esteem, decreased energy); (2) identification of factors that produce and maintain the target behaviors (e.g., inadequate social skills, dysfunctional cognitions, biochemical imbalance); (3) identification of an intervention which modifies the target behaviors and the maintaining factors; and (4) ongoing evaluation of target behavior (clinical progress) and of treatment outcome. Whereas the recent diagnostic systems (e.g., DSM-III, RDC) provide nomothetic suggestions about response covariation (characteristic of a depressive episode) and effective treatment for those disorders for which drug treatment is the treatment of choice, a behavioral analysis is an idiographic approach which offers an individualized assessment and behavioral treatment plan for the depressed client (Nelson & Barlow, 1981).

The use of operationalized diagnostic criteria for depressive disorders (e.g., DSM-III, RDC), together with a behavioral analysis of maladaptive behavior, helps the therapist to: (1) define depression in terms of specific behaviors that are problematic for the client, (2) differentiate among subtypes of depressive disorders; (3) identify factors in need of intervention; (4) select specific treatment interventions designed to modify the target behaviors; and (5) select measures to monitor the target behaviors and their response to treatment intervention and outcome. In the typical clinical situation, the therapist uses the data from the behavioral analysis to form hypotheses about the factors maintaining depression and shares these with the client. Then therapist and client agree upon treatment goals.

BEHAVIORAL–COGNITIVE FORMULATIONS OF DEPRESSION

A basic premise to behavioral–cognitive formulations of depression is that behavioral patterns are functionally related to depression and may result from one or more of the following factors: (1) Efforts to bring about positive reinforcement are inadequate; (2) perceptions of ability to control the world are distorted; or (3) the environment is unresponsive, offering few reinforcements. This section provides a brief overview of the three major behavioral and cognitive formulations of depression: social skills, cognitive, and learned helplessness. For each approach, we discuss the underlying theory, potential etiological and maintenance factors, specific assessment strategy, and treatment implications. Since it is beyond the scope of this chapter to examine each formulation in detail, the interested reader is referred to several excellent review articles (Blaney, 1977; Rehm & Kornblith, 1979; Wilcoxon, Schrader, & Nelson, 1976).

SOCIAL SKILLS FORMULATION

Social Skills Theory of Depression

One broad category of theory and treatment approaches in depression focuses on the training of social skills. In this approach, depression is considered to be the result of a reduced frequency of positive reinforcement (Ferster, 1965; Lazarus, 1968). More specifically, depression is said to occur either when there is little reinforcement, or when the available reinforcers are not contingent on the person's behavior (Lewinsohn, Biglan, & Zeiss, 1976). Although a change in the environment (e.g., the loss of an important reinforcer such as a job, or the death of a loved one) may initiate the depressive episode, the important factor from a treatment standpoint is that depressed people lack the social skills to cope effectively with the crisis and to elicit a satisfactory amount of positive reinforcement in their day-to-day living.

Lewinsohn and his colleagues have shown that depressed persons are less socially skillful than nondepressed persons (Libet & Lewinsohn, 1973; Lewinsohn & Schaffer, 1971; Sanchez & Lewinsohn, 1980). Operationally defining social skills as the ability to emit behaviors that are positively reinforced by others and to avoid behaviors that are punished, they have shown that socially skilled individuals are "active, quick to respond, relatively insensitive to an aversive person, do not miss chances to react, distribute their behaviors evenly across members in a group situation, and emit behaviors which are positively reinforcing" (Lewinsohn, Biglan, & Zeiss, 1976, p. 121). According to these empirically derived criteria, depressed persons are less socially skilled than nondepressed persons, and receive less positive reinforcement (MacPhillamy & Lewinsohn, 1974).

Assessment of Social Skills

The social skills literature concerns training in assertion, heterosexual skills, and communication. Assessment techniques used in studies of depressed populations include self-report and behavioral measures. Self-report measures are most easily administered, and there are several such questionnaires for the assessment of assertiveness (Wolpe–Lazarus Assertiveness Questionnaire, 1966; Rathus Assertiveness Scale, 1973; Galassi, DeLo, Galassi, & Bastien's College Self-Expression Scale, 1974; Gambrill & Richey's Assertion Inventory, 1975). Although the face validity of these scales is clear, there has been insufficient evaluation of their psychometric properties (Twentyman & Zimering, 1979). Since depressed individuals may not be aware of their behavior patterns, whether skillful or deficient, objective behavioral assessment is important. Several coding systems have been developed specifically for the behavior of depressed individuals (e.g., Williams, Barlow, & Agras, 1972).

Hersen, Bellack, and Himmelhoch (1982) developed a 16-item roleplay test which samples several target areas of social skills, in varying social contexts and with different social partners. Dependent measures include variables such as duration of eye contact, number of smiles, duration of reply, and loudness of speech. One difficulty with such behavioral assessment devices is their possible effect on training (Hersen & Bellack, 1978). Moreover, the concept of "social skill" is a broad one. Since there does not appear to be a significant transfer of training across target behaviors in social situations, it is important to sample broadly and to specify precise targets for change.

Another commonly used assessment instrument is the Pleasant Events Schedule (MacPhillamy & Lewinsohn, 1974). This daily self-report checklist assesses the frequency and reinforcement potential of pleasant events. Events that correlate with positive mood can be targets for increased frequency during treatment.

Treatment Implications of a Social Skills Model

According to this model, depression can be alleviated by improving social skills and increasing positive reinforcement. Investigators have attempted to do this using treatment strategies that vary from simple programs which focus on one behavior (e.g., positive assertion) to elaborate programs which target a broad spectrum of social functioning. We will describe some features of the more complete packages.

Lewinsohn, Biglan, and Zeiss (1976) describe a 3-month treatment program. Treatment is preceded by an extensive assessment period during which self-report measures of mood, activities, and interests are obtained during a home visit. Their treatment methods include systematic desensitization and modeling techniques for social situations that have become aversive because of the associated anxiety. They also have clients increase their experience of the reinforcing activities reported on the Pleasant Events Schedules.

McLean's (1976) treatment program is somewhat more structured. He characterizes it as an "interpersonal disturbance" model, in which depression results from an inability to control the interpersonal environment. Therapeutic intervention is aimed at teaching effective coping techniques to remedy situational life problems. Since prolonged marital discord has been identified as the primary etiological factor for 70% of the clients referred to their program, they stress the importance of including the spouse or significant other in treatment. Rather than focusing exclusive attention on the "symptom bearer" this orientation includes a functional analysis of the interaction patterns and power structure within the depressed person's immediate family or other relevant social network. A pretreatment questionnaire covering behavioral, somatic, and cognitive areas of functioning provides data for behavioral analysis. Based on this, together with information about social resources, specific goals are formulated. The treatment package has six components, each focusing on a different skill area: communication, behavioral productivity, social interaction, assertiveness, decision making and problem solving, and cognitive self-control. All clients receive training in the first three areas; the latter three are optional, depending upon the client's behavioral analysis. Each skill area is broken down into several problem areas, with accompanying treatment interventions and improvement criteria. A variety of interventions are used, including scheduled, structured "talk time," graduated performance assignments, therapist modeling of desired responses, behavior rehearsal and several cognitive self-control techniques. McLean's emphasis on the quality of the marital relationship in the treatment of depression is particularly relevant for women. For many women, the role of wife and mother is primary; an unhappy marriage can precipitate a significant loss of self-esteem (Bardwick & Douvan, 1972) and depression. There is evidence that a woman who has a confiding relationship, particularly with her husband, has much less chance of developing depression when she experiences a severe loss than a married woman without such a relationship (Brown & Harris, 1978). Thus, for many women a focus on the marital relationship is an important treatment component.

In an evaluation of this treatment package, McLean and Hakstian (1979) compared it with insight-oriented psychotherapy, a deep-muscle relaxation training control, and chemotherapy. Treatment was provided in 10 weekly outpatient visits to 196 men and women. At posttreatment evaluation, the behavioral group scored significantly better than one or more of the other treatment groups in 6 of 10 self-report measures of outcome, but at the 3-month follow-up, the behavioral group was significantly superior on only two of the measures. Moreover, the relaxation control group was a relatively successful treatment, an indication that a large number of nonspecific factors influenced treatment outcome.

Of all the behavioral programs, the treatment package developed by Hersen et al. (1982) borrows most consciously from the general social skills training literature. The program focuses on three types of social skills which they feel have special relevance for depressed women: (1) positive assertion (the expression of positive feelings to others); (2) negative assertion (the expression of displeasure and standing up for one's rights; and (3) conversational skill, including the ability to initiate, maintain, and gracefully end conversations. Each skill is broken down into several components, and training focuses on content of verbalizations as well as nonverbal variables such as quality of voice intonation and amount of eye contact. They assume that social skills are situationally specific and therefore target the particular social interactions (e.g., strangers, friends, family members, work, or school) that are problematic for a given client. After an assessment of problematic social contexts, persons, and types of social interactions, training focuses on a hierarchy of these scenes. The target behavior and its rationale is described for the client; instructions, role play, feedback and positive reinforcement, as well as repetition are used during skills training.

Evaluation of this treatment package is in progress. Pilot data on four depressed female outpatients showed that all were improving on behavior ratings of assertiveness, self-report measures of assertiveness and depression, and psychiatric ratings of depressive symptoms (Wells, Hersen, Bellack, & Himmelhoch, 1979). Similarly positive results were obtained with five more depressed female outpatients (Hersen et al., 1982). The program by Hersen and his colleagues is notable for its detailed specification of target responses. During training, the therapist makes clear to the client what elements of a "skillful response" they are working toward, and the rationale for performing the response in the desired manner. An example: "The next thing we need to work on is eye contact. It is important that you look straight at people when you tell them that you are displeased. If you do, they'll know you are serious and not to be taken lightly. If you don't, they'll think that you are unsure of yourself and can be bullied" (Hersen et al., 1982).

The social skills research, including the more circumscribed assertion training, has burgeoned in the past 10 years. Since the rationale for using social skills training for depressives rests on the assumption that depressives lack important skills and that this type of training effectively provides those skills, it is appropriate to inquire about the efficacy of skills training. In a recent review of the social skills literature (including primarily assertion training and heterosexual skills) Twentyman and Zimering (1979) concluded that when compared to a waiting-list or no-treatment control, behavioral training is clearly superior in training new social skills. When compared to other treatment modalities such as traditional psychotherapy or support groups, however, the evidence is not as clear. They noted that a common element in many therapies is information about acceptable and effective social behavior. Since behavioral training has not consistently been shown superior to other therapies, they suggest that social skills methods may be successful mainly because of their information value. Social skills involve many subtle and complex behaviors, however, and it is also possible that trainers and programs have differed in their ability to impart these skills.

Recent reviews of social skills training (including assertion and marital skills programs) as a treatment specifically for depression (Blaney, 1981; Rehm & Kornblith, 1979) show mixed results in comparison with other treatments. Among the seven assertion training studies reviewed by Blaney (1981), three found social skills training more effective than other treatments, while four did not. With one exception, the studies that found no differences between social skills training and other treatments involved less disturbed subjects than did studies showing social skills training to be more effective. It may be that subjects with fewer social skills deficits respond equally well to most types of intervention, while severely depressed and skill-impaired individuals require a more structured and systematic treatment for alleviation of their depression.

Because of the preponderance of women among depressives, women have been well represented in these social skills studies. The subjects in most studies have been either exclusively female or a combination of males and females. In the few studies that have looked at sex differences in the response to treatment, none have been found (McLean & Hakstian, 1979; McLean, 1981).

COGNITIVE FORMULATION

Cognitive Theory of Depression

Although a number of cognitive formulations have been developed which attribute an important role to cognition for the occurrence of maladaptive behavior (Ellis, 1962; Valins & Nisbett, 1971; Rehm, 1976), Beck has made the most effort to elucidate the cognitive component specific to depression. We will review briefly the major assumptions of the model and the supporting data. (For a detailed review, see Beck, 1967; Rush & Beck, 1978; Blaney, 1977.)

Briefly, Beck's model asserts that depression results from the activation of three interrelated patterns of thought which distort the depressed person's perception of reality. The "cognitive triad" consists of negative views of self, of present experiences, and of the future (Beck, 1967). That is, depressed people tend to believe: (1) that they are defective, inadequate, deprived (Beck, Rush, Shaw, & Emery, 1979, p. 11); (2) that their present experiences are primarily negative; and (3) that their current difficulties or suffering will continue indefinitely (Beck *et al.*, 1979, p. 12). According to Beck, the cognitive triad is based on "stable cognitive patterns" (i.e., schemata) which constitute the basis for screening, categorizing, and evaluating past, present, and future experiences. Combining the construct of schema and the beliefs of the cognitive triad, Beck also asserts that the depressed person systematically makes cognitive errors (e.g., arbitrary inference, selective abstractions, overgeneralization) such that information consistent with the depressed schema is distorted so that it either fits the schema or is disregarded.

For example, consider the woman who developed from early experiences the schema: "To be accepted, valued, and successful, I must be perfect." Although she has been successful as a junior accountant in a large business firm, she would overgeneralize (i.e., make predictions based upon a single incident), and selectively abstract (i.e., focus on a detail taken out of context, while ignoring other salient features of the situation) when she received corrections from her supervisor. Although she rarely received corrections from her supervisor, whenever this occurred, she would react to her supervisor's correction with: "Unless I do a perfect job, I am a failure. I am incompetent." These maladaptive cognitions could result in dysphoric mood and/or related symptoms of depression. Thus, according to this formulation, although environmental events may precipitate depression, it is the depressed person's idiosyncratic perception and appraisal of the event that renders them depression-inducing. Maladaptive cognitions are considered the primary causes of depression, while other depressive behaviors (e.g., overt, somatic, affective) are regarded as secondary manifestations resulting from maladaptive cognitions.

Research support of Beck's model of depression has been adequately reviewed elsewhere (Blaney, 1977; Craighead, 1980; Eastman, 1976) and will be briefly summarized. According to Beck, the cognitive triad consists of the individual's percepts of the self, prior experiences, and the future. The major distinguishing characteristic of depressive self-percepts is their negative valence. Several experimental studies support the notion that depressed persons tend to attribute failures at tasks to defects in themselves (e.g., effort, ability) to a greater degree than nondepressed controls (Rizley, 1978; Klein, Fencil-Morse, & Seligman, 1976). In addition studies have demonstrated that depression is associated with more frequent and rapid recall of negative events (Lishman, 1972; Lloyd & Lishman, 1975), which is consistent with the notion of negative cognitive set. Other studies have demonstrated that depressed individuals tend to distort positive feedback in a negative direction (Nelson & Craighead, 1977; DeMonbreun & Craighead, 1977; Hammen & Krantz, 1976). Finally, a number of studies report that depressed individuals engage in excessive self-blame (Abramson & Sackeim, 1977) and recall negative feedback more accurately than nondepressed persons (Nelson & Craighead, 1977). Although the generalizability of these results may be limited due to the population sampled (college students), they are consistent with the prediction of Beck's cognitive model and suggest that a person's vulnerability to depression may depend on the individual's idiosyncratic schemata. Within this framework, women are no more predisposed to suffer from depression than men. According to Beck and Greenberg (1974), "What distinguishes male from female depression is simply that the events which typically 'trigger' depression tend to be sex-typed" (p. 129). However, if women, as a class, are exposed to more environmental disadvantages, as Gove (1979, 1980) and others (Chesler, 1972; Radloff, 1980; Lemkau, 1980) assert, we would expect that these factors would activate maladaptive schemata more often in women than men.

Assessment of Dysfunctional Cognitions

Although Beck's cognitive model of depression has provided the impetus for a great deal of research concerning the role of dysfunctional cognitions in depression, relatively few standardized procedures assess cognitive distortion. Hammen and her colleagues (Hammen & Krantz, 1976; Krantz & Hammen, 1979) have developed one standardized measure—the Cognitive Bias Questionnaire (CBQ), which encompasses several of the thinking errors (e.g., arbitrary inference) noted by Beck (1967). In a series of studies comparing depressed and nondepressed individuals, including inpatients and outpatients, Krantz and Hammen (1979) report that the CBQ has moderate test–retest reliability, and reliably differentiates depressed and nondepressed individuals. These results have been replicated by Norman, Miller, and Klee (in press). In both the Krantz and Hammen (1979) and Norman et al. (in press) studies, there were no depressed–distortion differences due to gender. Watkins and Rush (1978) have developed the Cognitive Response Test (CRT), which aims at assessing the instantaneous automatic thoughts that occur in conjunction with specific situations. Preliminary results suggest that outpatients diagnosed as having a major depressive disorder have significantly higher scores for irrational–depressed responses than nondepressed psychiatric outpatients, nondepressed medical patients, and nonde-pressed nonpatients. Irrational–depressed response differences due to gender were not investigated. Additional work is underway to evaluate test reliability and to identify the most discriminating test tems.

Several instruments assess the irrational beliefs (Jones, 1968) and dysfunctional attitudes (Weissman & Beck, 1978) that are assumed to be basic assumptions of individuals experiencing emotional problems (e.g., depression). Lewinsohn and his associates (Lewinsohn, Muñoz, & Larson, 1978; Muñoz & Lewinsohn, 1975; Zeiss, Lewinsohn, & Muñoz, 1979) also have developed several questionnaires to assess personal beliefs, subjective probability of positive and negative present–future events, as well as cognitive events. Although preliminary support for these tests is promising, studies to cross-validate these measures have not been conducted.

Cognitive Therapy for Depression

Cognitive therapy is designed to identify, challenge and correct distorted conceptualizations and dysfunctional beliefs (schemata). The cognitive therapist helps clients think and act more realistically and adaptively about their psychological problems and thus reduce their symptoms (Beck et al., 1979). More specifically, cognitive therapy endeavors to teach the client: (1) to monitor negative, automatic thoughts; (2) to recognize the connections between cognitions, affect, and behavior; (3) to examine the evidence for and against distorted automatic thoughts; (4) to substitute more realistic interpretations for the dysfunctional cognitions; and (5) to identify and alter the dysfunctional beliefs which encourage distortion of personal experience (Beck et al., 1979).

The basic premise of cognitive therapy is that depressed clients systematically misconstrue their experience. It is the task of the therapist to elicit the automatic thoughts that accompany various events (e.g., "I must always be successful at work"). The therapist attempts to: (1) identify target symptoms and their accompany cognitions; (2) describe these cognitions to the client as hypotheses; (3) help the client evaluate the validity of each hypothesis; and (4) help the client generate new hypotheses. The target symptoms addressed in therapy fall into one or more categories: affect, cognition, behavioral, and somatic complaints. The behavioral–cognitive techniques applied to these target behaviors have been described at length by Beck et al. (1979) and include: scheduling activities, mastery and pleasure techniques, graded task assignments, cognitive rehearsal, monitoring and reality testing of automatic thoughts, and homework assignments.

A number of controlled outcome studies comparing the efficacy of cognitive therapy with other treatments of depression have shown cognitive therapy to be effective with a variety of depressed populations, including college students (Shaw, 1977), depressed outpatients (Rush, Beck, Kovacs, & Hollon, 1977), and hospitalized depressed patients (Shaw, 1981). Rush et al. (1977) compared cognitive therapy and antidepressant medication (imipramine). Although both groups improved, the cognitive therapy group made significantly more improvement. More people dropped out of the antidepressant group before the end of therapy. This study was the first to show a relative advantage of any psychotherapy over chemotherapy in the treatment of moderate to severely depressed outpatients. In the Rush et al. (1977) study the cognitive treatment package included a substantial behavioral component which may have enhanced its efficacy. In fact, Taylor and Marshall (1977) found that a combined cognitive and behavior treatment package to be superior than either component alone. In summary, these studies have shown that cognitive (or combined cognitive–behavioral) therapy, as described by Beck et al. (1979), is an effective treatment approach to depression.

LEARNED HELPLESSNESS FORMULATION

Learned Helplessness Theory of Depression

The reformulated learned helplessness model of depression as presented by Miller and Norman (1979) and Abramson, Seligman, and Teasdale (1978) proposed the following etiology for depression. Due to some combination of early learning experiences or repeated exposure to uncontrollable events, the individual adopts a depressive attributional style. A depressive attributional style is a tendency to make internal, stable, and general attributions for uncontrollable aversive outcomes, and to make external, variable, and specific attributions for controllable success outcomes. The presence of many aversive events, and a depressive attributional style, produce a generalized expectancy for uncontrollable aversive outcomes which precipitates depression. Once the individual has become depressed, this depressive attributional style maintains the depression by minimizing the impact that controllable outcomes have on the individual's general expectancies for uncontroll-ability.

For example, consider the woman who has had a satisfactory mar-riage for several years and then has her first child. She finds herself increasingly involved in motherhood and child care and her husband starts to complain about her lack of time and affection for him. She attempts to pay more attention to her husband, but finds he still feels neglected. As time passes, her husband becomes increasingly angry and distant and ultimately she discovers that he is having an affair. If this woman attributes her husband's behavior to her being a "bad wife" (an internal, stable, and general attribution), as did Lori, a case history described by Scarf (1980), she is likely to become chronically depressed. On the other hand, if she attributes her husband's behavior to "his inability to deal with being a parent" (an external, variable, and specific attribution), she probably would not become significantly or chronically depressed.

Research support for the reformulated model of learned helpless-ness has been amply reviewed elsewhere (Garber & Seligman, 1980; Abramson et al., 1978; Miller & Norman, 1979) and will be briefly sum-marized here. A number of studies have reported differences in attri-butions between depressed and nondepressed college students (Seligman, Abramson, Semmel, & von Baeyer, 1979; Kuiper, 1978; Rizley, 1978; Blaney, Behar, & Head, 1980; Golin, Sweeney, & Shaeffer, 1981), out-patients (Gong-Guy & Hammen, 1980), and inpatients (Miller, Klee, & Norman, 1982). Other studies have demonstrated that a prior depressive attributional style predicts later depression (Golin et al., 1981; Seligman, 1981). Finally, a number of studies report that exposing nondepressed individuals to uncontrollable aversive outcomes induces depression and performance deficits (Miller & Seligman, 1973, 1975, 1976; Hiroto & Se-ligman, 1975).

The reformulated learned helplessness model is particularly relevant to depressed women. Traditionally, women have been trained to be less mastery-oriented than men. If socialization predisposes women to a depressive attributional style and these factors produce depression, then we should find evidence for the following propositions.

1. There should be differences in the interactions of adults with girls and boys. Adults should interact with girls in a helplessness-inducing fashion. That is, adult–child interactions should foster depressive attri-butional style and/or expectancies of uncontrollability in female children. A recent study by Dweck and her colleagues has obtained just these

kinds of data (Dweck, Davidson, Nelson, & Enna, 1978). They report that while grade school teachers tended to give negative feedback to boys which focused on their conduct (internal, variable, and specific attribution) their negative feedback to girls focused on their intellectual ability (internal, stable, and general attribution). Thus, girls received feedback which reinforced an internal, stable, and general attribution for negative events—a depressive attributional style. Serbin, O'Leary, Kent, and Tonick (1973) also report that boys received more contingent reinforcement than did girls.

2. Girls and boys should differ in the degree of helplessness and depressive attributional style. Again, studies by Dweck and her colleagues have provided supporting data. Girls are more likely to attribute failure outcomes to lack of ability (internal, stable, and general) while boys tended to attribute failure to task difficulty or to the teacher (external, variable, and specific). Moreover, following failure, girls show less persistence (i.e., increased helplessness) and lower expectancies for future success than boys (Dweck & Bush, 1976; Dweck & Gillard, 1975; Dweck & Reppucci, 1973).

3. As adults, women should be more susceptible to learned helplessness than men. Thus, when compared to men, women should show: (a) a more depressive attributional style, (b) a lower expectancy for controllability; and (c) greater learned helplessness when exposed to uncontrollable aversive events. While the research on these predictions is relatively sparse, there is some support for them. Most studies of attributional style have not investigated sex differences, but Deaux and Emswiller (1974) report that good performance is attributed to skill (internal, stable, general) by men but to luck (external, variable, specific) by women. Additionally, women have been reported to have a more external locus of control (Phares, 1976). However, the few studies which analyzed sex differences in reaction to uncontrollable aversive outcomes found no differences between men and women (e.g., Gatchel & Proctor, 1976; Miller & Seligman, 1976).

In summary, there is some empirical evidence that females' early learning experiences predispose them to a depressive attributional style and learned helplessness. However, if increased susceptibility is due to early experience, the type of early experience rather than gender should be the best predictor of susceptibility. Individuals who manifest feminine sex-typed traits (presumably developed by early experiences) should be most susceptible to learned helplessness. Several relevant studies have reported that compared to more androgynous individuals, individuals with feminine sex-typed traits were more susceptible to learned help-lessness and depression (Ray & Bristow, 1978; Berzins, Welling, & Wetter, 1978; Baucom & Danker-Brown, 1979).

The implications of the learned helplessness model for treatment of depression in women are fairly straightforward. Basically this line of research suggests that women with feminine sex-typed traits may be predisposed to depression by a set of maladaptive attributions and expectancies which inhibit development of adaptive skills. If the refor-mulated model is applicable to some depressed women, how does the clinician go about assessing the role of these constructs in a given in-dividual's depression? This question is the subject of the next section.

Assessment of Learned Helplessness

Assessment techniques for the learned helplessness model have received less attention and research than the etiological concerns. Originally, learned helplessness was assessed by performance on tasks such as anagrams, instrumental learning, or by changes in expectancies follow-ing success or failure experiences. These tasks, however, lack normative data. There have been several recent attempts to develop self-report scales of uncontrollability (Evans & Dinning, 1978; Glass, 1977) and depressive attributional style (Seligman et al., 1979; Hammen, Krantz, & Cochran, in press; Miller, Klee, & Norman, 1982). While there is preliminary evidence for the utility of these scales, definitive studies of reliability, validity, and normative values have yet to be published. Thus, these scales are not ready for clinical use.

Treatment Implications of the Learned Helplessness Model

Research on the treatment implications of the learned helplessness model has also been neglected. Four theoretical approaches to treatment of depressed individuals derived from the learned helplessness model have been outlined by Abramson et al. (1979) and Seligman (1981).

1. *Change the individual's expectancy from uncontrollability to controlla-bility.* Changing an individual's expectancy could be accomplished in one of three ways. First, an uncontrollable circumstance might be mod-ified, with consequent changes in the individual's expectancies. For ex-ample, financial assistance or job placement could be found for parents who are depressed because of their inability to care for their families. This approach has been investigated in analogue studies in which stu-

dents who were made helpless by exposure to uncontrollable outcomes were "treated" by repeated exposure to controllable outcomes (Klein & Seligman, 1976; Klein, Fencil-Morse, & Seligman, 1976). A second way to modify an expectancy of uncontrollability is to teach new skills so that a previously uncontrollable situation becomes controllable. For example, a woman who is depressed because of an inability to meet men could be taught social skills, while the woman who is depressed because of her domineering husband could be taught assertiveness skills. While we have previously discussed the effectiveness of social skills training programs in the treatment of depression, none of the studies reviewed have concomitantly evaluated expectancies of uncontrollability or depressive attributional styles. A third way to change expectancies is to modify an inaccurate expectancy that events are uncontrollable. Thus, a single woman's belief that she will have no social life without a permanent male companion could be challenged and modified. Again, while no direct evidence for this treatment approach is available, a cognitive-based treatment for depression (Beck et al., 1979; Ellis, 1962) may be seen as providing support for this hypothesis.

2. *Reattribution training*. This approach involves changing the depressed individual's attributional style. For example, the attribution of a rejection by a boyfriend to "lack of attractiveness to men" can be modified to, "he just wasn't ready for a long-term relationship with anyone." Several studies have reported that experimental manipulations designed to change attributions decrease the level of learned helplessness and depression (Dweck, 1975; Klein, Fencil-Morse, & Seligman, 1976; Miller & Norman, 1981). While all of these studies changed only one attribution and not an attributional style, they do suggest that changes in attributions produce changes in helplessness and depressed mood.

3. *Make important outcomes less important*. If helplessness and depression are due to the uncontrollability of important outcomes, treatment might decrease the subjective importance of the outcome (i.e., "Although I'm not the most productive person in my profession, I can still be successful"). There is no evidence of the efficacy of this approach.

In summary, the learned helplessness model of depression could contribute to the treatment of depressed women. However, more investigations of the clinical applications of this model are needed. Issues of control and attributions of causality are probably significant factors in the depression of men and women. In the absence of well-validated measures of these constructs, clinical applications of the learned helplessness model depends on the acumen of the therapist. The development of clinically useful measures of control and attributional style will be a major step forward.

The learned helplessness model offers few treatment recommendations for the therapist. Although this seems to limit the clinical applicability of the learned helplessness model, Seligman (1981) suggested that the learned helplessness model explains the efficacy of established therapies for depression (e.g., cognitive therapy, social skills training). Even if Seligman is correct, research must demonstrate that: (1) constructs postulated by the learned helplessness model mediate improvement during treatment, and (2) the learned helplessness model aids in matching individual clients with specific treatment approaches. Until this research is accomplished, the learned helplessness model will represent a heuristically interesting but clinically limited model for the treatment of depression.

CONCLUSIONS AND RECOMMENDATIONS

VALUE ISSUES

One criticism of psychotherapy for women has been that the woman client is in a typically helpless role vis-à-vis the powerful therapist, thus perpetuating (particularly in the case of depression) an important source of the problem. Moreover, there is concern over the subtle or obvious influence of the therapists' values, particularly when they favor different standards of mental health for women and for men, or when they encourage passive adjustment to difficult or oppressive environmental conditions, rather than active mastery and change (Kravetz, 1980; Chesler, 1972). We believe that a behavioral approach *has the potential* to minimize these dangers, or at least to make value issues more available for open discussion between the therapist and client, through appropriate behavioral assessment of treatment.

When treatment goals are explicitly discussed by clinician and client, conflicting beliefs and values can be addressed. Once there is some agreement on goals, work can begin. It has been argued that behavior therapists are technicians who use their expertise to aid clients in obtaining goals they request (Bandura, 1969, p. 101). This argument minimizes the complexity of the goal-selection process. Specification of goals may be one of the most difficult, and important, parts of treatment. In social skills training, for instance, the components of a skillful response must be identified. This issue is side-stepped to a certain extent by defining a skillful response in terms of its potential for eliciting reinforcement. This seems reasonable, since the ultimate goal of treatment is to increase the client's frequency of positive reinforcement. But at some point, someone makes judgments about what kinds of behaviors are likely to be reinforced, and what behaviors are likely to be punished. This is a complex decision, since what is appropriate can be influenced by situational as well as subject variables. In this regard, Linehan and Egan (1979) discuss the difficulties posed for women by the style and content of many assertion training programs. They suggest that many assertion training programs favor an interpersonal style of directness and brevity which is typical of persons with high power and influence, and achieves immediate objectives. This style, however, tends *not* to be associated with interpersonal attractiveness and relationship enhancement, and in some situations may be detrimental to those kinds of goals. Thus, personal values dictate what interpersonal style will provide lasting gratification.

Therapists must make judgments about treatment goals, yet these decisions may be difficult with women clients. In many cases, direct observation of behavior will indicate necessary goals. The depressed woman who shows little affect, has a retarded speech pattern, and initiates little activity in situations will receive more reinforcement for a livelier affect and more initiative. But for clients with less severe disorders, the choice of treatment goals is more difficult, and more likely to be influenced by the therapist's personal experience and values. Assessment throughout treatment provides feedback about goal attainment and permits the client to request adjustments in treatment techniques.

Finally, we believe that the behavioral formulations of depression guide clinicians in a manner beneficial to women clients. The focus on mastery and skills development, as opposed to passivity and adjustment is helpful, as is the focus on interpersonal, and intrapersonal targets for change.

Three formulations of depression (social, cognitive, and learned helplessness) were presented, and for each the underlying theory, the specific assessment strategy, and the treatment implications were discussed. These formulations offer two major advantages for treatment of depressed women. The social and learned helplessness formulations explain the greater prevalence of depression among women. Secondly, these formulations offer a theoretical perspective and a treatment technology which consider the interplay of environmental and intrapersonal factors in depression. Although substantial empirical data have demonstrated the effectiveness of behavioral and behavioral–cognitive treatments for depression, research in this area has neglected diagnostic issues and demographic characteristics of depressed subjects. Future research should examine treatment outcome in relation to specific subtypes of depression, client profiles, and treatment interventions.

REFERENCES

Abramson, L. Y., & Sackeim, H. A. A paradox in depression: Uncontrollability and self-blame. *Psychological Bulletin*, 1977, 84, 838–851.

Abramson, L. Y., Seligman, M. E. P., & Teasdale, J. Learned helplessness in humans: Critique and reformulation. *Journal of Abnormal Psychology*, 1978, 87, 49–74.

Adams, P. W., Rose, D. P., & Folkard, J. Effects of pyridoxine hydrochloride upon depression associated with oral contraception. *Lancet*, 1973, 2, 897–904.

Amenson, C. F., & Lewinsohn, P. M. An investigation into the observed sex difference in prevalence of unipolar depression. *Journal of Abnormal Psychology*, 1981, 90, 1–13.

Bandura, A. *Principles of behavior modification*. New York: Holt, Rinehart & Winston, 1969.

Bardwick, J. M., & Douvan, E. Abivalence: The socialization of women. In J. M. Bardwick (Ed.), *Readings in the psychology of women*. New York: Harper & Row, 1972.

Baucom, D. H., & Danker-Brown, P. Influence of sex roles on the development of learned helplessness. *Journal of Consulting and Clinical Psychology*, 1979, 47, 928–936.

Beck, A. T. *Depression: Clinical, experimental and theoretical aspects*. New York: Hoeber, 1967.

Beck, A. T., & Greenberg, R. L. Cognitive therapy with depressed women. In V. Franks & V. Burtle (Eds.), *Women in therapy: New psychotherapies for a changing society*. New York: Brunner/Mazel, 1974.

Beck, A. T., Kovacs, M., & Weissman, A. Hopelessness: An indicator of suicidal risk. *Suicide*, 1975, 5, 98–103.

Beck, A. T. Rush, A. J., Shaw, B. F., & Emery, G. *Cognitive therapy of depression*. New York: Guilford, 1979.

Beck, A. T., Weissman, A., Lester, D., & Trexler, L. The measurement of pessimism: The hopelessness scale. *Journal of Consulting and Clinical Psychology*, 1974, 42, 861–865.

Becker, J. *Depression: Theory and research*. Washington, D.C.: Winston, 1974.

Berzins, J. R., Welling, M. A., & Wetter, R. E. A new measure of psychological androgyny based on the personality research form. *Journal of Consulting and Clinical Psychology*, 1978, 46, 126–138.

Blaney, P. H. Contemporary theories of depression: Critique and comparison. *Journal of Abnormal Psychology*, 1977, 86, 203–223.

Blaney, P. H. The effectiveness of cognitive and behavioral therapies. In L. P. Rehm, (Ed.), *Behavior therapy for depression*. New York: Academic, 1981.

Blaney, P. H., Behar, V., & Head, R. Two measures of depressive cognitions: Their association with depression and with each other. *Journal of Abnormal Psychology*, 1980, 89, 678–682.

Brown, G. W., & Harris, T. *Social origins of depression*. New York: Free Press, 1978.

Burglass, D., & Horton, J. A scale for predicting subsequent suicidal behavior. *British Journal of Psychiatry*, 1974, 124, 573–578.

Chesler, P. *Women and madness*. Garden City, N.Y.: Doubleday, 1972.

Clancy, K., & Gove, W. Sex differences in mental illness: An analysis of response bias in self-reports. *American Journal of Sociology*, 1974, *80*, 205–216.

Craighead, W. E. Away from a unitary model of depression. *Behavior Therapy*, 1980, *11*, 122–128.

Deaux, K., & Emswiller, T. Explanations of successful performance on sex-linked tasks: What is skill for the male is luck for the female. *Journal of Personality and Social Psychology*, 1974, *29*, 80–85.

DeMonbreun, B. G., & Craighead, W. E. Distortion of perception and recall of positive and neutral feedback in depression. *Cognitive Therapy and Research*, 1977, *2*, 311–329.

Depue, R. A., & Monroe, S. M. Learned helplessness in the perspective of the depressive disorders: Conceptual and definitional issues. *Journal of Abnormal Psychology*, 1978, *87*, 3–20.

Depue, R. A., & Monroe, S. The unipolar–bipolar distinction in the depressive disorders: Implications for stress-onset interaction. In R. A. Depue (Ed.), *The psychobiology of depressive disorders: Implications for the effects of stress.* New York: Academic, 1979.

Diagnostic and statistical manual of mental disorders (2nd ed.). Washington, D.C.: American Psychiatric Association, 1968.

Diagnostic and statistical manual of mental disorders (3rd ed.). Washington, D.C.: American Psychiatric Association, 1980.

Dweck, C. S. The role of expectations and attributions in the alleviation of learned helplessness. *Journal of Personality and Social Psychology*, 1975, *31*, 674–685.

Dweck, C. S., & Bush, E. S. Sex differences in learned helplessness: I. Differential debilitation with peer and adult evaluators. *Developmental Psychology*, 1976, *12*, 147–156.

Dweck, C. S., Davidson, W., Nelson, S., & Enna, B. Sex differences in learned helplessness: The contingencies of evaluated feedback in the classroom and experimental analysis. *Developmental Psychology*, 1978, *14*, 268–276.

Dweck, C. S., & Gilliard, D. Expectancy statements as determinants of reactions to failure: Sex differences in persistence and expectancy change. *Journal of Personality and Social Psychology*, 1975, *32*, 1007–1084.

Dweck, C. S. & Reppucci, N. D. Learned helplessness and reinforcement responsibility in children. *Journal of Personality and Social Psychology*, 1973, *25*, 109–116.

Eastman, C. Behavioral formulations of depression. *Psychological Review*, 1976, *83*, 277–291.

Ellis, A. *Reason and emotion in psychotherapy.* New York: Lyle Stewart, 1962.

Endicott, J., & Spitzer, R. L. A diagnostic interview: The schedule for affective disorders and schizophrenia. *Archives of General Psychiatry*, 1978, *35*, 837–844.

Evans, R. G., & Dinning, W. D. Reductions in experienced control and depression in psychiatric inpatients: A test of the learned helplessness model. *Journal of Clinical Psychology*, 1978, *34*, 609–613.

Ferster, C. B. Classification of behavior pathology. In L. Krasner & L. P. Ullmann (Eds.), *Research in behavior modification.* New York: Holt, Rinehart & Winston, 1965.

Friedman, R. J., & Katz, M. M. *The psychology of depression: Contemporary theory and research.* Washington, D. C.: Winston, 1974.

Galassi, J. P., DeLo, J. S., Galassi, M. D. & Bastien, S. The College Self-Expression Scale: A measure of assertiveness. *Behavior Therapy*, 1974, *5*, 165–171.

Gambrill, E. D., & Richey, C. A. An assertion inventory for use in assessment and research. *Behavior Therapy*, 1975, *6*, 550–561.

Garber, J., & Seligman, M. E. P. *Human helplessness: Theory and application.* New York: Academic, 1980.

Gatchel, R. J., & Proctor, J. D. Physiological correlates of learned helplessness in man. *Journal of Abnormal Psychology*, 1976, *85*, 27–34.

Glass, D. R. *Measures of helplessness in research on depression.* Paper presented at the Annual Meeting of the Western Psychological Association, Seattle, Wash., 1977.

Goldman, N., & Ravid, R. Community surveys: Sex differences in mental illness. In M. Guttentag, S. Salasin, & D. Belle (Eds.), *The mental health of women*. New York: Academic, 1980.

Golin, S., Sweeney, P. D., & Shaeffer, D. E. The causality of causal attributions in depression: A cross-lagged panel correlational analysis. *Journal of Abnormal Psychology*, 1981, *90*, 14–22.

Gong-Guy, E., & Hammen, C. Causal perceptions of stressful events in depressed and nondepressed outpatients. *Journal of Abnormal Psychology*, 1980, *89*, 662–669.

Gove, W. Sex roles, marital roles, and mental illness. *Social Forces*, 1972, *51*, 34–44.

Gove, W. Sex differences in the epidemiology of mental disorder. In E. Gomberg & V. Franks (Eds.), *Gender and disorder behavior: Sex differences in psychopathology*. New York: Brunner/Mazel, 1979.

Gove, W. Mental illness and psychiatric treatment among women. *Psychology of Women Quarterly*, 1980, *4*, 345–362.

Gove, W., & Tudor, J. Sex differences in mental illness: A comment on Dohrenwend and Dohrenwend. *American Journal of Sociology*, 1977, *82*, 1327–1336.

Grinker, R., Miller, J., Sabshin, M., Nunn, R., & Nunnally, J. *The phenomena of depression*. New York: Hoeber, 1961.

Hamilton, M. A. A rating scale for depression. *Journal of Neurology, Neurosurgery and Psychiatry*, 1960, *23*, 56–61.

Hammen, C. L., & Krantz, S. Effect of success and failure on depressive cognitions. *Journal of Abnormal Psychology*, 1976, *85*, 577–586.

Hammen, C., Krantz, S., & Cochran, S. Relationship between depression and causal attributions about stressful life events. *Cognitive Therapy and Research*, in press.

Hammen, C. L., & Padesky, C. A. Sex differences in the expression of depressive responses on the Beck Depression Inventory. *Journal of Abnormal Psychology*, 1977, *86*, 609–614.

Hersen, M., & Bellack, A. S. (Eds.). *Behavior therapy in the psychiatric setting*. Baltimore: Williams & Wilkins, 1978.

Hersen, M., Bellack, A. S., & Himmelhoch, J. M. Skills training with unipolar depressed women. In J. P. Curran & P. M. Monti (Eds.), *Social skills training: A practical handbook for assessment and treatment*. New York: Guilford, 1982.

Hiroto, D. S., & Seligman, M. E. P. Generality of learned helplessness in man. *Journal of Personality and Social Psychology*, 1975, *31*, 311–327.

Jones, R. G. A factored measures of Ellis' irrational beliefs systems. Wichita, Kans.: Test Systems, 1968.

Klein, D. C., Fencil-Morse, E., & Seligman, M. E. P. Learned helplessness, depression, and the attribution of failure. *Journal of Personality and Social Psychology*, 1976, *33*, 508–516.

Klein, D. C., & Seligman, M. E. P. Reversal of performance deficits and perceptual deficits in learned helplessness and depression. *Journal of Abnormal Psychology*, 1976, *85*, 611–619.

Krantz, S., & Hammen, C. L. The assessment of cognitive bias in depression. *Journal of Abnormal Psychology*, 1979, *88*, 611–619.

Kravetz, D. Consciousness-raising and self-help. In A. M. Brodsky & R. T. Hare-Mustin, (Eds.), *Women and psychotherapy*. New York: Guilford, 1980.

Kuiper, N. A. Depression and causal attributions for success and failure. *Journal of Personality and Social Psychology*, 1978, *36*, 236–246.

Lazarus, A. A. Learning theory and the treatment of depression. *Behaviour Research and Therapy*, 1968, *6*, 83–89.

Lemkau, J. P. Women and employment: Some emotional hazards. In C. L. Heckerman (Ed.), *The evolving female*. New York: Human Sciences, 1980.

Lettieri, D. J. Research issues in developing prediction scales. In C. Neuringer (Ed.),

Psychological assessment of suicidal risk. Springfield, Ill.: Thomas, 1974.

Levitt, E. E., & Lubin, B. *Depression: Concepts, controversies and some new facts.* New York: Springer, 1975.

Lewinsohn, P. M., Biglan, A., & Zeiss, A. M. Behavioral treatment of depression. In P. O. Davidson (Ed.), *The behavioral management of anxiety, depression and pain.* New York: Brunner/Mazel, 1976.

Lewinsohn, P. M., Muñoz, R., & Larson, D. *Measurement of expectations and cognitions in depressed patients.* Paper presented at the 12th Annual Meeting of the Association for Advancement of Behavior Therapy, Chicago, November 1978.

Lewinsohn, P. M., & Lee, W. M. L. Assessment of affective disorders. In D. H. Barlow (Ed.), *Behavioral assessment of adult disorders.* New York: Guilford, 1981.

Lewinsohn, P. M., & Schaffer, M. Use of home observations as an integral part of the treatment of depression: Preliminary report and case studies. *Journal of Consulting and Clinical Psychology,* 1971, *37,* 87–94.

Libet, J., & Lewinsohn, P. M. Concept of social skill with special reference to the behavior of depressed persons. *Journal of Consulting and Clinical Psychology,* 1973, *40,* 304–312.

Linehan, M. M., & Egan, K. J. Assertion training for women. In A. S. Bellack & M. Hersen (Eds.), *Research and practice in social skills training.* New York: Plenum, 1979.

Lishman, W. A. Selective factors in memory: II. Affective disorders. *Psychological Medicine,* 1972, *2,* 248–253.

Lloyd, C. G., & Lishman, W. A. Effect of depression on the speed of recall of pleasant and unpleasant experiences. *Psychological Medicine,* 1975, *5,* 173–180.

MacPhillamy, D. J., & Lewinsohn, P. M. Depression as a function of levels of desired and obtained pleasure. *Journal of Abnormal Psychology,* 1974, *83,* 651–657.

Makosky, V. P. Stress and the mental health of women: A discussion of research and issues. In M. Guttentag, S. Salasin, & D. Belle (Eds.), *The mental health of women.* New York: Academic, 1980.

McLean, P. Therapeutic decision-making in the behavioral treatment of depression. In P. O. Davidson (Ed.), *The behavioral management of anxiety, depression and pain.* New York: Brunner/Mazel, 1976.

McLean, P. D. Matching treatment to patient characteristics in an outpatient setting. In L. P. Rehm, (Ed.), *Behavior therapy for depression.* New York: Academic, 1981.

McLean, P. D., & Hakstian, A. R. Clinical depression: Comparative efficacy of outpatient treatments. *Journal of Consulting and Clinical Psychology,* 1979, *47,* 818–836.

Miller, I. W., Klee, S., & Norman, W. H. Depressed and nondepressed inpatients cognitions of hypothetical events, life events and experimental tasks. *Journal of Abnormal Psychology,* 1982, *91,* 78–81.

Miller, I. W., & Norman, W. H. Learned helplessness in humans: A review and attribution theory model. *Psychological Bulletin,* 1979, *86,* 93–118.

Miller, I. W., & Norman, W. H. The effects of attributions for success on the alleviation of learned helplessness and depression. *Journal of Abnormal Psychology,* 1981, *90,* 113–124.

Miller, W. R., & Seligman, M. E. P. Depression and the perception of reinforcement. *Journal of Abnormal Psychology,* 1973, *82,* 62–73.

Miller, W. R., & Seligman, M. E. P. Depression and learned helplessness in man. *Journal of Abnormal Psychology,* 1975, *84,* 228–238.

Miller, W. R., & Seligman, M. E. P. Learned helplessness, depression, and the perception of reinforcement. *Behaviour Research and Therapy,* 1976, *14,* 7–17.

Muñoz, R. F., & Lewinsohn, P. M. *The Cognitive Events Schedule.* Unpublished manuscript, University of Oregon, 1975.

Nathan, P. E. Symptomatic diagnosis and behavioral assessment: A synthesis. In D. H. Barlow (Ed.), *Behavioral assessment of adult disorders.* New York: Guilford, 1981.

Nelson, R. E., & Craighead, W. E. Selective recall of positive and negative feedback, self-control behaviors and depression. *Journal of Abnormal Psychology*, 1977, 86, 279–288.

Nelson, R. O., & Barlow, D. H. Behavioral assessment: Basic strategies and initial procedures. In D. H. Barlow (Ed.), *Behavioral assessment of adult disorders*. New York: Guilford, 1981.

Norman, W. H., Miller, I. W., & Klee, S. Assessment of cognitive distortion in a clinically depressed population. *Cognitive Therapy and Research*, in press.

Norman, W. H., & Nelson, R. E. *Cross validation of self-report and behavioral measures of depression*. Paper presented at the meeting of the Association for Advancement of Behavior Therapy, Chicago, 1978.

Padfield, M. The comparative effects of two counseling approaches on the intensity of depression among rural women of low socioeconomic states. *Journal of Counseling Psychology*, 1976, 23, 209–214.

Paykel, E. S. Recent life events in the development of the depressive disorders. In R. A. DePue (Ed.), *The psychology of the depressive disorders: Implications for the effects of stress*. New York: Academic, 1979.

Paykel, E. S., Myers, J. K., Diendelt, M. N., Klerman, G. L., Lindenthal, J. J., & Pepper, M. P. Life events and depression: A controlled study. *Archives of General Psychiatry*, 1969, 21, 753–760.

Phares, E. J. *Locus of control and personality*. Morristown, N. J.: General Learning Press, 1976.

President's Commission on Mental Health, Special Population Subpanel on Mental Health in Women. Washington, D.C.: U.S. Government Printing Office, 1978.

Radloff, L. Sex differences in depression: The effects of occupation and marital status. *Sex Roles*, 1975, 1, 249–265.

Radloff, L. S. Risk factors for depression: What do we learn from them? In M. Guttentag, S. Salasin, & D. Belle (Eds.), *The mental health of women*. New York: Academic, 1980.

Raskin, A., Schulterbrandt, J. G., Reatig, N., Crook, T. H., & Odle, D. Depression subtypes and response to phenelzine, diazepam, and a placebo. *Archives of General Psychiatry*, 1974, 30, 66–75.

Rathus, S. A. Instigation of assertive behavior through videotape-mediated assertive models and directed practice. *Behaviour Research and Therapy*, 1973, 11, 57–65.

Ray, E. P., & Bristow, A. R. *Sex role identities in depressed women*. Paper presented at the meeting of the Western Psychological Association, New Orleans, 1978.

Rehm, L. Assessment of depression. In M. Hersen & A. S. Bellack (Eds.), *Behavioral assessment*. New York: Pergamon, 1976.

Rehm, L. P., & Kornblith, S. J. Behavior therapy for depression: A review of recent developments. In M. Hersen, R. M. Eisler, & P. M. Miller (Eds.), *Progress in behavior modification* (Vol. 7). New York: Academic, 1979.

Ripley, H. S. Depression and the life span epidemiology. In G. Usden (Ed.), *Depression: Clinical, biological and psychological perspectives*. New York: Brunner/Mazel, 1977.

Rizley, R. C. Depression and distortion in the attribution of causality. *Journal of Abnormal Psychology*, 1978, 87, 32–48.

Robins, L. N., Helzer, J. E., Croughan, J., & Ratcliffe, F. S. National Institute of Mental Health diagnostic interview schedule. *Archives of General Psychiatry*, 1981, 38, 381–389.

Rush, A. J., & Beck, A. T. Adults with affective disorders. In M. Hersen & A. S. Bellack (Eds.), *Behavior therapy in the psychiatric setting*. Baltimore: Williams & Wilkins, 1978.

Rush, A. J., Beck, A. T., Kovacs, M., & Hollon, S. Comparative efficacy of cognitive therapy and imipramine in the treatment of depressed outpatients. *Cognitive Therapy and Research*, 1977, 1, 17–37.

Sanchez, V., & Lewinsohn, P. M. Assertive behavior and depression. *Journal of Consulting* and Clinical Psychology, 1980, 48, 119–120.

Scarf, M. Unfinished business: Pressure points in the lives of women. Garden City, N.Y.: Doubleday, 1980.

Schuyler, D. The depressive spectrum. New York: Aronson, 1974.

Schuyler, D., & Katz, M. M. The depressive illnesses: A major public health problem. Washington, D. C.: U. S. Government Printing Office, 1974.

Seligman, M. E. P. A learned helplessness point of view. In L. P. Rehm (Ed.), Behavior therapy for depression. New York: Academic, 1981.

Seligman, M. E. P., Abramson, L. Y., Semmel, A., & vonBaeyer, C. Depressive attributional style. Journal of Abnormal Psychology, 1979, 88, 242–247.

Serbin, L. A., O'Leary, K. D., Kent, R. N., & Tonick, I. J. A comparison of teacher response to problems and pre-academic abilities of boys and girls. Child Development, 1973, 44, 796–804.

Shaw, B. F. Comparison of cognitive therapy and behavior therapy in the treatment of depression. Journal of Consulting and Clinical Psychology, 1977, 45, 543–551.

Shaw, B. F. Matching treatment to inpatient characteristics. In L. P. Rehm (Ed.), Behavior therapy for depression: Present status and future directions. New York: Academic, 1981.

Spitzer, R. L., Endicott, J., & Robins, E. Research diagnostic criteria: Rationale and reliability. Archives of General Psychiatry, 1978, 35, 773–782.

Stewart, A. J., & Salt, P. Life stress, life styles, depression and illness in adult women. Journal of Personality and Social Psychology, 1981, 40, 1063–1069.

Taylor, F. G., & Marshall, W. L. A cognitive-behavior therapy for depression. Cognitive Therapy and Research, 1977, 1, 59–72.

Turns, D. The epidemiology of major affective disorders. American Journal of Psychotherapy, 1978, 32, 5–19.

Twentyman, C. T., & Zimering, R. T. Behavioral training of social skills: A critical review. In M. Hersen, R. M. Eisler, & P. M. Miller, (Eds.), Progress in behavior modification, (Vol. 7). New York: Academic, 1979.

Valins, S., & Nisbett, R. E. Attribution process in the development and treatment of emotional disorders. New York: General Learning, 1971.

Watkins, J. T., & Rush, A. J. Cognitive response test. Paper presented at the meeting of the Association for Advancement of Behavior Therapy, Chicago, 1978.

Weissman, A. N., & Beck, A. T. Development and validation of the Dysfunctional Attitude Scale. Paper presented at the 12th Annual Meeting of the Association for Advancement of Behavior Therapy, Chicago, November, 1978.

Weissman, M. M., & Klerman, G. L. Sex differences and the epidemiology of depression. Archives of General Psychiatry, 1977, 34, 98–111.

Weissman, M. M., & Myers, J. K. Affective disorders in a U.S. urban community. Archives of General Psychiatry, 1978, 35, 1304–1411.

Weissman, M. M., & Slaby, A. E. Oral contraceptives and psychiatric disturbance, evidence from research. British Journal of Psychiatry, 1973, 123, 513–518.

Wells, K. C., Hersen, M., Bellack, A. S., & Himmelhoch, J. M. Social skills training in unipolar nonpsychotic depression. American Journal of Psychiatry, 1979, 136, 1331–1332.

Wessman, A. E., & Ricks, D. F. Mood and personality. New York: Holt, Rinehart & Winston, 1966.

Wilcoxon, L. A., Schrader, S. L., & Nelson, R. E. Behavioral formulations of depression. In W. E. Craighead, A. E. Kazdin, & M. J. Mahoney (Eds.), Behavior modification: Principles, issues and application. Boston: Houghton Mifflin, 1976.

Williams, J. G., Barlow, D. H., & Agras, W. S. Behavioral measurement of severe depression. Archives of General Psychiatry, 1972, 27, 330–333.

Wing, J. K., Cooper, J. E., & Sartorius, N. Measurement and classification of psychiatric symptoms. Cambridge, England: Cambridge University Press, 1974.

Winston, F. Oral contraceptives, pyridoxine, and depression. *American Journal of Psychiatry*, 1973, *130*, 1217–1221.

Wolpe, J., & Lazarus, A. A. *Behavior therapy techniques: A guide to treatment of neuroses.* New York: Pergamon, 1966.

Zeiss, A. M., Lewinsohn, P. M., & Muñoz, R. F. Nonspecific improvement effects in depression using interpersonal skills training, pleasant activity schedules or cognitive training. *Journal of Consulting and Clinical Psychology*, 1979, *47*, 427–439.

Zung, W. A self-rating depression scale. *Archives of General Psychiatry*, 1965, *12*, 63–70.

12

PHYSIOLOGICAL AND REPRODUCTIVE DISORDERS

KAREN S. CALHOUN
ELLIE T. STURGIS

OVERVIEW

Recent research suggests that earlier models of the physiological and reproductive disorders have been incomplete and guided by erroneous assumptions. This chapter reviews the status of research on the behavioral treatment of the most common physiological and reproductive disorders in women and suggests directions for future research.

BACKGROUND

Until recently, the psychophysiological and reproductive disorders have comprised the "ugly duckling" of the medical and psychological professions. The term "psychophysiological disorder" refers to diseases which involve disruptions in function or damage to physical structures of the body, and which are caused or affected by psychological factors including stress. In the third edition of the *Diagnostic and Statistical Manual of Mental Disorders* (DSM-III, 1980), this diagnostic category has been eliminated and replaced with the category "psychological factors affecting physical disease." This occurred primarily because recent data have indicated that most, if not all, physical diseases are affected by psychological factors. The term reproductive disorder refers to disruptions in

Karen S. Calhoun. Department of Psychology, University of Georgia, Athens, Georgia.

Ellie T. Sturgis. Department of Psychiatry and Human Behavior, University of Mississippi Medical Center, Jackson, Mississippi.

reproductive functions that may involve pain and physiological manifestations such as hot flashes and edema. The most common of these
are menstrual cycle and menopausal disorders.

The reasons for the inferior status of these disorders are numerous.
First, the disorders present diagnostic problems, since the symptoms
are variable in appearance (e.g., present at certain times and absent at
others). The course of symptom appearance is often accompanied by
changes in stress experienced by the individual, suggesting a marked
psychological component in the disorder. Second, the majority of the
disorders are accompanied by complaints of pain. Pain cannot be directly
observed but must be inferred from emotional expressions. Symptoms
which cannot be easily validated frustrate the diagnostician and clinician.
Complaints of pain are also frequently viewed as signs of malingering.
Third, these disorders often resist traditional medical or psychological
procedures. Finally, with the exception of cardiovascular disease and
peptic ulcers, more women than men report psychosomatic disorders.
Reproductive disorders occur primarily in women. Disorders occurring
more often in women have traditionally been viewed by the predominantly male medical world as hysterical or imaginary entities.

Treatment of psychophysiological disorders has been narrow in
perspective. Medical treatments have ignored psychological components
of the dysfunctions while psychological treatments have minimized the
physiological components. Research and treatment efforts have been
guided by psychodynamic hypotheses about behavior. For most disorders, these hypotheses were proposed during the early 20th century and
accepted uncritically by researchers and clinicians. Recent research has
not supported traditional assumptions, especially in regard to headaches
and dysmenorrhea. Basic and interdisciplinary research may improve
the understanding and treatment of psychophysiological disorders.

Rational treatments for the disorders covered in this chapter are
lacking, even though they are extremely common. Unfortunately, when
physicians do not understand the physiological processes underlying
medical disorders, they tend to use psychogenic explanations (Seiden,
1979) which blame the sufferer for her own problems.

Physiological and reproductive disorders are discussed separately
in this chapter. In the section on psychophysiological disorders, the
tension headache is used as a prototype. The disorder is defined, theoretical data and research concerning etiology are presented, and treatment strategies are reviewed. We argue that widely accepted theories
are fallacious and have interfered with treatment. The migraine headache

and Raynaud's phenomenon are reviewed briefly, and the status of treatment is discussed. The section ends with suggestions for clinical management. The remainder of the chapter focuses on reproductive disorders. Etiological theories of dysmenorrhea are presented followed by a discussion of medical and behavioral treatments. Premenstrual tension and menopause are briefly discussed, and suggestions regarding clinical management are presented.

PHYSIOLOGICAL DISORDERS

TENSION HEADACHE

Tension or muscle contraction headaches are the garden variety headache, causing problems for over 60% of the population and significant difficulties for over 20% of the population (Friedman, 1962). The public and the health professions assume these headaches predominate in women. However, epidemiological studies reveal no apparent sex difference in incidence. As is true for many other disorders, women with tension headaches receive more mental health treatment while men with serious tension headaches receive more comprehensive medical work-ups including evaluations by neurologists and neurosurgeons (Ryan & Ryan, 1978). The Ad Hoc Committee on the Classification of Headaches (Friedman, 1962) defined the tension headache as follows:

> Ache or sensation of tightness, pressure, or constriction widely varied in intensity, frequency, and duration sometimes long-lasting commonly suboccipital. It is associated with sustained contraction of the skeletal muscles in the absence of permanent structural change, usually as part of the individual's reaction during life stress. (p. 379)

This definition and traditional assumptions about the muscle contraction headache have hindered understanding of tension headaches. Phillips (1978) criticized the definition and the related assumptions on several points.

First, the definition indicates that sustained contraction of the musculature of the neck and head is a necessary condition for the development of a muscle contraction headache. While early research supported this, more recent findings have been inconsistent. We reviewed 14 psychophysiological investigations comparing electromyographic (EMG) activity in normal, tension headache, and migraine headache subjects.

Seven studies reported elevations in frontalis electromyographic activity for the tension headache group while seven did not.[1] To confuse the picture even further, when the EMG data sampled from migraine and muscle contraction subjects were compared, five studies showed migraineurs to have higher elevations in EMG activity than did the muscle contraction subjects, while three did not. These data suggest that the muscle contraction headache is not reliably characterized by high levels of frontalis EMG activity.

Phillips (1978) expected to find high and significant correlations among headache intensity, headache frequency, EMG activity, and pain behavior. When she examined only the tension headache subjects, she found a high Pearson correlation between headache intensity and headache frequency ($r = .71; p < .01$) and headache intensity and medication intake ($r = .85; p < .01$). Electromyographic activity showed a high correlation with headache frequency ($r = .66; p < .01$), while only a weak correlation was found between muscle tension and headache intensity ($r = .32$). No relationship was found between levels of muscle tension and medication intake. Subsequent investigators have not found strong relationships between EMG and pain levels (Epstein, Abel, Collins, Parker, & Cinciripini, 1978; Epstein & Blanchard, 1977; Haynes, Griffin, Mooney, & Parise, 1975; Vaughn, Pall, & Haynes, 1977), again supporting Phillips's findings and challenging the traditional hypotheses about headache. Similar evidence of desynchrony among multiple measures of one complaint (phobic behavior) has been described by Beck and Barlow (Chapter 2) and by Padawer and Goldfried (Chapter 13) in this volume.

The hypothesis that the tension headache involves an abnormality in the resting or tonic levels of the EMG response has persisted despite a lack of empirical support. Recent challenges to this hypothesis (Phillips, 1977; Gannon, Haynes, Hamilton, & Safranek, in press; Thompson & Adams, 1980) have demonstrated greater transient increases in muscular activity when the individuals were exposed to or were asked to imagine personally relevant stressors. Sturgis (1980) found higher EMG levels in muscle contraction subjects than in normals and in migraineurs when subjects kept eyes open during baseline. There were no group differences when subjects closed their eyes. Thus, the relative increase in EMG levels may be periodic and phasic rather than tonic.

----

[1] A list of these articles can be obtained from the second author.

Although the Ad Hoc Committee's definition (Friedman, 1962) did not specify a psychological component of chronic tension headaches, many clinicians have considered psychological stress to be an antecedent to tension headache (Bakal, 1979). Psychodynamic therapists viewed the headache as a symbolic attempt to resolve a mental conflict (Friedman, 1979). Bakal (1979) indicated that life experiences which produce anger, frustration, anxiety, and interpersonal difficulties precipitate tension headaches. Phillips (1976), in an investigation of the personality characteristics of tension headache patients, found that the headache sufferers were not more neurotic on the Eysenck Personality Inventory than were the normal controls. Nontreated males and females did not differ either. However, when the patients were subdivided into high and low medication-takers, high-medicating females had significantly more neurotic symptoms than the other groups while high medicating males did not differ from the average patients. Phillips (1976) challenged the assumption that all tension headache patients are neurotic as an instance of overgeneralization from a minority of subjects who exaggerate their difficulties when talking to their physicians and therapists. The majority of tension headache patients apparently do not seek treatment for their headaches and score in the normal range on personality measures.

Treatment of Tension Headache

Treatment of tension headache has not been successful with a large number of patients. A variety of treatments including psychoanalysis, muscle relaxants, tranquilizers, biofeedback, relaxation training, cognitive restructing, assertiveness training, and stress management have helped some tension headache subjects, but no treatment has been found to be beneficial for all patients. We suggest that ignorance about the disorder results in inadequate assessment and failure to match relevant treatments to specific behavioral complexes. Instead, groups of heterogeneous patients have received homogeneous treatments. A review of the behavioral treatment is presented below.

Medical management has been the most frequent treatment for the muscle contraction headache. Pharmacotherapy has relied on mild analgesics (e.g., aspirin or Tylenol), potent analgesics, centrally acting tranquilizers, and muscle relaxants. These drugs have usually reduced headache activity (e.g., frequency, intensity, and duration); however, the psychological and physical side effects of frequent medication ingestion made adjunct treatments necessary. Behavioral treatments for headache are relatively recent. Prior to Bakal's (1975) review of headache, there were only five reports of nonmedical treatments. There are now more than 30 studies of behavioral approaches to the treatment of tension headaches, including relaxation training, biofeedback training, or both together.

The use of relaxation training to treat muscle contraction headache is based on the assumption that individuals with tension headache show elevated levels of EMG activity, and that training in general relaxation skills will decrease EMG levels and will thereby alter the headache activity. As noted earlier, this assumption has questionable validity. There have been no controlled group studies examining the effectiveness of relaxation training for tension headaches (Blanchard, Ahles, & Shaw, 1979). Three group studies using an AB design reported a substantial reduction in headache activity following progressive relaxation training (Fichtler & Zimmerman, 1973; Tasto & Hinkle, 1973; Warner & Lance, 1975).

Biofeedback treatments have generally used EMG biofeedback to reduce tonic (or resting) levels of cephalic EMG activity. While the electrodes are typically placed over the frontalis muscles, these sites also reflect the activity of other muscles in the face, head, and upper trunk (Basmajian, 1976). Numerous studies of EMG biofeedback (Budzynski, Stoyva, & Adler, 1970; Budzynski, Stoyva, Adler, & Mullaney, 1973; Kondo & Canter, 1977; Phillips, 1977) have shown that true EMG biofeedback, used alone or together with relaxation training, yields significantly greater reductions in headache activity than does false feedback or self-monitoring of headache activity.

At least five studies have compared relaxation training and EMG feedback in the treatment of tension headaches (Chesney & Shelton, 1976; Cox, Freundlich, & Meyer, 1975; Haynes, Griffin, Mooney, & Parise, 1975; Hutchings & Reinking, 1976; Martin & Mathews, 1978). A comparison of biofeedback, relaxation training, and a medication placebo found the active treatments to be superior to the medical placebo in reducing tension headache (Cox et al., 1975). Two studies found no differences in treatment efficacy for biofeedback and relaxation training (Haynes et al., 1975; Martin & Mathews, 1978). Hutchings and Reinking (1976) reported that biofeedback was superior to relaxation training at the end of treatment, that at 3-month follow-up a combination of the two treatments was superior to receiving either biofeedback or relaxation training alone, and that at 1-year follow-up there were no differences among the three treatments. At follow-up those subjects who continued to practice some relaxation strategy regardless of their initial treatment, reported significantly fewer headaches than those who did not practice regularly. Both relaxation and biofeedback appear to be effective ways of reducing muscle contraction headache frequency, intensity, and duration.

Since it is not clear what type of control patients learn during behavioral treatments of headaches, it is impossible to prescribe an effective treatment for the individual patient. In tension headache, the role of the EMG activity of the cervical and cranial muscles has not been definitively demonstrated. Both EMG biofeedback and relaxation training aim to reduce tonic levels of muscle tension; yet, data from two sources suggest the dysfunction is episodic or phasic, rather than tonic (Phillips, 1978; Thompson & Adams, 1980). These treatments aim to reduce general elevations in EMG activity even though the elevations may be specific and time limited. Assessment of multiple EMG sites during headache, headache onset, and headache-free states will clarify this issue. The biofeedback treatments have provided the same number of treatment sessions to all patients; they have not aimed for a standard criterion of reduced EMG activity (Belar, 1979). Since some patients take longer than others to achieve the same reduction in EMG activity, the conventional method of conducting studies of biofeedback treatment hinders outcome assessment. It would be preferable for outcome studies to extend treatment until all patients achieve voluntary control over a specified response. Few studies have adequately assessed the pathophysiological responses of the individual or how biofeedback or relaxation training affects the individual's control over these responses (Thompson, Raczynski, Haber, & Sturgis, 1981). If future research demonstrates no difference between response to biofeedback and relaxation training in treatment outcome, relaxation training will be the preferred treatment since biofeedback equipment is expensive, mysterious to the client, and physiological control achieved with biofeedback does not readily generalize to sites outside the laboratory.

Behavioral self-control treatments for tension headache have focused on modifying cognitive responses to stressful situations (Holroyd, Andrasik, & Westbrook, 1977). Underlying these approaches is the assumption that aberrant EMG activity is caused by maladaptive cognitive or behavioral responses to stressful situations. Holroyd et al. (1977) taught patients to identify their current reactions to stress and to problem solve during stressful situations. Cognitive treatment worked better than a biofeedback-assisted relaxation treatment when subjects were led to expect no improvement with the latter condition (counterdemand instructions) and led to expect changes from the cognitive treatment. It is unclear whether biofeedback would have worked better than cognitive treatment if subjects had been led to expect no improvement from the latter treatment. While biofeedback treatment reduced EMG activity, no reductions in headache activity occurred. The cognitive treatment group reported decreased headache activity with no changes in EMG activity, again supporting the independence of tonic EMG levels and pain behavior. The patient's headache symptoms were not accompanied by increased EMG levels during the assessment sessions for either group. After treatment the biofeedback group showed borderline reductions in EMG levels but these were not accompanied by fewer headache symptoms. The multiple differences in treatment procedures make it difficult to interpret why the headache changes resulted.

Thompson (1981) has argued that most behavioral studies of headache treatment use inappropriate criteria for subject selection. By definition, muscle contraction headaches are associated with elevations in EMG activity. If the subjects provided with experimental treatments do not show EMG elevations, then they are not tension headache subjects. To further substantiate his argument, Thompson (1981) reviewed 50 recent treatment studies of chronic pain and found no cases of diagnosed psychogenic or hypochondriacal headache. He suggests that many of the low level EMG responders are psychogenic headache sufferers who also experience depression or anxiety, or both. For the psychogenic headache sufferer, anxiety management and cognitive behavioral training are appropriate. Research in progress in our laboratory at the University of Mississippi Medical Center examines differential symptom patterns and treatment responses of subjects with and without elevations in EMG activity and evaluates sex differences in headache types. In Chapter 11, on depression, in this volume, Norman, Johnson, and Miller have also emphasized the relevance of diagnostic information to the assessment of treatment outcome.

MIGRAINE HEADACHE

The migraine headache is experienced by 3–12% of the general population. The Ad Hoc Committee (Friedman, 1962) defined the migraine headache as:

Recurrent attacks of headache widely varied in intensity, frequency, and duration. The attacks are commonly unilateral in onset, and usually associated with anorexia, and sometimes, with nausea and vomiting; occasionally are preceded by, or associated with, conspicuous sensory, motor, or mood disturbances; and are often familial. (p. 378)

Migraine or vascular headaches are either of the classic or common type. The accompaniments of the classic group are sensory and motor prodromal symptoms prior to the onset of the head pain, unilateral pain, and sensations of nausea before and during the headache attack. The common migraine is a bilateral headache with no prodromal symptoms.

Epidemiological research generally indicates that most migraine sufferers are women (Bakal, 1975). Refsom (1968) cited several studies in which female–male ratios of incidence varied from 1.7:1 to 4.0:1. However, these epidemiological studies of prevalence among medical patients may have been biased by sex-differences in help sought for migraines. Studies of the general population have found that women are more often diagnosed as migraineurs and treated for migraine, even though men and women are equally represented in the migraine population (Adams, Feuerstein, & Fowler, 1980).

Theories of the Etiology of Migraine Headache

Several factors have been implicated in the development of migraine headaches. To date, no comprehensive theory accounts for the pathological condition, even though biological, psychological, and psychophysiological processes all appear to be involved. The traditional theory of migraine (Dalessio, 1972) emphasizes the role of extracranial vasodilation (enlargement or dilation of the blood vessels in the cranial area), even though classic migraineurs exhibit extracranial vasoconstriction followed by rebound vasodilation. Migraine has been attributed to vascular substances including serotonin, plasmakinin, histamine, and hormones. Migraine has also been attributed to psychological factors including repressed anger (Harrison, 1967), and to behavior tendencies such as excessive and rigid orderliness and morality (Friedman, von Storch, & Merritt, 1954). By and large, the data have not confirmed the contribution of psychological factors to the migraine headache (Bakal, 1975; Adams et al., 1980). In the psychophysiological view of the migraine headache, during times of stress and/or hormonal imbalance, migraine sufferers exhibit greater reactivity in the vasomotor system, especially the temporal arteries. Environmental or internal events trigger a vasomotor reaction via an abnormal orienting or defensive response. The integrity of the cerebral vascular system changes and painful neurochemicals are released (Ryan & Ryan, 1978).

Treatment of Migraine Headache

Biofeedback-assisted temperature training is often used to treat migraine headaches (Ray, 1980). The usefulness of temperature was serendipitously discovered by Sargent, Walters, and Green (1973) who used biofeedback to train a woman to raise the temperature of her hand, and observed that her migraine headaches decreased. In a follow-up study of 110 patients treated at the Menninger Clinic, Solbach and Sargent (1977) reported that 74 subjects completed training and 55 (74%) were rated as moderately improved, markedly improved, or asymptomatic. A controlled study designed to assess the active ingredients in biofeedback (Mullinix, Norton, Hack, & Fishman, 1978) compared true and false feedback in the treatment of migraine headaches. The true biofeedback group showed greater increases in hand temperature than did the false feedback group; however, there was no difference in headache activity between groups.

Two studies have compared hand temperature training with relaxation training as treatments for migraine headache. In one study (Andreychuk & Skriver, 1975) the relaxation training group had a 36% improvement rate and the temperature biofeedback group had a 75% improvement rate. In a second study (Blanchard, Theobald, Williamson, Silver, & Brown, 1978) both training groups improved significantly more than the waiting-list control group; however, the relaxation training group reduced headaches slightly more than the temperature biofeedback group. At 1-year follow-up both treatment groups maintained their posttreatment improvement, even though subjects did not practice their new skills regularly.

A second biofeedback technique commonly employed in the treatment of migraine headache is designed to cause vasoconstriction of the cranial arteries. Friar and Beatty (1976) trained one group of migraineurs to reduce the pulse amplitude in the finger. The extracranial group showed marked reductions in headache activity. Similar findings have been reported in research conducted at the University of Georgia (Bild & Adams, 1980; Feuerstein & Adams, 1977; Sturgis, Tollison, & Adams, 1978; Sturgis & Adams, 1979). In these studies, pulse volume amplitude feedback was more effective than EMG feedback in reducing migraine activity. There are differences of opinion about the physiological mechanisms which underlie successful temperature and pulse amplitude biofeedback training (Adams, Brantley, & Thompson, 1982; Adams *et al.*, 1980). Temperature and relaxation training appear to be effective because the individual learns a generalized relaxation strategy which inhibits sympathetic nervous system activity. Adams *et al.* (1982) hypothesize that pulse volume feedback actually alters the tonus of the extracranial vasculature, reducing vascular instability and headache activity.

Mitchell and his colleagues have attempted to use nonbiofeedback self-control strategies in the treatment of migraine headaches. Mitchell and Mitchell (1971) assigned 17 migraine patients to a relaxation training only, a relaxation training plus systematic desensitization, or a waiting-list control group. Relaxation training alone produced 24% reduction in frequency and a 50% reduction in duration, the waiting list brought about no change. Mitchell and White (1976) compared nonbiofeedback training procedures with 12 migraineurs. Self-monitoring brought about no change in headache activity, whereas training in a set of coping strategies (progressive muscle relaxation, mental relaxation, self-desensitization, and problem solving) markedly reduced headache activity. It is unclear which components of the treatment package were most effective.

RAYNAUD'S SYNDROME

Raynaud's syndrome is a vasomotor phenomenon characterized by decreased blood flow to the periphery of the body, particularly the hands, feet, and head. Primary Raynaud's symptoms which are not caused by any other physical condition are relatively benign, but secondary Raynaud's symptoms which result from another physical cause may have serious, even fatal consequences. Other disorders which need to be considered in a differential diagnosis of Raynaud's include chronic arterial diseases, the collagen vascular disorders, occupational exposure to vibrating instruments, lead or arsenic poisoning, drug ingestion (particularly the ergotamine preparations, methysergide, and propranolol), hematologic disorders, occult carcinoma, late sequelae of cold injury, and primary pulmonary hypertension (Isselbacher, Adams, Braunwald, Petersdorf, & Wilson, 1980). Thus, before any type of psychological intervention is considered for Raynaud's symptoms, a physical examination and medical clearance are imperative.

The term "Raynaud's disease" describes a peripheral vascular condition of at least 2 years' duration characterized by three sequential stages of skin color changes including pallor or white color, cyanosis or blue color, and hyperemia or red color (Taub & Stroebel, 1978). Raynaud described these symptoms in 1862 along with diagnostic criteria including: (1) intermittent attack of changes in color of the acral or peripheral parts of the body; (2) a symmetrical or bilateral involvement of the body; (3) an absence of clinical evidence of occlusive lesions of the peripheral arteries; and (4) the presence of gangrene or nutritionally induced changes in large portions of the skin. The fourth criterion was later retracted. Allen and Brown (1932) added two diagnostic criteria: (5) the presence of the disease for a minimum of 2 years; and (6) the presence of a disease process which could not be accounted for by other causes. Symptoms which have existed for less than 2 years are termed "Raynaud's phenomena." Raynaud's phenomena are a precursor to the more chronic disorder, Raynaud's disease.

In its mildest form of cold hands, Raynaud's symptoms have been noted in about 20% of the population. Raynaud's symptoms occur in women about five times as often as they do in men. Signs of the disorder are typically observed within the first two decades of life and rarely emerge for the first time after the age of 30 (Sappington, Fiorito, & Brehony, 1979). The hands are the part of the body most frequently affected; however, the feet and head may also display the symptoms. Raynaud's symptoms are most common in cool, temperate climates where efforts to maintain a warm indoor temperature are thought to be unnecessary; they are less common in warm or extremely cold climates (Sappington et al., 1979).

Theories of Raynaud's Disease

Raynaud's disease has been attributed to excessive sympathetic nervous system innervation, vascular organ damage, and psychological exacerbation. None of these theories has adequately explained the phenomenon (Isselbacher et al., 1980). Raynaud's belief that sympathetic nervous system overreactivity causes the disease (1862) is supported by evidence that emotional stress precipitates vasospastic (vasoconstrictive) attacks (Graham, 1955; Graham, Stern, & Winokur, 1958; Mittleman & Wolff, 1939). Lewis (1949) suggested that the disorder was caused by a structural fault in the peripheral vasculature, and he demonstrated that the blood was initially absent from the capillaries during a vasospasm. However, whether the spasm occurred at an arterial, arteriolar, or capillary level remains uncertain (Willerson, Thompson, Hookman, Herdt, & Decker, 1970). Langer and Crocell (1960) hypothesized that during a vasomotor attack, the blood was shunted away from the outermost layer of skin and pooled in the junctions between the arteries and veins (ateriovenous anastomoses); only one subgroup of Raynaud's patients shows signs of vascular obstruction (Mendlowitz & Naftchi, 1959).

Both neurogenic and psychogenic factors appear to be involved in the pathophysiology of Raynaud's. Prolonged exposure to cold temperatures, emotional stress, deep inhalation, prolonged and rapid inhalation of tobacco smoke, and exposure to novel stimuli increase the frequency or intensity of the vasospasms (Sappington et al., 1979). Emotional stress may be the most important contributor to Raynaud's. Pain, pallor, and cyanosis do not result when vasoconstriction and decreased skin temperature occur without increased autonomic arousal (Mittleman & Wolff, 1939). A physiological assessment recorded during a stress interview indicated the greatest amount of vasoconstriction, reduction in decreased temperatures, and increase in pain, occurred during periods of greatest arousal.

Treatment of Raynaud's Disease

Behavioral treatment of Raynaud's disease has included: (1) vasomotor feedback to increase peripheral circulation; (2) skin temperature feedback to lower sympathetic arousal and to facilitate circulation; (3) EMG biofeedback to facilitate relaxation; (4) autogenic or relaxation training to facilitate relaxation and decrease sympathetic activity; and (5) hypnosis and psychotherapy.

Shapiro and Schwartz (1972) used vascular feedback to increase skin temperature in two case studies. A male client initially succeeded in increasing blood flow and skin temperature and experienced decreased pain, while the female client was unsuccessful. At 15-month follow-up, treatment was reinstated for the first client, since symptoms had returned. It is unclear whether the sex of the client affected the clinical outcome. Surwit (1973) pioneered the use of temperature biofeedback coupled with relaxation and autogenic training in the treatment of Raynaud's disease in the first report of successful behavioral treatment of a woman with Raynaud's disease. After 74 treatment sessions, the client increased basal skin temperature from 23° to 26.6°C and reported fewer Raynaud's attacks. However, these gains were not maintained at follow-up. Blanchard and Haynes (1975) tested skin temperature training with a 28-year-old female in an ABAB single-case design. Biofeedback training to increase finger skin temperature relative to forehead skin temperature was more effective in teaching hand warming than relaxation training. The only clinical evidence presented was the client's report that it was easier to warm her hands when they were cold. Frequency, duration, and intensity of vasospastic attacks were not reported.

A group study randomly assigned 30 female patients to four treatment groups (Surwit, Pilon, & Fenton, 1978). Subjects received either home or laboratory exposure to autogenic training or autogenic training with skin temperature biofeedback. All treated subjects demonstrated the ability to increase skin temperature both in the laboratory and home, were able to maintain digital skin temperature in the presence of a cold stress challenge, and reported significant reductions in frequency and intensity of vasospastic attacks. No such changes occurred over time without training. Finally, the investigators found no added clinical benefit from the combination of skin temperature feedback and autogenic training. A 1-year follow-up study (Keefe, Surwit, & Pilon, 1979) reported on 19 of the original 30 patients, including 86% of those trained in the laboratory and 44% of those trained at home. The self-reported posttreatment reduction in vasospastic attacks was maintained at follow-up but skin temperature response to a cold-challenge test deteriorated to the pretreatment baseline level. Most subjects reported they no longer practiced the relaxation or the skin temperature exercises.

Jacobson, Manschrek, and Silverberg (1979) provided either progressive muscular relaxation or skin temperature training combined with relaxation training to nine females and three male patients with idiopathic Raynaud's disease. Both treatments resulted in consistent finger temperature increases during treatment. The relaxation training produced significantly greater skin temperature increases during treatment than the biofeedback group. At the end of 2-year follow-up, 7 of 11 patients contacted reported less severe and less frequent vasospasms; 6 of the 7 indicated they practiced relaxation regularly.

SUMMARY

Interdisciplinary study of physiological disorders waned in the mid-1950s because earlier research led to few treatment alternatives. With the advent of biofeedback during the 1960s interest increased about the mechanisms of the physiological disorders, the relationships among physical and psychological, causal and modulation factors, and the design of new treatments.

Many questions about the psychophysiological disorders need to be asked. First, the physiological and psychological causes of the disorders are not well understood. Further research must determine what physiological processes are dysfunctional for each case, under what conditions the process attenuates, how the system can be restored to a state of homeostasis or appropriate operation. Second, the role of sex differences in the disorders is unclear. Available data do not indicate whether there is a sex difference in incidence, and whether sex differences are caused by biological or environmental variables. Third, there appear to be marked individual differences in the characteristics of the disorders. Refinement of assessment procedures will clarify individual differences and guide the selection of treatment procedures. Finally, methods of early detection and early treatment of these disorders must be developed.

RECOMMENDATIONS FOR TREATMENT

In order to improve the behavioral treatment of psychophysiological disorders, the following treatment suggestions are made.

Tension Headache

    1. Medical clearance for treatment is desirable.

    2. A self-monitoring baseline of 4 weeks is necessary.

    3. Assessment should include daily self-reported headache activity, results of psychophysiological assessment (particularly frontalis EMG activity) taken during the headache and nonheadache condition, and diaries of daily stressors. From this assessment, a functional analysis of headache activty, its precipitants, and its consequences can be made.

    4. If elevations of EMG activity are noted, relaxation training and/or EMG biofeedback are appropriate interventions. If no pathophysiology is noted, a behavioral analysis of precipitants and consequences of the headache activity is necessary to determine the appropriate treatment strategy.

Migraine Headache

1. Medical clearance for treatment is necessary.

2. Because of the frequent relationship of migraine and menstrual phenomena and the relatively infrequent occurrence of the migraine, self-monitoring baseline periods should include a minimum of three headache attacks and be at least 1 month in duration.

3. Self-reports of headache activity, physiological recordings (EMG levels and digital skin temperature, and/or cephalic blood volume pulse), and diaries of events preceding and following headache activity should be used to evaluate the phenomenon.

4. If digital skin temperature is abnormally low, autogenic relaxation exercises and/or skin temperature biofeedback is appropriate. If blood volume pulse activity is abnormal, pulse volume biofeedback is an appropriate strategy. If the individual reports difficulty handling life stress, stress management training with both cognitive and behavioral management emphasis is appropriate.

Raynaud's Phenomena

1. Medical clearance for treatment is necessary.

2. Because of the relationship between weather changes and symptom severity, self-monitoring data should include a period of decreased environmental temperature.

3. Self-reports of pain level, skin coloration, and skin lesions; psychophysiological assessment of digital skin temperature; and diaries of events preceding and following pain episodes should be employed as assessment devices.

4. Autogenic relaxation exercises, skin temperature biofeedback, and stress management training appear to be effective intervention strategies.

REPRODUCTIVE DISORDERS

Until recently, research into the causes and treatment of the most common reproductive disorders in women was neglected by the biomedical sciences. Considering the high incidence of disorders such as dysmenorrhea, menopausal and postpartum complaints, this neglect is remarkable. The reasons are many; they include absence of an obvious disease process and the assumption that these disorders are psychologically based and that women who present them are neurotic. Unfortunately the latter assumption has been supported by assertions of psychologists. As a result, women have had to live with their pain or submit to tranquilizers or hormone treatment with adverse side effects. Many women are no longer willing to accept the status quo, more women are in medical practice and research, and the technology and acceptance of preventive medicine has improved. For all these reasons, contemporary research on menstrual cycle disorders has blossomed, with promising results.

Psychology and psychiatry have hindered the development of effective treatments by labeling reproductive disorders as psychosomatic, psychogenic, and hysteric in origin. What little basic research has been done, has assumed that conflict about reproduction and about fulfillment of the feminine role underlies the reproductive disorders and impairs behavior and affect (Berry & McGuire, 1972), or that women with reproductive complaints are neurotic in many respects (Bloom, Skelton, & Michaels, 1978; Coppen & Kessel, 1963; Gruba & Rohrbaugh, 1975; Halbreich & Kas, 1977; Hirt, Kurtz, & Ross, 1967). Treatment procedures also have focused on the acceptance of reproduction and the female role. Gannon (1981) pointed out several flaws in this research, including the tendency to infer from correlational findings that neuroticism or maladjustment causes menstrual distress. Gannon also pointed to evidence of experimenter bias in several studies, and to the tendency of subjects to fill out restrospective menstrual symptom questionnaires on the basis of cultural stereotypes rather than personal experience.

A shift in the focus of study has resulted from a feminist influence within the field of psychology and a trend toward behavioral research and treatment. Basing their work on nonsexist theories and using technology that is neutral as to social values (Blechman, 1980), behaviorists should be able to view reproductive disorders unobstructed by psychodynamic assumptions. When this happens, women's reports of pain and discomfort can be respected and treatment can aim for direct relief. This is not to say that behaviorists should ignore psychological factors, but that they regard them no more heavily in reproductive disorders than in other physiological dysfunctions. Though most of the relevant behavioral treatment techniques are in a rudimentary stage of development, many show promise.

This section focuses on two examples of reproductive disorders: menstrual cycle disorders and menopausal disorders. These are the areas of greatest research activity, and they offer the most valuable contributions. Postpartum depression and other disorders of childbirth have yet to receive systematic attention from behaviorists.

MENSTRUAL CYCLE DISORDERS

Menstrual cycle disorders usually are divided into two types: dysmenorrhea—painful uterine cramps that may be accompanied by nausea, diarrhea, and/or backache; and premenstrual syndrome (or tension) —symptoms which vary widely from one woman to the next but which may include water retention, weight gain, and irritability prior to and ending with onset of the menstrual period (Dalton, 1964, 1969). Dysmenorrhea can occur secondary to a disease process such as endometriosis, but the majority of cases occur in the absence of disease. It is primary dysmenorrhea that concerns us. Estimates of its prevalence vary, but it is clear that over 50% of young women report dysmenorrhea (Kessel & Coppen, 1963). Kistner (1971) estimated that 140 million annual work hours are lost in this country due to menstrual distress. The prevalence of premenstrual problems is more difficult to estimate because of the lack of clear diagnostic criteria. In fact, the notion of a "syndrome" has been seriously criticized and it has been suggested that the reported problems could result from social reinforcement and cultural expectation (Paige, 1973; Parlee, 1974; Shainess, 1961). The relationship between premenstrual and menstrual distress is unclear although Cox, McMahon, and Pennebaker (1977) reported a correlation of .69 between scores for the two types of disorders, with a great deal of overlap in the items subjects ranked high for each disorder. Premenstrual problems are usually attributed to water retention and treatment consists almost exclusively of diuretics and analgesics (along with tranquilizers in some cases).

Theories of Menstrual Cycle Disorders

Theories abound concerning the physiological mechanisms involved in menstrual cycle changes (Ruble, Brooks-Gunn, & Clarke, 1980; Southam & Gonzaga, 1965). However, research in the area has been inconclusive because of inconsistent findings and methodological problems (Ruble et al., 1980).

Dalton (1969) used the terms spasmodic and congestive dysmenorrhea to describe dysmenorrhea and premenstrual syndrome, respectively. Congestive dysmenorrhea begins about 4 days prior to the period and ends abruptly with the onset of the period. Chesney and Tasto (1975a) developed a self-report instrument, the Menstrual Symptom Questionnaire (MSQ), to measure the two types. The instrument is used for baseline and outcome measurement. The Moos (1968) Menstrual Distress Questionnaire (MDQ) and the MSQ are the most widely used measures of menstrual symptoms. The Menstrual Distress Question-naire is a 47-item scale that is filled out to describe the most recent menstrual, premenstrual, and intermenstrual periods. Since retrospec-tive descriptions differ substantially from daily ratings (Moos, Kopell, Melges, Yalom, Lunde, Clayton, & Hamburg, 1969), a daily rating form is now available (Moos, 1977). (See Ruble *et al.*, 1980, for a review of the forms of bias in self-report studies of menstrual-related changes.)

Dysmenorrhea (spasmodic type) has been the focus of most of the recent psychological and medical research on reproductive disorders. Though the pathophysiology of dysmenorrhea is still not completely understood, the past two decades have seen an increase in knowledge (Akerlund, 1979). It has long been known that oral contraceptive pills can eliminate dysmenorrhea, apparently because they suppress ovula-tion and its accompanying hormonal cycle. In fact, the pill was the treatment of choice for dysmenorrhea, prior to general awareness of adverse side effects. The pill's effect is not a simple one, and birth-control pills with certain compositions can actually increase dysmenor-rhea in some women (Dalton, 1969). Surprisingly little research on dys-menorrhea followed the discovery of the pill's effect. However, a new assessment device unexpectedly increased understanding of the path-ophysiology of dysmenorrhea. Filler and Hall (1970) used an intrauterine balloon device to study uterine motility. Contrary to previous assump-tions, they reported that pain was correlated with dysrhythmic con-tractions and with elevated tonus of the uterine muscle, not with intense contractions. They concluded that elevated tonus interferes with ade-quate blood supply to the uterine muscle, allowing toxic wastes to build up in the muscle, and contributing to pain. However, recent research leads to the conclusion that almost all dysmenorrhea is accompanied by hyperactivity of the uterus and the pain is associated with the general pattern of hyperactivity (Akerlund, 1979; Akerlund, Andersson, & In-gemarsson, 1976; Csapo, Pulkkinen, & Henz, 1977). Restricted blood flow from blood vessels compressed by uterine hyperactivity seems to be a direct cause of pain (Akerlund, 1979).

The role of prostaglandins in stimulating uterine hyperactivity and dysmenorrhea has been the focus of much recent research. Prostaglan-dins are hormone-like substances produced by the uterine lining as well as in many other tissues of the body. They are thought to increase uterine hypercontractility as well as having systemic effects such as nausea and dizziness. A number of studies have examined the effects of drugs that inhibit the synthesis of prostaglandins. For example, Lundstrom, Green, and Svanborg (1979) found that 9 of 10 women suffering from dysmenorrhea showed significantly higher blood levels of prostaglandin PGF2a than nondysmenorrheic controls. Naproxen, a prostaglandin synthesis inhibitor, reduced these blood levels as well as the self-report of pain significantly more than a placebo. Because of such studies, prostaglandin-inhibiting drugs are being hailed as a breakthrough in the treatment of dysmenorrhea (e.g., *Consumer Reports*, 1981). However, oral contraceptives were hailed as a breakthrough in their day. Long-term side effects of prostaglandin inhibitors have not been fully assessed, and most prostaglandin studies have methodological problems, including small, select samples, no active placebo, and no objective assessment of side effects. In addition, some dysmenorrhea suffers do not show elevated prostaglandin levels, indicating that other mechanisms may be responsible.

Treatment

New directions are being taken with the behavioral treatment of dysmenorrhea. In a recent review Denney and Gerrard (1981) categorized these procedures in four subgroups: hypnotherapy, Lamaze exercises, desensitization-based procedures, and biofeedback procedures. However, because hypnotherapy and Lamaze exercises have been reported only in a few uncontrolled multiple-case studies, their potential usefulness cannot be evaluated. Hypnotherapy usually combines relaxation and suggestions of painlessness, but frequently has involved hypnoanalysis as well (Leckie, 1964). There have been no recent reports of its use with dysmenorrhea. Lamaze exercises emphasize relaxation and self-control. Elements of this elaborate procedure have not been separately evaluated.

The most commonly used behavioral methods for the treatment of dysmenorrhea are based on desensitization. The first report was a case study (Mullen, 1968) of a 31-year-old married woman who had been suffering from severe dysmenorrhea for 21 years. Systematic desensitization combined with the husband's ignoring pain behavior resulted in reduced self-report of pain, medication use, and invalid hours, with results maintained at 6-month follow-up. Mullen (1971) reported that five college students given 4–6 sessions of systematic desensitization showed significantly less severe self-reported menstrual symptoms than an untreated control group. Chesney and Tasto (1975b) found group systematic desensitization effective in reducing the severity of dysmenorrhea symptoms in nonparous women, compared to placebo (discussion) and waiting-list control groups. Groups were matched on severity of symptoms and type of dysmenorrhea (congestive or spasmodic). Treatment was effective only for spasmodic dysmenorrhea. Cox and Meyer (1978) treated 14 college students with systematic desensitization; the students reported significant decreases in severity of symptoms, negative attitudes toward menstruation, medication use, and invalid hours, compared to pretreatment baseline. They maintained improvement at 6-month follow-up on all measures except for their attitudes toward menstruation, which regressed to pretreatment levels.

These and other studies (Reich, 1972; Tasto & Chesney, 1974) provide evidence that without lengthy treatment, desensitization and relaxation strategies can reduce menstrual pain and discomfort among relatively healthy college students. No differences were found between male and female or experienced and inexperienced therapists (Mullen, 1971; Cox & Meyer, 1978).

Though desensitization appears to be a useful strategy in the treatment of dysmenorrhea, questions about its effects remain. One question concerns the persistence of these effects. Only Mullen (1968) and Cox and Meyer (1978) used follow-ups as long as 6 months. The pretreatment baselines were also brief—1 or 2 months in all cases. Systematic pre- and posttreatment assessment over several consecutive menstrual periods is needed given fluctuations in symptoms due to uncontrolled individual or environmental variables. Another question about desensitization concerns the separation of placebo from treatment effects. Of the studies mentioned above, only Chesney and Tasto's (1975b) used placebo control groups. Plausible placebo treatment controls in all studies would strengthen the conclusions drawn from findings. They would also address the most troublesome remaining problem—identifying the active ingredient in the desensitization treatment. The typical procedure is to train subjects to relax, and muscle relaxation is then paired with imagery of pain, discomfort, and inconvenience associated with menstrual periods. In some studies, however, relaxation was paired with scenes associated with menstrual pain reduction (Tasto & Chesney, 1974). Most of the recent studies emphasize self-control as an important goal of treatment, indicating that learning to use relaxation as a coping strategy may be the active ingredient. If so, active mastery achieved through cognitive–behavioral or other strategies might produce equivalent results. In addition, desensitization procedures have not been compared to relaxation training alone.

The role of anxiety in dysmenorrhea needs further clarification. It is usually thought to be associated more with the premenstrual than the menstrual period (Golub, 1976), but the experience of pain and inconvenience along with the negative stereotypes taught by society should lead to the expectation of increased anxiety during the period itself. Stress is a known factor in some cases of amenorrhea and menstrual irregularity; thus it would not be surprising to find that stress and anxiety lowered pain thresholds in dysmenorrheic women. However, Reich (1972) found desensitization more effective for low-anxious than for high-anxious subjects. Future research should address the interaction between treatment effects and individual difference variables such as levels of anxiety.

Biofeedback, usually combined wth relaxation training, has been examined in a few exploratory studies. For example, Tubbs and Carnahan (1976) reported that a client trained in hand warming unexpectedly experienced a cessation of menstrual cramps. They then gave eight dysmenorrheic women hand temperature biofeedback training, EMG feedback training for muscle relaxation, and home practice in systematic relaxation. Four women were able to relieve their cramps and two showed moderate improvement. No studies to date have attempted to separate the effects of biofeedback from those of relaxation training.

Heczey (1978) used autogenic training combined with biofeedback of vaginal temperature (which she assumed to be correlated with uterine blood flow). She randomly assigned subjects to one of four groups: (1) individual relaxation training; (2) group relaxation training plus discussion; (3) hand and vaginal temperature biofeedback plus relaxation training; (4) no treatment. All groups, including the control group, were given written self-help advice. All three treatment groups improved significantly compared to controls, although the combined treatment group showed a trend toward greater improvement than the other treatment groups. Whether biofeedback augments the effectiveness of relaxation training is still in doubt, as Heczey's (1975) study demonstrated. She gave one group autogenic relaxation training plus vaginal temperature feedback and a second group relaxation training plus false feedback. False feedback resulted in consistent lowering of vaginal temperature. However, both groups reported improvement in dysmenorrhea symptoms.

Biofeedback treatment strategies are in the infant stage of development, and whether they will prove more effective or cost beneficial than desensitization or relaxation cannot be seen without more carefully controlled studies. Such studies should include plausible placebo treatment groups. Comparisons of hand temperature and vaginal temperature training are also needed. Both are aimed at increasing blood flow, but the rationale for increasing peripheral blood flow in the case of dysmenorrhea is unclear. However, relaxation reduces sympathetic arousal and is accompanied by vasodilation in the skeletal muscles (Engel & Chism, 1967). If this effect can be shown to include internal structures as well, relaxation training may be the treatment of choice.

Thus far, few behavioral treatment studies have focused on premenstrual problems, perhaps because of the vagueness of the complaints (irritability, water retention, depressed feelings), and the fact that women are not encouraged to report these problems to professionals. For the same reasons, accurate estimates of prevalence are not available, but the problems are very common. Rees (1958) found an incidence of 79%, although estimates depend on the criteria used. Etiology is unknown as well, with theories centering around estrogen/progesterone imbalance (Dalton, 1969) and electrolyte metabolism (Vila & Beech, 1980). Social expectation also appears to play a strong role in reporting of symptoms (Parlee, 1974). This is supported by the findings of Vila and Beech (1980) that women tested either premenstrually or intermenstrually reported no differences in mood states when the purpose of the study was disguised, though their retrospective reports indicated negative premenstrual moods.

Dalton (1977) suggested that a high-protein/low-carbohydrate diet helps control mood swings which she thinks are due to altered sugar metabolism during the premenstrual period. In more extreme cases, she recommends progesterone treatment, though no double blind studies have supported its effectiveness.

Behavioral treatment studies have been few. Chesney and Tasto (1975b) and Cox and Meyer (1978) included premenstrual subjects in their outcome studies of desensitization. Chesney and Tasto found the treatment to be ineffective for subjects with premenstrual problems (congestive dysmenorrhea) though effective for (spasmodic) dysmenorrhea. Cox and Meyer (1978), compared the two types post hoc and found the treatment equally effective for both. However, their results were based on a small number of subjects. Further research is needed to clarify the effectiveness of relaxation training and desensitization for premenstrual problems. Behavioral techniques of other kinds might be helpful as well. For example, assertiveness training might aid in the control of behavior stemming from irritability. Biofeedback methods could prove useful in treating the headaches some women report, and perhaps even the swelling due to edema. Cognitive coping strategies might also be useful, as well as environmental controls such as Mullen's (1968) having the client's husband ignore pain-related behavior.

MENOPAUSE

The term "menopause" has been used very loosely in the literature to refer to physiological changes, psychological problems, a combination of the two, or to the general midlife stage of women. There is no agreement on a definition of the term or criteria for examining the phenomena associated with it. The term means, strictly speaking, the end of menstruation, but some studies have included women in the general age range of 45 to 55, while others have carefully grouped women according to the progress of menstrual cessation (McKinlay & Jefferys, 1974). This confusion, along with neglect of the menopause in medical literature, results in little certainty about the syndrome. There is agreement that it occurs on the average about the age of 50 (McKinlay, Jefferys, & Thompson, 1972). The ovaries gradually cease to function and endocrine changes result; a decline in the level of estrogen decreases vaginal lubrication (Mason, 1976). Although a number of other physical and psychological changes are popularly thought to be associated with this process (hot flashes, night sweats, insomnia, headaches, irritability, anxiety, depression, etc.), only hot flashes and night sweats have been shown to be associated unquestionably with the cessation of menstruation (McKinlay & Jefferys, 1974). The sweats are considered nighttime manifestations of hot flashes—a sudden feeling of warmth in all or a part of the body with accompanying sweating and possible redness. Increased pulse and respiration may also occur. Molnar (1975), in a case study of one woman, found that tachycardia and electrocardiographic changes preceded the hot flashes. Hot flashes are reported by up to 75% of menopausal women and may continue for 5 years or more (McKinlay & Jefferys, 1974). The other physiological problems women sometimes report (headaches, insomnia, weight gain, dizziness) are less common (McKinlay & Jefferys, 1974) and may be associated with social changes in individual women's lives and with the general aging process (Notman & Nadelson, 1980).

Psychological changes, including such severe problems as depressive and psychotic reactions, have long been included in the popular descriptions of menopause, in spite of early evidence that only a few women experience such changes (Stern & Prados, 1946). Studies using modern endocrinologic methods have found no correlations between endocrine states and clinical states such as depression. For example, Winokur (1973) found women to be at no greater risk for depression during menopause than during other life cycles. Weissman and Klerman (1977), reviewed the literature and concluded that there is no good statistical evidence that menopause affects rates of depression. Subclinical levels of depression and anxiety may be experienced by women who don't seek treatment (only one fifth of the 638 subjects in the McKinlay and Jefferys [1974] study sought medical treatment), but major changes in women's family and social lives as well as hormonal changes characterize the perimenopausal period.

A variety of drugs including psychotropic medication have been used to treat menopause. The most common form of treatment, estrogen "replacement therapy," appears to reduce hot flashes and sweats (Detre, Hayashi, & Archer, 1978), but it also may increase the risk of endometrial cancer (Ziel & Finkle, 1975). Combining estrogen with progestin may decrease this risk (Detre et al., 1978), but women should exercise caution in using such drugs until the risks are more fully assessed.

Alternatives to drug treatment are greatly needed in this area. Until now these alternatives have consisted largely of traditional psychotherapies that focus on internal states and unresolved conflicts as the source of problems such as mood changes and anxiety (Notman, 1980). A woman with no children left to raise, no occupational skills, and a disinterested husband needs more immediate and direct coping skills. Therefore, behavioral approaches to treatment appear to have much to offer women at midlife. That so little has been done in this direction is consistent with society's general neglect of middle-aged women.

Some suggestions for behavioral intervention with menopausal women include assertiveness training to help women cope with life changes, communicate better with others, and express their own needs in relationships; social skills training to help women expand their social networks; relaxation training for insomnia; systematic desensitization for anxieties that limit activities and lead to depression; reinforcement programs to decrease secondary gains such as undue attention to complaints; weight-control programs; biofeedback training for headaches. It may be possible to teach women self-control of hot flashes and sweats through biofeedback. Coping strategies could be developed, if women can learn to identify cues that trigger hot flashes, such as hot rooms, angry encounters, or anxiety producing situations. Treatment should emphasize teaching women to exert control over their own behavior and over their surroundings so that they are not at the mercy of their hormones. Acquired control over hormone levels should not be discounted. Male rhesus monkeys have been shown to alter their testosterone levels in response to environmental changes, including presentation and removal of less dominant animals from the group (Rose, Gordon, & Bernstein, 1972). Contrary to earlier beliefs, such studies indicate a reciprocal relationship between hormones and behavior, with intriguing implications for new treatment techniques.

SUMMARY

Like the physiological disorders, reproductive disorders of women are becoming popular topics of medical and psychological research, in contrast to their neglect in the past. This is a welcome trend, although the etiology and course of these disorders is still poorly understood. Especially unknown are the physiological and psychological processes specific to the menopause. Behavioral treatment methods have been applied with some success to menstrual cycle disorders, but menopausal, postpartum, and other reproductive disorders have been almost completely neglected by behavioral researchers. However, advances in knowledge of the processes underlying these disorders point to possible intervention strategies, for example, biofeedback of skin temperature for controlling hot flashes.

Premenstrual and menopausal disorders suffer from a lack of definition and consequently from an absence of outcome measures by which to evaluate effects of treatment. A search for physiological correlates of self-report is indicated for all the reproductive disorders. In addition, psychological correlates such as stress and anxiety should be explored.

Recommendations for Treatment

Although behavioral treatments for reproductive disorders are in very early stages of development, the following suggestions for treatment can be made.

1. Medical evaluation to rule out disease processes should precede any behavioral intervention.

2. Since reported symptoms may vary over time, stable pretreatment baselines may require lengthy evaluation. For dysmenorrhea and premenstrual disorders, it is recommended that baseline data cover three complete cycles.

3. For the same reason, evaluation of treatment outcome should include follow-ups of at least 3 to 6 months.

4. Multiple outcome measures should be used instead of relying on self-report alone.

5. The common element in treatment studies for reproductive disorders has been some form of relaxation training. Until dismantling research evaluates the role of various treatment components, relaxation training appears to be the most promising technique.

CONCLUSION

Increasing research interest in physiological disorders common among women, has dispelled stereotypes about psychogenic causes. Contemporary behavioral treatment procedures enhance women's control over their own physiological processes. These treatments may change the socialization process, so that women expect self-control and demand that psychological treatments aim for more self-control.

However, contemporary behavioral treatments for physiological and reproductive problems are flawed. Treatment is hindered by ignorance about etiology and about the relationship between psychological and physiological factors, inadequate diagnostic criteria, and crude assessment techniques. Because pain is subjective, treatment outcome has been measured by self-report, despite obvious bias. For example, many women believe that their intellectual performance fluctuates with their menstrual cycles, despite contrary findings on objective measures (Sommer, 1973). Improved diagnostic criteria, and objective and valid outcome measures are needed to test behavioral treatment strategies. More information about individual differences is needed to fit treatment to individual clients.

Research designs used to study physiological and reproductive disorders could be improved. The most popular design is the clinical trial; while relatively unsophisticated, the clinical trial can generate hypotheses and refine treatment techniques. More dismantling studies, which test individual elements of complex treatment packages, are needed. More comparisons of behavioral and drug treatments are needed in light of charges that women are overmedicated (Stein, Del Gaudio, & Ansley, 1976). Although past evaluations of behavioral treatments for physiological and reproductive disorders have not been well controlled, most recent research uses sound methodology. Continuation of this trend should result in important treatment advances for disorders that afflict millions of women.

REFERENCES

Adams, H. E., Brantley, P. J., & Thompson, K. Biofeedback and headache: Methodological issues. In L. White & B. Tursky (Eds.), *Clinical biofeedback: Efficacy and mechanisms.* New York: Guilford, 1982.

Adams, H. E., Feuerstein, M., & Fowler, J. L. Migraine headache: Review of parameters, etiology, and intervention. *Psychological Bulletin,* 1980, *87,* 217–237.

Akerlund, M. Pathophysiology of dysmenorrhea. *Acta Obstetrica et Gynecologica Scandinavia (Supplement),* 1979, *87,* 27–32.

Akerlund, M., Andersson, K. I., & Ingemarsson, I. Effects of terbutaline on myometrial activity, uterine blood flow and lower abdominal pain in women with primary dysmenorrhea. *British Journal of Obstetrics and Gynaecology,* 1976, *83,* 673.

Allen, E. V., & Brown, G. E. Raynaud's disease: A clinical study of one hundred and forty-seven cases. *Journal of the American Medical Association,* 1932, *99,* 1472–1478.

Andreychuk, T., & Skriver, C. Hypnosis and biofeedback in the treatment of migraine headache. *International Journal of Clinical and Experimental Hypnosis,* 1975, *23,* 172–183.

Bakal, D. A. Headache: A biopsychological perspective. *Psychological Bulletin,* 1975, *82,* 369–382.

Bakal, D. A. *Psychology and medicine: Psychobiological dimensions of health and illness.* New York: Springer, 1979.

Basmajian, J. V. Facts vs. myth about EMG biofeedback. *Biofeedback and Self-Regulation,* 1976, *1,* 369–371.

Belar, C. D. A comment on Silver and Blanchard's (1978) review of the treatment of tension headache via EMG feedback and relaxation training. *Journal of Behavioral Medicine,* 1979, *2,* 215–220.

Berry, C., & McGuire, F. L. Menstrual distress and acceptance of sexual role. *American Journal of Obstetrics and Gynecology,* 1972, *114,* 83–87.

Bild, R., & Adams, H. E. Modification of migraine headaches by cephalic blood volume pulse and EMG biofeedback. *Journal of Consulting and Clinical Psychology,* 1980, *48,* 51–57.

Blanchard, E. B., Ahles, T. A., & Shaw, E. R. Behavioral treatment of psychophysiological disorders. *Behavior Modification,* 1979, *3,* 518–549.

Blanchard, E. B., & Haynes, M. R. Biofeedback treatment of a case of Raynaud's disease. *Journal of Behavior Therapy and Experimental Psychiatry,* 1975, *6,* 230–234.

Blanchard, E. B., Theobald, D. E., Williamson, D. A., Silver, B. V., & Brown, D. A. Temperature biofeedback in the treatment of migraine headaches: A controlled evaluation. *Archives of General Psychiatry,* 1978, *35,* 581–588.

Blechman, E. A. Behavior therapies. In A. M. Brodsky & R. T. Hare-Mustin (Eds.), *Women and psychotherapy.* New York: Guilford, 1980.

Bloom, L. J., Skelton, J. L., & Michaels, A. C. Dysmenorrhea and personality. *Journal of Personality Assessment,* 1978, *42,* 272–276.

Budzynski, T., Stoyva, J., & Adler, C. Feedback-induced muscle relaxation: Application to tension headache. *Journal of Behavior Therapy and Experimental Psychiatry*, 1970, *1*, 205–211.

Budzynski, T., Stoyva, J. M., Adler, C. S., & Mullaney, D. J. EMG biofeedback and tension headache: A controlled outcome study. *Seminar in Psychiatry*, 1973, *5*, 397–410.

Chesney, M. A., & Shelton, J. L. A comparison of muscle relaxation and electromyogram biofeedback treatment for muscle-contraction headache. *Journal of Behavior Therapy and Experimental Psychiatry*, 1976, *7*, 221–225.

Chesney, M. A., & Tasto, D. L. The development of the Menstrual Symptom Questionnaire. *Behaviour Research and Therapy*, 1975, *13*, 237–244. (a)

Chesney, M. A., & Tasto, D. L. The effectiveness of behavior modification with spasmodic and congestive dysmenorrhea. *Behaviour Research and Therapy*, 1975, *13*, 245–253. (b)

Consumer Reports. Finally, drugs that work for menstrual pain. February 1981, pp. 92–93.

Coppen, A., & Kessel, N. Menstruation and personality. *British Journal of Psychiatry*, 1963, *109*, 711–721.

Cox, D., Freundlich, A., & Meyer, R. Differential effectiveness of electromyograph feedback, verbal relaxation instructions, and medication placebo with tension headaches. *Journal of Consulting and Clinical Psychology*, 1975, *43*, 892–898.

Cox, D. J., McMahon, E., & Pennebaker, J. W. *Distribution and covariance of premenstrual symptoms among college students.* Paper presented at the Southeastern Psychological Association, Atlanta, 1977.

Cox, D. J., & Meyer, R. G. Behavioral treatment parameters with primary dysmenorrhea. *Journal of Behavioral Medicine*, 1978, *3*, 297–310.

Csapo, A. I., Pulkkinen, M. O., & Henz, M. R. The effect of naproxensodium on the intrauterine pressure and menstrual pain of dysmenorrheic patients. *Prostaglandins*, 1977, *13*, 193.

Dalessio, D. J. *Wolff's headache and other pain.* New York: Oxford University Press, 1972.

Dalton, K. *The premenstrual syndrome.* Springfield, Ill.: Thomas, 1964.

Dalton, K. *The menstrual cycle.* New York: Pantheon, 1969.

Dalton, K. *The premenstrual syndrome and progesterone therapy.* London: Heinemann, 1977.

Denney, D. R., & Gerrard, M. Behavioral treatments of primary dysmenorrhea: A review. *Behaviour Research and Therapy*, 1981, *19*, 303–312.

Detre, T., Hayashi, T. T., & Archer, D. F. Management of the menopause. *Annals of Internal Medicine*, 1978, *88*, 373–378.

Diagnostic and statistical manual of mental disorders (3rd ed.). Washington, D.C.: American Psychiatric Association, 1980.

Engel, B. T., & Chism, R. A. Effect of increases and decreases in breathing rate on heart rate and finger pulse volume. *Psychophysiology*, 1967, *4*, 83–39.

Epstein, L. H., Abel, G., Collins, F., Parker, L., & Cinciripini, P. M. The relationship between frontalis muscle activity and self-reports of headache pain. *Behaviour Research and Therapy*, 1978, *16*, 153–160.

Epstein, L. H., & Blanchard, E. B. Biofeedback, self-control, and self-management. *Biofeedback and Self-Regulation*, 1977, *2*, 201–211.

Feuerstein, M., & Adams, H. E. Cephalic vasomotor feedback in the modification of migraine headache. *Biofeedback and Self-Regulation*, 1977, *2*, 241–254.

Fichtler, H., & Zimmerman, R. Changes in reported pain from tension headaches. *Perceptual and Motor Skills*, 1973, *36*, 712.

Filler, W. W., & Hall, W. C. Dysmenorrhea and its therapy. *American Journal of Obstetrics and Gynecology*, 1970, *106*, 20–26.

Friar, L., & Beatty, J. Migraine: Management by trained control of vasoconstriction. *Journal of Consulting and Clinical Psychology*, 1976, *44*, 46–53.

Friedman, A. P. Ad Hoc Committee on Classification of Headache: Classification of headaches. *Neurology*, 1962, *12*, 378–380.

Friedman, A. P. Characteristics of tension headache: A profile of 1420 cases. *Psychosomatics*, 1979, *20*, 451–461.

Friedman, A. P., von Storch, T. J. C., & Merritt, H. H. Migraine and tension headaches: A clinical study of two thousand cases. *Neurology*, 1954, *4*, 773–788.

Gannon, L. Evidence for a psychological etiology of menstrual disorders: A critical review. *Psychological Reports*, 1981, *48*, 287–294.

Gannon, L., Haynes, S., Hamilton, J., & Safranek, R. A psychophysiological investigation of muscle contraction and migraine headache. *Journal of Psychosomatic Research*, in press.

Golub, S. The effect of premenstrual anxiety and depression on cognitive function. *Journal of Personality and Social Psychology*, 1976, *34*, 99–105.

Graham, D. T. Cutaneous vascular reactions in Raynaud's disease and in states of hostility, anxiety, and depression. *Psychosomatic Medicine*, 1955, *17*, 201–207.

Graham, D. T., Stern, J. A., & Winokur, G. Experimental investigation of the specificity of the attitude hypothesis in psychosomatic disease. *Psychosomatic Medicine*, 1958, *20*, 446–457.

Gruba, G. H., & Rohrbaugh, M. MMPI correlates of menstrual distress. *Psychosomatic Medicine*, 1975, *37*, 265–273.

Halbreich, U., & Kas, D. Variations in the Taylor MAS of women with premenstrual syndrome. *Journal of Psychosomatic Research*, 1977, *31*, 391–393.

Harrison, R. Psychological testing in headache: A review. *Headache*, 1967, *1*, 62–73.

Haynes, S. N., Griffin, P., Mooney, D., & Parise, M. Electromyographic biofeedback and relaxation instruction in the treatment of muscle-contraction headaches. *Behavior Therapy*, 1975, *6*, 672–678.

Heczey, M. D. *Effects of autogenic temperature training on dysmenorrhea and other menstrual discomforts.* Unpublished Master's thesis, Hunter College, City University of New York, 1975.

Heczey, M. D. Effects of biofeedback and autogenic training on dysmenorrhea. In A. Dan et al. (Eds.), *The menstrual cycle: Synthesis of interdisciplinary research.* New York: Springer, 1978.

Hirt, M., Kurtz, R., & Ross, W. D. The relationship between dysmenorrhea and selected personality variables. *Psychosomatics*, 1967, *8*, 350–353.

Holroyd, K. A., & Andrasik, F. Coping and the self-control of chronic tension headache. *Journal of Consulting and Clinical Psychology*, 1978, *46*, 1036–1045.

Holroyd, K. A., Andrasik, F., & Westbrook, T. Cognitive control of tension headache. *Cognitive Therapy and Research*, 1977, *1*, 121–133.

Hutchings, D., & Reinking, R. Tension headaches: What form of therapy is most effective? *Biofeedback and Self-Regulation*, 1976, *1*, 182–190.

Isselbacher, K. J., Adams, R. D., Braunwald, E., Petersdorf, R. G., & Wilson, J. D. *Harrison's principles of internal medicine* (9th ed.). New York: McGraw-Hill, 1980.

Jacobson, A. M., Manschrek, T. C., & Silverberg, E. Behavioral treatment of Raynaud's Disease: A comparative study with long-term follow-up. *American Journal of Psychiatry*, 1979, *136*, 884–886.

Keefe, F. J., Surwit, R. S., & Pilon, R. N. A 1-year follow-up of Raynaud's patients treated with behavioral therapy techniques. *Journal of Behavioral Medicine*, 1979, *2*, 285–391.

Kessel, N., & Coppen, A. The prevalence of common menstrual symptoms. *Lancet*, 1963, *61*, 14–17.

Kistner, R. W. *Gynecology: Essentials of clinical practice.* Chicago: Year Book, 1971.

Kondo, C., & Canter, A. True and false electromyographic feedback: Effect on tension headache. *Journal of Abnormal Psychology*, 1977, *86*, 93–95.

Langer, P., & Crocell, L. *Le phénomène de Raynaud: Aspects cliniques, étiopathogéniques, et thérapeutiques.* Paris: L'expansion Scientifique Française, 1960.

Leckie, F. H. Hypnotherapy in gynecological disorders. *International Journal of Clinical and Experimental Hypnosis,* 1964, *12,* 121–145.

Levitt, E. E., & Lubin, B. Some personality factors associated with menstrual complaints and menstrual attitude. *Journal of Psychosomatic Research,* 1967, *11,* 267–270.

Lewis, T. *Vascular disorders of the limbs: Described for practitioners and students.* London: Macmillan, 1949.

Lundstrom, V., Green, K., & Svanborg, K. Endogenous prostaglandins in dysmenorrhea and the effect of prostraglandin synthetase inhibitors on uterine contractability. *Acta Obstetrica et Gynecologica Scandinavia (Supplement),* 1979, *87,* 51–56.

McKinlay, S. M., & Jefferys, M. The menopausal syndrome. *British Journal of Preventive and Social Medicine,* 1974, *28,* 108–115.

McKinlay, S., Jefferys, M., & Thompson, B. An investigation of the age at menopause. *Journal of Biosocial Science,* 1972, *4,* 161–173.

Martin, P. R., & Mathews, A. M. Tension headaches: Psychophysiological investigation and treatment. *Journal of Psychosomatic Research,* 1978, *22,* 389–399.

Mason, A. S. The events of the menopause. *Royal Society of Health Journal,* 1976, *96,* 70–71.

Mendlowitz, M., & Naftchi, N. The digital circulation in Raynaud's disease. *American Journal of Cardiology,* 1959, *5,* 580–584.

Mitchell, K. R., & Mitchell, D. M. An exploratory treatment application of programmed behavior therapy. *Journal of Psychosomatic Research,* 1971, *15,* 137–157.

Mitchell, K. R., & White, R. G. Self-management of tension headaches: A case study. *Journal of Behavior Therapy and Experimental Psychiatry,* 1976, *7,* 387–389.

Mittleman, B., & Wolff, H. G. Affective states and skin temperature: Experimental studies of subjects with "cold hands" and Raynaud's syndrome. *Psychosomatic Medicine,* 1939, *1,* 271–292.

Molnar, G. W. Body temperatures during menopausal hot flashes. *Journal of Applied Physiology,* 1975, *38,* 499–503.

Moos, R. H. The development of the Menstrual Distress Questionnaire. *Psychosomatic Medicine,* 1968, *30,* 853–867.

Moos, R. H. *Menstrual Distress Questionnaire manual.* Palo Alto, Calif.: Social Ecology, 1977.

Moos, R. H., Kopell, B. S., Melges, F. T., Yalom, I. D., Lunde, D. T., Clayton, R. B., & Hamburg, D. A. Fluctuations in symptoms and moods during the menstrual cycle. *Journal of Psychosomatic Research,* 1969, *13,* 27–44.

Mullen, F. G. The treatment of a case of dysmenorrhea by behavior therapy techniques. *Journal of Nervous and Mental Disease,* 1968, *147,* 371–376.

Mullen, F. G. *Treatment of dysmenorrhea by professional and student behavior therapists.* Paper presented at meeting of the American Psychological Association, Washington, D. C., September 1971.

Mullinix, J. M., Norton, B. J., Hack, S., & Fishman, M. A. Skin temperature biofeedback and migraine. *Headache,* 1978, *18,* 242–244.

Notman, M. Adult life cycles: Changing roles and changing hormones. In J. E. Parsons (Ed.), *The psychobiology of sex differences and sex roles.* New York: McGraw-Hill, 1980.

Notman, M. T., & Nadelson, C. Reproductive crises. In A. M. Brodsky & R. T. Hare-Mustin (Eds.), *Women and psychotherapy.* New York: Guilford, 1980.

Paige, K. E. Women learn to sing the menstrual blues. *Psychology Today,* 1973, *7,* 41–46.

Parlee, M. B. Stereotypic beliefs about menstruation: A methodological note on the Moos menstrual distress questionnaire and some new data. *Psychosomatic Medicine,* 1974, *36,* 229–240.

Phillips, C. Headache and personality. *Journal of Psychosomatic Research,* 1976, *20,* 535–542.

Phillips, C. The modification of tension headache pain using EMG biofeedback. *Behaviour Research and Therapy*, 1977, 15, 119–129.

Phillips, C. Tension headache: Theoretical problems. *Behaviour Research and Therapy*, 1978, 16, 249–261.

Ray, W. J., Raczynski, J. M., Rogers, T., & Kimball, W. H. *Evaluation of clinical biofeedback.* New York: Plenum, 1980.

Raynaud, A. G. *De l'asphyxie locale et de la gangrène symétrique des extrémités.* Paris: Rigoux, 1862.

Rees, L. *Psychoendocrinology.* London: Grune & Stratton, 1958.

Refsom, S. Genetic aspects of migraine. In P. J. Vinkin & G. W. Broyn (Eds.), *Handbook of clinical neurology* (Vol. 5). New York: Wiley, 1968.

Reich, S. K. *The effects of group systematic desensitization on the symptoms of primary dysmenorrhea.* Unpublished doctoral dissertation, University of New Mexico, 1972.

Rose, R. M., Gordon, T. P., & Bernstein, I. S. Plasma testosterone levels in the male rhesus: Influence of sexual and social stimuli. *Science*, 1972, 178, 643–645.

Rouse, P. Premenstrual tension: A study using the Moos Menstrual Questionnaire. *Journal of Psychosomatic Research*, 1978, 22, 215–222.

Ruble, D. M., Brooks-Gunn, J., & Clarke, A. Research on menstrual-related psychological changes: Alternative perspectives. In J. E. Parsons (Ed.), *The psychobiology of sex differences and sex roles.* Washington, D. C.: Hemisphere, 1980.

Ryan, R. F., & Ryan, Jr., R. E. *Headache and head pain: Diagnosis and treatment.* St. Louis, Mo.: Mosby, 1978.

Sappington, J. T., Fiorito, E. M., & Brehony, K. A. Biofeedback as therapy in Raynaud's disease. *Biofeedback and Self-Regulation*, 1979, 4, 155–169.

Sargent, J. D., Walters, E. D., & Green, E. E. Psychosomatic self-regulation of migraine headaches. *Seminars in Psychiatry*, 1973, 5, 415–428.

Seiden, A. M. Gender differences in psychophysiological illness. In E. S. Gomberg & V. Franks (Eds.), *Gender and disordered behavior.* New York: Brunner/Mazel, 1979.

Shainess, N. A reevaluation of some aspects of femininity through a study of menstruation: A preliminary report. *Comprehensive Psychiatry*, 1961, 64, 20–26.

Shapiro, D., & Schwartz, G. E. Biofeedback and visceral learning: Clinical applications. *Seminars in Psychiatry*, 1972, 4, 171–184.

Solbach, P., & Sargent, J. D. A follow-up evaluation of the Menninger pilot migraine study using thermal training. *Headache*, 1977, 17, 198–202.

Sommer, B. The effect of menstruation on cognitive and perceptual–motor behavior: A review. *Psychosomatic Medicine*, 1973, 33, 411–428.

Southam, H. L. & Gonzaga, F. P. Systematic changes during the menstrual cycle. *American Journal of Obstetrics and Gynecology*, 1965, 91, 142–165.

Stein, L. S., Del Gaudio, A. C., & Ansley, M. Y. A comparison of male and female neurotic depressives. *Journal of Clinical Psychology*, 1976, 32, 19–21.

Stern, K., & Prados, M. Personality studies in menopausal women. *American Journal of Psychiatry*, 1946, 103, 358.

Sturgis, E. T. *Liability and reactivity in the headache response.* Paper presented at meeting of the Association for Advancement of Behavior Therapy, New York, November 1980.

Sturgis, E. T., & Adams, H. E. Use of cephalic vasomotor and electromyogram feedback in treatment of migraine, muscle-contraction, and combined headaches. In N. Birbaumer & H. D. Kimmel (Eds.), *Biofeedback and self-regulation.* New York: Erlbaum, 1979.

Sturgis, E. T., Tollison, C. D., & Adams, H. E. Modification of combined migraine–muscle contraction headaches using BVP and EMG feedback. *Journal of Applied Behavior Analysis*, 1978, 22, 215–223.

Surwit, R. Biofeedback: A possible treatment for Raynaud's disease. In L. Birk (Ed.), *Biofeedback: Behavioral medicine*. New York: Grune & Stratton, 1973.

Surwit, R., Pilon, R., & Fenton, C. Behavioral treatment of Raynaud's disease. *Journal of Behavioral Medicine*, 1978, *1*, 323–335.

Tasto, D. L., & Chesney, M. A. Muscle relaxation treatment for primary dysmenorrhea. *Behavior Therapy*, 1974, *5*, 668–672.

Tasto, D., & Hinkle, J. Muscle relaxation treatment for tension headaches. *Behaviour Research and Therapy*, 1973, *11*, 347–349.

Taub, E., & Stroebel, C. F. Biofeedback in the treatment of vasoconstrictive syndromes. *Biofeedback and Self-Regulation*, 1978, *3*, 363–373.

Thompson, J. K. *Diagnosis of head pain: An idiographic approach to assessment and classification*. Unpublished manuscript, University of Georgia, 1981.

Thompson, J. K., & Adams, H. E. *Physiological reactivity to stressful and nonstressful imagery for normals, migrainers, and individuals with muscle contraction headaches*. Paper presented at meeting of the Association for Advancement of Behavior Therapy, New York, November 1980.

Thompson, J. K., Raczynski, J. M., Haber, J. D., & Sturgis, E. T. *The control issue in biofeedback training*. Unpublished manuscript, University of Mississippi Medical Center, 1981.

Tubbs, W., & Carnahan, C. *Clinical biofeedback for primary dysmenorrhea: A pilot study*. Paper presented at 2nd Annual Convention of the Biofeedback Society of California, Berkeley, December 1976.

Vaughn, R., Pall, M. L., & Haynes, S. N. Frontalis EMG response to stress in subjects with frequent muscle contraction headaches. *Headache*, 1977, *16*, 313–317.

Vila, J., & Beech, H. R. Premenstrual symptomatology: An interaction hypothesis. *British Journal of Social and Clinical Psychology*, 1980, *19*, 73–80.

Warner, G., & Lance, J. Relaxation therapy in migraine and chronic tension headache. *Medical Journal of Australia*, 1975, *1*, 298–301.

Weissman, M., & Klerman, G. Sex differences and the epidemiology of depression. *Archives of General Psychiatry*, 1977, *34*, 98–111.

Willerson, J. T., Thompson, R. H., Hookman, P., Herdt, J., & Decker, J. L. Reserpine in Raynaud's disease and phenomenon: Short-term response to intra-arterial injection. *Annals of Internal Medicine*, 1970, *72*, 17–27.

Winokur, G. Depression in the menopause. *American Journal of Psychiatry*, 1973, *130*, 92–93.

Ziel, H. K., & Finkle, W. D. Increased risk of endometrial carcinoma among users of conjugated oestrogens. *New England Journal of Medicine*, 1975, *293*, 1167.

13

ANXIETY-RELATED DISORDERS, FEARS, AND PHOBIAS

WENDY J. PADAWER
MARVIN R. GOLDFRIED

The anxiety-related problems, fears, and phobias experienced by women are, in part, a function of their prescribed sex roles in our society. The primary focus of this chapter is to describe how kowledge of societal sex-role constraints on women can be helpful to the clinician, both in conducting a behavioral analysis of the anxiety-related disorders of women, and in designing and implementing appropriate intervention procedures. The chapter begins with a discussion of the traditional conceptions of femininity and masculinity and the more recent notion of androgyny. We present a cognitive–behavioral analysis of sex roles, describing sex-role stereotypes as a function of modeling, reinforcement, and punishment and their ultimate manifestation in women's beliefs and cognitive self-schemata. The concepts of locus of control and helplessness, and their contribution to stress in women, are analyzed. We then review in detail specific anxiety-related problems, including simple phobias, agoraphobia, interpersonal assertiveness anxiety, and work-related anxiety, making suggestions for relevant therapeutic intervention. We conclude by noting some general considerations about behavioral intervention with women. Although this chapter and Chapter 2 in this volume by Beck and Barlow discuss sex roles, the chapters' emphases are radically different. Whereas Beck and Barlow's concern is with the motor component of the sex-role construct, our interest is in its cognitive and interpersonal manifestations.

Wendy J. Padawer and Marvin R. Goldfried. Department of Psychology, State University of New York at Stony Brook, Stony Brook, New York.

BACKGROUND

ON FEMININITY AND MASCULINITY

The traditional stereotypes of women and men in our society (Bakan, 1966; Parsons & Bales, 1955; Rosenkrantz, Bee, Vogel, & Broverman, 1968) have had a significant impact on the behavioral, emotional, and cognitive experiences of women. Much of the literature on sex-role stereotypes has its bases in personality trait theories, which have been used to blame women for their inherent pathologies. To avoid any misunderstandings concerning our frequent references to the sex-role literature, it is important to emphasize that:

  1. Stereotypes are beliefs that may not reflect reality.
  2. Although they may be false, stereotypes point to important situational influences on both men and women.

One of our goals is to determine how popular stereotypes, regardless of their accuracy, can aid the behavior therapist.

Parsons and Bales (1955) equated femininity and masculinity with "expressiveness" and "instrumentality," respectively. Expressiveness encompasses emotional and supportive responses, directed toward nurturance of others, whereas instrumentality involves goal directedness and accomplishment. In discussing the "duality of human existence," Bakan (1966) characterized femininity by "communion" and masculinity by "agency." Communion involves concern with the group, and is manifested by contact, openness, cooperation, and feeling. Agency, on the other hand, refers to a concern for the self and is manifested in self-protection, self-assertion, isolation, mastery, and the repression of feeling. These theoretical conceptualizations of femininity and masculinity are consistent with empirical findings concerning sex roles and sex-role stereotypes. Rosenkrantz et al. (1968) found that both men and women described the "typical woman" to be gentle, quiet, expressive of tender feelings, overly emotional and excitable, conceited about appearance, not self-confident, passive, submissive, subjective, illogical, and dependent. The "typical male" was viewed as aggressive, unemotional, rough, blunt, self-confident, dominant, objective, logical, and independent. Despite the fact that women preferred masculine characteristics, they nonetheless incorporated the less desirable attributes into their self-concepts (Rosenkrantz et al., 1968).

Although the term "sex role" often appears in the literature on the psychology of women, its meaning varies. According to role theory, *role expectations* are subjective beliefs about the "rights and privileges, the duties and obligations of any occupant of a social position in relation to persons occupying other positions in the social structure" (Sarbin & Allen, 1968, p. 497). Role expectations vary in their clarity. A person who is presented with ambiguous role expectations cannot predict the demands of the situation or decide how to act. Ambiguous role expectations are equivalent to unpredictable reinforcement schedules in their detrimental effects on psychological well-being, and their induction of anxiety. *Role enactment* refers to observable conduct in a particular setting, and its dimensions include: (1) the *number* of roles in the person's repertoire; with more roles, there are more options for dealing with situational demands; (2) organismic involvement, referring to the *intensity* or effort exerted in role enactment; and (3) preemptiveness, or the amount of *time* spent in role enactment. Many life circumstances demand enactment of multiple roles (e.g., wife, mother, professional), which may be complementary or in conflict. *Interrole conflict* occurs when a person occupies different roles simultaneously (e.g., mother and career woman), whereas *intrarole conflict* exists when the individual is caught between differing expectations concerning the same role (e.g., the preemptiveness of motherhood for a full-time mother vs. a working mother). The psychological distress associated with role conflict (Gyllstrom & Herman, 1977; Powell & Reznikoff, 1976) has been blamed for symptom formation in women (Fodor, 1974a), including agoraphobia (Fodor, 1974b).

The *sex-role stereotype* summarizes common beliefs about the personality traits of "typical" men and women. The assumption that masculinity and femininity are mutually exclusive traits has been challenged by the view that these are actually unrelated characteristics, which can coexist in the androgynous person (Bem, 1974; Block, 1973; Constantinople, 1973; Kelly & Worell, 1977; Spence, Helmreich, & Stapp, 1975; Spence & Helmreich, 1978). The presumed benefit of androgyny is the capacity to deal with a range of situations, each of which demands different skills (Bem, 1975). Because the construct of androgyny refers to appropriate male and female attributes, use of the construct could be seen as perpetuating stereotypes or endorsing the belief that certain characteristics *are* objectively male or female. Stereotypes do not reflect the behavioral heterogeneity that exists among women; moreover, they tend to devalue women, as the stereotype of femininity is characterized by more negative and fewer positive characteristics than is masculinity.

An advantage of such a typology, on the other hand, is that women who understand how stereotypes function are prepared to evaluate the likely consequences of various behavior patterns.

As psychologists, when we hear terms "role" or "stereotype," we tend to think of these as abstract sociological concepts without concrete referents. Sex roles have been described as the differing characteristics and behaviors that are socially desirable for men and women. However, standards of social desirability have directly observable consequences, such as may be seen in the contingencies of social reinforcement. Early socialization involves differential reinforcement for boys' and girls' behavior. Lenney (1979) has suggested that feminine-typed women experienced a pattern of contingencies in which gender-appropriate behaviors were reinforced and cross-gender behaviors were punished or extinguished (Block, 1973; Fagot, 1977). As adults, women continue to be selectively reinforced for behaviors congruent with the female role, and punished for behaviors appropriate to the male role. Although the feminine woman may benefit from social acceptance, she may acquire limited coping skills. For example, a newly divorced feminine sex-typed woman, while experiencing the pain and grief from feeling alone, may suddenly confront unfamiliar tasks (e.g., finances, house repairs) and feel anxious about the absence of her former husband's masculine-typed coping skills. Such deficient behavioral repertoires add to the poverty, marginal social status, and double work load of child rearing and income maintenance as a source of stress.

BELIEFS AND SELF-SCHEMATA

Sex-role stereotypes, which reflect consensual beliefs about the typical woman and typical man, are particularly interesting in light of the growing emphasis in behavior therapy on cognitive mediators of emotional upset. Inasmuch as the stereotypic female role contains undesirable attributes, women who perceive themselves as typical will endorse negative beliefs about their abilities, and by implication, are likely to evidence anxiety and other dysphoric mood states. Stereotypes provide a way of organizing one's experience of the world (Ashmore & Del Boca, 1979), and resist contradictory information (Tajfel, 1969). Social psychology's stereotype resembles cognitive psychology's "schema," a structure of knowledge that selectively organizes perception, storage, and retrieval of information about the environment (Neisser, 1976). If those individuals with whom a woman frequently interacts are operating with their own schemata for "female" that includes the concepts "competent, rational, and emotionally sensitive," this network of associations may ultimately affect the self-schema of that woman. More pessimistically, if a woman is repeatedly confronted by others whose schemata for "female" closely parallel some of the more negative characteristics of the sex-role stereotype, such as "dependent, overly emotional, illogical, and clinging," she is likely to develop a more negative self-schema that will in turn influence her future beliefs and actions.

Research on self-role orientation and cognitive schemata has been integrated by Bem (1981), who has proposed a "gender schema theory." As a result of differential socialization, girls and boys learn different sex-linked sets of associations, or "gender schemata," which affect the processing of new information. Masculine or feminine sex-typed individuals rely more on gender schemata during information processing, than androgynous individuals. In support of gender schema theory, Bem (1981) reported that sex-typed subjects clustered more words according to gender in a free-recall task than did cross-sex-typed, undifferentiated, or androgynous subjects. The findings are consistent with those of Markus, Crane, and Siladi (cited by Markus & Sentis, 1980). The relationship between sex-role stereotypes and women's information processing has implications for therapeutic intervention. Women who rely on feminine self-schemata before therapy will evaluate themselves according to the female sex-role stereotype, even after they have acquired new skills. Corrective experiences, self-monitoring, and feedback directed at the feminine schema will be needed before therapy succeeds. As noted by Goldfried and Robins (1982) male and female clients often discount actual behavioral improvement, demonstrating the impermeability of self-schemata.

LOCUS OF CONTROL: REALITY AND PERCEPTION

Locus of control (Rotter, 1966), which affects psychological well-being and seems to be differentially distributed between men and women, refers to the belief that life is controlled by the self (internal control) or by society (external control). Perception of personal control reduces the aversiveness of stimuli (Geer, Davison, & Gatchel, 1970; Glass, Singer, Leonard, Krantz, Cohen, & Cummings, 1972), even without overt attempts to cope with the situation (Glass, Singer, & Friedman, 1969).

Women have higher average externality scores than men (Strickland & Haley, 1980). Thus, some women believe that the consequences of their actions are controlled by others more than by themselves; these women may be relatively incapable of tolerating aversive stimuli. Inasmuch as men in our society are generally in control of important contingencies, it is not surprising that many women perceive events as externally controlled. Hence, if women's tendency to an external locus of control reflects an accurate appraisal of social reality, attempts to change perceptions of control may provide a distorted view of the world. When people cannot exercise control, but act as if they should be able to do so, decreased coping abilities and increased depression and anxiety result (Glass, 1977). In the long run, then, realistic appraisal of the limits of one's control, although stressful, is probably more adaptive.

Abramson, Seligman, and Teasdale (1978) have proposed that styles of explaining success and failure are associated with learned helplessness and depression. The attributional style of socially anxious subjects has been found to parallel that of depressives (Sutton-Simon & Goldfried, 1982), as socially anxious subjects blamed failure on themselves while less anxious subjects attributed the same failure to environmental interference. Moreover, anxious people attributed success to the environment, while less anxious subjects gave themselves credit for success. Presented with a hopeless situation (Baucom & Danker-Brown, 1979), androgynous and undifferentiated subjects were unaffected, while feminine and masculine sex-typed subjects showed cognitive, motivational, and mood deficits. Sex-typed subjects may have lacked the coping strategies needed to deal with the experimental task, which required both masculine- and feminine-typed behaviors.

Although many women demonstrate an external locus of control, they blame themselves for failures. After successful task completion, girls and women tend to credit external causes (e.g., luck) more than boys and men; after failure, girls and women tend to credit an internal cause, such as lack of ability (Dweck & Goetz, 1978; Deaux & Farris, 1977; Ickes & Layden, 1978). This self-blaming pattern of thinking seems to produce depression and anxiety.

Having discussed the female sex role and its relationship to anxiety among women, we will now consider in further detail some of the various manifestations of anxiety, including simple phobias, agoraphobia, interpersonal assertiveness anxiety, and anxiety associated with work.

ANXIETY-RELATED DISORDERS IN WOMEN

Fear is a normal response to an imagined or actual threat (Marks, 1969). The physiological symptoms of fear include trembling, dizziness, rapid heart rate, palpitation, nausea, diarrhea, desire to urinate, and feelings of suffocating or choking (Barlow & Mavissakalian, 1981). The cognitive component is a fearful idea, or self-report (e.g., "What if I see a dog and I can't cope? What if I get hurt?"), although behavioral avoidance does not always accompany fearful ideas. "Synchrony" describes a condition in which reported fear, physiological reactivity, and behavioral avoidance covary with each other; "desynchrony" refers to little or no association among response modes (Barlow & Mavissakalian, 1981). Participants in a recent NIMH research conference on anxiety-related disorders (Barlow & Wolfe, 1981) agreed that evaluation of all three response systems was advisable, and that this approach might unravel the complex interactions among response systems.

Fear can be useful if it leads to quick action and a return to safety. A phobia is fear that is excessive, inappropriate to the situation, out of control, and not readily altered by reason (Marks, 1969). By definition, fears are rational and adaptive, phobias are irrational and maladaptive. Anxiety is closely related to fears and phobias and describes feelings of apprehension, uneasiness, nervousness, and tension.

Goldfried and Davison (1976) classified anxiety according to its probable causes: (1) classical or vicarious conditioning; (2) instrumental deficits; (3) self-generated anxiety-eliciting statements; (4) self-induced behaviors; and (5) an untenable aspect of one's life situation. When women seek therapy for anxiety, it is important to determine what conditions maintain anxiety and to differentiate between the rational and irrational sources of anxiety. For example, work-related anxiety is often a rational response and its treatment proceeds differently from the treatment of phobias.

SIMPLE PHOBIAS

Phobias are mostly a female problem. Marks (1969) reported that women experience 95% of specific animal phobias, and 75% of specific situational phobias. Typical small-animal phobias are directed toward cats, dogs, birds, and snakes, and specific situational phobias often involve heights, or such natural phenomena as thunderstorms and darkness. Blood and injury phobias include fears of doctor and dentist visits, hospitals, the sight of blood, and such specific illnesses as cancer and heart attack. Both animal and situational phobias begin in childhood and are chronic problems if they remain untreated, whereas blood and injury phobias tend to decline with age (Barlow & Mavissakalian, 1981). Marks (1969) has described simple phobic clients as timid, dependent, and immature. Both the phobia and the personality style of simple phobic clients are relevant treatment goals. For example, one client described a fear of dogs; during treatment it became apparent that her fear of dogs caused her to stay home close to her parents, and prevented her from looking for a job. She was unassertive with her parents and angry about their overprotectiveness, and much of her excess, irrational anxiety seemed to be the result of interpersonal deficits.

Participants in a state-of-the-art conference on anxiety-related disorders (Barlow & Wolfe, 1981) agreed that *exposure* is the treatment of choice for phobias and compulsions. For those individuals who complete treatment, exposure procedures have a 65% to 75% success rate, based on follow-ups of up to 9 years. De Silva and Rachman (1981) define "exposure" as "exposure of the subject to the fear-evoking stimulus, either in real life (*in vivo* exposure) or in fantasy (imaginal exposure)" (p. 227). This definition, however, does not address the issue of what has been referred to as "functional" exposure (Barlow & Wolfe, 1981). It seems that some phobics employ selective attentional strategies to avoid complete exposure to the anxiety-provoking situation. For example, a snake-phobic client who is gradually observing and approaching snakes during treatment, may imagine herself somewhere else, avoid anxious feelings, and prevent the extinction of her fear. When avoidance strategies are covert, the therapist cannot have complete control over functional exposure.

Some of the recent work by Lang (1979) on emotional imagery has important implications for exposure procedures. Lang contends that emotional arousal does not result merely from imaginal exposure to the feared stimulus; activation of emotional responses (e.g., feelings of muscle tension and attention to increased heart rate) are also needed. When *both* the stimulus and response components are emphasized in the imaginal presentation of aversive scenes, more arousal results. Lang, Melamed, and Hart (1970) found greater fear reduction in desensitization for those individuals who displayed more emotional reactivity. Taken together, these findings would suggest that imaginal exposure that deals with both stimulus and responses aspects is more likely to result in arousal, and hence is more likely to be "functional" in nature. The question of exposure to the internal feelings of anxiety, versus exposure only to the external phobic stimulus, has important implications for the use of psychotropic medication as an adjunct to treatment. As psychotropic medication can decrease the amount of anxiety experienced, it may limit functional exposure to the aversive stimulus and thereby jeopardize treatment outcome.

There are several ways to conduct exposure treatment. The client can imagine confronting the phobic stimulus or can confront the stimulus *in vivo*. Prolonged exposure to the phobic stimuli is called "flooding" and can be conducted either *in vivo* or in fantasy. Flooding is very aversive and prohibits avoidance. Systematic desensitization (Wolpe, 1958), on the other hand, involves graded exposure to a hierarchy of fear-evoking situations. Graded exposure elicits little anxiety, as the client imagines scenes while deeply relaxed until each scene elicits no anxiety. Goldfried's (1971) modification of desensitization teaches clients to actively deal with aversive images by means of relaxation as a coping skill. Another form of exposure that elicits little anxiety is "fading" (Ost, 1978). The client controls the presentation of calming and phobic slides by fading the phobic and calming slides in and out, gradually increasing the amount of time spent looking at the phobic slide. In another variation of exposure treatment, reinforced practice (Leitenberg, 1976), clients are praised for each approach to the phobic stimulus. In a review of the variants of behavioral treatment for phobias, Marks (1978) has reached several conclusions:

    1. *In vivo* exposure has generally been shown to be more effective than imaginal exposure.
    2. The optimal duration for exposure is as yet unknown.
    3. Relaxation adds little to exposure.
    4. High levels of arousal are not crucial during the exposure procedure.

Some research has addressed the issue of cognitive processes in the treatment of simple phobias. Sutton-Simon and Goldfried (1979) found that acrophobia was weakly associated with irrational thinking ($r = .26$), and strongly related to negative self-statements about high places ($r = .62$). Landau (1980) found that in comparison to nonphobics, dog phobics have a more impoverished meaning structure of dogs, and overemphasize characteristics associated with their ferocity. In comparison to nonphobics, phobics generate frightening thoughts that exacerbate autonomic nervous system responding (May, 1977a, 1977b). Furthermore, self-generated phobic thoughts produce more physiological activity and subjective anxiety than phobic thoughts elicited by such external stimuli as pictures and statements. Phobics with extreme physiological reactions may benefit when maladaptive phobic cognitions are addressed by cognitive therapy (Odom, Nelson, & Wein, 1978), as seen when snake phobics were treated with guided participation, systematic desensitization, verbal extinction, cognitive restructuring, or attention placebo. The four experimental treatments were superior to the placebo and a no-treatment control condition. Although guided participation led to most improvement in behavioral avoidance and self-reported fear, cognitive restructuring was more effective than guided participation on the physiological (heart rate) measure.

Tailor-made treatment plans require attention to the unique characteristics of the phobia, and to the interplay between the phobia and other difficulties. Since fainting is relatively common among blood, injury, and illness phobics, steps should be taken to prepare the client and to prevent injury (Connolly, Hallam, & Marks, 1976). Inasmuch as *in vivo* exposure to real thunderstorms is difficult to arrange, desensitization must rely on ingenious simulations of lightning and thunder (Leitenberg, Agras, Allen, Butz, & Edwards, 1975; Lubetkin, 1975). The thunderstorm phobic's fear is omnipresent, and is accompanied by obsessive worrying and compulsive rituals (Liddell & Lyons, 1978; Ost, 1978). Thunderstorm-phobic women have been described as incapable of enjoying summertime and good weather; they listen to every weather forecast, constantly search for approaching storms, and plan their days to avoid being away from home in a storm.

A woman who avoided public transportation (Hayes & Barlow, 1977) demonstrated a phobia maintained by unassertiveness, and illustrates how an active coping strategy dispels fear. This woman feared riding on buses, as people tended to comment on her facial anomaly, a cleft palate. In *flooding relief* treatment, the client practiced responding assertively to strangers' comments, while the therapist described strangers looking at and commenting on her hairlip. Aversive scenes were terminated when the client made an appropriately assertive statement. Until she acted assertively, the scene was described ever more aversively by the therapist. The importance of active coping is supported by evidence that active coping response practice improved rat phobics more than desensitization (Newman & Brand, 1980). During active coping training the women rehearsed approach behavior and instrumental problem solving with the goal of approaching and calming the frightened rat. As many women have been taught it is acceptable to be afraid of certain animals, they may never have had the opportunity to learn active coping skills, such as how to handle a rat or snake. This study nicely demonstrates the importance of dealing directly with this issue clinically.

Suggestions for the Treatment of Simple Phobias

1. Determine what general cognitions and specific negative self-statements contribute to the phobias, as cognitive therapy techniques could be used to challenge faulty thinking. Repeated "functional" exposure to the feared stimulus is a necessary feature of successful treatment.

2. If a phobic fears losing consciousness, gather historical data about fainting. In the case of blood, injury, or illness phobics, prevent the occurrence of fainting or the resulting injury.

3. Determine whether dependent behavior is a general problem for the client. Be prepared to treat problems other than the phobia, such as difficulties in close relationships, and a lack of confidence.

4. Assess whether the simple phobia involves instrumental deficits, such as ability to handle animals, or a disabled car. Women with a traditionally feminine upbringing may need training in relevant coping skills along with exposure treatment.

AGORAPHOBIA

Agoraphobia, or "fear of the marketplace," is often described as a fear of being away from home or in open and enclosed places; agoraphobics are either housebound or panic easily when away from home. Like simple phobics, most agoraphobics (75%) are women (Marks, 1969). Unlike other phobias, however, agoraphobia is a complex and heterogeneous syndrome, and successful treatment requires an assessment of the interplay among the client's many problems. When an agoraphobic improves, new problems often come to light. Fodor (1974a) has suggested that agoraphobics epitomize the stereotyped, oversocialized, ultrafeminine woman. Agoraphobia exemplifies the maladaptive nature of extreme femininity, with its dependency, passivity, and avoidance. Therapy must deal with the maladaptive style of the agoraphobic, not just the phobia, and impart instrumental, problem-solving behavior through role playing, marital intervention, consciousness-raising groups, assertion training, and modeling of independent behavior.

Goldstein and Chambless (1978) distinguish between "simple" and "complex" agoraphobia, and the recommended treatment differs with the type of agoraphobia. Simple agoraphobics are "clients whose symptoms are precipitated by panic attacks produced by drug experiences or physical disorders such as hypoglycemia. They do not necessarily present the same personality characteristics as other agoraphobics and usually recover more quickly when any contributing physical disorder is controlled" (pp. 50–51). Most clients are "complex" agoraphobics, with a syndrome rather than a simple phobia. Goldstein and Chambless (1978) describe four necessary and sufficient elements for this classification: (1) a central phobic element of "fear of fear," or fear of physiological symptoms of anxiety; (2) low levels of self-sufficiency, due to anxiety and/or lack of skills; (3) no understanding of the cause of the anxiety, which is believed to come "out of the blue," rather than from interpersonal conflicts; and (4) the onset of the problem is associated with conflict, typically interpersonal in nature. This complex agoraphobic conforms to stereotypes about the excessively feminine woman. She fears she can not control her own emotions (fear of fear), and she is emotionally dependent (Weiss, 1964). She cannot understand why she is afraid, employing a hysterical cognitive style (Shapiro, 1965) that provides vague impressions rather than specific facts. Finally, she is too unassertive to manage the interpersonal conflict that makes her fearful.

Chambless and Goldstein (1981) involve husbands in the treatment of agoraphobia, as they often reinforce maladaptive helplessness. Some husbands do household chores that would take their wives away from home, and ignore or punish independent behavior. This may often be done unwittingly, by a man who has been socialized to "take over." Under such circumstances, the agoraphobic cannot be described as reacting totally unrealistically, as her behavior is, in part, a function of reinforcement contingencies. This becomes evident when an agoraphobic wife improves and her husband's confidence wanes. At such times husbands may undermine progress (e.g., forbidding wives to look for a job), or marital conflict may erupt. Hence, it is important to consider the environmental situation in the treatment of complex agoraphobics, with particular attention to the feminine and masculine sex-role patterns within the dyad that may be contributing to the problem.

The interpersonal difficulties of agoraphobics—particularly their marital problems—have often been noted (Emmelkamp, 1974; Hafner

& Marks, 1976; Hand, Lamontagne, & Marks, 1974; Hand & Lamontagne, 1976). Among agoraphobics in treatment, 66% perceived their
marriages as unsatisfactory before treatment; of the clients with unhappy
marriages, 50% experienced acute marital difficulties after treatment
(Hand *et al.*, 1974). Hafner (1976) similarly found that agoraphobic clients
with marital distress showed the most relapse and deterioration after
treatment. At a 3-month follow-up, when the agoraphobic women
showed maximum improvement, the husbands of the most hostile
clients reported decreased self-satisfaction and increased neuroticism
(Hafner, 1977a, 1977b). At a 6-month follow-up, the wives became more
symptomatic and their husbands' neuroticism scores decreased. One
husband attempted suicide, and reported that he felt useless now that
his wife was no longer dependent on him; other husbands became jeal-
ous and argumentative as their wives improved. Milton and Hafner
(1979) found that although all agoraphobic clients responded to an intensive 1-week *in vivo* flooding treatment, women who were satisfied
with their marriages before treatment had better symptom scores after
treatment than dissatisfied women. Six couples reported more marital
satisfaction after treatment, and nine couples reported more distress.
Bland and Hallam (1981) found maritally satisfied agoraphobics maintained treatment gains at follow-up whereas maritally dissatisfied
women relapsed.

A treatment program for use with female agoraphobics, which was
based in the home and actively involved the husband, was designed
and evaluated by Mathews, Teasdale, Munby, Johnston, and Shaw
(1977). By requiring the husband to participate in planning and encouraging practice attempts, they hoped to maintain his role of "being
needed" while at the same time assisting his wife to become more self-
sufficient and independent. Results found this program to be most effective. Barlow, Mavissakalian, and Hay (1981) also involved husbands
as cotherapists; their group treatment program used *in vivo* exposure,
cognitive restructuring, and covert rehearsal of coping with anxiety, and
attempted to prevent husbands from encouraging dependency. Four
couples experienced improvement in phobic symptomatology and marital satisfaction, while two couples experienced increased phobic severity
and decreased marital satisfaction. Taken together, studies in this area
show that although agoraphobic symptomatology appears related to
marital satisfaction, it is unclear which couples need adjunct marital
treatment to prevent relapse in the agoraphobic client.

Given that fear of fear appears to be central to the agoraphobic

syndrome (Goldstein & Chambless, 1978), functional exposure to physiological fear stimuli may be necessary for treatment success (cf. Lang,
1979). One potential source of avoidance during exposure involves *psychotropic medication*. Thus, agoraphobic patients made anxious by flooding treatment improved significantly more than patients who received
the same treatment without anxiety because of Brevital injections
(Chambless, Foa, Groves, & Goldstein, 1979). Because psychotropic
medications decrease the panic attacks experienced by phobics, some
believe that drugs help agoraphobics enter phobic situations (e.g., Zitrin,
Klein, & Woerner, 1978). Klein and Fink (1962) found that although
imipramine reduced acute panic attacks, it did not improve anticipatory
anxiety or phobic avoidance behavior. Klein (1974) reported similar results with monoamine oxidase (MAO) inhibitors. Imipramine-treated
patients (combined with either supportive psychotherapy or *in vivo* exposure) showed greater improvement at the end of treatment than those
receiving a placebo, but the relapse rate 1 year later was higher for the
imipramine than for the placebo groups. Moreover, 23% of the imipramine groups dropped out of treatment, compared to 9% dropout from
the behavior therapy–placebo group (Zitrin, Klein, & Woerner, 1978).
According to Zitrin (1981), imipramine-treated patients use the drug
"as a crutch" and do not exert themselves to deal with their fear on their
own. When the medication is withdrawn, they once again become susceptible to panic attacks. When agoraphobics practice exposure under
a drug-induced calm state, they are likely to attribute their success to
the drug, and the success experience is unlikely to facilitate future effort
(cf. Davison & Valins, 1969; Valins & Nisbett, 1971; Whalen & Henker,
1976).

   Cognitive strategies can also function like psychotropic medication,
by providing the agoraphobic with a "cognitive crutch" during the *in
vivo* exposure. The agoraphobic may try to maintain control by "fighting"
the anxiety, or by distracting herself by talking with the therapist. One
client used medication and a cognitive strategy to avoid functional exposure, by reassuring herself with the thought, "If I get too anxious, I
can always talke Valium when I get home." According to Weekes (1976),
the fear of fear has two parts. There is an initial physiological reaction
(e.g., heart racing, trembling, nausea) followed by an automatic cata-
strophic thought (e.g., "What if the feeling gets worse?" "What if I
panic?"). Agoraphobics sometimes avoid functional exposure with coun-
tercatastrophic cognitions (e.g., "If I drink some water, I'll be safe," or
"My therapist will save me if I have a heart attack"). The agoraphobic

must learn that a normal anxiety reaction to daily life stress does not signal a catastrophe. Toward this end, coping self-statements should be rehearsed during *in vivo* exposure (e.g., "It's just a feeling. Even though it's scary, it's not dangerous. Adrenalin will run its course if I let it" [adapted from Weekes, 1976]).

Inasmuch as many agoraphobics suffer from avoidant behavior, defeating cognitions, lack of confidence, and depression, Fishman (1981) has developed a "multiform behavoral treatment plan" which includes relaxation training, imaginal and *in vivo* exposure, simulated anxiety attacks, independence and assertion training, cognitive restructuring, bibliotherapy, and medication.

Outcome research in agoraphobia has demonstrated the superiority of *in vivo* exposure over systematic desensitization (e.g., Gelder, Marks, & Wolff, 1967; Marks & Gelder, 1965; Marks, Boulougouris, & Marset, 1971), and of *in vivo* over imaginal exposure (Emmelkamp & Wessels, 1975; Mathews *et al.*, 1977; Stern & Marks, 1973; Watson, Mullett, & Pillay, 1973). In one study, prolonged *in vivo* exposure has been found superior to cognitive restructuring (Emmelkamp, Kuipers, & Eggeraat, 1978). A second study (Emmelkamp & Kuipers, 1979) compared cognitive restructuring, prolonged *in vivo* exposure, and the two together. Although the combined treatment and the exposure-alone treatment were superior to cognitive restructuring at posttest, these differences disappeared at follow-up, due to the continued improvement of the cognitive restructuring group.

Suggestions for the Treatment of Agoraphobia

1. During the early sessions, let the agoraphobic know that you are sensitive to her difficulties in traveling from home to receive treatment. Acknowledge, accept, and discuss nonverbal signs of discomfort.

2. Prepare the client for *in vivo* exposure by providing a rationale, and predicting an increase and then a gradual decrease in the anxiety.

3. Have the client monitor feelings and thoughts before and during exposure, and recognize the first and second fear. Ask her to generate counterthoughts to the second fears (e.g., "It's just a feeling. I only *think* it's dangerous but it really isn't") as a part of the written self-monitoring exercise, and to practice these thoughts during *in vivo* exposure.

4. Discuss cognitive avoidance techniques and discourage crutches (e.g., a glass of water, a Lifesaver candy) during the homework assignment.

5. The exposure contract may have to be quite specific, to consider many dimensions of anxiety. For example, concerning a bus ride: Will you take the first bus that comes by? Will you take a crowded one, or one that is relatively empty? Will the therapist sit together with the client? Will you sit near or far from the door? How many stops will you go? How many times will you repeat the bus ride?

6. To reduce anticipatory anxiety (which may be worse than the anxiety experienced during *in vivo* practice), ask the client to self-monitor anxiety before and during the exposure sessions. In this way, the agoraphobic learns that contrary to her belief, anticipatory anxiety is *not* predictive of either anxiety during exposure, or of her ability to cope with anxiety.

7. If a "trusted companion" functions as a crutch with whom the agoraphobic feels no anxiety, make sure that person does not accompany the woman on her practice outings.

8. Discuss dependency and sabotage with spouse, family, and friends, and encourage active uninvolvement.

9. Because agoraphobic couples are often unwilling to acknowledge marital dissatisfaction, probe for signs of conflict slowly and in a nonthreatening manner.

10. Provide expressiveness or assertiveness training to agoraphobics who express angry feelings with difficulty and panic during interpersonal conflict.

11. When treatment is at an impasse, assess what conditions reinforce staying home, and identify potentially gratifying activities outside the home that could compete with housecrafts.

12. Combine agoraphobics into groups of people who live close to each other. Practice sessions in groups can augment the effectiveness of exposure and help socially isolated agoraphobics build a social network (Sinnott, Jones, Scott-Fordham, & Woodward, 1981).

INTERPERSONAL ASSERTIVENESS ANXIETY

In contrast to agoraphobia, anxiety in interpersonal situations is more evenly distributed between the sexes. Yet there are sex differences for specific types of social anxiety. College men have more difficulties than college women in heterosocial interaction (Borkovec, Stone, O'Brien, & Kaloupek, 1974; Schmurak, cited in Glass, Gottman, & Schmurak, 1976), and women experience more problems when an instrumental, assertive response is required (Linehan & Egan, 1979). In a study of sex-role orientation and interpersonal effectiveness, Kelly, O'Brien, Hosford, and Kinsinger (1976) found that feminine women gave less effective responses than androgynous women when they had to refuse unreasonable demands. Androgynous men were more effective than masculine or undifferentiated men when they had to be warm and approving. In Chapter 6 on assertiveness in this volume, Linehan focuses on remediation of unassertive behavior. Our concern is with cognitive and emotional aspects of unassertiveness, and with the remediation of interpersonal anxiety.

To reconcile different definitions of "assertiveness" (Linehan, 1979; Rich & Schroeder, 1976), McFall (1976) equated assertiveness with effective and reinforcing responses. Effectiveness is situation specific and reflects personal values. Goldstein (1976) proposed that the term "appropriate expressiveness" replace "assertiveness." Clients who express their feelings and desires, to themselves and others, are much more likely to be effective and avoid anxiety. As has been discussed by Blechman in Chapter 1 of this volume, competence reflects the attainment of *interpersonal* and *achievement* oriented goals. Interpersonal goals include receiving the approval of others, being liked, and being considered attractive. Achievement goals are exemplified by such events as receiving a raise, successfully negotiating a lease, and obtaining more help in household tasks from a significant other.

Three models have been proposed to explain the etiology and maintenance of unassertiveness: conditioned anxiety, skills deficits, and inhibiting cognitions (Goldfried & Davison, 1976; Linehan & Egan, 1979; Twentyman & Zimering, 1979). In the *conditioned anxiety* model, anxiety is classically conditioned to aversive stimuli (e.g., rejection and failure) associated with interpersonal experiences (Arkowitz, 1977). Even the individual with adequate social skills avoids social interaction due to conditioned anxiety. The conditioned anxiety explanation of unassertiveness is indirectly supported by evidence that general social anxiety is improved by systematic desensitization (Curran, 1975; Curran & Gilbert, 1975), response practice with *in vivo* exposure (Christensen, Arkowitz, & Anderson, 1975), and self-reinforcement for approach behavior (Rehm & Marston, 1968). However, most of these findings have dealt with social anxiety in general, and little if any research stemming from this model has dealt directly with unassertiveness.

The *skills deficit* model assumes that the unassertive person has inadequate social skills (Curran, 1977), and that frequent rejection by others produces fear and avoidance. According to Arkowitz (1977), this fear is a realistic appraisal of potentially aversive consequences of social interaction. Although skills training procedures are commonly used to treat unassertiveness, consensus about the components of assertive behavior has not been achieved (Goldfried & Linehan, 1977; Linehan & Egan, 1979; McFall & Marston, 1970; Rich & Schroeder, 1976). If characteristics of the specific situation dictate the form of an effective response (Linehan & Egan, 1979; Rich & Schroeder, 1976), and effective assertive behavior differs for women and men, perhaps a generalized assertive response tendency is a fiction.

Skills training programs generally assume that the trainer can identify the verbal and nonverbal components of assertive responses. Assertive verbal behavior is said to be "direct" and "open" (Galassi & Galassi, 1977; Lange & Jakubowski, 1976) and sensitive to the personal values of the client and therapist, societal values, and the demands of the specific situation (Rich & Schroeder, 1976). Assertive, paralinguistic behavior includes quick, loud, long, responses, with appropriate affect (Eisler, Miller, & Hersen, 1973). Skills training programs generally include one or more component procedures: (1) rehearsal, (2) modeling, (3) coaching, and (4) feedback and/or reinforcement. Rehearsal through overt or covert (imagined) practice of the new responses has been found effective alone, and in combination with other components (Gormally, Hill, Otis, & Rainey, 1975; Kazdin, 1974; McFall & Marston, 1970; McFall & Twentyman, 1973; Nietzel, Martorano, & Melnick, 1977; Rathus, 1973; Turner & Adams, 1977; Winship & Kelly, 1976). Rehearsal time can be increased with homework assignments, and improvised practice in a variety of environments should facilitate generalization of new skills (Twentyman & Zimering, 1979). Modeled demonstrations of effective assertive behavior by live, audiotaped, or videotaped experimenters, therapists, or confederates are frequently included in training packages (Friedman, 1971; Kazdin, 1974; McFall & Twentyman, 1973; Nietzel *et al.*, 1977; Turner & Adams, 1977), but apparently they do not augment the efficacy of behavioral rehearsal or coaching. Coaching by the therapist, audiotape, or videotape provides clients with information concerning appropriate assertive behavior (Hersen *et al.*, 1973; McFall & Twentyman, 1973). Feedback and reinforcement provide specific information, positive and negative, about the effectiveness of behavior (Gormally *et al.*, 1975; Kazdin, 1974, 1976; McFall & Marston, 1970; Melnick & Stocker, 1977).

According to the *cognitive* view of interpersonal assertiveness anxiety, the anxious person fears negative evaluation (Watson & Friend, 1969). In unassertiveness, this fear of negative evaluation often seems tied to various beliefs concerning the imagined negative consequences of assertive behavior, such as one's inability to change the difficult situation, and the belief that an assertive response will result in rejection. On the basis of clinical observations, Goldfried and Davison (1976) and Lange and Jakubowski (1976) have suggested that unassertiveness may be maintained by irrational beliefs (Ellis, 1962) about the importance of approval, perfection, and having things go one's own way. Schwartz and Gottman (1976) found that individuals who varied in assertiveness did not differ in physiological anxiety, knowledge of the content of an appropriately assertive response, or performance of a competent assertive response in a hypothetical, nonthreatening situation; yet unassertive subjects perceived more tension and endorsed fewer positive and more negative self-statements in assertion-related situations than moderately or highly assertive individuals. These findings have since been replicated (Alden & Safran, 1978; Bordewick & Bornstein, 1980; Robinson & Calhoun, 1981). The clinical observations (Goldfried & Davison, 1976; Lange & Jakubowski, 1976) that unassertiveness may be maintained by irrational beliefs have been supported by Alden and Safran (1978), who found endorsement of irrational beliefs to be positively correlated with unassertiveness. In comparison to assertive women, unassertive women were less accurate in evaluating the reactions of males to assertive behavior (Robinson & Calhoun, 1981), and more likely to anticipate negative consequences from an assertive response (Fiedler & Beach, 1978).

The inclusion of cognitive components (e.g., rational–emotive therapy, cognitive self-statement training, and cognitive restructuring) appears to enhance the outcome of assertiveness skills training (Carmody, 1978; Derry & Stone, 1979; Jacobs & Cochran, 1982, Linehan, Goldfried, & Goldfried, 1979; Wolfe & Fodor, 1977). Perhaps the client's pretreatment anxiety level should determine the inclusion of cognitive or skill components in assertiveness training. Safran, Alden, and Davidson (1980) studied this interaction and found that cognitive restructuring and skills training were equally effective for less anxious clients and that anxious clients showed significantly more behavior change after skills training. In contrast, Hammen, Jacobs, Mayol, and Cochran (1980) found no evidence that dysfunctional cognitions differentially affected response to skills training versus cognitive–behavioral intervention. Although the available research suggests that cognitive interventions can facilitate assertiveness, the nature of the interaction between client variables and treatment modality has yet to be determined.

Above and beyond the particular intervention technique used to facilitate assertiveness among women is the issue of how to prepare them for possible negative reactions from others. Woolfolk and Dever (1979) found that audiotaped and written descriptions of assertive behavior were considered appropriate and efficacious; however, an assertive actor was considered hostile, impolite, and neurotic. Hull and Schroeder (1979) had the rater interact with a confederate, and obtained similar results. Some evidence exists that assertive men and women are evaluated differently. Kelly, Kern, Kirkley, and Patterson (1980) found that assertive individuals were judged higher in ability and achievement but less likeable interpersonally than their unassertive counterparts. Moreover, observers of both sexes judged an assertive woman to be less likeable, competent, able, and attractive than an assertive man. Rose and Tryon (1979) showed observers identical samples of assertive behavior enacted by men and women, and found that judges of both sexes considered the women more aggressive. It is not surprising that in situations requiring assertive behavior, women experience anxiety. Inasmuch as assertive women may meet with social disapproval, it seems important to innoculate them against rejection by providing practice in both overt behavior (e.g., after disagreement, restate the position in a calm, firm voice) and cognitive coping (e.g., "I can still feel good about myself even though someone is annoyed with me") (Goldfried, 1979; Linehan, 1979; Linehan et al., 1979).

Suggestions for the Treatment of Interpersonal Assertiveness Anxiety

1. Assess behavioral and cognitive factors to design a treatment plan tailored to the individual woman's assertiveness difficulties.

2. Consider training the client to discriminate between assertive and aggressive behavior, and demonstrate how to offset potential negative reactions with empathic statements (Lange & Jakubowski, 1976; Woolfolk & Dever, 1979).

3. Determine which beliefs about the negative consequences of assertion are irrational and which are realistic in her life situation.

4. Keep in mind that treatment emphasizing interpersonal goals (e.g., being liked) and neglecting achievement goals encourages conventional feminine sex-role behavior.

5. Prepare the woman for social disapproval so that she does not then abandon her assertive behavior. Cognitive restructuring concerning the irrational belief of needing to be liked by everyone may be particularly warranted where achieving instrumental goals via assertive behavior concurrently results in negative interpersonal consequences.

6. When the woman's goals involve changing aspects of her marital or familial life via assertive behavior, it may be more effective to include significant others.

7. Therapists should examine their own personal values about assertive women, so that biases are less likely to interfere with the client's values and treatment goals.

WORK-RELATED ANXIETY

Forty percent of women in our society choose traditional wife and mother roles (Marecek & Ballou, 1981) and are more likely to display psychopathology than unmarried women (Gove & Tudor, 1973). The "housewife" has one role and one major source of gratification, the family. In contrast, married men have their work *and* their family. For many women the tasks of keeping house and raising children are frustrating, lacking in intellectual challenge, and low in prestige. When asked what they "do," these women say, "Nothing, I don't work," or "I'm just a housewife." Many housewives without children incur social disapproval, and many with children feel overburdened and underappreciated. Compared to men and to working women, housewives are likely to feel they have not pursued their true interests. Housewives with few outside interests and friends are particularly vulnerable to stress. The combination of social isolation and poverty has been implicated as a major contributing factor to child abuse (Garbarino, 1977; Wahler, 1980; Wahler, Leske, & Rogers, 1979).

Although prevalence rates for mental illness are higher for housewives than for women working outside the home, working women are nonetheless confronted by numerous stresses, most of which are functionally connected to the female sex role. Women are discriminated against in the job market, and often work in positions far below their educational attainment (Gove & Tudor, 1973). "Pink-collar" (Marecek & Ballou, 1981) jobs such as clerical positions provide low pay, prestige, and little room for advancement. Over 50% of the working women in 1981, as contrasted with only 15.2% of the working men, occupied clerical or service jobs (U.S. Department of Labor, 1982). Working mothers must also care for their children, and adequate day care is either unavailable (Dunlop, 1981) or too expensive, particularly for single mothers. Misconceptions about the harm done to children by working mothers adds social disapproval to the burden of such women (Dunlop, 1981).

Role conflict can be particularly acute for career women. Powell and Reznikoff (1976) found that androgynous high-achieving women had significantly higher symptom scores than traditional women. The career woman faces *intrarole* conflict (Darley, 1976), caught between the values of two reference groups: the minority of people whose values support her nontraditional role, and traditional friends and family who may perceive her as an inadequate wife and mother. Career women and working mothers also face an *interrole* dilemma (Darley, 1976), with too little time and energy to juggle the demands of mother/wife and worker. Many women are overburdened by their attempts to be "superwomen."

Rapoport and Rapoport (1971, 1976) have analyzed several dilemmas experienced by dual-career families which include: (1) dividing household responsibilities between husband and wife; (2) little time for socializing with relatives; and (3) conflicts about the importance of career versus family demands. In dual-career marriages, Rice (1979) noted a tendency to deny conflicts about: (1) career competition, and (2) power struggles in decision making. Women in dual-career families experience heightened stress when a job offer to one spouse requires changing locations, or when the husband presses his wife to remain at home fulfilling traditional sex-role expectations.

More than ever, women are now experiencing the negative effects of the traditional male role (see Goldfried & Friedman, 1982). One hazard is the hard-driving, ambitious, competitive, Type A coronary-prone behavior pattern (Waldron, 1978). Type A behavior is most prevalent among women who are employed full-time in high-status jobs and have been working for more than half of their adult lives. Socialization into a nontraditional female role may include training in Type A behavior (Chesney, 1979; Waldron, 1978). There is reason to believe that Type A women are particularly sensitive to situations that demand stereotypically feminine relationship skills, while Type A men are most sensitive to demands for stereotypically masculine, problem-solving behavior. Type A males have been found to be more physiologically responsive to impersonal reaction time tasks than Type B males; however, Type A women are more reactive during an interview than Type B women

(Dembrowski, cited in Chesney, 1979). As sex roles become less rigid and women pursue more challenging careers, a wider range of situations may elicit Type A behavior in women.

Before concluding this section, one other issue should be mentioned, namely fear of success. Fear of success, as described by Horner (1972), occurs when women avoid intellectual achievement rather than risk being considered unfeminine and unattractive. In behavioral terminology, their fear has been conditioned to the socially undesirable experience of success. Horner's theory has been criticized for its emphasis on "inner motives," rather than culturally prescribed roles, and for its inadequate conceptualization of males' fear of success as well. Cherry and Deaux (1978) suggest that the syndrome represents a rational fear of gender-inappropriate behavior, by *both* women and men. The perceived consequences of gender inappropriate behavior include rejection by peers, challenge to sexual adequacy, and poor prospects for dating.

Suggestions for the Treatment of Work-Related Anxiety

1. Information that the client's anxiety is a function of stressful life circumstances can encourage her to make appropriate external attribution and reduce self-blame.

2. Help "superwomen" to establish realistic goals that consider available time and energy, and to choose appropriate standards of comparison for their achievements.

3. Women who experience many kinds of work-related stress can be trained in the use of relaxation as a general coping skill.

4. In dual-career couples, assess unresolved conflicts concerning competition and decision-making power, and consider open discussion of these issues. Communication training and problem solving are appropriate tools for such purposes.

5. Because of the severity of the problem of social isolation for some women, and its association with child abuse among poor women, one should explore potential sources of social support.

6. Homemakers whose anxiety is the result of an unfulfilling role may need to find gratification outside the home, at school, or on the job. Assertiveness training may facilitate these changes.

7. Should a change in either sex-role identity or sex-role enactment be indicated in dealing with the woman's anxiety level, the therapist should carefully explore with the client any possible consequences to

her various social systems, especially that of the family. Whenever necessary, other family members should be involved before, during, and after the change process.

CONCLUSIONS

Because of early social learning experiences and current environmental contingencies, many women have a limited repertoire of skills for coping with anxiety. Behavior therapy offers procedures for broadening the range of the coping repertoire, and for modifying belief systems and external contingencies. Clinicians must be sensitive to negative aspects of sex-role stereotypes for treatment to succeed. Women with anxiety-related disorders must learn to cope actively with stressors, and to feel competent and independent. This is not to suggest that all anxious women are passive, avoidant, and irrational. Many women who cope effectively experience anxiety from environmental stressors produced by our predominantly male-oriented society. For these women, an awareness of environmental hazards can promote an external attribution of causality, and decrease self-blame.

The contribution of sex-role stereotypes to anxiety in women is apparent during treatment. Therapists and simple-phobic clients struggle with the conventional belief that women are too delicate to face a caged mouse, garter snake, or harmless spider. The helplessness of housebound agoraphobics has more far-reaching consequences, as the family often maintains the agoraphobic syndrome. For interpersonally anxious women, becoming more assertive requires instrumental, non-traditional, rather than traditional, interpersonal goals. However, when significant others have traditional values, increased assertiveness may be punished. These women may need to learn to value being effective rather than lovable. Full-time homemakers, women working out of necessity in traditional and low-paying female jobs, and the more atypical woman in a high-paying/high-status career, experience work-related stress. Many of these women should attribute more of their stress to the environment, and decrease their overly high expectations of themselves.

Given the typically feminine pattern of internal attributions for failure and external attributions for success experiences, women are particularly prone to a perpetuating cycle of self-blame for their life difficulties. Although clients need to "take responsibility" for their problems in order to be motivated to work constructively for change, women can benefit from "blaming the victim" a little less and blaming society's sex-role expectations a little more. Information that her problems are not unique to herself, and that many women experience comparable problems due to their similar life experiences, can help a woman overcome difficulties susceptible to her own control. Ultimately, to ensure the psychological well-being of women, social change is needed. Perhaps as sex-role stereotypes become less rigid, women and men will develop their full potential with less anxiety and stress.

ACKNOWLEDGMENTS

Preparation of this chapter was supported in part by Grant MH 24327 from the National Institute of Mental Health. The authors are grateful to Elaine A. Blechman, Anita Powers Goldfried, and Clive Robins for their comments on an earlier draft of this chapter.

REFERENCES

Abramson, L. Y., Seligman, M. E. P., & Teasdale, J. D. Learned helplessness in humans: Critique and reformulation. *Journal of Abnormal Psychology*, 1978, *87*, 49–74.

Alden, L., & Safran, J. Irrational beliefs and non-assertive behavior. *Cognitive Therapy and Research*, 1978, *2*, 357–364.

Arkowitz, H. Measurement and modification of minimal dating behavior. In M. Hersen, R. Eisler, & P. Miller (Eds.), *Progress in behavior modification* (Vol. 5). New York: Academic, 1977.

Ashmore, R. D., & Del Boca, F. K. Sex stereotypes and implicit personality theory: Toward a cognitive–social psychological conceptualization. *Sex Roles*, 1979, *5*, 219–248.

Bakan, D. *The duality of existence.* Chicago: Rand-McNally, 1966.

Barlow, D. H., & Mavissakalian, M. Directions in the assessment and treatment of phobia: The next decade. In M. Mavissakalian & D. H. Barlow (Eds.), *Phobia: Psychological and pharmacological treatment.* New York: Guilford, 1981.

Barlow, D. H., Mavissakalian, M., & Hay, L. R. Couples treatment of agoraphobia: Changes in marital satisfaction. *Behaviour Research and Therapy*, 1981, *19*, 245–255.

Barlow, D. H., & Wolfe, B. E. Behavioral approaches to anxiety disorders: A report on the NIMH-SUNY, Albany research conference. *Journal of Consulting and Clinical Psychology*, 1981, *49*, 448–454.

Baucom, D. H., & Danker-Brown, P. Influence of sex roles on the development of learned helplessness. *Journal of Consulting and Clinical Psychology*, 1979, *47*, 929–936.

Bem, S. L. The measurement of psychological androgyny. *Journal of Consulting and Clinical Psychology*, 1974, *42*, 155–162.

Bem, S. L. Sex role adaptability: One consequence of psychological androgyny. *Journal of Personality and Social Psychology*, 1975, *31*, 634–643.

Bem, S. L. Gender schema theory: A cognitive account of sex typing. *Psychological Review*, 1981, *88*, 354–364.

Bland, K., & Hallam, R. S. Relationship between response to graded exposure and marital satisfaction in agoraphobics. *Behaviour Research and Therapy*, 1981, *19*, 335–338.

Block, J. H. Conceptions of sex role: Some cross-cultural and longitudinal perspectives. *American Psychologist*, 1973, *28*, 512–526.

Bordewick, M. C., & Bornstein, P. H. Examination of multiple cognitive response dimensions among differentially assertive individuals. *Behavior Therapy*, 1980, *11*, 440–448.

Borkovec, T. D., Stone, N. M., O'Brien, G. T., & Kaloupek, D. G. Evaluation of a clinically relevant target behavior for analogue outcome research. *Behavior Therapy*, 1974, *5*, 503–511.

Carmody, T. Rational–emotive, self-instructional, and behavioral assertion training: Facilitating maintenance. *Cognitive Therapy and Research*, 1978, *2*, 241–253.

Chambless, D. L., Foa, E. B., Groves, G. A., & Goldstein, A. J. Flooding with Brevital in the treatment of agoraphobia: Countereffective. *Behaviour Research and Therapy*, 1979, *17*, 243–251.

Chambless, D. L., & Goldstein, A. J. Clinical treatment of agoraphobia. In M. Mavissakalian & D. H. Barlow (Eds.), *Phobia: Psychological and pharmacological treatment*. New York: Guilford, 1981.

Cherry, F., & Deaux, K. Fear of success versus fear of gender-inappropriate behavior. *Sex Roles*, 1978, *4*, 97–101.

Chesney, M. *Cultural and sex differences*. Paper presented at the Annual Meeting of the American Psychological Association, New York, 1979.

Christensen, A., Arkowitz, H., & Anderson, J. Practice dating as treatment for college dating inhibitions. *Behaviour Research and Therapy*, 1975, *13*, 65–68.

Connolly, J., Hallam, R. S., & Marks, I. M. Selective association of fainting with blood–injury–illness fear. *Behavior Therapy*, 1976, *7*, 8–13.

Constantinople, A. Masculinity–femininity: An exception to a famous dictum? *Psychological Bulletin*, 1973, *80*, 389–407.

Curran, J. P. An evaluation of a skills training program and a systematic desensitization program in reducing dating anxiety. *Behaviour Research and Therapy*, 1975, *13*, 65–68.

Curran, J. P. Skills training as an approach to the treatment of heterosexual–social anxiety: A review. *Psychological Bulletin*, 1977, *84*, 140–157.

Curran, J. P., & Gilbert, F. S. A test of the relative effectiveness of a systematic desensitization program and an interpersonal skills training program with date anxious subjects. *Behavior Therapy*, 1975, *6*, 510–521.

Darley, S. A. Big-time careers for the little woman: A dual-role dilemma. *Journal of Social Issues*, 1976, *32*, 85–98.

Davison, G. C., & Valins, S. Maintenance of self-attributed and drug-attributed behavior change. *Journal of Personality and Social Psychology*, 1969, *11*, 25–33.

Deaux, K., & Farris, E. Attributing causes for one's own performance: The effects of sex norms and outcome. *Journal of Research in Personality*, 1977, *22*, 59–72.

Derry, P., & Stone, G. Effects of cognitive-adjunct treatment on assertiveness. *Cognitive Therapy and Research*, 1979, *3*, 213–221.

De Silva, P., & Rachman, S. Is exposure a necessary condition for fear-reduction? *Behaviour Research and Therapy*, 1981, *19*, 227–232.

Dunlop, K. H. Maternal employment and child care. *Professional Psychology*, 1981, *12*, 67–75.

Dweck, C. S., & Goetz, T. F. Attribution and learned helplessness. In J. H. Harvey, W. Ickes, & R. F. Kidd (Eds.), *New directions in attribution research* (Vol. 2). Hillsdale, N.J.: Erlbaum, 1978.

Eisler, R. M., Miller, P. M., & Hersen, M. Components of assertive behavior. *Journal of Clinical Psychology*, 1973, *29*, 295–299.

Ellis, A. *Reason and emotion in psychotherapy*. New York: Lyle Stuart, 1962.

Emmelkamp, P. M. G. Self-observation versus flooding in the treatment of agoraphobia. *Behaviour Research and Therapy*, 1974, *12*, 229–237.

Emmelkamp, P. M. G., & Kuipers, A. Agoraphobia: A follow-up study four years after treatment. *British Journal of Psychiatry*, 1979, *134*, 352–355.

Emmelkamp, P. M. G., Kuipers, A. C. M., & Eggeraat, J. B. Cognitive modification versus prolonged exposure *in vivo:* A comparison with agoraphobics as subjects. *Behaviour Research and Therapy*, 1978, *16*, 33–41.

Emmelkamp, P. M. G., & Wessels, H. Flooding in imagination versus flooding *in vivo:* A comparison with agoraphobics. *Behavior Research and Therapy*, 1975, *13*, 7–15.

Fagot, B. I. *How parents reinforce feminine role behaviors in toddler girls.* Paper presented at the meeting of the Association for Women in Psychology, St. Louis, February 1977.

Fiedler, D., & Beach, L. R. On the decision to be assertive. *Journal of Consulting and Clinical Psychology*, 1978, *46*, 537–546.

Fishman, S. T. *Multiform behavioral treatment of agoraphobia.* New York: BMA Audio Cassettes, 1981.

Fodor, I. G. The phobic syndrome in women. In V. Franks & V. Burtle (Eds.), *Women in therapy.* New York: Brunner/Mazel, 1974. (a)

Fodor, I. G. Sex role conflict and symptom formation in women: Can behavior therapy help? *Psychotherapy: Theory, Research and Practice*, 1974, *11*, 22–29. (b)

Galassi, M. D., & Galassi, J. P. *Assert yourself! How to be your own person.* New York: Human Sciences, 1977.

Garbarino, J. The price of privacy in the social dynamics of child abuse. *Child Welfare*, 1977, *56*, 565–575.

Geer, J. H., Davison, G. C., & Gatchel, R. I. Reduction of stress in humans through nonveridical perceived control of aversive stimulation. *Journal of Personality and Social Psychology*, 1970, *16*, 731–738.

Gelder, M. G., Marks, I. M., & Wolff, H. H. Desensitization and psychotherapy in the treatment of phobic states: A controlled enquiry. *British Journal of Psychiatry*, 1967, *113*, 53–73.

Glass, D. C. *Behavior patterns, stress, and coronary disease.* Hillsdale, N.J.: Erlbaum, 1977.

Glass, C. R., Gottman, J. M., & Shmurak, S. H. Response-acquisition and cognitive self-statement modification approaches to dating-skills training. *Journal of Consulting Psychology*, 1976, *23*, 520–526.

Glass, D. C., Singer, J. E., & Friedman, L. N. Psychic cost of adaptation to an environmental stressor. *Journal of Personality and Social Psychology*, 1969, *12*, 200–210.

Glass, D. C., Singer, J. E., Leonard, H. S., Krantz, D., Cohen, S., & Cummings, H. Perceived control of aversive stimulation and actual arousal as determinants of emotion. *Journal of Personality and Social Psychology*, 1972, *21*, 41–51.

Goldfried, M. R. Systematic desensitization as training in self-control. *Journal of Consulting and Clinical Psychology*, 1971, *37*, 228–234.

Goldfried, M. R. Anxiety reduction through cognitive–behavioral intervention. In P. C. Kendall & S. D. Hollon (Eds.), *Cognitive–behavioral interventions: Theory, research, and procedures.* New York: Academic, 1979.

Goldfried, M. R., & Davison, G. C. *Clinical behavior therapy.* New York: Holt, Rinehart & Winston, 1976.

Goldfried, M. R., & Linehan, M. M. Basic issues in behavioral assessment. In A. R. Ciminero, K. S. Calhoun, & H. E. Adams (Eds.), *Handbook of behavioral assessment.* New York: Wiley-Interscience, 1977.

Goldfried, M. R., & Friedman, J. M. Clinical behavior therapy and the male sex role. In K. Solomon & N. B. Levy (Eds.), *Men in transition: Theories and therapies for psychological health.* New York: Plenum, 1982.

Goldfried, M. R., & Robins, C. On the facilitation of self-efficacy. *Cognitive Therapy and Research*, 1982, *6*, 361–379.

Goldstein, A. Appropriate expression training: Humanistic behavior therapy. In A. Wandersman, P. Poppen, & D. Ricks (Eds.), *Humanism and behaviorism: Dialogue and growth.* Elmsford, N.Y.: Pergamon, 1976.

Goldstein, A. J., & Chambless, D. L. A reanalysis of agoraphobia. *Behavior Therapy,* 1978, 9, 47–59.

Gormally, J., Hill, C. E., Otis, M., & Rainey, L. A microtraining approach to assertion training. *Journal of Counseling Psychology,* 1975, 22, 299–303.

Gove, W. R., & Tudor, J. F. Adult sex roles and mental illness. *American Journal of Sociology,* 1973, 78, 812–832.

Gyllstrom, K. K., & Herman, J. B. Working men and women: Inter and intra-role conflict. *Psychology of Women Quarterly,* 1977, 1, 319–333.

Hafner, R. J. Fresh symptom emergence after intensive behaviour therapy. *British Journal of Psychiatry,* 1976, 129, 378–383.

Hafner, R. J. The husbands of agoraphobic women: Assortative mating or pathogenic interaction? *British Journal of Psychiatry,* 1977, 130, 233–239. (a)

Hafner, R. J. The husbands of agoraphobic women and their influence on treatment outcome. *British Journal of Psychiatry,* 1977, 131, 289–294. (b)

Hafner, R. J., & Marks, I. Exposure *in vivo* of agoraphobics: Contributions of diazepam, group exposure, and anxiety evocation. *Psychological Medicine,* 1976, 6, 71–88.

Hammen, C. L., Jacobs, M., Mayol, A., & Cochran, S. D. Dysfunctional cognitions and the effectiveness of skills and cognitive behavioral assertion training. *Journal of Consulting and Clinical Psychology,* 1980, 48, 685–695.

Hand, I., & Lamontagne, Y. The exacerbation of interpersonal problems after rapid phobia-removal. *Psychotherapy: Theory, Research and Practice,* 1976, 13, 405–441.

Hand, I., Lamontagne, Y., & Marks, I. M. Group exposure (flooding) *in vivo* for agora-phobics. *British Journal of Psychiatry,* 1974, 124, 588–602.

Hayes, S. C., & Barlow, D. H. Flooding relief in a case of public transportation phobia. *Behavior Therapy,* 1977, 8, 742–746.

Hersen, M., Eisler, R. M., Johnson, M. B., & Pinkston, S. G. Effects of practice, instructions, and modeling on components of assertive behavior. *Behaviour Research and Therapy,* 1973, 11, 443–451.

Hersen, M., Eisler, R. M., & Miller, P. M. Development of assertive responses: Clinical measurement, and research considerations. *Behaviour Research and Therapy,* 1973, 11, 505–521.

Horner, M. S. Toward an understanding of achievement-related conflicts in women. *Journal of Social Issues,* 1972, 28, 157–175; 253–255.

Hull, D. B., & Schroeder, H. E. Some interpersonal effects of assertion, nonassertion, and aggression. *Behavior Therapy,* 1979, 10, 20–28.

Ickes, W., & Layden, M. A. Attributional styles. In J. Harvey, W. Ickes, & R. Kidd (Eds.), *New directions in attribution research* (Vol. 2). Hillsdale, N.J.: Erlbaum, 1978.

Jacobs, M. K., & Cochran, S. D. The effects of cognitive restructuring on assertive behavior. *Cognitive Therapy and Research,* 1982, 6, 63–76.

Kazdin, A. E. Effects of covert modeling and model reinforcement on assertive behavior. *Journal of Abnormal Psychology,* 1974, 83, 240–252.

Kazdin, A. E. Effects of covert modeling, multiple models, and model reinforcement on assertive behavior. *Behavior Therapy,* 1976, 7, 211–222.

Kelly, J. A., Kern, J. M., Kirkley, B. G., & Patterson, J. N. Reactions to assertive versus unassertive behavior. Differential effects for males and females and implications for assertive training. *Behavior Therapy,* 1980, 11, 670–682.

Kelly, J. A., O'Brien, C. G., Hosford, R. C., & Kinsinger, E. C. *Sex roles and social skills: A behavioral analysis of "masculinity," "femininity," and "psychological androgyny."* Paper presented at the Association for Advancement of Behavior Therapy, New York, December 1976.

Kelly, J. A., & Worell, J. New formulations of sex roles and androgyny: A critical review. *Journal of Consulting and Clinical Psychology*, 1977, 45, 1101–1115.

Klein, D. F. Delineation of two drug-responsive anxiety syndromes. *Psychopharmacologia*, 1964, 5, 397–408.

Klein, D. F., & Fink, M. Psychiatric reaction patterns to imipramine. *American Journal of Psychiatry*, 1962, 119, 432–438.

Landau, R. J. The role of semantic schemata in phobic word interpretation. *Cognitive Therapy and Research*, 1980, 4, 427–434.

Lang, P. J. A bio-informational theory of emotional imagery. *Psychophysiology*, 1979, 16, 495–511.

Lang, P. J., Melamed, B. G., & Hart, J. A psychophysiological analysis of fear modification using an automated desensitization procedure. *Journal of Abnormal Psychology*, 1970, 76, 220–234.

Lange, A. J., & Jakubowski, P. *Responsible assertive behavior: Cognitive/behavioral procedures for trainers.* Champaign, Ill.: Research, 1976.

Leitenberg, H. *Handbook of behavior modification and behavior therapy.* Englewood Cliffs, N.J.: Prentice-Hall, 1976.

Leitenberg, H., Agras, W. S., Allen, R., Butz, R., & Edwards, J. Feedback and therapist praise during treatment of a phobia. *Journal of Consulting and Clinical Psychology*, 1975, 43, 396–404.

Lenney, E. Androgyny: Some audacious assertions toward its coming of age. *Sex Roles*, 1979, 5, 703–719.

Liddell, A., & Lyons, M. Thunderstorm phobias. *Behaviour Research and Therapy*, 1978, 16, 306–308.

Linehan, M. M. Structured cognitive–behavioral treatment of assertion problems. In P. C. Kendall & S. D. Hollon (Eds.), *Cognitive–behavioral interventions: Theory, research, and procedures.* New York: Academic, 1979.

Linehan, M. M., & Egan, K. J. Assertion training for women. In A. S. Bellack & M. Hersen (Eds.), *Research and practice in social skills training.* New York: Plenum, 1979.

Linehan, M., Goldfried, M., & Goldfried, A. Assertion therapy: Skill training or cognitive restructuring. *Behavior Therapy*, 1979, 10, 372–388.

Lubetkin, B. The use of a planetarium in the desensitization of a case of bronto- and astra-phobia. *Behavior Therapy*, 1975, 6, 276–277.

Marecek, J., & Ballou, D. J. Family roles and women's mental health. *Professional Psychology*, 1981, 12, 39–46.

Marks, I. M. *Fears and phobias.* New York: Academic, 1969.

Marks, I. M. Behavioral psychotherapy of adult neurosis. In S. L. Garfield & A. E. Bergin (Eds.), *Handbook of psychotherapy and behavior change.* New York: Wiley, 1978.

Marks, I. M., Boulougouris, J., & Marset, P. Flooding versus desensitization in the treatment of phobic patients: A cross-over study. *British Journal of Psychiatry*, 1971, 119, 353–375.

Marks, I. M., & Gelder, M. G. A controlled retrospective study of behaviour therapy in phobic patients. *British Journal of Psychiatry*, 1965, 111, 571–573.

Markus, H., & Sentis, K. The self in social information processing. In J. Suls (Ed.), *Social psychological perspectives.* Hillsdale, N.J.: Erlbaum, 1980.

Mathews, A. M., Teasdale, J. D. Munby, M., Johnston, D. W., & Shaw, P. M. A home-based treatment program for agoraphobia. *Behavior Therapy*, 1977, 8, 915–924.

May, J. R. Psychophysiology of self-regulated phobic thoughts. *Behavior Therapy*, 1977, 8, 150–159. (a)

May, J. R. A psychophysiological study of self and externally regulated phobic thoughts. *Behavior Therapy*, 1977, 8, 849–861. (b)

McFall, R. M. Behavioral training: A skill-acquisition approach to clinical problems. In J.

T. Spence, R. C. Carson, & J. W. Thibaut (Eds.), *Behavioral approaches to therapy* (Vol. 1). Morristown, N.J.: General Learning, 1976.

McFall, R. M., & Marston, A. An experimental investigation of behavioral rehearsal in assertive training. *Journal of Abnormal Psychology,* 1970, *76,* 295–303.

McFall, R. M., & Twentyman, C. T. Four experiments on the relative contributors of rehearsal, modeling, and coaching on assertion training. *Journal of Abnormal Psychology,* 1973, *81,* 199–218.

Melnick, J., & Stocker, R. B. An experimental analysis of the behavioral rehearsal with feedback technique in assertiveness training. *Behavior Therapy,* 1977, *8,* 222–228.

Milton, F., & Hafner, J. The outcome of behavior therapy for agoraphobia in relation to marital adjustment. *Archives of General Psychiatry,* 1979, *36,* 807–811.

Neisser, U. *Cognition and reality.* San Francisco: Freeman, 1976.

Newman, A., & Brand, E. Coping response training versus *in vivo* desensitization in fear reduction. *Cognitive Therapy and Research,* 1980, *4,* 397–407.

Nietzel, M., Martorano, R. D., & Melnick, J. The effects of covert modeling with and without reply training on the development and generalization of assertive responses. *Behavior Therapy,* 1977, *8,* 183–192.

Odom, J. V., Nelson, R. O., & Wein, K. S. The differential effectiveness of five treatment procedures on three response systems in a snake phobia analogue study. *Behavior Therapy,* 1978, *9,* 936–942.

Ost, L. G. Fading vs. systematic desensitization in the treatment of snake and spider phobia. *Behaviour Research and Therapy,* 1978, *16,* 379–389.

Parsons, T., & Bales, R. E. *Family socialization and interaction process.* Glencoe, Ill.: Free Press, 1955.

Powell, B., & Reznikoff, M. Role conflict and symptoms of psychological distress in college-educated women. *Journal of Consulting and Clinical Psychology,* 1976, *44,* 473–479.

Rapoport, R., & Rapoport, R. *Dual-career families.* Baltimore, Md.: Penguin, 1971.

Rapoport, R., & Rapoport, R. *Dual-career families re-examined.* New York: Harper, 1976.

Rathus, S. A. Instigation of assertive behavior through videotape-mediated assertive models and directed practice. *Behaviour Research and Therapy,* 1973, *11,* 57–65.

Rehm, L., & Marston, A. Reduction of social anxiety through modification of self-reinforcement: An instigation therapy technique. *Journal of Consulting and Clinical Psychology,* 1968, *32,* 565–574.

Rice, D. G. *Dual-career marriage.* New York: Free Press, 1979.

Rich, A. R., & Schroeder, H. E. Research issues in assertiveness training. *Psychological Bulletin,* 1976, *83,* 1081–1096.

Robinson, W. L., & Calhoun, K. S. *Assertiveness and cognitive processing in interpersonal situations.* Unpublished manuscript, DePaul University, 1981.

Rose, V. J., & Tryon, W. W. Judgments of assertive behavior as a function of speech loudness, latency, content, gestures, inflection, and sex. *Behavior Modification,* 1979, *3,* 112–123.

Rosenkrantz, P., Bee, H., Vogel, S., & Broverman, I. Sex-role stereotypes and self-concepts in college students. *Journal of Consulting and Clinical Psychology,* 1968, *32,* 287–295.

Rotter, J. B. Generalized expectancies for internal versus external control of reinforcement. *Psychological Monographs,* 1966, *80* (1, Whole No. 609).

Safran, J. D., Alden, L. E., & Davidson, P. O. Client anxiety level as a moderator variable in assertion training. *Cognitive Therapy and Research,* 1980, *4,* 189–200.

Sarbin, T. R., & Allen, V. L. Role theory. In G. Lindzey & E. Aronson (Eds.), *The handbook of social psychology* (Vol. 1). Reading, Mass.: Addison-Wesley, 1968.

Schwartz, R., & Gottman, J. Toward a task analysis of assertive behavior. *Journal of Consulting and Clinical Psychology,* 1976, *44,* 910–920.

Shapiro, D. *Neurotic styles.* New York: Basic, 1965.

Sinnott, A., Jones, R. B., Scott-Fordham, A., & Woodward, R. Augmentation of *in vivo* exposure treatment for agoraphobia by the formation of neighborhood self-help groups. *Behaviour Research and Therapy*, 1981, *19*, 339–347.

Spence, J. T., & Helmreich, R. L. *Masculinity and femininity*. Austin, Tex.: University of Texas Press, 1978.

Spence, J. T., Helmreich, R. L., & Stapp, J. Ratings of self and peers on self-role attributes and their relation to self-esteem and conceptions of masculinity and femininity. *Journal of Personality and Social Psychology*, 1975, *32*, 29–39.

Stern, R. S., & Marks, I. M. A comparison of brief and prolonged flooding in agoraphobics. *Archives of General Psychiatry*, 1973, *28*, 270–276.

Strickland, B. R., & Haley, W. E. Sex differences on the Rotter I-E Scale. *Journal of Personality and Social Psychology*, 1980, *39*, 930–939.

Sutton-Simon, K., & Goldfried, M. R. Faulty thinking patterns in two types of anxiety. *Cognitive Therapy and Research*, 1979, *3*, 193–203.

Sutton-Simon, K., & Goldfried, M. R. *Cognitive processes in social anxiety*. Unpublished manuscript, Oberlin College, 1982.

Tajfel, H. Cognitive aspects of prejudice. *Journal of Social Issues*, 1969, *25*, 79–97.

Turner, S. M., & Adams, H. E. Effects of assertive training on three dimensions of assertiveness. *Behaviour Research and Therapy*, 1977, *15*, 475–483.

Twentyman, C. T., & Zimering, R. T. Behavioral training of social skills: A critical review. In M. Hersen, R. M. Eisler, & P. M. Miller (Eds.), *Progress in behavior modification*. New York: Academic, 1979.

U.S. Department of Labor, Bureau of Labor Statistics. *Employment and Earnings*, 1982, *29*(3), 139–141.

Valins, S., & Nisbett, R. E. Attribution processes in the development and treatment of emotional disorders. In E. Jones, D. E. Kanouse, H. H. Kelly, R. E. Nisbett, S. Valins, & B. Weiner (Eds.), *Attribution: Perceiving the causes of behavior*. New York: General Learning, 1971.

Wahler, R. G. The insular mother: Her problems in parent–child treatment. *Journal of Applied Behavior Analysis*, 1980, *13*, 207–219.

Wahler, R. G., Leske, G., & Rogers, E. S. The insular family: A deviance support system for oppositional children. In L. A Hamerlynck (Ed.), *Behavioral systems for the developmentally disabled (I: School and family environments)*. New York: Brunner/Mazel, 1979.

Waldron, I. The coronary-prone behavior pattern, blood pressure, employment and socioeconomic status in women. *Journal of Psychosomatic Research*, 1978, *22*, 79–87.

Watson, D., & Friend, R. Measurement of social-evaluative anxiety. *Journal of Consulting and Clinical Psychology*, 1969, *33*, 447–457.

Watson, J. P., Mullett, G. E., & Pillay, H. The effects of prolonged exposure to phobic situations upon agoraphobic patients treated in groups. *Behaviour Research and Therapy*, 1973, *11*, 531–546.

Weekes, C. *Simple, effective treatment of agoraphobia*. New York: Hawthorn, 1976.

Weiss, E. *Agoraphobia in the light of ego psychology*. New York: Grune & Stratton, 1964.

Whalen, C. K., & Henker, B. Psycho stimulants and children: A review and analysis. *Psychological Bulletin*, 1976, *83*, 1113–1130.

Winship, B. J., & Kelly, J. A. A verbal response model of assertiveness. *Journal of Counseling Psychology*, 1976, *2*, 55–84.

Wolfe, J., & Fodor, I. Modifying assertive behavior in women: A comparison of three approaches. *Behavior Therapy*, 1977, *8*, 567–574.

Woolfolk, R. L., & Dever, S. Perceptions of association: An empirical analysis. *Behavior Therapy*, 1979, *10*, 404–411.

Wolpe, J. *Psychotherapy by reciprocal inhibition*. Stanford, Calif.: Stanford University Press, 1958.

Zitrin, C. M. Combined pharmacological and psychological treatment of phobias. In M.

Mavissakalian & D. H. Barlow (Eds.), *Phobia: Psychological and pharmacological treatment*. New York: Guilford, 1981.

Zitrin, C. M., Klein, D. F., & Woerner, M. C. Behavior therapy, supportive psychotherapy, imipramine and phobia. *Archives of General Psychiatry*, 1978, *35*, 307–316.

14

WEIGHT DISORDERS: OVERWEIGHT AND ANOREXIA

IRIS GOLDSTEIN FODOR
JODI THAL

OVERVIEW

"It would seem advantageous to categorize weight and eating disorders along two separate and partially independent dimensions. The first of these is the extent to which the body weight deviates from population norms. The second dimension is the extent to which the desire to lose weight becomes a chronic focus of effort and worry, with adverse effects on well-being and overall functioning" (Wooley & Wooley, 1980, p. 136). This chapter addresses behavioral treatments for the two most prevalent weight disorders: overweight (obesity) and anorexia nervosa. Women constitute the majority of people in therapy for these problems (over 90%).

Behavioral treatments for both overweight and anorexia have focused on treatment of the weight disorders by targeting for change the eating behaviors that are assumed to contribute to the weight gain or loss. Hence, for the overweight woman, a standard behavior package has been developed for self-control of overeating, while for the anorectic use of contingent reinforcement (access to privileges, activity, etc.) has been tried to increased eating and weight gain. These behavioral programs have ignored the second variable highlighted by the Wooleys, namely, the extent to which the "desire to lose weight become a chronic focus of effort and worry" (1980, p. 136). While behavioral programs stressing increasing or decreasing food intake do have some positive

Iris Goldstein Fodor and Jodi Thal. Department of Educational Psychology, School Psychology Program, New York University, New York, New York.

short-term effects (in the case of anorectics they may be lifesaving), maintenance of these changes has typically not occurred. Neglected in behavioral programs is the focus on the obsessive wish to be thinner.

Since we have not yet designed programs for effective long-term weight loss, and since we are mainly serving female clients, it may be time to examine the interplay of women's issues with weight problems. In particular, we need to explore the relationship between societal conditioning about the undesirability of overweight and women's preoccupation with dieting and weight loss. There has been remarkable standardization of behavioral programs, which only work for the short term. It may be time to redirect our efforts to focus on other target behaviors (the obsession with thinnness, self-esteem, body image, and the focus on dieting as an avoidance of age-appropriate issues) and design different, more effective programs for the large number of women who are asking for help.

BACKGROUND

In our culture the yardstick for overweight is the average weight of people of the same age, sex, height, and body frame in the Metropolitan Life Insurance Tables (Bray, 1973; Stuart & Jacobson, 1979). According to these tables (1960, 1977, 1980), males and females differ at various points in the life cycle in degree of underweight, normal weight, and overweight. (These guidelines are soon to be revised upward by approximately 10%.) Females have more body fat than males, with increases following puberty, childbirth, and in the mid-30s. If 20% over average weight from the Metropolitan Life Insurance Tables is overweight (the criterion used in most behavioral studies), then until age 40, 32% of men and 40% of women are so classified. However, by the age of 60, 29% of the men and 45% of the women, almost half the female population, is classified as overweight. Further, while older women are overweight, young women are more likely to be classified as underweight.

The terms "overweight" and "obese" are often used interchangeably. Obesity is usually defined as a greater than average amount of body fat (Powers, 1980). Body weight is a far less reliable criterion for obesity than skin fold measurement. (Keys, Fidanza, Karvonen, Kimura, & Taylor, 1972), and there is disagreement on the degree of overweight which constitutes obesity since there is a low correlation between weight and body fat (Bray, 1973; Leon, 1976; Mahoney, Mahoney, Rogers, & Straw, 1979). This chapter uses the term overweight since weight appears to be the central focus for therapists and their female clients.

THE DESIRE TO LOSE WEIGHT: WHO ARE THE CLIENTS?

"Some ladies smoke too much and some ladies drink too much and some ladies pray too much. But all ladies think they weigh too much" (Nash, 1962, p. 109). Women who think they weigh too much are the major consumers of the billion-dollar-a-year medical, pharmaceutical, and publishing industries. Each year, diet books are at the top of the best-seller lists. Women are also the major consumers of all treatments for overweight, and, in the past decade, they have turned to behavioral treaments. (Such treatments serve a population that is 80% to 95% female.) Issues common to all clients seeking help, regardless of the label of the "disorder," are the unacceptability of overweight and the desire to do what is necessary to control it. The four categories of women who seek help, range from severely overweight to anorectic: for example, women who are overweight and wish to reduce; thin women who worry that they are too fat; bulimics who periodically binge and then vomit to remain thin; and anorectics who are preoccupied with becoming even thinner.

Overweight Women

Mild to moderately overweight women represent the majority of clients seeking behavioral treatment (at least 20% overweight by the Metropolitan Life Insurance Tables). While overweight per se does not warrant classification as a mental disorder by the third edition of the *Diagnostic and Statistical Manual of Mental Disorders* of the American Psychiatric Association (DSM-III, 1980), many of these women are so obsessed with their weight that they become compulsive dieters.

> The dieting efforts . . . may number in the dozen, over spans of from 10 to 40 years, and include repeated hospitalizations, stays at reducing spas, multiple forms of outpatient treatment and self-help groups. In its most extreme form, the effort to be slender becomes so central to self-acceptance that all other life activities are relegated to relative unimportance. If weight is too high, the patient will avoid seeing friends, refuse to attend social events, avoid sex, and postpone or drop out of training or careers. The

plan is always to begin or resume these activities once weight is lost, but for many that day never comes, or, if it does, it is short-lived. (Wooley & Wooley, 1980, p. 137)

Thin Women

Another category of women seeking help for their overweight are women of normal weight who sincerely believe they are overweight. Bruch (1980) calls them "thin–fat people." Silverstone (1968) reports that as many as 33% of normal-weight females in contrast to 10% of normal-weight males consider themselves overweight. They represent about 20% of the first author's self-referred clients for overweight groups, and others note a similar trend (Wooley & Wooley, 1980).

Bulimia

Bulimia usually begins in adolescence with heightened concern about body appearance and weight. The seriousness of bulimia is highlighted by its inclusion in the category of mental disorders by the American Psychiatric Association: "Episodic binge eating accompanied by an awareness that the eating pattern is abnormal, fear of not being able to stop eating" (DSM-III, 1980, p. 69). The women make repeated attempts to control the binge eating by "dieting, vomiting or the use of cathartics or diuretics. Frequent weight fluctuations due to alternating binges and fasts are common" (DSM-III, 1980, p. 70). Attention to bulimia in the popular press may affect prevalence statistics. In recent surveys, 4–20% of college women seeking help at university counseling centers were bulimic, while a British Broadcasting Corporation (BBC) program on bulimia is reported to have drawn 10,000 letters from people asking for help (Brody, 1981).

Anorexia Nervosa

Anorexia nervosa typically occurs in young adolescent women; it is estimated that from 12–18 years of age, as many as 1 in 250 will develop this disorder. Ninety-five percent of the cases of anorexia are female. This syndrome is also classified as a mental disorder and defined as follows: "The essential features are intense fear of becoming obese, disturbance of body image, significant weight loss, refusal to maintain normal body weight and amenorrhea (in females). . . . Individuals with this disorder say they 'feel fat' when they are of normal weight or even emaciated. They are preoccupied with their body size" (DSM-III, 1980, pp. 67–68). Unlike other weight disorders, anorexia can be deadly. It is estimated that 5–20% of anorectics die from prolonged fasting (Moldofsky & Garfinkel, 1974). In addition, many anorectics develop bulimia or become overweight as part of their postanorectic phase (Bemis, 1978; DSM-III, 1980) Anorexia and bulimia have often been viewed as similar syndromes in the clinical literature. Only recently have there been systematic attempts to distinguish them (Boskind-Lodahl & Sirlin, 1977; Crisp, 1977b; Russell, 1979).

SOCIAL CONDITIONING OF ACCEPTABLE BODY TYPES

Although 30% of men are overweight, women are the majority of clients seeking help for weight problems. Further, the major aim of this struggle to be thin is enhancement of physical attractiveness (Stuart & Jacobson, 1979). The overrepresentation of females in weight-reduction programs, the irrational beliefs of normal-sized women that they are overweight, the self-inflicted starvation of the anorectics, and the self-torture of bulimics have one common element: the belief that to be considered physically attractive and socially acceptable as a woman, one must be thin.

Until early in this century, a somewhat larger, mature figure was favored (Dyer, Feldman, & Mayer, 1970), so aptly described by the Victorian "beauty expert," Alexander Walker, in 1836 (cited by Reichman, 1977, p. 23): "Her face is round, her shoulders are softly rounded, her bosom, in its luxuriances, seems literally to protrude on the space occupied by her arms; her waist, though sufficiently marked, is as it were encroached on the lushness of all the contiguous parts . . . the whole figure is soft and voluptuous in the extreme." (He then goes on to describe excessive leanness as repulsive.)

In the 1920s this standard changed. The flapper era emancipated women from restrictive clothing and introduced a new, but equally restrictive, ideal. Since then the standard for beauty has been a tall, thin, flat-chested young girl. The top fashion model of the 1980s is likely to be an anorectic 12-year-old (Juffe & Haden-Guest, 1980). Venus di Milo, Rubens's models, and Marilyn Monroe would be unacceptable to the male-dominated design and fashion photography circles who would rather see clothes on boyish girls than on shapely women. The media not only focus on young, undeveloped thin females, they also under-represent normal overweight females. In a survey of popular TV shows, only one overweight female was featured among 131 females roles (O.W. Wooley & Wooley, 1979). When overweight women appear in films or novels, they are often singled out for ridicule and derision. This was done by characters in Doctorow's (1979) recent best-seller *Loon Lake* and by Lina Wertmüller in several of her films.

Overweight people have internalized our society's prejudices. Reports of low self-esteem, dislike of their bodies, and depression are common among the overweight (Bruch, 1973; Powers, 1980; Stunkard, 1976). Many normal weight women who compare themselves to ano-rectic models believe they are too fat. Adolescents are particularly vulnerable. By late adolescence, 75% of females and 25% of males are reported to dislike their bodies and feel they are too fat (Stuart & Jacobson, 1979).

While overweight is devalued, thinness is believed to attract material benefits and happiness. In fact, overweight among women is related to acculturation, ethnicity, race, social class, and age. Immigrant women of Eastern European descent, Black women, elderly women, women of lower socioeconomic class, and women who have lost social status are likely to be overweight; while upper-class and upwardly mobile women are likely to be thin (Goldblatt, Moore, & Stunkard, 1965). Physical attractiveness influences men's choices of dates; for most women, partnership with a male fends off low social status and poverty (Berscheid & Walster, 1974). Therefore, it is no wonder women are so concerned about their appearance.

OVEREATING AS A PRIME CAUSE OF OVERWEIGHT

Central to our culture's obsession with remaining thin is the belief that excess weight is caused by overeating and underexercising; that you can weigh less if you eat less and exercise more. Behavior therapists, in particular, have based their self-control treatment programs for over-eating on Schachter's stimulus-bound model which emphasizes the difference between obese and nonobese eating styles (e.g., Mahoney, 1975, p. 416). Other factors which play a crucial role in the development and maintenance of weight problems are generally ignored. These factors include: constitutional variables (if both parents are overweight, there is a very high risk of the child being overweight); childhood environment (80% of overweight girls become overweight women); hormonal and metabolic irregularities (Bray, 1973; Powers, 1980; Stunkard, 1977, Wooley, Wooley, & Dyrenforth, 1979).

SELF-CONTROL AS THE CURE FOR OVERWEIGHT

Conventional wisdom holds that anybody with enough willpower can learn to exercise, control overeating behavior, and regulate weight. Our protestant ethic values self-control of impulses and asserts that self-regulation must be beneficial. Lack of control manifested by body fat suggests an immorality which invites retribution (Maddox & Liederman, 1979). Thus, the anorectic who is able to resist food and lose weight feels virtuous. This moralistic attitude toward dieting and exercise is of recent origin. Victorian women's magazines advised women to wear corsets, since the shape of a woman's body was unlikely to change. Until recently, women have been actively discouraged from full participation in athletic programs (Zegman, 1982). Today, overweight women are expected to control body fat and weight, and they blame themselves when they do not lose weight by diet or exercise.

TREATMENT OF OVERWEIGHT AND ANOREXIA

MEDICAL AND TRADITIONAL PSYCHOTHERAPY TREATMENTS

Therapists of all persuasions have responded to pleas for help from overweight women. While the popular press has promoted willpower for weight reduction, traditional therapies have encouraged women to be patient recipients of the doctor's treatments. There is a remarkable parallel in medical and psychoanalytic approaches to the overweight patients who lack self-control, and to the anorectics, who exercise too much willful control. Medical treatments for overweight have included appetite suppressants, hospitalization for fasting, amphetamines, and, in extreme cases, intestinal bypass surgery and jaw wiring (Powers, 1980). For the anorectic who refuses to eat, there has been hospitalization with variations of forced feeding (tube or intravenous), prescriptions of chlorpromazine and insulin, hormones and corticosteroids, and in a few resistant cases, electroconvulsive therapy and prefrontal leukotomy (Bemis, 1978; Moldofsky & Garfinkel, 1974).

Most traditional psychotherapy aims for understanding of unconscious impulses; as with medical treatments, the result is a loss of client autonomy. The client cannot be autonomous because the causes of overweight and anorexia are of deep origin and out of the patient's conscious control. They involve pre-Oedipal fixations, fantasies of oral impregnation, and fears of sexuality (Bushkirk & Swan, 1977; Rollins & Blackwell, 1968). Bruch (1970, 1973, 1979) has described with sensitivity the complex psychodynamics of overweight and anorexia, their unresponsiveness to psychoanalysis, and the need for individualized treatment focused on interpersonal issues. Stunkard (1958) aptly summed up the prospects for weight reduction through medical and traditional therapy treatments: "Most obese persons will not remain in treatment. Of those that remain in treatment, most will not lose weight, and of those that do lose weight, most will regain it" (p. 79). Anorectics have a 25–50% relapse rate; 38% require a second hospitalization within two years; their mortality rate varies from 5–20% (Moldofsky & Garfinkel, 1974). Bemis (1978) summed up the prospects for recovery as follows: "Optimistic outcomes in anorexia are in the minority, with most long term surveys emphasizing the chronic nature of physical and emotional symptoms" (p. 596).

BEHAVIORAL TREATMENT FOR OVERWEIGHT

Behavior therapy for overweight, with its focus on self-control, has proved an attractive alternative to medical and traditional psychotherapeutic treatments. The basic, behavioral, self-control package for overweight has appealed to the many women who value their autonomy. In 1 year, as many as 1 million people each week (over 90% of them female) may have participated in some form of behavioral, weight-focused treatment (Brownell, 1981). "Major behavioral treatment centers have sprung up around the United States, behavioral self-help programs in the form of cassette tapes and books are widely available, and Weight Watchers, the most popular commercial weight control program, has modified its basic program to incorporate behavioral self-help procedures" (Wilson & Brownell, 1980, p. 49).

THE BASIC SELF-CONTROL PROGRAM

The first behavioral program for overweight, applied operant techniques to break the chain of responses leading to overeating (Ferster, Nurnberger, & Levitt, 1962). Stuart (1967) adapted Ferster's techniques and reported astounding success for eight female patients. Three of the women lost more than 40 pounds, and the rest over 30. These were among the best results ever reported for the outpatient treatment of overweight (Stunkard, 1977). In 1972, Stuart and Davis elaborated their basic program for overeating; their book *Slim Chance in a Fat World* became a universal primer for behavioral self-control. The step-by-step behavioral program emphasizes self-monitoring of food intake, setting goals to alter eating behavior by limiting external food related cues, changing eating behaviors, altering patterns of exercise, and providing social reinforcement for the changed behaviors.

The basic Stuart and Davis package has seen wide clinical and research use mostly with female clients (80–100% in most published studies). Early reviews of the basic self-control package were enthusiastically positive (Abramson, 1973; Bellack, 1977; Hall & Hall, 1974; Leon, 1976; Stunkard, 1975b; Stunkard & Mahoney, 1976).

The basic self-control program is usually carried out in a group, for 8–16 weeks (Wilson & Brownell, 1980), by leaders who explain principles of behavior therapy, design individualized programs, and encourage group support. Clients begin by recording their eating—and sometimes their exercise—behaviors, urges to eat, and the date, time, place, and mood accompanying these urges; whether they actually ate or engaged in some other activity, and the amount of calories consumed. After a week or more of *self-monitoring*, *goals* are set for alteration of problematic baseline behaviors, rather than for weight loss. To implement these goals, clients learn to *limit external food-related cues* and to *change their manner of eating*.

To eliminate stimuli that cue overeating and to develop cues for appropriate eating, the client follows a list of very specific rules. Sample rules are: Separate eating from all other activities. Eat in a specified room at a designated time. Do not engage in other activities when you are eating—no television viewing, studying, or pleasure reading. Make high-caloric foods unavailable, inconspicuous, or hard to prepare. Always shop for groceries after a meal, not before. In restaurants decide in advance what to order, do not look at the menu (Ferster *et al.*, 1962; Stuart & Davis, 1972; Stunkard & Mahoney, 1976).

Instructions are also provided about how to limit food intake. Such instructions (Ferster *et al.*, 1962; Stuart & Davis, 1972) include: Eat three meals a day. Follow a set schedule. Use shallow bowls or small plates. Put small portions of food on each plate. Eat slowly. Swallow one bite before putting the next one on the fork. Count bites to slow eating (Water Pik, 1977). Patterns of exercise are noted, and the clients are given exercises to engage in and taught the caloric expenditure involved in each activity (Stuart & Davis, 1972).

Finally, a schedule of points earned by altered eating and exercise is arranged. The points are converted into concrete rewards such as a vacation, and into opportunities for approval from significant others. Contracts may be written which schedule punishment for persistent, problem behavior, or inadequate weight loss (Brownell & Stunkard, 1980; Stuart & Davis, 1972; Stunkard & Mahoney, 1976).

COMMUNITY-BASED WEIGHT CONTROL GROUPS

Leading behavior therapists extended the basic self-control program to nationwide, commercial groups for overweight clients: Weight Watchers, with a membership of 350,000, and Take Off Pounds Sensibly (TOPS), with a membership of 300,000 (Levitz & Stunkard, 1974; Stuart, 1977). These groups made behavioral consultation part of their basic philosophy (Levitz & Stunkard, 1974; Stuart, 1977). Using similar principles, behavior therapists consulted with community health maintenance organizations (Heckerman & Prochaska, 1977). Stuart (1977) described the basic program at TOPS as follows: "Members are privately weighed-in at each meeting and their weekly weight changes are announced to the group. Losers are recognized with applause, occasional cash prizes and the opportunity to become 'queen' for the week by achieving the greatest loss. Gainers are reprimanded, occasionally fined or asked to perform embarrassing activities. In addition, they are sometimes labeled 'pig' of the week for recording a large weight gain" (pp. 293–294). Stuart (1977) developed behavioral modules for the Weight Watchers basic program; Stuart and Mitchell (1980) reported that Weight Watchers members found the techniques "relevant," "helpful," and "easy to use." Stunkard (1976) was particularly optimistic about these developments: "Private industry may well be the most potent agent for the widespread control of obesity in this country. . . . We may . . . witness a phenomenon unprecedented in the history of medicine: management of a major health problem passing out of medical hands into those of private industry" (p. 231).

REAPPRAISAL OF THE BASIC BEHAVIORAL PACKAGE

"Effective control of obesity is, above all, long term control. . . . The process of repeatedly losing and then gaining weight has more deleterious effects upon health than maintenance of obesity" (Stunkard, 1977, p. 329). By the mid-1970s, appraisals of behavioral techniques for overweight were increasingly skeptical. While clients lost a pound a week, most behavioral programs were short term, and the average weight loss was only 11 pounds. For even a moderately overweight women, this loss was not clinically meaningful (Jeffery & Coates, 1978). Yates (1975, p. 149) was the first to call attention to issues of maintenance of weight loss; by the late 1970s, many researchers agreed with Yates. Stunkard (1977) retreated from his earlier endorsement, noting that at a 5-year follow-up his clients tended to return to their pretreatment weight, and to continually fluctuate in body weight. To improve maintenance, clinicians and researchers expanded on the basic Stuart and Davis (1972) self-control package. Mahoney and Mahoney (1976) added a cognitive treatment component, family members were involved as auxiliary therapists, booster sessions and social support systems were developed (Wilson & Brownell, 1980).

COGNITIVE SELF-CONTROL TREATMENT

In 1976, in keeping with the cognitive trend in behavior therapy, Mahoney and Mahoney described a cognitive component for the basic self-control package, in their popular primer *Permanent Weight Control*. Their self-control model, given the acronym SCIENCE because it was modeled after a study of the alteration of theoretical belief systems of scientists, involved six stages. (1) *S*pecify the general problem: Is it food quality (high caloric foods) or food quantity (extra large portions)? (2) *C*ollect data about your problem behavior. (3) *I*dentify patterns. Under what circumstances does the problem behavior occur? (4) *E*xamine possible solutions. What alternative behaviors are possible? (5) *N*arrow the options to one that is likely to succeed, and experiment. (6) *C*ompare current and past data, with a graph of self-collected information. (7)

Extend, revise, or replace your solution. Central to the Mahoneys' self-control package is the notion that the "cognitive ecology" of negative monologues can be replaced with self-statements. The Mahoneys (1976) have provided excellent examples of negative monologues and alternative positive monologues.

ADDITIONAL REFINEMENTS TO THE SELF-CONTROL PACKAGE

The self-control package has been expanded to focus on family support systems by including female members in training sessions, giving them homework assignments, instructing them to act as auxiliary therapists, and encouraging them to provide social support for the dieter (Brownell, Heckerman, Westlake, Hayes, & Monti, 1978; Weisz & Bucher, 1980; Wilson & Brownell, 1978; Zitter & Fremouw, 1978). Wilson and Brownell (1980) added periodic booster sessions during follow-up to the basic package. Wilson (1979, 1980) listed a number of refinements to the basic package, including exercise, drugs for rapid initial weight loss, and self-programming (Loro, Fisher, & Levenkron, 1979).

APPRAISAL OF THE BASIC SELF-CONTROL PACKAGE

In a comprehensive review of controlled and uncontrolled clinical studies, Wilson and Brownell (1980) evaluated self-control procedures for weight reduction, and concluded:

1. Behavioral techniques are superior to traditional medical and psychotherapeutic treatments in helping clients lose weight. The average weight loss is 10.4 pounds; the average treatment length is 12.8 weeks.

2. The results for 1-year follow-up are mixed. In most studies, subjects do not lose additional weight following treatment but they do maintain their initial weight loss.

3. One year after treatment clients tend to regain the weight lost during treatment.

4. There are mixed results for extensions of the basic self-control package. The Mahoneys' (1976) cognitive program had poor outcomes while Rodin's (1980) similar program was remarkably successful at the 2-year follow-up. When spouses are included in treatment, the results are mixed. Positive findings result when treatment relies on the social support of family and friends, and stresses exercise.

5. Behavioral programs have markedly reduced attrition rates (12–20%), compared to the rates of traditional (80%) and self-help (50%) programs.

6. There is marked interindividual variability in outcome during treatment and follow-up. "Attempts to identify predictor variables for outcome have been unsuccessful . . . subject variables, demographic and background data and personality measures have not been reliably related to treatment outcomes" (Wilson & Brownell, 1980, p. 60). The severely obese appear to benefit least from behavioral programs.

7. Program administrators have ranged from naive peers to experienced therapists; experienced therapists tend to get better results.

8. The effects of booster sessions on maintenance have been mixed. There is some evidence that regularly scheduled booster sessions enhance maintenance. (Booster sessions are not a common feature in behavioral weight loss programs.)

NEW DIRECTIONS IN BEHAVIORAL TREATMENT OF OVERWEIGHT

The concepts which gave rise to the basic self-control program may be invalid (Jeffery & Coates, 1978). The assumption that overeating causes overweight may be fat fiction (Mahoney, 1975). Several reviewers (Gaul, Craighead, & Mahoney, 1975; Leon, 1976; Mahoney, 1978) agree with S. C. Wooley and Wooley's (1979) conclusion that on "the average the obese eat no more than the lean," and that there is no distinctive obese eating style. Finally, client adherence to behavioral instructions may not lead to weight loss (Johnson, Wildman, & O'Brien, 1980). Brownell (1981) reported no relationship between behavior change (adherence to program) and weight change.

Behavioral techniques have been prematurely disseminated to the public in advance of careful assessment of relevant variables (Brownell, 1981). Behavior therapists, by focusing on self-control, have made a common assessment error, selecting as the target behavior, the "first identifiable problem, especially one for which an intervention is readily available" (Nelson & Barlow, 1981, p. 16). It is time to acknowledge the lack of success of the basic self-control program, and to design more varied behavioral treatments for weight problems. Overweight is a complex, multifaceted problem that like other addictive disorders is characterized by high rates of relapse (Wilson & Brownell, 1980). The resistance of clients to sustained weight loss suggests the existence of a homeostatic control mechanism which returns weight to a physiologically determined set point (Stunkard, 1977). Future research may clarify central mechanisms common to all obese clients; for the present, a shift from standard programs to individualized ones is in order. Other methods of assessment should be used (Wolpe, 1977), such as Straw's questionnaire (Straw, Mahoney, Straw, Rogers, Mahoney, Craighead, & Stunkard, 1980). Cultural and psychological influences peculiar to overweight women deserve much more attention, and methods of assessing and altering the obsessive wish to lose weight should be developed.

ANOREXIA: THE OBSESSION WITH THINNESS

The thin–fat, bulimic, and anorectic young women share the overweight woman's obsession. Each group has its own way of handling the obsession, the overweight, and self-perceived overweight try to diet, the bulimics binge and purge, while the anorectics diet and exercise to the point of starvation and exhaustion. There is little behavioral literature on bulimia and the self-perceived overweight person's obsession with dieting. However, anorexia has attracted much attention.

ANOREXIA: THE CLINICAL PICTURE

"It is such a terrible disease because you watch your child deliberately hurting herself, and obviously suffering, and yet you are unable to help her . . . her thinness has become her pride and joy and the main object of our life" (letter from a mother of an anorectic writing to ask for help; Bruch, 1979, p. 1). Anorectics do what few overweight women can, they diet and lose weight. Their fear of being fat resembles a phobic reaction. Unlike phobics who passively avoid the feared stimulus, anorectics actively ward off fatness by constant exercise and by dieting often to the point of starvation and death.

There is remarkable agreement in the medical psychoanalytic, and behavioral literatures about the characteristics of the anorectic (Bemis, 1978; Bruch, 1979; Halmi & Larson, 1977; National Clearing House for Mental Health Information, 1981). She is usually a young adolescent, living at home with her parents, White and upper middle class, seen as a good or perfect child, a high achiever. Her family is concerned with appearances, the mother is concerned about her own weight and attractiveness, and the father values an attractive daughter. Anorexia often begins in a somewhat chubby adolescent who begins to diet after a remark (sometimes by her father) that she is getting too fat. At first, parents and peers praise the girl for weight loss; it is a while before the parents notice that things have gone too far. The girl becomes increasingly preoccupied with strenuous exercise, jogging miles each day, hoarding or hiding food, and denying that her behavior is unusual, even though menstruation has stopped. A power struggle ensues, everyone in the family tries to get the girl to eat. Soon the family doctor and school personnel lend their efforts. A therapist is typically consulted after the emaciated child has rendered significant adults powerless through her overdieting. Behavior therapists are generally consulted at the point of crisis when the young girl is hospitalized and the medical staff is preoccupied with the possibility of death or enduring physiological damage. Even at this stage, some anorectics stubbornly insist they are too fat, take pride in their diet achievements, and continue to fast if permitted.

THE OPERANT APPROACH FOR SHAPING EATING BEHAVIORS

An operant analysis of anorexia was first presented by Ayllon, Haughton, and Osmond (1964) in their description of hospitalized schizophrenics who refused to eat: "In conditioning terms, food rejecting behavior is reinforced by the attention it produces" (p. 151). The following year, Bachrach, Erwin, and Mohr (1965) described the treatment of a 47-pound anorectic woman. The patient was kept in a bare room and had to earn privileges by increasing her eating behavior. Positive reinforcement, including praise and privileges, was contingent on behavior such as picking up a fork and eating. Since then, numerous single-case reports and single-case design studies of hospitalized patients have used variants of the basic treatment in which anorectics earn privileges contingent on each kilogram of weight gain. Some studies gave patients feedback about weight gain, others did not (Agras, Barlow, Chapin, Abel, & Leitenberg, 1974; Azzerad & Stafford, 1969; Bianco, 1974, Stunkard, 1975a; Garfinkel, Kline, & Stancer, 1973; Halmi, Powers, & Cunningham, 1975). Blinder, Freeman, and Stunkard (1970) exploited the hyperactivity of anorectics by making access to physical activity contingent on weight gain.

Most studies report gains of 2–3 pounds a week during hospitalization (Bemis, 1978; Halmi et al., 1975; Kellerman, 1977; Pertschuk, 1977). It is difficult to assess the outcome of operant treatments, since they are usually combined with drug treatments and psychotherapy. A comparison of behavioral treatments with other inpatient interventions found similar results for all treatment (Eckert, Goldberg, Halmi, Casper, & Davis, 1979).

While most anorectic patients are discharged close to normal weight following operant treatment, maintenance of weight after discharge appears no better than in conventional therapy (Bemis, 1978). Operant programs have not reduced the suicide risk, the recurrence of symptoms, and the development of new problems which are common in the posttreatment phase of anorexia (Bemis, 1978; Blinder et al., 1970; Ollendick, 1979). Pertschuk (1977) reviewed the posttreatment progress of 27 recipients of inpatient operant treatment and found that only two were completely recovered. The remainder were readmitted for depression, eating problems, and suicide attempts. While no bulimia was reported prior to treatment, as many as 10 patients reported bulimia and compulsive vomiting after treatment. Since one third to one fourth of anorectic patients later become compulsive overeaters, Bemis (1978) criticized the emphasis on large weight gains which necessitate a gargantuan daily intake, a kind of officially endorsed bulimia. While operant methodology deals with the immediate crisis of near starvation, the typical, long-term problems for anorectics are their obsession with thinness and dieting, adolescent self-determination, and coping with familial, school, and peer pressures (Bruch, 1974).

EXPANDED BEHAVIORAL TREATMENT FOR WEIGHT DISORDERS

In this section, we describe, in some detail, how behavioral treatment for women with weight disorders can be improved. Comparison of proposed improvements with the basic self-control package is the next step.

TREATMENTS FOR BODY IMAGE DISTURBANCES

Body image distortions have been noted in both the overweight and the anorectic (Bruch, 1973; Button, Fransella, & Slade, 1977; Dyrenforth, Wooley, & Wooley, 1980; Fransella & Crisp, 1979; Stunkard & Mendelson, 1967). A methodology developed to study body image distortion

(Garner, Garfinkel, & Moldofsky, 1978) has anorectics estimate their real size compared to a full-length, distorted photograph. Five of nine anorectics overestimated their body size; and they had poor treatments outcomes. The four who had good outcomes underestimated their size. Perceptual training, videotape and feedback (Biggs, Rosen, & Summerfield, 1980), desensitization, and cognitive restructuring could be used to shape realistic body images. Information about women's bodies throughout the life cycle might help weight-obsessed clients develop healthy body images.

Consistent with the notion that anorectics are obsessed with the ideal of thinness, Leitenberg, Agras, and Thomson (1968) suggested that the anorectic's refusal of food is a form of avoidance behavior. Others viewed anorexia as a weight phobia (Crisp, 1977a) and a fear of fatness (Bemis, 1978). Hallsten (1965) and Hauserman and Lavin (1977) used systematic desensitization for a weight phobia and a food phobia. Crisp (1977b) incorporated desensitization for weight gain in a comprehensive package since he assumed that as anorectics gain weight they are exposed to a feared situation; this approach proved successful in a large clinical study.

AVOIDANCE OF AGE-APPROPRIATE TASKS

Rarely addressed by behavioral programs is the client's fear of growing, changing, and moving on to the next age-appropriate developmental level or task. Anorexia permits physical, social, and academic escape from the demanding tasks of adolescence. The adolescent avoids age-appropriate tasks by putting a brake on biological development, and focusing on weight (Crisp, 1979). Although these issues have been left to psychoanalysts, behavior therapists have relevant treatment techniques. Lang (1965) used systematic desensitization to treat fear of criticism in an adult female anorectic; Wolpe (1975) advised treatment for anorectics' social anxieties. Social-anxiety treatment and assertiveness training have been successful in the posthospitalization phase of anorexia (Crisp, 1977a; Hauserman & Lavin, 1977). While the emphasis in this chapter has been on adolescent anorexia, anorexia can appear at any stage of life. Individualized treatments should address issues relevant to the married anorectic or to the elderly woman in a nursing home.

Many overweight women also avoid age-appropriate growth and

development. A young overweight adult may sit at home waiting for her life to begin, fearing dating, sex, and expression of feelings, and clinging to fantasies about how marvelous life could be if she were thinner. A middle-aged overweight woman may not risk leaving an unhappy marriage or searching for a better job. Overweight women, who once were thin, focus on dieting as a return to youth. They resent growing older and believe their age-appropriate weight gives a matronly appearance. Behavioral techniques can address developmental-stage issues for such women (Fodor, 1977).

A 28-year-old woman who weighed 200 pounds came to therapy with the first author for behavioral treatment of her weight problem. During the first interview, I discovered that the client had never dated, had a clerical job in the back of a local store, wished to go to college, and had never traveled beyond her small suburban town. She lived at home with her parents and her social life revolved around the family. For this young woman, overweight functioned as a form of agoraphobia. Since the client was bright, curious, and adventurous, I agreed to design a program for weight reduction if the client listed and gradually participated in previously avoided activities. When the standard self-control program was initiated (Stuart & Davis, 1972), the client was told that she might not lose as much weight as she wished and that maintenance could be a problem. The client joined a daily exercise class and enrolled at a community college. Three months into treatment, the client heard of a Halloween contest offering a trip to Mexico for the best costume. She stayed up all night, sewed a Mexican outfit, and won the prize. She was still overweight, but she was beginning to enjoy life.

COMBINED OPERANT AND FAMILY SYSTEMS APPROACH

In the family systems approach, anorexia is viewed as a "pathological organization of the family around the symptom which provides a mechanism through which family members can avoid interpersonal conflicts" (Rosman, Minuchin, & Liebman, 1975, p. 850). Treatment involves family lunch sessions during which new patterns of interaction develop. This approach has been combined with operant treatment and parent training to improve maintenance of weight gain. Parents learn to require that the anorectic gain 2 pounds a week for participation in weekend activities. As the patient continues to gain weight, treatment shifts from weight gain, interpersonal, and intrafamilial issues, to peer-group and school issues. The success rate for the combined treatment approach is promising, 85% of patients have been found improved 3 months to 4 years after treatment in the few studies conducted to date (Bemis, 1978).

When significant others are involved in behavioral treatment for overweight, they generally monitor their partners' behavior, model prescribed eating habits, and assist their partners in high-risk situations that are incompatible with eating (Brownell et al., 1978). The results of such interventions are mixed. A therapist working with an overweight woman and her husband might prefer to redefine the problem as one involving a couple system. After all, the husband may or may not want a thinner wife, the wife may or may not want to please her husband. Issues of the roles of the wife and husband may also be relevant. The traditional wife is responsible for food shopping, and meal preparation. It may be difficult for a woman to buy and prepare her husband's and family's favorite foods, but still control her eating behavior. Stuart and Davis's (1972) program may require a level of self-controlled eating that is unreasonable for a homemaker. It is like asking an alcoholic to tend bar (Kaplan, 1980). More research is needed on how reallocation of shifting food-preparation roles within the family affects weight control.

RAISING CONSCIOUSNESS ABOUT THE OBSESSION WITH THINNESS

Consciousness-raising techniques borrowed from the women's movement have rarely been tried with adolescent anorectics. Many young people in the community need such help. Garner and Garfinkel (1978) and Druss and Silverman (1979) report similarities between ballet dancers and anorectics. Boskind-Lodahl and Sirlin (1977) used consciousness-raising techniques with a group of anorectics and bulimics. Several preventive measures seem in order: empirically based information modules for schools, pressure on the media to stop idealizing the physique of ballerinas and other dancers for normal-weight people, and so on.

Consciousness-raising techniques might encourage overweight women (as well as their spouses) to acknowledge how prejudice fuels the preoccupation with dieting; these techniques might help their therapists realize that failure in weight reduction programs is the common experience, success a rarity (Aldebaran, 1977; Flack & Grayer, 1975; Orbach, 1978). Both clients and therapists must question the assumptions of such programs. "The very existence of [such] treatments participate in the cultural designation and definition [of overweight as a physical and emotional disorder], thereby shaping the way people feel about themselves and what they do" (Wooley & Wooley, 1980, p. 135).

RAISING CONSCIOUSNESS ABOUT THE ACCEPTANCE OF
OVERWEIGHT

Given our current behavioral technology, the best we can offer many overweight women is an inconsequential weight loss. Therapists need to develop programs for self-acceptance of unavoidable or trivial overweight to help weight-obsessed clients give up their compulsive dieting and obsession with thinness. After all, according to the Metropolitan Life Insurance Tables, almost half the female population may expect to be classified as overweight at some point in their life cycle.

The first author (Fodor, 1980, 1982) outlined a self-acceptance training program, which begins by providing information about the current status of behavioral treatment programs, and about societal conditioning of negative attitudes to overweight. For example, a woman client complained that when she was sick, her doctor relentlessly urged her to lose weight. As evidence that doctors dislike fat patients and view them as weak-willed and ugly (Powers, 1980), medical journal advertisements for diet pills were presented. An advertisement on the front page of every 1979 issue of *Obesity and Bariatric Medicine* showed an overweight woman with a childish hairstyle staring at a television, and eating a candy bar. A feather duster and soda can were on top of the television; the caption read, "Keep a diet from dying of hunger." The client then practiced assertiveness, so that she could point out to her doctor that it is not unhealthy to be moderately overweight (Fodor, 1982; Mann, 1975; Metropolitan Life Insurance Tables, 1980).

Next the therapist challenged the client's negative personal beliefs with steps from Ellis's (1962) rational–emotive therapy. (1) *Belief:* If my body doesn't conform to the charts, then I'm fat. (2) *Evaluation of belief:* It is horrible to be fat. I am an undesirable person because I can't lose weight. (3) *Disputing techniques:* Where is the evidence that you don't deserve to enjoy life as a fat person? Why can't fat people be happy? Finally, the therapist encouraged the client to "love yourself fat," with training in sensuality, and a search for social-support networks. The focus on favorable views of overweight women was aided by Reichman's

(1977) *Great Big Beautiful Doll* which presents a large woman as beautiful and appealing.

CONCLUSIONS AND RECOMMENDATIONS

It is time for behavior therapists to devise alternative programs for women with weight disorders. In focusing on weight loss for the overweight and weight gain for the anorectic, we have neglected our clients' obsession with thinness. The basic behavioral weight programs may not only fail to reduce the gap between real and ideal weights, they may also lower self-esteem by convincing clients that their self-control is inadequate. Recommendations for improved treatment of women's weight disorders follow.

1. Current information suggests that the best weight program is individualized, guided by experienced therapists, focuses on exercise, and considers familial role assignments and social support networks. Maintenance of weight loss is most likely when the program helps the client set more limited goals, develops programs for other problematic areas in the client's life, shifts the family's system's focus away from weight, and includes regularly scheduled booster sessions over a long follow-up period.

2. Combinations of pharmaceutical and behavioral treatments should be done cautiously (Wilson & Brownell, 1980). In a recent comparison, the combined behavioral/pharmaceutical group had poorer maintenance than did the behavioral group (Craighead, Stunkard, & O'Brien, 1981).

3. Clients who have repeatedly failed to lose weight may benefit from self-acceptance of overweight, (Fodor, 1980, 1982; Stuart & Jacobson, 1976; Wooley & Wooley, 1980) which uses consciousness raising, cognitive restructuring, and alternative role models.

4. More emphasis must be placed on prevention of the weight obsessions, common to all the weight disorders. The targets of prevention might be the families most likely to rear overweight or anorectic children. Most parents need education about how to deal with overweight teenagers, teach proper eating habits, develop family physical fitness, and cope with necessary dieting.

5. At school, children and adolescents need to be taught proper eating patterns, healthy acceptance of different body types, the variety of ways to be attractive, and the necessity for lifelong physical exercise.

6. In the interest of women's health, the mass media should be encouraged to employ average-weight, as well as older and larger women, as models and as actresses.

REFERENCES

Abramson, E. A review of behavioral approaches to weight control. *Behaviour Research and Therapy*, 1973, *11*, 547–556.

Agras, W. S., Barlow, D. H., Chapin, H. N., Abel, G. G., & Leitenberg, H. Behavior modification of anorexia nervosa. *Archives of General Psychiatry*, 1974, *30*, 270–286.

Aldebaran. Fat liberation—a luxury? An open letter to radical (and other) therapists. *State and Mind*, 1977, *5*, 34–38.

Ayllon, T., Haughton, E., & Osmond, H. O. Chronic anorexia: A behavior problem. *Canadian Psychiatric Association Journal*, 1964, *9*, 147–154.

Azzerad, J., & Stafford, R. Restoration of eating behavior in anorexia nervosa through operant conditioning and environmental manipulation. *Behaviour Research and Therapy*, 1969, *7*, 165–171.

Bachrach, A. J., Erwin, W. J., & Mohr, J. P. The control of eating behavior by operant conditioning techniques. In L. Ullmann & L. Krasner (Eds.), *Case studies in behavior modification*. New York: Holt, Rinehart & Winston, 1965.

Bellack, A. Behavioral treatment for obesity: Appraisal and recommendations. In M. Hersen, R. Eisler, & P. Miller (Eds.), *Progress in behavior modification*. New York: Academic, 1977.

Bemis, K. M. Current approaches to the etiology and treatment of anorexia nervosa. *Psychological Bulletin*, 1978, *85*, 593–617.

Berscheid, E., & Walster, E. Physical attractiveness *Advances in Experimental Social Psychology* 1974, *7*, 157–215.

Bianco, F. J. Rapid treatment of two cases of anorexia nervosa. *Journal of Behavior Therapy and Experimental Psychiatry*, 1974, *3*, 223–224.

Biggs, S. J., Rosen, B., & Summerfield, A. B. Videofeedback and personal attribution in anorexic, depressed and normal viewers. *British Journal of Medical Psychology*, 1980, *53*, 249–254.

Blinder, B. J., Freeman, D. M. A., & Stunkard, A. J. Behavior therapy of anorexia nervosa: Effectiveness of activity as a reinforcer of weight gain. *American Journal of Psychiatry*, 1970, *126*, 1093–1098.

Boskind-Lodahl, M., & Sirlin, J. The gorging–purging syndrome. *Psychology Today*, 1977, *10*, 50–52.

Bray, G. (Ed.). *Obesity in perspective* (DHEW Publication No. [NIH] 75-708). Washington, D.C.: U.S. Government Printing Office, 1973.

Brody, J. E. An eating disorder of binges and purges reported widespread. *The New York Times*, October 20, 1981.

Brownell, K. D., Heckerman, C. L., Westlake, R. J., Hayes, S. C., & Monti, P. M. The effects of couples training and partner cooperativeness in the behavioral treatment of obesity. *Behaviour Research and Therapy*, 1978, *16*, 323%333.

Brownell, K. D. Assessment of eating disorders. In D. H. Barlow, (Ed.), *Behavioral assessment of adult disorders*. New York: Guilford, 1981.

Brownell, K. D., & Stunkard, A. J. Physical activity in the development and control of obesity. In A. J. Stunkard (Ed.), *Obesity*. Philadelphia: Saunders, 1980.

Bruch, H. Psychotherapy in primary anorexia nervosa. *Journal of Nervous Mental Disorders*, 1970, *150*, 51–67.

Bruch, H. *Eating disorders, obesity, anorexia nervosa, and the person within.* New York: Basic, 1973.

Bruch, H. Perils of behavior modification in the treatment of anorexia nervosa. *Journal of the American Medical Association*, 1974, *230*, 1419–1422.

Bruch, H. *The golden cage: The enigma of anorexia nervosa.* New York: Vintage, 1979.

Bruch, H. Thin fat people. In J. R. Kaplan (Ed.), *A woman's conflict: The special relationship between women and food.* Englewood Cliffs, N.J.: Prentice-Hall, 1980.

Bushkirk, V., & Swan, S. A two-base perspective on the treatment of anorexia nervosa. *Psychological Bulletin*, 1977, *84*, 529–538.

Button, E. J., Fransella, F., & Slade, P. C. A reappraisal of body perception in anorexia nervosa. *Psychological Medicine*, 1977, *7*, 235–243.

Craighead, L. W., Stunkard, A. J., & O'Brien, R. M. Behavior therapy and pharmacotherapy for obesity. *Archives of General Psychiatry*, 1981, *38*, 763–767.

Crisp, A. H. Diagnosis and outcomes of anorexia nervosa: The St. George's view. *Proceedings of the Royal Society of Medicine*, 1977, *70*, 464–469. (a)

Crisp, A. H. The differential diagnosis of anorexia nervosa. *Proceedings of the Royal Society of Medicine*, 1977, *70*, 686–690. (b)

Crisp, A. H. Early recognition and prevention of anorexia nervosa. *Developmental Medicine and Child Neurology*, 1979, *21*, 393–395.

Diagnostic and statistical manual of mental disorders (3rd ed.). Washington, D.C.: American Psychiatric Association, 1980.

Doctorow, E. L. *Loon lake.* New York: Random House, 1979.

Druss, R. G., & Silverman, J. Body image and perfectionism of ballerinas: Comparison and contrast with anorexia nervosa. *General Hospital Psychiatry*, 1979, *1* (2), 115–121.

Dyer, J., Feldman, J., & Mayer, J. The social psychology of dieting. *Journal of Health and Social Behavior*, 1970, *11*, 269.

Dyrenforth, S. R., Wooley, O. W., & Wooley, S. C. A woman's body in a man's world: A review of findings on body image and weight control. In J. A. Kaplan (Ed.), *A woman's conflict: The special relationship between women and food.* Englewood Cliffs, N.J.: Prentice-Hall, 1980.

Eckert, E. D., Goldberg, S. C., Halmi, K. A., Casper, R. C., & Davis, J. M. Behavior therapy in anorexia nervosa. *British Journal of Psychiatry*, 1979, *134*, 55–59.

Ellis, A. *Reason and emotion in psychotherapy.* New York: Lyle Stuart, 1962.

Ferster, C. B., Nurnberger, J. L., & Levitt, E. B. The control of eating. *Journal of Mathematics*, 1962, *1*, 87–109.

Flack, R., & Grayer, E. D. Consciousness raising for obese women. *Social Work*, 1975, *20* (6), 484–485.

Fodor, I. G. A cognitive behavioral approach to helping the overweight woman. *Scandinavian Journal of Behavior Therapy*, 1977, *6* (4), 60. (Abstract)

Fodor, I. G. *Issues in treating the overweight woman.* Paper presented at International Congress of Behavior Therapy, Jerusalem, 1980.

Fodor, I. G. Behavior therapy for the overweight woman: A time for re-appraisal. In M. Rosenbaum & C. Franks (Eds.), *Perspectives on behavior therapy in the eighties: Selected and updated proceedings from the First World Congress on Behavior Therapy.* New York: Springer, 1982.

Fransella, F., & Crisp, A. H. Comparisons of weight concepts in groups of neurotic, normal and anorexic females. *British Journal of Psychiatry*, 1979, *134*, 76–86.

Garfinkel, P. E., Kline, S. A., & Stancer, H. C. Treatment of anorexia nervosa using operant conditioning techniques. *Journal of Nervous Mental Disorders*, 1973, *157* (6), 428–433.

Garner, D. M., Garfinkel, P. E., & Moldofsky, H. Perceptual experiences in anorexia nervosa and obesity. *Canadian Psychiatric Association Journal,* 1978, *23* (4), 249–263.

Garner, D. M., & Garfinkel, P. E. Sociocultural factors in anorexia nervosa. *Lancet,* 1978, *8091,* 674.

Gaul, D. J., Craighead, W. E., & Mahoney, M. J. Relationship between eating rates and obesity. *Journal of Consulting and Clinical Psychology,* 1975, *43,* 123–126.

Goldblatt, P. B., Moore, E., & Stunkard, A. J. Social factors in obesity. *Journal of the American Medical Association,* 1965, *192,* 1039.

Hall, S. M., & Hall, R. G. Outcome and methodological considerations in behavioral treatment for obesity. *Behavior Therapy,* 1974, *5,* 352–364.

Hallsten, E. A., Jr. Adolescent anorexia nervosa treated by desensitization. *Behaviour Research and Therapy,* 1965, *3,* 87–91.

Halmi, K. A., & Larson, L. Behavior therapy in anorexia nervosa. In S. Feinstein (Ed.), *Adolescent psychiatry: Developmental and clinical studies.* New York: Aronson, 1977.

Halmi, K. A., Powers, P., & Cunningham, S. Treatment of anorexia nervosa with behavior modification. *Archives of General Psychiatry,* 1975, *32,* 93–96.

Hauserman, N., & Lavin, P. Post-hospitalization continuation treatment of anorexia nervosa. *Journal of Behavior Therapy and Experimental Psychiatry,* 1977, *8,* 309–313.

Heckerman, C. L., & Prochaska, J. O. Development and evaluation of weight reduction procedures in a health maintenance organization. In R. B. Stuart (Ed.), *Behavioral self-management: Strategies, techniques and outcomes.* New York: Brunner/Mazel, 1977.

Jeffery, R., & Coates, R. J. Why aren't they losing weight? *Behavior Therapy,* 1978, *9* (5), 856–860.

Johnson, W. G., Wildman, H. A., & O'Brien, T. The assessment of program adherence: The Achilles heel of behavioral weight reduction. *Behavioral Assessment,* 1980, *2,* 297–302.

Juffe, M., & Haden-Guest, A. Pretty babies. *New York Magazine,* September 29, 1980.

Kaplan, J. R. Beauty and the feast. In J. R. Kaplan (Ed.), *A woman's conflict: The special relationship between women and food.* Englewood Cliffs, N.J.: Prentice-Hall, 1980.

Kellerman, J. Anorexia nervosa: The efficacy of behavior therapy. *Journal of Behavior Therapy and Experimental Psychiatry,* 1977, *8,* 387–390.

Keys, A. Fidanza, F., Karvonen, M. J., Kimura, N., & Taylor, H. L. Indices of relative weight and obesity. *Journal of Chronic Disease,* 1972, *25,* 329–343.

Lang, P. Behavior therapy with a case of nervous anorexia. In L. Ullmann & L. Krasner (Eds.), *Case studies in behavior modification,* New York: Holt, Rinehart & Winston, 1965.

Leon, G. Current directions in the treatment of obesity. *Psychological Bulletin,* 1976, *83,* 557–578.

Leitenberg, H. Agras, W. S., & Thomson, L. E. A sequential analysis of the effect of selective positive reinforcement in modifying anorexia nervosa. *Behaviour Research and Therapy,* 1968, *6,* 211–218.

Levitz, L. S., & Stunkard, A. J. A therapeutic coalition for obesity: Behavior modification and patient self-help. *American Journal of Psychiatry,* 1974, *131,* 423–427.

Loro, A. D., Fisher, E. B., & Levenkron, J. Comparison of established and innovative weight-reduction procedures. *Journal of Applied Behavior Analysis,* 1979, *2,* 141–155.

Maddox, G. L., & Liederman, V. Overweight as a social disability with medical implications. *Journal of Medical Education,* 1979, *44,* 214–220.

Mahoney, M. Fat fiction. *Behavior Therapy,* 1975, *6,* 416–418.

Mahoney, M. Behavior modification in the treatment of obesity. *Psychiatric Clinics of North America,* 1978, *1,* 651–660.

Mahoney, M., & Mahoney, K. *Permanent weight control.* New York: Norton, 1976.

Mahoney, M., Mahoney, K., Rogers, T., & Straw, M. Assessment of human obesity: The measurement of body composition. *Journal of Behavioral Assessment*, 1979, 1.

Mann, G. V. The influence of obesity on health. *New England Journal of Medicine*, 1975, 291, 226–232.

Metropolitan Life Insurance Company. Frequency of overweight and underweight. *Statistical Bulletin*, 1960, 41, 1–8.

Metropolitan Life Insurance Company. Trends in average weights and heights among insured men and women. *Statistical Bulletin*, 1977, 58, 3–5.

Metropolitan Life Insurance Company. Mortality differentials favor women. *Statistical Bulletin*, 1980, 61, 2–3.

Moldofsky, H., & Garfinkel, P. E. Problems of treatment of anorexia nervosa. *Canadian Psychiatric Association Journal*, 1974, 19, 169–175.

National Clearinghouse for Mental Health Information, Division of Scientific and Public Information. *Anorexia nervosa* (Literature Survey Series, No. 1). U.S. Department of Health and Human Services, Public Health Service, Alcohol, Drug Abuse and Mental Health Administration, 1981.

Nash, O. Curl up and diet. In *The pocketbook of Ogden Nash*. New York: Pocket Books, 1972.

Nelson, R. O., & Barlow, D. H. Behavioral assessment: Basic strategies and initial procedures. In D. Barlow (Ed.), *Behavioral assessment of adult disorders*. New York: Guilford, 1981.

Ollendick, T. H. Behavioral treatment of anorexia nervosa: A five-year study. *Behavior Modification*, 1979, 3 (1), 124–135.

Orbach, S. *Fat is a feminist issue*. New York and London: Paddington, 1978.

Pertschuk, M. Behavior therapy: Extended follow-up. In R. A. Vigersky (Ed.), *Anorexia nervosa*. New York: Raven, 1977.

Powers, P. *Obesity: The regulation of weight*. Baltimore: Williams & Wilkins, 1980.

Reichman, S. *Great big beautiful doll*. New York: Dutton, 1977.

Rodin, J. *The Yale weight control program*. Unpublished manuscript, Yale University, 1980.

Rollins, N., & Blackwell, A. The treatment of anorexia nervosa in children and adolescents: Stage 1. *Journal of Child Psychology and Psychiatry*, 1968, 9, 81–91.

Rosman, B. L., Minuchin, S., & Liebman, R. Family lunch session: An introduction to family therapy in anorexia nervosa. *American Journal of Orthopsychiatry*, 1975, 45, 846–853.

Russell, G., Bulimia nervosa: An ominous variant of anorexia nervosa. *Psychological Medicine*, 1979, 9 (3), 429–448.

Silverstone, J. T. Psychosocial aspects of obesity. *Proceedings of the Royal Society of Medicine*, 1968, 61, 371–375.

Straw, M. K., Mahoney, M. J., Straw, R. B., Rogers, T., Mahoney, B. K., Craighead, L., & Stunkard, A. *The master questionnaire: An obesity assessment device*. Unpublished manuscript, Pennsylvania State University, 1980.

Stuart, R. Behavioral control of overeating. *Behaviour Research and Therapy*, 1967, 5, 357–365.

Stuart, R. B., Self-help group approach to self-management. In R. B. Stuart (Ed.), *Behavioral self-management: Strategies, techniques and outcomes*. New York: Brunner/Mazel, 1977.

Stuart, R. B., & Davis, B. *Slim chance in a fat world*. Ill.: Research, 1972.

Stuart, R. B., & Jacobson, B. Sex differences in obesity. In E. Gomberg & V. Franks (Eds.), *Gender and disordered behavior: Sex differences in psychopathology*. New York: Brunner/Mazel, 1979.

Stuart, R. B., & Mitchell, C. Self-help groups in the control of body weight. In A. J. Stunkard (Ed.), *Obesity*. Philadelphia: Saunders, 1980.

Stunkard, A. J. The management of obesity. *New York State Journal of Medicine*, 1958, 58, 79–87.

Stunkard, A. J. Anorexia nervosa. In J. P. Sanford (Ed.), *The science and practice of clinical medicine*, New York: Grune & Stratton, 1975. (a)

Stunkard, A. J. From explanation to action in psychosomatic medicine: The case of obesity. *Psychosomatic Medicine*, 1975, *37* (3), 195–236. (b)

Stunkard, A. J. *The pain of obesity*. Palo Alto, Calif.: Bull, 1976.

Stunkard, A. J. Behavioral treatment of obesity: Failure to maintain weight loss. In R. B. Stuart (Ed.), *Behavioral self-management: Strategies, techniques and outcomes*. New York: Brunner/Mazel, 1977.

Stunkard, A. J., & Mahoney, M. J. Behavioral treatment of the eating disorders. In H. Leitenberg (Ed.), *Handbook of behavior modification and behavior therapy*. Englewood Cliffs, N.J.: Prentice-Hall, 1976.

Stunkard, A. J., & Mendelson, M. Obesity and the body image: I. Characteristics of disturbances in the body image of some obese persons. *American Journal of Psychiatry*, 1967, *123*, 1296–1300.

Water Pik. *Countdown: Guide book to permanent weight loss*. Ft. Collins, Col.: Teledyne Water Pik, 1977.

Weisz, G., & Bucher, B. Involving husbands in treatment of obesity—Effects on weight loss, depression and marital satisfaction. *Behavior Therapy*, 1980, *11*, 643–650.

Wilson, G. T. Behavioral treatment of obesity: Maintenance strategies and long term efficacy. In P. Sjoden, S. Bates, & W. Dockens (Eds.), *Trends in behavior therapy*. New York: Academic, 1979.

Wilson, G. T. Behavior modification and the treatment of obesity. In A. J. Stunkard (Ed.), *Obesity*. Philadelphia: Saunders, 1980.

Wilson, G. T., & Brownell, K. Behavior therapy for obesity: Including family members in the treatment process. *Behavior Therapy*, 1978, *9* (5), 943–945.

Wilson, G. T., & Brownell, K. D. Behavior therapy for obesity: An evaluation of treatment outcome. *Advances in Behavior Research and Therapy*, 1980, *3*, 49–86.

Wolpe, J. Letter. *Journal of the American Medical Association*, 1975, *233*, 317–318.

Wolpe, J. Inadequate behavior analysis: The Achilles' heel of outcome research in behavior therapy. *Journal of Behavior Therapy and Experimental Psychiatry*, 1977, *8*, 1–4.

Wooley, O. W., & Wooley, S. C. Obesity and women: II. A neglected feminist topic. *Women's Studies International Quarterly*, 1979, *2*, 81–92. (b)

Wooley, S.C., & Wooley, O. W. Obesity and women: I. A closer look at the facts. *Women's Studies International Quarterly*, 1979, *2*, 69–79.

Wooley, S. C., & Wooley, O. W. Eating disorders: Obesity and anorexia. In A. M. Brodsky & R. T. Hare-Mustin (Eds.), *Women and psychotherapy: An assessment of research and practice*. New York: Guilford, 1980.

Wooley, S. C., Wooley, O. W., & Dyrenforth, S. R. Theoretical, practical and social issues in behavioral treatments of obesity. *Journal of Applied Behavior Analysis*, 1979, *12*, 3–25.

Yates, A. *Theory and practice in behavior therapy*. New York: Wiley, 1975.

Zegman, M. Women, weight and health. In V. Franks & E. Rothblum (Eds.), *Sex role stereotypes and women's mental health*. New York: Springer, 1982.

Zitter, R. E., & Fremouw, W. J. Individual versus partner consequation for weight loss. *Behavior Therapy*, 1978, *9*, 808–813.

IV

NEGLECTED POPULATIONS

The final four chapters of this book concern populations of women who have been neglected by traditional and by behavioral researchers and clinicians: female delinquents, alcoholic women, elderly women, and mentally retarded mothers.

Female delinquency is increasingly prevalent, although young women have yet to equal young men's record of criminal behavior. Warburton and Alexander's review of current theories of female delinquency (Chapter 15) suggests the need for experimental field tests of theories about presumed antecedents and consequences of female criminal behavior. Some of these theories may have to be disregarded simply because as stated they are irrefutable. Warburton and Alexander utilize their intimate knowledge of behavioral family interventions to suggest methods of treating female delinquents and their families and to point out the need for program development and evaluation. Since the Utah group is one of only a few in the United States to apply behavioral strategies to female delinquents, the detailed exposition of this group's approach to treatment makes an important addition to the literature on delinquency treatment.

Behavioral intervention with problems of alcohol addiction is an established and respected behavior modification specialty. McCrady (Chapter 16) argues convincingly that women drinkers have been ignored both in basic research on addiction mechanisms and in applied research on intervention strategies. Data on the incidence and prevalence of alcoholism among women are elusive because women hide their drinking more readily than men. Nevertheless, this chapter emphasizes that the proportion of women with drinking problems is large enough to constitute a public health problem and to warrant the attention of applied researchers. Regarding a cutoff for the diagnosis of alcoholism, McCrady proposes that presence and severity of alcoholism be measured by the extent to which drinking interferes with a woman's major responsibilities at home and on the job. In Chapter 8 on parent training, Strauss and Atkeson hint at the usefulness of parent training as a treatment for the depression of mothers. In similar fashion, McCrady depicts the boredom and frustration of the homemaker who drinks, and suggests that some practical skill training might be more relevant to the treatment of women drinkers than stimulus control procedures currently recommended for male problem drinkers.

As Wisocki makes very clear in Chapter 17, aging women are accorded extremely low status in our society, despite their increasing numbers. The primary characteristic by which women judge themselves, and are judged by others, is physical attractiveness. When youth and beauty wane, women tend to lose social power and self-esteem. This notion, central to Wisocki's presentation, is also discussed by Fodor and Thal (Chapter 14) and by Foreyt and Goodrick (Chapter 9) in this volume. Little attention has been paid to behavioral assessment or intervention with aging women. Thus, as Calhoun and Sturgis point out in Chapter 12, the problem of menopause has been neglected, despite relevant behavioral intervention strategies. In the face of a dearth of information about behavioral gerontology, Wisocki acquaints the reader with available data, clarifies questions that need to be addressed by researchers, and makes practical recommendations for prevention and intervention with elderly women.

The unique problems of mentally retarded women begin with puberty, and concern sexuality, reproduction, and child rearing. Although there has been public debate about the ethics of sterilizing mentally retarded women against their will, in Chapter 18 Budd and Greenspan provide the first discussion of this issue for behaviorists in the field of retardation. This chapter focuses on a core problem of mentally retarded women—child rearing. Budd and Greenspan argue that the differences in parenting behavior between women who have been labeled retarded, and women with an IQ of a few more points, are often trivial. Moreover, they point out that motherhood takes on a special significance in the lives of retarded women who feel deficient in so many respects. When parent-training procedures are altered to suit these women's special needs, retarded women who love their children can learn to be as successful at child rearing as many untutored parents. After reviewing the most recent evidence about training of retarded mothers, Budd and Greenspan discuss their own survey of therapist experiences with this population.

15

FEMALE DELINQUENTS

JANET R. WARBURTON
JAMES F. ALEXANDER

OVERVIEW

Adolescence brings traumatic change in hormone levels, peer relationships, role demands, and family relationships. These changes often create problems for adolescents, parents, and authority figures. Unfortunately,
adolescence is also a time when delinquent behavior emerges. This chapter focuses on delinquency, the contexts in which delinquency develops,
and the issues involved in treatment. In particular, the chapter emphasizes delinquency among female offenders. Despite the voluminous delinquency research and treatment literature, relatively little attention has
been paid to the female delinquent. Instead, delinquency has been
viewed as the product of a ubiquitous process such as emancipation, or
seen as a male phenomenon. In the past, adolescent males committed
delinquent acts at a considerably higher rate than adolescent females.
However, the ratio of female to male delinquency has increased in recent
years, so that female delinquency is no longer infrequent or inconsequential (Adler, 1975; Campbell, 1977; Cernkovich, & Giordano, 1979a;
Hindelang & McDermott, 1981; Simons, Miller, & Aigner, 1980; U.S.
Department of Justice, 1980). The relatively sparse theoretical, research,
and treatment literature on female delinquency can produce untoward
consequences which include inappropriate treatment goals, inappropriate assumptions about causal or maintaining variables, and inappropriate treatment technologies. The purpose of this chapter is to evaluate
the available literature on delinquency, compare female and male delin-

Janet R. Warburton. Western States Family Institute, Salt Lake City, Utah.
James F. Alexander. Department of Psychology, University of Utah, Salt Lake City,
Utah.

quency, and consider current and future treatment goals and techniques in light of client gender.

BACKGROUND: STEREOTYPES AND DATA

FEMALE DELINQUENCY

"I'd rather deal with 10 of the boys than one of the girls." The belief that female delinquents are particularly devious, deceitful, and more difficult to treat than males is often expressed in youth correction circles. Juvenile justice system workers and therapists who prefer male delinquents will often be disappointed since they will have to deal with an increasingly visible population of female delinquents. To do so effectively requires knowledge about female delinquency, its predominant modes of expression, and the variables that produce, maintain, and modify its expression. This chapter reviews various sources of information relevant to female delinquency. These sources include recent statistics about female delinquency rates, psychological research on sex differences, writings from the women's movement, and attempts by social scientists to explain the recent increase in female delinquency. Because the rates of female crime remained relatively stable prior to the mid-1970s, a historical survey of etiologies is not included. Such surveys appear elsewhere (Adler, 1975; Sarri, 1979; Simon, 1975; Smart, 1977) and cover theories from Lombroso and Ferrero (1895) through the work of Glueck and Glueck (1934), Konopka (1966), and Pollak (1950).

FEMALE CRIME RATES

Three major sources used to describe crime rates include arrest data, victimization surveys, and self-report statistics. Each source makes important contributions to knowledge about criminal behavior, yet each has serious conceptual and practical limitations. Taken together, however, these sources provide important clues about the nature of female delinquency.

Arrest Data

Arrest rates are derived from the *Uniform Crime Reports* for adults and juveniles, and from juvenile court records of referrals for juveniles. While females appear in official statistics about one seventh as frequently as boys (Campbell, 1977) the recent percentage increases of female participation in crime are large. Between 1960 and 1973 the arrest rate of females under 18 years of age increased 265% for all offenses, 393% for violent crimes, and 334% for property crimes. This compares with increases of 124%, 236%, and 82%, respectively, for males in the same age group (Giordano, 1978). Thus, while males continue to commit, or are at least arrested for, more criminal offenses, the frequency of female involvement in serious crime seems to have increased much more rapidly than male involvement, particularly in the area of property crime. The dramatic increase in violent crimes is largely a function of the extremely low base rate in 1960. In actual numbers, the increase has been small.

It has been suggested that the *apparent* differences in male and female crime rates are largely the result of unequal processing of males and females by the juvenile justice system (Adler & Simon, 1979; Datesman & Scarpetti, 1980). The juvenile justice system, including judges, lawyers, and police officers, was thought to have a paternalistic stance when it came to arresting female juveniles. If girls were involved in a serious crime, but had families to whom they could be released, they were often diverted from the juvenile justice system. If girls were runaways or sexual offenders, they were judged to be in need of court supervision, leading to formal processing and incarceration to protect their virtue. As a result, more males were apprehended and detained for serious crimes, while more females were apprehended and detained for status offenses. To the extent that police and court decisions were affected by the offender's gender, misrepresentation of juvenile offense rates would result. However, paternalistic attitudes affect processing of juveniles in the system more than they affect arrest data. Further, the victimization surveys and self-report statistics cited below add information about female offense rates, and verify that the sex difference in crime rates is more than the result of unequal processing.

Victimization Survey Data

The most recent comprehensive report of victimization survey data was compiled by Hindelang and McDermott for the Office of Juvenile Justice and Delinquency Prevention (1981). Victimization surveys use subjective data since they depend on victims' visual recognition of global characteristics of an offender such as age, sex, and ethnicity. At the same time, victimization data correct for the unequal processing of female and male delinquents, and they eliminate status offenses or victimless crimes, which inflate male and female delinquency statistics. Hindelang and McDermott grouped rates of offending according to demographic characteristics, including age, race, and sex, for the years 1973–1977. The face-to-face crimes they examined included rape, robbery, assault, and personal larceny. While Hindelang and McDermott found more males than females in each group, a breakdown of offense rates by age and race provided detailed, useful, information about patterns of delinquency. For example, the ratio of male to female crime was 4 to 1 for ages 12 through 17, 15 to 1 for ages 18 to 20, and 14 to 1 for ages 21 and above. Among older adolescents the offense rate is dramatically higher for males; among younger adolescents, male and female rates are more similar. The data also demonstrate that the offense rate peaks at a younger age for females than for males. An examination of the data as a function of race provides additional information. For White females the offense rate remains constant across the entire range of age from 12 to 21. Black females, on the other hand, have significantly higher offense rates than their White counterparts at ages 12 through 17, while there is little differences between Black and White females' rates by age 21.

The data showing sex differences in both magnitude and peak age of delinquency rates suggest different processes may be operating for males and females. However, race differences among females at some ages suggest that gender alone cannot fully explain the variations and manifestations of female delinquency. Additional perspectives of opportunity theory and association theory, which are described below, seem necessary to understand this phenomenon.

Hindelang and McDermott also described the victims of juvenile offenders. Juveniles tend to victimize members of their own age group and sex. Male offenders of all ages victimize males in about 7 out of 10 of their crimes. Female offenders generally victimize females but as female offender age increases, male victims become more likely. Only 1 out of 10 victims of juvenile females was male, whereas 3 of 10 victims of adult females were male. Familiarity between offenders and victims also differs by sex. Female offenders and their female victims often know each other (only 45% are strangers), while male offenders and their male victims are often strangers (75%).

Self-Report Data

In self-report studies investigators generally sample large populations of high school students and administer self-report questionnaires. Although males admit offenses more frequently than females, the patterns of male and female delinquency are similar since both males and females report many status offenses such as runaway and ungovernable (Bowker, 1978; Cernkovich & Giordano, 1979a; Simons, Miller, & Aigner, 1980). Further, there tends to be a smaller sex difference in self-reported delinquency rates than is generally assumed (Cernkovich & Giordano, 1979a). For example, in the Simons, Miller, and Aigner (1980) survey, 8.8% of males and 3.5% of females reported high involvement in delinquent activity. This is consistent with evidence, discussed above, that under 18 years of age, the ratio of male to female offenders may be as low as 3 to 1. Females report a particularly large increase in property crimes. Only in the violent offense category do females consistently comprise 10% of offenders (Balkan & Berger, 1979; Bowker, 1978).

SUMMARY AND IMPLICATIONS

It is not surprising that males commit delinquent acts at a higher rate than females. However, the small sex difference in offense rates among younger adolescents is surprising since almost all major treatment programs emphasize male delinquency. The paucity of research and treatment programs that target young women seems inappropriate in light of the recent increase in female delinquency described above. This paucity could mean that many treatment programs for female delinquents are guided more by stereotypes and unwarranted assumptions than by empirical data. If rates and types of male and female delinquency are comparable or converging, it may be profitable to examine common experiences of male and female adolescents. The struggle for emancipation, for example, is encountered by all adolescents and their families. Delinquency may represent one response to this ubiquitous relationship issue which is similar for males and females.

Within the larger context of emancipation, the differences between male and female delinquents may be more important than the similarities. Differences in the ages at which offense rates peak, and differences in the typical sex of the victim and in the relationship between victim and offender, suggest male and female delinquency represent different processes. Age and race differences among female delinquents further suggest that explanations of delinquency based solely on gender will not suffice. Several explanations of the differences and similarities in male and female delinquency have been offered by a number of theorists, including association theory, opportunity theory, and biological theories. These theories will be reviewed, along with relevant sociological data, since they provide a background for the discussion of the behaviorally oriented treatment approaches to female delinquency.

EXPLANATORY MODELS

BIOLOGICAL AND INTRAPERSONAL THEORIES

Biological and intrapersonal theories posit that individuals have innate characteristics which account for sex differences in delinquency. Fairly large and consistent sex differences in aggression were described by Maccoby and Jacklin (1974) and later by Block (1976). Boys and girls show sex differences in aggressive tendencies at a very early age. Numerous studies of aggression in play situations have found clear sex differences by age 3 (cf., for review, Maccoby & Jacklin, 1974; Pederson & Bell, 1970). Boys spend more time in aggressive play than girls, and boys' aggression tends to be more vigorous, destructive, and hurtful than that of girls (Serbin, O'Leary, Kent, & Tonick, 1973). Much higher rates of hyperactivity are reported among boys (cf., for review, Maccoby & Jacklin, 1974).

By adolescence, Maccoby and Jacklin (1974) report some sex differences in aggression, but there were fewer relevant studies. According to Block (1976) the Maccoby and Jacklin review of the adolescent aggression literature underestimates sex differences. Studies of juvenile and adult violent crime definitely indicate sex differences. Ninety percent of violent crime is committed by juvenile and adult males; these statistics support the assumption that higher rates of child and adult male aggression have a biological cause. This supposition is corroborated as well by evidence from other mammalian species (Moyer, 1974).

Most reports of biologically based sex differences in aggression come from hormonal studies on mammals. In her classic experiment, Beeman (1947) found that male mice showed considerable aggression when placed together after a period of isolation. Mice who were castrated in prepuberty did not develop intermale aggression. When testosterone pellets were implanted in the castrated mice, aggressive behavior appeared, only to disappear when the pellets were removed. The female hormones of estrogen and progesterone, most notably estrogen, have inhibited male aggression (Moyer, 1974). A few studies on humans, primarily prison inmates, yielded similar results. Both castration (Hawke, 1950) and female hormones (Golla & Hodge, 1949) have been reported to control aggressive tendencies in males.

While these studies suggest a biological base for higher rates of male aggression, females nevertheless do develop some degree of aggressive behavior. Interestingly, though, in the adolescent literature a duality of terminology is found. The adolescent literature describes females' aggressive behavior as irritability. Several studies suggest that female irritability increases prior to the onset of menses. Increases in female crime at the time of menstruation have often been noted in the social science and medical literature (Dalton, 1964; Ellis & Austin, 1971; Shah & Roth, 1975). The irritability in women during premenstrual periods has been described by Ivey and Bardwick (1968) and Cooke (1945). A study of prison records revealed that 62% of crimes of violence were committed during the premenstrual week and only 2% at the end of the period (Morton, Addison, Addison, Hunt, & Sullivan, 1953).

However, these data can also be interpreted to emphasize the positive effect of female hormones. When female hormone levels are high, women exhibit very low rates of aggressive/irritable behavior. It is as if when their hormone levels are relatively low their behavior more closely approximates male behavior (Frieze, Parsons, Johnson, Ruble, & Zellman, 1978). Similarly, as Parlee (1973) pointed out, the fact that women are most likely to commit their crimes when premenstrual, does not mean normal women become criminal when premenstrual. In fact, the increase of female hormones may elicit increases in positively valued behaviors.

While these studies have found significant sex differences in aggression, they do not seem to explain the current increase in female crime. Maccoby and Jacklin (1974) concluded that the sex difference in aggression has a biological foundation, yet then emphasized that the mode of expression of aggression is learned. We must turn to psychological and sociological learning theories to understand the increased rates of female crime.

SUBCULTURAL OR ASSOCIATION THEORIES

Subcultural or association theories became popular in the 1950s when peer groups were seen as an important cause of delinquent behavior (Cohen, 1955). Sutherland and Cressey (1978) posit a relationship between people's associates and their values and behavior. From this perspective, the female delinquent has been seen as a passive accomplice of male delinquents, rather than a perpetrator or initiator of crime. All females are assumed to be motivated by affiliative needs, and the deviant female adolescent is assumed to seek her boyfriend's love through co-operation in his criminal activities. Thus female crimes have friendship and sexuality as motivating forces.

While association theory emphasizes the contribution of relation-ships with males to female delinquency, Giordano (1978) argues that friendships with females are at least as influential to female participation in both minor and serious crime. Giordano's study on friendships and delinquency found that White females are more likely to commit delin-quent acts in mixed-sex groups, with significant correlations between approval from *girl friends* and participation in delinquency. In contrast, Black females are more likely to commit crimes in same-sex groups. Giordano suggests that White females may be apprenticed to male and female friends, learning delinquent skills by participating in mixed-sex group crimes, while inner-city Black females are exposed to crime at earlier ages and need fewer examples of criminal behavior. In both White and Black subsamples, the most perceived approval for engaging in illegal activities came from girl friends; the least approval came from boyfriends. Female offenders were more likely to perceive approval from males with whom they had no romantic involvement, rather than from potential sexual partners. Thus, romantic notions about female accompl-ices in Bonnie and Clyde teams derive less support than explanations which take female and male peer relationships into account.

The finding that female delinquency most frequently occurs in mixed-sex groups seems to conflict with reanalyzed data from the mid-1960s showing that the presence of females decreases the likelihood of male delinquent activity (Bowker, 1978; Bowker, Gross, & Klein, 1980). The conflict in findings is superficial. Males and females may respond differently to a mixed sex group, with females' presence decreasing males' crimes, and males' presence increasing females' crimes. Since females commit 57% of their offenses in groups, while males commit 36% of their offenses in groups (Altman, 1980), peer groups appear to be highly influential to female delinquents, but do not account for all of the variance. The percentages indicate that 43% of these young women act alone.

OPPORTUNITY THEORY

According to opportunity theory, delinquent behavior results when le-gitimate channels to opportunity are blocked (Cloward & Ohlin, 1960).

Adolescents who are young, poor, and from minority ethnic and racial groups enter delinquency because they are unlikely to achieve goals that are universally desired in this society. Possibly because opportunity theory assumes that delinquency results from unequal treatment of an oppressed population, the theory was popularized by female criminologists as an explanation for the increase in female delinquency (Adler & Simon, 1975; Smart, 1977; Miller, 1979). According to this view, since the 1960s, women have entered legitimate and illegitimate economic enterprises as nontraditional female role options have expanded and traditional role options have shrunk. In the contemporary economy, more women work for pay than ever before and more women are forced to support themselves and their children. When legitimate means of self-sufficiency are unavailable, women may seek illegitimate means for success. Jesse Bernard echoes this view: "As more and more women enter the labor force the opportunities for more profitable property crimes may increase" (Bernard, 1981, p. 223). Political reaction to opportunity theory is evident in the written proceedings of the National Conference on Women and Crime (Loving & Olson, 1976). Participants argued that a primarily middle-class and adult women's movement has little impact on the lower-class and adolescent females who commit the majority of criminal and status offenses.

Cernkovich and Giordano (1979b) tested the opportunity theory of female delinquency, by surveying adolescents' perceptions of general and gender-based blocked opportunities for White and non-White males and females. Contrary to previous findings, non-White reported that many legitimate opportunities were blocked, yet they were unlikely to get involved in delinquent acts because of this perception. Reports of blocked opportunity were strongly associated with reports of delinquent involvement by male and female White adolescents. Liberated sex-role attitudes and reports of female delinquency were associated with perceptions of general blocked opportunity but not with perceptions of gender-blocked opportunity. These findings do not support Adler (1975) who posited that gender-based blocked opportunity contributed to the rise in female crime. The rise of crime among adolescent females who have experienced few economic pressures also detracts from Adler's support.

Expectations about opportunities for education and work differ for White males, White females, and for members of ethnic minorities. A decade of affirmative action plans devised to equalize opportunities is based on this assumption, and labor statistics confirm this perception.

While White males are raised to believe that an almost endless array of opportunities await them, females and minority group members gradually realize that their opportunities are more limited. When White males' aspirations are blocked, delinquency may seem justified to them. On the other hand, the delinquency of females and minority group members who have always expected limited opportunities probably results from conditions other than frustrated expectations.

IMPLICATIONS

Opportunity theory, association theory, and biological theories all suggest reasons for different types and rates of delinquency among males and females. Only opportunity theory, which addresses recent social phenomena, can explain the dramatic absolute and relative rise in female delinquency rates. However, perceptions of blocked opportunities do not adequately explain rises in delinquency among young women. As older female adolescents and adults experience educational and vocational discrimination because of their gender, their frustration could embitter them and encourage deviant behavior. Although consciousness raising by the women's movement has made women aware of blocked opportunities, the conclusion that this awareness has increased criminal behavior in adolescent females is mere speculation. It is unlikely that younger adolescents of either sex have experienced a history of blocked opportunities long enough to cause a dramatic rise in the female delinquency rate. Although some White males and females attribute their delinquency to perceived, general blocked opportunity, the early peak in female delinquency and its interpersonal nature (e.g., familiarity with victims) suggests precipitants other than opportunity. For younger delinquents, these precipitants may be found in the family and in the transition to peer relationships that occur during emancipation.

FAMILIAL CONTRIBUTIONS TO DELINQUENCY

The family has long been accorded a central role in the delinquency literature. Early correlational studies led to the view that the family can prevent or precipitate delinquent behavior. Family size, number of parents in the home, mother's mental illness, and parental criminality have all been correlated with delinquency (Andrew, 1976; Duke & Duke, 1978;

Glueck & Glueck, 1934; James & Thornton, 1980; Offord, Abrams, Allen, & Poushinsky, 1978). Female delinquency has been explained as an attempt by girls, in conflict with parents or in a father-absent home, to gain compensatory affection and acceptance from young males (Heatherington, 1972; Gibbons, 1976). Similarly, male delinquency is often attributed to a family that fails to meet boys' needs for affection and approval (Glueck & Glueck, 1934; Gold, 1963; Rodman & Grams, 1967). This tends to occur in large, chaotic families with little parent–child contact (Offord et al., 1978). Simons, Miller, and Aigner (1980) found that the relationship between parental rejection and delinquency is similar for the two sexes. However, rejection apparently occurs under different family conditions (single-parent vs. large two-parent family) for the two sexes. Correlation of a variable with delinquent behavior does not imply causality, and caution must be used when interpreting individual correlates. Taken together, these correlates do hint at the family background as an important variable in the understanding of delinquent females. Datesman and Scarpetti (1980) reported that differences in rates of female and male delinquency were due to the overrepresentation of father-absent girls in the status offense categories. The implication that father-absent homes may produce delinquent daughters must be weighed against evidence that in some instances young females fare better in single-parent homes on variables such as achievement. However, there is clear evidence that proportionately more female than male delinquents come from single-parent homes.

In an effort to add to the available literature about the effect of father absence on adolescent daughters, Malouf (1979) compared successful single-mother families with successful two-parent families. She found that 14- to 17-year-old daughters of single mothers were more coercive in terms of demands than daughters of married mothers, sons of single mothers, or sons of either married parent. These findings about nondelinquent girls suggest the importance of the father–daughter relationship.[1] At the same time, it is unclear whether father absence causes delinquency and how lasting its effects are (Blechman, 1982; Heatherington, 1972). Nevertheless, the differential impact of family process and structure on adolescent females must be considered in behavioral interventions.

---

[1] *Editor's note.* These data also support another conclusion—that socialization by a single mother encourages active, assertive, achievement-oriented behavior in girls, while socialization in the father-dominant two-parent family has a similar effect on boys.

CONTRIBUTIONS OF PUBERTY TO FEMALE DELINQUENCY

Behavioral treatment programs must also consider sex differences when treating adolescents as opposed to younger children. It has long been hypothesized that adolescence is more difficult for females while childhood is more difficult for males. Social norms restrict young girls less than young boys (Locksley & Douvan, 1979). These more lenient standards of socialization for girls have been termed bisexual socialization (Bardwick, 1971). The result can be a higher prevalence of behavior problems in young boys who are expected to be independent, aggressive, and yet self-controlled. Not until puberty is female behavior restricted by narrow sex-role expectations. Task achievement, at which girls excel during grade school, becomes less important to the adolescent girl than affiliation because she sees marriage as her best chance for economic and social success. (In Chapter 14 of this volume, Fodor & Thal explain adolescent and adult women's unhealthy preoccupations with weight in just these terms.) During childhood most mental health referrals are males, from adolescence and through adulthood most referrals are females (Locksley & Douvan, 1979). Female adolescents have traditionally expressed their symptoms via depression, anxiety, eating disorders, and abuse of legitimate drugs. Delinquency may simply be a new way of expressing old problems of emancipation and autonomy.

TREATMENT APPROACHES

Behaviorally oriented treatment programs have typically approached delinquency as a combination of deficiencies in individual response repertoires, peer relationships, parenting skills, communication and negotiation skills, and family relationships. To remedy these deficiencies, behavioral programs have treated the delinquent: (1) directly with behavior modification principles (Shostock, 1977); (2) in the context of peer relationships (Schwitzgebel, 1964); (3) in the natural environment through the agency of parents and teachers (Tharp & Wetzel, 1969) who learn behavior management strategies and techniques (Patterson & Reid, 1973); (5) by training parent–child dyads and whole families in communication, contracting, and problem-solving skills (Blechman, 1977, 1980b; Blechman & Olson, 1976; Robin, 1980; Robin, Kent, O'Leary, Foster, & Prinz, 1977; Stuart & Lott, 1972); (6) by using a range of therapeutic and behaviorally oriented educational techniques to modify family relationship patterns (Alexander & Barton, 1980; Alexander & Parsons, 1982; Barton & Alexander, 1980; Shostak, 1977); and (7) by instituting behavior change programs in alternative living environments such as group homes and institutions (Kirigin, Braukmann, Atwater, & Wolf, 1982; Ross & McKay, 1976).

Not all these programs will be reviewed. Instead, the chapter will focus on programs that have received wide dissemination and systematic evaluation, and that have taken into account issues raised earlier: the unique nature of female delinquency, family and peer (same- and opposite-sex) relationships, perceptions of available opportunities and resources, and the emancipation process. Behavioral treatment approaches to female delinquency must take all these issues into account to understand individual delinquents and to individualize treatment plans. For example, methods of parental control that are effective and appropriate for young children are often ineffective and inappropriate for emancipating teenagers. This is a major reason why contingency *management* is often used with younger children, whereas contingency *contracting* is more frequently used with adolescents (Blechman, 1977; Lutzker, 1980). Emancipation is a biologically and socially mandated process, which intervention programs should not reverse or terminate. Nevertheless, delinquent manifestations of emancipation can and should be modified. The following programs have formally attempted to do so.

TRAINING IN COMMUNICATION AND FAMILY PROBLEM SOLVING

Stuart's (1971) classic work demonstrated the promise of behavioral contracting with families of delinquents. Subsequent careful research, however, led Stuart and Lott (1972) to conclude that establishment of a contract, or of the elements of a contract per se, is not sufficient for successful intervention. Instead, they suggest families are helped most by learning the *process* of contract negotiation and group problem solving. Two programs that target such processes are family problem solving and problem solving–communication training. These behaviorally oriented family treatment programs are designed for use by both one- and two-parent families with in-home problems of children and youth.

In family problem-solving training (Blechman, 1980b) family members interact as they play the family contract game (Blechman & Olson, 1976) to write agreements and practice effective problem solving. The game uses clear, specific step-by-step directions for interpersonal problem solving to guide the family as they identify displeasing behavior, then choose, monitor, and reward desired alternative behaviors (Blechman, Kotanchik, & Taylor, 1981; Blechman, Taylor, & Schrader, 1981). Therapists do not participate during family problem solving, but do introduce and monitor the procedures. After problem-solving strategies are learned in the context of the game, and contracts are carried out with therapist supervision, the same strategies can be used (with or without the game's structure) to resolve serious complaints at home after treatment ends.

Family problem solving differs from many of the parent training programs utilized with younger children because it legitimizes the youth's influence strategies as well as those of the parent. During successful emancipation, parents function as effective, but democratic leaders (Blechman, 1980b), who enhance teenagers' ability to influence their social environment. Helping teenagers establish symmetrical influence strategies through approaches such as family problem solving not only resolves specific problems at home, but also increases the likelihood of appropriate, effective adult–peer interaction away from home (Morton, Alexander, & Altman, 1976).

Problem solving–communication training (Robin, 1980; Robin, Kent, O'Leary, Foster, & Prinz, 1977) is based on similar assumptions. Families experiencing parent–adolescent conflict are seen by therapists who employ modeling, behavior rehearsal, and feedback techniques to teach problem solving and communication skills. Families are helped to resolve issues they have generated, and for homework they practice negotiating solutions using their new problem-solving and communication skills.

Steps in problem solving–communication training include: (1) defining the problem in nonaccusatory terms; (2) brainstorming alternative solutions; (3) evaluating the benefits and costs of each solution, resulting in a negotiated agreement; and (4) planning to implement the solution. As they learn these procedures, families replace negative communication styles (e.g., verbal hostility, inattention, overgeneralization) with positive communication skills (e.g., active listening, I-messages). Preliminary data from a study that randomly assigned subjects to conditions suggest the clear superiority of problem solving–communication training over waiting-list controls, and the possible superiority of problem solving–communication training over other forms of family therapy on some process and outcome measures, including parent satisfaction (Robin, 1980).

BEHAVIOR CHANGE PROGRAMS IN ALTERNATIVE TREATMENT SETTINGS

Achievement Place is a community-based residential program for delin-quents, which provides (1) skill training; (2) a token economy reinforce-ment system; (3) student government; and (4) relationship building. Drawing on both association and social learning theory, these homes aim for a family-like environment run by teaching-parents who are skilled in behavior modification (Kirigin *et al.*, 1982; Minkin, Braukmann, Minkin, Timbers, Timbers, Fixsen, Phillips, & Wolf, 1976; Minkin, Minkin, Goldstein, Braukmann, Kirigin, & Wolf, 1982).

A recent evaluation of the teaching-family model emphasizes dif-ferential treatment of male and female populations (Kirigin *et al.*, 1982). In both male and female delinquent populations the number of youth involved in offenses during treatment was significantly lower than that of similar residents of non-teaching-family comparison programs. While boys entered the Achievement Place and comparison programs with similar pretreatment offense rates, females sent to Achievement homes had slightly higher offense rates than those sent to non-teaching-family homes. This suggests a preference by judges and court personnel for the Achievement Place model. Although they entered with higher of-fense rates than females in comparison homes, at Achievement Place females were involved in fewer offenses during treatment. Unfortu-nately, boys' and girls' posttreatment offense rates were no different in Achievement Place than they were in the comparison residential pop-ulations.

Within Achievement Place residences, girls' offense rates were con-siderably lower than those of boys, although patterns of offenses were similar for female and male delinquents. The *Supplement to the Handbook for Teaching Parents in Girls' Homes* describes a typical resident of a girls' home as a status offender in placement because of running away from home (Schumaker, 1980). The manual emphasizes reintegrating the girl into her family, and implies that the family is more important for the female offender than for the male offender.

Girls enter Achievement Place homes more skilled than boys in four areas: social skills, academic skills, self-care skills, and household main-tenance skills, making it more difficult to pinpoint deficit skill areas for females (Schumaker, 1980). In spite of these apparent assets, the pro-gram aims for improved conversational and interpersonal skills, dating behavior, and sexual reputations (Minkin et al., 1976, 1982; Schumaker, 1980). To the authors' credit, small sections of the manual discuss the need for nontraditional female role models. The manual's traditional sex-role orientation may reflect the personal values of program developers, gender differences in the base rates of problem behaviors, or the demands of the communities to which delinquent girls must return.

Ross and McKay (1976) compared four methods of improving postresidential adjustment: (1) a token economy system; (2) behavior modification with rewards contingent only on prosocial behavior; (3) token economy system plus a peer therapy program in which girls were trained to reward peers' prosocial behavior; and (4) peer therapy alone. Peer therapy alone produced the best institutional, and postinstitutional adjustment. Note that peer therapy influenced cognitions as well as behavior, since it relabeled the female residents as competent at eliciting prosocial behavior from their peers. Such attribution of positive characteristics through labeling has been shown to be effective in eliciting and maintaining prosocial behavior (Miller, Brickman, & Bolen, 1975).

MODIFYING FAMILY RELATIONSHIP PATTERNS

The cognitive–behavioral technique of positive relabeling used by Ross and McKay (1976) represents a deviation from traditional behavior modification principles which aim to change overt behavior. Functional Family Therapy is a major program which has used this technique extensively with delinquent families and has demonstrated considerable and replicated success with male and female delinquents (Alexander & Parsons, 1982). A study with rigorous methodological controls demonstrated that 1 year after treatment, male and female status offenders in the Functional Family Therapy condition reduced their recidivism rates from one half to one third below the rate of randomly assigned no treatment and alternative treatment controls (Alexander & Parsons, 1973). These results have been replicated (Alexander, Barton, Schiavo, & Parsons, 1976) and the model has been extended to hard-core delinquents. With this older and more criminally active population (averaging over 20 prior offenses leading to arrest), recidivism rates 16 months after treatment were 33% lower in the Functional Family Therapy group than in alternative treatments (Technical Report to the Utah State Division of Youth Corrections, 1981).

The focus on family attributional sets as a precursor to communication training, sets the Functional Family model apart from traditional behavior modification approaches, as do the following assumptions:

1. Behavior change technologies do not account for most of the variance in positive therapeutic change.

2. Therapist characteristics, including gender, powerfully influence intervention process and outcome (Alexander, Barton, Schiavo, & Parsons, 1976; Warburton, Alexander, & Barton, 1980).

3. Delinquent behavior must be assessed and modified in terms of the interpersonal relationships it maintains.

4. The behavior change technologies must be tailored to "fit" individual relationship functions (Alexander & Parsons, 1982; Barton & Alexander, 1980).

5. Relationship functions are defined and maintained by phenomenological, affective, and attributional processes as well as by overt response patterns (Barton & Alexander, 1979).

The Functional Family model did not emphasize these differences from traditional behavioral intervention at the outset. Instead, it began as a skills-training approach which emphasized communication, negotiating and contracting, and problem solving (Parsons & Alexander, 1973), because of evidence that skills deficiences (Alexander, 1973; Parsons & Alexander, 1973) contributed to delinquency. Other research (Stuart, 1971) had suggested that this type of skills training could significantly reduce delinquent behavior. Clinical experience soon demonstrated that despite common, problematic communication styles, delinquent families differ markedly from one another, in: (1) gender (i.e., male and female delinquents); (2) race and ethnicity; (3) value systems (i.e., conservative and/or religious vs. liberal and/or nonreligious); (4) structure (i.e., patriarchal vs. matriarchal vs. egalitarian); and (5) integration (i.e., highly interdependent—enmeshed, in Minuchin's [1974] terms—vs. fragmented or disengaged). Because of such differences, reactions to a uniform skills training approach varied widely. These reactions included enthusiasm ("This is the first time we've been able to talk together in years.") and extreme resistance ("What the hell is this? I'm not going to bribe her. As long as she's in this house—which, believe me, may not be long—she's gonna obey the rules!"). These varied family characteristics and reactions force therapists to make technical decisions which unavoidably involve values and life-styles. For example, when a delinquent female creates distance and independence in her relationships with conservative parents by adopting a nontraditional female role, should we attempt to change the daughter so she becomes more dependent and traditional, or should we attempt to change the parent(s) so they can facilitate female autonomy? Both goals are technically difficult to achieve, since people generally resist fundamental changes in value systems. Further, such goals encourage therapists to impose their values on clients in an ethically questionable and potentially damaging process.

The interaction process goals of Functional Family Therapy are to:

> 1. Identify the value systems, interpersonal functions, and behavioral manifestations of all members in delinquent families or other natural living systems.
> 2. Apply motivational and attributional techniques that will help *all* members of those systems to be willing to change.
> 3. Apply behavioral technologies, such as communication and problem-solving training, that will help all members change their behavioral styles, but will at the same time allow them to retrain preferred value systems and interpersonal functions.

In doing so, therapists also consider intrafamilial and extrafamilial variables that will enhance generalization and maintenance of these changes. In the Functional Family model these goals are met in the Assessment, Therapy, and Education phases, respectively. Assessment and Therapy phases begin simultaneously at the first point of contact between the family and the therapist. The Education phase begins after the successful initiation of Assessment and Therapy. Assessment of all family members identifies critical overt behavioral sequences and phenomenologically defined affective and cognitive reactions. Functions and values are derived from what people do, how they feel, and how they explain their own and others' motivations (Barton & Alexander, 1979). In the Therapy phase, attributional and motivational changes are primarily accomplished through relabeling and relationship focus techniques (Alexander & Parsons, 1982). Using these techniques, therapists focus on the impact of behavior sequences on relationships rather than on behavior change. Relationship focus and relabeling provide positive, benign, and nonblaming messages that all members of the system are victims, and none are at fault. When, and only when, each family member has adopted a new and positive attributional set, educational change techniques are presented, modeled, prompted, and shaped by therapists. Educational techniques fall into three classes: (1) communication skills (e.g., concreteness, providing alternatives, source responsibility; see Alexander, 1973); (2) technical aids (e.g., charts, message centers, home–school feedback system, scripts; see Alexander & Parsons, 1982); and (3) interpersonal tasks (e.g., home practice, allowing transition times, and competency builders; see Alexander & Parsons, 1982). The selection of educational techniques which fit the interpersonal functions of behavior (Barton & Alexander, 1980) produces new, specific behavioral sequences consistent with the individual family's unique pattern of values and interpersonal functions, while it imparts general problem-solving and communication patterns useful to all families (Parsons & Alexander, 1973).

The general and specific process goals of Functional Family Therapy are consistent with our review of theories and data about delinquency. The interaction process goals provide adaptive ways for families of all adolescents to successfully engage in and resolve the ubiquitous crisis of emancipation.

SOCIAL AND POLITICAL IMPLICATIONS OF INTERVENTION WITH FEMALE DELINQUENTS

Biased therapeutic judgment (Broverman, Broverman, Clarkson, Rosenkrantz, & Vogel, 1970; Warburton *et al.*, 1980), unclarified client and therapist values, the interplay of client, therapist, employer, and teacher status characteristics, all affect treatment outcome. If these influential variables are ignored, well-designed behavioral strategies will be undermined. We are reminded of a young woman at the Youth Development Center outside Salt Lake City, Utah, who had a long string of status offenses. Upon leaving the institution she was referred to a program for young female offenders with a nontraditional job skills component. After one day there, she refused further involvement. Her reason: "They have decided what I'll be. I have always wanted to grow up to wear tight skirts in an office and wiggle my ass, and *they* want me to be a carpenter." Since we had made the referral we had to look at our own reason for wanting to transform this bright young woman into a nontraditional female against her will. She did not see her delinquent behavior as rebellion against culturally imposed sex roles. She wanted a legitimate but traditional job.

VALUE CLARIFICATION

Clinicians must avoid the temptation to set a priori treatment outcomes which ignore individual differences among women. This advice does not preclude consciousness raising during treatment. Traditionalism is at its height during adolescence, particularly among female delinquents; yet it is during adolescence that life-shaping decisions about work and family life are made. It is the duty of the therapist to convey facts about adult life in a compelling manner. Information about the different salaries of a secretary and a heavy-machine operator, statistics about women in the work force, and data on the increase of impoverished, single-parent households, increase the probability that the female delinquent will make thoughtful decisions about her future. Exposure to competent adult women broadens the female delinquent's vision of her own future. At the same time, the therapist must beware of confusing the political issue of female emancipation with the developmental phase of adolescent emancipation. Client values and the functions of the delinquent behavior should be the primary determinants of therapeutic process.

The era of unquestioned traditionalism, when improved functioning with home and family was the only goal for female clients, has passed. Even so, a job is not the solution for every contemporary female client. As therapists we must clarify client goals, and make a conscious decision as to whether we will comply with clients' stated objectives. The expectation that therapists remain value free has proven unrealistic; their examination of their own personal values is essential.

TREATMENT GOALS

The increase in female crime is seen by some writers as a necessary evil (Adler, 1975; Adler & Simon, 1979; Miller, 1980), a minor, undesirable side effect of social emancipation of women. Even if this assumption is correct, it provides no practical direction for the therapist. Information about the distinctive behavior of nondelinquent peers of delinquent girls would provide a fund of practical guidance for therapists, since it would suggest appropriate treatment goals. Skills training has been suggested as the behavior technology of choice for the treatment of women when necessary environmental change is impossible (Blechman, 1980a). Criteria for the construction of skills training repertoires have yet to be clearly defined. As Blechman pointed out, since skills training should result in demonstrable competence in specific areas of deficiency, the therapist must know what it is the client lacks. Thus we need to know how delinquent females differ from nondelinquent females. Selection of a nondeviant criterion sample of adolescent females is difficult. Since females referred to therapists and school counselors may show role-deviant behavior, a nonreferred, criterion sample may be biased in the direction of traditional behavior. It is our contention that the criterion sample of nondelinquent teens must include young women with non-traditional values.

MATCHING-TO-SAMPLE OF TREATMENT GOALS

In our opinion, the increase in female delinquency does seem to have occurred in response to the political climate of the 1960s, most likely through the filtering down process outlined by James and Thornton (1980). They attribute the increase to more lenient parental control over adolescent females and to increasing peer support for delinquency rather than to the liberated sex-role attitudes of adolescent females. Female delinquents pass through the developmental stage of emancipation in a deviant manner; only some of them experience sex-role strain. The choice of intervention strategies should be based on information about females exposed to both social and developmental change. A matching-to-sample strategy could then be used to select treatment and outcome criteria, from the repertoires of the nondeviant sample (Parsons & Alexander, 1973).

Use of the matching-to-sample strategy in family therapy has been criticized as perpetuating traditional female roles (Gurman & Klein, 1980, Chapter 7, this volume; Hines & Hare-Mustin, 1978). This criticism shows misunderstanding of the matching-to-sample concept. Alexander and Parsons (1973) used a matching-to-sample approach to narrow the gap between families of delinquent and normal teenagers in clarity and precision, reciprocity, and generation of alternative solutions during family discussions. The dependent measures used in the Alexander and Parsons' study were value-free interpersonal process variables, such as talk time, number of interruptions, and defensiveness/supportiveness ratios. Treatment aimed to move the family toward the symmetry characteristic of healthier families rather than toward complementarity and traditional role distribution (Watzlawick, Beavin, & Jackson, 1967). Alexander and Parsons found that treatment produced: (1) more equality of talk time among family members; (2) more family activity; and (3) more interruptions. Mischler and Waxler (1968) found that high rates of interruption were characteristic of normal families. Thus, use of a matching-to-sample strategy did not produce the hierarchical authority structure that Schuham (1970) idealized.

Behavioral parent training approaches may produce hierarchical power structures, but not because of the matching-to-sample strategy. Given the centrality of emancipation to healthy adolescent development, perhaps delinquent teens, male and female, should be helped to be more assertive and to engage in more symmetrical relationships with authority figures, particularly parents. The effects of treatments which aim to enhance emancipation need to be tested. At the same time, assumptions about the process of emancipation can be tested in studies which contrast female delinquent with nondelinquent family and peer interaction patterns. Gaffney and McFall (1981) recently reported that responses to the Problem Inventory for Adolescent Girls significantly discriminated between delinquent and nondelinquent girls, and that delinquency is related more to skills deficits in interaction with adult authority figures than to skills deficits with peers. These findings, which highlight the adolescent female's emancipation struggle, illustrate the utility of measures of process in the study of female delinquency.

CONCLUSIONS AND RECOMMENDATIONS

Adolescence is a period of traumatic change and a time when delinquent behavior may occur. For male and female delinquents deviant behavior may be a response to the emancipation process. The recent upsurge in female delinquency warrants a closer look at what precipitates and maintains this deviancy. Biology, peer relationships, and opportunity all play their part. Emancipation from family of origin and the interpersonal processes necessary to achieve autonomy point to behavioral explanations for problematic behavior.

In order to develop treatment programs appropriate for delinquent females, therapists must understand how female deviancy differs from male deviancy. Programs developed exclusively for male delinquents must be reevaluated when applied to females. A first step in setting treatment goals for the female delinquent is to determine what interactional process measures distinguish female delinquents from nondelinquents.

In the meantime therapists treating adolescent females must view female delinquency within the context of family, peers, and community. For females, delinquency occurs primarily during the early adolescent years when females face emancipation from family of origin and move toward careers and families of their own. In approaching treatment, therapists must:

1. Review each family member and identify critical behavioral, affective, and cognitive reactions within the family system. Identify unclear relationships and hypothesize potential payoffs for the maintenance of the behavior of each family member.

2. Develop intermediate and long-range goals that will maintain family functions (e.g., emancipation) but change the family patterns that produce dysfunctional delinquent behavior.

3. Review and develop specific educational techniques that will produce intermediate and long-term goals. Assertiveness training and negotiation skills may replace running away from home. Attention must be paid to parental payoffs which might sabotage the adolescent's new skills.

4. Assist the female delinquent in coping with new peer, school, and vocational systems. Values clarification may be an important component of this phase for the delinquent female client.

5. Delay termination until spontaneous problem solving and cessation of problematic behavior occur. Be certain that new interaction styles benefit all family members, as well as significant others outside the family system.

REFERENCES

Adler, F. *Sisters in crime: The rise of the new female criminal.* New York: McGraw-Hill, 1975.

Adler, F., & Simon, R. J. *The criminology of deviant women.* Boston: Houghton Mifflin, 1979.

Alexander, J. F. Defensive and supportive communication in normal and deviant families. *Journal of Consulting and Clinical Psychology,* 1973, *40,* 223–231.

Alexander, J. F., & Barton, C. Systems–behavioral intervention with delinquent families. In J. Vincent (Ed.), *Advances in family intervention: Assessment and theory.* Greenwich, Conn.: JAI, 1980.

Alexander, J. F., Barton, C., Shiavo, R. S., & Parsons, B. V. Behavioral intervention with families of delinquents: Therapist characteristics, family behavior, and outcome. *Journal of Consulting and Clinical Psychology,* 1976, *44* (4), 656–664.

Alexander, J. F., & Parsons, B. V. Short-term behavioral intervention with delinquent families: Impact on family process and recidivism. *Journal of Abnormal Psychology,* 1973, *51,* 219–233.

Alexander, J. F., & Parsons, B. V. *Functional family therapy: Principles and procedures.* Monterey, Calif.: Brooks/Cole, 1982.

Altman, M. G. Group involvement in delinquent acts—A study of offense types and male–female participation. *Criminal Justice and Behavior,* 1980, *7* (2), 85–192.

Andrew, J. M. Delinquency, sex, and family variables. *Social Biology,* 1976, *23,* 168–171.

Balkan, S., & Berger, L. The changing nature of female delinquency. In C. B. Kapp & M. Kirkpatrick (Eds.), *Becoming female: Perspectives on development.* New York: Plenum, 1979.

Bardwick, J. *The psychology of women: A study of bio-cultural conflict.* New York: Harper & Row, 1971.

Barton, C., & Alexander, J. F. *Delinquent and normal family interaction in competitive and cooperative conditions.* Paper presented at the American Psychological Association meeting, New York, 1979.

Beeman, E. A. The effect of male hormones on aggressive behavior in mice. *Physiological Zoology,* 1947, *20,* 373–405.

Bernard, J. *The female world.* New York: Free Press, 1981.

Blechman, E. Behavior therapies. In A. M. Brodsky & R. T. Hare-Mustin (Ed.), *Women and psychotherapy: An assessment of research and practice.* New York: Guilford, 1980. (a)

Blechman, E. A. Family problem-solving training. *American Journal of Family Therapy,* 1980, *8,* 3–22. (b)

Blechman, E. A. Are children with one parent at psychological risk: A methodological review. *Journal of Marriage and the Family,* 1982, *44,* 179–195.

Blechman, E. A., Kotanchik, N., & Taylor, C. J. Families and schools together: Early behavioral intervention with high-risk students. *Behavior Therapy,* 1981, *12,* 308–319.

Blechman, E. A., & Olson, D. H. L. The family contract game: Description and effectiveness. In D. H. L. Olson (Ed.), *Treating relationships.* Lake Mills, Iowa: Graphic, 1976.

Blechman, E. A., Taylor, C. J., & Schrader, S. M. Family problem solving vs. home notes as early intervention with high-risk children. *Journal of Consulting and Clinical Psychology,* 1981, *49,* 919–926.

Block, J. Issues, problems, and pitfalls in assessing sex differences: A critical review of the psychology of sex differences. *Merrill–Palmer Quarterly,* 1976, *22,* 283–309.

Bowker, L. H. The incidence of female crime and delinquency: A comparison of official and self-report statistics. *International Journal of Women's Studies,* 1978, *1* (2), 178–192.

Bowker, L. H., Gross, H. S., & Klein, M. W. Female participation in delinquent activities. *Adolescence,* 1980, *15,* 509–519.

Brodsky, A. M. (Ed.). *The female offender.* Beverly Hills, Calif.: Sage, 1975.

Broverman, I. K., Broverman, D. M., Clarkson, F. E., Rosenkrantz, P. S., & Vogel, S. Sex role stereotypes and clinical judgments of mental health. *Journal of Consulting and Clinical Psychology,* 1970, *34,* 1–7.

Campbell, A. What makes a girl turn to crime? *New Society,* 1977, *39,* 172–73.

Cernkovich, S. A., & Giordano, P. C. A comparative analysis of male and female delinquency. *Sociological Quarterly,* 1979, *20* (1), 131–145.(a)

Cernkovich, S. A., & Giordano, P. C. Criminology: Delinquency, opportunity, and gender. *Journal of Criminal Law and Criminology,* 1979, *70* (2), 145–151. (b)

Cloward, R. A., & Ohlin, L. E. *Delinquency and opportunity.* Glencoe, Ill.: Free Press, 1960.

Cohen, A. K. *Delinquent boys: The culture of the gang.* Glencoe, Ill.: Free Press, 1955.

Cooke, W. R. The differential psychology of the American woman. *American Journal of Obstetrics and Gynecology,* 1945, *49,* 457–472.

Dalton, K. *The premenstrual syndrome.* Springfield, Ill.: Thomas, 1964.

Datesman, S. K., & Scarpetti, F. R. *Women, crime, and justice.* New York: Oxford University Press, 1980.

Duke, D. S., & Duke, P. M. The prediction of delinquency in girls. *Journal of Research and Development in Education,* 1978, *11,* 18–33.

Duke, M. P., & Fenhazen, E. Self–parental alienation and locus of control in delinquent girls. *Journal of Genetic Psychology,* 1975, *127,* 103–107.

Ellis, D., & Austin, P. Menstruation and aggressive behavior in a correctional center for women. *Journal of Criminal Law—Criminology and Police Science,* 1971, *62,* 388–395.

Frieze, I. H., Parsons, J. E., Johnson, P. B., Ruble, P. N., & Zellman, G. L. *Women and sex roles: A social psychological perspective.* New York: Norton, 1978.

Gaffney, L. R., & McFall, R. M. A comparison of social skills in delinquent and nonde-
    linquent adolescent girls using a behavioral role-playing inventory. *Journal of Con-
    sulting and Clinical Psychology*, 1981, *49*, 959–967.
Gibbons, D. C. *Delinquent behavior.* Englewood Cliffs, N.J.: Prentice-Hall, 1976.
Giordano, P. C. Girls, guys, and gangs: The changing social context of female delinquency.
    Journal of Criminal Law and Criminology, 1978, *69* (1), 126–132.
Glueck, S., & Glueck, E. *Five hundred delinquent girls.* New York: Alfred Knopf, 1934.
Gold, M. *Status forces in delinquent boys.* Ann Arbor, Mich.: Institute of Social Research,
    1963.
Golla, F. L., & Hodge, R. S. Hormone treatment of the sexual offender. *Lancet*, 1949, *1*,
    1006.
Gurman, A. S., & Klein, M. H. Marital and family conflicts. In A. M. Brodsky & R. T.
    Hare-Mustin (Ed.), *Women and psychotherapy: An assessment of research and practice.*
    New York: Guilford, 1980.
Hawke, C. C. Castration of mentally deficient male offenders. *American Journal of Mental
    Deficiency*, 1950, *55*, 220.
Heatherington, E. M. Effects of father absence on personality development in adolescent
    daughters. *Developmental Psychology*, 1972, *7*, 313–326.
Hindelang, M. J., & McDermott, M. J. *Juvenile criminal behavior: An analysis of rates and
    victim characteristics.* U. S. Department of Justice, Criminal Justice Research Center,
    New York, 1981.
Hines, P., & Hare-Mustin, R. T. Ethical concerns in family therapy. *Professional Psychology*,
    1978, *9*, 165–171.
Ivey, M. E., & Bardwick, J. M. Patterns of affective fluctuation in the menstrual cycle.
    Psychosomatic Medicine, 1968, *30*, 336–345.
James, J., & Thorton, W. Women's liberation and the female delinquent. *Journal of Research
    in Crime and Delinquency*, *17* (2), 1980, 230–244.
Kirigin, K. A., Braukmann, C. J., Atwater, J., & Wolf, M. M. An evaluation of teaching-
    family (Achievement Place) group homes for juvenile offenders. *Journal of Applied
    Behavior Analysis*, 1982, *15*, 1–16.
Konopka, G. *The adolescent girl in conflict.* Englewood Cliffs, N.J.: Prentice-Hall, 1966.
Locksley, A., & Douvan, E. Problem behavior in adolescents. In E. S. Gomberg & V.
    Franks (Eds.), *Gender and disordered behavior: Sex differences in psychopathology.* New
    York: Brunner/Mazel, 1979.
Lombroso, C., & Ferrero, W. *The female offender.* New York: D. Appleton, 1895.
Loving, N., & Olson, F. (Eds.). *Proceedings of the National Conference on Women and Crime.*
    National League of Cities, U.S. Conference of Mayors. Washington, D.C.: U.S.
    Government Printing Office, 1976.
Lutzker, J. R. Deviant family systems. In B. B. Lahey & A. E. Kazdin (Eds.), *Advances in
    clinical child psychology* (Vol. 3). New York: Plenum, 1980.
Maccoby, E. E., & Jacklin, C. N. (Eds.). *Psychology of sex differences.* Palo Alto, Calif.:
    Stanford University Press, 1974.
Malouf, R. E. *Social bases of power and two-parent families.* Unpublished doctoral dissertation,
    University of Utah, 1979.
Miller, P. Y. Female delinquency: Fact and fiction. In M. Sugar (Ed.), *Female adolescent
    development.* New York: Brunner/Mazel, 1979.
Miller, R. L., Brickman, P., & Bolen, D. Attribution versus persuasion as a means for
    modifying behavior. *Journal of Personality and Social Psychology*, 1975, *31*, 430–441.
Minkin, N., Braukmann, C., Minkin, B., Timbers, G., Timbers, B., Fixsen, D., Phillips,
    E., & Wolf, M. The social validation and training of conversational skills. *Journal
    of Applied Behavior Analysis*, 1976, *9*, 127–139.
Minkin, N., Minkin, B. L., Goldstein, R. S., Braukmann, C. J., Kirigin, K. A., & Wolf, M.

M. Analysis, validation, and training of peer-criticism skills with delinquent girls. In W. Upper & S. M. Ross (Eds.), *Behavioral group therapy*. Champaign, Ill.: Research, 1982.

Minuchin, S. *Families and family therapy*. Cambridge, Mass.: Harvard University Press, 1974.

Mischler, E., & Waxler, N. *Interaction in families*. New York: Wiley, 1968.

Morton, J. H., Addison, H., Addison, R. G., Hunt, L., & Sullivan, J. J. A clinical study of premenstrual tension. *American Journal of Obstetrics and Gynecology*, 1953, *65*, 1182–1191.

Morton, T. L., Alexander, J. F., & Altman, I. Communication and relationship definition. In G. R. Miller (Ed.), *Annual review of communication research* (Vol. V: *Interpersonal communication*). Beverly Hills, Calif.: Sage, 1976.

Moyer, K. E. Sex differences in aggression. In R. C. Friedman, R. M. Richart, & R. L. Vande Wiele (Eds.), *Sex differences in behavior*. New York: Wiley, 1974.

Offord, D. R., Abrams, N., Allen, N., & Poushinsky, M. Broken homes, parental psychiatric illness, and female delinquency. *American Journal of Orthopsychiatry*, 1979, *49* (2), 252–264.

Parlee, M. B. The premenstrual syndrome. *Psychological Bulletin*, 1973, *80*, 454–465.

Parsons, B. V., & Alexander, J. F. Short-term family intervention: A therapy outcome study. *Journal of Consulting and Clinical Psychology*, 1973, *41*, 195–201.

Patterson, G. R., & Reid, J. B. Intervention for families of aggressive boys: A replication study. *Behaviour Research and Therapy*, 1973, *11*, 383–394.

Pederson, F. A., & Bell, R. Q. Sex differences in preschool children without histories of complications of pregnancy and delivery. *Developmental Psychology*, 1970, *3*, 10–15.

Pollak, O. *The criminality of women*. New York: Barnes, 1950.

Robin, A. L. Parent–adolescent conflict: A skill training approach. In D. P. Rathjen & J. P. Foreyt (Ed.), *Social competence: Interventions for children and adults*. New York: Pergamon, 1980.

Robin, A. L., Kent, R. N., & O'Leary, K. D., Foster, S., & Prinz, R. J. An approach to teaching parents and adolescents problem-solving communication skills: A preliminary report. *Behavior Therapy*, 1977, *8*, 639–643.

Rodman, H., & Grams, P. Juvenile delinquency and the family: A review and discussion. In *Task Force report: Juvenile delinquency and youth crime*. Washington, D.C.: U.S. Government Printing Office, 1967.

Ross, R. A., & McKay, H. B. A study of institutional treatment programs. *International Journal of Offender Therapy and Comparative Criminology*, 1976, *20*, 165–173.

Sarri, R. Crime and the female offender. In E. S. Gomberg & V. Franks (Eds.), *Gender and disordered behavior*. New York: Brunner/Mazel, 1979.

Schuham, A. I. Power relations in emotionally disturbed and normal family triads. *Journal of Abnormal Psychology*, 1970, *75*, 30–37.

Schumaker, J. B. *Supplement to the handbook for teaching parents in girls' homes*. Lawrence, Kans.: Achievement Place, 1980.

Schwitzgebel, R. *Street corner research: An experiential approach to the juvenile delinquent*. Cambridge, Mass.: Harvard University Press, 1964.

Serbin, L. A., O'Leary, K. D., Kent, R. N., & Tonik, I. J. A comparison of teacher response to the pre-academic and problem behavior of boys and girls. *Child Development*, 1973, *44*, 796–804.

Shah, S. A., & Roth, L. H. Biological and psychophysiological factors in criminality. In D. Glaser (Ed.), *Handbook of criminology*. Chicago: Rand McNally, 1975.

Shostak, D. A. *Family versus individual oriented behavior therapy as treatment approaches to juvenile delinquency*. Unpublished doctoral dissertation, University of Virginia, 1977.

Simon, R. J. *The contemporary woman and crime*. Washington, D.C.: U.S. Government Printing Office, 1975.

Simons, R. L., Miller, M. G., & Aigner, S. M. Contemporary theories of deviance and female delinquency. *Journal of Research on Crime*, 1980, *17* (1), 42–57.

Smart, C. *Women, crime, and criminology: A feminist critique*. London: Routledge & Kegan Paul, 1977.

Stuart, R. B. Behavioral contracting within the families of delinquents. *Journal of Behavior Therapy and Experimental Psychiatry*, 1971, *2*, 1–11.

Stuart, R. B. & Lott, L. A., Jr. Behavioral contracting with delinquents: A cautionary note. *Journal of Behavior Therapy and Experimental Psychiatry*, 1972, *3*, 161–169.

Sutherland, E. H., & Cressey, D. R. *Criminology* (10th ed.). Philadelphia: Lippincott, 1978.

Technical report to the Utah state division of youth corrections. Salt Lake City: Western States Family Institute, 1981.

Tharp, R. G., & Wetzel, R. J. *Behavior modification in the natural environment*. New York: Academic, 1969.

United States Department of Justice. *Crime in the United States, 1960–1973 (Uniform Crime Reports*, Federal Bureau of Investigation). Washington, D.C.: U.S. Government Printing Office, 1980.

Wahler, R. G. Oppositional children: A guest for parental reinforcement control. *Journal of Applied Behavior Analysis*, 1969, *2*, 159–170.

Warburton, J. R., Alexander, J. F., & Barton, C. *Sex of client/sex of therapist: Variables in a family process study*. Paper presented at the American Psychological Association Meeting, Montreal, 1980.

Watzlawick, F., Beavin, J. H., & Jackson, D. D. *Pragmatics of human communication*. New York: Norton, 1967.

16

WOMEN AND ALCOHOLISM

BARBARA S. MCCRADY

OVERVIEW

This chapter considers behavioral treatment of women who experience problems as a consequence of their use of alcohol. The objective of the chapter is to stimulate others to consider directions which the behaviorally oriented clinician or clinical researcher could take in treating and studying the treatment of women with alcohol abuse problems. Women who experience problems from the use of other drugs are a secondary concern of the chapter. The discussion focuses on *treatment* issues, and does not address the process of alcoholism or drinking behavior in women. Furthermore, the emphasis is on treatment for individual women with drinking problems, rather than on the meaning of patient roles for women, the contributions of societal attitudes and socialization experience to the development of behavior problems, or methods of social change. While these issues are extremely important they are addressed in introductory chapters to this book. Following a general discussion of substance abuse problems in women, the remainder of the chapter focuses on five areas: (1) ways in which behavioral research can contribute to the identification of drinking problems in women; (2) strategies to help women remain in behavioral alcoholism treatment; (3) behavioral assessment of women's drinking problems; (4) directions for behavioral interventions with women; and (5) issues in outcome evaluation which are unique to women. Most of the comments and suggested clinical interventions are the author's current ideas about women and substance abuse, and must be subjected to rigorous scientific evaluation.

Barbara S. McCrady. Brown University/Butler Hospital, Providence, Rhode Island.

BACKGROUND

In the last 5 years, there has been an increasing interest in women with drinking problems. Research, treatment, and prevention programs for women are a high priority of the National Institute on Alcohol Abuse and Alcoholism (NIAAA). A professional workshop on alcoholism and women was recently sponsored by the NIAAA, several major review articles and books have appeared on the topic in recent years (e.g., Beckman, 1975; Gomberg, 1976; Greenblatt & Schuckit, 1976; NIAAA, 1980), and a number of new research projects have been undertaken to study prevalence, incidence, and problems associated with drinking in women.

This increased attention to substance abuse issues in women is important in light of recent epidemiological data on women substance abusers. For example, in a recent review of the epidemiological literature, Celentano, McQueen, and Chee (1980) cite several survey studies which suggest that the ratio of female to male alcohol abuse is about 1:4 or 1:5. However, in analyzing alcohol-related death figures, they noted that this ratio drops to approximately 1:2. This discrepancy may be accounted for by the fact that many female problem drinkers and alcoholics are hidden, because of negative attitudes toward female drunkenness, secret home drinking, the woman's own shame and embarrassment about her drinking, and her husband's or family's shame and desire to protect her. Coupling these findings with the NIAAA estimates of 10 million alcohol abusers and alcoholics in this country suggests that the problems of identification and treatment of women with alcohol problems are immense.

When women who use or abuse other drugs are considered, the data, while scanty, are equally troubling. Celentano and colleagues (1980) point out that most studies of drug abusers focus on adolescents, male veterans, or narcotics addicts. Such studies tend to underrepresent women because women are more often abusers of prescription drugs than street drugs. For example, approximately twice as many women as men use psychotropic drugs, and almost 70% of psychotherapeutic drug prescriptions are written for women. An estimated 1 to 2 million women have problems because of their use of prescription drugs (Nellis, Hager, Potope, & Harkins, 1978).

Despite the general increase in research and treatment programs for women problem drinkers, behavioral researchers have been deafeningly silent on the issue. This is true in spite of major advances in the behavioral alcoholism research field. Some of these advances have included: experimental wards to study drinking behavior (e.g., Mello, 1972); treatment goals other than abstinence (e.g., Sobell & Sobell, 1973); blood alcohol level discrimination studies (e.g., Nathan, 1978); alternate skills training for alcoholics (e.g., Miller, 1972); behavioral marital therapy for alcoholics (e.g., Paolino & McCrady, 1977); abstinence violation studies (e.g., Marlatt, 1978a); studies of craving (e.g., Hodgson, Rankin, & Stockwell 1978); and development of behavioral assessment techniques (e.g., Nathan & Briddell, 1977). Unfortunately, most of these advances have been accompanied by little or no consideration of women with drinking problems. The only areas of behavioral alcoholism research in which women have consistently been considered are studies of the interaction of expectancies and alcohol on behavior and emotions (e.g., Abrams & Wilson, 1979), sexual arousal studies (e.g., Wilson & Lawson, 1978), and studies of social influence and drinking (e.g., Hendricks, Sobell, & Cooper, 1978).

To more thoroughly examine the representation of women in behavioral alcoholism research, a search was made of several major journals for the years 1977 to 1979. The journals selected, including *Addictive Behaviors, Behaviour Research and Therapy, Behavior Therapy, Journal of Abnormal Psychology, Journal of Consulting and Clinical Psychology,* and *Journal of Studies on Alcohol,* are not an exhaustive list of all journals which publish behavioral alcoholism research. Journals selected are either widely read by behavioral psychologists, or represent major publication outlets for alcoholism research. Of the 56 behavioral alcoholism studies reported in these journals, 61% used only male subjects while 7% used only female subjects. Both sexes were studied in 28% of the studies; of these, only 31% analyzed the data separately by sex. In 4% of the studies, the sex of the subjects was unclear.

The behavioral drug abuse treatment field has lagged behind the alcohol abuse field in general, and in particular has done little to consider the special issues of drug-abusing women. A recent review of behaviorally oriented drug treatment studies (Götestam, Melin, & Öst, 1976) revealed that 69% of the subjects studied were male; only 31% were female. The subjects were primarily opiate abusers, with small proportions of subjects who abused amphetamines, hallucinogens, or sedatives. Several behavioral treatment approaches have been attempted with drug abusers, including aversion therapies, extinction procedures, systematic desensitization, convert conditioning, contingency contracting, broad spectrum behavior therapy, and ward programs. These studies have rarely analyzed data separately for male and female subjects, and only 8 of 52 group or single-case studies focused exclusively on women.

This search of the recent literature suggests that women are sadly underrepresented in the behavioral alcoholism and drug abuse literatures. However, women are underrepresented in the general alcoholism and drug abuse research literature, and a polemical statement that behavioral researchers also neglect women is of rather trivial import. Therefore, the remainder of the chapter will focus on an examination of directions which the behavioral field could take in the study of the treatment of women and substance abuse, with the main focus on alcohol.

IDENTIFICATION OF DRINKING PROBLEMS IN WOMEN

Behavioral alcoholism researchers have rarely addressed the difficult issue of how to identify alcohol problems. Since drinking is a problem for about 1 in 10 adult Americans, for about 25% of patients in psychiatric hospitals, and for 30–50% of patients in general medical hospitals, detection is a crucial issue. Standard diagnostic systems, such as the National Council on Alcoholism (NCA) criteria (1976) for the diagnosis of alcoholism (1972), or the third edition of the *Diagnostic and Statistical Manual of Mental Disorders* (DSM-III, 1980), use a broad range of criteria. The Michigan Alcoholism Screening Test (MAST) (Moore, 1972), and the health habits survey (Wilkins, 1974) inquire about consequences commonly associated with drinking problems, and are used to screen large populations of potential alcoholics; they have high false positive rates, but extremely low false negative rates. Both screening and diagnostic instruments rely exclusively on interviewee self-reports and on interviewer judgment, and treat alcoholism as a disease entity with a set of common recognizable symptoms.

An alternative to the disease/diagnosis model is a functional approach, which emphasizes the relationship between drinking behavior and its consequences. If negative consequences occur, then drinking may be a problem behavior. For example, alcohol use is a problem if it interferes with a woman's social or familial relationships, her job or financial status, her emotional well-being or her physical health (DSM-III, 1980). Similarly, drug use is abuse if it results in mental disturbance, impairment of social functioning, behavior dangerous to self or others, interference with personal or social development, or physical damage or disability (Balter, 1974).

Using a functional definition of substance abuse, how can behavioral clinicians increase their detection of substance abuse problems among women clients? First, behavioral clinicians should include detailed drinking and drug use histories in their routine, interview assessment of women clients, even if substance abuse is not presented as a problem area. Simple paper-and-pencil screening instruments such as the MAST and reported observations of family members are also useful steps in identification. However, clients often do not recognize the functional relationship between their substance use and the problems for which they are seeking treatment. For example, it is estimated that as many as 25% of women alcoholics also have diagnosable affective disorders (e.g., Schuckit, Pitts, Reich, King, & Winokur, 1969). Since alcohol has central nervous system depressant effects, many women experience depression as a consequence of their alcohol consumption. Not understanding this relationship, they incorrectly label their primary problem as depression. Similarly, one of the after effects of heavy drinking is central nervous system overarousal. After heavy drinking, a woman may have difficulty sleeping, be tense, anxious, or restless. As with the depressed woman alcohol abuser, the anxious woman incorrectly labels her primary problem as anxiety, rather than alcohol abuse. When a woman drinks heavily and regularly, her efficiency and productivity may decrease. She may receive poor job evaluations, or have trouble completing her household responsibilities. She may experience subtle neuropsychological deficits as a result of her drinking (e.g., Parsons, 1980), with resultant problems in memory or abstract conceptual abilities. She may be physically ill because of her drinking. She may develop problems that most clinicians recognize as alcohol related such as liver disease, peripheral neuropathies, or pancreatitis. Or, she may develop medical problems less commonly recognized by clinicians as alcohol related such as ulcers, gastritis, diabetes, or seizures.

Whenever a woman client is troubled by depression, anxiety, suicidal ideation, car accidents, certain medical problems, memory problems, problems at work, marital problems, or management problems with children (Wilkins, 1974), further assessment of her substance use patterns is essential. Assessment can include self-monitoring of drinking and drug use, and can be embedded in general health habits monitoring, with daily recording of the presenting problems, and monitoring of the woman's use of alcohol, tobacco, caffeine, licit and illicit drugs, and food. Self-monitoring as a screening procedure for alcohol problems is untested, and needs evaluation with heterogeneous samples, but it is the best procedure available to the clinician. If drinking regularly precedes high self-ratings of anxiety, then alcohol may be a cause of this anxiety. If the woman often drinks on days when she records high depression ratings, it may be that she uses alcohol to cope with depression. More serious drinking problems may develop, if the relationship between depression and drinking is ignored during treatment.

REMAINING IN TREATMENT

Barriers that may prevent women from entering alcoholism treatment (Beckman, 1978) include: prejudice against women with drinking problems, low self-esteem of women alcoholics, inadequate child care for women in treatment, lack of programs designed for women clients, and few women therapists in the alcohol field (Nellis et al., 1978). Once a woman begins treatment, there are obstacles to treatment completion. Methods which motivate male alcoholics for treatment may not help women. For example, men often are directed to treatment after being arrested for driving under the influence (DUI), or as a requirement of continued employment. Women are rarely arrested for DUI (Argeriou & Paulino, 1976), both because of the greater frequency of home drinking among many women, and because of police officers' reluctance to recognize and ticket women for DUI. Therefore, this external sanction rarely is available to help a woman stay in treatment. Occupational specialists[1] believe that when confronted about drinking by an employer, women often transfer to a similar position in another company rather than remain on the job. Thus, employers' sanctions may rarely help women seek and remain in treatment.

Even when external contingencies force a woman to stay in alcoholism treatment, the clinical appropriateness of coercion is questionable. Many women enter treatment believing that they should act in certain ways to fulfill others' expectations. This assumption may contribute to the woman's alcoholism and low self-esteem. Coerced treatment provides one more example that "I have to do what people say;

[1] Personal communication from Mary Cahill of the Planners Studio, Newton Upper Falls, Mass., who is conducting research on occupational alcoholism programming for women.

I have to please them." Thus, while the threatened contingency might keep her in treatment, the long-term impact might be countertherapeutic. Although difficult, it is advisable to help a woman develop her own treatment contract and generate her own contingencies. The contract could include attendance and homework compliance, with self-reinforcement for completion and agreed upon negative consequences for not complying with the contract. The self-generated contract could increase a woman's commitment to treatment, and reinforce reliance on her own, rather than on others' judgments.

Finally, the woman's relationship with her therapist and the degree of therapist authority affect her decision to remain in treatment. If the practitioner is authoritarian and uses power as the vehicle for change, the woman will have another experience of being in a one-down, coercive relationship. Because behavioral clinicians often act as consultants helping clients discover solutions to their problems, they are more likely to have an impact on women drinkers. The clinician who functions as a problem-solving consultant teaches the client coping skills while involving the client in treatment.

BEHAVIORAL ASSESSMENT

Four types of behavioral assessment procedures have been used to analyze drinking behavior: analogue tasks in laboratory settings, observations on experimental wards, physiological measures, and self-report measures (Nathan & Briddell, 1977). Few laboratory tasks are useful in clinical programs and there are no empirical data about their usefulness with women drinkers. For example, laboratory tasks which use an operant console to deliver alcohol as a reinforcer may not apply to women. Since women tend to drink heavily when alone but moderately in social settings, the laboratory analogue task may reveal little about actual drinking behavior. To minimize the woman's feeling that she is being observed, videotapes and automated operant consoles might be used. To encourage a woman to believe that she is obtaining alcohol surreptitiously, taste rating tasks such as those used by Marlatt and his colleagues (Marlatt, 1978b) might be used. A drink dispenser might "accidently" be unlocked, or a bottle of alcohol could be left in a partly visible spot. Such deception rauses ethical concerns which must be dealt with by careful debriefing.

Experimental drinking wards have primarily been used to study the behavior of male alcoholics. In one notable exception, Tracey and Nathan (1976) found that alcoholic women drank more like social drinking men than like alcoholic males. Women worked longer at their operant consoles than men, and spent more points to engage in activities with others. Women reported that they preferred to drink with others, even though they usually were solitary drinkers. The authors suggest that negative societal values about women drinking heavily might keep many women solitary drinkers. Since the women's drinking patterns were so different on the ward and at home, clinicians and researchers who use the experimental drinking ward must verify the representativeness of their findings.

Because analogue tasks and experimental wards have limited usefulness, *in vivo* observations, self-monitoring, the observations of significant others, and self-report questionnaires may be the most useful assessment procedures for the clinical behavior therapist. Unfortunately, self-observations and those of others are filtered through personal experiences. A woman may self-record negative self-statements, negative emotions, or poor coping responses as the immediate antecedents to drinking behavior. These might be accurate perceptions of the effective antecedents to drinking, or they might reflect her belief that her own flaws cause her problems. She might be insensitive to an oppressive, restrictive relationship, and to the absence of satisfying, self-affirming experiences. Thus, while self-monitoring of drinking behavior and thoughts about drinking may provide extremely informative clinical data, the therapist needs to structure the self-recording to capture data about settings, persons, and immediate prior interpersonal interactions, as well as the woman's own cognitions and affective responses to these settings and events. These self-recording data have to be examined regularly with a critical eye to the woman's attributions about the causes of her problems. There are only a few studies of the reliability and validity of self-monitoring either of drinking behavior or of thoughts about drinking alcohol. Satisfactory reliability and validity of self-reports of drinking behavior and drinking consequences has been reported (e.g., McCrady, Paolino, & Longabaugh, 1978; Miller, Crawford, & Taylor, 1979; Sobell & Sobell, 1978), but no study has analyzed the data by sex, establishing the validity of women's self-reports of drinking. It is quite possible that the reliability and validity of self-monitoring differs with gender.

The behavioral assessment questionnaire is commonly used for assessment. The Drinking Profile (Marlatt, 1975) is a structured interview which assesses the development of the client's drinking problems, environmental and cognitive antecedents to drinking, and negative consequences of drinking behavior. The questionnaire has serious limitations for women since it does not assess the negative consequences of drinking for women who work in the home, including uncompleted household responsibilities, poor parenting, and child behavior problems. Based on this interview, the drinking behavior of some women might appear quite innocuous, both to the interviewer and to the woman interviewed. In addition, the Drinking Profile's free-response format assumes that clients accurately observe and recall significant antecedents, cognitions, and consequences of drinking. This is a questionable assumption, since clinical experience suggests that women erroneously attribute too many of their problems to internal deficits while ignoring environmental obstacles. A forced-choice format which surveys a broad range of cues, cognitions, and consequences of drinking helps women report more about the environment than they would in a free-response format. The Drinking Patterns Questionnaire (Zitter & McCrady, 1979), which is currently being tested with male and female clients, is designed to accomplish a wide-ranging assessment of drinking behavior, without requiring the client to explain why drinking occurs. It promotes response to many cues that a woman might recognize as salient, even if she could not generate these items on her own. Figure 16-1 samples items from the questionnaire.

ASSESSMENT OF BIOLOGICAL FACTORS IN DRINKING

Until the mid-1970s, behavioral clinicians and researchers paid limited attention to the role of biological factors in assessment and treatment. Lately, researchers have begun to study the role of hormonal fluctuations in women's drinking, and have suggested that behavioral intervention consider the central nervous system properties of abused substances. For example, Jones and Jones (1976) studied alcohol absorption rates at different points in the menstrual cycle of young social drinkers, and found that the highest peak blood alcohol levels occurred during the premenstrual phase. Their findings have several interesting research and treatment implications. After these findings are replicated and extended to alcoholics and older women, other questions can be addressed. Naturalistic studies of the temporal relationships between menstrual

I. Environmental Items
———— 9. I seem to drink or get an urge to drink more on particular days of the week. Please specify:

———— 13. I sometimes enjoy having a drink with certain meals. Please specify:

II. Work
———— 4. I sometimes go drinking with friends straight from work before stopping home.
———— 13. I sometimes drink or get an urge to drink when I feel that I'm not getting anywhere in my job or career.

III. Financial
———— 7. I sometimes drink or get an urge to drink when a family member makes a purchase that I know we can't afford.
———— 11. I sometimes drink or get an urge to drink when I get angry over who controls the money.

IV. Physiological
———— 2. I sometimes drink or get an urge to drink when I feel tired or fatigued.
———— 5. I sometimes drink or get an urge to drink when I get restless.

V. Interpersonal
———— 10. I sometimes think that I don't relate well to others and drinking helps me do so.
———— 13. I sometimes find that I drink or get an urge to drink after I become angry at someone.

VI. Marital
———— 14. I sometimes drink or get an urge to drink when I want to enjoy sexual relations more.
———— 26. I sometimes drink or get an urge to drink when I am not happy with my role in the family.

VII. Parents
———— 3. I sometimes drink with my parents or in-laws. (Remember, *circle* parents, in-laws, or both.)
———— 8. I sometimes drink or get an urge to drink when I feel that my parents or in-laws don't respect me as an adult.

VIII. Children
———— 9. I sometimes drink or get an urge to drink after my children get in trouble at school or with legal authorities.
———— 20. I sometimes drink or get an urge to drink when I feel that my children don't need me any longer.

IX. Emotional
———— 6. Lonely
———— 22. Self-confident

X. Life Stresses
———— 11. Pregnancy
———— 20. Major change in usual social/recreational activities

FIGURE 16-1. Sample items from the Drinking Patterns Questionnaire. A complete copy of the questionnaire is available from the author on request.

cycle phase and quantity of alcohol consumed would reveal whether social drinking and alcoholic women vary in their consumption at different points in the menstrual cycle to compensate for the differing peak blood alcohol levels achieved, and whether certain women increase alcohol consumption premenstrually, further increasing their peak blood alcohol levels. In a similar vein, the clinician should routinely investigate the relationship between menstrual cycle phase, negative consequences due to drinking, and amount of alcohol consumed. When a client is particularly vulnerable at a certain phase of her cycle, treatment should modify drinking at those times. As a prevention measure, health education programs could include materials on menstrual cycling and blood alcohol levels, and teach social drinking women how to decrease their premenstrual alcohol consumption.

Alterman and McLellan (1981) have suggested that patterns of drug abuse, and the substances selected may reflect the client's effort to induce a "particular psychophysiological effect" (p. 25). Rather than focusing exclusively on *what* drug is abused (as in the DSM-III), assessment should consider what psychophysiological class of drugs is abused. They suggest a five-category classification: (1) single-substance abusers of psychodepressant drugs (e.g., alcohol, narcotics); (2) single-substance abusers of psychostimulants (e.g., amphetamines); (3) multiple, similar-substance abusers of psychodepressants; (4) multiple, similar-substance abusers of psychostimulants; and (5) multiple, dissimilar-substance abusers. This model can enrich the assessment of women's drinking. The model suggests inquiry about other substances in the same psychoactive class as the first substance mentioned. For example, if a woman states that alcohol use is a problem, the presence of barbiturates and minor tranquilizers should be assessed through inquiry and blood tests. Inquiry about the effects of abused substances has a variety of practical advantages. It may reveal the need for detoxification from several substances. It may uncover information about how she obtained these drugs, thereby assisting in plans for a social system intervention, such as education of the woman's physician. When a woman regularly abuses drugs of one type, the biological effects of this class of drugs will probably reinforce continued use, unless the woman learns to obtain similar effects without drugs (e.g., through meditation or relaxation for persons who use psychodepressant drugs). When a woman uses several classes of drugs, an analysis of the circumstances of use of each class of drugs will provide information about a necessary range of interventions.

BEHAVIORAL INTERVENTIONS WITH WOMEN DRINKERS

Functional analysis of behavior should be used to design interventions which take into account the life circumstances of alcoholic women. Interventions tailor-made for alcoholic women must consider antecedents to drinking, organismic variables, the drinking response, and the consequences of drinking.

ANTECEDENTS

Stimulus control procedures, alternate skills training and behavioral marital therapy are behavioral treatments which aim to alter the antecedents to drinking. All of these approaches search for discriminative stimuli (S^Ds), whose occurrence increases the future probability of drinking. Stimulus control interventions aim to change or eliminate the presence of these cues (Miller & Muñoz, 1976). Discussions of stimulus control incorrectly assume that most people with alcoholic problems drink with others, outside the home. The literature repeatedly describes interventions which succeed because the client car pools to get home from work and no longer stops at the neighborhood bar, carries limited money, or gets involved in activities incompatible with drinking (e.g., Miller, 1978). Because many women are isolated home drinkers, popular examples of stimulus control procedures are simply irrelevant.

Examples of interventions relevant to solitary women drinkers are not difficult to describe. A woman who drinks when her children leave for school might plan an outside activity during school hours which involves a friend. Women who are solitary drinkers often feel bored with house cleaning, laundry, and chauffeuring children. Although rearranging the daily schedule would relieve unpleasant feelings which often precede drinking, such major changes in life-style are difficult to introduce. The clinician can begin by helping the woman to organize her household and child-care responsibilities to free time for alternate activities so that she does not feel that her whole life revolves around unpleasant tasks.

Alternate skills training teaches the client to respond differently to cues that generally prompt drinking; it includes drink refusal training (Foy, Miller, Eisler, & O'Toole, 1976), relaxation training (Miller & Mastria, 1977), social skills training (Chaney, 1977), and problem-solving training (Marlatt & Gordon, 1979). In drink refusal training, the client learns how to say "no" when offered a drink. Target skills are usually taught through behavioral rehearsal. They include direct eye contact, a firm tone of voice, making it clear that the person does not want a drink, and offering a constructive alternative such as a soft drink or suggesting going to a movie instead of a nightclub. In relaxation training, the client learns deep-muscle relaxation, which can be used in tension-producing situations, or as a regular means of relaxing. In social skills training, the client learns to express positive and negative feelings, give and receive compliments, and initiate and carry on conversations through modeling and behavioral rehearsal. In problem-solving training, the client learns to identify and specify problems, generate a wide range of solutions, evaluate the viability of the solutions, and implement and evaluate solutions.

Alternate skills, no matter how they are acquired, may change a maladaptive stimulus constellation. A woman who is consistently assertive with a critical boss may be criticized less, and eliminate this cue for drinking. Although alternate skills training seems to be crucial for alcoholic women, it has *never* been systematically applied to female populations. Developing skills which enable women to alter their environments, could increase the self-efficacy of these women who are chronically low in self-esteem (e.g. Beckman, 1978).

Troublesome marital interaction is a common antecedent to drinking. Poor communication and inept problem solving characterize alcoholic couples (Paolino & McCrady, 1977), regardless of the sex of the alcoholic (McCrady & Wiener, 1978). Female alcoholics often report that marital conflicts exacerbate their drinking problems (e.g., Rosenbaum, 1958) and are antecedent to drinking episodes. Despite the obvious relevance of behavioral marital therapy to female alcoholics, it has *never* been systematically applied to this population. In the author's current research[2] married male and female alcoholics receive behavioral marital therapy in an attempt to identify effective ingredients in conjoint alcoholism treatment. Couples learn to increase their rates of positive behavior exchanges, communicate, and solve problems together.

Approximately one third of alcoholic women are married to alcoholic men (e.g., Miller, Hedrick, & Taylor, 1979). At times the husband's

[2] *Marital, Spouse, and Self-Control Treatment of Alcoholism* (NIAAA Grant No. 5 R01 AA03984-03), B. S. McCrady, Principal Investigator.

drinking precedes his wife's drinking, because he pressures her to drink, or because she evaluates her situation as hopeless, and thinks, "Why bother, what choice do I have?" when he drinks. Rational–emotive therapy, directed at hopeless thoughts, might help the woman recognize realistic choices. Skills deficits and a true lack of alternatives keep many women married to alcoholics. Women who do not want to divorce and women who fear violent retaliation if they leave home can be helped. Family members, friends, employers, other women with drinking problems, and self-reinforcement can be called on to support improvements in her drinking behavior. To accomplish this, the clinician explains the relationship between social support and improved drinking behavior, helps the woman identify people with whom she might develop supportive and enjoyable relationships, and helps the woman discuss her needs with others and ask for help. Problem solving to identify helpful behavior, and role playing with the therapist before talking with the friend may help. Some women select friends to call on the phone at times when they want to drink, and coach the friends by telling them supportive things to say when called for help. Some women plan a regular, mutually enjoyable date with a friend to talk, play handball, swim, or shop.

A woman married to an actively drinking alcoholic man needs interpersonal survival skills, so she can deal with her husband when he is drinking, pressuring her to drink, or acting belligerent. Saying no to drinks in a calm, positive tone, and talking quietly to her belligerent mate may help. These women must learn how to leave the scene in a safe manner if their husbands' behavior threatens their abstinence or their physical safety.

ORGANISMIC VARIABLES

The thoughts and feelings of women drinkers generally have been ignored by behavioral treatment packages, even though depression and low self-esteem appear to be common problems among women alcoholics (Beckman, 1978). An exception is a program designed to increase the general self-esteem of alcoholic women (Burtle, Whitlock, & Franks, 1974). Treatment programs which investigate specific links between external events and internal reactions have not been developed for alcoholic women. Such links are important since depression and low self-esteem may come about in several ways. Social skills deficits lead some alcoholic women to believe they are only competent in social situations when drinking. They overgeneralize from their social failures to unrelated situations, or conclude that they will never improve and become depressed. For such women, treatment should enhance social skills, and challenge beliefs about incompetence. Some women receive little positive reinforcement from family, self, or others, and little recognition for their accomplishments and abilities, while at the same time they often are locked into interaction patterns characterized by aversive control. Yelling, threats, and punishment from husbands and employers have little effect on drinking behavior, but reinforce beliefs of incompetence. The aim of treatment might be the establishment of relationships with friends, family, and fellow employees which provide positive reinforcement. Husbands might compliment their wives on their abstinence (e.g., "I really enjoyed this evening," "You look so healthy since you haven't been drinking"); or couples might make mutually enjoyable activities contingent on the women's abstinence. So that these women can maintain independence and a sense of control in therapy, the husband's role must be supportive, and the initiative must come from the client. If therapists merely teach the husbands to provide differential reinforcement for behaviors they value, their wives will once again feel manipulated and helpless. Women who experience aversive control in relationships and chide themselves with negative self-statements, can also learn to reinforce themselves for abstinence. They might think, "I did well," when they accomplish a task, or do something nice for themselves after they refuse to drink under pressure. The positive side effect of self-reinforcement is its focus on the woman's accomplishments.

THE DRINKING RESPONSE

Because contemporary treatments which focus on the drinking response generally aim to modify the style of drinking behavior, they do not apply to alcoholic women, whose style of drinking (e.g., sip rate, intersip interval) is similar to that of social drinkers (Tracey & Nathan, 1976). It is unclear whether abstinence or controlled social drinking is a better goal for women. Marlatt and Gordon (1979) suggest that alcoholics continue to drink after consuming one drink because of cognitive reactions to drinking which they have called the abstinence violation effect (AVE). The AVE includes thoughts such as "I've blown it," "I'm drinking again," "As long as I'm going to catch it for one I might as well have a few," and a general change in self-perception from nondrinker to drinker. Yet, Miller and Joyce (1979) recently found that women problem drinkers return to moderate social drinking significantly more often than do alcoholic men. It may be that the abstinence violation effect is less salient for women, or that women experience less social pressures to drink than do men. Clinical observations also suggest that many women initially present a pattern of limited, appropriate drinking in social situations along with extremely heavy, solitary drinking. If a woman can maintain control of her alcohol consumption in certain settings but not others, her drinking goal might be abstinence in high-risk situations, and limited drinking in lower-risk environments.

Drinking response treatments have also ignored dual addictions to alcohol and other drugs (such as minor tranquillizers or barbiturates), and the substitution of drug abuse by women who previously had alcohol problems. Programs should anticipate drug use and drug substitution during treatment, rather than waiting for it to emerge 6 months after treatment. Alternate skills training might eliminate the need for mood-altering drugs, while cognitive treatments might encourage women to realize that they can cope with their environment without drugs. Intervention may have to include educating a personal physician who reaches for the prescription pad whenever the client describes psychological discomfort.

CONSEQUENCES

Developing support systems such as employers and families who provide positive reinforcement for nondrinking and none for drinking are the goal of the community reinforcement programs (Hunt & Azrin, 1973; Azrin, 1976), and of programs emphasizing behavioral contracting with spouses (e.g., Miller, 1972), employers, and the court (e.g., Miller, 1975). Men may have salient, intact reinforcement systems, so that employers, spouses, and judges need only to learn how to appropriately consequate drinking and nondrinking to support abstinence or controlled drinking. Unfortunately, most women lack such natural reinforcement systems, either because they are not employed outside their homes, or because they transfer to a similar position in another company if confronted by the employer. Because supervisors put off identifying and acting upon alcoholism problems in women, the impact of the natural reinforcement system may be diluted. Employers and supervisors could learn to discuss drinking problems with female employees. Support from other female or male employees with drinking problems might be harnessed to facilitate entrance into treatment. The relative effectiveness of confrontation by male versus female supervisors needs to be determined.

Behavioral treatment often uses the family reinforcement system to alter drinking behavior. For many female alcoholics, major changes in intimate relationships must precede such a treatment approach. Since the female alcoholic's husband often is an alcohol or drug abuser, he is unlikely to reinforce a change in his wife's drinking behavior. Even nonalcoholic husbands of female alcoholics may encourage passivity and deference to their decisions. The possibility of altered family reinforcement is unavailable to many women because the separation and divorce rates of alcoholic women are extremely high (Paolino & McCrady, 1977).

The legal system is a major resource in the treatment of alcoholic men, but not in the treatment of alcoholic women. The rate of arrest for drunken driving, drunk and disorderly, or drunk in public is much lower for women than men (Argeriou & Paolino, 1976). Women appear to be less likely to drive when drinking than men. Also, women's drunk driving occurs primarily in the afternoons, rather than the evening, when men are more often arrested. Since many police departments have special DUI units, and patrol the highways more heavily on evenings and weekends, it is less likely that drunken women driving in the afternoons will be stopped. Even if stopped, police officers are less likely to charge women with DUI than men.

Reinforcement systems commonly manipulated in behavioral alcoholism treatment programs are rarely effective with women. Clinicians and researchers need to explore the reinforcement systems which maintain women's drinking, and to modify these systems so that they reinforce adaptive drinking behavior.

EVALUATION OF TREATMENT OUTCOME FOR WOMEN ALCOHOLICS

Improved methods have been developed to evaluate the outcomes of alcoholism treatment (e.g., Sobell, 1978). Good outcome studies include: retrospective reports of daily drinking gathered for the 12 months before treatment, monthly follow-ups for at least 12 months following treatment, and a convergent validity approach, in which information is collected about legal problems, job functioning, interpersonal functioning, psychological well-being, and physical health. Daily drinking behavior is categorized as none, light (1–2 drinks/day), moderate (3–6 drinks/day), or heavy (greater than 6 drinks/day).

This methodology is insufficient to evaluate women's progress in treatment. The first problem lies in defining impaired functioning for women who are not employed outside of their homes. Days when the homemaker was unable to complete her responsibilities at home because of her drinking are analogous to days missed from work, but their presence can only be validated by another family member or roommate, who may have a very different definition of what possibilities *should* be completed. The woman may think that TV dinners equal a meal cooked from scratch; her husband may not. Brief rating scales could be developed with agreement from the woman and her family about the meaning of anchor points. Functioning could be rated as "no change in completing responsibilities," "completed basic responsibilities, but quality decreased," or "unable to complete any basic responsibilities on that day." These rating scales might decrease discrepancies between self- and correspondent-reports.

Convergent validity data often include: hospitalizations, arrests, days missed from work, and evaluations of significant others, as well as self-reports or other job-related measures. Since women with dependent children may be less willing than their male counterparts to accept hospitalization or residential treatment, lack of hospitalization during posttreatment follow-up may not mean that she is functioning well, but may instead mean that she is afraid, alone, and not using the services which she needs. Contacts with the legal system are not useful in validating outcomes, because women have less alcohol-related legal consequences than men. The problems of gathering meaningful data at work have already been discussed. For many women, the family may be the only source of validation data, even though there may be systematic distortions in the reports of the families of women alcoholics. Although the convergent validity approach is useful, more relevant sources of information must be located. These could include liver function studies, records of doctor visits for medical complaints, and reports from close friends, neighbors, AA sponsors, and clergy. Measures of children's functioning might also be of value, since children often show behavioral problems when an alcoholic parent is actively drinking.

Current definitions of light, moderate, and heavy drinking also impede evaluation of the outcomes of treatment for women alcoholics. Given the differences in weight between the average man and average woman, for 6 drinks, a woman's blood alcohol level (BAL) is 40–50 mg%

higher on the average than is a man's BAL (e.g., Miller & Muñoz, 1976). The woman who drinks 6 drinks per day may reach the same level of intoxication, with the same potential legal, familial, occupational, and health risks as a man who drinks 8–9 drinks per day. Current usage would categorize her drinking quantity as moderate, even though it may be functionally equivalent to heavy drinking by a man.

A desirable alternative to current classification methods is the alcohol metabolism curve (Matthews & Miller, 1979). Self-reports of hourly consumption are combined with blood alcohol consumption cutoffs, taking body weight into account. Light, moderate, heavy, and very heavy drinking days can then be defined as days in which the blood alcohol consumption levels were: less than 50 mg%, 50–100 mg%, 100–150 mg%, and more than 150 mg%. The primary limitation of this approach is that few clients persist with recording hourly self-report data over long periods of time.

Lower quantity cutoffs for women could also be set, defining light drinking as 1–2 drinks, moderate as 3–5 drinks, and heavy as greater than 5 drinks per day. Finally, body weight at the beginning of a study could be used to identify how many drinks correspond to light, moderate, or heavy blood alcohol consumption. Weight would have to be monitored throughout the study, and weight changes of 10 pounds would require readjustment of the individual's drinking cutoffs.

CONCLUSIONS AND RECOMMENDATIONS

The behavioral treatment of substance-abusing women presents unique challenges. These include the need for reliable means of detecting alcohol and drug problems, and valid ways of assessing the relationship between drinking or drug-taking and other areas of functioning. Studies of the most effective ways of engaging women in treatment and maintaining their involvement are needed. The contribution of interpersonal relationships, coping skills, and reinforcement systems to the maintenance of treatment gains remains to be evaluated. A social learning framework could yield objective assessments and effective treatments for women as whole persons. The need to *systematically evaluate* procedures as they are developed cannot be emphasized enough. The empirical study of the issues of *women and of men*, in any behavioral substance abuse treatment, is a major challenge for the 1980s.

Throughout the chapter, many suggestions are offered for clinicians and clinical researchers. Some of the suggestions have been offered by other authors writing about the assessment and treatment of female alcohol abusers. Of the new suggestions, the following five seem particularly important to pursue in clinical practice and through controlled research:

1. The use of self-monitoring for assessing the relationship between drinking and other problem areas.

2. The use of alternate skills training in treatment.

3. The development of alternative support or reinforcement systems.

4. Developing a valid and reliable means of measuring impaired functioning for homemakers.

5. Evaluating the appropriateness of controlled drinking and abstinence goals, as related to previous drinking patterns.

REFERENCES

Abrams, D. B., & Wilson, G. T. Effects of alcohol on social anxiety in women: Cognitive versus physiological processes. *Journal of Abnormal Psychology,* 1979, *88* (2), 161–173.

Alterman, A. I., & McLellan, A. T. A framework for refining the diagnostic categorization of substance abusers. *Addictive Behaviors,* 1981, *6,* 23–27.

Argeriou, M., & Paulino, D. Women arrested for drunken driving in Boston: Social characteristics and circumstances of arrest. *Journal of Studies on Alcohol,* 1976, *37,* 648–658.

Azrin, N. J. Improvements in the community-reinforcement approach to alcoholism. *Behaviour Research and Therapy,* 1976, *14,* 339–348.

Balter, M. B. Drug abuse: A conceptual analysis and overview of the current situation. In C. E. Josephson & E. E. Carroll (Eds.), *Drug use: Epidemiological and sociological approaches,* New York: Wiley, 1974.

Beckman, L. J. Women alcoholics: A review of sociological and psychological studies. *Journal of Studies on Alcohol,* 1975, *36,* 797–824.

Beckman, L. J. Self-esteem of women alcoholics. *Journal of Studies on Alcohol,* 1978, *39* (3), 491–498.

Burtle, V., Whitlock, D., & Franks, V. Modification of low self-esteem in women alcoholics: A behavior treatment approach. *Psychotherapy: Theory, Research and Practice,* 1974, *11* (1), 35–40.

Celentano, D. D., McQueen, D. V., & Chee, E. Substance abuse by women: A review of the epidemiologic literature. *Journal of Chronic Diseases,* 1980, *33,* 383–394.

Chaney, E. F. *Skill training with alcoholics.* Unpublished doctoral dissertation, University of Washington, 1976.

Diagnostic and Statistical Manual of Mental Disorders (3rd ed.). Washington, D.C.: American Psychiatric Association, 1980.

Foy, D. W., Miller, P. M., Eisler, R. M., & O'Toole, D. H. Social skills training to refuse drinks effectively. *Journal of Studies on Alcohol,* 1976, *37,* 1340–1345.

Gomberg, E. S. The female alcoholic. In R. E. Tarter & A. A. Sugarman (Eds.), *Alcoholism: Interdisciplinary approaches to an enduring problem.* Reading, Mass.: Addison-Wesley, 1976.

Götestam, K. G., Melin, L., & Öst, L. G. Behavioral techniques in the treatment of drug abuse: An evaluative review. *Addictive Behaviors*, 1976, *1*, 205–225.

Greenblatt, M., & Schuckit, M. A. *Alcoholism problems in women and children*. New York: Grune & Stratton, 1976.

Hendricks, R. D., Sobell, M. B., & Cooper, A. M. Social influences on human consumption in an analogue situation. *Addictive Behaviors*, 1978, *3*, 253–259.

Hodgson, R., Rankin, H., & Stockwell, T. Craving and loss of control. In P. E. Nathan, G. A. Marlatt, & T. Løberg (Eds.), *Alcoholism: New directions in behavioral research and treatment*. New York: Plenum, 1978.

Hunt, G. M., & Azrin, N. H. A community-reinforcement approach to alcoholism. *Behaviour Research and Therapy*, 1973, *11*, 91–104.

Jones, B. M., & Jones, M. K. Alcohol effects in women during the menstrual cycle. *Annals of the New York Academy of Sciences*, 1976, *273*, 576–587.

Marlatt, G. A. The drinking profile: A questionnaire for the behavioral assessment of alcoholism. In E. J. Mash & L. G. Terdal (Eds.), *Behavior therapy assessment: Diagnosis and evaluation*. New York: Springer, 1975.

Marlatt, G. A. Craving for alcohol, loss of control, and relapse: A cognitive–behavioral analysis. In P. E. Nathan, G. A. Marlatt, & T. Løberg, (Eds.), *Alcoholism: New directions in behavioral research and treatment*. New York: Plenum, 1978. (a)

Marlatt, G. A. Behavioral assessment of social drinking and alcoholism. In G. A. Marlatt & P. E. Nathan (Eds.), *Behavioral approaches to alcoholism*. New Brunswick, N.J.: Rutgers Center of Alcohol Studies, 1978. (b)

Marlatt, G. A., & Gordon, J. R. Determinants of relapse: Implications for the maintenance of behavior change. In P. Davidson (Ed.), *Behavioral medicine: Changing health lifestyles*. New York: Brunner/Mazel, 1979.

Matthews, D. B., & Miller, W. R. Estimating blood alcohol concentration: Two computer programs and their applications in therapy and research. *Addictive Behaviors*, 1979, *1*, 55–60.

McCrady, B. S., Paolino, T. J., & Longabaugh, R. L. Correspondence between problem drinker and spouse report of drinking behavior and impairment. *Journal of Studies on Alcohol*, 1978, *39*, 1252–1257.

McCrady, B. S., & Wiener, J. *Verbal and nonverbal marital interactions in male and female alcoholics*. Paper presented at the Annual Meeting of the Association for Advancement of Behavior Therapy, Chicago, November 1978.

Mello, N. K. Behavioral studies of alcoholism. In B. Kissin & H. Begleiter (Eds.), *The biology of alcoholism*. New York: Plenum, 1972.

Miller, P. M. The use of behavioral contracting in the treatment of alcoholism: A case report. *Behavior Therapy*, 1972, *3*, 593–596.

Miller, P. M. A behavioral intervention program for chronic drunkeness offenders. *Archives of General Psychiatry*, 1975, *32*, 915–918.

Miller, P. M. Alternative skills training in alcoholism treatment. In P. E. Nathan, G. A. Marlatt, & T. Løberg (Eds.), *Alcoholism: New directions in behavioral research and treatment*. New York: Plenum, 1978.

Miller, P. M., & Mastria, M. A. *Alternatives to alcohol abuse: A social learning model*. Champaign, Ill.: Research, 1977.

Miller, W. R., Crawford, V. L., & Taylor, C. A. Significant others as corroborative sources for problem drinkers. *Addictive Behaviors*, 1979, *4* (1), 67–70.

Miller, W. R., Hedrick, K. E., & Taylor, C. A. *Relationship between alcohol consumption and related life problems before and after behavioral treatment of problem drinkers*. Paper presented at the Annual Meeting of the Association for Advancement of Behavior Therapy, San Francisco, 1979.

Miller, W. R., & Joyce, M. A. Prediction of abstinence, controlled drinking, and heavy drinking outcomes following behavioral self-control training. *Journal of Consulting and Clinical Psychology*, 1979, 47, (4), 773–775.

Miller, W. R., & Muñoz, R. F. *How to control your drinking*. Englewood Cliffs, N.J.: Prentice-Hall, 1976.

Moore, R. A. The diagnosis of alcoholism in a psychiatric hospital: A trial of the Michigan alcoholism screening test (MAST). *American Journal of Psychiatry*, 1972, 128 (12), 1565–1569.

Nathan, P. E. Studies in blood alcohol level discrimination. In P. E. Nathan, G. A. Marlatt, & T. Løberg (Eds.), *Alcoholism: New directions in behavioral research and treatment*. New York: Plenum, 1978.

Nathan, P. E., & Briddell, D. W. Behavioral assessment and treatment of alcoholism. In B. Kissin & H. Begleiter (Eds.), *The biology of alcoholism* (Vol. 5). New York: Plenum, 1977.

National Council on Alcoholism, Criteria Committee. Criteria for the diagnosis of alcoholism. *American Journal of Psychiatry*, 1972, 129, 127–135.

National Institute on Alcohol Abuse and Alcoholism. *Alcoholism and alcohol abuse among women: Research issues* (DHEW Publ. No. [ADM] 79–835). Washington, D.C.: U.S. Government Printing Office, 1980.

Nellis, M., Hager, M., Potope, P., & Harkins, C. *Final report on drugs, alcohol and women's health*. National Institute on Drug Abuse, DHEW, 1978.

Paolino, T. J. & McCrady, B. S. *The alcoholic marriage: Alternative perspectives*. New York: Grune & Stratton, 1977.

Parsons, O. A. Cognitivie dysfunction in alcoholics and social drinkers. *Journal of Studies on Alcohol*, 1980, 41, 105–118.

Rosenbaum, B. Married women alcoholics at the Washingtonian hospital. *Quarterly Journal of Studies on Alcohol*, 1958, 19, 79–89.

Schuckit, M. A., Pitts, F. N., Reich, T., King, L. J., & Winokur, G. Alcoholism: Two types of alcoholism in women. *Archives of General Psychiatry*, 1969, 20, 301–306.

Sobell, L. C. Alcohol treatment outcome evaluation: Contributions from behavioral research. In P. E. Nathan, G. A. Marlatt, & T. Løberg (Eds.), *Alcoholism: New directions in behavioral research and treatment*. New York: Plenum, 1978.

Sobell, M. B., & Sobell, L. C. Alcoholics treated by individualized behavior therapy: One year treatment outcome. *Behaviour Research and Therapy*, 1973, 11, 599–618.

Sobell, M. B., & Sobell, L. C. Alternatives to abstinence: Evidence, issues and some proposals. In P. E. Nathan, G. A. Marlatt, & T. Løberg (Eds.), *Alcoholism: New directions in behavioral research and treatment*. New York: Plenum, 1978.

Tracey, D. A., & Nathan, P. E. Behavioral analysis of chronic alcoholism in four women. *Journal of Consulting and Clinical Psychology*, 1976, 44 (5), 832–842.

Wilkins, R. H. The alcoholic at risk register. In *The hidden alcoholic in general practice*. London: Elek, 1974.

Wilson, G. T., & Lawson, D. M. Expectancies, alcohol, and sexual arousal in women. *Journal of Abnormal Psychology*, 1978, 87 (3), 358–367.

Zitter, R., & McCrady, B. S. *The Drinking Patterns Questionnaire*. Unpublished manuscript, Brown University/Butler Hospital, 1979.

17

AGING WOMEN

PATRICIA A. WISOCKI

OVERVIEW

There is no literature on the topic "behavior therapy with elderly women." There are several reasons for this state of affairs. First of all, behavior therapists have not included the elderly (men or women) in a significant amount of their research. A recent survey of the primary journals devoted to behavioral research and therapy (Wisocki & Mosher, 1982) indicated that the elderly were used as subjects in .6% of the articles published. When other professional journals were examined along with behavioral journals, only 107 articles were found in a 16-year period which concerned treatment-relevant behavioral-gerontological work. Further, in 75% of these articles, the population sample of elderly was an institutionalized one. Gender differentiations were rarely made. Thus, issues pertinent to the aging woman have not been explored in the behavioral literature. To some extent, this lack of involvement with elderly as subjects reflects the fact that age per se has never been considered an important determinant of behavioral procedures. Historically, behavior therapists have shown little regard for diagnoses, gender, or population variables in prescribing treatment methods, preferring instead to focus on the problems presented in a given situation.

This chapter provides an opportunity to describe the problems which exist for elderly women, drawing primarily from work which has compared both elderly men and elderly women in a variety of areas. Often, however, no separation is possible between the genders, since the aging process affects us all in much the same way. Three specific problem areas have been addressed as particularly relevant to the clinical

Patricia A. Wisocki. Department of Psychology, University of Massachusetts, Amherst, Massachusetts.

treatment of elderly women: drug abuse, depression, and hypochondriasis.

The second part of this chapter covers the current behavioral research with elderly populations. The research is reviewed as it concerns institutionalized elderly in the areas of social interaction and participation, self-care, and environmental manipulation programs. Behavioral work with community-dwelling elderly is also reviewed, with particular focus on studies describing the modification of physical and cognitive changes in the aging process.

Finally, there is a brief review of some of the problems involved in conducting gerontological research and suggestions for future directions.

BACKGROUND

THE IMPORTANCE OF BEING A STATISTIC

In considering the topic of "the elderly" it is customary to begin by presenting the statistical data which place the elderly in perspective to the rest of society. The statistics (taken from U.S. Department of Health, Education and Welfare report, 1975) serve as forceful reminders of the fact that the elderly constitute a significant percentage of the population (22 million people in the United States are over 65 years of age) and that they will be around for many years (the life expectancy for elderly White men is 68 years and for elderly White women it is 76 years; for elderly Black men and women, the corresponding numbers are 60 years and 67 years). Elderly women number approximately 13 million and constitute 6% of the total U.S. population and 59% of the total elderly population.

The statistics also serve to dispel some popular misconceptions about the elderly. For instance, 95% of the elderly live in the community; the rest reside in state and federal hospitals and in nursing homes. Of those elderly in institutional placements, 58.3% are women. About 1 million elderly women make up 1% of the U.S. labor force, many of them employed for the first time in their lives. Ninety percent of elderly women are registered voters, most of whom vote regularly.

These bits of data only provide the skeletal bones of the population under consideration. They do not hint at the individual variability of the group. It is left to us to recall stories of our mothers, grandmothers, or elderly aunts who performed daring and exciting feats (such as rafting down the Colorado River, running for controversial political office, demonstrating against the draft) or who carried on more commonplace activities that took us years to appreciate fully (such as taking in grandchildren after the death of an adult son or daughter, returning to college for an advanced degree, or supporting adult children through life crises).

Everyone knows an elderly woman who defies the stereotypes promulgated in the media, in social policy statements, or even in daily conversation. Yet the individual personalities we know as colorful, dynamic women who happen to be over 65 disappear from view when we consider the mass population called "elderly women." Since they live longer than any other population and have been exposed to more changes and a greater mix of environmental variables, it is likely that elderly women are the most heterogeneous of all populations. Indeed, Maas and Kuypers (1974) suggest that women in general are more responsive than men to environmental events and have had more variation in their life-styles over the years. This responsivity has been attributed to the changing requirements of a mother's role as her children develop (Breed & Huffine, 1979). These authors contend that if a woman's role has been defined by her child-rearing experiences, she not only has greater variability in her life, but in the course of it she learns effective coping skills for later use.

Given their numbers, their longevity, and their adaptability, it is odd to think of this population as a "neglected" one. Yet there is little doubt that elderly women can lay legitimate claim to that unfortunate categorization. For example, most medical practitioners reportedly dislike working with the elderly (Field, 1970), expecting them to be uncooperative and frustrating (Barrow, 1971). Trained to believe that aging is a natural disease process (Hazell, 1960), physicians use fewer preventative medical procedures with the elderly (Barrow, 1971). Some physicians may also believe that their skills are "wasted" with a population who have few years left to live. There is also a fear that an elderly patient might die during treatment, a factor seen as a challenge to the practitioner's sense of self-worth (Group for the Advancement of Psychiatry, 1971).

There is no reason to assume that the attitude of clinical psychologists is any different. Less than 400 clinical psychologists are now providing services to elderly clients (Storandt, Siegler, & Elias, 1978), although it has been estimated that there are at least 2.5 million elderly in need of some kind of mental health service (Kramer, Taube, & Redick,

1973). Kahn (1975) has pointed out that the U.S. mental health system actually serves a small proportion of older persons today than in previous decades. He reports a 45% reduction in the number of patient care episodes for the aged from 1966 to 1971 at psychiatric units in general hospitals. In 1971 the elderly in community mental health centers represented only 7% of inpatient service and only 3% of the outpatient cases. Clinical psychologists, like physicians, are reluctant to be associated with such low status clients either because such an association may lower the clinician's self-esteem and professional repute (Kastenbaum, 1978) or because the elderly arouse feelings of inadequacy, helplessness, and anxiety in the therapist (Goldfarb, 1956).

The elderly are also neglected by government agencies, employers, and the social systems we depend upon for life support. For example, upon retirement women who have worked all their lives have usually earned less than men in comparable positions and have thus earned lower retirement benefits (Bernstein, 1974). This lower income level combined with a longer life span, means that a woman's income must be stretched over more years than is necessary for men. Many of the jobs held by older women, such as waitressing, hospital work, and domestic service, have only recently been covered under Social Security. Employers have generally been reluctant to hire older women because they fear they will be unable to adapt to new technology, be sick frequently, be cantankerous, and be unattractive. Yet, the research evidence (as cited by Butler & Lewis, 1977) indicates that older women have a lower turnover rate, higher productivity, and less absenteeism than men or younger women.

More important, elderly women themselves are neglectful of their own rights and privileges, perhaps due to a fear of self-assertion and years of practice in being submissive to male figures. The aging woman is often biased against women, having been culturally conditioned to see only males as sources of reinforcement and authority, and women as competitors and less desirable companions than men (Jacobs, 1979). This attitude may influence the elderly woman to avoid association with female peers and female professionals who are likely to be sympathetic and helpful. The same attitude influences them to seek associations with men. In making important decisions about investments or methods of increasing capital, for example, women are often encouraged to turn their money over to men for management (e.g., lawyers, sons, bank officers), instead of developing their own investment programs. Thus, in spite of their large numbers, elderly women are victims of two kinds of discrimination: age and sex. They have not yet recognized their unified strength and in many ways they are their own worst enemies.

EMPIRICAL DATA ABOUT THE ELDERLY

The elderly have also been neglected as a research population. A survey by the American Psychological Association (cited by Birren & Woodruff, 1973) indicated that for every 73,000 people over the age of 65 there was one psychologist engaged in an activity relevant to aging. A comprehensive survey of doctoral dissertations in the field of aging between 1934 and 1969 indicated that only 69 universities in the United States had awarded one or more degrees for a dissertation in aging research (Moore & Birren, 1971). The remedy of this apparent lack of interest is unknown. While gerontologists want to increase the involvement of psychologists and other mental health professionals with the elderly, some are reluctant to encourage an emphasis on chronological age as a variable in therapeutic practice and research. They suggest that such an emphasis might further segregate the elderly population from the rest of society. Others, including behaviorists, maintain that available research with younger populations can be generalized to the elderly and that it is not necessary to replicate research to demonstrate its applicability to a new population. The assumption behind both these notions is that the elderly are represented in research and therapeutic practice, in proportion to their numbers in the general population. Unfortunately, this assumption is false.

One positive solution has been posed by Kastenbaum (1978) who recommends that instead of cultivating a special field of geriatric psychotherapy, we examine the specific characteristics of a given individual (e.g., a recently widowed woman who is depressed over her loss), or a particular group with common characteristics (e.g., persons who are in significant life transitions, such as elderly persons facing retirement and young adults experiencing divorce), or a predominant distress syndrome (e.g., depression). Research and therapy would then proceed on the basis of our best knowledge concerning each of the areas presented. Kastenbaum (1978) also points out that this approach might "protect us from formulating theory and techniques that have more to do with one particular generation of people who have grown old at one particular time in our social history than with problems that are intrinsic to aging and the aged" (p. 206).

It is also possible to argue that the elderly should be singled out as a separate population group for researchers and clinicians. Consider the following points. The elderly are different physically from younger subjects. The physiological effects of aging must influence treatment prescriptions, response to treatment, and length of time required for treatment. As people age, they experience gradually diminishing efficiency on all levels, both physiological and behavioral. Decrements are greater in the performance of more complex coordinated activities involving connections between nerves and glands and muscles. Older people are less able to respond to both physical and psychological stress, and they need more time to return to their prestress levels than younger people (Shock, 1974). This breakdown in homeostatic efficiency is also demonstrated in poor adjustment to environmental temperature changes, particularly heat stress. Older people experience significantly less water loss when exposed to hot temperatures, which means a reduction in the body's ability to cool itself by evaporation (Burch, Cohn, & Neumann, 1942). With diminished regenerative capacity of certain body cells (e.g., skin, kidneys, liver, and bone marrow), and the death of other body cells, a large number of biochemical reactions occur in every tissue and organ system of the body, possibly producing some change in function associated with age in brain, kidney, heart, and other muscle tissue (Weg, 1975).

Other physical changes occurring in old age are detailed in Table 17-1. It is reasonable to suppose that within each area of physical decline behavioral effects will occur which may either produce a specific problem behavior or may influence a strategy of treatment. For example, the physical changes occurring in skin, bones, and muscles are likely to contribute to the development of cautiousness in the elderly, slowing them down in numerous ways. Such changes could easily lead an elderly woman to develop agoraphobia or an intense fear of falling, driving, or leaving home. Such changes may make one reluctant to be seen in public, visit a therapist, or practice therapeutic assignments.

Secondly, the elderly have some unique health problems. If these are not singled out for attention they may not be treated. For instance, while disease is not an inevitable condition of aging, diseases are more likely to occur in elderly people and be more debilitating for them. Eighty-six percent of old people have some chronic health problem

TABLE 17-1. Effects of Aging

Physical changes	Effects on body
Skin	
1. Grows thinner	1. Breaks more easily; loss of elasticity, resulting in more wrinkles
2. Becomes drier	2. More subject to irritation
3. Loss of fat cells below skin surface	3. Less insulation for body, producing increased sensation of cold; eyes sink deeper into skull cavity
4. Cells lose ability to regenerate	4. Wounds heal more slowly
5. Changes occur in pigmentation	5. "Liver spots" may develop
6. Some cells turn into connective tissue which gets tough and fibrous	6. Finger and toenails become hard and thick; general drying out of tissue
Bones	
1. Calcium is withdrawn from cartilage and ligaments	1. Bones become more porous and brittle; break more easily and mend more slowly
2. Degeneration of joint cartilage	2. Loss of elasticity in certain joints; experience of pain with movement; frame settles and becomes shorter
3. Decrease in bone mass	3. Increased stress in weight-bearing areas, predisposing one to fractures
Muscles	
1. Increase in interstitial fat and lipid within muscle fiber	1. Some loss of ability to control movements; walk becomes slower
2. Diminished size, strength, tone of muscles	2. May cause prolapse of bladder or anus, resulting in incontinence
Hair	
1. Hormonal changes occur	1. Thins and becomes gray
	2. Increased facial hair on women
Senses	
1. Gradual loss of visual acuity	1. Person requires glasses, more light to see
2. Cataracts may develop	2. Eyes more sensitive to glare; vision is poorer

TABLE 17-1. *(Continued)*

Physical changes	Effects on body

Senses *(Continued)*

3. Loss in audition, especially of higher frequencies	3. Inability to distinguish some voices, sounds; may require hearing aid
4. Loss of taste buds; diminished ability to smell	4. Lack of interest in food; poor nutritional habits
5. Impairment of proprioception	5. Impaired coordination and balance
6. Decreases in sensation of touch	6. Decrease in responsivity, adaptation to environmental stimuli, increase in "clumsy" behavior (e.g., dropping objects)
7. Increased pain threshold	7. Greater susceptibility to accidents, especially from hot objects and fire

Teeth and gums

1. Decrease in salivary flow	1. Food more likely to stick between teeth, resulting in decay around roots of teeth; mouth more prone to friction from rough food; retards rapid softening of coarse food stuff; swallowing is impeded
2. Breakdown of supporting tissues	2. Gums recede, exposing more tooth surface which is less resistant to decay and more sensitive to temperature changes
3. Loss of bone	3. Teeth loosen, wear down, abrade, and fracture
4. Tissues covering ridges and palate become thinner and more fragile	4. Palate is more susceptible to lesions from mechanical stimuli (e.g., toothbrush)
5. Tooth extraction or ill-fitting dentures	5. Facial muscles relax, causing wrinkles and lines; changes in speech patterns

Systemic changes

1. Decline in overall function of nervous system	1. Diminished reaction time; overall loss of speed, flexibility, reserve, and coordination
2. Reduction in breathing capacity, residual lung volume, total capacity, and basal oxygen consumption	2. Decrease in reserves for all body functions, affecting overall health maintenance
3. Heart pump works harder	3. Breathlessness, tires more easily
4. Increases in peripheral resistance, circulation time, diastolic and systolic blood pressure	4. Hands and feet become cold easily; arteries and veins become clogged and less elastic
5. Decreases in renal blood flow, glomerular filtration, and tubular excretion rates	5. Lowered efficiency and servicing of bodily needs

(continued)

TABLE 17-1. *(Continued)*

Physical changes	Effects on body

Systemic changes (Continued)

6. Decrease in hormones which promote immunity responses	6. Greater susceptibility to diseases
7. Lowered levels or changes in the digestive juices	7. Decreased appetite, possible malnutrition
8. Reduction in persistalsis	8. Weight gain
9. System more subject to stress	9. Constipation or diarrhea
10. Deficiencies in mineral, protein, and vitamin intake	10. Periodontal disease which leads to loss of teeth; reduced bone, thyroid, and heart muscle function

Sexual changes

1. Decrease in gonadal hormones	1. Changes in genital tissue; reduction, and finally loss of fertility
2. In women, gradual atrophy of ovarian, uterine, and vaginal tissues and a decreased level of lubrication	2. Experience of some pain upon intromission of penis; need longer time for lubrication of vaginal and vulval areas and for clitoral response (*Note.* Climax is as effective as in younger years)
3. In men, a lower rate of spermatogenesis; a decrease in viable sperm; smaller and firmer testes; prostate enlarges; decrease in volume and viscosity of seminal fluid	3. Reduction in frequency of intercourse, force of ejaculation, speed of attaining erection; ability to maintain erection longer

which requires visits to a physician; old people get sick more often than young; they stay in hospitals for longer periods; they spend more money on health care (Butler & Lewis, 1977). Some disease states which occur more frequently with increasing age, constitute the major cripplers and killers of the elderly. One major disease is cardiovascular failure due to arteriosclerosis in which blood vessels narrow, and the heart works harder to achieve less. For each decade over 45 years of age, the mortality risk from heart disease doubles for males and triples for females, but males have a higher incidence in middle age (Weg, 1975). Cerebrovascular accidents account for 200,000 deaths each year in the United States; 80% are among people over 65 years of age. Those who survive are often debilitated in speech and movement. Half of all deaths from cancer occur in the over-65 group (Weg, 1975). There is a greater incidence of lung cancer and neoplasia of the prostate among men, and breast and uterine cancer among women. Arthritis of all kinds is a significant problem in medicine (Smith & Bierman, 1973), affecting about 14% of males and 23% of females beyond 45 years of age. Similarly, osteoporosis, a loss of total bone mass, is not only a common problem in elderly, but is four times more common in women than men. On the other hand, four times as many men as women succumb to pulmonary diseases, such as chronic bronchitis, fibrosis, and emphysema, most likely because of a higher frequency in cigarette smoking and direct experience with pollution among men. Nutritional and metabolic dysfunctions are expressed in the form of gallbladder disease, obesity, and anemia. These dysfunctions not only become debilitating in old age, but they interact with other dysfunctions, such as diabetes, arteriosclerosis, varicose veins, hernia, osteoarthritis, cardiovascular disease, peptic ulcer, and hypertension. Elderly overweight persons are also high risks for respiratory problems, thromboembolisms, infection, and wound breakdown from surgery.

Physiological changes occurring in the aging woman may affect sexual functioning to some extent. In some postmenopausal women, hormonal changes, leading to a loss of expansive ability and lubrication in the vagina, may be responsible for the experience of painful intercourse and an increase in vaginal infection. As Masters and Johnson (1966) point out, however, the vasocongestive increase in clitoral shaft diameter and the retraction of the clitoral shaft and glans during high arousal does not change with age. This finding is particularly important when one considers the major role of the clitoris in reaching orgasm (Hite, 1976). Kleigman (1959) has reported that orgasmic response still occurs in women over the age of 70. This finding has been supported by the work of Masters and Johnson (1966) who concluded that a woman's capacity for sexual enjoyment remains intact all her life, especially if regular stimulation occurs.

Data indicate, however, that fewer women than men remain sexually active (Newman & Nichols, 1960; Verwoerdt, Pfeiffer, & Wang, 1969). Among older women, a higher incidence of sexual activity is found among the married than in the unmarried (Christenson & Gagnon, 1965), and among the divorced more than the widowed (Gebhard, 1971). The amount of sexual activity of older women is highly dependent on the interest and availability of men. Loss of a partner was given as a reason for ending intercourse by 48% of women in a study by Pfeiffer, Verwoerdt, and Wang (1968) while only 10% of the men indicated that reason. Spouse behavior, such as illness or lack of sexual interest or ability, was given as reasons by 48% of the women and by 30% of the men. Personal illness or lack of personal sexual interest or ability were given by 14% of the women and approximately 58% of the men.

Older men not only seem to influence strongly the sexual activity of women, but they are at a premium in U.S. society. At age 65 and over, there are about 69 men per 100 women (U.S. Bureau of the Census, 1977). Sixty-three percent of older women are unmarried, while only 27% of older men are unmarried (U.S. Bureau of the Census, 1977). Older women tend to select partners older than they are while older men select younger women. Thus, for many of those women who wish to marry, the choices are few.

In the area of psychological or emotional distress the elderly have a considerable need for psychological services. Redick and Taube (1980) have stated that "at any one point in time approximately 10 percent of the total U.S. population may have a mental disorder . . . and that over a one year period of time as much as 15 percent of the population may have . . . need of treatment services" (p. 60). If this projection accurately applies to the elderly, approximately 3.4 million people are in need of psychological service. This is, however, a minimum number. Most estimates of the prevalence of mental illness among the elderly are higher. For example, Roth (1976) estimates that 18–25% of older people have significant mental health symptoms. Bergmann (1971) studied a random sample of 300 aged subjects and found that 51% were suffering from mild to moderately severe neurotic symptoms. Incapacitating anxiety and depression were found in approximately 14% of one community sample of elderly (Kay, Bergmann, Foster, McKechnie, & Roth, 1970). Cohen (1977) has concluded that the over-65 age group has a greater prevalence of mental disorders than any other age group in the population.

Despite these numbers, the elderly generally do not avail themselves of psychological services. Cohen (1976) has reported that at best only 4% of clients seen at mental health clinics and only 2% at private psychiatric clinics have been elderly. The majority of those elderly utilizing outpatient services are women. Redick and Taube (1980) estimate a ratio of 28 males to every 100 females. Using these numbers, Cohen (1980) has calculated that in 1974, 1.3% of the funds for direct care of mental illness was allocated for community-dwelling elderly. There is no question that the population is severely underserved.

SURVEY DATA

The clinical picture is not as gloomy as the statistical data suggest. When the elderly have spoken for themselves in surveys, they have not reported feeling miserable. Riley and Foner (1968) determined that only about one fifth of elderly subjects scored low on various happiness and morale scales, a figure not significantly different from that for younger subjects. In a 1975 Harris survey, 25% of people over 65 responded affirmatively to the statement, "This is the dreariest time of my life." A majority said, "I am just as happy as when I was younger." Only 17% reported problems in keeping busy. This lack of boredom among the elderly was corroborated by another survey (Dean, 1962) with a different elderly population.

The majority of old people has not reported feeling socially isolated or lonely (Dean, 1962; Harris, 1975). Most older persons visit close relatives frequently (Binstock & Shanas, 1976), often socialize with their friends (Harris, 1975), are active members of a church or synagogue (Erskine, 1964), and belong to voluntary organizations (Hausknecht, 1962). In addition, although attitudes stabilize with age, most elderly adapt to the many major changes in their lives: retirement, children leaving home, widowhood, moving to new homes, serious illness (Palmore, 1977). Their political and social attitudes also tend to shift with those of the rest of society, although at a somewhat slower rate than for younger people (Cutler & Kaufman, 1975; Glenn & Hefner, 1972).

These data are derived from limited samples and are based on self-report measures with problems of verification and bias. Thus, the data are only suggestive. Research on maladaptive and positive adaptive behaviors is sparse. Any conclusions reached from these data are confounded by problems of diagnosis, stereotypic attitudes, and the interplay of physical and social factors.

SELECTED CLINICAL PROBLEMS OF ELDERLY WOMEN

There are some clinical problems which occur frequently for older women and deserve specific attention. In the following section, the problems of drug abuse, depression, and hypochondriasis are described.

DRUG ABUSE

Elderly men are more likely than elderly women to be alcoholics (e.g., McCusker, Cherubin, & Zimberg, 1971); elderly women are more likely than elderly men to be addicted to drugs (Schuckit & Moore, 1979). Persons over 60 receive 25% of all prescribed drugs (Batalden, 1974). In addition, the elderly frequently self-medicate (Lenhart, 1976), hoard out-dated medication, share prescriptions with friends (Gibson & O'Hare, 1968), and use over-the-counter drugs and combine them with alcohol (Capel & Stewart, 1971). The elderly are twice as likely to react adversely to medications even in normal doses (Cooper, 1975) and they experience side effects from a wider variety of medications than do the young (Morrant, 1975). The ability to metabolize drugs slows down with age. Loss of body weight and loss of fluid impair absorption, distribution, excretion, and metabolism (Lenhart, 1976). Barbiturates and tranquil-izers are the classes of drugs most abused by the elderly. Sleeping pills and antianxiety medications decrease alertness and may result in con-fusion, increasing the possibility of a misdiagnosis of organic brain syn-drome. Another effect of decreased alertness is hypotension which can precipitate falls. Lethargy and apparent sadness may occur and may be misdiagnosed as depression. Abuse of over-the-counter drugs, espe-cially aspirins, bromides, and laxatives, is especially common among elderly women. Each of these drugs has physical effects on the aging body which may appear as behavior disorders, neurologic manifesta-tions, or mental changes.

DEPRESSION

Depression is the diagnosis given to 45% of new admissions over 65 years of age to mental hospitals (Myers, Sheldon, & Robinson, 1963). Pfeiffer and Busse (1973) found significant depressive symptoms in 65% of a population over 60. Elderly subjects differ from younger subjects in the types of depressive symptoms they express (Fisch, Goldfarb, Shahinian, & Post, 1962); they exhibit more physical complaints, less guilt (Schwab, Holzer, & Warheit, 1973), and more apathy (Levin, 1963). Elderly also more often express paranoid behaviors, ranging from sus-piciousness and irritability to delusions.

The diagnosis of depression is unreliable. It may be influenced by a variety of factors including the time of onset of the disorder, the

physical condition of the person, residence inside or outside an institution, the diagnostic measure, and prevalent social conditions. Butler
and Lewis (1977) explicate a wide variety of factors which may contribute
to the misdiagnosis of depression in the elderly: feelings of helplessness,
guilt, loneliness, boredom, sadness, lack of vitality, personal devaluation, constipation, sexual disinterest, suicidal thoughts, grief, insomnia,
early morning fatigue, marked loss of appetite, hypochondriasis, and
somatic symptoms. With a decline in sensory acuity, particularly in the
areas of hearing and vision, elderly persons often experience depression,
paranoid ideation, inactivity, and a reluctance to socialize with others.
There is evidence of physiological concomitants of depression in the
aged, due for instance, to viral diseases or Parkinson's disease (Birren,
Butler, Greenhouse, Sokoloff, & Yarrow, 1963). Tranquilizers and drugs
for hypotension can cause depression (Butler & Lewis, 1977), while
antidepressant medication may cause agitation.

There has been some speculation that depression should follow the
experience of menopause. The decrease of estrogens, which inhibit
monoamine oxidase, an enzyme implicated in the etiology of depression,
certainly supports this notion. Indeed, estrogens have been shown effective in alleviating the depressive symptoms of menopausal women
(Verwoedt, 1976). Studies of the rates of depression in postmenopausal
populations, however, have not provided evidence to support the notion
that depression following menopause was greater than chance (Weeke,
Bille, Videbach, Dupont, & Juel-Nielsen, 1975).

HYPOCHONDRIASIS

Many elderly women receive the diagnosis of hypochondriasis. The
diagnosis is made when a woman is preoccupied with physical functions
and bodily processes, and interprets minor pains or intermittent aches
as signs of serious disease. A woman who believes she is ill may seek
corroboration from a physician, worry about her symptoms privately,
or discuss them endlessly with friends and family. If the older woman
complains to her physician, she may find the physician unresponsive
or unwilling to give her more than a cursory examination. The physician
may dismiss such complaints as natural artifacts of the aging process
for which no treatment is possible. The elderly woman may be told to
expect discomfort and accept it as indicative of aging. This attitude is
reflected in the following story:

An old woman makes her yearly visit to her physician and complains that her left knee is bothering her terribly. Her physician airily waves his hand and says, "It's because you're old, Annie. There's nothing to be done." After a moment's thought, Annie asks, "Then can you tell me, doctor, why my left knee is older than my right knee?"

Many elderly worry over the meaning of the pain they experience. Some truly fear consulting a physician because they equate disease with old age (MacDonald, 1973) and impending death. Most people use physical health as the primary index of age in themselves and others (Kastenbaum, 1964). Fear may prompt these elderly to ruminate more and more about their bodies to the point that psychological or physical decline occurs. Some elderly use their states of health as a primary source of conversation and as a way of eliciting involvement from others. Blum and Weiner (1979) propose that physical complaints represent the displacement of anxiety from more threatening issues, such as society's rejection of an unproductive, low-status, inactive, passive old person. Extensive discussion of physical complaints may gratify guilt feelings and atone for hostile feelings against family members or friends (Fenichel, 1945); or they may indicate "regressive autoeroticism," narcissistic pleasure derived from caring for the body (Verwoerdt, 1976). When the body images of older and younger subjects were evaluated, Plutchik, Weiner, and Conte (1971) found that regardless of age, those scoring highest on measures of bodily worries and discomforts received little attention from others and were not actively involved with others.

ELDERLY IN INSTITUTIONS

There is one group of elderly who have been given research and treatment attention. These are the institutionalized elderly who number about 1 million and receive 14% of the total expenditures in national health funds (Cohen, 1977). Female admissions outnumber male admissions to private and general psychiatric hospital inpatient units, but male admissions to state and county mental hospitals are nearly double those for females (Redick & Taube, 1980). Those elderly in mental hospitals are usually in advanced old age (over 80 years), poor, and suffering from impaired mental and physical functioning, multiple chronic disabilities, and a loss of family. More than 40% have lived in the institution longer than 10 years; they comprise 30% of the total institutional population. Only 17%, however, were admitted after age 65 (Butler & Lewis,

1977). Thus the majority of elderly mental hospital residents who grew old during their institutional stay and became accustomed to the custodial role, would be considered chronic schizophrenics. Behaviors they typically exhibit, such as apathy, withdrawal from social stimulation, hoarding, and poor self-maintenance skills, are signs of institutionalization, not of aging. In fact, these behaviors are probably due to environmental factors in the institution.

Those elderly residing in nursing homes are recipients of the form of service most associated with the aged and often the most dreaded. Nursing homes are presently used by the terminally ill who require intensive nursing care, patients recuperating from an illness, those infirm who lack sufficient social resources to manage themselves in the community, and former residents of state mental hospitals who were transferred to make room for younger patients. By far, the majority of nursing home residents are considered senile, mentally retarded, or mentally ill.

A major factor influencing the status of elderly living in institutions is the sense of futility experienced by providers of health care to geriatric populations, and expressed in attitudes toward service delivery. One attitude, "Let Them Rest in Peace," assumes that people who have survived beyond 65 years have earned the right to be kept in comfort for their remaining years. They should not be required to dress themselves, or lose weight, or give up their cigarettes. The second attitude, "You Can't Teach an Old Dog New Tricks," assumes it is a waste of time and energy to try to teach people who cannot or will not learn. At face value, neither attitude is particularly evil. These attitudes are consistent with our humanitarian and liberal economic traditions. Nevertheless, people who express these attitudes, whether they are themselves elderly or service personnel in geriatric units, are generally pessimistic about the outcome of change efforts.

BEHAVIORAL INTERVENTIONS WITH THE ELDERLY

INSTITUTIONAL POPULATIONS

A substantial amount of behavioral gerontological research has been conducted with institutional populations. With this group, behavioral researchers have worked primarily in three overlapping areas: increasing social interaction and participation; increasing self-care behaviors; and environmental manipulation programs which involve changing a physical factor in the client's environment and measuring the behavioral effects. A host of programs aim to stimulate activities and social participation among the institutionalized elderly through positive reinforcement and prompting (Ince, 1969; Jenkins, Felce, Lund, & Powell, 1977; McClannahan & Risley, 1974, 1975; Newkirk, Feldman, Bickett, Gipson, & Lutzker, 1976; Quilitch, 1974); heightened stimulus control (Quattrochi-Tubin & Jason, 1980); and social skills training (Berger & Rose, 1977; Lopez, 1980; Lopez, Hoyer, Goldstein, Gershaw, & Sprafkin, 1980). Self-care programs target behaviors in the domains of continence (Atthowe, 1972; Collins & Planka, 1975; Grosicki, 1968; Pollock & Liberman, 1974); self-feeding (Baltes & Zerbe, 1976; Blackman, Gehle, & Pinkston, 1979; Geiger & Johnson, 1974); independent walking (Burt, Law, Machan, Macklin, Nesbitt, Read, & Wiebe, 1974; MacDonald & Butler, 1974); and self-bathing (Rinke, Williams, Lloyd, & Smith-Scott, 1978). As would be expected, investigators have found that geriatric residents can increase their level of social involvement, participation, and self-care activities. Sometimes change has occurred only with a great deal of effort. For example, Wisocki and Mosher (1980) required 48 weeks to teach basic sign language to a chronic brain-damaged aphasic patient and 56 weeks to increase social interaction among six geriatric men in a Veterans Administration hospital (Wisocki & Mosher, 1978). In many cases, however, change occurred with a minimum of effort. Work on environmental programming, which has demonstrated that the institutionalized elderly are extremely responsive to physical changes in the environment, provide beer and wine (Black, 1969; Carroll, 1978; Chien, 1971; Mishara & Kastenbaum, 1974; Volpe & Kastenbaum, 1967); encourage indoor gardening (Powell, Felce, Jenkins, & Lund, 1979) and furniture arranging (Peterson, Knapp, Rosen, & Pither, 1977; Sommer & Ross, 1958); provide a store for shopping (McClannahan & Risley, 1973); and supply opportunities for letter writing (Goldstein & Baer, 1976).

While some of this research has been criticized by Kahn (1977) as "trivial," and of limited relevance to treatment for the elderly, the value of this research may lie in its closer look at the physical qualities of institutions for the elderly. Likened to the isolation and sensory deprivation elements of the experimental chamber used by Pavlov to induce sleep in animals (Cautela, 1966), the institutional environment is often characterized by individual isolation, repetitive stimuli, and a dearth of reinforcement. Not only is reinforcement for social interaction between the patients on an extinction schedule, but reinforcement is often contingent on depressive and dependent behaviors. It is quite likely that some of the undesirable behaviors of the institutionalized geriatric patient (such as complaining and poor eating) are operants for attention and interactions with the staff. If staff do not respond to their elderly clients unless they demonstrate maladaptive behaviors, we might seriously question the ethics of using behavioral procedures to lessen maladaptive behaviors. A good deal of the positive effects obtained in these studies has been attributed to the process of making the staff aware of the relevant contingencies and monitoring their use of those contingencies (Barton, Baltes, & Orzeck, 1980; Lester & Baltes, 1978; Mikulic, 1971). McReynolds and Coleman (1972) pointed out that staff attitudes contributed to the success of a token-economy program. They found that improvement in the behavior of severely regressed institutionalized psychiatric patients was accompanied by an increase in staff enthusiasm.

Several attempts have been made to modify staff attitudes and behavior toward elderly patients. Hickey (1974) and Heller and Walsh (1976) designed broad-ranging training programs involving role playing and practical exercises for direct care staff. Positive changes in attitude were measured by self-report questionnaires. Wisocki and Telch (1980) compared the effects of direct experience (overt reinforcer sampling) and covert reinforcer sampling on the attitudes of undergraduate students toward geriatric patients, and found positive gains from both techniques.

COMMUNITY-DWELLING ELDERLY

Behavioral work with the large population of community-dwelling elderly is sparse. Aside from those articles advocating behavior therapy as a useful approach with elderly persons (e.g., Baltes & Barton, 1977; Cautela, 1966; Lane, 1966), the majority of behavioral work with this population falls into three categories: (1) increasing participation in community activities, such as meal programs (Bunck & Iwata, 1978), recreational events (Pierce, 1975), and the foster grandparent program (Fabry & Reid, 1978); (2) the therapeutic strategies for clinical problems of the elderly, such as depression (Falloon, 1975), phobia (Friedman, 1966; Wellman, 1978), grief (Flannery, 1974), and obsessive–compulsive behavior (O'Brien, 1978); and (3) modification of physical and cognitive changes in elderly clients. This third category is fairly well developed. It is important both to the design of treatment programs for elderly and to help dispel the myth of aging as an inevitable disease process. For these reasons I will expand on those studies in some detail.

MODIFICATION OF PHYSICAL AND COGNITIVE CHANGES IN AGING

Many of the specific biological and physical changes which occur with aging individuals are modifiable, suggesting that one's physiological age may be extended somewhat beyond one's chronological age. Loss of functions occur at varying rates in the different organs and systems of the body. Even within the same person, different systems will probably not age at the same rate (Weg, 1975). One common factor in aging is indicated by the slowing of the dominant brain rhythm. By age 60, the dominant brain wave rhythm is around 9 cps; for young adults the dominant rhythm is 10.2 to 10.5 cps. While this decelerating rate is related to some pathological states, such as cerebral arteriosclerosis or severe brain atrophy, even healthy elderly persons demonstrate the slower brain wave rhythms (Birren, 1964). An experiment by Woodruff (1972), in which old subjects demonstrated an ability to increase the abundance of EEG alpha activity as well as young subjects, suggests that at least some of the alpha slowing occurring in old age may be reversible. DeVries (1970) also found that with an exercise program, physiological change occurred in blood pressure, oxygen transport capacity, amount of body fat, and the capacity for work. Others (Pastalan, Mantz, & Merrill, 1973), found an increase in visual capacity with exercise. The value of physical exercise for increasing the cognitive functioning of geriatric institutionalized patients has been suggested by Powell (1974) who found that, compared with control subjects, patients given exercise and "social therapy" treatment improved on measures of cognitive activity, but not on behavioral ratings.

Reaction time also slows down with age and does not appear to be related to a disease process. There is evidence that psychomotor performance in older persons can be improved with practice (Murrell, 1970) and that the amount of slowing in reaction time is dependent on a variety of variables, including the nature of the task and the investigator. In test performances in other areas, the behavior of the elderly was affected by motivational and structural factors, such as fatigue (Furry & Baltes, 1973), task meaningfulness (Arenberg, 1973), and the novelty of the testing situation (Goulet, 1972). Speed of responding to test items was increased with practice (Hoyer, Labouvie, & Baltes, 1973) and reinforcement (Hoyer, Hoyer, Treat, & Baltes, 1978–1979). Accuracy of responding was improved with feedback training (Schultz & Hoyer, 1976); cautiousness in elderly test performance was improved by differential reinforcement (Birkhill & Schaie, 1975).

Continuation of work in this area is vitally important to the elderly. The interplay of biomedical and psychological issues is more apparent with the elderly than with any other age group (Cohen, 1980). Applications to the elderly of current findings in behavioral medicine will improve knowledge of the diseases closely linked to aging, and of compliance with treatment and medication, a notorious problem for elderly. Application of the behavioral model to an analysis of the effects of psychotropic medication on older people is also warranted. They not only use more drugs than younger people, but their altered metabolism rates influence responses to drugs. Many of the diseases associated with aging may be arrested with medication and health care. Many more may never occur if good health maintenance occurs. Changes in diet and nutrition, exercise as an integral part of daily life, a reduction in environmental stresses, maintenance of intellectual and affective pursuits, elimination of habitually excessive use of alcohol and cigarettes, will prolong health and life. These are all areas in which behavioral technology is particularly suitable.

PROBLEMS IN RESEARCH WITH THE ELDERLY

Research with elderly clients is often a difficult process. The factors of fatigue, type of test items used, meaningfulness of the test items, and placebo have a significant effect on research with an aging population (Botwinick, 1967). Severe impairment of vision or hearing, medications, and stress of the testing situation are additional factors to be considered. Tests currently in use have generally not been standardized on an elderly population. Even the Wechsler Adult Intelligence Scale (WAIS), a frequently used measure of declining intelligence, was standardized with a limited geographic sample and did not include sufficient numbers of elderly (Wechsler, 1955). The institutionalized have been shown to be so responsive to small changes in the physical environment and in staff attention, that no research design can ignore these factors. Changes in one area are likely to lead to collateral, generalized changes in other areas. Because of this difficulty in isolating the effects of the independent variable, some researchers (e.g., Hoyer, 1974) have suggested that reversal designs and multiple-baseline designs be avoided in behavioral-gerontological research in favor of multielement designs in which behaviors are repeatedly measured under alternating conditions of the independent variable. The concurrent schedule design, in which several independent variables are manipulated simultaneously, has also been recommended (Rebok & Hoyer, 1977) because it closely approximates conditions existing in the natural environment.

CONCLUSIONS AND RECOMMENDATIONS

Treatment-oriented research must be expanded in behavioral gerontology. Researchers have only begun to explore the possibilities for behavior change with the elderly, and have barely knocked at the doors of the elderly in their communities. The elderly in institutions challenge us to develop effective staff training programs and generalization programs, and to expose the modifiable components of disease and aging. Work with the elderly in any setting challenges us to develop a technology for slowing the aging process and preserving life. The age-limits of behavioral techniques have not yet been reached. We do not know what environmental conditions hasten and delay the biological deterioration of aging. There has been too much emphasis on alleviating deficits in the elderly and too little emphasis on prevention of future loss.

Work with elderly populations offers us a chance to expand our research strategies to include: (1) consideration of complex variables and their interactions; (2) the long-range effects of interventions; (3) conceptualization of adaptive mechanisms in evolutionary terms over the life span; (4) projects which are more generalizable to naturalistic contexts and involve the use of existing resources; (5) involvement with professionals from other disciplines; (6) discoveries of new dimensions to psychological problems and their treatment strategies. Focusing research attention on the elderly population will probably lead to improved services, better treatment and living conditions, and greater understanding. Because we are all aging women and men, the work we do with the aged will soon benefit us as well as the current elderly.

REFERENCES

Arenberg, D. Cognition and aging: Verbal learning, memory, and problem solving. In C. Eisdorfer & M. P. Lawton (Eds.), *The psychology of adult development and aging.* Washington, D.C.: American Psychological Association, 1973.

Atthowe, J. M. Controlling nocturnal enuresis in severely disabled and chronic patients. *Behavior Therapy*, 1972, *3*, 232–239.

Baltes, M. M., & Barton, E. M. New approaches toward aging: A case for the operant model. *Educational Gerontology: An International Quarterly*, 1977, *2*, 383–405.

Baltes, M. M., & Zerbe, M. B. Independence training in nursing home residents. *The Gerontologist*, 1976, *16*, 428–432.

Barrow, G. M. Physicians' attitudes toward aging and the aging process. *Dissertation Abstracts International*, 1971, *32*, 2205.

Barton, E. M., Baltes, M. M., & Orzeck, M. J. Etiology of dependence in older nursing home residents during morning care: The role of staff behavior. *Journal of Personality and Social Psychology*, 1980, *38*, 423–431.

Batalden, P. *Working with older people* (Vol. 2: *Biological, psychological, and sociological aspects of aging*) (DHEW Publ. No. HRA 74-3117). Washington, D.C.: U.S. Government Printing Office, 1974.

Berger, R. M., & Rose, S. D. Interpersonal skill training with institutionalized elderly patients. *Journal of Gerontology*, 1977, *32*, 346–353.

Bergmann, K. The neuroses of old age. In D. Kay & A. Wolk (Eds.), *Recent developments in psycho-geriatrics, a symposium*. *British Journal of Psychiatry*, Special Publ. No. 6, 1971.

Bernstein, M. C. Forecast of women's retirement income: Cloudy and colder; 25% chance of poverty. *Industrial Gerontology*, 1974, *1*, 1–13.

Binstock, R., & Shanas, E. (Eds.). *Handbook of aging and the social sciences*. New York: Van Nostrand, 1976.

Birkhill, W. R., & Schaie, K. W. The effect of differential reinforcement of cautiousness in intellectual performance among the elderly. *Journal of Gerontology*, 1975, *30*, 578–583.

Birren, J. *The psychology of aging*. Englewood Cliffs, N.J.: Prentice-Hall, 1964.

Birren, J., Butler, R., Greenhouse, S., Sokoloff, L., & Yarrow, M. Summary and interpretations. In *Human aging*. Washington, D.C.: U.S. Government Printing Office, 1963.

Birren, J., & Woodruff, D. Academic and professional training in the psychology of aging. In D. Eisdorfer & M. P. Lawton (Eds.), *The psychology of adult development and aging*. Washington, D.C.: American Psychological Association, 1973.

Black, A. L. Altering behavior of geriatric patients with beer. *Northwest Medicine*, 1969, *68*, 453–456.

Blackman, D. K., Gehle, C., & Pinkston, E. M. Modifying eating habits of the institutionalized elderly. *Social Work Research and Abstracts*, 1979, 18–24.

Blum, J. E., & Weiner, M. Neurosis in the older adult. In O. Kaplan (Ed.), *Psychopathology of aging*. New York: Academic, 1979.

Botwinick, J. *Cognitive processes in maturity and old age*. New York: Springer, 1967.

Breed, W., & Huffine, C. Sex differences in suicide among older white Americans. In O. Kaplan (Ed.), *Psychopathology of aging*. New York: Academic, 1979.

Bunck, T. J., & Iwata, B. A. Increasing senior citizen participation in a community-based nutritious meal program. *Journal of Applied Behavior Analysis*, 1978, *11*, 75–86.

Burch, G., Cohn, A., & Neumann, C. A study of the rate of water loss from the surfaces of the fingertips and toe tips of normal and senile subjects and patients with arterial hypertension. *American Heart Journal*, 1942, *23*, 185–196.

Burt, B., Law, M., Machan, L., Macklin, C., Nesbitt, D., Read, B., & Wiebe, C. Mildred Jones walks again. *Canadian Nurse*, 1974, *70*, 37.

Butler, R., & Lewis, M. *Aging and mental health*. St. Louis, Mo.: Mosby, 1977.

Capel, W., & Stewart, G. The management of drug abuse in aging populations: New Orleans findings. *Journal of Drug Issues*, 1971, *1*, 114–120.

Carroll, P. J. The social hour for geropsychiatric patients. *Journal of the American Geriatrics Society*, 1978, *26*, 32–35.

Cautela, J. R. Behavior theory and geriatrics. *Journal of Genetic Psychology*, 1966, *108*, 9–17.

Chien, C. P. Psychiatric treatment for geriatric patients: "Pub or drug?" *American Journal of Psychiatry*, 1971, *127*, 110–115.

Christenson, C., & Gagnon, J. Sexual behavior in a group of older women. *Journal of Gerontology*, 1965, *20*, 351–356.

Cohen, G. Mental health services and the elderly: Needs and options. *American Journal of Psychiatry*, 1976, *133*, 65–68.

Cohen, G. Approach to the geriatric patient. *Medical Clinics of North America*, 1977, *61*, 855–866.

Cohen, G. Prospects for mental health and aging. In J. Birren & R. Sloan (Eds.), *Handbook of mental health and aging*. Englewood Cliffs, N.J.: Prentice-Hall, 1980.

Collins, R. W., & Plaska, T. Mowrer's conditioning treatment for enuresis applied to geriatric residents of a nursing home. *Behavior Therapy*, 19765, *6*, 632–638.

Cooper, J. W. Implications of drug reactions: Recognition, incidences, and prevention. *Rhode Island Medical Journal*, 1975, *58*, 274–280.

Cutler, S., & Kaufman, R. Cohort changes in political attitudes. *Public Opinion Quarterly*, 1975, *39*, 69–81.

Dean, L. Aging and decline of affect. *Journal of Gerontology*, 1962, *17*, 440–446.

deVries, H. A. Physiological affects of an exercise training regimen upon men aged 52–88. *Journal of Gerontology*, 1970, *24*, 325–336.

Erskine, H. The polls. *Public Opinion Quarterly*, 1964, *28*, 679.

Fabry, P. L., & Reid, D. H. Teaching foster grandparents to train severely handicapped persons. *Journal of Applied Behavior Analysis*, 1978, *22*, 111–123.

Falloon, I. R. The therapy of depression: A behavioral approach. *Psychotherapy and Psychosomatics*, 1975, *25* (1–6), 69–75.

Fenichel, O. *The psychoanalytic theory of neurosis*. New York: Norton, 1945.

Field, M. *Depth and extent of the geriatric problem*. Springfield, Ill.: Thomas, 1970.

Fisch, M., Goldfarb, A., Shahinian, S., & Post, F. *The significance of affective symptoms in old age*. London: Oxford, 1962.

Flannery, R. B. Behavior modification of geriatric grief: A transactional perspective. *International Journal on Aging and Human Development*, 1974, *5*, 197–203.

Friedman, D. Treatment of a case of dog phobia in a deaf mute by behaviour therapy. *Behaviour Research and Therapy*, 1966, *4*, 141.

Furry, C., & Baltes, P. The effect of age differences in ability: Extraneous performance variables on the assessment of intelligence in children, adults, and the elderly. *Journal of Gerontology*, 1973, *28*, 73–80.

Gebhard, P. Postmarital coitus among widows and divorcees. In P. Bohannan (Ed.), *Divorce and after*. Garden City, N.Y.: Doubleday, 1971.

Geiger, O. G., & Johnson, L. A. Positive education for elderly persons: Correct eating through reinforcement. *The Gerontologist*, 1974, *14*, 432–436.

Gibson, S., & O'Hare, M. Prescription of drugs for old people at home. *Gerontologica Clinica*, 1968, *10*, 271–280.

Glenn, N., & Hefner, T. Further evidence on aging and party identification. *Public Opinion Quarterly*, 1972, *36*, 31–47.

Goldfarb, A. The rationale for psychotherapy with older persons. *American Journal of Medical Science*, 1956, *232*, 181–185.

Goldstein, R. S., & Baer, D. M. A procedure to increase the personal mail and number of correspondents for nursing home residents. *Behavior Therapy*, 1976, *7*, 348–354.

Goulet, L. R. New directions for research on aging and retention. *Journal of Gerontology*, 1972, *27*, 52–60.

Grosicki, J. P. Effect of operant conditioning on modification of incontinence in neuro-psychiatric geriatric patients. *Nursing Research*, 1968, *17*, 304–311.

Group for the Advancement of Psychiatry. *The aged and community mental health: A guide to program development.* Vol. 8, Series No. 81, November 1971.

Harris, L. *The myth and reality of aging in America.* Washington, D.C.: National Council on Aging, 1975.

Hausknecht, M. *The joiners.* New York: Bedminster, 1962.

Hazell, K. *Social and medical problems of the elderly.* London: Hutchinson, 1960.

Heller, B., & Walsh, F. Changing nursing students' attitudes toward the aged: An experimental study. *Journal of Nursing Education*, 1976, *15*, 9–17.

Hickey, T. In-service training in gerontology. *The Gerontologist*, 1974, *14*, 57–64.

Hite, S. *The Hite report.* New York: Macmillan, 1976.

Hoyer, F. W., Hoyer, W. J., Treat, N. J., & Baltes, P. B. Training response speed in young and elderly women. *International Journal of Aging and Human Development*, 1978–1979, *9*, 247–253.

Hoyer, W. J. Aging as intraindividual change. *Developmental Psychology*, 1974, *10*, 821–826.

Hoyer, W. J., Labouvie, G. V., & Baltes, P. B. Modification of response speed deficits and intellectual performance in the elderly. *Human Development*, 1973, *16*, 233–242.

Ince, L. P. A behavioral approach to motivation in rehabilitation. *Psychological Record*, 1969, *19*, 105–111.

Jacobs, R. *Life after youth.* Boston: Beacon, 1979.

Jenkins, J., Felce, D., Lund, B., & Powell, L. Increasing engagement in activity of residents in old people's homes by providing recreational materials. *Behaviour Research and Therapy*, 1977, *15*, 429–434.

Kahn, R. L. The mental health system and the future aged. *The Gerontologist*, 1975, *15*, 24–31.

Kahn, R. L. Perspectives in the evaluation of psychological mental health programs for the aged. In W. D. Gentry (Ed.), *Geropsychology: A model of training and clinical service.* Cambridge, Mass.: Ballinger, 1977.

Kastenbaum, R. (Ed.). *New thoughts on old age.* New York: Springer, 1964.

Kastenbaum, R. Personality theory, therapeutic approaches, and the elderly client. In M. Storandt, I. Siegler, & M. Elias (Eds.), *The clinical psychology of aging.* New York: Plenum, 1978.

Kay, D., Bergmann, K., Foster, E., McKechnie, A., & Roth, M. Mental illness and hospital usage in the elderly: A random sample followed up. *Comprehensive Psychiatry*, 1970, *1*, 26–35.

Kleigman, S. Frigidity in women. *Quarterly Review of Surgery, Obstetrics, and Gynecology*, 1959, *16*, 243–248.

Kramer, M., Taube, C. A., & Redick, R. W. Patterns of uses of psychiatric facilities by the aged: Past, present, and future. In D. Eisdorfer & M. P. Lawton (Eds.), *The psychology of adult development and aging.* Washington, D.C.: American Psychological Association, 1973.

Lane, G. Adjustment to aging: Some applications of learning theory. *The Gerontologist*, 1966, *6*, 88–89.

Lenhart, D. The use of medications in the elderly population. *Nursing Clinics of North America*, 1976, *22*, 135–143.

Lester, P. B., & Baltes, M. M. Functional interdependence of the social environment and the behavior of the institutionalized aged. *Journal of Gerontological Nursing*, 1978, *4*, 22–27.

Levin, S. Depression in the aged: A study of the salient external factors. *Geriatrics*, 1963, *18*, 302–307.

Lopez, M. Social-skills training with institutionalized elderly: Effects of precounseling, structuring, and overlearning on skill acquisition and transfer. *Journal of Counseling Psychology*, 1980, *27*, 286–293.

Lopez, M. A., Hoyer, W. J., Goldstein, A. P., Gershaw, N. J., & Sprafkin, R. P. Effects of overlearning and incentive on the acquisition and transfer of interpersonal skills with instituionalized elderly. *Journal of Gerontology*, 1980, *35*, 403–408.

Maas, H. S., & Kuypers, J. A. *From thirty to seventy*. San Francisco: Jossey-Bass, 1974.

MacDonald, M. The forgotten Americans: A sociopsychological analysis of aging and nursing homes. *American Journal of Community Psychology*, 1973, *1*, 272–294.

MacDonald, M. L., & Butler, A. K. Reversal of helplessness: Producing walking behavior in nursing home wheelchair residents using behavior modification procedure. *Journal of Gerontology*, 1974, *29*, 97–101.

Masters, W., & Johnson, V. *Human sexual response*. Boston: Little, Brown, 1966.

McClannahan, L. E., & Risley, T. R. A store for nursing home residents. *Nursing Homes*, 1973, *22*, 10–11.

McClannahan, L. E., & Risley, T. R. Design of living environments for nursing home residents: Recruiting attendance at activities. *The Gerontologist*, 1974, *14*, 236–240.

McClannahan, L. E., & Risley, T. R. Activities and materials for severely disabled geriatric patients. *Nursing Homes*, 1975, *24*, 10%13.

McCusker, J., Cherubin, C., & Zimberg, S. Prevalence of alcoholism in general municipal hospital populations. *New York State Journal of Medicine*, 1971, *71*, 751–754.

McReynolds, W. T., & Coleman, J. Token economy: Patient and staff charges. *Behaviour Research and Therapy*, 1972, *10*, 29–34.

Mikulic, M. Reinforcement of independent and dependent patient behavior by nursing personnel: An exploratory study. *Nursing Research*, 1971, *20*, 162–163.

Mishara, B. L., & Kastenbaum, R. Wine in the treatment of long-term geriatric patients in mental institutions. *Journal of the American Geriatrics Society*, 1974, *22*, 88–94.

Moore, J., & Birren, J. Doctoral training in gerontology: An analysis of dissertations on problems of aging in institutions of higher learning in the United States: 1934–1969. *Journal of Gerontology*, 1971, *26*, 249–257.

Morrant, J. Medicines and mental illness in old age. *Canadian Psychiatric Association Journal*, 1975, *20*, 309–312.

Murrell, F. H. The effect of extensive practice in age differences in reaction time. *Journal of Gerontology*, 1970, *25*, 268–274.

Myers, J., Sheldon, D., & Robinson, S. A study of 138 elderly first admissions. *American Journal of Psychiatry*, 1963, *120*, 244–249.

Newkirk, J. M., Feldman, S., Bickett, A., Gipson, T. T., & Lutzker, J. R. Increasing extended care facility residents' attendance at recreational activities with convenient locations and personal invitations. *Journal of Applied Behavior Analysis*, 1976, *9*, 207.

Newman, G., & Nichols, C. Sexual activities and attitudes in older person. *Journal of the American Medical Association*, 1960, *173*, 33–35.

O'Brien, J. S. The behavioral treatment of a thirty-year smallpox obsession and hand washing compulsion. *Journal of Behavior Therapy and Experimental Psychiatry*, 1978, *9*, 365–368.

Palmore, E. Facts on aging. *The Gerontologist*, 1977, *17*, 315–320.

Pastalan, L., Mantz, R., & Merrill, J. The stimulation of age related nursing homes: A new approach to the study of environmental barriers. In W. Preissen (Ed.), *Environmental design research*. Stroudsburg, Pa.: Dowden, Hutchinson, & Ross, 1973.

Peterson, R. F., Knapp, T. J., Rosen, J. C., & Pither, B. F. The effects of furniture arrangement on the behavior of geriatric patients. *Behavior Therapy*, 1977, *8*, 464–467.

Pfeiffer, E., & Busse, E. Mental disorders in later life—affective disorders; paranoid, neurotic, and situational reactions. In E. Busse & E. Pfeiffer (Eds.), *Mental illness in later life*. Washington, D.C.: American Psychiatric Association, 1973.

Pfeiffer, E., Verwoerdt, A., & Wang, H. Sexual behavior in aged men and women. I. Observations on 254 community volunteers. *Archives of General Psychiatry*, 1968, *19*, 753–758.

Pierce, C. H. Recreation for elderly: Activity participation at a senior citizen center. *The Gerontologist*, 1975, *15*, 202–205.

Plutchik, R., Weiner, M., & Conte, H. Studies of body image: I. Body worries and body discomforts. *Journal of Gerontology*, 1971, *26*, 334–350.

Pollock, D. D., & Liberman, R. P. Behavior therapy of incontinence in demented in patients. *The Gerontologist*, 1974, *14*, 488–491.

Powell, L., Felce, D., Jenkins, J., & Lund, B. Increasing engagement in a home for the elderly by providing an indoor gardening activity. *Behaviour Research and Therapy*, 1979, *17*, 127–135.

Powell, R. R. Psychological effects of exercise therapy upon institutionalized geriatric mental patients. *Journal of Gerontology*, 1974, *29*, 157–161.

Quattrochi-Tubin, S., & Jason, L. A. Enhancing social interactions and activity among the elderly through stimulus control. *Journal of Applied Behavior Analysis*, 1980, *13*, 159–163.

Quilitch, H. R. Purposeful activity increased on a geriatric ward through programmed recreation. *Journal of the American Geriatrics Society*, 1974, *22*, 226–229.

Rebok, G., & Hoyer, W. The functional context of elderly behavior. *The Gerontologist*, 1977, *17*, 27–32.

Redick, R., & Taube, C. Demography and mental health care of the aged. In J. Birren & R. Sloan (Eds.), *Handbook of mental health and aging*. Englewood Cliffs, N.J.: Prentice-Hall, 1980.

Riley, M., & Foner, A. *Aging and society* (Vol. 1: *An inventory of research findings*). New York: Russell Sage Foundation, 1968.

Rinke, C. L., Williams, J. J., Lloyd, K. E., & Smith-Scott, W. The effects of prompting and reinforcement on self-bathing by elderly residents of a nursing home. *Behavior Therapy*, 1978, *9*, 873–881.

Roth, M. The psychiatric disorders of later life. *Psychiatric Annals*, 1976, *6*, 417–445.

Schuckit, M., & Moore, M. Drug problems in the elderly. In O. Kaplan (Ed.), *Psychopathology of aging*. New York: Academic, 1979.

Schultz, N. R., & Hoyer, W. J. Feedback effects on spatial egocentrism in old age. *Journal of Gerontology*, 1976, *31*, 72–75.

Schwab, J., Holzer, C., & Warheit, G. Depressive symptomotology and age. *Psychosomatics*, 1973, *14*, 135–141.

Shock, N. W. Physiological theories of aging. In R. Rockstein (Ed.), *Theoretical aspects of aging*. New York: Academic, 1974.

Smith, D., & Bierman, E. (Eds.). *The biologic ages of man*. Philadelphia: Saunders, 1973.

Sommer, R., & Ross, H. Social interaction on a geriatrics ward. *International Journal of Social Psychology*, 1958, *4*, 128–132.

Storandt, M., Siegler, I., & Elias, M. (Eds.). *The clinical psychology of aging*. New York: Plenum, 1978.

U.S. Bureau of the Census. *Statistical abstracts of the United States* (98th ed.). Washington, D.C.: U.S. Government Printing Office, 1977.

U.S. Department of Health, Education and Welfare. *Facts about older Americans* (Publ. No. OHD 75-20006B). Washington, D.C.: U.S. Government Printing Office, 1975.

Verwoerdt, A. *Clinical geropsychiatry*. Baltimore: Williams & Wilkins, 1976.

Verwoerdt, A., Pfeiffer, E., & Wang, H. Sexual behavior in senescence. Changes in sexual activity and interest in aging men and women. *Journal of Geriatric Psychiatry*, 1969, *2*, 163–180.

Volpe, A., & Kastenbaum, R. Beer and TLC. *American Journal of Nursing*, 1967, *67*, 101–103.

Weeke, A., Bille, M., Videbach, T., Dupont, A., & Juel-Nielsen, N. Incidence of depressive symptoms in a Danish county. *Acta Psychiatrica Scandinavica*, 1975, *51*, 28–41.

Weg, R. Changing physiology of aging: Normal and pathological. In D. Woodruff & J. Birren (Eds.), *Aging: Scientific perspectives and social issues*. New York: Van Nostrand, 1975.

Wisocki, P. A., & Mosher, P. M. *Effect of individual attention and recreational activities on improving the social skills of institutionalized geriatric men*. Paper presented at the Association for Advancement of Behavior Therapy, Chicago, 1978.

Wisocki, P. A., & Mosher, P. M. Peer-facilitated sign language training for a geriatric stroke victim with chronic brain syndrome. *Journal of Geriatric Psychiatry*, 1980, *13*, 89–102.

Wisocki, P. A., & Mosher, P. The elderly: An understudied population in behavior research. *International Journal of Behavioral Geriatrics*, 1982, *1*, 5–14.

Wisocki, P. A., & Telch, M. Modifying attitudes toward the elderly with the use of sampling procedures. *Scandanavian Journal of Behavior Therapy*, 1980, *9*, 87–96.

Wechsler, D. *Manual for the Wechsler Adult Intelligence Scale*. New York: Psychological Corp., 1955.

Woodruff, D. S. *Biofeedback control of EEG alpha rhythm and effect on reaction time in young and old*. Doctoral dissertation, University of Southern California, 1972.

18

MENTALLY RETARDED MOTHERS

KAREN S. BUDD
STEPHEN GREENSPAN

OVERVIEW

Of all the women who may receive behavior therapy, few present as many target areas for behavior change as the mentally retarded. As Bijou's (1966) functional definition of retardation indicates, mentally retarded individuals have "a limited repertoire of behavior shaped by events that constitute [their] history" (p. 2). We could, therefore, focus on many arenas—including work, social skills, and self-maintenance—in which behavior therapists have helped mentally retarded women cope with adult life. Instead we have restricted our focus to the issue of mentally retarded women as parents. This chapter discusses the role of mentally retarded women as parents, surveys the literature on behavioral interventions with mentally retarded parents, and indicates factors that may be related to successful parenting by such individuals.

BACKGROUND

TABOOS PREVENTING MENTALLY RETARDED WOMEN FROM BECOMING PARENTS

The decision to limit our focus to the issue of mentally retarded women as parents reflects our view that there is something about being a parent

Karen S. Budd. Meyer Children's Rehabilitation Institute, University of Nebraska Medical Center, Omaha, Nebraska.

Stephen Greenspan. Boys Town Center for Study of Youth Development, Omaha, Nebraska.

which represents the most fundamental strivings of mentally retarded women to be accepted as fully functioning adults. If one were to ask middle-aged mildly mentally retarded women, as we have done, "Why were you institutionalized?," a common answer would be, "When I was seventeen the boys used to follow me around and my mother thought I was boy crazy" (Greenspan & Budd, 1981a). And if one were to ask about the events immediately preceding their release from the institution years later, it would not be surprising to hear, "They told me I had a tumor and they operated on me. But I found out later, by accident, that I had been sterilized" (Greenspan & Budd, 1981b). Almost without exception, these women feel anger and hurt over being restricted from exercising what they believe to be their right to give birth to children and to rear those children to adulthood (Andron & Sturm, 1973).

The majority of mentally retarded people are mildly handicapped individuals who can live in the community with the help of specialized support services. Today, institutions are reserved mainly for the most severely and multiply handicapped individuals, or those with serious behavior problems. Until the early 1970s, however, most retarded people, regardless of severity level, were institutionalized. Mildly retarded women typically entered institutions after puberty and left after menopause, unless they were sterilized. Furthermore, rigid sexual segregation was enforced. Therefore, it is easy to agree with Wolfensberger's (1975) contention that one of the main functions of these institutions was to guard against the possibility that mentally retarded individuals would procreate.

Until recently, taboos about procreation by mentally retarded women reflected concerns about genetic transmission of low intelligence. The early history of institutions for the mentally retarded in this country is largely intertwined with the eugenics movement, which was quite powerful around the turn of the century (cf. Bass, 1963). Eugenic considerations no longer have much credibility, and civil liberty safeguards now inhibit involuntary sterilization. Nevertheless, mentally retarded women are not always free to exercise their desire to function as parents. As Hertz (1979) and Wald (1975) indicated, in many states parental rights can be terminated on the grounds that a parent bears the label "mental retardation." Even if a mentally retarded woman retains custody of her child, she is likely to be monitored closely by child protective workers, who can seek removal of the child from the home if the quality of parental care does not measure up to community standards. Thus, while the taboos preventing mentally retarded women from functioning as parents have lifted, they have not disappeared. The locus of fear has shifted from a concern over the genetic transmission of inferiority to concerns that mentally retarded women cannot meet the physical, emotional, and cognitive needs of developing children.

Concern that mentally retarded women will be inadequate parents is not unjustified. Mental retardation is, by definition, a condition marked by relatively widespread incompetence; effective child rearing demands the judgment and flexibility that many mentally retarded individuals lack. Yet, many mentally retarded people are not globally incompetent; some of them may function adequately as parents and benefit from training in child-rearing skills. An IQ score, particularly at the upper levels of the retardation range, does not always accurately predict how an individual will discharge specific life tasks. The burden is now on clinicians and legal authorities to approach each parent as an individual, without overgeneralizing from a label which may provide limited information about the individual's capabilities and deficits.

DIFFICULTIES IN DEFINING MENTAL RETARDATION

As with many nosological categories in education and psychiatry, the definition of mental retardation has undergone considerable change and is the subject of some controversy today. Central to this debate is the appropriate role of standardized tests of intelligence. The official definition of the American Association on Mental Deficiency (AAMD) (Grossman, 1973) states: "Mental retardation refers to significantly subaverage general intellectual functioning existing concurrently with deficits in adaptive behavior, and manifested during the developmental period" (p. 11). The last proviso, concerning the age of onset, excludes from the definition individuals of average intelligence as children and adolescents whose intelligence was impaired in adulthood through an accident or other means. The criterion for "significantly subaverage general intellectual functioning" is usually an IQ score two standard deviations or more below the mean on a standardized intelligence test (typically either the Wechsler or the Stanford–Binet). Thus, the cutoff would be an IQ score of 70 or less on the Wecshler Scales and 68 or less on the now less widely used Stanford–Binet.

Four levels of mental retardation are defined, with each level corresponding to an IQ standard deviation range (15 points on the Wechsler Scales). Mild mental retardation is an IQ between 70 (two standard deviations below the mean) and 55 (three standard deviations below the mean); moderate mental retardation is a score from 55 to 40; severe mental retardation is a score from 40 to 25; and profound mental retardation is a score below 25. The "borderline mental retardation" category (Heber, 1961), which was defined as an IQ score between 85 (one standard deviation below the mean) and 70, is no longer in official use. The borderline category misclassified too many culturally disadvantaged people whose IQ scores were close to the mean for individuals of low socioeconomic status (SES) even though they were one standard deviation below the norm for the population at large. Mercer has devised the System of Multicultural Pluralistic Assessment (SOMPA) for recomputing IQ scores on the WISC-R to take account of a child's cultural background (Mercer & Lewis, 1978). Development of this system was motivated by a concern that traditional diagnostic methods often lead to inappropriate assignment of the mental retardation label. This point is emphasized because a significant percentage of currently diagnosed "mentally retarded" parents received that designation when diagnostic criteria were looser than they are today.

The second criterion in the AAMD definition of mental retardation—"deficits in adaptive behavior"—reflects the view that low IQ alone is too narrow a basis for diagnosing someone as retarded. This criterion codifies the views of Tredgold (1937) and Doll (1941) that only the socially incompetent should be considered mentally retarded. The IQ index, while a good predictor of academic achievement, is only moderately predictive of success in vocational and community adaptation. Individuals whose low IQ resulted from cultural–familial rather than organic causes may have an IQ lower than two standard deviations below the mean and still function adequately in most respects other than classroom achievement. This is the phenomenon of the "6-hour retarded child" (President's Committee on Mental Retardation, 1970), the child who is retarded in the classroom but normal in the schoolyard (Jensen, 1970). Many individuals viewed as retarded in childhood (when school performance is the most widely used criterion) will not be considered retarded in adulthood, when occupational success is the significant criterion (Mercer, 1973).

Specific medical etiologies—chromosomal disorders (such as Down's syndrome), perinatal anoxia, prenatal and postnatal infections—can be identified for only a minority of cases of mental retardation. Furthermore, individuals whose retardation has a clear medical basis are clustered in the moderately to profoundly retarded end of the IQ spectrum.

Since most individuals with IQs in the mild mental retardation range do not have an identifiable medical basis for their low IQ and often have a completely natural physical appearance, an "adaptive behavior" criterion is needed to complement the diagnostic use of the IQ score. The adaptive behavior construct, as originally conceptualized by Heber (1961), has two components: (1) the ability to maintain oneself independently in the community, and (2) the ability to abide by socially accepted standards of interpersonal behavior. Measures of adaptive behavior, such as the AAMD Adaptive Behavior Scale (Nihira, Foster, Shellhaas, & Leland, 1975), are not fully satisfactory as diagnostic tools, because their scores discriminate only people at the lower end of the retardation continuum and their test items do not assess the full range of abilities required for independent living. Given the inadequacies of existing measures, many clinicians ignore adaptive behavior altogether when diagnosing mental retardation (Smith & Polloway, 1979); others have called for a return to exclusive reliance on IQ (Clausen, 1972).

In short, mental retardation is difficult to diagnose, especially when IQ is above 55, as is the case for virtually all mentally retarded parents. There is nothing magical about the 70 IQ cutting score. Many individuals with IQs below 70 function adequately in a variety of social roles (including socialization of children) while many others do not. Furthermore, many individuals with IQs above 70 are far more "retarded" (in the sense of being globally handicapped in performing normal social roles) than others with IQs below 70. Thus, there are no dramatic discontinuities between "mentally retarded" parents and parents of low SES and low (but not lower than 70) IQ. Mentally retarded parents have the same problems of living and potential for growth as do many other parents who are not mentally retarded.

Historical changes in the definition of mental retardation, and inconsistent usage of diagnostic criteria, obstruct a coherent review of the literature. To deal with these difficulties, we have adopted a "social systems" (Mercer, 1973) perspective, in which the main diagnostic criterion is whether significant persons within a woman's social world consider her to be mentally retarded. For purposes of this chapter, an individual is considered mentally retarded if the cited clinician or researcher says she is. While such an approach has obvious limitations, it incorporates the most important element in any definition, namely, the perception that an individual is unable to cope—because of cognitive limitations—with tasks and roles considered to be within the basic behavioral repertoire of most adults.

RESEARCH ON MENTALLY RETARDED PARENTS

ADEQUACY OF MENTALLY RETARDED PARENTS

A review of the research literature on the competence of mentally retarded parents sheds light on the clinical problems that these parents
present and their capacity to benefit from intervention. However, a
discussion of the competence of mentally retarded parents is hindered
by the absence of clear and widely accepted definitions of "adequate"
parental care (Plamondon & Soskin, 1978; Wald, 1975). There are no
clear-cut minimum parenting standards for socialization of personality
(via parental discipline) and intellect (via parental stimulation). Research
has provided equivocal evidence concerning the effects on children of
inadequacies in these areas. Criticisms of mentally retarded parents
usually focus on physical neglect, because the standards for neglect are
relatively well defined, and because the consequences of neglect —particularly on infants and young children—are more obvious. Provision
of adequate physical care can be a major problem for mentally retarded
parents in that they often are poor, live in substandard housing, and
experience numerous environmental crises. Like nonretarded neglecting
parents, retarded parents often come from lower socioeconomic back-
grounds. Since mentally retarded parents have deficits in judgment and
information processing, they are likely to encounter problems meeting
medical emergencies, avoiding safety hazards, and providing adequate
nutrition.

As pointed out by Fotheringham (1980), research on mentally retarded parents has suffered from a failure to anticipate methodological
confounds. These include: (1) social class (since most retarded parents
are poor, and poor people in general have lower IQs, it is difficult to separate out the effects of low IQ and poverty); (2) biased sampling procedures (most studies have used subjects who were either formerly
institutionalized or on the caseloads of child protective agencies, thus
excluding more competent parents from the sample); and (3) discrimi-
natory legal and social work practices (since public agencies are less
likely to give mentally retarded parents the benefit of the doubt, interventions have been more frequent and extreme than might otherwise
be the case). Also, most studies in this area lack direct methods of data
collection, standardized measurement instruments, reliability procedures, and experimental designs (Mira & Roddy, 1980). In spite of these
methodological difficulties, sufficient evidence exists to support three
general conclusions.

The first conclusion is that *mentally retarded parents are very likely to be considered inadequate, and their children are very likely to be viewed as troubled.* Epidemiological studies by Mickelson (1947) and Shaw and Wright (1960) found that approximately one third of formerly institutionalized parents were considered by child protective agencies to be grossly incompetent or neglecting, and an equal number were considered to be providing marginal or questionable care. Mitchell (1947) reported that a majority of mentally retarded mothers had problems as parents, a view echoed by Kugel and Parsons (1967) and Berry and Shapiro (1975).

The at-risk status of mentally retarded parents also is reflected in evidence that their offspring often have serious difficulties (see Mira & Roddy, 1980, for a review). For example, Kugel and Parsons (1967) found physical growth abnormalities suggestive of inadequate nutrition in a large percentage of children of mentally retarded parents. Numerous studies, reviewed by Fotheringham (1980), have found that children of mentally retarded parents typically are of higher intelligence than their parents yet have a higher than average likelihood of being mentally retarded.

A second conclusion which can be drawn from the research literature is that *mentally retarded parents share many of the characteristics of nonretarded at-risk parents.* There is no sharp, qualitative distinction between parents who fall on either side of the mental retardation cutting score. For example, Sheridan (1956) found that neglectful mothers in general have below average IQs (mean of 80), although most have not been diagnosed mentally retarded. This finding, replicated in various studies, indicates considerable overlap in the distributions of inadequate mothers who are retarded and those who are not. Borgman (1969) found that, among low-SES adults, IQ alone is not predictive of parental adequacy except in cases of extremely low intelligence (IQ less than 50). Fotheringham (1980) has argued, on the basis of these and other studies, that much of the child-rearing inadequacy observed among mentally retarded parents may be attributed purely to the product of poverty. When judging the adequacy of a mentally retarded parent, it is important to keep in mind the family's cultural milieu. It would be unfair to assess adequacy of a poor, mentally retarded parent by applying middle-class standards, which might not be so readily used as a yardstick were the parent poor but of higher intelligence.

A third, and most important, conclusion drawn from the research literature is that *a surprisingly large percentage of mentally retarded adults are reasonably competent as parents* and are able to meet minimum standards for the provision of adequate care to children. All relevant investigations support this conclusion. For example, Mickelson (1947) found that 42% of children living with a mentally retarded parent (typically the mother) were receiving satisfactory care. Berg and Nyland (1975) found that while 45% of children of a mentally retarded parent no longer lived with that parent, over 60% of those who did, received good or satisfactory care. Mattinson (1970) found children living with retarded parents to be in generally good health, as did Floor, Baxter, Rosen, and Zisfein (1975). Brandon (1957), in an epidemiological study of 73 mildly retarded mothers, found that most of the 150 children were developing adequately. In short, considerable individual differences characterize parents who bear the mentally retarded label. Many of them, including the clients of protective service agencies, can adequately meet the physical, emotional, and developmental needs of their children.

EFFECTS OF INADEQUATE EXPERIENCE ON CHILDREN

The three conclusions listed in the preceding section were drawn from the limited research on mentally retarded parents. A fourth conclusion about the competence of mentally retarded parents comes from the voluminous literature on low-SES parents, which has been comprehensively reviewed (Clarke-Stewart & Apfel, 1979; Sameroff & Chandler, 1975). This conclusion can be stated as follows: *One cannot accurately predict the effect that a given environment, even an inadequate one, will have on a given child; many children from inadequate environments become competent adults.* It is not that environmental differences are unimportant in influencing a child's development. Numerous studies have shown that maternal characteristics, prevalent in affluent and educated families, are associated with positive child outcomes. These favorable characteristics include an affectionate and accepting attitude toward the child; a less restrictive, controlling, and punitive disciplinary style; frequent mother–child interaction, especially verbal exchanges and interactive play with materials; and prompt, consistent, and rewarding responses to child behavior (Clarke-Stewart & Apfel, 1979). At the same time, investigations of the effects of early environment have demonstrated important exceptions to the environment–outcome link that limit the predictive usefulness of the findings. These exceptions are of three types, as discussed below.

First, there is wide diversity among low-SES mothers in child-rearing practices. Clarke-Stewart and Apfel (1979) noted that despite *mean* differences between classes, the *modal* behavior of parents and children is similar across SES levels, and heterogeneity generally is greater within than between classes. Most studies correlated scores between classes, ignoring variation within groups that indicate how environment affects child development. Thus, SES predicts neither specific parenting patterns nor child outcomes.

Second, there is evidence that children's behavior and temperament contribute to their development in ways that may, at times, supersede the influence of parental factors. There appears to be a reciprocal relationship between the behavior of children and their parents, such that "good" babies elicit positive caretaking responses, and difficult children disrupt parents' normal caretaking abilities (Bell, 1968; Thomas, Chess, & Birch, 1968). Also, some children have an apparent "invulnerability" (Garmezy, 1971) to negative environmental characteristics that allow them to flourish as competent individuals despite disturbed parenting practices. This resilience in the face of environmental stress may reflect an inherent adaptability of the child or undocumented benefits of the child's environment (such as a neighbor who takes responsibility for a child and provides love and stimulation not available at home). An understanding of which of these explanations is correct has important implications for the study of environmental influences on child development. In either case, the child's healthy development is a pleasant contradiction to the expected negative influences of deviant parenting practices.

A third factor complicating the relationship between environment and child behavior is the changing nature of environmental conditions. Although early environment is important, the effects of experiences in infancy often are reversed by later childhood experiences. Clarke and Clarke (1976b) concluded from an extensive literature review that the effects of early experience are determined largely by what follows the experience and thus prolongs what would otherwise by transitory effects, good or bad. Environmental change occurs by the moment, hour, day, and month, as parent and child interact in a dynamic, interdependent manner. Sameroff and Chandler (1975) proposed a "transactional" model of development in which this progressive interplay of the child and the environment determines long-range child outcomes. Since the child and environment affect one another over time, any conclusion about how a child will turn out based on an early assessment of the environment is likely to be inaccurate.

FACTORS CONTRIBUTING TO INADEQUACIES OF MENTALLY RETARDED PARENTS

Why are mentally retarded women generally less adequate parents than nonretarded women, and why are some mentally retarded women more adequate parents than others? These questions have not been addressed directly by researchers, but they may be the key to understanding the problems and prospects of mentally retarded women as parents. Of course, there are as many differences among mentally retarded women as among nonretarded women (Heber, 1964), and no single factor can explain why an individual is a ompetent parent. Researchers already have gained some understanding about the failure of low-IQ and low-SES parents to stimulate the linguistic and cognitive development of young children (Clarke-Stewart & Apfel, 1979). The ensuing discussion focuses on individual differences among retarded women in their ability to discipline children and provide physical care, since problems in these areas frequently are brought to the attention of behavior therapists and child guidance clinics.

A useful starting point for this discussion is to explore how intelligence may contribute to one's effectiveness in meeting the physical and socioemotional needs of children. The answer could lie not in that aspect of intelligence measured by IQ tests (which may predict successful socialization of linguistic and cognitive competence) but in the two other aspects of intelligence referred to by Thorndike (1920) as "social intelligence" and "practical intelligence." These other two aspects of intelligence have important implications for success in the respective socialization realms of discipline and physical care. These aspects of intelligence—referred to by Guilford (1967) as "behavioral" (social) and "figural" (practical) ability—are only moderately correlated with IQ. Thus, many retarded adults with relatively good social or practical intelligence may be more adequate as socialization agents than their IQ scores suggest.

Social intelligence, or better yet social judgment, refers to a person's ability to understand and to deal effectively with social and interpersonal objects and events (Greenspan, 1979). An adult with good social judgment knows what others are thinking or feeling, reflects on the motives underlying another's behavior, anticipates the interpersonal consequences of actions, and understands how to influence others to behave in desired ways. Social judgment may account for success in managing the behavior of children, dispensing rewards or punishments contingently, knowing when to ignore diversionary tactics, and understanding the meaning of child behavior. Clinical experience has indicated that when mentally retarded parents are found wanting as disciplinarians, it usually is not because of a lack of love or caring but rather because of the disorganized and ineffective quality of their management of contingencies. Perhaps mentally retarded women are poor disciplinarians because of their poor social judgment.

The term "practical intelligence" refers to the ability to care for housekeeping, hygienic, and vocational aspects of daily life. It is that aspect of intelligence which is captured in the first part of the operational definition of "adaptive behavior" referred to earlier (and measured in Part I of the AAMD Adaptive Behavior Scale). Accurately diagnosed mentally retarded people tend to have difficulty in dealing with daily tasks in an organized, planful, and skillful manner; their households often appear chaotic, unhygienic, and neglectful. Accusations of neglect usually result from a crisis during which poor judgment is used to handle a dangerous situation (Pelton, 1981). Poor judgment might include leaving an infant unattended in a hazardous place, substituting solid foods when baby formula is unavailable, or failing to seek prompt medical attention when an infant is ill. Mentally retarded women low in practical intelligence may be judged incompetent parents because of failure to anticipate the consequences of their actions to the child. Deficiencies in both social and practical judgment tend to multiply the mother's problems. We have learned of mothers who had difficulty meeting their children's physical needs, who didn't realize how serious the situation seemed to outsiders, and who didn't act contrite when told of their errors. This chain of events, a product of poor judgment rather than ill will, can lead to removal of a child from the retarded mother's care.

In addition to the role of intelligence in contributing to the failure or success of mentally retarded parents, at least three other factors may be relevant. One factor, which has been addressed in research on personality processes of mentally retarded adults, but not specifically in research on parenting processes, has been referred to as the mother's self-esteem. Low self-esteem, resulting from a lifetime of being viewed and treated as deficient, is endemic among mentally retarded adults (Schurr, Joiner, & Towne, 1970). It has been noted anecdotally (Landesman-Dwyer, 1981), that some mentally retarded adults feel threatened when children acquire skills (such as reading) which are beyond their

parents' capabilities, and when they do better in school than their retarded parents did. Individual differences in parents' perceptions of
themselves and their children may, in turn, result in differences in their
behavior toward the children.

The quantity and quality of prior experience with children also may
explain why some women are more competent than others as parents.
One mentally retarded woman we interviewed played the role of sur-
rogate mother to her younger siblings and their children. Other mentally
retarded women acquired considerable experience with children in the
nurseries of institutions where they were unpaid workers during years
of enforced institutionalization. For some women, experience could have
a detrimental effect, if the nature of previous experience was with models
of inadequate or bizarre parenting practices, as is the case for women
whose own parents were incompetent.

Finally, the amount of stress faced by the parent and the support
network that exists to help her cope with that stress probably affect
parenting competence. Many mentally retarded parents are fairly adequate when dealing with one child but are less adequate in coping with
the greater responsibilities of additional children (Mickelson, 1947; Shaw
& Wright, 1960). Marriage stability, physical and mental health, and
financial resources also are sources of stress or support that relate to the
quality of child care by retarded parents (Mickelson, 1947).

Given the inadequate way in which adaptive behavior is defined
and measured, and the variable way in which the criterion is applied,
the only thing one can say for certain about mentally retarded parents
is that they have low IQ scores. Most mentally retarded mothers will
show some inadequacies as teachers and stimulators of language and
cognitive development. These deficiencies may not be large in comparison to low-SES families, and the long-term impact on children of these
deficiencies cannot be accurately predicted. Whether the parent is deficient in providing physical care or discipline cannot be predicted from
IQ alone and may depend on the mother's practical and social judgment,
perceptions of herself and her child, prior experience with children,
ambient stress, and available social support. If few generalizations can
be made about the parenting abilities of mentally retarded women, then
each family deserves to be examined on an individual basis for specific
child-rearing strengths and weaknesses. The following section discusses
the promise of a behavioral approach for assessing and enhancing the
skills of mentally retarded parents.

BEHAVIORAL INTERVENTIONS WITH MENTALLY RETARDED MOTHERS

DESCRIPTIONS OF SEVERAL INTERVENTION PROGRAMS

Behavioral parent training approaches dysfunctional family interactions by teaching parents to apply procedures of child management in everyday interactions. Deviant parent–child interactions are viewed as a product not only of maladaptive child behavior but also of unwitting errors in parents' initiations and reactions to child behavior. These errors strengthen and maintain maladaptive child behavior. Rather than attributing parents' ineffective management efforts to permanent character flaws, a behavioral approach assumes that parents can learn to change how they interact with their children and thereby modify the children's deviant behavior. The program of intervention becomes one of identifying specific parent and child behaviors in need of change and methods of teaching parents the new techniques.

Because a behavioral approach is based on a theoretical framework of social learning principles, the choice of behaviors to be changed typically involves an analysis of the ongoing contingencies operating between parent and child behaviors, and training is oriented toward restructuring the nature and/or timing of contingent parent responses. However, the provision of more global child-rearing skills also can be construed within a behavioral approach if one considers the new parent skills to be antecedents and consequences for child behavior. In this review, behavioral parent training refers to parenting interventions via contingency management as well as more comprehensive enhancement of child-rearing skills.

A behavioral approach has obvious applicability to mentally retarded adults, who may display a broad range of deficits in parenting skills. Yet little mention has been made in the behavioral parent training literature of interventions directed specifically at mentally retarded parents. This absence may be due in part to the general antilabeling bias of behavioral clinicians, but it also may reflect a lack of interest, ability, or experience in dealing with mentally retarded parents and few successful parent training outcomes with this population. Of necessity, this section includes unpublished clinical accounts to illustrate recent efforts at behavioral intervention with mentally retarded women and their children. Two types of programs are reviewed: (1) parent training programs that have developed modifications in the standard training format to accommodate the needs of mentally retarded parents, and (2) parent training programs devised specifically for mentally retarded parents.

Szykula, Haffey, and Parsons (1981) described supplementary treatment methods used in their behavioral treatment program for families of socially aggressive children. One procedure, a parenting salary, was effective with a mildly retarded women who had been inconsistent in implementing a time-out procedure with her 5-year-old daughter. A salary of one dollar per day was paid to the mother contingent on instituting the recommended treatment procedures, recording data on child behavior and use of time out, and calling the caseworker daily on schedule to report the data. The authors observed an immediate change in the mother's participation in the treatment program that maintained after the 4-week period the parenting salary was in effect, although the duration of effects was not indicated. This case report extends to a mentally retarded mother the findings of Fleischman (1979) that parenting salaries are effective in increasing the cooperation of some families in behavioral treatment. Fleischman found the most consistent positive effects of parenting salaries with low-income as opposed to middle- or upper-income families.

Eyberg (1979) described a training program for parents of 2- to 7-year-old children with conduct problems at the University of Oregon Health Sciences Center based on a modification of Hanf's two-stage training model (Hanf & Kling, 1973). During a child-directed activity, parents were taught to describe and praise ongoing child behavior while refraining from questions, commands, and other directive responses. During a parent-directed activity, they learned to provide clear instructions, praise for child compliance, and implement time out for noncompliance. Eyberg (1981) reported that the program has been used successfully with mildly retarded parents by extending the number of training sessions from an average of 9 for regular cases to 15 to 20 sessions with mentally retarded parents. She surmised that lower functioning parents were able to master the interaction skills because of the intensive *in vivo* coaching provided and the relatively simple rules involved in parents' application of the treatment program.

Another parent training program that has been adapted to mentally retarded adults is that of Embry and her colleagues at the University of Kansas. The standard program (Embry, Kelley, Herbert-Jackson, & Baer, 1978; Embry, Schilmoeller, Kelley, & O'Malley, 1975) was a 10-week behavior management course for a small group of parents; individualized instruction and feedback on the application of techniques to free-play and instructional situations were provided in families' homes. Program modifications made for mentally retarded clients (Embry, 1981) include (1) audiotaping the readings and lectures so parents could review them; (2) giving oral quizzes; (3) writing out parents' oral answers to home assignments; (4) simplifying the data collection procedures parents use for home projects; and (5) enhancing the structure of in-home training by using more modeling and behavioral rehearsal. In addition to programming changes, occasional assistance was provided in other spheres such as helping a mother enroll her child in a preschool program to insure that the child was exposed to appropriate models for language stimulation. Embry (1981) trained 10 mentally retarded parents using the modified program. Their progress, as measured by direct observations in the home free-play and instructional situations, was no different from the progress of other, nonretarded parents with such family and environmental handicaps as low income, social isolation, marital instability, and health problems. Parents' commitment to their children's growth and development seemed a better predictor of success than intellectual functioning. An objective measure of parental commitment, which could test this observation, has yet to be developed.

In addition to their inclusion in general parent training programs, mentally retarded clients have participated in programs designed for abusive or neglectful families. One such program is Project 12-Ways, a comprehensive service program for abusive and neglectful parents and their children (cf. Lutzker, Frame, & Rice, 1982). Therapists in Project 12-Ways described a program developed for a mildly retarded mother whose 4-year-old child had been placed in foster care due to neglect (Sarber, Messmer, Halasz, & Bickett, 1981). The mother was taught basic nutrition skills as a precursor to returning the child to the home. Because the mother was illiterate, color-coded food cards and a menu planning chart were used to teach her how to plan menus and purchase groceries. The mother demonstrated better nutrition skills during training, but it is unclear whether she used these skills after her daughter returned home.

Another program for abusive and neglectful families that was tailored to serve mentally retarded parents is that of Rosenberg, McTate, and Robinson (1981). In this program, a mother's concern for her child, and willingness to put the child's needs ahead of her own immediate desires, seemed to be more important predictors of her ability to improve child-care skills than the mother's level of intelligence (Rosenberg &

McTate, 1982). Comprehensive services to mentally retarded parents were provided, including training in basic child care and in parent–child interactions, assistance in obtaining community resources, and development of supportive social networks. A unique training problem presented by retarded parents was rigid overgeneralization of training instructions. For example, one mother was taught how to fix pancakes in a cooking skills program and then proceeded to fix pancakes for breakfast, lunch, and dinner. Another mother was taught to play games with her 9-month-old infant; one year later she was still attempting to engage the child in these same games. Although Rosenberg and his colleagues provide no data on differential training effects for retarded versus nonretarded parents, their summary comments on outcome are similar to those reported informally by Embry (1981), whose experimental training program allowed for direct observational comparisons of mentally retarded parents with other parents in the program. One difference between these programs was the extent of assistance in basic child care, resource provision, and support provided within the programs. Rosenberg and McTate's program was designed to be comprehensive in nature, whereas Embry's program collaborated with other social service agencies and focused on behavior management skills.

The intervention programs discussed above were those that developed modifications in the standard parent training format to accommodate the needs of mentally retarded parents. A review of the published literature and informal contacts with parent training colleagues brought to our attention four additional behavioral intervention programs designed specifically for mentally retarded parents and their children. Also, Madsen (1979) briefly described a training curriculum for use by nurses in a 5-week parenting class for mentally retarded adults; however, her report included no other descriptive information regarding the training program and no report of outcome.

In recent years, the best known intervention program for mentally retarded parents and their children was the Milwaukee Project. This multifaceted treatment program operated throughout much of the 1970s in the poorest area of Milwaukee (Heber & Garber, 1975). The program was an intensive experimental effort to prevent "cultural–familial" retardation in the children of poor Black mothers, who themselves scored below 75 on standardized intelligence tests. The 20 children in the experimental group ranged in age from 3 to 6 months when intervention began. Until they entered first grade, they participated in daily educational programs away from home while their mothers learned academic, vocational, home management, and child-care skills. At age 5½, a comparison of 20 children in the experimental condition and 20 in the control condition showed IQ differences averaging as high as 31 points, more advanced learning and performance scores on structured tasks, and more sophisticated language development for the experimental group of children. However, Page (1972) issued a methodological critique of the study and questioned its findings, while Clarke and Clarke (1976a) reported that the children's gains diminished after the intervention program ended. In contrast to the marked (albeit disputed and temporary) gains for children as a result of intervention, Heber and Garber (1975) found no differences between experimental and control group mothers in their teaching abilities as assessed in mother–child interactions. They reported informally that various problems were encountered in training homemaking and child-care skills, although the specific nature of the problems was not described. In general, they reported greater success with vocational training than other areas. However, not all mothers received training in all areas, so it is not possible to evaluate mother or child gains as a function of specific maternal training provided. The Milwaukee Project was the first major intervention program to focus on mentally retarded parents and their children. Despite the limitations of the project as a research endeavor, the results require consideration because they suggest that children of retarded parents made gains equal to or better than disadvantaged families in other intervention programs (Bronfenbrenner, 1974).

Another program designed to provide training for mentally retarded mothers was the Homemaker Service Program operated by the Home Services Association of St. Paul, Minnesota (Halpern & Fraser, 1975). Nineteen mothers informally identified as retarded were involved in the program. Ten mothers were married, and five of these husbands were retarded. Each family included one child below age 7 and one or more older children. Training focused on parents' homemaking skills, including meal preparation, budgeting, and use of the phone, and on child-care skills including limit setting and responding to a child's crying. Parents and staff chose specific training goals together. A unique feature of this program was its use of paraprofessionals as treatment agents under the direction of professional staff. Parents received the paraprofessionals more openly than they did the professionals. The paraprofessionals visited families' homes an average of 4 to 6 hours per week for several months to demonstrate target skills, discuss implementation, and provide feedback on parents' performance. Evaluation of the training's effects was based on the subjective reports of the project coordinator. Of the 17 families with sufficient involvement in the program at the time of the report to estimate outcome, 6 (35%) were perceived to have made substantial gains, 4 (24%) moderate gains, 6 (35%) minimal gains, and 1 (6%) no gain. In the two-parent families, almost all of the fathers were reported to have emotional difficulties that necessitated their involvement so that they would not sabotage the treatment program. Intervention seemed more successful when the paraprofessional shared some characteristics with the mother (e.g., age, life experiences), interacted with the mother both as a friend and a teacher, and did not exert control by doing things for the mother (such as cleaning up the house) during home visits. Although this outcome assessment was subjective, it suggests that intervention can help some mentally retarded parents. The report's case illustrations and practical suggestions on intervention provide useful background reading for therapists interested in working with mentally retarded parents.

A third project for mentally retarded parents is the Specialized Family Program developed by Pomerantz and his colleagues in Buffalo (Pomerantz, 1981; Pomerantz, Towne, & Pomerantz, 1979, 1980). For 2 years, the program served 30 families in which there was at least one mentally retarded parent. Of the 40 children in these families, nearly half were handicapped or had serious health problems. Training took from 3 weeks to 20 months; its mean length was 5 months. The program included direct community intervention on the clients' behalf and training in effective skills related to use of community resources. The outcome of intervention seemed to depend in part on how well the clients interacted with people in the community, such as caseworkers at social agencies, landlords, and store merchants. Training covered a wide range of topics, including basic childcare, behavior amanagement, parent–parent interaction, home management, and community management. As in the Home Services program, parents participated in the selection of goals, for which specific intervention plans were devised. Family aides (often social work students) visited clients' homes at least twice a week to provide on-site training and spent an additional 5–10 hours per week in agency and community contacts as client advocates. Evaluation measures consisted of parents' consumer satisfaction ratings, family aides' case records of parent progress on each intervention plan, and records of children's intellectual development, health, and community placement before and after intervention. Parents had positive reactions to the program; they especially liked the home visiting and the family aides' dedicated approach. Parents were more equivocal about the aides' teaching effectiveness and the program's effectiveness outside the home. A total of 160 intervention plans (with a range of 1–12 per family) were implemented. For 104 plans (65%), aides judged that the criterion goal of intervention was met; for 35 plans (22%), aides reported some progress toward the criterion; and for 21 plans (13%), aides reported no progress. Children's progress, as measured by Bayley test scores, was comparable to the gains of a group of at-risk infants whose parents were not retarded and who received services in a related family intervention program. Of 11 children with serious health problems at referral, all but one was in good health following intervention. Most important, in 27 of the 30 families, the children were still living with their parents at the end of the program. The Specialized Family Program is an impressive example of an intervention program for mentally retarded parents, by virtue of its program design and its apparent success. Its evaluation procedures were more comprehensive and somewhat more objective than those used in the Home Services project, although neither project is methodologically sufficient as a research investigation.

The final project reviewed here is a Boston day-care center developed as a training environment for mentally retarded parents by Robb, Weiss, Geelen, and others (Bradley, Attaliades, Fisher, Geelen, & Hamad, 1981; Robb, Attaliades, Bradley, Fisher, Mann, & Weiss, 1981; Weiss, 1981). The day-care program was an outgrowth of several individual home-based projects, in which these therapists and their colleagues taught retarded parents to use extinction (Mills, Stortecky, & Bass, 1981), token reinforcement (Goldstein & Weiss, 1981), and time out (Robb & Weiss, 1981). In all cases, the home-based interventions met with some success. However, due to the extensive time devoted to individual cases, the similarity of basic child-rearing deficits across families, and the problems encountered in getting parents to apply the skills outside training sessions, the day-care center seemed a more efficient site for training retarded parents. The day-care center provides care to a few normally developing children, aged 1 to 3 years, whose parents work as staff members of social service programs. Three mentally retarded mothers and one other retarded adult are paid one dollar per hour to serve as day-care workers and receive training in child-care skills. At present, their own children are not served at the day-care center. Graduate students in applied behavior analysis are used as supervisors and trainers. Workers are taught to implement child-care routines (such as diaper checks and changes) in a standard sequence that

includes performing the component behaviors, self-recording completion of the routine, and setting a timer to cue themselves to reinitiate
the sequence. Because the program has been in operation for only a
short time, data are not yet available on its success in teaching childcare
skills. Its novel approach to training mentally retarded parents certainly
deserves careful evaluation. A measure of the program's importance will
be its ability to develop parenting skills that generalize to the home.

SURVEY OF THERAPIST EXPERIENCES WITH MENTALLY
RETARDED MOTHERS

In view of the meager research literature to date on interventions with
mentally retarded parents, we surveyed behaviorally oriented therapists
to obtain informal reports of their experiences with mentally retarded
parents and their children (Budd, 1982). Questionnaires were sent to 20
professionals involved in parent training programs with high-risk families, primarily psychologists at community mental health centers or
university-based clinics. Respondents were asked to complete one questionnaire per family on up to five families meeting these criteria: (1) the
mother was considered mentally retarded; (2) some form of behavioral
or educational parenting skill intervention was attempted with the family; and (3) the therapist had sufficient contact with the family (even if
the case was ongoing) to be able to estimate the outcome of treatment.
    The Parent Training Questionnaire contained 56 items. Twenty-nine
items requested demographic and historical information about the family
(e.g., number of children, referral problems, income) and individual
family members (e.g., age, education, occupation, institutional history).
It was expected that standardized measures of intellectual functioning
would be available for only a few cases; thus, respondents were requested to estimate intellectual functioning for individual family members at one of five levels: average or above average, low average or
borderline, mildly retarded, moderately retarded, severely or profoundly retarded. Therapists described the type of treatment provided
(content, location, duration, current status), and they rated each parent's
involvement (defined as attending sessions and participating in treatment) on 2 4-point scales from not involved to extensively involved.
Therapists rated the outcome of treatment (success on referral problems,
generalized benefits, negative changes, eventual likelihood of adequate

family functioning) on 4 4-point scales from none to extensive. They rated each parent's competence and resources on 13 4-point scales from very incompetent to "as competent as an average family" in three areas of child interaction (caring for child's physical needs, discipline, teaching) and 10 adult activities (e.g., housekeeping, grooming, making and keeping friends, job stability). On three open-ended items, therapists described things parents did (or did not do) that would cause a protective service agency to question parental custody of the children, reasons for the success or failure of treatment, and recommendations for treatment with mentally retarded parents.

A total of 52 questionnaires were returned by 16 parent training programs (mean of 3.25 questionnaires returned per program). Responses to all but the three open-ended questions were coded numerically according to explicit response categories, rechecked independently by a second coder, and computer analyzed for frequency distributions on individual items. Statistical analyses identified relationships between family and treatment items and parent performance on outcome variables. Content analyses identified recurrent comments or themes on the open-ended items. Because of occasional missing data, numbers of subjects varied across analyses.

The survey results indicated that in almost all cases intervention involved training parents in behavior management procedures, educating parents about basic child care and development, or both. Although intervention sometimes included other components (e.g., family communication and problem solving, social and advocacy support, and stimulation of child skills), the contingency-management and educational focus predominated. Training more often took place in the home (83%) than in the clinic (17%); but over half of the home-based interventions were supplemented by training in clinics, schools, and other community facilities. The length of treatment varied from 1 month to 4 years (median of 30 weeks). Since one third of the cases were still in progress when the questionnaires were returned, these figures underestimate treatment length.

In all cases, mothers participated in intervention; their level of involvement was rated as slight in 17% of the cases, moderate in 21% of the cases, and extensive in 62% of the cases. Fathers were present in 30 (58%) of the 52 families. In these two-parent families, 22% of the fathers were not involved in treatment, 39% were slightly involved, 13% were moderately involved, and 26% were extensively involved. Although mothers were rated as more active participants in intervention than fathers, there was some father involvement in three-quarters of the two-parent families.

Therapist ratings of intervention on the four outcome measures are summarized in Table 18-1. The most optimistic finding was that in 43% of the cases therapists judged a moderate or extensive amount of change to have occurred in the referral problems as a result of treatment. However, only 18% of the families showed moderate or extensive generalized benefits of intervention. A relatively encouraging prognosis regarding the adequacy of eventual family functioning was given for 34% of the cases. Negative changes were perceived in only a few cases.

Three types of statistical tests were used to identify relationships between selected family and treatment items and the combined level of parent performance on three outcome variables (success on referral problems, generalized benefits, and adequacy of family functioning). T-tests were used for eight items in which the responses could be grouped for analysis into two levels. These items were the mother's and father's functioning levels; presence of the father in the family; the mother's and father's involvement in treatment; the mother's and father's institutional history; and treatment location. Analyses of variance were used for five variables: number of children in the family, children's functioning level, family income, and mother's and father's ages. Correlational tests were used with six variables: the mother's and father's educational levels, and each parent's combined level of competence and resources in three child activities and 10 adult activities. Univariate analyses were employed because of the small number of subjects relative to the number of var-

TABLE 18-1. Therapist Ratings of Outcome: Percentage of Total Cases Rated at Each Outcome Level

Outcome measures	Level of outcome			
	None	Slight	Moderate	Extensive
Success in helping family with referral problems	20	37	25	18
Generalized benefits beyond problems and settings treated	33	49	8	10
Unexpected negative changes correlated with treatment	85	8	2	2
Eventual likelihood of adequate family functioning	18	48	28	6

iables; multivariate procedures would have been preferable as a means for determining the relative contribution made by the independent variables to outcome. Given the small number of cases, the data analyses are considered preliminary and should be interpreted cautiously regarding their predictive value.

Of the 19 items tested, 5 were associated significantly with treatment outcome. The largest associations were found with parental intelligence, parental adaptive functioning, and maternal involvement in intervention. A comparison of 21 mothers with low average or borderline intellectual functioning to 26 mothers with mild or moderate mental retardation revealed a trend for more favorable treatment outcome among higher functioning mothers ($t = 1.91$, $p < .06$). An even stronger relationship emerged when clusters of maternal competence and resource items were correlated. The mother's competence in child interacions (caring for physical needs, discipline, teaching) was highly correlated with successful intervention ($r = .483$, $p < .001$). Similarly, the mother's competence in adult activities (e.g., housekeeping, grooming, making and keeping friends, job stability) covaried positively with treatment outcome ($r = .306$, $p < .05$). Twenty-seven cases in which the mother was involved extensively in intervention were rated overall as significantly more successful than 20 cases where the mother was only slightly or moderately involved ($t = 2.60$, $p < .05$). The father's intellectual functioning level and his involvement in treatment did not predict outcome, but, as in the case of mothers, his competence in areas of child interaction and adult activities was correlated with better intervention effects ($r = .538$, $p < .01$, and $r = .365$, $p < .05$, respectively).

In summary, the parent training programs for mentally retarded clients we surveyed were more directive, intensive, and longer than the typical program for nonhandicapped parents. Slightly less than half of the families made substantial improvement on referral problems, and in only one third of the cases were therapists optimistic about the family's ability to function adequately without extensive continued assistance. There was limited generalization of effects beyond the specific problems and settings treated, despite the comprehensiveness of treatment. While outcome levels were lower than those reported by behavioral clinicians working with nonretarded parents (Miller, 1975; O'Dell, 1982), one very important point emerges: Some mentally retarded parents made considerable improvements as a result of intervention. Contrary to the traditional view of mentally retarded people as globally and permanently incompetent parents, the questionnaire data indicate that some retarded individuals benefit substantially from training in parenting skills. The most success in treatment was shown by parents with high levels of child care and adaptive functioning, and by mothers who were actively involved in the treatment program.

Therapists' open-ended responses provide insights about the causes of success and failure in interventions with mentally retarded parents. When describing the clients' parenting deficiencies, it is striking how often they defined the referring problem in terms of neglect—that is, inadequate provision for physical needs of children—rather than in terms of abuse or inadequate intellectual stimulation. In 57% of the cases, they mentioned seriously inadequate attention to children's medical, nutritional, or safety needs, while in 20% they noted serious physical or psychological abuse. Therapists frequently mentioned that neglect reflected ignorance about the developmental needs and capabilities of young children, rather than a lack of love or interest in children. For example, a therapist wrote about one mother that there were "general problems involving judgment, such as leaving unsafe items on the floor where her child was crawling, leaving the child alone in the bath or in the apartment. . . . This mother was very committed to her child and would do whatever people suggested. However, she would not generalize, anticipate, or plan well at all." Other clients misunderstood the health needs of young children and, for example, substituted water for infant formula if they ran out, or failed to contact a physician when the child was ill or not thriving. Poor judgment and ignorance was also mentioned as a major impediment to the success of parenting interventions. In 27% of the cases, intellectual or communication deficits made it difficult for clients to apply their newly acquired skills. For example, a therapist noted about one client that "the primary reason for continued services is because we could not find a way to teach judgment." Several respondents mentioned that clients often did not grasp the responsibilities of being a parent and did not see their impact on the child's development. Such parents put their own needs before the child's and saw little reason for therapy.

As an adaptation to the cognitive limitations of mentally retarded parents, 25% of the respondents noted that intervention must be more concrete than usual, with much repetition and practice and few verbal instructions and explanations. There were differences of opinion about the utility of individual rather than group training for parents. One point was made frequently—persistence and patience are needed together with lengthy therapeutic contact, sometimes lasting several years. One third of the therapists stressed the crucial role of the client's extended family and social network in aiding as well as in undermining treatment success. These clients were often dependent on others' advice and approval, and would quickly cease following the therapist's advice when support from significant others was lacking. Therefore, therapists had to enlist the support of the client's spouse, her parents, neighbors, and even nontarget children. Therapists also had to be more active than usual in enlisting the cooperation of other agencies. Thirty-nine percent of the respondents noted that mentally retarded parents have so many problems that the therapist must act as an advocate or team coordinator, helping the client to cope with a variety of crises and problems, which have little to do with parenting. While therapist assistance was mentioned occasionally as encouraging excessive dependency, global therapist involvement often was required to stablize the home situation enough for parent training to succeed. On a more positive note, 23% of the respondents mentioned that the clients were motivated and cooperative and viewed the relationship with the therapist enthusiastically. Many respondents stated that interventions with mentally retarded parents can succeed if the therapist is supportive and patient and provides a great deal of encouragement and positive reinforcement.

CONCLUSIONS

We support the conclusions of Mickelson (1949), who stated that "the mentally deficient parent emerges . . . not as a different kind of parent but as a more vulnerable one" (p. 532). While mentally retarded women often are viewed as inadequate parents, their skills vary, and many of them function adequately, especially when compared to nonretarded women with similar demographic characteristics. The experiences of intervention programs indicate that standard behavioral approaches need to be modified for these women.

Intervention programs have emphasized these elements: parenting salaries, longer training, *in vivo* coaching, simple verbal presentations, home visits, advocacy to secure vital economic and social services for families, training in basic child-care skills such as nutrition, use of paraprofessionals, and training many skills not directly related to childcare. Success rates were lower than those reported for nonretarded parents, despite the increased efforts of these programs, and improvements often failed to generalize beyond the specific focus of the intervention. Never-

theless, a significant percentage of women derived substantial immediate benefit from therapy. Success of intervention was related to
mothers' initial levels of childcare and adaptive competence and to the
extent of their involvement in therapy. A major obstacle to the success
of interventions was these mothers' extremely poor judgment when
faced with novel child-rearing situations.

Working with mothers who have been labeled "mentally retarded"
is a challenging, often frustrating, experience but one which is not without rewards. The behaviorally oriented therapists we surveyed reported
considerable progress, even in cases that initially seemed hopeless. Our
message to therapists who work with such women is: keep an open
mind and don't underestimate their ability to change. These women
have been the victims of enforced sterilization, lengthy institutionalization, and termination of parental rights—all based on the assumption
that they could not possibly make fit parents. As more and more people
with intellectual handicaps demonstrate the ability to live in the community and fulfill various normal social roles, it is incumbent upon us
as professionals and as human beings to give mentally retarded women
who are parents every benefit of our expertise and support.

ACKNOWLEDGMENTS

We are indebted to many people who provided valuable assistance in our preparation
of this chapter. We are grateful to the following therapists (and their colleagues) who
completed our survey questionnaire and provided thoughtful comments on their experiences in working with mentally retarded parents: Lois Dixon, Lynne Embry, Sheila
Eyberg, Pam Fabry, Ann Garner, Karen Geelen, J. Gouse-Sheese, John Lutzker, Ted
Maloney, Mary Mira, David Pomerantz, Linda Riner, Steve Rosenberg, Robert Schilling,
Steve Szykula, and Robert Wahler. We would also like to thank the various advisors of
the Eastern Nebraska Community Office on Retardation (ENCOR), especially Barb Jessing,
who facilitated our interviews with mentally retarded mothers. We are especially grateful
to those ENCOR clients who agreed to be interviewed. We appreciate very much the
valuable help of our Boys Town Center colleagues Tom Green, Bonnie Shoultz, Marsha
Weir, and Kathy Whitmore, and the staff of the Center's word processing unit. We also
appreciate the helpful comments of our editor, Elaine Blechman, and of Stan O'Dell on
earlier versions of the manuscript. This project was supported in part by Project 405 from
Maternal and Child Health Services to the Meyer Children's Rehabilitation Institute of the
University of Nebraska Medical Center and by core support provided to the Research
Program on Personal Competence in At-Risk Youth by Father Flanagan's Boys' Home.

The Parent Training Questionnaire was adapted with permission from the Pre-AABT
Conference Demographic Questionnaire designed by Elaine Blechman of Wesleyan University. Additional content material was obtained from the Washington Family Role Inventory developed by F. Ivan Nye and Victor Gecas at Washington State University, by
permission of the authors and the university. We gratefully acknowledge their contributions.

REFERENCES

Andron, L., & Sturm, M. L. Is "I do" in the repertoire of the retarded? A study of the functioning of married retarded couples. *Mental Retardation*, 1973, *11*, 31–34.

Bass, M. S. Marriage, parenthood, and prevention of pregnancy. *American Journal of Mental Deficiency*, 1963, *68*, 320–335.

Bell, R. W. A reinterpretation of the direction of effects in studies of socialization. *Psychological Review*, 1968, *75*, 81–95.

Berg, E., & Nyland, D. Marriage and mental retardation in Denmark. In D. A. A. Primrose (Ed.), *Proceedings of the Third Congress of the International Association for the Scientific Study of Mental Deficiency* (Vol. 1). Warsaw: Polish Medical Publishers, 1975.

Berry, J. D., & Shapiro, A. Married mentally handicapped patients in the community. *Proceedings of Royal Society of Medicine*, 1975, *68*, 795–798.

Bijou, S. W. A functional analysis of retarded development. In N. R. Ellis (Ed.), *International review of research in mental retardation* (Vol. 1). New York: Academic, 1966.

Borgman, R. D. Intelligence and maternal inadequacy. *Child Welfare*, 1969, *48*, 301–304.

Bradley, D., Attaliades, E., Fisher, S., Geelen, K., & Hamad, C. *Specialized day care: A training environment for retarded caregivers.* Poster presentation at conference of Association for Behavior Analysis, Milwaukee, May 1981.

Brandon, M. W. G. The intellectual and social status of children of mental defectives. *Journal of Mental Science*, 1957, *103*, 710–738.

Bronfenbrenner, U. *A report on longitudinal evaluations of preschool programs* (Vol. 2: *Is early intervention effective?*) (DHEW Publ. No. 75-25). Washington, D.C.: Department of Health, Education & Welfare, 1974.

Budd, K. S. *Factors contributing to successful interventions with mentally retarded parents.* Paper presented at the meeting of the American Association on Mental Deficiency, Boston, June 1982.

Clarke, A. M., & Clarke, A. D. B. Some contrived experiments. In A. M. Clarke & A. D. B. Clarke (Eds.), *Early experience: Myth and evidence.* New York: Free Press, 1976. (a)

Clarke, A. M., & Clarke, A. D. B. The formative years? In A. M. Clarke & A. D. B. Clarke (Eds.), *Early experience: Myth and evidence.* New York: Free Press, 1976. (b)

Clarke-Stewart, K. A., & Apfel, N. Evaluating parental effects on child development. In L. S. Shulman (Ed.), *Review of research in education* (Vol. 6). Itasca, Ill.: Peacock, 1979.

Clausen, J. Quo vadis, AAMD? *Journal of Special Education*, 1972, *6*, 51–60.

Doll, E. A. The essentials of an inclusive concept of mental deficiency. *American Journal of Mental Deficiency*, 1941, *46*, 214–219.

Embry L. H. Personal communication, March 23, 1981.

Embry, L. H., Kelley, M. L., Herbert-Jackson, E., & Baer, D. M. *Group parent training: An analysis of generalization from classroom to home.* Paper presented at convention of the Association for Advancement of Behavior Therapy, Chicago, November 1978.

Embry, L. H., Schilmoeller, G. L., Kelley, M. L., & O'Malley, J. *A parent class for training parents as their children's therapists.* Paper presented at convention of the American Psychological Association, Chicago, August 1975.

Eyberg, S. *A parent–child interaction model for the treatment of psychological disorders in early childhood.* Paper presented at the meeting of the Western Psychological Association, San Diego, April 1979.

Eyberg, S. Personal communication, March 1981.

Fleischman, M. J. Using parenting salaries to control attrition and cooperation in therapy. *Behavior Therapy*, 1979, *10*, 111–116.

Floor, L., Baxter, D., Rosen, M., & Zisfein, L. A survey of marriages among previously institutionalized retardates. *Mental Retardation*, 1975, *13*, 33–37.

Fotheringham, J. B. *Mentally retarded persons as parents*. Unpublished manuscript, 1980. (Available from North York General Hospital, 4001 Leslie St., Willowdale, Ontario M2K 1E1.)

Garmezy, N. Vulnerability research and the issue of primary prevention. *American Journal of Orthopsychiatry*, 1971, *41*, 101–116.

Goldstein, W., & Weiss, F. C. *The effects of training a retarded mother to implement a token reinforcement procedure on her son's compliance*. Unpublished manuscript, 1981. (Available from Eunice Kennedy Shriver Center, 200 Trapelo Rd., Waltham, Mass. 02154.)

Greenspan, S. Social intelligence in the retarded. In N. R. Ellis (Ed.), *Handbook of mental retardation: Psychological theory and research* (2nd ed.). Hillsdale, N.J.: Erlbaum, 1979.

Greenspan, S., & Budd, K. S. Interview with mentally retarded mother, Omaha, Nebraska, July 19, 1981. (a)

Greenspan, S., & Budd, K. S. Interview with mentally retarded mother, Omaha, Nebraska, July 20, 1981. (b)

Grossman, H. (Ed.). *Manual on terminology and classification in mental retardation*. Washington, D.C.: American Association on Mental Deficiency, 1973.

Guilford, J. P. *The nature of human intelligence*. New York: McGraw-Hill, 1967.

Halpern, P., & Fraser, L. *Homemaker service for developmentally disabled mothers*. Unpublished manuscript, 1975. (Available from Home Services Association, Inc., 1954 University Ave., St. Paul, Minn. 55104.)

Hanf, C., & Kling, F. *Facilitating parent–child interaction: A two-stage training model*. Unpublished manuscript, 1973. (Available from University of Oregon Medical School, Portland, Ore. 97201.)

Heber, R.A. *A manual on terminology and classification in mental retardation*. Washington, D.C.: American Association on Mental Deficiency, 1961.

Heber, R. Personality. In H. A. Stevens & R. Heber (Eds.), *Mental retardation: A review of research*. Chicago: University of Chicago Press, 1964.

Heber, R., & Garber, H. The Milwaukee project: A study in the use of family intervention to prevent cultural–familial mental retardation. In B. Z. Friedlander, G. M. Sterritt, & G. E. Kirk (Eds.), *Exceptional infant* (Vol. 3: *Assessment and intervention*). New York: Brunner/Mazel, 1975.

Hertz, R. A. Retarded parents in neglect proceedings: Erroneous assumptions of parental inadequacy. *Stanford Law Review*, 1979, *31*, 785–805.

Jensen, A. R. A theory of primary and secondary familial mental retardation. In N. R. Ellis (Ed.), *International review of research in mental retardation* (Vol. 4). New York: Academic, 1970.

Kugel, R. B., & Parsons, M. H. *Children of deprivation: Changing the course of familial retardation*. Washington, D.C.: U.S. Government Printing Office, 1967.

Landesman-Dwyer, S. Personal communication, April 1981.

Lutzker, J. R., Frame, R. E., & Rice, J. M. Prject 12-Ways: An ecobehavioral approach to the treatment and prevention of child abuse and neglect. *Education and Treatment of Children*, 1982, *5*, 141-155.

Madsen, M. K. Parenting classes for the mentally retarded. *Mental Retardation*, 1979, *17*, 195–196.

Mattinson, J. *Marriage and mental handicaps*. Pittsburgh: University of Pittsburgh Press, 1970.

Mercer, J. R. *Labelling the mentally retarded: Clinical and social system perspectives on mental retardation*. Berkeley: University of California Press, 1973.

Mercer, J. R., & Lewis, J. R. *System of multi-cultural pluralistic assessment*. New York: Psychological Corp., 1978.

Mickelson, P. The feebleminded parent: A study of 90 family cases. *American Journal of*

Mental Deficiency, 1947, *51*, 644–653.

Mickelson, P. Can mentally deficient parents be helped to give their children better care? *American Journal of Mental Deficiency*, 1949, *53*, 516–534.

Miller, W. H. *Systematic parent training: Procedures, cases and issues.* Champaign, Ill.: Research, 1975.

Mills, D. M., Stortecky, E. A., & Bass, R. W. *Training a retarded mother as a behavior change agent via videotape modeling and corrective feedback.* Unpublished manuscript, 1981. (Available from Eunice Kennedy Shriver Center, 200 Trapelo Rd., Waltham, Mass. 02154.)

Mira, M., & Roddy, J. *Parenting competencies of retarded persons: A critical review.* Unpublished manuscript, 1980. (Available from Children's Rehabilitation Unit, University of Kansas Medical Center, Kansas City, Kans. 66103.)

Mitchell, S. B. Results in family casework with feebleminded clients. *Smith College Studies in Social Work*, 1947, *18*, 21–36.

Nihira, K., Foster, R., Shellhaas, M., & Leland, H. *American Association on Mental Deficiency Adaptive Behavior Scale* (1975 rev.). Washington, D.C.: American Association on Mental Deficiency, 1975.

O'Dell, S. L. Enhancing parent involvement in training: A discussion. *The Behavior Therapist*, 1982, *5*, 9-13.

Page, E. B. Miracle in Milwaukee: Raising the IQ. *Educational Researcher*, 1972, *1*, 8–16.

Pelton, L. H. Child abuse and neglect and protective intervention in Mercer County, New Jersey. In L. H. Pelton (Ed.), *The social context of child abuse and neglect.* New York: Human Sciences, 1981.

Plamondon, A. L., & Soskin, R. M. Handicapped parents: Can they call their children their own? *Amicus*, 1978, *3* (6), 24–31.

Pomerantz, D. J. Personal communication, July 13, 1981.

Pomerantz, D. J., Towne, R. C., & Pomerantz, P. B. *Evaluation reports on the specialized family program for urban, developmentally disabled parents* (Supplements to Grant No. G007701809). U.S. Department of Health, Education & Welfare, Bureau of Education for the Handicapped, November 1979 and December 1980.

President's Committee on Mental Retardation. *The six-hour retarded child.* Washington, D.C.: U.S. Government Printing Office, 1970.

Robb, W., Attaliades, E., Bradley, D., Fisher, S., Mann, P., & Weiss, F. *Teaching parenting skills to retarded parents in a supervised day care environment.* Poster presentation at conference of Association for Behavior Analysis, Milwaukee, May 1981.

Robb, W., & Weiss, F. C. *Training retarded parents as behavior change agents.* Unpublished manuscript, 1981. (Available from Eunice Kennedy Shriver Center, 200 Trapelo Rd., Waltham, Mass. 02154.)

Rosenberg, S. A., & McTate, G. A. Intellectually handicapped mothers: Problems and prospects. *Children Today*, 1982, *11*, 24–26.

Rosenberg, S. A., McTate, G. A., & Robinson, C. C. *Final report: Intensive services to families at risk project* (Grant No. 90-C-1266). U.S. Department of Health & Human Services, Agency for Children, Youth, & Families, September 1981.

Sameroff, A. J., & Chandler, M. J. Reproductive risk and the continuum of caretaking casualty. In F. D. Horowitz, E. M. Hetherington, S. Scarr-Salapatek, & G. M. Siegel (Eds.), *Review of child development research* (Vol. 4). Chicago: University of Chicago Press, 1975.

Sarber, R. E., Messmer, M. C., Halasz, M. M., & Bickett, A. D. *In-home training of nutrition skills to a mentally retarded parent to prevent child neglect.* Paper presented at convention of the Association for Behavior Analysis, Milwaukee, May 1981.

Schurr, K. T., Joiner, L. M., & Towne, R. C. Self-concept research on the mentally retarded:

A review of empirical studies. *Mental Retardation,* 1970, *8,* 39–43.

Shaw, C. H., & Wright, C. H. The married mental defective: A follow-up study. *Lancet,* 1960, *30,* 273–274.

Sheridan, M. D. The intelligence of 100 neglectful mothers. *British Medical Journal,* 1956, *1,* 91–93.

Smith, J. D., & Polloway, E. A. The dimension of adaptive behavior in mental retardation research: An analysis of recent practices. *American Journal of Mental Deficiency,* 1979, *84,* 203–206.

Szykula, S. A., Haffey, A. P., & Parsons, D. E. Two treatment supplements to standard behavior modification for socially aggressive children. In M. Bryce & J. C. Lloyd (Eds.), *Treating families in the home: An alternative to placement.* Springfield, Ill.: Thomas, 1981.

Thomas, A., Chess, S., & Birch, H. G. *Temperament and behavior disorders in children.* New York: New York University Press, 1968.

Thorndike, E. L. Intelligence and its uses. *Harper's Magazine,* 1920, *140,* 227–235.

Tredgold, A. F. *A textbook of mental deficiency.* Baltimore: William Wood, 1937.

Wald, M. State intervention on behalf of "neglected" children: A search for realistic standards. *Stanford Law Review,* 1975, *27,* 985–1040.

Weiss, F. C. Personal communication, May 30, 1981.

Wellman, R. J. Fear of solo driving treated with sequentially arranged behavioral methods: A case study. *Behavior Therapy,* 1978, *9,* 290–292.

Wolfensberger, W. *The origin and nature of our institutional models.* Syracuse, N.Y.: Human Policy Press, 1975.

AUTHOR INDEX

Abarbanel, A.R., 125, 127, 139n.
Abel, G., 311, 336n.
Abel, G.G., 387, 394n.
Abramowitz, C.V., 171, 186n.
Abramowitz, S.I., 26, 29 n.
Abrams, D.B., 430, 447n.
Abrams, N., 411, 426n.
Abramson, E., 381, 394n.
Abramson, L.Y., 18, 27n., 32n., 292, 294, 295, 297, 301n., 306n., 346, 365n.
Achenbach, T., 5, 27n.
Adams, H.C., 118, 128, 133, 142n.
Adams, H.E., 74, 89n., 311, 314, 316–318, 335n., 336n., 339n., 340n., 358, 371n.
Adams, N.E., 19, 28n.
Adams, P.W., 281, 301n.
Adams, R.D., 318, 337n.
Addison, H., 407, 426n.
Addison, R.G. 407, 426n.
Adler, C.S., 313, 336n.
Adler, F., 401–403, 409, 420, 423n.
Afton, A.D., 208, 210, 220n.
Agras, W.S., 52, 53, 57n., 283, 286, 306n., 350, 369n., 387, 389, 394n., 396n.
Aguar, D., 196, 215n.
Ahles, T.A., 313, 335n.
Aiello, J.R., 50, 57n.
Aiello, T.D., 50, 57n.
Aigner, S.M., 401, 405, 411, 427n.
Akerlund, M., 326, 335n.
Alberti, R.E., 144, 150, 158, 163n.
Aldebaran, 391, 394n.
Alden, L., 359, 365n., 359, 370n.
Alexander, J.F., 171, 172, 175, 186n., 189n., 192, 193, 196, 210, 213n., 218n., 227, 399, 401–427, 413–419, 421, 423n., 424n., 426n., 427n.
Alford, B.A., 203, 218n.
Alkema, F., 145, 163n.
Allen, D.R., 205, 214n.
Allen, E.V., 319, 335n.
Allen, N., 411, 426n.

Allen, R., 350, 369n.
Allen, V.L., 343, 370n.
Alpert, R., 47, 59n.
Alterman, A.I., 438, 447n.
Altman, I., 414, 426n.
Altman, M.G., 408, 423n.
Amaro-Plotkin, H.D., 48, 59n.
Amenson, C.F., 283, 301n.
Amir, M., 247, 248, 270n.
Anastasi, A., 62, 65–67, 69, 79, 86, 89n.
Andberg, M.M., 70, 71, 92n.
Anderson, J., 357, 366n.
Anderson, S.D., 226, 242n.
Anderson, K.I., 326, 335n.
Andrasik, F., 314, 337n.
Andrew, J.M., 410, 423n.
Andreychuk, T., 317, 335n.
Andron, L., 478, 503n.
Angle, H.V., 75, 91n.
Annon, J.S., 127, 134, 139n.
Ansley, M.Y., 26, 32n., 335, 339n.
Anspach, D.F., 207, 213n.
Apfel, N., 484–486, 503n.
Appenzeller, O., 228, 242n.
Archer, F.F., 332, 336n.
Arenberg, D., 468, 470n.
Argeriou, M., 433, 444, 447n.
Argyle, M., 145, 158, 163n.
Aries, E., 147, 164n.
Arkowitz, H., 357, 358, 365n., 366n.
Armstrong, P.M., 192, 214n.
Arnkoff, D.B., 233, 244n.
Arnold, S., 192, 195, 201, 213n.
Aronson, E., 88, 89n.
Arvey, R.D., 15, 27n.
Asarnow, J., 156, 167n.
Ascher, M.L., 131, 133, 135, 139n.
Ascione, R.F., 193, 219n.
Ash, P., 70, 89n.
Asher, S.J., 17, 28n., 207, 214n.
Ashmore, R.D., 344, 365n.
Astrand, I., 230, 242n.

507

Atkeson, B.M., 98, 102, 105, 106, 110, 190–220, 191, 193, 199, 209, 210, 213n., 214n., 249–251, 270n., 271n., 339
Attaliades, E., 495, 503n., 505n.
Atthowe, J.M., 466, 471n.
Atwater, J., 413, 425n.
Austin, N., 144, 158, 168n.
Austin, P., 407, 424n.
Axelrod, S., 192, 215n.
Ayllon, T., 191, 213n., 387, 394n.
Azrin, N.H., 190, 192, 213n., 443, 448n.
Azzerad, J., 387, 394n.

Bachrach, A.J., 387, 394n.
Baer, D.M., 95, 99, 101–106, 107n., 108n., 194, 200, 216n., 217n., 219n., 466, 472n., 490, 503n.
Baer, J., 144, 158, 164n.
Bagley, R.W., 228, 243n.
Bailey, D.A., 223, 242n.
Bailey, J.S., 191, 200, 213n., 217n.
Bakal, D.A., 312, 313, 316, 335n.
Bakan, D., 342, 365n.
Baker, B.L., 210, 213n.
Bales, R.E., 342, 370n.
Balkan, S., 405, 423n.
Ballou, D.J., 361, 369n.
Balter, M.B., 432, 447n.
Baltes, M.M., 84, 89n., 466, 467, 471n., 473n.
Baltes, P.B., 468, 472n., 473n.
Bandura, A., 6, 19, 27n., 28n., 116, 139n., 147, 153, 164n., 198, 213n., 263, 270n., 299, 301n.
Bane, M.J., 207, 213n.
Bank, B.J., 14, 28n.
Barbach, L., 115, 132, 137, 139n.
Bardwick, J.M., 288, 301n., 407, 412, 424n., 425n.
Barkley, R.A., 197, 213n., 214n.
Barloon-Noble, R., 194, 216n.
Barlow, D.H., 1, 34–59, 36, 37, 40, 43, 46, 48–50, 52–55, 57n., 58n., 70n., 74, 76, 89n., 92n., 97, 124, 139n., 274, 283, 284, 286, 305n., 306n., 311, 341, 347, 348, 350, 353, 365n., 368n., 385, 387, 394n., 397n.
Barnard, J.C., 192, 209, 213n.
Barron, N., 147, 164n.
Barrow, G.M., 452, 471n.
Barry, H., 5, 29n.

Barry, W.A., 173, 183, 186n.
Bart, P.B., 18, 28n., 264, 270n.
Barthell, C.N., 145, 164n.
Barton, C., 171, 172, 174, 175, 186n., 413, 416, 417, 419, 423n., 424n., 427n.
Barton, E.M., 467, 471n.
Barton, R., 18, 31n.
Basmajian, J.V., 313, 335n.
Bass, M.S., 478, 503n.
Bass, R.W., 495, 505n.
Batalden, P., 462, 471n.
Bates, J.E., 48, 58n.
Baucom, D.H., 297, 301n., 346, 365n.
Baumrind, D., 17, 28n.
Bauske, B., 196, 220n.
Baxter, D., 484, 503n.
Beach, L.R., 156, 165n., 359, 367n.
Beatty, J., 317, 336n.
Beavin, J.H., 421, 427n.
Beck, A.T., 18, 28n., 249, 255–257, 270n., 272n., 276, 283, 290–294, 298, 301n., 305n., 306n.
Beck, J.G., 1, 34–59, 97, 124, 139n., 274, 311, 341
Becker, J., 261–263, 270, 270n., 275, 301n.
Becker, W.C., 194, 213n.
Beckman, L.J., 16, 28n., 429, 433, 440, 441, 447n.
Bedrosian, R.C., 238, 243n.
Bee, H., 342, 370n.
Beech, H.R., 330, 340n.
Beeman, E.A., 406, 424n.
Behan, P.O., 70, 92n.
Behar, V., 295, 301n.
Beiman, J., 75, 89n.
Belar, C.D., 314, 335n.
Bell, R.W., 197, 198, 213n., 485, 503n.
Bell, R.Q., 406, 426n.
Bellack, A.S., 74, 80, 89n., 91n., 144, 145, 149, 156–158, 160, 164n., 166n., 168n., 169n., 236, 242n., 286, 289, 303n., 306n., 381, 394n.
Bellamy, G.T., 209, 216n.
Bem, D.J., 171, 186n.
Bem, S.L., 6, 28n., 36, 43, 49, 54, 56, 57n., 171, 186n., 343, 345, 365n.
Bemis, K.M., 72, 79, 82, 91n., 377, 380, 386–389, 391, 394n.
Benlolo, L., 200, 201, 218n.
Bentler, P.M., 192, 213n.
Berg, E., 484, 503n.
Berg, J.H., 16, 28n.

Berger, L., 405, 423n.
Berger, M., 185, 186n.
Berger, R.M., 466, 471n.
Bergin, A.E., 170, 174, 183, 185, 186n., 187n.
Bergmann, K., 460, 471n., 473n.
Berkowitz, B.P., 190, 213n.
Bernal, M.E., 191, 200, 209, 213n.
Bernard, J., xii, xiiin., 17, 22, 28n., 147, 164n., 172, 186n., 409, 424n.
Bernhill, E.A., 94, 107n.
Bernstein, I.S., 333, 339n.
Bernstein, M.C., 453, 471n.
Bernstein, M.H., 249, 271n.
Berry, C., 324, 335n.
Berry, J.D., 483, 503n.
Berscheid, E., 378, 394n.
Berzins, J.R., 297, 301n.
Bialer, I., 11, 28n.
Bianco, F.J., 387, 394n.
Bickett, A., 466, 474n., 491, 505n.
Biddle, B.J., 14, 28n.
Bieber, M., 265, 268, 272n.
Bieliauskas, L.A., 9, 30n.
Bierman, E., 459, 475n.
Biggs, S.J., 389, 394n.
Biglan, A., 285–287, 304n.
Bijou, S.W., 477, 503n.
Bild, R., 317, 335n.
Bille, M., 463, 476n.
Biller, H.B., 207, 213n.
Binstock, R., 461, 471n.
Birch, H.G., 485, 506n.
Birdwhistell, R., 48, 57n.
Birkhill, W.R., 469, 471n.
Birren, J., 454, 463, 468, 471n., 474n.
Black, A.L., 466, 471n.
Blackman, D.K., 466, 471n.
Blackwell, A., 380, 397n.
Blackwell, C.J., 194, 200, 218n.
Blair, S.N., 227, 242n.
Blanchard, E.B., 145, 159, 164n., 165n., 311, 313, 317, 321, 335n., 336n.
Blanchard, R., 82, 90n.
Bland, K., 353, 365n.
Blaney, P.H., 285, 290, 291, 295, 301n.
Blashfield, R., 70, 89n.
Blau, P.M., 8, 28n.
Blechman, E.A., xi, xiiin., 3–33, 11, 20, 28n., 52, 54, 56, 57n., 146, 164n., 171, 174, 179, 187n., 192–194, 196, 200, 207, 208, 214n., 216n., 324, 335n., 357, 411–414, 420, 424n.

Blinder, 387, 388, 394n.
Block, J., 25, 29n., 181, 188n., 406, 424n.
Block, J.E., 181, 188n.
Block, J.H., 147, 164n., 343, 344, 366n.
Blood, R.O., 173, 187n.
Bloom, B.L., 17, 28n., 207, 214n.
Bloom, L.J., 324, 335n.
Bloom, L.Z., 144, 158, 164n.
Blum, J.E., 464, 471n.
Blumenthal, J.A., 231, 233, 243n.
Blyth, D., 101, 107n.
Bolen, D., 416, 425n.
Bolstad, O.D., 86, 91n., 209, 210, 216n.
Bordewick, M.C., 359, 366n.
Borg, G.A.V., 231, 242n.
Borgman, R.D., 483, 503n.
Borkovec, T.D., 356, 366n.
Bornstein, P.H., 149, 166n., 359, 366n.
Boskind-Lodahl, M., 377, 391 394n.
Boswell, P.C., 10, 28n.
Botwinick, J., 469, 471n.
Boulougouris, J., 263, 271n., 355, 369n.
Bower, G.H., 144, 158, 164n.
Bower, S.A., 144, 158, 164n.
Bowker, L.H., 405, 408, 424n.
Bradley, D., 495, 503n., 505n.
Bradlyn, A.S., 203, 218n.
Brady, J.P., 128, 136, 139n.
Brand, E., 350, 370n.
Brandon, M.W.G., 484, 503n.
Brantley, P.J., 318, 335n.
Braukmann, C.J., 413, 415, 425n.
Braunwald, E., 318, 337n.
Bray, G., 374, 375, 379, 394n.
Breed, W., 452, 471n.
Brehony, K.A., 319, 339n.
Breiner, J., 196, 215n.
Brennan, N.J., 101, 107n.
Brickman, P., 416, 425n.
Briddell, D.W., 430, 434, 449n.
Bridgwater, C.A., 149, 166n.
Bristow, A.R., 297, 305n.
Broderick, J., 205, 218n.
Brodsky, A.M., xi, 72n., 76, 89n., 170, 187n.
Brody, J.E., 376, 394n.
Bronfenbrenner, U., 493, 503n.
Bronheim, S., 162, 167n.
Brooks-Gunn, J., 325, 339n.
Broverman, D.M., 419, 424n.
Broverman, I.K., 342, 370n., 419, 424n.
Brown, B., 15, 29n.
Brown, B.S., 95, 107n.

Brown, D., 47, 57n.
Brown, D.A., 317, 335n.
Brown, G., 75, 91n.
Brown, G.E., 319, 335n.
Brown, G.W., 279, 288, 301n.
Brown, N., 162, 168n.
Brown, S.H., 149, 167n.
Brownell, K.D., 226, 227, 229, 242n., 380–385, 391, 393, 394n., 398n.
Bruch, H., 376, 378, 380, 386, 388, 395n.
Bruch, M.A., 155, 157, 164n.
Bruner, J.S., 4, 29n.
Bryant, B.M., 162, 169n.
Bryant, N.D., 15, 30n.
Bucher, B., 193, 194, 214n., 384, 398n.
Budd, K.S., 98, 99, 104, 202, 215n., 400, 477–506, 478, 496, 503n., 504n.
Budzynski, T., 313, 336n.
Bukstel, L.H., 206, 219n.
Bunch, G., 192, 220n.
Bunck, T.J., 467, 471n.
Burch, G., 455, 471n.
Burgess, A.W., 247–249, 263, 265, 270n.
Burgess, D., 129, 131, 133, 139n.
Burglass, D., 283, 301n.
Burke, E.J., 231, 242n.
Burnap, D., 119, 139n.
Burns, B.J., 191, 213n.
Burt, B., 466, 471n.
Burtle, V., ix, ixn., 441, 447n.
Busemeyer, J., 206, 219n.
Bush, E.S., 296, 302n.
Bushkirk, V., 380, 395n.
Busse, E., 462, 474n.
Butler, A.K., 466, 474n.
Butler, C.A., 130, 132, 139n.
Butler, L., 155, 167n.
Butler, P.E., 144, 158, 164n.
Butler, R., 453, 458, 463, 464, 471n.
Button, E.J., 388, 395n.
Butz, R., 350, 369n.

Caird, W., 118, 123, 126, 137, 138, 139n.
Calhoun, K.S., 74, 89n., 249–251, 260, 270n., 271n., 273, 308–340, 359, 370n., 400
Callner, D.A., 145, 164n.
Campbell, A., 401, 403, 424n.
Campbell, D.T., 85, 86, 89n., 93n.
Campbell, S., 197, 214n.
Canter, A., 313, 337n.
Capel, W., 462, 471n.
Carlsmith, J.M., 88, 89n.

Carmody, T., 359, 366n.
Carnahan, C., 329, 340n.
Carney, R., 195, 220n.
Carpenter, C.J., 22–24, 28n.
Carroll, P.J., 466, 471n.
Cartelli, L., 192, 214n.
Casper, R.C., 388, 395n.
Catalano, R., 10, 32n.
Caudill, S., 6, 30n.
Cautela, J.R., 466, 467, 472n.
Celentano, D.D., 429, 447n.
Cernkovich, S.A., 401, 405, 409, 424n.
Chambless, D.L., 173, 187n., 352, 354, 366n., 368n.
Chandler, M.J., 484, 485, 505n.
Chaney, E.F., 439, 447n.
Chapin, H.N., 387, 394n.
Chaplin, W., 18, 31n.
Chee, E., 429, 447n.
Cheek, D.K., 144, 164n.
Cherry, F., 363, 366n.
Cherubin, C., 462, 474n.
Chesler, P., 51, 57n., 172, 187n., 292, 299, 301n.
Chesney, M.A., 313, 325, 328, 330, 336n., 340n., 362, 363, 366n.
Chess, S., 485, 506n.
Chien, C.P., 466, 472n.
Chism, R.A., 330, 336n.
Christensen, A., 176, 187n., 209, 216n., 357, 366n.
Christophersen, E.R., 192, 213n., 214n.
Christy, J., 270, 271n.
Ciminero, A.R., 74, 76, 77, 89n., 209, 214n.
Cinciripini, P.M., 311, 336n.
Clancy, K., 283, 302n.
Clark, E.V., 158, 164n.
Clark, H.B., 192, 216n.
Clark, H.H., 158, 164n.
Clark, R.A., 147, 166n.
Clarke, A., 325, 339n.
Clarke, A.D.B., 485, 493, 503n.
Clarke, A.M., 485, 493, 503n.
Clarke-Stewart, K.A., 484–486, 503n.
Clarkson, F.E., 419, 424n.
Clausen, J., 481, 503n.
Clayton, R.B., 326, 338n.
Clifford, R.E., 131, 133, 135, 139n.
Cloward, R.A., 408, 424n.
Coates, R.J., 383, 385, 396n.
Cobb, J.A., 195, 218n.
Coburn, K., 100, 164n.

Cochran, S.D., 297, 303*n*., 359, 368*n*.
Coe, R.M., 94, 107*n*.
Cohen, A.K., 407, 424*n*.
Cohen, E.S., 70, 72*n*., 90*n*.
Cohen, G., 460, 464, 469, 472*n*.
Cohen, J.A., 85, 89*n*.
Cohen, S., 345, 367*n*.
Cohn, A., 455, 471*n*.
Coleman, J., 467, 474*n*.
Coletti, G., 203, 214*n*.
Collins, F., 311, 336*n*.
Collins, R.W., 466, 472*n*.
Compton, J.V., 75, 93*n*.
Cone, J.D., 74, 80, 90*n*.
Conger, J.J., 211, 214*n*.
Connolly, J., 350, 366*n*.
Connolly, K.J., 4, 29*n*.
Connor, J.M., 149, 164*n*.
Constantinople, A., 36, 57*n*., 343, 366*n*.
Conte, H., 464, 475*n*.
Conway, J.B., 194, 214*n*.
Cook, S., 86, 93*n*.
Cooke, W.R., 407, 424*n*.
Cookerly, J.R., 179, 187*n*.
Cooper, A.J., 127, 128, 139*n*.
Cooper, A.M., 430, 448*n*.
Cooper, J., 158, 169*n*.
Cooper, J.W., 462, 472*n*.
Cooper, K.B., 222–224, 230, 242*n*.
Coopersmith, S., 11, 29*n*.
Coppen, A., 324, 325, 336*n*.
Corwin, B.J., 149, 166*n*.
Cox, D.J., 313, 325, 328, 330, 336*n*.
Cox, M., 206, 216*n*.
Cox, R., 206, 216*n*.
Craighead, L., 386, 393, 395*n*., 397*n*.
Craighead, W.E., 144, 164*n*., 291, 292, 302*n*., 305*n*., 385, 396*n*.
Cranston, S.S., 191, 215*n*.
Crawford, V.L., 435, 448*n*.
Cressey, D.R., 407, 427*n*.
Crisp, A.H., 377, 388, 389, 395*n*.
Cristler, C., 191, 215*n*.
Crocell, L., 320, 338*n*.
Cronbach, L.J., 78*n*., 90*n*.
Croughan, J., 282, 305*n*.
Crook, T. H., 283, 305*n*.
Crowley, C.P., 192, 214*n*.
Crowne, D.P., 81, 90*n*.
Crozier, J., 192, 194, 214*n*.
Csapo, A.I., 326, 336*n*.
Cummings, H., 345, 367*n*.

Cunningham, C.E., 198, 213*n*., 214*n*.
Cunningham, S., 387, 396*n*.
Curran, J.P., 145, 160, 165*n*., 357, 366*n*.
Curtis, R., 16, 29*n*.
Cutler, S., 461, 472*n*.

Dalessio, D.J., 316, 336*n*.
Dalton, K., 325, 326, 330, 336*n*., 407, 424*n*.
Danker-Brown, P., 297, 301*n*., 346, 365*n*.
Darley, S.A., 362, 366*n*.
Datesman, S.K., 403, 411, 424*n*.
Davidson, C. V., 26, 29*n*.
Davidson, N., 171, 180, 181, 187*n*.
Davidson, P.O., 359, 370*n*.
Davidson, T., 265, 266, 271*n*.
Davidson, W., 14, 29*n*., 296, 302*n*.
Davis, B., 239, 244*n*., 381–383, 390, 391, 397*n*.
Davis, H.R., 100, 108*n*.
Davis, J.M., 388, 395*n*.
Davison, G.C., 144, 159, 161, 165*n*., 345, 347, 354, 357, 359, 366*n*., 367*n*.
Dean, L., 461, 472*n*.
Deaux, K., 43, 59*n*., 296, 302*n*., 346, 363, 366*n*.
DeBakey, M.E., 235, 243*n*.
Decker, J.L., 320, 340*n*.
Del Boca, F.K., 344, 365*n*.
DelGaudio, A.C., 26, 32*n*., 335, 339*n*.
DeMonbreun, B.G., 292, 302*n*.
Denney, D.R., 327, 336*n*.
Depue, R.A., 9, 32*n*., 282, 302*n*.
DeRisi, W.J., 144, 166*n*.
Derogatis, L.R., 121, 122, 141*n*.
Derry, P., 359, 366*n*.
De Silva, P., 348, 366*n*.
Detre, T., 332, 336*n*.
Deur, J.L., 207, 216*n*.
Deutsch, M., 86, 93*n*.
Dever, S., 360, 371*n*.
deVries, H.A., 468, 472*n*.
deWolf, V.A., 15, 29*n*.
Diament, C., 203, 214*n*.
Diendett, M.N., 279, 305*n*.
DiMascio, A., 260, 272*n*.
Dinning, W.D., 297, 302*n*.
Divasto, P., 270, 271*n*.
Dobes, R.W., 84, 90*n*.
Doctorow, E.L., 378, 395*n*.
Dodson, M., 16, 28*n*.
Doering, C.R., 70, 90*n*.
Doleys, D., 192, 214*n*.

Doll, E.A., 480, 503n.
Dollard, J., 6, 31n.
Donovan, D.M., 145, 168n.
Dooley, D., 10, 32n.
Doster, J., 192, 214n.
Dotemoto, S., 198, 220n.
Douvan, E., 288, 301n., 412, 425n.
Drabman, R.S., 209, 214n.
Druss, R.G., 391, 395n.
Duffy, B., 249, 271n.
Duke, D.S., 410, 424n.
Duke, P.M., 410, 424n.
Duncan, O.D., 8, 10, 28n.
Dunlop, K.H., 362, 366n.
Dupont, A., 463, 476n.
Duryee, J.S., 191, 213n.
Dweck, C.S., 14, 29n., 295, 296, 298, 302n.,
    346, 366n.
Dyer, J., 377, 395n.
Dyrenforth, S.R., 235, 244n., 379, 388, 395n.,
    398n.
D'Zurilla, T.J., 150, 165n.

Eagly, A.H., 146, 147, 165
Eastman, C., 291, 302n.
Eckert, E.D., 388, 395n.
Edney, J.J., 50, 57n.
Edwards, A.L., 36, 58n.
Edwards, J., 350, 369n.
Egan, K.J., 145, 147, 148, 150, 156, 158,
    167n., 300, 304n., 357, 358, 369n.
Eggeraat, J.B., 355, 367n.
Ehrhardt, A., 47, 59n.
Eischens, R.R., 228, 231, 243n.
Eisler, R.M., 71, 90n., 145, 157–159, 161,
    162, 165n.–167n., 358, 366n., 439,
    447n.
Ekehammer, B., 73, 90n.
Elias, M., 452, 475n.
Ellis, A., 127, 139n., 156, 165n., 290, 298,
    302n., 359, 366n., 392, 395n.
Ellis, D., 407, 424n.
Ellis, E.M., 249, 251, 270n.
Ellsworth, N.M., 227, 242n.
Embry, L.H., 194, 217n., 490–492, 503n.
Eme, R.F., 18, 29n.
Emery, G., 238, 243n., 256, 272n., 290, 301n.
Emmelkamp, P.M.G., 352, 355, 366n., 367n.
Emmons, M.L., 144, 150, 158, 163n.
Emswiller, T., 296, 302n.
Ender, R.A., 149, 164n.
Endicott, J., 66, 70n., 93n., 249, 272n., 278,
    282, 302n., 306n.
Endler, N.S., 69, 90n.
Engel, B.T., 330, 336n.
Enna, B., 14, 29n., 296, 302n.
Epstein, L.H., 231, 233, 243n., 311, 336n.
Epstein, N., 149, 154, 165n.
Epstein, R.C., 144, 165n.
Erbaugh, J., 249, 270n.
Erickson, M.T., 84, 85, 93n.
Erskine, H., 461, 472n.
Erwin, W.J., 387, 394n.
Eshleman, R., 235, 243n.
Espenshade, T.J., 207, 214n.
Etaugh, C., 15, 29n.
Evans, I.M., 60, 90n.
Evans, M., 136, 142n.
Evans, R.G., 297, 302n.
Eyberg, S.M., 190, 194, 200, 209, 210, 214n.,
    490, 503n.

Fabry, P.L., 467, 472n.
Fagot, B.I., 344, 367n.
Fairweather, G.W., 94, 107n.
Falloon, I.R., 467, 472n.
Farina, A., 5, 9, 29n.
Faris, J.W., 228, 243n.
Farquhar, J.W., 227, 242n.
Farris, E., 346, 366n.
Faustman, W.O., 202, 210, 218n.
Fawcett, S.B., 104, 107n.
Featherman, D.L., 10, 29n.
Feinleib, M., 234, 243n.
Felce, D., 466, 473n., 475n.
Feldman, J., 377, 395n.
Feldman, S., 466, 474n.
Fencil-Morse, E., 291, 298, 303n.
Fenichel, O., 6, 29n., 464, 472n.
Fenton, C., 321, 340n.
Ferber, H., 203, 204, 214n.
Ferguson, L.R., 205, 214n.
Ferrero, W., 402, 425n.
Ferster, C.B., 285, 302n., 381, 382, 395n.
Fertel, N.S., 125, 127, 139n.
Feuerstein, M., 75, 82, 83, 89n., 91n., 316,
    317, 335n., 336n.
Fezler, W.D., 127, 140n.
Fichtler, H., 313, 336n.
Fidanza, F., 374, 396n.
Fiedler, D., 156, 165n., 359, 367n.
Field, M., 452, 472n.
Filler, W.W., 326, 336n.
Finch, B.E., 161, 162, 165n.

Fineberg, B.L., 173, 187n.
Fink, M., 354, 369n.
Finkle, W.D., 332, 340n.
Fiorito, E.M., 319, 339n.
Firestone, S., 172, 187n.
Fisch, M., 462, 472n.
Fisher, E.B., 384, 396n.
Fisher, S., 130, 139n., 495, 503n., 505n.
Fishman, M.A., 317, 338n.
Fishman, S.T., 355, 367n.
Fixsen, D., 415, 425n.
Flack, R., 391, 395n.
Flannery, R.B., 467, 472n.
Fleischman, M.J., 180, 181, 189n., 196, 205, 214n., 218n., 490, 503n.
Fletcher, R.K., 104, 107n.
Floor, L., 484, 503n.
Flowers, J.V., 26, 33n.
Flynn, J., 200, 201, 218n.
Foa, E.B., 354, 366n.
Foch, T.T., 15, 32n.
Fodor, I.G., 55, 96, 99, 144, 145, 161, 162, 165n., 169n., 171, 187n., 221, 223, 227, 234, 241, 274, 343, 351, 359, 367n., 371n., 373–398, 390, 392, 393, 395n., 400, 412
Folkard, J., 281, 301n.
Foner, A., 461, 475n.
Fontaine, C.M., 46, 58n.
Fontaine, P., 235, 243n.
Forehand, R.L., 191–196, 199–202, 204–206, 209–211, 213n–220n.
Foreyt, J.P., 102, 105, 109, 221–244, 223, 224, 234, 235, 239, 243n., 274, 400
Foster, E., 460, 473n.
Foster, R., 481, 505n.
Foster, S., 6, 7, 29n., 85, 86, 91n., 193, 219n., 412, 414, 426n.
Fotheringham, J.B., 482, 483, 504n.
Fowler, J.L., 316, 335n.
Fowler, R., 116, 139n.
Fox, R.A., 193, 215n.
Foxx, R.M., 235, 243n.
Foy, D.W., 439, 447n.
Frame, R.E., 491, 504n.
Frangia, G.W., 205, 219n.
Frank, E., 98, 110, 245–272, 249, 271n., 274
Frank, J., 71, 72, 72n., 90n.
Franklin, B.A., 230, 243n.
Franks, V., ix, ixn., 441, 447n.
Fransella, F., 388, 395n.
Fraser, L., 493, 504n.

Fraser, S.C., 45, 58n.
Freedman, D., 65, 90n.
Freedman, J.L., 45, 58n.
Freeman, D.M.A., 387, 394n.
Fremouw, W.J., 384, 398n.
French, B.D., 101, 107n.
Freud, S., 6, 29n., 114, 130, 139n.
Freund, K., 82, 90n.
Freundlich, A., 313, 336n.
Friar, L., 317, 336n.
Friedan, B., 9, 29n.
Friedman, A.P., 310, 312, 315, 316, 337n.
Friedman, D., 467, 472n.
Friedman, J.M., 362, 367n.
Friedman, L.N., 345, 367n.
Friedman, P.H., 161, 162, 165n.
Friedman, R.J., 275, 302n.
Friend, R., 359, 371n.
Frieze, I.H., 266, 271n., 407, 424n.
Fruge, E., 75, 89n.
Fuchs, K., 126, 127, 139n.
Fuller, M., 50, 58n.
Furry, C., 468, 472n.

Gaffney, L.R., 422, 425n.
Gagnon, J., 459, 472n.
Galassi, J.P.,. 144, 148, 158, 161, 165n., 358, 367n.
Galassi, M.D., 144, 148, 158, 161, 162, 165n., 358, 367n.
Galligan, P., 18, 32n.
Gallimore, R., 191, 217n.
Gambrill, E.D., 144, 149, 158, 161, 165n.
Gannon, L., 311, 324, 337n.
Garbarino, J., 361, 367n.
Garber, H., 492, 493, 504n.
Garber, J., 295, 302n.
Garber, S., 191, 213n.
Garfield, S.L., 170, 186n., 187n.
Garfinkle, P.E., 377, 380, 387, 389, 391, 395n.–397n.
Garmezy, N., 5, 29n., 485, 504n.
Garner, A., 200, 217n.
Garner, D.M., 389, 391, 396n.
Garron, D.C., 9, 30n.
Gatchel, R.I., 345, 367n.
Gatchel, R.J., 296, 302n.
Gaul, D.J., 385, 396n.
Gayford, J.J., 266, 271n.
Gebhard, P.H., 114, 140n., 459, 472n.
Geelen, K., 495, 503n.
Geer, J., 82, 90n., 124, 142n., 345, 367n.

Gehle, C., 466, 471n.
Geiger, O.G., 466, 472n.
Gelbart, P., 162, 169n.
Gelder, M.G., 355, 367n., 369n.
Gelles, R.J., 265, 266, 271n.
Gerrard, M., 327, 336n.
Gershaw, N.J., 466, 474n.
Gewirtz, J.L., 6, 29n.
Gholson, B., 21, 33n.
Gibbons, D.C., 411, 425n.
Gibson, D.M., 209, 213n.
Gibson, S., 462, 472n.
Giebenhain, J.E., 203, 218n.
Gilbert, F.S., 357, 366n.
Gillard, D., 296, 302n.
Gillespie, H.G., 123, 129, 139n.
Gilmore, S., 209, 220n.
Gilmour, R., 145, 163n.
Giordano, P.C., 401, 403, 405, 408, 409, 424n., 425n.
Gipson, T.T., 466, 474n.
Giraldo, Z.I., 15, 29n.
Glaser, E.M., 101, 107n.
Glass, C.R., 356, 367n.
Glass, D.C., 345, 346, 367n.
Glass, D.R., 297, 302n.
Glasser, W., 225, 231, 243n.
Glenn, N., 461, 472n.
Gleser, R., 68, 90n.
Glogower, F., 195, 200, 201, 203, 209, 215n.
Glueck, E., 402, 411, 425n.
Glueck, S., 402, 411, 425n.
Goetz, T.E., 14, 29n., 346, 366n.
Goklaney, M., 260, 272n.
Gold, M., 411, 425n.
Goldberg, S.C., 388, 395n.
Goldblatt, P.B., 378, 396n.
Golden, J., 119, 135, 139n., 140n.
Golden, M.A., 135, 140n.
Golden, M.M., 8, 32n., 145, 168n.
Goldfarb, A., 453, 462, 472n.
Goldfried, A., 359, 369n.
Goldfried, M.R., 55, 72, 90n., 98, 109, 144, 150, 159, 161, 165n., 227, 263, 273, 274, 311, 341–372, 345–347, 349, 357–360, 362, 367n., 369n., 371n.
Goldman, H., 75, 91n.
Goldman, N., 280, 303n.
Goldstein, A., 173, 187n., 352, 354, 357, 366n.–368n.
Goldstein, A.P., 161, 166n., 466, 474n.
Goldstein, R.S., 415, 425n., 466, 472n.

Goldstein, W., 495, 504n.
Golin, S., 295, 303n.
Golla, F.L., 406, 425n.
Golub, S., 329, 337n.
Gomberg, E.S., 429, 447n.
Gong-Guy, E., 295, 303n.
Gonzaga, F.P., 325, 339n.
Good, T.L., 14, 28n.
Goodenough, F.L., 69, 90n.
Goodrick, G.K., 102, 105, 109, 221–244, 223, 224, 228, 234, 243n., 274, 400
Gordon, J.R., 241, 244n., 440, 442, 448n.
Gordon, M., 135, 140n.
Gordon, S., 74, 91n., 171, 180, 181, 187n.
Gordon, T.P., 333, 339n.
Gormally, J., 358, 368n.
Götestam, K.G., 430, 448n.
Gotlib, I.H., 10, 29n.
Gottfredson, G.D., 15, 29n.
Gottman, J.M., 157, 168n., 172, 175, 187n., 356, 359, 367n., 370n.
Gotto, A.M., 235, 243n.
Gould, C.F., 71, 92n.
Goulet, L.R., 468, 472n.
Gove, W., 17, 29n., 145, 165n., 173, 187n., 279, 280, 283, 292, 302n., 303n., 361, 368n.
Graham, D.T., 319, 337n.
Grame, C., 195, 220n.
Grams, P., 411, 426n.
Gray, J., 193, 215n.
Grayer, E.D., 391, 395n.
Graziano, A.M., 190, 213n., 215n.
Greden, J.F., 235, 243n.
Green, D.R., 202, 215n., 216n.
Green, E.E., 317, 339n.
Green, K., 196, 215n., 327, 338n.
Green, R., 37, 50, 58n., 119, 140n.
Greenberg, R.L., 292, 301n.
Greenblatt, M., 429, 448n.
Greenhouse, S., 463, 471n.
Greenspan, S., 98, 99, 104, 400, 477–506, 478, 486, 504n.
Greist, J.H., 228, 231, 243n.
Grey, S.,. 36, 53, 59n.
Grief, E., 192, 203, 209, 215n.
Griest, D.L., 192, 194–197, 200, 204, 205, 215n., 217n., 219n., 220n.
Griffin, P., 311, 313, 337n.
Grimes, P.S., 101, 107n.
Grinker, R., 276, 283, 303n.
Grosicki, J.P., 466, 472n.

Gross, H.S., 408, 424n.
Gross, N.C., 94, 108n.
Grossman, H., 479, 504n.
Grossnickle, W.F., 149, 166n.
Groves, G.A., 354, 366n.
Gruba, G.H., 324, 337n.
Gruson, L., 155, 167n.
Guilford, J.P., 486, 504n.
Gullion, E., 194, 218n.
Gurel, L., 145, 166n.
Gurman, A.S., xii, xiiin., 104, 110, 170–189, 170, 171, 174, 176, 179–185, 187n., 188n., 210, 421, 425n.
Guthrie, K.M., 101, 107n.
Gwaltney, M.K., 100, 101, 108n.
Gwinup, G., 227, 243n.
Gyllstrom, K.K., 343, 368n.

Haan, N., 25, 29n.
Haber, J.D., 314, 340n.
Haccoun, D.M., 26, 29n.
Hack, S., 317, 338n.
Haden-Guest, A., 377, 396n.
Haffey, A.P., 490, 506n.
Hafner, R.J., 352, 353, 368n., 370n.
Hagen, E.P., 21, 32n.
Hager, M., 429, 449n.
Hagerman, S., 18, 30n.
Hakstian, A.R., 288, 290, 304n.
Halasz, M.M., 491, 505n.
Halberstadt, A.G., 11, 30n.
Halbreich, U., 324, 337n.
Haley, W.E., 346, 371n.
Hall, G., 231, 233, 244n.
Hall, J.A., 11, 30n.
Hall, K., 147, 165n.
Hall, R.G., 381, 396n.
Hall, R.V., 191–193, 200, 215n.
Hall, S.M., 381, 396n.
Hall, W.C., 326, 336n.
Hallam, R.S., 350, 353, 365n., 366n.
Halleck, .L., 249, 271n.
Hallsten, E.A., Jr., 389, 396n.
Halmi, K.A., 386–388, 395n., 396n.
Halpern, P., 493, 504n.
Halpert, H.P., 102, 107n.
Hamad, C., 495, 503n.
Hamburg, D.A., 326, 338n.
Hamilton, H., 94, 107n.
Hamilton, J., 311, 337n.
Hamilton, M.A., 250, 271n., 283, 303n.
Hammen, C.L., 26, 30n., 129, 141n., 283,

292, 295, 297, 303n., 359, 368n.
Hand, I., 353, 368n.
Hanf, C., 196, 200, 216n., 490, 504n.
Harbin, H.T., 70, 72n., 90n.
Hardy, A.B., 19, 28n.
Hare-Mustin, R.T., xi, 72n., 76, 89n., 170, 174, 180, 187n., 188n., 421, 425n.
Hargis, K., 192, 216n.
Harkins, C., 429, 449n.
Harris, G.G., 144, 145, 158, 168n.
Harris, L., 222–225, 228, 243n., 461, 473n.
Harris, T., 279, 288, 301n.
Harrison, R., 316, 337n.
Hart, J., 348, 369n.
Harter, S., 5, 22, 30n.
Hartshorne, H., 69, 90n.
Hartup, W.W., 145, 165n.
Haskell, W.L., 227, 242n.
Hastings, D.W., 128, 140n.
Hathaway, S.R., 35, 58n., 70, 90n.
Hathorn, S., 6, 30n.
Haug, M.R., 15, 30n.
Haughton, E., 387, 394n.
Hauser, R.M., 10, 29n.
Hauserman, N., 389, 396n.
Hausknecht, M., 461, 473n.
Hawke, C.C., 406, 425n.
Hawkins, R.P., 74, 84, 90n.
Hay, L.R., 50, 58n., 75, 91n., 353, 365n.
Hay, W.M., 50, 58n., 75, 91n.
Hayashi, T.T., 332, 336n.
Hayes, S.C., 37, 40, 44–46, 48, 50, 51, 57n., 58n., 70n., 72, 73, 92n., 229, 242n., 350, 368n., 384, 394n.
Haynes, K.F., 162, 167n.
Haynes, M.R., 321, 335n.
Haynes, S.G., 234, 243n.
Haynes, S.N., 66, 68, 73–75, 78–80, 82, 87, 91n., 190, 209, 210, 216n., 311, 313, 337n., 340n.
Hazell, K., 452, 473n.
Head, R., 295, 301n.
Heatherington, E.M., 411, 425n.
Heber, R.A., 480, 481, 486, 492, 493, 504n.
Heckerman, C.L., 43, 58n., 229, 242n., 382, 384, 394n., 396n.
Heczey, M.D., 329, 337n.
Hedges, D., 201, 219n.
Hedrick, K.E., 440, 448n.
Hefner, T., 461, 472n.
Heifetz, L.J., 210, 213n.
Heiman, J.R., 124, 141n.

Heimberg, J.S., 150, 165n.
Heimberg, R.G., 150, 165n.
Heinzelman, F., 228, 243n.
Heller, B., 467, 473n.
Helmreich, R.L., 36, 59n., 343, 371n.
Helzer, J.E., 282, 305n.
Hemmes, N.S., 238, 244n.
Hendler, J., 50, 58n.
Hendricks, R.D., 430, 448n.
Henker, B., 198, 220n., 354, 371n.
Henley, N.M., 42, 58n.
Henz, M.R., 326, 336n.
Herbert, E., 200, 216n.
Herbert-Jackson, E., 490, 503n.
Herdt, J., 320, 350n.
Herjanic, B., 75, 91n.
Herjanic, M., 75, 91n.
Herman, J.B., 343, 368n.
Hersen, M., 53, 58n., 69, 74, 80, 89n., 91n.,
    144, 145, 157–162, 164n., 166n., 169n.,
    191, 216n., 286, 288, 289, 303n., 306n.,
    358, 366n., 368n.
Hertz, R.A., 478, 504n.
Herzog, E., 207, 216n.
Hess, E.P., 149, 158, 166n.
Hetherington, E.M., 206, 207, 216n.
Hewes, G.W., 37, 48, 58n.
Hickey, T., 467, 473n.
Hicks, M.W., 173, 188n.
Hilberman, E., 246, 265–267, 271n.
Hill, C.E., 358, 368n.
Hill, G., 162, 168n.
Hilpert, F., 147, 166n.
Himmelhoch, J.M., 286, 289, 303n., 306n.
Hindelang, M.J., 401, 403, 404, 425n.
Hines, P.M., 174, 188n., 421, 425n.
Hinkle, J., 313, 340n.
Hiroto, D.S., 295, 303n.
Hirt, M., 324, 337n.
Hite, S., 133, 140n., 459, 473n.
Hodge, R.S., 406, 425n.
Hodgson, R., 36, 53, 59n., 430, 448n.
Hoffman, E.G., 205, 219n.
Hogan, D.R., 135, 136, 140n.
Hogan, J.L., 194, 200, 218n.
Hollon, S.D., 72, 79, 82, 91n., 224, 238,
    243n., 256, 272n., 294, 305n.
Holmes, D.S., 145, 164n.
Holmstrom, L.L., 247–249, 263, 265, 270n.
Holroyd, J., 126, 128, 140n.
Holroyd, K.A., 314, 337n.
Holstein, C.E., 25, 30n.

Holt, W., 23, 28n.
Holzer, C., 462, 375n.
Hookman, P., 320, 340n.
Hoon, E.F., 96, 109, 111, 113–142, 122, 124,
    140n., 142n.
Hoon, P.W., 118, 122, 124, 140n., 142n.
Hops, H., 178, 188n.
Horner, M.S., 363, 368n.
Horowitz, J., 208, 219n.
Horton, J., 283, 301n.
Horton, W.G., 202, 218n.
Hosford, R.C., 6, 30n., 357, 368n.
Hovell, M.F., 191, 219n.
Howells, G.N., 19, 28n.
Hoyer, F.W., 468, 473n.
Hoyer, W.J., 466, 468–470, 473n.–475n.
Huffine, C., 452, 471n.
Hughes, H.M., 190, 209, 216n.
Hull, D.B., 26, 30n., 360, 368n.
Humphreys, L, 210, 216n.
Hunt, G.M., 443, 448n.
Hunt, J. McV., 69, 90n.
Hunt, L., 407, 426n.
Hunt, M., 119, 130, 140n.
Huston, A.C., 22–24, 28n.
Huston-Stein, A., 23, 28n.
Hutchings, D., 313, 337n.
Hyde, J.S., 15, 30n.

Iammaring, N.K., 223, 243n.
Ickes, W., 346, 368n.
Ince, L.P., 128, 140n., 466, 473n.
Ingemarsson, I., 326, 335n.
Inkeles, A., 4, 30n.
Inwold, R.H., 15, 30n.
Isselbacher, K.J., 318, 319, 337n.
Ivey, M.E., 407, 425n.
Iwata, B.A., 231, 233, 244n., 467, 471n.

Jacklin, C.N., 6, 15, 21, 31n., 47, 58n., 146,
    147, 167n., 406, 407, 425n.
Jackson, D.D., 181, 188n., 421, 427n.
Jacobs, M., 359, 368n.
Jacobs, M.J., 137, 140n.
Jacobs, R., 453, 473n.
Jacobson, A.M., 321, 337n.
Jacobson, B., 374, 377, 378, 393, 397n.
Jacobson, E., 252, 271n.
Jacobson, N.S., 171, 174–178, 180, 182, 183,
    188n.
Jahoda, M., 6, 30n., 86, 93n.
Jakubowski, P., 144, 148, 158, 166n., 358–360,
    369n.

Jakubowski-Spector, P., 145, 166n.
James, J., 411, 421, 425n.
Jason, L.A., 193, 216n., 466, 475n.
Jefferys, M., 331, 332, 338n.
Jeffery, R., 383, 385, 396n.
Jehu, D., 133, 140n.
Jenkins, J., 466, 473n., 475n.
Jenkins, R.L., 145, 166n.
Jenni, D.A., 48, 58n.
Jenni, M., 48, 58n.
Jensen, A.R., 480, 504n.
Jensen, B.J., 74, 75, 91n.
Jewett, J., 192, 216n.
Johnson, B.A., 55, 102, 227, 255, 273, 275–307, 315
Johnson, J.S., 173, 189n.
Johnson, L.A., 466, 472n.
Johnson, M., 162, 166n., 194, 202, 215n., 216n.
Johnson, P.B., 407, 424n.
Johnson, S., 75, 89n.
Johnson, S.M., 86, 91n., 190, 194, 197, 200, 204, 205, 209, 210, 214n., 216n., 217n.
Johnson, V.E., 96, 107n., 114, 115, 119, 125, 127, 128, 130, 131, 133, 136, 141n., 459, 474n.
Johnson, W.G., 385, 396n.
Johnston, D.W., 353, 369n.
Joiner, L.M., 487, 505n.
Jones, B.M., 436, 448n.
Jones, D.I.R., 146, 166n.
Jones, F.C., 192, 215n.
Jones, M.K., 436, 448n.
Jones, R.B., 356, 370n.
Jones, R.G., 293, 303n.
Jordan-Edney, N.L., 50, 57n.
Joyce, M.A., 443, 449n.
Juel-Nielsen, N., 463, 476n.
Juffe, M., 377, 396n.

Kahn, R.L., 453, 466, 473n.
Kallman, W.M., 82, 83, 91n.
Kaloupek, D.G., 356, 366n.
Kanfer, F.M., 18, 30n., 75, 91n., 157, 161, 166n.
Kaplan, H.S., 125, 126, 128–133, 140n.
Kaplan, J.R., 391, 396n.
Karlen, A., 119, 140n.
Karoly, P., 209, 217n.
Karvonen, M.J., 374, 396n.
Kas, D., 324, 337n.

Kasch, F.W., 228, 243n.
Kasnetz, M., 193, 203, 218n.
Kastenbaum, R., 453, 454, 464, 466, 473n.–475n.
Katz, E., 94, 107n.
Katz, M.M., 275, 302n., 306n.
Katz, R.C., 192, 194, 214n.
Katz, S., 247, 251, 271n.
Kaufman, A., 270, 271n.
Kaufman, R., 461, 472n.
Kay, D., 460, 472n.
Kazdin, A.E., 67, 91n., 144, 145, 159, 162, 164n., 166n., 182, 188n., 210, 217n., 358, 368n.
Keane, T.M., 148, 166n.
Keefe, F.J., 74, 91n., 231, 233, 243n., 321, 337n.
Keeley, S.M., 203, 214n.
Kegel, A.H., 134, 140n.
Kellerman, J., 387, 396n.
Kelley, M.L., 194, 217n., 490, 503n.
Kelly, J.A., 6, 30n., 44, 58n., 148, 166n., 343, 357, 358, 360, 368n., 369n., 371n.
Kelly, J.B., 207, 217n., 220n.
Kenigsberg, M.I., 223, 227, 244n.
Kent, R.N., 72, 85, 86, 90n., 91n., 93n., 193, 219, 296, 306n., 406, 412, 414, 426n.
Kern, J.M., 88, 91n., 148, 166n., 360, 368n.
Kerr, M.A., 145, 168n.
Kessel, N., 324, 325, 336n.
Keys, A., 374, 396n.
Kilmann, P.R., 130, 132, 140n., 142n., 206, 219n.
Kilpatrick, D.G., 248–251, 260, 261, 271n.
Kimura, N., 374, 396n.
King, H.E., 193, 194, 196, 215n.
King, L.J., 432, 449n.
King, L.W., 144, 166n.
Kinsey, A.C., 114, 130, 140n.
Kinsinger, E.C., 357, 368n.
Kirigin, K.A., 413, 415, 425n.
Kirkley, B.G., 148, 166n., 360, 368n.
Kistner, R.W., 26, 30n., 325, 337n.
Kitchener, R.F., 185, 188n.
Klee, S., 292, 295, 297, 304n., 305n.
Kleigman, S., 459, 473n.
Klein, A.R., 48, 58n.
Klein, D.C., 291, 298, 303n.
Klein, D.F., 354, 369n., 372n.
Klein, M.H., 104, 110, 170–189, 170, 173, 180, 182, 184, 187n., 188n., 210, 228, 243n., 421, 425n.

Klein, M.W., 408, 424n.
Kleinman, K.M., 75, 91n.
Klemesrud, J., 26, 30n.
Klerman, G.L., 18, 33n., 173, 189n., 204, 220n., 260, 272n., 278–280, 283, 305n., 306n., 332, 340n.
Kline, S.A., 387, 395n.
Kling, F., 196, 200, 216n., 490, 504n.
Knapp, M.L., 158, 166n.
Knapp, T.J., 466, 474n.
Knight, M.R., 192, 217n.
Knight, R., 10, 32n.
Kniskern, D.P., 171, 174, 180–184, 187n., 188n.
Knott, J., 99, 107n.
Knudson, R.M., 171, 174, 176, 188n.
Koch, J., 178, 188n.
Koch, L., 178, 188n.
Kohlberg, L., 8, 10, 20, 30n., 49, 58n.
Kolotkin, R.A., 159, 166n.
Kondo, C., 313, 337n.
Konopka, G., 402, 425n.
Kopel, S.A., 74, 91n.
Kopell, B.S., 326, 338n.
Kornblilth, S.J., 285, 290, 305n.
Kornreich, M., 170, 189n.
Korol, B., 75, 91n.
Kostrubala, T., 225, 230, 231, 243n.
Kotanchik, N., 11, 28n., 414, 424n.
Kovacs, M., 256, 272n., 283, 294, 301n., 305n.
Kramer, C., 147, 166n.
Kramer, M., 452, 473n.
Krantz, D., 345, 367n.
Krantz, S., 292, 297, 303n.
Krasner, L, 69, 72, 93n., 116, 142n., 177, 189n.
Kraus, H., 224, 243n.
Kravetz, D., 299, 303n.
Kroger, W.S., 127, 140n.
Krop, H.D., 96, 109, 111, 113–142, 129, 131, 133, 139n.
Krug, W.W., 193, 202, 203, 210, 218n.
Kugel, R.B., 483, 504n.
Kuiper, N.A., 295, 303n.
Kuipers, A., 355, 367n.
Kuntzleman, C.T., 225, 243n.
Kuriansky, J., 121, 141n.
Kurtz, R., 324, 337n.
Kuypers, J.A., 452, 474n.

Labouvie, G.V., 468, 473n.

Lacey, B.C., 83, 91n.
Lacey, J.I., 83, 91n.
LaCrosse, J., 8, 10, 20, 30n.
Lamont, H., 125, 140n.
Lamontagne, Y., 353, 368n.
Lance, J., 313, 340n.
Landau, R.J., 349, 369n.
Landesman-Dwyer, S., 487, 504n.
Lane, G., 467, 473n.
Lang, P.J., 36, 58n., 87, 91n., 348, 354, 369n., 389, 396n.
Lang, S., 202, 215n.
Lange, A.J., 144, 148, 158, 166n., 358–360, 369n.
Langer, E., 156, 166n.
Langer, P., 320, 338n.
Lanyon, B.P., 144, 166n.
Lanyon, R.I., 144, 166n.
Lao, R.C., 149, 166n.
LaPointe, C., 123, 129, 139n.
Larcen, S.W., 194, 200, 218n.
Larsen, J.K., 95, 99, 102, 107n.
Larson, D., 293, 304n.
Larson, L., 386, 396n.
Lathan, G.P., 25, 31n.
Laval, R.A., 206, 219n.
Lavigueur, H., 26, 29n., 193, 194, 201, 217n.
Lavin, P., 389, 396n.
Law, M., 466, 471n.
Laws, J.L., 173, 189n.
Lawson, D.M., 430, 449n.
Layden, M.A., 346, 368n.
Lazarus, A.A., 75, 91n., 128, 140n., 145, 166n., 171, 189n., 263, 271n., 285, 303n.
Lazere, R., 200, 217n.
Lazovik, A.D., 87, 91n.
Leahy, R.L., 25, 30n.
Leavitt, P., 9, 30n.
Leckie, F.H., 327, 338n.
Lee, W.M.L., 283, 304n.
Lefkowitz, M.M., 9, 11, 31n.
Leiblum, S.R., 115, 138, 140n.
Leibman, N., 50, 58n.
Leitenberg, H., 349, 350, 369n., 387, 389, 394n.
Leland, H., 481, 505n.
Lemkau, J.P., 292, 303n.
Lenhart, D., 462, 473n.
Lennane, K.J., 26, 31n.
Lennane, R.J., 26, 31n.
Lenney, E., 15, 31n., 43, 57n., 344, 369n.

Leon, G., 375, 381, 385, 396n.
Leonard, H.S., 345, 367n.
Leonard, S.R., 44–46, 51, 53, 58n.
Leske, G., 361, 371n.
Lester, D., 283, 301n.
Lester, P.B., 467, 473n.
Lettieri, D.J., 283, 303n.
Levenkron, J., 384, 396n.
Levin, M.L., 94, 107n.
Levin, S., 462, 473n.
Levine, A.G., 195, 213n.
Levine, J., 5, 33n.
LeVine, R.A., 4, 31n.
Levine, S.B., 136, 140n.
Levis, D., 263, 272n.
Levitt, E.B., 381, 395n.
Levitt, E.E., 278, 283, 304n.
Levitz, L.S., 382, 396n.
Lewine, R.R.J., 11, 31n.
Lewinsohn, P.M., 9, 18, 31n., 145, 149,
    167n., 168n., 283, 285–287, 293, 301n.,
    304n., 305n., 307n.
Lewis, C.C., 25, 31n.
Lewis, J.R., 480, 504n.
Lewis, M., 453, 458, 463, 464, 471n.
Lewis, T., 319, 338n.
Liberman, R.P., 144, 166n., 192–194, 220n.,
    466, 475n.
Libet, J.M., 9, 18, 31n., 149, 167n., 286,
    304n.
Liddell, A., 350, 369n.
Lieberknecht, K., 265, 268, 271n.
Liebman, R., 390, 397n.
Liederman, V., 379, 396n.
Lief, H., 119, 122, 140n., 141n.
Lifton, N., 265, 268, 272n.
Lillesand, D.B., 162, 167n.
Lindenthal, J.J., 279, 305n.
Lindsley, O., 77, 91n.
Linehan, M.M., 46, 55, 74, 76, 91n., 96, 109,
    110, 143–169, 145, 147–150, 154–156,
    158–160, 162, 167n., 300, 304n.,
    357–360, 367n., 369n.
Lipinsky, D.P., 76, 77, 89n.
Lishman, W.A., 291, 304n.
Litz, M.C., 161, 165n.
Lloyd, C.G., 9, 31n., 291, 304n.
Lloyd, K.E., 466, 475n.
Lobitz, G.K., 118, 120, 141n., 197, 204, 205,
    210, 216n., 217n.
Lobitz, W.C., 118, 120, 123, 133, 141n.
Locke, E.A., 25, 31n.

Locke, H.J., 122, 141n., 183, 189n.
Locksley, A., 412, 425n.
Loevinger, J., 69, 91n.
Lombroso, C., 402, 425n.
Longabough, R., 116, 139n., 435, 448n.
Longfellow, C., 207, 217n.
Lopez, M.A., 466, 473n., 474n.
LoPiccolo, J., 114, 121, 123, 132, 133, 135,
    141n., 142n.
LoPiccolo, L., 121, 128, 129, 132, 141n., 142n.
Lorber, R., 192, 218n.
Loro, A.D., 384, 396n.
Lott, D.F., 50, 58n.
Lott, L.A., Jr., 412, 413, 427n.
Lovaas, O.I., 48, 50, 59n.
Loving, N., 409, 425n.
Low, B.P., 48–50, 59n.
Lowman, J., 173, 187n.
Lubetkin, B., 350, 369n.
Lubetsky, M., 235, 243n.
Lubin, B., 278, 283, 304n.
Luckey, E.B., 173, 189n.
Luiselli, J.K., 192, 217n.
Lund, B., 466, 473n., 475n.
Lunde, D.T., 326, 338n.
Lundstrom, V., 327, 338n.
Lutzker, J.R., 190, 217n., 413, 425n., 466,
    474n., 491, 504n.
Lyons, M., 350, 369n.

Maas, H.S., 452, 474n.
Maccoby, E.E., 6, 15, 21, 31n., 47, 58n., 146,
    147, 167n., 406, 407, 425n.
MacDonald, G., 191, 217n.
MacDonald, J.M., 247, 271n.
MacDonald, M.L., 1, 60–93, 66–68, 73, 76,
    79–81, 87, 88, 92n., 93n., 96, 98, 103,
    104, 106, 145, 148, 150, 151, 159, 160,
    167n., 464, 466, 474n.
MacDonald, W.S., 191, 217n.
Machan, L., 466, 471n.
Macklin, C., 466, 471n.
MacPhillamy, D.J., 10, 31n., 286, 287, 304n.
Maddox, G.L., 379, 396n.
Madsen, C.H., 150, 165n.
Madsen, M.K., 492, 504n.
Magnus, E.C., 171, 189n.
Mahoney, B.K., 223, 227, 244n., 386, 397n.
Mahoney, K., 375, 383–385, 396n.
Mahoney, M.J., 76, 77, 92n., 144, 156, 164n.,
    167n., 223, 227, 233, 237, 243n., 244n.,
    375, 378, 381–386, 396n.–398n.

Mahoney, N.D., 202, 218n.
Makosky, V.P., 279, 304n.
Malouf, R.E., 411, 425n.
Mann, G.V., 392, 397n.
Mann, P., 495, 505n.
Manschrek, T.C., 321, 337n.
Mantz, R., 468, 474n.
Marecek, J., 361, 369n.
Margolin, G., 174, 175, 178, 188n., 189n.
Markle, A., 145, 168n.
Marks, I.M., 263, 271n., 347–351, 353, 355, 366n.–369n., 371n.
Markus, H., 345, 369n.
Marlatt, G.A., 241, 244n., 430, 434, 435, 440, 442, 448n.
Marlowe, D., 81, 90n.
Marset, P., 263, 271n., 355, 369n.
Marshall, W.L., 294, 306n.
Marston, A., 157, 162, 167n., 357, 358, 370n.
Martin, B., 196, 217n.
Martin, C.E., 114, 140n.
Martin, P.R., 313, 338n.
Martorano, R.D., 358, 370n.
Martyna, W., 43, 57n.
Mash, E.J., 74, 92n., 200, 217n.
Mason, A.S., 331, 338n.
Massad, C.M., 6, 31n.
Masters, J.C., 145, 149, 161, 168n., 252, 272n.
Masters, W.H., 96, 107n., 114, 115, 119, 125, 127, 128, 130, 131, 133, 136, 141n., 459, 474n.
Mastria, M.A., 439, 448n.
Masur, F., 119, 141n.
Mathews, A.M., 313, 338n., 353, 355, 369n.
Matthews, D.B., 446, 448n.
Mattinson, J., 484, 504n.
Mavissakalian, M., 36, 57n., 347, 348, 353, 365n.
May, J.R., 350, 369n.
May, M.A., 69, 90n.
Mayer, J., 227, 244n., 377, 395n.
Mayol, A., 359, 368n.
Mazur, M.A., 247, 251, 271n.
McCann, M., 144, 166n.
McClannahn, L.E., 466, 474n.
McCrady, B.S., 96, 97, 99, 103, 104, 146, 167n., 339, 428–449, 430, 435, 436, 440, 444, 448n., 449n.
McCusker, J., 462, 474n.
McDermott, M.J., 401, 403, 404, 425n.
McFall, R.M., 6, 7, 31n., 149, 157, 162,

167n., 357, 358, 369n., 370n., 422, 425n.
McGovern, K.B., 132, 141n.
McGuire, F.L., 324, 335n.
McKay, H.B., 413, 416, 426n.
McKechnie, A., 460, 473n.
McKenzie, H.S., 192, 217n.
McKinlay, S.M., 331, 332, 338n.
McKinley, J.C., 35, 58n., 70, 90n.
McLean, P.D., 287, 288, 290, 304n.
McLellan, A.T., 438, 447n.
McMahon, E., 325, 336n.
McMahon, R.J., 191, 194–197, 200–202, 204, 205, 215n.–217n., 219n.
McQueen, D.V., 429, 447n.
McReynolds, P., 62–64, 92n.
McReynolds, W., 191, 219n.
McReynolds, W.T., 467, 474n.
McTate, G.A., 491, 492, 505n.
McWhorter, A., 200, 219n.
Mednick, M.T.S., 16, 32n.
Meehl, P.E., 70, 90n.
Meeler, M.E., 37, 40, 48, 57n., 58n.
Mehrabian, A., 48, 59n.
Meichenbaum, D.H., 155, 156, 167n.
Melamed, B.G., 348, 369n.
Melges, F.T., 326, 338n.
Melin, L., 430, 448n.
Mello, N.K., 430, 448n.
Melnick, J., 358, 370n.
Meltzoff, J., 170, 189n.
Mendelson, M., 249, 270n., 388, 398n.
Mendlowitz, M., 320, 338n.
Mercer, J.R., 480, 481, 504n.
Merritt, H.H., 316, 337n.
Merrill, J., 468, 474n.
Messmer, M.C., 491, 505n.
Meyer, J.K., 122, 139n.
Meyer, R.G., 313, 328, 330, 336n.
Michael, G., 50, 59n.
Michaels, A.C., 324, 335n.
Mickelson, P., 483, 484, 488, 501, 504n., 505n.
Mikulic, M., 467, 474n.
Miles, C., 36, 59n.
Milich, R., 195, 220n.
Miller, I.V., 145, 165n.
Miller, I.W., 18, 31n., 55, 102, 227, 255, 273, 275–307, 292, 294, 295, 297, 298, 304n., 305n., 315
Miller, J., 270, 271n., 276, 283, 303n.
Miller, M.G., 401, 405, 411, 427n.

Miller, N.E., 6, 31n.
Miller, P.M., 145, 158, 159, 161, 162, 165n.–167n., 358, 366n., 430, 439, 443, 447n., 448n.
Miller, P.Y., 409, 420, 425n.
Miller, R.L., 416, 425n.
Miller, W.H., 499, 505n.
Miller, W.R., 18, 31n., 122, 141n., 249, 271n., 295, 296, 304n., 435, 439, 440, 443, 446, 448n., 449n.
Mills, D.M., 495, 505n.
Mills, J.R., 37, 40, 53, 57n.
Milton, F., 353, 370n.
Minkin, B.L., 415, 425n.
Minkin, N., 415, 416, 425n.
Minuchin, S., 390, 397n., 417, 426n.
Mira, M., 194, 203, 217n., 482, 483, 505n.
Mischel, W., 6, 18, 19, 31n., 36, 44, 59n., 69, 70, 72, 73, 81, 92n., 156, 167n.
Mischler, E., 421, 426n.
Mishara, B.L., 466, 474n.
Mitchell, C., 382, 397n.
Mitchell, D.M., 318, 338n.
Mitchell, K.R., 318, 338n.
Mitchell, S.B., 483, 505n.
Mittleman, B., 319, 320, 338n.
Mock, J., 249, 270n.
Moeller, D., 270, 271n.
Mohr, J.B., 387, 394n.
Moldofsky, H., 377, 380, 389, 396n., 397n.
Molnar, G.W., 331, 338n.
Molnar, J.M., 5, 31n.
Money, J., 37, 47, 53, 58n., 59n.
Monroe, M.M., 18, 32n.
Monroe, S.M., 282, 302n.
Montgomery, D., 150, 165n.
Monti, P.M., 145, 165n., 229, 242n., 384, 394n.
Moon, T.H., 66, 92n.
Mooney, D., 311, 313, 337n.
Moore, B.L., 200, 217n.
Moore, D., 144, 167n.
Moore, E., 378, 396n.
Moore, J., 454, 474n.
Moore, M., 462, 475n.
Moore, R.A., 432, 449n.
Moos, R.H., 326, 338n.
Morgan, S.R., 14, 31n.
Morgan, W.P., 228, 244n.
Morganstern, K.P., 74, 75, 92n.
Morokoff, P.J., 124, 141n.
Morrant, J., 462, 474n.

Morrison, D.C., 194, 220n.
Morrison, R.L., 156, 168n.
Morton, J.H., 407, 426n.
Morton, T.L., 414, 426n.
Mosher, P.M., 450, 466, 476n.
Moss, H., 48, 59n.
Mountjoy, P., 116, 141n.
Moyer, K.E., 406, 426n.
Mueller, C.W., 10, 15, 32n.
Mullaney, D.J., 313, 336n.
Mullen, F.G., 327, 328, 331, 339n.
Mullett, G.E., 355, 371n.
Mullinix, J.M., 317, 338n.
Munby, M., 353, 369n.
Munjack, D., 119, 141n.
Muñoz, R.F., 293, 304n., 307n., 439, 446, 449n.
Munson, F.C., 99, 108n.
Munson, M., 265–267, 271n.
Murphy, D.M., 210, 213n.
Murray, E.J., 10, 28n.
Murray, S.R., 16, 32n.
Murrell, F.H., 468, 474n.
Myers, J.K., 278, 279, 305n., 306n., 462, 474n.

Nadelson, C., 331, 338n.
Naftchi, N., 320, 338n.
Nash, O., 375, 397n.
Nathan, P.E., 70, 71, 92n., 284, 304n., 430, 434, 435, 442, 449n.
Nay, W.R., 73, 87, 92n., 193, 202, 217n.
Neath, J.F., 23, 28n.
Neisser, U., 344, 370n.
Nellis, M., 429, 433, 449n.
Nelson, R.E., 283, 285, 292, 305n., 306n.
Nelson, R.O., 37, 40, 48, 54, 57n., 58n., 70n., 72, 73, 75–79, 89n., 91n., 92n., 284, 305n., 350, 370n., 385, 397n.
Nelson, S., 14, 29n., 296, 302n.
Nesbitt, D., 466, 471n.
Neu, C., 260, 272n.
Neumann, C., 455, 471n.
Newkirk, J.M., 466, 474n.
Newman, A., 350, 370n.
Newman, G., 459, 474n.
Nichols, C., 459, 474n.
Nielsen, S.L., 149, 167n.
Nies, D.C., 176, 187n.
Nietzel, M., 358, 370n.
Nihira, K., 481, 505n.
Nilson, L.B., 15, 32n.

Nisbett, R.E., 290, 306n., 354, 371n.
Nock, S.L., 10, 32n.
Norman, W.H., 18, 31n., 55, 102, 227, 255,
    273, 275–307, 283, 292, 294, 295, 297,
    298, 304n., 305n., 315
Norton, B.J., 317, 338n.
Norval, J.D., 234, 244n.
Notman, M.T., 331, 332, 338n.
Nowinski, J., 121, 132, 141n.
Nunn, R., 276, 283, 303n.
Nunnally, J., 276, 283, 303n.
Nurnberger, J.L., 381, 395n.
Nyland, D., 484, 503n.

Oberman, A., 228, 244n.
O'Briant, A.L., 203, 218n.
O'Brien, C.G., 6, 30n., 357, 368n.
O'Brien, G.T., 356, 366n.
O'Brien, J.S., 467, 474n.
O'Brien, R.M., 393, 395n.
O'Brien, T., 385, 396n.
O'Connor, D., 121, 141n.
O'Dell, S.L., 190, 193, 194, 200–203, 210,
    218n., 499, 505n.
Odle, D., 283, 305n.
Odom, J.V., 350, 370n.
Offord, D.R., 411, 426n.
Ogbu, J.U., 4, 32n.
O'Hare, M., 462, 472n.
Ohlin, L.E., 408, 424n.
O'Leary, D.E., 145, 168n.
O'Leary, K.D., 68, 72, 73, 79, 81, 86, 93n.,
    177, 189n., 193, 205, 218n., 219n.,
    296, 306n., 406, 412, 414, 426n.
O'Leary, M.R., 145, 168n.
Ollendick, T.H., 388, 397n.
Olny, K., 149, 167n.
Olson, D.H.L., 412, 413, 424n.
Olson, F., 409, 425n.
Oltmanns, T., 205, 218n.
O'Malley, J., 390, 503n.
O'Neill, P., 75, 89n.
O'Quin, J.A., 193, 203, 218n.
Ora, J.P., 192, 219n.
Orbach, S., 391, 397n.
Orzeck, M.J., 467, 471n.
Osborn, S.M., 144, 145, 158, 168n.
Osborne, J.G., 193, 218n.
Osmond, H.O., 387, 394n.
Öst, L.G., 349, 350, 370n., 430, 448n.
Otis, M., 358, 368n.
O'Toole, D.H., 439, 448n.

Oziel, L., 119, 131, 132, 141n.

Padawer, W.J., 55, 98, 109, 150, 227, 263,
    273, 274, 311, 341–372
Padesky, C.A., 283, 303n.
Padfield, M., 280, 305n.
Page, E.B., 493, 505n.
Paige, K.E., 325, 338n.
Pall, M.L., 311, 340n.
Palmore, E., 461, 474n.
Paolino, T.J., 430, 435, 440, 444, 449n.
Parcel, T.L., 10, 15, 32n.
Paris, B.L., 173, 189n.
Parise, M., 311, 313, 337n.
Parker, L., 311, 336n.
Parlee, M.B., 325, 330, 338n., 407, 426n.
Parloff, M.B., 184, 189n.
Parsons, B.V., 172, 189n., 192, 193, 196,
    213n., 218n., 413, 416–419, 421, 423n.,
    426n.
Parsons, D.E., 490, 506n.
Parsons, J.E., 407, 424n.
Parsons, M.H., 483, 504n.
Parsons, T., 342, 370n.
Pasquella, M.J., 16, 32n.
Pastalan, L., 468, 474n.
Patch, V.D., 70, 92n.
Pathak, D., 270, 271n.
Patterson, G.R., 180, 181, 188n., 189n., 191,
    193–196, 198, 200, 205, 209, 211,
    213n., 218n., 220n., 412, 426n.
Patterson, J.N., 148, 166n., 202, 210, 218n.,
    360, 368n.
Patterson, V., 181, 188n.
Patton, M.W., 101, 107n.
Paul, G.L., 136, 141n., 252, 272n.
Paulino, D., 433, 444, 447n.
Pauly, I.B., 53, 59n.
Paykel, E.S., 10, 32n., 204, 220n., 279, 305n.
Pearlman, J., 144, 164n.
Pederson, F.A., 406, 426n.
Peed, S., 191, 193, 196, 215n., 218n.
Pelton, L.H., 487, 505n.
Pelz, D.C., 94, 99, 100, 108n.
Pennebaker, J.W., 325, 336n.
Pepper, M.P., 279, 305n.
Perlin, L.I., 173, 189n.
Pertschuk, M., 387, 388, 397n.
Pervin, L.A., 115, 138, 140n.
Pesses, D.I., 209, 213n.
Peters, J.J., 249, 272n.
Peters, S.D., 26, 30n.

Petersdorf, R.G., 318, 337n.
Peterson, D.R., 69, 72, 93n.
Peterson, G.B., 135, 141n.
Peterson, L.R., 135, 141n.
Peterson, L.W., 201, 217n.
Peterson, R.F., 194, 201, 217n., 220n., 466, 474n.
Petrowsky, K., 23, 28n.
Pettus, C., 70, 93n.
Pfeiffer, E., 459, 462, 474n., 475n.
Phares, E.J., 296, 305n.
Phelps, S., 144, 158, 168n.
Phillips, C., 310–314, 338n., 339n.
Phillips, E., 191, 213n., 415, 425n.
Phillips, L., 5, 33n., 71, 93n.
Pierce, C.H., 467, 475n.
Pillay, H., 355, 371n.
Pilon, R.N., 321, 337n., 340n.
Pinkston, E., 202, 215n., 466, 471n.
Pinkston, S., 162, 166n.
Pisani, R., 65, 90n.
Pisor, K., 191, 213n.
Pither, B.F., 466, 474n.
Pitts, F.N., 432, 449n.
Plamondon, A.L., 482, 505n.
Planka, T., 466, 472n.
Platt, J.J., 145, 156, 168n.
Platt, M., 173, 188n.
Plomin, R., 15, 32n.
Plutchik, R., 464, 475n.
Polak, P.R., 71, 90n.
Pollak, O., 402, 420n.
Pollock, D.D., 466, 475n.
Polloway, E.A., 481, 506n.
Polly, S., 231, 233, 244n.
Pomerantz, D.J., 494, 505n.
Pomerantz, P.B., 494, 505n.
Pomeranz, D.M., 72, 90n.
Pomeroy, W.B., 114, 140n.
Post, F., 462, 472n.
Post, M., 162, 169n.
Potope, P., 429, 449n.
Poushinsky, M., 411, 426n.
Powell, B., 343, 362, 370n.
Powell, L., 466, 473n., 475n.
Powell, L.K., 23, 28n.
Powell, R.R., 468, 475n.
Powers, P., 374, 378, 379, 387, 392, 396n., 397n.
Powers, R.B., 193, 218n.
Prados, M., 332, 339n.
Primrose, C., 53, 59n.

Prinz, R.J., 193, 219n., 412, 414, 426n.
Pritikin, N., 235, 244n.
Prochaska, J.O., 382, 396n.
Proctor, J.D., 296, 302n.
Pruett, H.L., 191, 213n.
Prusoff, B.A., 260, 272n.
Pulkinen, M.O., 326, 336n.
Purves, R., 65, 90n.

Quade, D., 70, 93n.
Quattrochi-Tubin, S., 466, 475n.
Quilitch, H.R., 466, 475n.

Rachman, S., 36, 53, 59n., 348, 366n.
Raczynski, J.M., 82, 83, 93n., 314, 340n.
Radloff, L.S., 10, 17–20, 32n., 173, 189n., 280, 292, 305n.
Rae, D.S., 10, 17–20, 32n.
Rainey, L., 358, 368n.
Rankin, H., 430, 448n.
Rapoport, R., 362, 370n.
Raskin, A., 283, 305n.
Ratcliffe, F.S., 282, 305n.
Rathus, S.A., 162, 168n., 358, 370n.
Rau, L., 47, 59n.
Raume, J., 193, 214n.
Ravid, R., 280, 303n.
Ray, E.P., 297, 305n.
Ray, R.S., 195, 218n.
Ray, W.J., 82, 83, 93n., 317, 339n.
Raynaud, A.G., 310, 318-320, 323, 339n.
Razin, A.M., 170, 188n.
Read, B., 466, 471n.
Reatig, N., 283, 305n.
Rebok, G., 470, 475n.
Reddan, W., 228, 244n.
Redick, R.W., 452, 460, 464, 473n., 475n.
Rees, L., 330, 339n.
Refsom, S., 316, 339n.
Rehm, L.P., 18, 32n., 283, 285, 290, 305n., 357, 370n.
Reich, S.K., 328, 329, 339n.
Reich, T., 432, 449n.
Reichman, S., 377, 392, 397n.
Reid, D.H., 467, 472n.
Reid, J.B., 192, 196, 198, 200, 209, 211, 218n., 220n., 412, 426n.
Reid, R.L., 26, 32n.
Reinking, R., 313, 337n.
Reisinger, J.J., 192, 205, 219n.
Reiss, I.L., 122, 141n.
Rekers, G.A., 48–50, 59n.
Reppucci, N.D., 296, 302n.

Resick, P.A., 200, 201, 219n., 248–251, 261, 271n.
Reynolds, E.J., 52, 57n.
Reznikoff, M., 343, 362, 370n.
Rice, D.G., 170, 189n., 362, 370n.
Rice, J.K., 170, 189n.
Rice, J.M., 491, 504n.
Rice, R.E., 104, 108n.
Rich, A., 172, 189n.
Rich, A.R., 148, 150, 168n., 357, 358, 370n.
Richey, C.A., 144, 158, 165n.
Rickard, K.M., 204, 219n.
Ricks, D., 8, 10, 20, 30n.
Ricks, D.F., 276, 306n.
Riddle, P.K., 228, 244n.
Riger, S., 18, 32n.
Riley, M., 461, 475n.
Rimm, D.C., 145, 149, 161, 162, 168n., 252, 272n.
Rinke, C.L., 466, 475n.
Rinn, R.C., 145, 168n.
Riordan, M., 231, 233, 244n.
Ripley, H.S., 278, 305n.
Risley, T.R., 95, 99, 107n., 466, 474n.
Ritchey, W.L., 6, 7, 29n.
Rizley, R.C., 291, 295, 305n.
Robb, W., 495, 505n.
Roberts, M., 191, 201, 216n., 218n.
Robertson, P., 71, 92n.
Robertson, R., 192, 215n.
Robin, A.L., 193, 194, 196, 219n., 412, 414, 426n.
Robins, C., 345, 367n.
Robins, E., 66, 70n., 93n., 249, 272n., 278, 306n.
Robins, L.N., 282, 305n.
Robinson, C.C., 491, 505n.
Robinson, S., 462, 474n.
Robinson, W.L., 359, 370n.
Roddy, J., 482, 483, 505n.
Rodin, J., 384, 397n.
Rodman, H., 411, 426n.
Roessner, J.D., 100, 108n.
Roff, M., 8, 10, 32n., 145, 168n.
Rogers, E.M., 104, 108n.
Rogers, E.S., 361, 371n.
Rogers, M., 191, 213n.
Rogers, T., 223, 227, 244n., 375, 386, 396n., 397n.
Rohrbaugh, M., 324, 337n.
Rollins, N., 380, 397n.
Romano, J.M., 149, 156, 158, 168n.

Rook, K.S., 129, 141n.
Rose, D.P., 281, 301n.
Rose, R.M., 333, 339n.
Rose, S.D., 161, 162, 168n., 446, 471n.
Rose, V.J., 360, 370n.
Rose, Y., 46, 59n., 149, 168n.
Roseen, D.L., 193, 215n.
Rosen, A.C., 48, 49, 59n.
Rosen, B., 389, 394n.
Rosen, G.M., 135, 142n.
Rosen, J.C., 466, 474n.
Rosen, L.W., 238, 244n.
Rosen, M., 484, 503n.
Rosenbaum, B., 440, 449n.
Rosenbaum, S., 132, 141n.
Rosenberg, S.A., 491, 492, 505n.
Rosenkrantz, P., 342, 370n., 419, 424n.
Rosenthal, M., 209, 217n.
Rosman, B.L., 390, 397n.
Ross, H., 466, 475n.
Ross, J., 192, 204, 219n.
Ross, R.A., 413, 416, 426n.
Ross, S.M., 145, 164n.
Ross, W.D., 324, 337n.
Rossi, P.H., 10, 32n.
Roth, L.H., 407, 426n.
Roth, M., 71, 92n., 460, 473n., 475n.
Rotter, J.B., 345, 370n.
Rounsaville, B., 265, 267, 268, 272n.
Roy, M., 265, 272n.
Rozensky, R., 236, 242n.
Rubenfire, M., 230, 243n.
Rubinoff, A., 235, 243n.
Ruble, D.M., 325, 326, 339n.
Ruble, P.N., 407, 424n.
Rudd, S., 202, 215n.
Rush, A.J., 255, 256, 272n., 290, 292, 294, 301n., 305n., 306n.
Russell, G., 377, 397n.
Rutley, B.R., 50, 58n.
Rutter, M., 204, 219n.
Ryan, B., 94, 108n.
Ryan, R.E., Jr., 310, 317, 339n.
Ryan, R.F., 310, 317, 339n.
Ryback, D., 191, 219n.

Saari, L.M., 25, 31n.
Sabshin, M., 276, 283, 303n.
Sackeim, H.A., 292, 301n.
Sadd, S., 130, 142n.
Safran, J., 359, 365n., 370n.
Safranek, R., 311, 337n.

Sajwaj, T., 201, 204, 219*n*.
Sakheim, D.K., 124, 139*n*.
Salasin, S.E., 100, 108*n*.
Salt, P., 279, 306*n*.
Salter, A., 145, 168*n*.
Sameroff, A.J., 484, 485, 505*n*.
Sampen, S.E., 193, 220*n*.
Sanchez, V., 145, 168*n*., 286, 305*n*.
Sanders, D.H., 94, 107*n*.
Sandifer, M.G., Jr., 70, 93*n*.
Sanok, R.L., 193, 219*n*.
Sappington, J.T., 319, 320, 339*n*.
Sarber, R.E., 491, 505*n*.
Sarbin, T.R., 343, 370*n*.
Sargent, J.D., 317, 339*n*.
Sarri, R., 402, 426*n*.
Sartory, B., 36, 53, 59*n*.
lSaslow, G., 75, 91*n*.
Scarf, M., 295, 306*n*.
Scarpetti, F.R., 403, 411, 424*n*.
Schaffer, M., 286, 304*n*.
Schaie, K.W., 469, 471*n*.
Sheri, D.J., 248, 249, 272*n*.
Schiavi, R.C., 121, 141*n*.
Schiavo, R.S., 416, 417, 423*n*.
Schilmoeller, G.L., 490, 503*n*.
Schinke, S.P., 161, 162, 168*n*.
Schlenker, B.R., 16, 32*n*.
Schmurak, S.H., 356, 367*n*.
Schoen, S., 43, 58*n*.
Schrader, S.L., 285, 306*n*.
Schrader, S.M., 11, 28*n*., 414, 424*n*.
Schroeder, H.E., 26, 30*n*., 357, 358, 360, 368*n*., 370*n*.
Schroeder, H.W., 148, 150, 168*n*.
Schuckit, M.A., 429, 432, 448*n*., 449*n*., 462, 475*n*.
Schuham, A.I., 422, 426*n*.
Schulterbrandt, J.G., 283, 305*n*.
Schultz, N.R., 469, 475*n*.
Schumaker, J.B., 191, 219*n*., 415, 416, 426*n*.
Schurr, K.T., 487, 505*n*.
Schuyler, D., 275, 278, 306*n*.
Schwab, J., 462, 475*n*.
Schwartz, G.E., 320, 339*n*.
Schwartz, J., 236, 242*n*.
Schwartz, R.D., 85, 93*n*.
Schwartz, R.M., 157, 168*n*., 359, 370*n*.
Schwitzgebel, R., 412, 426*n*.
Scott, L.W., 235, 243*n*.
Scott, P.D., 265, 266, 272*n*.
Scott-Fordham, A., 356, 370*n*.

Scovern, A., 130, 142*n*.
Scovern, A.W., 206, 210, 219*n*.
Sears, R.R., 6, 32*n*., 47, 59*n*.
Sechrest, L., 85, 93*n*.
Seeman, J., 10, 32*n*.
Seiden, A.M., 309, 339*n*.
Seifert, R., 149, 154, 167*n*.
Selder, D.J., 228, 244*n*.
Seligman, M.E.P., 18, 27*n*., 31*n*., 32*n*., 291, 294–299, 302*n*.–304*n*., 306*n*., 346, 365*n*.
Sella, S.B., 8, 32*n*., 145, 168*n*.
Selltiz, C., 86, 93*n*.
Semmel, A., 18, 32*n*., 295, 306*n*.
Sentis, K., 345, 369*n*.
Serber, M., 123, 141*n*.
Serbin, L.A., 149, 164*n*., 296, 306*n*., 406, 426*n*.
Shaeffer, D.E., 295, 303*n*.
Shaffer, D.R., 46, 59*n*.
Shah, S.A., 407, 426*n*.
Shahinian, S., 462, 472*n*.
Shainess, N., 325, 339*n*.
Shanas, E., 461, 471*n*.
Shankweiler, P.J., 135, 140*n*.
Shapiro, A., 483, 503*n*.
Shapiro, D., 320, 339*n*., 352, 370*n*.
Sharpe, L., 121, 141*n*.
Shaw, B.F., 256, 272*n*., 290, 294, 301*n*., 306*n*.
Shaw, C.H., 483, 488, 506*n*.
Shaw, E.R., 313, 335*n*.
Shaw, K.N., 25, 31*n*.
Shaw, P., 162, 169*n*.
Shaw, P.M., 353, 369*n*.
Sheese, G., 201, 217*n*.
Sheldon, D., 462, 474*n*.
Shellhaas, M., 481, 505*n*.
Shelton, J.L., 313, 336*n*.
Shemberg, K.M., 203, 214*n*.
Sheridan, M.D., 483, 506*n*.
Sherman, A.R., 231, 233, 244*n*.
Sherman, J.A., 191, 219*n*.
Sherwood, D.E., 228, 244*n*.
Shields, S.A., 56, 59*n*.
Shinn, M., 207, 219*n*.
Shock, N.W., 455, 475*n*.
Shore, B., 249–251, 272*n*.
Shores, R.E., 145, 168*n*.
Shostock, D.A., 412, 413, 426*n*.
Shure, M.B., 156, 168*n*.
Shuttleworth, F.K., 69, 90*n*.
Siegel, J.M., 145, 168*n*.

Siegler, I., 452, 475n.
Silver, B.V., 317, 335n.
Silverberg, E., 321, 337n.
Silverman, J., 391, 395n.
Silverstone, J.T., 376, 397n.
Simmons, R., 224, 244n.
Simon, R.J., 402, 403, 409, 420, 423n., 427n.
Simons, R.L., 401, 405, 411, 427n.
Simpson, H.F., 71, 92n.
Singer, J.E., 345, 367n.
Sinnott, A., 356, 370n.
Sintchak, G., 124, 142n.
Sirlin, J., 377, 391, 394n.
Skelton, J.L., 324, 335n.
Skinner, B.F., 76n., 93n., 110, 111n., 177, 189n.
Skriver, C., 317, 335n.
Slaby, A.E., 281, 306n.
Slade, P.C., 388, 395n.
Slater, J., 9, 32n.
Sloane, H.N., 193, 220n.
Sloop, E.W., 195, 200, 201, 203, 209, 215n.
Smart, C., 402, 409, 427n.
Smith, D., 191, 213n., 459, 475n.
Smith, E.L., 228, 244n.
Smith, J.D., 481, 506n.
Smith, M., 25, 29n.
Smith, V., 206, 219n.
Smith-Scott, W., 466, 475n.
Snow, M.Y., 75, 91n.
Snyder, A., 132, 142n.
Sobell, L.C., 430, 435, 444, 449n.
Sobell, M.B., 430, 435, 448n., 449n.
Sokoloff, L., 463, 471n.
Solbach, P., 317, 339n.
Sommer, B., 334, 339n.
Sommer, R., 50, 58n., 466, 475n.
Sorg, D.A., 129, 142n.
Soskin, R.M., 482, 505n.
Sotile, W.M., 130, 142n.
Southam, H.L., 325, 339n.
Sowell, T., 62, 93n.
Spanier, G.B., 122, 142n.
Spence, J.T., 36, 59n., 343, 371n.
Spitzer, R.L., 66, 70n., 93n., 249, 272n., 278, 282, 302n., 306n.
Spivack, G., 145, 156, 168n.
Sprafkin, R.P., 466, 474n.
Staats, A.W., 191, 219n.
Stableford, W., 192, 219n.
Stafford, R., 387, 394n.
Stampfl, T., 263, 272n.

Stancer, H.C., 387, 395n.
Stanley, J.C., 86, 89n.
Stapp, J., 36, 59n., 343, 371n.
Steele, D.L., 37, 40, 48, 57n., 58n.
Steger, J.C., 121, 141n.
Stein, L.S., 26, 32n., 335, 339n.
Steinberg, L.D., 10, 32n.
Steinman, D.L., 53, 57n.
Stephan, W.G., 16, 28n.
Stern, J.A., 319, 337n.
Stern, K., 332, 339n.
Stern, M.P., 227, 242n.
Stern, R.S., 355, 371n.
Stewart, A.J., 279, 306n.
Stewart, B.D., 98, 110, 245–272, 249, 271n., 274
Stewart, G., 462, 471n.
Stewart, R., 132, 141n.
Stingle, K.G., 6, 29n.
Stocker, R.B., 358, 370n.
Stockwell, T., 430, 448n.
Stokes, T.F., 99, 101–106, 108n., 194, 219n.
Stolz, S.B., 2, 94–108, 99–101, 104, 108n.
Stone, G., 359, 366n.
Stone, N.M., 356, 366n.
Storandt, M., 452, 475n.
Stortecky, E.A., 495, 505n.
Stout, R.L., 145, 165n.
Stoyva, J.M., 313, 336n.
Strain, P., 145, 168n., 208, 219n.
Strauss, C.C., 97, 102, 105, 106, 110, 190–220, 399
Straw, M.K., 223, 227, 244n., 375, 386, 396n., 397n.
Straw, R.B., 386, 397n.
Strickland, B.R., 346, 371n.
Stroebel, C.F., 319, 340n.
Strong, E.K., 36, 59n.
Stuart, J., 162, 168n.
Stuart, R.B., 73, 93n., 193, 219n., 239, 240, 244n., 374, 377, 378, 381–383, 390, 391, 393, 397n., 412, 413, 417, 427n.
Stunkard, A.J., 223, 226, 227, 242n., 244n., 378–383, 386–388, 393, 394n.–398n.
Sturdivant, S., 228, 244n.
Sturgis, E.T., 192, 196, 213n., 215n., 273, 308–340, 311, 314, 317, 339n., 340n., 400
Sturm, M.L., 478, 503n.
Sudia, C., 207, 216n.
Sullivan, J.J., 407, 426n.
Sultan, F., 127, 142n.

Summerfield, A.B., 389, 394n.
Surwit, R.S., 320, 321, 337n., 340n.
Sussman, A., 225, 244n.
Sutherland, E.H., 407, 427n.
Sutherland, S., 248, 249, 272n.
Sutton-Simon, K., 346, 349, 371n.
Svanborg, K., 327, 338n.
Swacker, M., 147, 168n.
Swan, G.E., 73, 93n.
Swan, S., 380, 395n.
Swatko, M.K., 15, 29n.
Sweeney, P.D., 295, 303n.
Sweeney, T.M., 149, 166n.
Szykula, S.A., 196, 214n., 490, 506n.

Tahmisian, J., 191, 219n.
Tajfel, H., 344, 371n.
Taplin, P., 192, 196, 209, 218n., 220n.
Tasto, D.L., 192, 220n., 313, 325, 328, 330, 336n., 340n.
Taub, E., 319, 340n.
Taube, C.A., 452, 460, 464, 473n., 475n.
Tavris, C., 130, 142n.
Taylor, C.A., 435, 440, 448n.
Taylor, C.J., 11, 28n., 414, 424n.
Taylor, F.G., 294, 306n.
Taylor, H.L., 374, 396n.
Taynor, J., 43, 59n.
Teasdale, J.D., 18, 27n., 294, 301n., 346, 353, 365n., 369n.
Telch, M., 467, 476n.
Tennov, D., 171, 189n.
Terdal, L., 74, 92n., 200, 217n.
Terman, L.M., 36, 59n.
Tesiny, E.P., 9, 11, 31n.
Tevlin, H.E., 74, 75, 92n.
Thal, J., 55, 96, 99, 221, 223, 227, 234, 241, 274, 373–398, 400, 412
Tharp, R.G., xii, xiiin., 190, 191, 220n., 412, 427n.
Theobald, D.E., 317, 335n.
Thienes, P.M., 190, 192, 213n.
Thomas, A. 485, 506n.
Thomas, L., 100, 108n.
Thompson, B., 331, 338n.
Thompson, J.K., 231, 233, 243n., 311, 314, 315, 340n.
Thompson, K., 318, 335n.
Thompson, R.H., 320, 340n.
Thomson, L.E., 389, 396n.
Thorndike, E.L., 486, 506n.
Thorndike, R.L., 21, 32n.

Thorne, G.L., 191, 220n.
Thornton, W., 411, 421, 425n.
Thorpe, G.L., 162, 168n.
Timbers, B., 415, 425n.
Timbers, G., 415, 425n.
Tollison, C.D., 118, 128, 133, 142n., 317, 339n.
Tonick, I.J., 296, 306n., 406, 426n.
Tornatzky, L.G., 94, 107n.
Touhey, J.C., 10, 33n.
Towne, R.C., 487, 494, 505n.
Tracey, D.A., 435, 442, 449n.
Treat, N.J., 468, 473n.
Tredgold, A.F., 480, 506n.
Trexler, L., 283, 301n.
Trickett, P.K., 20, 33n.
Trower, P., 155, 156, 158, 162, 168n.
Tryon, W., 46, 59n., 149, 168n., 360, 370n.
Tubbs, W., 329, 340n.
Tucker, B., 191, 215n.
Tudor, J.F., 145, 165n., 173, 187n., 279, 303n., 361, 368n.
Tumblin, A., 21, 33n.
Turkewitz, H., 177, 189n.
Turner, P.E., 202, 218n.
Turner, R.D., 231, 233, 244n.
Turner, S.M., 157, 160, 164n., 166n., 249, 271n., 358, 371n.
Turns, D., 278, 306n.
Twentyman, C.T., 157, 162, 167n., 169n., 286, 289, 306n., 357, 358, 370, 371n.
Tyler, L., 192, 215n.
Tyson, P.A., 88, 92n.

Ullmann, L.P., 69, 72, 93n., 116, 142n.
Unger, R.K., 34, 35, 59n., 63, 93n.
Upchurch, W.H., 149, 166n.

Valins, S., 290, 306n., 354, 366n., 371n.
Van Hasselt, V.B., 160, 169n.
Vaughn, R., 311, 340n.
Veronen, L.J., 248, 261, 271n.
Verwoerdt, A., 459, 463, 464, 474n., 475n.
Victor, B.S., 235, 243n.
Videbach, T., 463, 476n.
Vila, J., 330, 340n.
Vogel, S., 342, 370n., 419, 424n.
Vogler, R.E., 75, 93n.
Volpe, A., 466, 475n.
vonBaeyer, C., 18, 32n., 295, 306n.
Von Storch, T.J.C., 316, 337n.

Wachtel, D., 75, 89n.
Wahler, R.G., 190, 191, 194–196, 200, 204, 208–210, 220n., 361, 371n.
Wald, M., 478, 482, 506n.
Waldron, I., 362, 371n.
Walinder, J., 53, 59n.
Walker, A., 377
Walker, L.E., 265, 266, 272n.
Walker, R.O., 162, 167n.
Wallace, C.J., 161, 162, 165n.
Wallace, J.P., 228, 243n.
Wallace, K.M., 183, 189n.
Wallace, M., 162, 169n.
Wallace, R., 122, 141n.
Wallerstein, J.S., 207, 217n., 220n.
Walsh, F., 467, 473n.
Walster, E., 378, 394n.
Walter, H., 209, 220n.
Walters, E.D., 317, 339n.
Walters, R., 6, 28n.
Wang, H., 459, 474n., 475n.
Warbuton, J.R., 210, 227, 399, 401–427, 417, 419, 427n.
Ward, C.H., 249, 270n.
Warheit, G., 462, 475n.
Warner, G., 313, 340n.
Watkins, J.T., 292, 306n.
Watson, C., 43, 57n.
Watson, D., 359, 371n.
Watson, J.P., 355, 371n.
Watzlawick, F., 421, 427n.
Waxler, N., 421, 426n.
Weatherford, J.M., 15, 29n.
Weathers, L., 192–194, 220n.
Webb, E.J., 85, 86, 93n.
Wechsler, D., 469, 476n.
Weeke, A., 463, 476n.
Weekes, L., 354, 355, 371n.
Weg, R., 455, 459, 468, 476n.
Wegley, C., 46, 59n.
Wein, K.S., 350, 370n.
Weiner, M., 464, 471n., 475n.
Weinman, B., 162, 169n.
Weinrott, M., 196, 220n.
Weiss, C.H., 94–95, 101, 108n.
Weiss, E., 352, 371n.
Weiss, F.C., 495, 504n.–506n.
Weiss, J.A., 94–96, 108n.
Weiss, R.L., 174–178, 188n., 189n.
Weissback, T.A., 75, 93n.
Weissman, A., 283, 293, 301n., 306n.
Weissman, M.M., 10, 18, 32n., 33n., 173,

189n., 204, 220n., 260, 265, 267, 272n., 278–281, 283, 306n., 332, 340n.
Weisz, G., 384, 398n.
Weisz, J.R., 5, 31n.
Weitz, S., 56, 59n.
Welford, A.T., 156, 169n.
Welling, M.A., 297, 301n.
Wellman, R.J., 467, 506n.
Wells, K.C., 194, 196, 197, 200, 204, 205, 215n., 220n., 289, 306n.
Wertheim, E., 10, 32n.
Wessberg, H.W., 160, 165n.
Wessels, H., 355, 367n.
Wessman, A.E., 276, 306n.
West, C., 147, 169n.
Westbrook, T., 314, 337n.
Westlake, R.J., 229, 242n., 384, 394n.
Wetter, R.E., 297, 301n.
Wetzel, R.J., xii, xiiin., 190, 191, 220n., 412, 427n.
Whalen, C.K., 26, 33n., 198, 220n., 354, 371n.
Wheatt, T., 75, 91n.
White, B.L., 4, 33n.
White, R.G., 318, 338n.
White, S.W., 17, 28n., 207, 214n.
Whiteley, J.M., 137, 140n.
Whitlock, D., 441, 447n.
Whitman, T.L., 194, 216n.
Widholm, O., 26, 33n.
Wiebe, C., 466, 471n.
Wiener, J., 440, 448n.
Wiggins, J.S., 65, 69, 70, 76, 79, 80, 85, 87, 93n.
Wilcoxon, L.A., 285, 306n.
Wildavsky, A., 99, 107n.
Wildman, B.G., 84, 85, 93n.
Wildman, H.A., 385, 396n.
Wilkins, R.H., 431, 432, 449n.
Willerson, J.T., 320, 340n.
Williams, A.M., 249, 271n.
Williams, D.E., 209, 213n.
Williams, J.G., 283, 286, 306n.
Williams, J.J., 466, 475n.
Williamson, D.A., 317, 335n.
Willis, F.N., 50, 59n.
Willis, T.J., 48, 49, 59n.
Wills, T., 178, 188n.
Wilson, C.C., 74, 91n.
Wilson, G.T., 182, 188n., 380, 381, 383–385, 393, 398n., 430, 447n., 449n.
Wilson, J.D., 318, 337n.

Wiltz, N.A., 200, 220n.
Wincze, J.P., 96, 109, 111, 113–142, 116, 118, 120, 122–124, 126, 137, 138, 139n., 140n., 142n.
Wing, J.K., 282, 306n.
Wing, R.R., 231, 233, 243n.
Winkel, G.H., 194, 220n.
Winokur, G., 319, 332, 337n., 340n., 432, 449n.
Winship, B.J., 358, 371n.
Winston, F., 281, 307n.
Winston, M., 235, 243n.
Wisocki, P.A., 400, 450–476, 450, 466, 467, 476n.
Woerner, M.C., 354, 372n.
Wolf, M.M., 7, 33n., 95, 99, 107n., 191, 192, 210, 213n., 220n., 413, 415, 425n.
Wolfe, B.E., 347, 348, 365n.
Wolfe, D.M., 173, 187n.
Wolfe, J., 145, 148, 150, 161, 162, 169n., 359, 371n.
Wolfe, L., 246, 272n.
Wolfensberger, W., 478, 506n.
Wolff, H.G., 319, 320, 338n.
Wolff, H.H., 355, 367n.
Wolfgang, M.E., 265, 272n.
Wolpe, J., 72, 93n., 252, 253, 264, 272n., 349, 371n., 386, 389, 398n.
Wood, P.D., 227, 242n.
Wood, P.L., 246, 272n.
Woodruff, D.S., 454, 468, 471n., 476n.
Woodward, R., 356, 370n.
Wooley, O.W., 235, 244n., 373, 376, 378, 379, 385, 388, 392, 393, 395n., 398n.
Wooley, S.C., 235, 244n., 373, 376, 378, 379, 385, 388, 392, 393, 395n., 398n.
Woolfolk, R.L., 360, 371n.
Worchel, S., 158, 169n.
Worell, J., 343, 369n.
Worland, J., 195, 203, 209, 220n.
Wright, C.H., 483, 488, 506n.

Wright, D.F., 192, 220n.
Wright, L., 232, 244n.
Wright, M.J., 70, 72n., 90n.
Wysocki, T., 231, 233, 244n.

Yalom, I.D., 326, 338n.
Yardley, K., 162, 169n.
Yarrow, M., 463, 471n.
Yates, A., 383, 398n.
Yates, C.E., 48, 49, 59n.
Yen, S.S.C., 26, 32n.
Yevzeroff, H., 162, 167n.
Yin, R.K., 99–101, 108n.
Yoder, R., 193, 215n.
Youdin, R., 238, 244n.
Young, C.C., 208, 219n.

Zare, N.C., 71, 92n.
Zegman, M., 379, 398n.
Zeilberger, J., 193, 201, 220n.
Zeiss, A.M., 135, 142n., 285–287, 293, 304n., 307n.
Zeiss, R.A., 135, 142n.
Zellman, G.L., 407, 424n.
Zerbe, M.B., 466, 471n.
Ziel, H.K., 332, 340n.
Zigler, E., 5, 20, 27n., 30n., 33n., 71, 93n.
Zilbergeld, B., 136, 142n.
Zimberg, S., 462, 474n.
Zimering, R.T., 286, 289, 306n., 357, 358, 371n.
Zimmerman, D.H., 147, 169n.
Zimmerman, R., 313, 336n.
Zisfein, L., 484, 503n.
Zitrin, C.M., 354, 372n.
Zitter, R., 384, 398n., 436, 449n.
Zung, W., 283, 307n.
Zussman, L., 137, 142n.
Zussman, S., 137, 142n.
Zwick, W.R., 145, 165n.

SUBJECT INDEX

Abstinence violation effect (AVE), 442, 443
Achievement
  by children, 12–14
  decline in female, 14–20
    measuring incompetence in, 15–17
  gender and, 5, 9, 15–17
  as measurement of competence, 5, 7, 8
  single-parent homes and, 411
Achievement Place, 415, 416
Acrophobia, 349
Activity structure, 22–27
  defined, 23, 24
  gender and, 23, 23
  impact of, on competence, 25, 26
  level of, 23, 24
  manipulation of, 25
  problem-solving skill and, 24, 25
Ad Hoc Committee on the Classification of
    Headaches, 310–312, 315, 316
Adolescence
  avoiding age-appropriate tasks in, 389,
    390
  competence decline in, 16, 17, 25–27
  delinquency in (see Delinquency)
  depression in, 18, 20
  exercise in, 223, 224
  parent training and, 196
  sexual abuse in, 270
  social behavior in, 146
  weight disorders in, 376–377, 386–388
Age (see Elderly women)
Aggression, gender and, 406–407
Agoraphobia, 173, 351–356
  overweight as form of, 390
  treatment of, 355, 356
Alcoholism, 145, 146, 399, 428–449
  background on, 429–431
  behavioral assessment in, 434–438
  behavioral interventions in, 439–444
    antecedents to, 439–441
    consequences of, 443, 444
    drinking response and, 442, 443

organismic variables and, 441, 442
conclusions and recommendations on,
    446, 447
drug abuse and, 443, 462
of elderly persons, 462
evaluation of treatment outcome for,
    444–446
identifying drinking problems in, 431–433
overview on, 428
remaining in treatment for, 433, 434
wife abuse and, 266
Amenorrhea, 329
American Association on Mental Deficiency
    (AAMD), 479, 481, 487
American Heart Association, 235
American Psychological Association, 176,
    181, 454
Androgyny, 341, 343, 345, 346, 357, 362
  behavioral, 49–51, 54, 56
  competence and, 6, 7, 9, 14
  motor behavior in, 43, 49, 50
Anger, wife abuse and, 267
Anorexia nervosa, 373, 374, 376, 377, 386–388
  clinical picture of, 386, 387
  consciousness-raising in, 391, 392
  operant analysis of, 387, 388
  running and, 234
  treatment of
    body image disturbances in, 388, 389
    family treatment in, 390, 391
    issues in, 96
    medical and psychotherapeutic, 379, 380
Antidepressants, tricyclic, 282
Anxiety, 273-274
  alcoholism and, 432, 433
  classification of, 347
  conclusions on, 364, 365
  dysmenorrhea and, 329
  exercise and, 228
  interpersonal assertiveness, 356–361
  in mothers of behavior problem children,
    204, 205

Anxiety (continued)
  phobias and, 347–356
  rape and, 248–250, 253, 254, 258–261
  sexual, 124–128, 131, 136
  work-related, 361–364
Arrest data, 402, 403
Arthritis, 459
Assertion Inventory, 286
Assertiveness, 63, 143–169
  anxiety in interpersonal, 356–361
  background on, 144, 145
  conclusions and recommendations on,
      162, 163
  as defense against rape, 264
  depression and, 286–290
  exercise and, 228
  functional characteristics of, 149–153
    objectives effectiveness, 151, 152, 163
    relationship effectiveness, 152, 163
    self-respect effectiveness, 152, 153, 163
  gender and, 46, 47, 143–169
  maximizing skill in, 153, 154
    juggling goals, 153, 154
    time perspective for, 154
  overview on, 143, 144
  phobia treatment and, 350, 351
  sex differences in, 46, 47, 143–169
  topographical characteristics of, 148, 149
  training for, 96, 109, 110, 144, 145, 147,
      148, 151, 154–158, 300, 358–360
    assessment in, 159, 160
    autonomic arousal in, 157
    behavioral skills in, 158
    cognitive skills in, 155–157
    emotional skills in, 157, 158
    menopause and, 332
    strategies in, 160–162
Asthma, 226
Astrology, 63-64
Automatic negative thoughts, 256, 257
Autonomy, 176, 178-179

Beck Depression Inventory, 249, 283
Behavioral Assessment, 73, 74
Behavioral assessment, 60–93
  for alcoholism, 434–438
  for assertiveness training, 159, 160
  assumptions in, 62, 63
  conclusions on, 88, 89
  of dysfunctional cognitions, 292, 293
  emergence of and rationale for, 68–73

of learned helplessness, 297
overview on, 60–62
in parent training, 208–211
quantitative methods in, 64–68
after rape, 250, 251
for sexual dysfunction, 123
of social skills, 286, 287
strategies in, 73–88
  behavioral interviews, 74–76
  controlled observation, 86–88
  naturalistic observation, 83–86
  psychophysiological measures, 82, 83
  questionnaires, 79–82
  self-monitoring, 76–79
Behavioral Avoidance Tests, 65, 87
Behavioral marriage and family therapy
    (BMFT), 170–189
  assessing outcome of, 181–185
    effects of symptom removal in, 184
    normative criteria in, 182, 183
    treatment goals in, 184, 185
  clinical application of, 174–181
  conclusions and recommendations on,
      185, 186
  overview and background on, 170, 171
  views of dysfunction in, 171–174
Behaviorism, 43, 174
Bem Sex Role Inventory, 43, 53, 54
Biofeedback
  menopause and, 332, 333
  for menstrual cycle disorders, 329–331
  for migraine headache, 317, 318
  for Raynaud's syndrome, 320, 321
  tension headaches and, 313, 314, 322
Birth-control pills
  depression and, 281
  dysmenorrhea and, 326
Blood alcohol level (BAL), 445, 446
Body image
  acceptable types in, 377–379
  in adolescence, 223, 224
  age and, 464
  exercise and, 228, 229
  overweight and, 378
  rape treatment and, 262
  treatment for disturbances of, 388, 389
Bown Self-Report Inventory, 261
Brain activity of elderly persons, 468
Brevital, 128, 136, 354
Brief Behavioral Intervention Procedure
    (BBIP), 261
Bulimia, 376, 386, 388

Caffeine, 222, 235
Cardiovascular disease, 234, 235, 458
Children
    abuse of, 266, 267, 270, 361
    androgyny of, 14
    behavior problems in divorce, 206–208, 212
    depression and, 13, 14
    environment and behavior of, 484, 485
    social skills of, 12–14
Children's Locus of Control Scale, 11
Children's Personal Attributes Questionnaire, 11
Circus Test, 11, 12
Cognitive Bias Questionnaire (CBQ), 292
Cognitive Response Test (CRT), 292
Cognitive skills
    in assertiveness training, 155–157
        self-regulation skills, 157
        social adjustment, 156, 157
        social sensitivity, 155, 156
    in nutrition programs, 237, 238
Cognitive therapy
    for agoraphobia, 354, 355
    for depression, 293, 294
    in sexual assault treatment, 255–260
College Self-Expression Scale, 286
Communication
    in parent training, 193, 206
    sexuality and, 131, 132
    in treatment of delinquency, 414
Competence, 1, 3–33
    activity structure and, 22–26
    assertiveness and, 109
    decline in
        accompanying factors of, 17
        activity structure and, 25, 26
        in adolescence, 16, 17, 25–27
        depression and, 18–20
    definitions of, 4–11
        androgyny in, 6, 7, 9, 14
        fairness and, 9
        as mastery of challenging tasks, 5
        as mastery of culturally relevant tasks, 4, 7
        as mastery of daily life problems, 5–7
        operational, 7–11
        as social skill, 5–7
        validation of, 9, 10
    marriage and, 1, 3, 16, 25–27
    measurement of, in school-aged children, 11–14

    motor behavior and, 46
    problem-solving skill, 20–22, 24, 25
    psychopathology and lack of, 10, 11
    socioeconomic status and, 10
    work and, 1, 3
Conditioned anxiety, 357
Contingency management in nutrition programs, 239
Contracting
    in exercise programs, 233, 234
    in family problem-solving training, 414, 415
Coopersmith Self-Esteem Scale, 11
Coronary heart disease, 234, 235
Crime rates, 402–405
    arrest data in, 402, 403
    self-report data in, 404, 405
    victimization survey data in, 403, 404

Day-care centers, parent training and, 495, 496
Delinquency, 399, 401–427
    background on, 402–406
        female crime rates, 402–405
        female versus male, 402
        summary and implications of, 405, 406
    conclusions and recommendations on, 422, 423
    explanatory models of, 406–412
        biological and intrapersonal theories in, 406, 407
        contribution of puberty to, 412
        familial contributions to, 410, 411
        implications of, 410
        opportunity theory in, 408–410
        subcultural or association theories of, 407, 408
    modifying family relationship patterns in, 416–419
    overview on, 401, 402
    social and political implications of intervention in, 419–422
    treatment approaches to, 412–416
        behavior change programs in alternative treatment settings, 415, 416
        communication and family problem solving, 413, 414
Dependency, 148, 173, 176
    agoraphobia and, 352, 353, 356
    gender and, 22
    wife abuse and, 268
Depression, 102, 145, 273, 275–307

Depression (continued)
  in adolescence, 18, 20
  alcoholism and, 432, 433, 441
  assessment of, 281–283
    behavioral analysis in, 284, 285
    past and present symptoms in, 282
    physical examination, 281, 282
    severity in, 283
  child-rearing and, 110
  children and, 13, 14
  cognitive formulation of, 290–294
    cognitive theory of depression in, 290–292
    cognitive therapy in, 293, 294
    dysfunctional cognition in, 292, 293
  competence and, 10, 11
  conclusions and recommendations on, 299–301
  definition and clinical features of, 276–278
  of elderly women, 462, 463
  exercise and, 228, 230, 231
  health and, 222
  learned helplessness formation of, 18, 281, 294–299
    assessment of, 297
    theory of depression in, 294–296
    treatment implications of, 297–299
  marriage and, 17, 18, 110, 173, 287
  menopause and, 332, 463
  in mothers of behavior problem children, 204, 205
  motor behavior and, 53, 55, 56
  overview on, 275
  prevalence of, among women, 278–281
  rape and, 249, 250, 255–258, 260
  sex roles and, 279, 280, 346
  social learning theories of, 18–20
  social skills formulation of, 285–290
    assessment in, 286, 287
    theory of depression in, 285, 286
    treatment implications in, 287–290
  wife abuse and, 267, 268
Depressive Adjective Checklist, 283
Derogatis Sexual Function Inventory (DSFI), 122
Derogatis Symptom Checklist, 261
Desensitization
  in menstrual cycle disorders, 327, 328, 330
  in phobia treatment, 348–351, 354, 355
  after rape, 252–255, 258–260
  for weight gain, 389
Desynchrony, 36

Diagnostic Interview Schedule, 282
Diet and dieting (see Nutrition)
Divorce, child behavior problems and, 206–208, 212
Domestic violence (see Wife abuse)
Drinking Patterns Questionnaire, 436, 437
Drinking Profile, 435, 436
Driving, alcohol and, 433, 444
Drug abuse, 145, 429–431
  alcoholism and, 443, 462
  by elderly women, 462
  identification of, 431, 432, 438
DSM-II (Diagnostic and Statistical Manual of Mental Disorders, 2nd ed.), 282
DSM-III (Diagnostic and Statistical Manual of Mental Disorders, 3rd ed.), 120, 125, 128, 267, 278, 282, 284, 308, 375–377, 431
DUI (driving under the influence), 433, 444
Dyadic Adjustment Scale, 122
Dysmenorrhea, 325–331
  exercise and, 223, 228
Dyspareunia, 125–128, 262

Elderly women, 450–476
  behavioral interventions with, 465–470
    community dwellilng and, 467, 468
    institutional populations, 465–467
    modifying physical and cognitive changes in, 468, 469
    problems in research and, 469, 470
  clinical problems of, 461–465
    depression, 462, 463
    drug abuse, 462
    hypochondriasis, 463, 464
    institutionalization, 464–467
  conclusions and recommendations on, 470
  empirical data on, 454–461
    physical changes, 455–459
    psychological problems, 460
    sexual changes, 458–460
  neglect of, 453, 354
  statistics on, 451, 452
Electromyography (EMG)
  headaches and, 310, 311, 313–315, 322, 323
  in menstrual cycle disorders, 329
  for Raynaud's syndrome, 320, 321
Energy level, 235, 236
  caffeinism and, 235
  reducing intake of simple carbohydrates, 235, 236

Environment
  anxiety and, 364
  child behavior and, 484, 485
  competence and, 17
  motor behavior and, 54, 56
  sex-based differences in, 22
Estrogen "replacement therapy," 332
Eugenics, 478
Exercise, aerobic, 222–234
  benefits of, 222, 223
    physiological, 227, 228
    psychological, 228, 229
  cognitions about, 226, 227
  cultural attitudes toward, 223–225
  depression and, 228, 230, 231
  developing habit of, 231–234
    contracting, 233, 234
    running anorexia, 234
    self-monitoring in, 232
    stimulus control in, 232
  elderly persons and, 468
  establishing habits of, 229–231
    failure analysis in, 230
    feedback in, 230
    pacing in, 231
    social influences in, 229
    treatment schedule in, 230
  goals of programs in, 224, 225
  misconceptions and reservations about,
    225, 226
Eye contact, 288, 289
Eysenck Personality Inventory, 312

Family, 170–189
  activity structure in, 25
  alcoholism and, 444
  behavioral therapy and
    assessing outcome in, 181–185
    involvement in change process, 180, 181
    matching-to-sample, 175–177
    problem definition and treatment goals
      in, 177–180
  behavioral views of dysfunction in,
    171–174
  delinquency and, 410–414, 416–419, 42l,
    422
  extrafamilial support and child behavior
    problems, 207, 208
  in treatment of anorexia nervosa, 390, 391
Fantasy
  in rape treatment, 262
  in treatment of orgasmic problems, 135

Fathers (see also Parent training)
  absence of, and delinquency, 411
Fear, 274 (see also Phobias)
  of failure, 18
  pain and, 464
  rape and, 248–250, 261
  of success, 363
  symptoms of, 347
Feelings and Concerns Checklist, 283
Flooding relief treatment, 350
Functional Family Therapy, 416–419

Gender (see also Sex roles)
  achievement and, 5, 9, 15–17
  activity structure and, 22, 23
  aggression and, 406, 407
  alcoholism and, 429–431
  androgynous sex typing and, 6
  assertiveness and, 46, 47, 143–169
  defined, 35
  dependency and, 22
  depression and (see Depression)
  environmental differences in, 22
  hyperactivity and, 406
  interaction of masculinity and femininity
    in, 35, 36
  motor behavior and, 1, 48–51
  occupational achievement and, 15–17
  social skills and, 5, 6
Great Big Beautiful Doll (Reichman) 392, 393
Gynecology, behavioral, 273

Hamilton Psychiatric Rating Scale for
    Depression, 250, 283
Headache
  migraine, 315–318
    theories of etiology of, 316, 317
    treatment of, 317, 318, 323
  tension, 222, 310–315
    treatment of, 312–315, 322
Health maintenance, 221–244
  background on, 221, 222
  exercise in (see Exercise)
  nutrition in (see Nutrition)
  overview on, 221
Homemaker Service Program, 493, 494
Hospitalization
  alcoholism and, 445
  factors affecting, 5, 6
Hot flashes, 331–333
Human Sexual Inadequacy (Masters & John-
    son), 115

Hyperactivity
  gender and, 406
  parent training and, 197, 198
Hypnotherapy, 327
Hypochondriasis, 463, 464
Hysterical neurosis, 145

Imipramine, 354
Incest, 261, 263, 270
Infidelity, wife abuse and, 266, 267
Innovation
  dissemination of information on, 95–106
    explicit technology for, 99–101
    implicit technology for, 101–106
Innovations, 102
Insomnia, 222
  caffeine and, 235
Institutionalization
  of elderly women, 464–467
  mental retardation and, 483, 488
Intelligence (see also Mental retardation, pa-
    rental)
  practical, 487
  problem-solving skill and, 20, 21
  social, 486, 487
  socioeconomic status and, 480–483
  testing for, 69, 70, 96, 479–481
Interrole conflict, 343, 362
Intervention, behavioral, 94–108
  conclusion on, 106, 107
  explicit technology in, 99–101
  implicit technology in, 101–106
  information dissemination on, 94–99
Interviews
  in assessment of sexual dysfunction, 120,
    121
  pros and cons of, 74, 75
  reliability of, 75, 76
Intimacy, marital, 172, 173
Intrarole conflict, 343, 362
Isolation, 145
"It" Test, 47

Journal of Behavioral Assessment, 74

Kegel exercises, 127, 134

Lamaze exercises, 327
Learned helplessness
  depression and, 18, 281, 294–299
  sex roles and, 346

Lithium carbonate, 282, 284
Living Heart Diet, 235
Living with Children (Patterson & Gullion),
  194

Marital Interaction Coding System, 178, 179
Marriage, 170–189
  agoraphobia and, 352, 353, 356
  alcoholism and, 440–442
  behavioral therapy and, 174–181
    assessing outcome in, 181–185
    matching-to-sample, 175–177
    problem definition and treatment goals
      in, 177–180
  behavioral views of dysfunction in,
    171–174
  child behavior problems and, 205, 206
  competence and, 1, 3, 16, 25–27
  coronary heart disease and, 234, 235
  depression and, 17, 18, 110, 173, 287
  elderly women and, 459, 460
  exercise as issue in, 229
  role changes in, 148
  therapy for, 110
  wife abuse in (see Wife abuse)
  work-related anxiety and, 361–363
Marriage Inventory, 122
Masturbation, 114, 130, 131, 262
  in treatment of orgasmic problems, 133,
    134
Matching-to-sample philosophy
  application of, 173, 175–177, 182, 210
  in delinquency treatment, 421, 422
  described, 172
Measurement theory
  in behavioral assessment, 64–68
  reliability in, 70–72
Menopause, 331–333, 400
  depression and, 332, 463
Menstrual cycle disorders, 26, 324–331
  research on, 324
  theories of, 325–327
  treatment of, 327–331
Menstrual Distress Questionnaire (MDQ),
  326
Menstrual Symptom Questionnaire (MSQ),
  325, 326
Menstruation (see also Menstrual cycle dis-
    orders)
  aggression and, 407
  alcohol use and, 436–438
  amenorrhea, 329

dysmenorrhea, 223, 228, 325–331
  menopause, 331–333, 400, 463
  premenstrual syndrome, 325
Mental retardation, parental, 400, 477–56
  behavioral intervention in, 489–501
    parent training programs, 489–496
    survey of therapist experiences, 496–501
  conclusion on, 501, 502
  difficulties in defining, 479–481
  inadequacies of parents in, 486–488
  overview on, 477
  research on, 482–485
    adequacy as parents, 482–484
    effects on children, 484, 485
  taboos on, 477–479
Methylphenidate (Ritalin), 198
Methysergide, 318
Metropolitan Life Insurance Tables, 374, 392
Michigan Alcoholism Screening Test (MAST), 431, 432
Milwaukee Project, 492, 493
Minnesota Multiphasic Personality Inventory (MMPI), 70, 283
Modeling
  in assertiveness training, 358
  nutrition programs and, 240
Modesty, attributional, 16
Monoamine oxidase (MAO) inhibitors, 354
Mothers
  adjustment of, and parent training, 204, 205
  mental retardation of (see Mental retardation, parental)
  parent training and (see Parent training)
  social skills of, and child behavior, 208
  working, 361, 362
Motor behavior, 1
  in androgyny, 43, 49, 50
  assertiveness and, 155
  checklist for analyzing, 37–42
  clinical assessment of, 52–54
  depression and, 53, 55, 56
  sex-role
    in adults, 42–47
    in children, 47–52
  of transsexuals, 37–42, 52, 53

Naproxen, 327
National, Conference on Women and Crime, 409
National Council on Alcoholism (NCA), 431

National Institute of Mental Health, 102
National Institute on Alcohol Abuse and Alcoholism (NIAAA), 429
Neglect
  of elderly women, 453, 454
  mental retardation and, 482, 487
  parent training for, 490–496, 500
Nursing homes, 485
Nutrition, 221, 222, 234–240
  behavioral self-management of diet in, 237–240
    cognitive techniques and, 237, 238
    contingency management, 239
    maintaining good habits and, 240
    modeling and, 240
    problem solving and, 237
    stimulus control and, 239
    stress management and, 239, 240
    urge control and, 238, 239
  women's health and, 234–237
    caffeinism, 235
    qualitative dietary changes and, 236, 237
    reducing intake of simple carbohydrates, 235, 236

Obesity, 223, 373 (see also Overweight)
  defined, 374
  exercise and, 226, 227
  issues in treating, 96
Observation
  in behavioral assessment
    controlled, 86–88
    naturalistic, 83–86
Opportunity theory, 408–410
Orgasm, 114
  elderly women and, 459
  faking of, 132
  problems in attaining, 130–135
    description of, 130–132
    treatment of, 132–135
  rape and, 262
Osteoporosis, 459
Overweight (see also Obesity)
  acceptable body types and, 377–379
  avoiding age-appropriate tasks and, 389, 390
  body image disturbances in, 388, 389
  consciousness-raising in, 392, 393
  desire to lose weight and, 375, 376
  family treatment in, 391
  overeating as cause of, 378, 379

Overweight *(continued)*
  self-control as cure for, 379, 381–385
  standards for, 374, 375
  treatment for, 379–386
    behavioral, 380–386
    medical and traditional psychothera-
      peutic, 379, 380
    new directions in, 385, 386
    self-control program in, 381–385

Paranoia, 462, 463
Parents Are Teachers (Becker), 194
Parent training, 103, 106, 110, 111, 190–220,
    399, 400
  anorexia nervosa and, 390, 391
  assessment issues in, 208–211
  background on, 191–196
    intervention strategies, 194–196
    parenting skills, 192–194
    problem behaviors, 191, 192
    sample characteristics in, 192
  causal factors in child behavior and,
    197–197
  conclusions and recommendations on,
    211, 212
  cost effectiveness of treatment in, 202–204
  delinquency and, 412–414, 416–419, 421,
    422
  family variables in
    divorce, 206–208
    extrafamilial adjustment, 208
    marital adjustment, 205, 206
    maternal adjustment, 204, 205
  for mentally retarded persons, 98, 105,
    400, 489–501
  mother/father involvement in, 180, 181
  overview on, 190, 191
Parent Training Questionnaire, 496–499
Peer groups
  delinquency and, 407, 408
  of elderly women, 453
Peer Nomination Inventory of Depression, 11
Penis envy, 114
Permanent Weight Control (Mahoney & Ma-
    honey), 383
"Personal Science" procedure, 237
Phobias, 347–356
  agoraphobia, 173, 351–356, 390
  desensitization in treatment of, 348–351,
    354, 355
  of elderly women, 455
  sexual anxiety, 124–128, 131, 136

  simple, 347–351
    treatment of, 351
Pleasant Events Schedule, 287, 288
Pregnancy, 224
  after rape, 251
Premarital Sexual Permissiveness Scale, 122
Premenstrual syndrome, 325
Present State Examination, 282
Pritikin program, 235
Problem Inventory for Adolescent Girls, 422
Problem-solving skill, 20–22
  activity structure and, 24, 25
  for alcoholism, 440
  contracting in, 233, 234, 414, 415
  development of complex, 21–22
  environmental influences on, 22
  level of, 20, 21
  manipulation of, 25
  in nutritional program, 237
  in parent training, 193, 194, 200
Profile of Mood States Scale, 261
Progestin, 332
Project 12-Ways, 491
Propranolol, 318
Prostaglandins, 326, 327
Psychotherapy by Reciprocal Inhibition (Wolpe),
    72
Psychotropic medication, 354
Publication in information dissemination,
    102
Punishment in parent training, 193
  differential reinforcement, 193, 202, 203
  time out, 193, 202, 203
  token reinforcement, 193

Questionnaires
  in alcoholism assessment, 435–437
  in assessment of sexual dysfunction,
    121–123
  on parent training programs, 496–499
  requirements for using, 79–81
  validity of, 81, 82

Rape victimization, 110, 111, 245–264, 269,
    270 *(see also* Wife abuse)
  background on, 246–251
    epidemiologic data, 247, 248
    generalizability of findings, 250
    psychological distress, 248–250
    value of repeated assessment in, 250,
      251
  treatment for, 251–264

brief behavioral intervention, 261
cognitive therapy, 255–260
other behavioral strategies, 263, 264
sexual dysfunction, 261–263
systematic desensitization, 252–255, 258–260
Raskin Depression Scale, 283
Rathus Assertiveness Scale, 286
Raynaud's syndrome, 318–321
symptoms of, 319
theories of, 319, 320
treatment of, 320–321, 323
Reactivity in self-monitoring, 78, 79
Rehearsal in rape treatment, 263, 264
Reinforcement
in alcoholism treatment, 442–444
in nutrition programs, 239
in parent training, 193, 202, 203
symbolic, in exercise programs, 233
Relaxation techniques, 239, 240
for alcoholism treatment, 440
for menstrual cycle disorders, 327–329
for migraine headaches, 317, 318
rape and, 252
for tension headache, 314, 322
Research Diagnostic Criteria, 278
Ritalin (methylphenidate), 198
Role enactment, 343
Role expectations, 343
Running anorexia, 234

SCAT (School College Ability Test), 11, 12
Schedule for Affective Disorders and Schizophrenia, 282
Schizophrenia, 282, 387, 465
competence and, 11
depression and, 282
School, parent training and problems at, 191
School College Ability Test (SCAT), 11, 12
Self-control
overweight and, 379, 381–385
appraisal of basic package in, 384, 385
cognitive self-control treatment in, 383, 384
community-based weight control groups, 382–383
reappraisal of behavioral packages in, 383
refinements to self-control package in, 384
in parent training, 194, 195

Self-esteem, 151
alcoholism and, 433, 434, 441, 442
mental retardation and, 487, 488
Self-image, exercise and, 228
Self-monitoring
of alcohol/drug use, 432, 433, 435
in exercise programs, 232
in nutrition programs, 236–239
requirements of, 76–78
validity of, 79
in weight control programs, 381
Self-perception in depression, 290–292
Self-reporting, 404, 405
of alcohol consumption, 446
therapist intervention in, 177–180
Self-respect, assertiveness and, 152, 153, 163
Sequential Test of Educational Progress (STEP), 11, 12
Sex Knowledge and Attitude Test (SKAT), 122
Sex roles, 34–59 (see also Gender)
behavioral marriage and family therapy as a reinforcer of, 170–189
beliefs and self-schemata in, 344
conclusion on, 54–57
defined, 35
delinquency and, 412
depression and, 279, 280, 346
femininity and masculinity in, 342–344
locus of control in, 345, 346
measurement of
behavioral, 36, 37
masculinity and femininity in, 35, 36
motor behavior in
adult, 42–47
child, 47–52
clinical assessment of, 52–54
developing checklist for measurement of, 37–42
overview on, 34, 35
public policy and, 98, 99
sexuality and, 115
social skills and, 47, 146–148
stereotyped views of, 342–344
Sexual abuse, 270
Sexual Arousability Inventory (SAI), 122, 123
Sexual dysfunction, 111, 118–138
arousal problems, 128, 129
description of, 128, 129
treatment of, 129

Sexual dysfunction (continued)
    assessment of, 118–124
        behavior assessment in, 123
        clinical interview in, 120, 121
        medical examinations in, 118–120
        physiological measures in, 123, 124
        questionnaires in, 121–123
    behavioral model for, 116–118
    conclusions on, 135–137
    dyspareunia, 125–128, 262
    as learned characteristic, 115, 116
    orgasmic problems, 130–136
        description of, 130–132
        treatment of, 132–135
    rape and, 261–263
    recommendations to therapists in, 137, 138
    sexual anxiety, 124–128, 136
        description of, 124–126
        treatment of, 126–128, 136
    treatment for, 115, 116, 126–128, 132–136,
        261–263
    vaginismus, 125–127,136
Sexual Interaction Inventory (SII), 121, 122
Sexuality, 113–142
    attitudes to female, 114–116, 138
    behavioral model of, 116–118
    dysfunction in (see Sexual dysfunction)
    of elderly women, 458–460
    overview on, 113
    training in human, 119
Skills training
    alcoholism and, 439, 440
    delinquency and, 417, 418, 420, 421
Slim Chance in a Fat World (Stuart & Davis),
    381
Social Adjustment Scale–II (SAS-II), 258–260
Social skills
    alcoholism and, 440–442
    assertiveness in (see Assertiveness)
    of children, 12–14
    competence and, 5–7
    defined, 149–150
    depression and, 285–290
    of elderly persons, 466
    mental retardation and, 480, 481, 486, 487
    of mother and child behavior problems,
        208
    rape prevention and, 264
    sex roles and, 47, 146–148
Socioeconomic status (SES)
    child-rearing practices and, 484, 485
    competence and, 10

depression and, 280, 281
intelligence and, 480–483
touching behavior and, 42
wife abuse and, 265, 266
Specialized Family Program, 494, 495
Spouse abuse (see Wife abuse)
Spouse Observation Checklist (SOC), 175,
    175n., 176
Standardization samples, 66, 67
State–Trait Anxiety Inventory, 261
STEP (Sequential Test of Educational Prog-
    ress), 11, 12
Stimulus control
    in alcoholism treatment, 439
    in exercise programs, 232, 233
    in nutrition programs, 239
    in rape treatment, 263
Stress (see also Anxiety)
    depression and, 279, 280
    mental retardation and, 488
    nutrition and, 239, 240
    psychopathology and, 71
    wife abuse and, 267
Sugar
    consumption of, 236
    craving for, 238, 239
Suicide attempts, 146
Supplement to the Handbook for Teaching Par-
    ents in Girls' Homes, 415
System of Multicultural Pluralistic Assess-
    ment (SOMPA), 480

Take Off Pounds Sensibly (TOPS), 382
Target Complaints Assessment, 252, 252n.
Tests and testing (see also Behavioral as-
    sessment; specific tests)
    for alcoholism, 431, 432
    for assertiveness, 286, 287
    for assessment of sexual dysfunction,
        121–123
    for cardiovascular fitness, 230
    for depression, 283
    of elderly persons, 468, 469
    for intelligence, 69, 70, 96, 479–481
    for marital satisfaction, 178, 179, 181
    of problem-solving skills, 20, 21
Thinness, desire to lose weight and, 376
Thought-stopping, 264
Time management, exercise and, 225, 241
Time-Out Situation Test, 202
Traits
    defined, 69

intelligence as, 69, 70
Transsexuals, motor behavior of, 37–42, 52, 53
Type A behavior, 362, 363
Type B behavior, 362

Understanding the Rape Victim: A Synthesis of Research Findings (Katz & Mazur), 247
Uniform Crime Reports for the United States, 247, 402
Urge control in nutrition programs, 238, 239

Vaginismus, 125, 126, 127, 136
Values, delinquency and, 418–420
Venereal disease, 251
Veronen–Kilpatrick Modified Fear Survey Schedule, 261
Victimization survey data, 403, 404

Walden Two (Skinner), 110
Wechsler Adult Intellilgence Scale (WAIS), 469
Weight disorders, 274, 373–398 (*see also* Exercise, aerobic; Nutrition)
  anorexia nervosa (*see* Anorexia nervosa)
  bulimia, 376, 386, 388
  conclusion and recommendations on, 393, 394

expanded behavioral treatment for, 388–393
  acceptance of overweight and, 392, 393
  avoiding age-appropriate tasks, 389, 390
  body image disturbance, 388, 389
  obsession with thinness and, 391, 392
  operant and family systems approach in, 390, 391
overweight, 374–386
  acceptable body types, 377–379
  background on, 374–377
  treatment of, 379–386
Weight-reduction programs, 97, 240, 380, 382
Weight Watchers, 240, 380, 382
Wife abuse, 245, 265–270
  background on, 265–267
  treatment for, 267–269
Wolpe–Lazarus Assertiveness Questionnaire, 286
Work
  anxiety related to, 361–364
    treatment of, 363, 364
  assertiveness and, 46, 47
  competence and, 1, 3

Zung Depression Scale, 283